£4   hk 37

THE DIOCESE BOOKS
OF
SAMUEL WILBERFORCE

Cover illustration: Portrait of Bishop Samuel Wilberforce

Reproduced by kind permission of the Principal, Ripon College Cuddesdon, Oxfordshire

Photograph by Christopher Day

The Oxfordshire Record Society

VOLUME No. 66

2008

THE DIOCESE BOOKS OF SAMUEL WILBERFORCE

Bishop of Oxford 1845-1869

Transcribed and Edited
by
Ronald and Margaret Pugh

Berkshire Record Society

Volume 13

2008

This Edition © Oxfordshire Record Society 2008

Oxfordshire Record Society 2008
ISBN 0 902509 58 6

Berkshire Record Society 2008
ISBN 0 9548716 2 6

Produced for the Societies by
Past Historic, Kings Stanley, Gloucestershire
Printed in Great Britain by Henry Ling Limited, Dorchester

TABLE OF CONTENTS

page

FOREWORD (Oxfordshire Record Society) vi

FOREWORD (Berkshire Record Society) vii

LIST OF ABBREVIATIONS viii

INTRODUCTION ix

VOLUME I 1846 1

VOLUME II 1854 95

BIOGRAPHICAL APPENDIX 341

INDEX OF PERSONS AND PLACES 389

FOREWORD

Dr Ronald Pugh's edition of the *Letter Books of Samuel Wilberforce, 1843 – 68*, published in 1969, was a major contribution to the ecclesiastical history of the 19th century. This edition of the *Diocese Books* makes available documents which, though used previously by historians, are published in full for the first time; taken in conjunction with the *Letter Books*, Dr Pugh has therefore provided the wherewithal to reconstruct and analyse a remarkable episcopate yet more thoroughly if not, as he insists in his Introduction, in totality.

Anyone familiar with Wilberforce's appalling handwriting will feel a warm sense of sympathy with and gratitude towards Dr Pugh for his stamina and meticulous scholarship in making this material available to the general public. As he remarks laconically in his Introduction, he is after forty years uniquely familiar with its idiosyncrasies; even so he has on (very rare) occasion had to admit defeat. The societies publishing this volume are immensely grateful to Dr Pugh and to his wife Margaret who, as the Introduction makes clear, has played a significant part in the edition's preparation. As the Introduction also stresses, several other people have gone out of their way to assist the edition's progress. We would like to thank especially Carl Boardman and Rosemary Dunhill, the County Archivists of Oxfordshire and Hampshire respectively, and John Hardacre, Curator of Bishop Morley's Library, Winchester.

The Oxfordshire Record Society is grateful to its sister society in Berkshire which, in agreeing to offer the volume to its members, has greatly assisted in its publication.

General Editors of record societies are traditionally, and properly, inconspicuous. I shall break with convention on this occasion by noting that this volume will be the last to be published in my twenty-five years' tenure as General Editor of the Oxfordshire Record Society. Any sadness on my part is more than offset by the reassurance of knowing that future editions will be in the very capable hands of my successor, Dr William Whyte of St John's College, Oxford, who I take this opportunity of commending to our members.

Oxford, April 2008

Christopher Day
General Editor, ORS

FOREWORD

Berkshire Record Society is delighted to be associated with its sister society in Oxfordshire in the publication of this edition by Dr Ronald Pugh of the *Diocese Books* of Samuel Wilberforce. Wilberforce was a towering figure in the nineteenth-century church whose influence was felt far and wide. There can be few parts of his large diocese that were untouched by his energy and reforming zeal. In Berkshire alone he consecrated or re-consecrated over one hundred churches during his twenty-five years as bishop and attended the reopening after restoration of some 50 to 60 more. It is therefore both appropriate and pleasing that this edition should be given the wider circulation that joint publication allows.

As General Editor of the Berkshire Record Society I warmly endorse Chris Day's acknowledgement to Dr Pugh and his wife Margaret for undertaking the considerable labour involved in preparing this volume for publication.

Reading, April 2008

Peter Durrant
General Editor, BRS

ABBREVIATIONS
used in the text and in the Biographical Appendix

AKC	Theological Associate of King's College, London
B	Bachelor
BA	Bachelor of Arts
BD	Bachelor of Divinity
BNC	Brasenose College
B of K	Browne of Kiddington [*a source of advice in Diocese Book I*]
C	Curate; curacy
Ch Ch	Christ Church
D	Deacon; Duke
DC	District Chapel or Church
D&C	Dean and Chapter
DD	Doctor of Divinity
GM	[*possibly*] Good man
H	Hamlet
H Ch	Hamlet Chapel or Church
Ld C	Lord Chancellor
M	Married
MA	Master of Arts
P	Priest
PC	Perpetual Curate or Curacy
Pec	Peculiar [*an area or post outside Episcopal jurisdiction*]
Pus/Puss	Puseyite
R	Rector or Rectory
RC	Roman Catholic
RD	Rural Dean
SC	Senior Curate
V	Vicar or Vicarage

INTRODUCTION

The documents now published are not new discoveries. Their existence was well known to the original biographers of Bishop Samuel Wilberforce, and extensive use was made of them at the time. In particular the first of the two memoranda books provided Canon Ashwell with a panoramic sketch of the diocese which greatly helped his efforts to piece together the process though which Wilberforce not only initiated himself into the office and work of a Bishop but also inaugurated the newly enlarged Diocese of Oxford as he succeeded Charles Bagot in 1845 on his translation to the quieter waters of Bath and Wells.

Bagot had rather reluctantly accepted Berkshire from Salisbury in 1837 but had firmly refused to accept Buckinghamshire from Lincoln. Wilberforce had no such choice, and history records how he rose to the challenge. Not only did he press his authority and influence over the six hundred parishes for which he had become responsible but in the process made both the Church and the nation aware of the new standards and status which political as well as religious reformers required of the episcopate. Activity and efficiency were demanded by the radicals who opposed the Church as well as by the traditionalists who sought to defend it, whilst the Catholic revival both stimulated a more spiritual view of the Church and its leaders and aroused suspicions that reform might lead to the abandonment of the Anglican balance of Catholic and Protestant beliefs within a uniform liturgy. Becoming a Bishop in 1845, the year when Newman left the English Church, was a formidable step for the son of a revered Evangelical father who nevertheless had many Anglo-Catholics amongst his brothers and friends. Wilberforce was thus forced to walk a tightrope. His remedy was to seek to make the traditional Anglican Church work in all its aspects, liturgical, theological and pastoral, as the politicians who sympathised with it hoped he would.

The fruits of his labours have lasted until comparatively recent times. The Church of England which Wilberforce battled to defend and animate was recognisably the same Church as existed in the 1950s, but most of his achievements have now been thrown into the melting-pot. Though unfortunate in the ecclesiastical aspect, 1845 was a propitious date in secular and economic affairs: the dreaded Repeal of the Corn Laws occurred just as the agricultural community entered a generation of unparalleled prosperity, the demand for foodstuffs increasing as the urban population multiplied. As a result a rurally-based society was well able to overhaul its ecclesiastical arrangements – providing resident clergy in even the smallest communities and building or restoring countless churches. Oxford was a rural diocese, and Wilberforce was

THE DIOCESE OF OXFORD, c. 1869

Key
Main Parishes   WANTAGE
Parishes in the gift of the Bishop of Oxford   **BANBURY** / **Culham**
Railways
Roads
County boundaries

the man to build it up as the universally recognised model of what an Anglican diocese should be. These two books provide a unique insight into how he set about it.

The first of the two books, though a bound volume, consisted of systematic jottings about the parishes and their clergy which he acquired in a series of meetings at Cuddesdon with the archdeacons and rural deans of the new diocese in January 1846. Much of it consists of pairs of facing pages in which the two sets of comments were set out side by side. The jottings were assembled by deaneries in the Bishop's own hand, and in many cases the entries must have been made as he questioned his subordinates about the clergymen he had inherited and the situation he faced. There are attempts at an index at the end, as well as a section entitled Facienda, in which the immediate targets for action were listed. A few additional entries were inserted into the body of the text in the two or three years after this initial compilation early in 1846, but the volume remains essentially an analysis of the diocese in 1846. A degree of waywardness in the arrangement of the entries and some considerable difficulty in deciphering the various layers of handwriting makes any reconstruction in print technically challenging.

The second volume is entirely different. This is a large bound volume prepared in the diocesan office with a page for each parish in the diocese as it stood in 1854. By this time it had become apparent that the Bishop's heady rise to greatness had slowed to a stop, and that he was destined to remain at Oxford for some years to come. The Hampden controversy had lost him friends both at Court and in the Church; his efforts to improve his diocese by founding the colleges at Cuddesdon for the training of the clergy and at Culham for the training of teachers had awakened widespread suspicions that he was a covert Romanist, a view reinforced as one by one relatives and friends departed for the Roman fold and he alone remained faithful to the church of his fathers. The ascendancy of Palmerston, who took his ecclesiastical advice from Lord Shaftesbury, was an insuperable obstacle to Wilberforce's advancement. Meanwhile his active Parliamentary and public life, his wide circle of friendships, and his involvement in the development of the Anglican Communion overseas, demanded a great deal of his time and energies. Caring properly at the same time for his diocese entailed constant correspondence and travel, and made it a problem to keep track of the dealings he had with each parish and the succession of clergy who served them. By no means every page was used, but in several instances copious press cuttings were inserted, notably about the affairs of Boyne Hill and High Wycombe. Another curiosity is the inclusion of a series of cuttings from an antiquarian dictionary about the etymology of placenames and the ancient monuments of some parishes. The chief element remains the record in the Bishop's own often barely decipherable hand of visits to the parishes and relations with the clergy. Orders of service and architectural plans are also in evidence to mark the more memorable occasions in the Bishop's episcopal work.

Most of this second volume was compiled between 1854 and the early 1860s, by which time fatigue and a degree of disappointment were taking their toll, as the changing calligraphy bears witness. It was not until 1869 that the long-delayed promotion to Winchester was offered. London, Canterbury and York had all been filled more than once by premiers who were unsympathetic to Wilberforce or wary of the political fall-out which his higher preferment might have provoked. Gladstone, a loyal but open-eyed friend, had pressed on Palmerston the case for promoting him to York in 1862, but it was only when Gladstone himself succeeded to the premiership that he could offer the first significant advancement that came into his hands; and, as was his wont, offered his High-Church friends the posts with the hardest work. Winchester, fifth in the hierarchy and the scene of the happier experiences of Wilberforce's early career, was not a kind choice: the population and the number of parishes were both significantly greater than at Oxford, and an ageing widower with wayward clerical sons was not best equipped to deal with it. It had also been well administered by his old mentor Charles Richard Sumner, the personal records of whose episcopate have lamentably for the most part been lost. So the records that remain of Wilberforce's Winchester years are scanty, recording little more than the struggle to keep going. He could not even occupy Farnham Castle, where Sumner lived out the five years of his retirement, but had to make his centre his own house at Lavington in West Sussex.

His official papers in the Oxford diocese were duly stored by the Diocesan Registrar and found their way into the Bodleian Library when the floods of 1953 made that repository unsafe. (One parish box in eight was destroyed when the river broke into the cellars of the Registry in St. Aldates.) His personal papers, as might be expected, remained with his family, and mercifully escaped the destruction visited on the papers of Charles Sumner. The second Diocese Book was found in the papers of Bishop Ernest Roland Wilberforce of Newcastle and subsequently Chichester, and sent by his widow to the Bishop of Oxford, who presumably deposited it among the other diocesan papers. His other personal papers, including his correspondence books, remained in the care of Octavia Wilberforce, Ernest's great-niece, whom he confirmed in 1904; she deposited them in the Bodleian Library, which eventually purchased them from her executors. The Bodleian subsequently deposited all the diocesan papers in the Oxfordshire Record Office, where they now reside.

The current Editor of this volume became aware of the Memoranda Books when researching the Bishop's Oxford episcopate in the 1950s. The main source material for that study was the copious collection of administrative papers which were then in the Bodleian. Even these were so voluminous that a sampling method had to be adopted. The Memoranda Books had already been used and quoted by Ashwell and Wilberforce in their three-volume official biography, and at the time they seemed to offer little additional material. The eight volumes of correspondence, of which only one was known to the biographers, and several of which only came to light in Dr Octavia's attic, offered more useful insights for the purpose of the study; these were eventually transcribed, edited and published as volume XLVII in the Oxfordshire Record Society's publications, to mark the year 1869 as the centenary of Wilberforce's translation to Winchester. The project of transcribing the Memoranda Books came to the surface only in the 1990s, and their publication comes near the time of the bicentenary of the Bishop's birth in 1805.

The main reason offered for publishing these volumes is the light they cast on the state of the modern Diocese of Oxford at the time of its formation, and on the nature of the Bishop's relationships with his clergy. To have the complete archive enables the picture to be more comprehensive than quotations, however numerous, will allow. At this stage it is unlikely that they will throw much fresh insight on Wilberforce and his work, but they will certainly bear witness to his diligence and to his more human qualities. A further reason was the nature of the Bishop's handwriting, with which the current Editor had become uniquely familiar. Even so, there are many places where conjecture has to replace certainty, and a few where even conjecture is useless. Meanwhile, the custodians of the archives were increasingly reluctant, for reasons of conservation, to make them generally available. Transcription, as with the Letter Books, would thus serve to restore their accessibility to any who had reason to consult them.

The length of time taken up in the process has many causes, not least being the distance of sixty miles between Oxford and Winchester, where the Editor was engaged in a busy academic and examining career. (Even after retirement, a voluntary post proved equally restrictive.) This problem was met by the great courtesy of the County Archivists for Oxfordshire and Hampshire: Carl Boardman agreed to release the volumes into the temporary care of the County Archivist for Hampshire, who agreed to act as custodian of the volumes whilst they were being worked on. Even so, there would have been little progress without the involvement of the Editor's wife, who spent many hundreds of hours making an initial draft of the larger volume and subsequently embarked on the compilation of the Biographical Appendix, which it was realised would draw out connections between the clergy and their careers within and outside the Diocese of Oxford. Reducing the drafts to typescript and double-checking the text in the process was unsurprisingly slow, even with the aid of modern word-processing. At one point the County Archive was removed from Oxford to Cowley, and during this period the photocopies of Oldfield's *Clerus Diocesis Oxoniensis* were also lent to Winchester so that work could continue. Without the patience and understanding of Carl Boardman and of Rosemary Dunhill, then Hampshire County Archivist, and the staff of the splendid new Hampshire

Record Office, this volume would never have seen the light of day. The Chapter of Winchester, and their Curator, John Hardacre, in his capacity as custodian of Bishop Morley's Library, also provided Mrs Pugh with access to key reference works. In the final reckoning, the encouragement over these many years of Chris Day, General Editor for the Record Society, has been the determining factor in bringing the volume to publication.

Because the volumes had been accessioned by the Bodleian Library, the original pagination, which was in places very haphazard, had been replaced by a consistent series which it was decided to preserve in transcribing the text. Even the Bodleian pagination is not watertight: in Book II folios 341-400 and 534-554 are duplicated, and have been numbered 341a-400a, 341b-400b, 534a-554a and 534b-554b respectively. The order of entries in the text is unaffected, but readers who wish to refer to the originals may be glad to know of this anomaly. The original numeration stops at 591, but the Bishop inserted his own numbers in the remaining pages, which are mostly overflows from earlier entries or notes about new parishes or other miscellanea. Square brackets have been used where it is impossible to offer more than conjecture or where abbreviations have been amplified. Footnotes have been kept to a minimum. The original spellings and (somewhat idiosyncratic) syntax and punctuation have so far as possible been preserved as they stand. However, because the symbol @ now means something different in the age of electronic communication, its Victorian usage 'about' has been spelt out throughout the volume.

The Biographical Appendix has been compiled from a few key reference books which could be used in Winchester, notably Foster's *Alumni Universitatis Oxoniensis*, Venn's *Alumni Cantabrigienses*, a volume of the *Clergy List* for 1845, and early volumes of *Crockford's Clerical Directory*. It is not claimed to be complete or exhaustive. Those who have specific persons in view and have access to other reference books may well be able to supplement this basic information in many ways from other sources.

An overview of what these volumes may reveal is not easy to offer. That Wilberforce was diligent, concerned, and exacting needs little new exemplification. There are many touches of humour, and occasional records of tragedy. Although the personal qualities of the hundreds of clergy mentioned are the chief source of interest, the amount written about each is variable and often cryptic. As a whole, the volumes confirm the well-known facts that nearly all the clergy of the period were graduates of either Oxford or Cambridge, mostly in the era before university reform, and that not many had been subjected to the professional and vocational training coming into existence at the new Theological Colleges, such as Cuddesdon. It is also clear that pluralism was not wiped out at a stroke by Act of Parliament. The summary account of Wilberforce given in the Introduction to the O.R.S. edition of the Letter Books is probably still apposite, and it would be otiose to repeat it.

What has happened in the interim is the unravelling of most of the things which Wilberforce valued. Pluralism has been embraced with enthusiasm by diocesan authorities who cannot find either the men or the money to preserve the ideal of one resident priest for every community. The vigorous differentiation of Anglicanism from other forms of Christianity has disappeared thanks to the Ecumenical movement, and the jealous safeguarding of the Book of Common Prayer as the only legitimate form of worship is now regarded as a blinkered refusal to move with the times. This is partly the effect of radical social change: no more is the country parson a wealthy landowner with tithes to sustain his ministry. He and his Bishop must defer not to the resident landowner who was also the patron of the living but to the wealthy weekender who lives in the Old Rectory or Manor House, and who may have little inclination to part with his cash for the preservation of the historic building which may be the only surviving institution in an otherwise largely deserted village. What has mainly survived from Wilberforce's achievement has been the concept of the Bishop as the person around whom the religious life of the region revolves: the Dissenting competition has to a large extent diminished, though the Roman Church is much more visible than in the 1850s, whilst the responsibilities now accepted by Parochial Church Councils greatly resemble the autonomy which at that time marked the individual nonconformist churches. The creation of the General Synod, and its counterparts in Diocese and Deanery, have made the Church a labyrinthine compound of central and local bodies which perhaps has more in common with Methodism than with the Victorian Anglican Church. Within this strange scene the Diocese has become central, but the Bishop is not supreme within it: restrained by committees more numerous and active than anything the Victorian Parliament could have envisaged, today's Bishop has retained the bureaucratic functions but has to struggle to express a spiritual authority which may be as much disregarded by clergy and congregations as some of Wilberforce's calls to duty obviously were. Diocesan Secretaries are also immensely powerful, unlike John Davenport, who operated entirely as a legal assistant to the Bishop.

There are aspects of Wilberforce's episcopate which are not reflected in these volumes. The only record of Cuddesdon and the controversies it aroused are the lists of those who had supported public protests about the Bishop's alleged Romanist leanings. The work of the Diocesan Societies, for Education, Church Building, the Augmentation of Clergy Incomes, even for Bell Ringing, are hardly mentioned. Neither are the efforts to ordain clergy sufficiently prepared for the new concepts of the ministry. For a full picture of these aspects of diocesan life the administrative records remain the primary source, together with printed accounts of the proceedings of the Societies which can be read in the Bodleian. Confirmations were the most prominent occasions for the Bishop to maintain contact with his clergy and people, followed by the dedication of new or restored churches and churchyards. Efforts to improve standards of clerical behaviour, such as better observance of the liturgy, due residence, the appointment of curates where health or population dictated it, are quite frequent, but here too the diocesan records and the Letter Books offer fuller information.

Neither is there any coverage of the national aspects of the Bishop's work This is not in itself remarkable, and in any case much of this reflected Wilberforce the person raised to conspicuous public office through his family connections and obvious abilities, which had impressed the Queen and Prince Albert, as well as securing more cautious approval from Peel and Gladstone. Perhaps the main indicator of this aspect of his position is the occasional reference to his staying overnight on his Confirmation tours with the locally resident aristocracy rather than with even his more prominent clergy. Bishops ranked amongst the Earls, and Wilberforce lost no opportunity of cultivating influential dignitaries who as patrons of parishes or more generally as supporters of the Church could provide useful benefits to a zealous reformer.

These documents are therefore to be dipped into rather than read continuously, but any readers who do attempt a continuous perusal will surely emerge both breathless and impressed, even if aware that what they have read is inevitably only one aspect of a very complex story.

The Biographical Appendix was originally conceived along the lines of a database, from which interesting calculations might be made about the proportions of Oxford, Cambridge and other graduates, the career patterns which were available to the clergy, and even the part played by contact with the Diocese and its Bishop in later career moves. Even had the editors possessed the requisite skills and resources, this was soon shown to be a hopeless quest, in view of the haphazard quality of the material available. Those who are content with a more impressionistic approach will nevertheless find much to interest them in this section of the volume. The grip of family and college connections is revealed in the simpler biographies, which begin and end with a lengthy spell in one benefice, and there is, on a smaller scale, evidence for branching out into newer forms of ministry, usually embarked on by the less well-connected, whose careers included numerous curacies and chaplaincies before attaining, if ever, the security of a benefice. Readers may also be amazed at the amount of pluralism which can be detected well into the middle years of the century. For the innumerable gaps and errors the editors can only ask for pardon: interested parties will no doubt have access to more local and special knowledge than the reference books of Winchester could supply.

DIOCESE BOOK I

folio
1
                      Riseholme, Lincoln, August 14, 1844.

  My Lord Archbishop,
  I beg leave to state to your Grace that the official reasons for which I have granted a Licence of Non Residence[1] to the Reverend William Gurdon, Vicar of Westbury in the County of Buckingham, are detailed by him in a letter to me, of which I enclose a Copy.
  I have the Honor to be,
  My Lord Arch.Bishop,
       Your Grace's very faithful Servant
            J. Lincoln[2]

His Grace
The Arch-Bishop of Canterbury[3]

[*endorsed*: Bishop of Lincoln's Reasons for granting a Licence for Non-Residence to the Rev'd Wm. Gurdon [*sic*], Vic of Westbury Co Bucks Dat 14 Aug't 1844
No. 11]

2–3 [*original*] [*only in copy*: Westbury near Brackley, 16 July 1844]
My Lord
  As I have before stated to your Lordship, my situation here is so uncomfortable, from the conduct of my Brother, who is the chief proprietor of the Parish, that I am induced to apply to your Lordship for a licence of non-residence, (my place being supplied by a resident curate), the grounds on which I make the application are – that my Brother & his family totally absent themselves from the public worship, and declare their unalterable determination to persevere in that line of conduct during my residence in the Parish – that their influence and example have an injurious tendency, in general, with his dependants – that he has withdrawn all support from the Sunday schools – that he opposes church rates, and every other matter which is proposed by me, in parish matters – and that finally, he has gone

---

[1] The notification to the Archbishop of a Licence of Non-Residence was required under the Pluralities Act of 1838, as part of the campaign against plurality and non-residence. The Archbishop in turn had to notify Parliament annually of the number of licences issued. The effect was a very rapid reduction.

[2] John Kaye.

[3] William Howley, whose death in 1848 prevented the testing of his resolution to go to the Tower rather than consecrate Hampden as Bishop of Hereford.

so far, as to threaten to erect a dissenting chapel, in the parish – in short that he takes every method of rendering the discharge of my duties here, as uncomfortable & unsatisfactory, as he possibly can, with the intention, no doubt, of driving me from the parish.

In the hope that your Lordship will be pleased to take my case into consideration, –

I am, my Lord,
    Your Lordship's
    Most Obd't & Humb. Serv.
        Wm Guerdon
To the Lord Bishop of Lincoln

4–5 [*Office copy of the above letter*]

6–7   Holywell, Jan 14th, 1846.

My Dear Lord,

As you have expressed so lively an interest in the proceedings of the Vice Chancellor relative to Dr Pusey, it has occurred to me to send you the accompanying document which he put into my hands this morning. He at the same time kindly detailed to me the steps that he had taken in the matter, and his reasons, with which I need not trouble you, for consulting his Pro-Vice Chancellors, and not the Board of Heads of Houses and Proctors. The letter will probably be before the public by Friday next.

The following particulars which I have casually obtained this morning respecting two parishes in the neighbourhood of Deddington may possibly be useful to your Lordship on some future occasion.

<u>Steeple Barton</u>, – Pop. 640

Mr Oakeley the curate, an old man non–resident, but goes over to the parish once a week at least. Romanists diligent, and the parish going to ruin.

<u>North Aston</u> – Pop 289. No resident. Rev R Brown incumbent resides at Kidlington 11 miles off. No resident curate.

What you kindly told me the other day respecting what had passed at your Ordination has made a profound impression upon me. I trust that it will quicken me to renewed prayer for God's blessing on all your Labours.

        Believe me to be, my dear Lord,
           Yours most truly,
              Charles P Golightly[4]

The Right Rev
The Lord Bishop of Oxford

---

[4] The cordiality of this letter bears out the opinion of Burgon (*Lives of Twelve Good* Men) and others that Golightly, who later became something of a focus for the opposition aroused by

8   [*inserted letter, written on black-edged stationery*]
          Riseholme, Lincoln, February 15, 1847

My dear Lord,

I am sorry to learn that Mr Wynter has been obliged to quit Fenny Stratford: he appeared to me to be a man of an impracticable character, but I never heard him charged with intemperate habits. The additional £20 a year was paid out of Lady Conynghame's Bequest. She left £3333.6.8 £3 per cent [Invested]: the Interest to be divided into 5 equal parts, one of which to be paid to the Vicar of Hughenden for the time being: the other four to four beneficed Clergymen of the County of Buckingham deriving Incomes not exceeding £100 a year from their Benefices.

The present Annuitants are Mr Coxwell of Great Marlow, who was appointed[5] before I became Bishop of Lincoln, Mr Cox of Winchendon, Mr Wynter of Fenny Stratford: and Mr Hayton of Chearsley.

She left also £1000 £4 per cents, the interest to be paid to four Widows of Clergymen of the County of Buckingham. The present Annuitants are

> Mary Ann Barton, Widow of a Vicar of Lavendon,
> Eliza Gower, who was appointed by Bishop Pelham,
> Mary Archer, Widow of the late Vicar of Whitchurch,
> Mary [Woodd], Widow of the late Rector of Drayton Beauchamp.

The £4 per cents having been reduced to £3¼, in order to secure to each of the Widows £10 a year, I purchased, out of some savings which had accrued before, £200 stock: so that the Stock now standing in the £3¼ cents is £1200.

She also left £500 £4 per cents the Interest to be paid to the Vicar of Hughenden: and £100 for the Infirm of the Penn Union. This last Sum was expended about four years ago under the discretion of the Vicar.

It is clear that your Lordship's name should be inserted in the place of mine in this Trust: but this, I suppose, can only be done under an Act of Parliament. In the mean time, if you will be so good as to inform me whom you wish to be appointed in the place of Mr Wynter, I will direct Messrs Coutts, who receive the Dividends, to pay him £20 a year by half-yearly payments.

I will communicate with Mr Swan on the subject of the Letter of the

---

Cuddesdon College and the allegations that its students were a fifth column of Romanisers, (see *DNB* and Chadwick, *The Founding of Cuddesdon*) was not at heart hostile to Wilberforce. See also entries under Toot Baldon for his generous service to that small and ill-endowed parish. This letter is in marked contrast to the ambiguous letter of welcome the Bishop received from Dr Pusey (see Ashwell, vol 1, 300ff).

[5] In 1811.

Church–Warden of Shennington, and let you know the result. If the ground had been ready for consecration, as I believe that it might have been, in 1843, the year of my Visitation, the expense of Mr Swan's journey, which constitutes a large portion of the Bill, might have been saved.

    I am, my dear Lord,
    Yours very faithfully,
    J.Lincoln
The Lord Bishop of Oxford.

11   [*Blank*]

12–14   Walmer, November 6 1849
My dear Mr Wilberforce,[6]
I am sorry to be so late in answering your letter of the 2nd inst., but absence from home has prevented my acknowledging it sooner.

  Of Mr. Whitehead I know nothing personally: but I can tell you the circumstances under which the church which he serves was built, and you will be able to draw your own conclusion. When Harvey allowed the Church to speak for herself by establishing daily service and weekly Communion at Ramsgate, an outcry was raised against him by the worldly portion of his people, & a violent opposition to all his plans for good organized. An unworthy brother Mr. Sicklemore of St Lawrence lent himself to the feeling, & by means of subscriptions built a new Church within the parochial bounds of St Lawrence, but actually in the Town of Ramsgate, & was thus instrumental in fostering schism. To this Church, on its consecration, Mr. Whitehead was appointed, & has continued to minister there from that time until now; his congregation consisting almost entirely of the malcontents of the Town of Ramsgate. Another Church, at an opposite extremity of the Town has since been built under the auspices of Mr. Plumptre & a few others but whether this latter church originated in the notion that Mr. Whitehead did not go far enough towards the Dissenting extremes I do not know. In the meantime Harvey maintains his ground, & with the help of two curates, and a third as soon as he can find a suitable man, carries out the System of the Church in its entirety. With Mr. Whitehead I am unacquainted personally: nor have I ever heard him named by any of our brethren: but I believe he is liked by those who have attended his Church, but who, I need not say, are parties objecting to the real system of our Church. If I can be of any service to you in making enquiries on this or any other matter, do not hesitate to command my

---

[6] The Revd Henry Wilberforce, Rector of East Farleigh Kent, until his defection to Rome in 1850. The Bishop's youngest brother. Whitehead became incumbent of Gawcott, Beds, in 1849.

BOOK ONE 5

services. I find much to do in my new sphere of duty, tho' it is small as compared with Ash: & wish for my own sake that I had you in your former position at Walmer.

With earnest prayers for your continued usefulness & exertions in your present, or any position to which you may be called,
>Believe me to be,
>My dear Mr Wilberforce,
>>Your faithful and affec[tiona]te Brother,
>>Edward Penny[7]

Mr. Whitehead is the son of the Mr. W. who for some years has had a large School in Ramsgate, a layman.

15–16   [*inserted octavo paper*]

I Charles Mallard Bachelor of Arts of Trinity College Oxford, having lately been induced by the persuasion of certain persons to make profession of obedience to the Bishop of Rome, contrary to my bounden duty and previous engagements in the Church of England, do hereby declare and acknowledge that I sinned in so doing, and do hereby, so far as in me lies, revoke the said profession as unlawful and void.

And whereas I did at the same time profess my acceptance and belief, on the authority of the Church of Rome, of certain doctrines respecting Purgatory, the Invocation of Saints, Transubstantiation, The Supremacy of the Roman Church, &c, as articles of Faith, in addition to the Nicene Creed; I declare that I ought not to have accepted any such additions to the Faith, neither do I hold anything on any of these points contrary to the doctrine of the Church of England, as laid down in the XXXIX articles, and that I desire in these, as in other things, to submit myself humbly to the teaching of the Church of England, as the portion of Christ's Holy Catholic Church to which I belong.

And for these my faults and errors I humbly desire pardon of God and of His Church, and that I may be received back into the Communion of the Church of England so soon as I have given sufficient proof of a sincere return and amendment.

[*signed*] Chas.E.Mallard [*no date*]

16v, 17 [*blank*]

17v, 18 [*List of parishes in office hand (f.18), with jottings in pencil on facing page (f 17v)*]

---

[7] Curate of Ash, Kent, and Six Preacher in Canterbury Cathedral.

17v

Ambroseden – odd unmethodical energetic (Sportsman?)
Bletchingdon Dand Curate of Broughton. Shy. Good earnest man

Charlton Rigges. Inactive – drone – Bee in a bottle

Cottisford ... 1849. W Talman. Quiet. (Tall, soft-looking)

God[dington] Church about to be rebuilt at once. Mr H[averfield] to pay to Beedon towards Parsonage fund five pounds annually.

18

Bicester Deanery
Ardley R Lowe G. 56 M With me but scratchy – very good – moderate – if anything low.
Ambroseden V Dryden 40 B. PC Hamletts. Schematic.
Bletchingdon R Vane. Resigned for Lady Day
Bicester V
Bucknall R Master. 50 New Coll. New Rectory built by self.
Arch[deacon] very good man. Safe man. Active. Low.
Secretary to Eden. Moderate.
Charlton R

Chesterton V Aubrey Price 58. M. Once in gaol for debt. Safe – working well.
Elder Brother of Price of B.[8]
Cottisford R Hodgson Provost [of Eton] Dyke PC [corrected to SC] 40/M (oddish, moderate, attends)
Finmere R Mr Palmer R. Mr Wood resident eff[icient] Daily serv[ice] m & a
Fringford R Mr Roundell (a little huffish)
Fritwell V Mr Rawlings V. residing not in Parsonage wh[ich] getting. Does duty for [*illegible*]. Not gentleman. Rumours etc ... Mrs Willes [married lady]
Goddington R Pop 100 but Inc.334. No resident Curate. Haverfield.
Perkins Good. Steady

---

[8] Britwell Salome, where A Price, also rector of Down Ampney, is noted as being 92 years old.

Mr Perkins about 50. curate for 6 years residing at Twyford Parsonage.
2 services at Twy[ford] and 1 at God[dington].
2 in summer but only 1 sermon.

Hardwick Prater, "very high." Nervous. Fidgety yet sense

Kirtlington Curate "straight sound Churchman". The Rector a little priggish & finical. Likely to get into[trouble]

Hampton Poyle R Dodd G M. 40. M. (Very good man. Sound. North Country.)

Hampton Gay C Peculiar. Hill of St Edmund Hall.

Heyford Warren R Baker. 60. Violent. Poaches.

Heyford Bridge R Faithful 50. Pupils who hunt. V good about him. Hunter. Sub[tle?] clever, careful, farmers man.

Hethe R Slatter. Very good. Out of health
Resident at Cumnor. Curate Shurlock – not yet licensed.

Hardwick R Prater. (Should be joined to Tusmore).
Should have service once a day

Islip R

Kirtlington R Guillemard. Madman. Brother curate GM. Ch Tower £300 to Sir G. Dashwood

Launton R

Lillingston Lovell R Lloyd G M (A[rchdeacon:] very good man)

Merton R Stupart. Invalid.
Rumours of resign[ation].
Dissenters.
Rawlinson (anti–Gol[ightly])

Middleton Stoney R Pretyman .... Matthews PC (A[rchdeacon] Cricketer. Dull). Good gardener. Huge tulip.

Mixbury R Mr Palmer 2ce daily S[ervices]

18v, 19 [*spread across two pages*]
Newton Purcell R Meade. New Parsonage. Res[ident]. M. Deaf. Does well.
Oddington R Serle 58 m g Zel. Odd High & Dry – but takes pains. Scientific. Geologist.
Shelswell R Should be joined to Newton Purcell sm[all] Chur[ch] or Pop[ulation]
Somerton R <u>Clifton.</u> Manchester. nephew Young man. Rather unhappy, indiscreet.
"Young man favourable" <u>B of K</u> (Elder brother at Manchester, The Rector)
Souldern R Dr Stephenson 40 G M Pupils. "Cantab. Good. Very eccentric" <u>B of K</u>
Immoral 2 such returned, prosecution stopped. A[rchdeacon]. – eccentric, no influence in Parish. Lets all go their own way. Turns Church into Childrens & his own playground. Extempore Visitation Sermon Clear, Common Place. Views his own. Baptised 4 of his own children at once at 7 p.m. Great Servants [settlement–day] 1846
Stoke Lyne V Pop[ulation] 593. Net Inc[ome] 173. Caversfield Pop 123 Net Inc 69.
Mr Bullock to Mr C Marsham some 50 years ago. Service once a day – Disputed house at Caversfield – no resident clergyman at either.
Stratton Audley PC Owen Wife health Ch. Ch. P.C. [Clayton]
Piddington PC Cleobury 56 Well. Piddington (Cleobury) brother of surgeon, not intellectual, moderate, fair work –
Tusmore R [??Geckby] Should be with Hardwick. Never resident.
Wendlebury R Brown. 32. G. M. Brown "very good man" "takes sound views". Shy.
Weston on the Green V Matthews. <u>Good magistrate</u>. Connex[ion] of LordA[bingdon] High and Dry. Very kind hearted. Owner of land at Weston One of Lord A's trustees. Lost an eldest son, a young man traced to near London. Very poor. (Came back after year and ½ – more than 20 years ago – supposed insanity and half drowned)
2 Sons in orders – 1 Pretyman's curate at Middleton, one Beauchamp's curate.

BOOK ONE 9

19v [*pencil notes*]

Ascott & Leafield Together should be parted. Tolerable energy. Not so good as brother

Nov 27 1846 Langston a[bout] to build a School. NB the hamlet to be parted from Charlbury & with or better without Shorthampton made a separate cure with £300 per annum if St Johns will agree

[Diagram to show linkage between Chadlington, Langston, Shorthampton]

20 [*List in Wilberforce's own hand*]
Chipping Norton
Ascott PC joined with Leafield 3 miles apart Rev E [should be W] Williams. Gift of Vicar of Shipton.
Phillimore vicar of S. Brother of Dr Ph.
Rev E W about 40 PC dira paup[errimu]s: rather [moderate] Orthodox. Infirm in feet.
[*pencil note added*: Died 1848]
Charlbury Dr Silver. Poor. Full of Dissenters
Chiefly Dissenters. liberal.
NB excen[tri]c without influence
Chadlington. C[urate] Godfrey about 30. Nephew of Dr S. has been sailor. Forced into O[rders] by Dr S., pauperrimus. Clown in H[eave]n most good–tempered but!
[*pencil note, replacing whole entry*: Dismissed by me for Drunkenness Oct 1846]
Shorthampton
Finstock another chapelry. Bell ordained Dec 1845.
[Pencil note: £150 from Bazaar now £250. This is to be taken if possible to House]
[*Pencil note*: resigned 1848]

Chastleton Horatio Westmacott. Married Miss Poole (Copes people) a very excellent amiable man, Pleasing preacher, no twist.
[*Pencil note:* High Church. Rather Con[ciliatory]. Quite in earnest himself]

Chipping Norton (D[ea]n & Cap Gloster living) Robey Eldridge. [*pencil note:* Low Church, worn down] not up to situation as could Morell of Sibtoft. But respectable – dearly beloved by poor. Wholly given to his work. Long-sermoned & very fit for Country Par[ish]

20v **Church Hill, V.** held by Mr Barter. £75 raised to £200. Church built by Mr Langston &c. &c.
Cornwell, R. Do. (90) inhabitants. Held with for curate.
Enstone. Jordan. cum Brown[e] of Kiddington. Write to Lord Dillon [???] cum Curme Sandford
Fifield Merrymouth – Idbury Talmage – who had done great good at Finstock, married to Dr Silver's niece.
(*pencil note:* very industrious good man – simple minded – Draper's son in Ox[ford])
Heythrop ... Lord Shrewsbury's seat. Great R.C chapel. Chapel fell down & repairing. Rebuilt by Mr Barter. Mr Samuel came as curate to Chipping Norton. Indefatigable Much liked. about 35 Country bred. Steadying pretty well. Chaplain [Work] House of Chipping Norton [*Pencil note:* Weale]

21 **Hook Norton** Beautiful Church found to be falling down. Mr B 600 miles.... Given at Mr B's request to Curate of Banbury, Jn Rushton –very worthy man.
[*Pencil note:* A[rchdeacon] – very good Hardworking & from work health hurt]
Kingham Lockwood owns greater part of parish. Very respect[able] man, has repaired Church nicely at his own expense. Memorial to little girl. Some connexion with Pus[eyites]. Used to have Chelsea.
(A[rchdeacon]: Low, not very [much] so – very good)
Leafield
Rollright Great   BNC patron. Tench 80. "Church and King" man past. The Tithes let for his life: but a small pension out: Mr B to see if he can arrange for a tutor.
[*inserted note*: Dead 1848]
[*Pencil note:* Hill curate. Tench retiring 1846.] Eat up with Dissent.
Rollright Little. Held by Rector of Salford Mr Stevens [*Pencil note:* Poor creature] about 40. Worthy; takes pupils. Child drown *(sic)*. Miss her. Whole parish belongs to Sir John Reade and son.
Rich. One farm. Ch[urch]warden &c Dissenters. Very Pretty Ch: needing repair.

21v **Salford** [*pencil*] Stevens
Sarsden Mr Barter. This and Church Hill all belong to Mr Langstone, above.
550 pop: in the 2.
Shipton under Wychwood <u>Phillimore</u> vicar – Eccentric, no influence.
Patron Dr P[hillimore] Professor of Civil Law
Magistrate Much neglect
                }Leafield
Mr Williams }Ramsden with Finstock Mr Bell [*Pencil note:* strange]
above   }Ascott   unsatisfactory
Lyneham pop 300. Mr Langston would build & endow. Phillimore will not allow.
Spelsbury Pat[rons] Ch[rist] Ch[urch]. Mr Williams from Tring – an improvident match. Lord Dillon, Mr and Mrs Capt Evans proprietors. Licence for Non Res[idence] for two years from Bp Bagot, a quer[y] when intending to resign when elsewhere established. [*illegible*] of incumbent of Ch. Good Mr Tucker curate. Quiet, modest but well reported of.
Swerford R Magd Chambers (Rector) Old sportsman. Amiable. (Drives well)
Gentlemanlike. Chancel repaired. Very infirm. Mr Paterson (ordained Dec 1845) curate. Church falling down. Mr Walling professing all will be done
Banbury Mr Forbes has served & so entitled to new district of South Banbury

22v

23

Adderbury New [College] Charles Alcock N.L.C. Baring was curate 2 years. Independent meeting there. Church well
C Bodicott <u>To be separated.</u> <u>Land.</u> G[Warriner] 30 pretty good. indiff[eren]t [*pencil note:* Low Church takes pains.] Married man with invalid wife. Some means from 1st wife

Barford St John (Little) A little fat heavy man to be classed with Dryden – a peg or two below. I have great misgivings about Mr Hall – he would say, 'best be made ice'.

Barford C Little To be united to other Barford. H.W. Hall: Strange things. Bred Surgeon. Cynical. Endeavours. Irreverent. Resides at Deddington. Quere why not reside. Compounder of Sermons for lithograph. Buried not even baptised.

Alkerton Lord Jersey. R[ector] Rev. E Hughes:
74 [*dead*]. Rather Puss. Dr Bull's brother married his sister. Takes English Churchman. Good sort of man.
[*Pencil note:* Son has it now 1846. Fond of cricketing and shooting formerly]
Barford St Michaels Donative gift of Col Hall.
Held by H.W.Hall. of Little Barford above.
Bloxham P[opulation] 2000 £300 P[atron] Eton Coll[ege] G Bell 83 'I was afraid of Puseyism, I was afraid of Low Church & I have got hold of J[esus] C[hrist]. I abhor Low Churchmen'
G Saunders (very infirm) extreme Low Church. 50. Married. Paup[er]. Weaklier utinam devout (Son of dissenter & very weak)
Milcombe. hamlet served once a month by clergyman of Wigginton thrice a month by clergyman of Bloxham Bloxham Church "magnificent"
(Complaint from Mr Back June 2 1846. Wrote)
Broughton Rev C Wyatt. 53. no calibre but right–minded, not very devout, wealthy. Son Curate F Wyatt ordained Priest very promising. High Ch[urch] Puss: rather
North Newington Hamlet (No Church)
P[arish] a family living Church good. Parsonage d[itt]o & School. A man more to cast up accounts, but anxious to have good curates.

Rev. Halford B Burdett – at Broughton near Kettering Northamptonshire has been asked to shoot with Lord Douglas on his manor. Will give it up & in future not take certificate.
Rather Heavy. W Latimer 1849 not licensed

1 Cropredy[9] **& Bourton**
2 Wardington
3 Mollington & Claydon
W Holbeck Esq
Farnborough Park
Banbury

Drayton Lloyd. Magistrate absent some years ago on account of Diff[iculties]

Hanwell A good man. Little old fashioned.
Good man in Parish. Likes things to go on as they are. Low rather than high. Not remarkable. Plain minded good sort of man
Swaycliffe Very good man but crotchety on High Church De[ ] Visit[ation] sermon Anti-Hymns Service at same hours

Cropredy[10] Pec[ulia]r Jno Ballard, 65, Old school. Gentleman. (Moderate) Fine Church Excellent Parsonage
Wardington – 1 Service H[amlet] Ch[urch]
Ormerod fellow of BNC Dreadful stammer. Church quite empty
<u>From 500 to 30 (Old Mr Powys)</u>
Mollington H Ch Ballard
Claydon H Ch Ormerod Fellow of BNC
Gt Bourton H No Ch
Little Bourton H No Ch

Drayton Rev W Lloyd Lord Delaware Patron
Pop 206 Income £400. Not over accurate as to [money] &c. No influence. Not a man one likes to speak about
Hanwell <u>Pearce</u>. Not respected – a son of Magd[alen] demy. Respectable. Humdrum. No energy. No devotion. Pop 500 Lord Delawarr Patron

Swaycliffe New Coll: Rev E Payne a good man, active and efficient every way. High Church but quite right. Efficient – fit if need were for Rural Dean. Brother to Payne of Dunster
[*Pencil note:* M Payne – Scandal?]
Epwell & Shutford H C Rev C Thorpe
Not satisfactory, with an awkward [?sting]

---

[9] Actually spelt Croperdy.
[10] Actually spelt Croperdy.

Sibford T M A[rchdeacon]: I never heard that extreme

M (Michael) Harrison A[rch-deacon] "Dull man like Rawlings"

24v

Tadmarton R Lea A[rchdeacon] Comfortable looking man . Non Res[ident] for years. Middle aged and middling in every way

Wigginton A[rchdeaon] Williams. Good & very nice person, tending rather to low. Bad health, eyes bad. 'I and [? Harrington] contending for the body of Williams.'
Quere Curate?
[*ink note*: Mr Cookes Curate 1849 (efficient)]

Sibford (Mr Miller. Well) (T Morrell A more efficient man but Puss Puss [*crossed out*])
Pop 800 [*pencil note:* District Church taken from Swalcliffe]
Wroxton Rev T Wyatt. Man of considerable fortune. Non resident. Brother to C Wyatt.
Delicate health & better away. A good man but very singular uncouth.
Mr Harrison. Does his duty well.
Wroxton Col. & Lady Susan North Col. North a good supporter of Church.
Balscot H & Church in most miserable repair
Horley (Pec.) Sir Jno Seymour's living.
[*Pencil note:* Curate Pinwell 1849]

25

Banbury Deanery
Tadmarton R Lea, near 60 right–minded, well–affected man, not particularly devout

South Newington (A better creature does not live) Not quite a Puss [*pencil note*: An anti]
H D Harrington – was curate to late Rect[or] of Exeter
Evans "x x" B of K
Wigginton Rev. Jno Williams: a straight-minded man. His curate Dand a most excellent man
[*pencil note*: & now Bletchingdon]

Great Tew A[rchdeacon] High Church active

Great Tew J J Campbell. A very dour man.
Quite a [fancy plan about] – Bolton Little Tew greatly needs another Church
Worton Upper Incum[bent] just dead. Young Wilson to me
Worton Lower Claims to be extra Episcopal

26 **Deddington** [crossed out: Rev. W Risley. To reside in hired house curate in parsonage
Clifton H[amlet] Hempton H[amlet] Spurrell Going. Bad tempered.
Mr R wishes these endowed]
Brodgen 1847
Banbury Mardon was Baptist preacher. Unfit. Forbes good man –very.

28 [*Inserted page on Oxford parishes, in another hand*]
All Saints Revd. J Meredith just come Peculiar under Lincoln College. Two full services morn: & Evening. Pop: 560. No poor.
S. Aldates Revd. Mr Hawkins Rector non resident. Revd. John Ley Curate. Morn: & Aft: Services. Boys and Girls Schools. Pop: 2000.
Binsey Revd. Robert Hussey. 1 Service Morn: & Afternoon alternately. Peculiar. 60 Population.
S.Clements' Revd. J W Hughes. Two services. Schools endowed. Parish never visited. 20£ offered by the Small Livings Fund for a Curate, but not yet claimed. Pop: 1850.
S.Giles Revd. W Hunter. Pop: 2000 – rapidly increasing. Church not half large enough and no free seats. Services Morn: & Aft:. Boys and Girls Schools.
Summertown – Vacant. Hamlet of preceding. Pop about 700. Church built 15 years ago. School wanted.
S.Ebbe Old Church. Rector insane. Curates Revds. C. W.Heaton & W. F. Audland. Pop: 2000. 3 Services. 2 Schools.
S.Ebbe Holy Trinity Revd. J. West Pop: 2000. No schools at present. Services morn: & aftern:
S.John Baptist Merton Chaplains. Pop:120. No service.
S.Martin Revd. W. H. Cox. Pop: 400. No poor. Serv: Morn: & Evening. City Lecturers.
11. **S.Mary Magdalen** xx Revd. Jacob Ley Vicar. Revd.E Marshall Curate. Pop: 2600 Morn: & Aft: Service. 3 Schools.
12. **S.Mary the Virgin** xx Revd. C. P. Eden. Service Morn: & Aftern: Pop; 400.

13. **Littlemore** xx Revd. W Copeland, Curate. Service Morn: & Aft: Schools.
14. **S.Cross or Holywell** Revd. E. M. Goulburn. Serv: Morn: & Aftern: Few poor. Daily service given up last summer.
15. **S.Michaels** Revd. J. Calcot & M. J. Green Curates. Peculiar under Lincoln College.
16. **S.Peter le Bailey** Rector Mr. Penson xx non–resident. Curates Revd. W. Chepmell & J. H. Pollen. 3 Services. 3 Schools.
17. **S.Peter in the East** Revd. E. Hobhouse Vicar. H. Hansell Curate. xx 3 Services. Schools. Popn: 1200.
18. **S.Thomas** Revd. T[homas] C[hamberlain] Perp.Curate.
Revd. J.L. Patterson Curate.
3 services. 3 schools Pop: 2000
* Boatmen's Chapel Revd. A. P. Forbes – Chaplain
19. **S.Paul's** Revd. A. Hackman. Revd Mr Nott Curate. 3 Services. Girls' Schools. University School for Boys. Population 2500
20. **Wolvercote** Revd. Mr Judge, Chaplain of Mer[ton] 2 Services. A School.

  x Daily Service, once.
  xx Daily Services, twice.

29 [*missing, torn out*]

30 [*blank*]

30v   31

Cuddesdon Deanery

Albury with Tiddington New Church built by Lord Abingdon, Pat[ron] & Parsonage House. F. Bertie – always there, & magistrate. Lady Geor....

Baldon Toot Supposed to be a Donative, but no one instituted for many years. Golightly supposed to be. He has thoroughly repaired the Church. Service alternate with Marsh Baldon served by curate Mr. Macdougall

Baldon Marsh Pec:[uliar] of Dorchester Hugh Willoughby – nominally resident at another living. Sad quarrel.

Beckley. Old fashioned. Farmer. Painstaking

Beckley P.C. <u>Revd. T. Leigh Cooke</u> 65. Late fellow of Magd[alen] holds living in Essex. Resides at Beckley: where he has a large Farm. Liberal and kind. Church wants rest[or]ing. Mr C promises to do it having done the chancel well.

32 **Bensington** P.C. Ch[rist]Ch[urch] Least satisfactory popn. Parsons, Student of Ch Ch very good & active man. Rather inclining to Tra[ctarianism] "Strongest in our parts" but no introduct[io]n. Opinions stronger than practice. 35. Very anxious to do his duty.
Chislehampton cum Stadhampton Mr. Peers. United about 4 years ago. Perry most laborious & industrious in Parish. Churchman grafted on to Evangel:[ical]. Most tender conscience & much valued in Parish.
Clifton Hampden P.C. A very good man, Jos. Gibbs. Most attentive, & also to his Schools. Comfortably off. Everything in Parish very satisfactory.
Cowley P.C. * David Royce just come. Roof unsafe. The Rural Dean has named it to the Archdeacon. [*pencil*: Spoke to A Nov 3]

34 **Cuddesdon**
Culham Bp Oxon R Wintle (Father to Mrs Gilbert) Rich. Hypochondriac ("Mr Wingfield, you will give me cold") Walker 1849. Mr Coxe, curate, resides at Oxford & comes over constantly. A good Parsonage.
Dorchester P.C. Money raised for the House? Cooper Fellow of Wadham – a very good attentive man. resides const[ant]ly . J.F.Addison 1850.
Drayton PC Pec[uliar] of Dorchester Coley lives entirely out of society: vitae suspectae. Methodists complete command & he does nothing (Too much confirmed from Revelations of Housekeeper in Lunatic Asylum – children – & <u>gone</u> 1850)!*

33v Summoned him Sept 20 1850 Stated the charges, & inter alia, that during Service there had been charges thrown out. He denies absolutely & proposes that I should see his Farmers. Is to send them to me tomorrow.

33 [*small leaf inserted between 32v and 34*]
Drayton Farmers.
<u>Betteridge</u>. He goes to Stadhampton son and son's wife church.
<u>Dran.</u> – a most respectable well informed man: <u>believing the reports</u>
<u>Smith</u> – Farms half the Parish & is Mr C's Churchwarden. A poor nature. Good humoured Farmers.
Lord Abingdon & Trinity College the Proprietors. Patrons D & C of C Ch.

Has known the parish 40 years. Does not fear for his Character. Would like me to enquire of his farmers or any Parishioners.

34 (*continued*)
Elsfield V Lady S. North. Gordon. New parsonage house. None before. A very good clergyman. Might serve Woodeaton. Church not in good state. Presented by the Rural Dean to the Archdeacon.

35 **Forest Hill** P C Lincoln Coll. Mavor, probably insane – in Castle. All miserable. Served by Mr.Slight fellow of Corpus & apparently attentive. A New House built for living quite recently.
Garsington Annexed to Presid[en]t of Trinity. Mr Thurland, Chaplain of New Coll. resides in parsonage on very small means. Son of Chemist – a good man. Succeeded W Pusey.
[??] pop: Parsonage house & Church good.
Haseley – D[ean] of Windsor. Burkit curate – <u>Loquax</u>. Business. Clever man – writes Dr. Hobart's sermons. About Gilbert's standing.
Mr Hammersley anxious to do right. He too a most valuable man rel[igiousl]y minded man & very useful. Sister to Mr. Phillipps holds under the See at Culham.
Dissent rife at Haseley & a new meeting house of large size built. Independents?

36 **Headington** Most important in Deanery – poor preferment held by Chaplain of New Coll. Mr <u>Pring</u> resides at Bottom of Headington Hill – Quere if in the Parish – not very energetic. Respectable. No National School. R Dean been moving for it.
Holton Tyndale. Very attentive but x – Church and House repaired. Chancel [in] a very nice state.
Horse Path Held by Fellow of Magdalen. Held now by Mr Harris, Senr. Proctor. Lately there. Church in bad State. Magd: Coll. have <u>well</u> rebuilt the Chancel. Dr. Ellerton tried to get them to raise rate. This named to Arch[deacon]n.
Milton Great Pec[uliar] T Ellis Old man of 85 or 86 never very active. Method[ist] meeting late. Mr Shephard married his daughter & struck with

37 state of Parish went into Orders as Squire – to serve as Curate of Pa[rish]: Well off. Good active man. Opposed to Tractarians. Proper mean.
Milton Little New district Church – distinct Parish. <u>Ashurst,</u> son of Ashurst of Waterstock. A very excellent young man & the build[in]g the Church & conduct of young man done a great deal. Not at all Tract[aria]n. Resides close to Little Milton. Gr[eat] Milton tithes belong to Prebend of Milton Lincoln – extinct. Property merges in Eccl[esiastical] Comm[ission] yet on lease. Old Chapel in Litt. Milton – app[lication] to rebuild it. Fix.

[pencil entry] Nettlebed. ? Hazel. Low – Wallingford family. Good sort of man.
[pencil entry] Newington Pec[uliar] of Arch[bishop of Canterbury] A[rchdeacon:] Coles. Neighbours do not augur well. Something very odd. Thinks himself ruined, is very close.

38 **Nuneham:** Mr Baker. R[ural]Dean.
Noke Very retired. Near Islip. Carlyle. Retired country, respectable. A very poor place R.D. knows little.

37v Carlisle North Country man – respectable – was curate of Woodstock – supposed respectable.

38 **Sandford** Don[ative] Service done by someone for love of the work. Barker cousin of Puseys – ordained by the late B[isho]p for Sandford – lives at Puseys..
Stanton St John New Coll. Stonehouse a good serious man, very nervous, does little duty.
Warborough White a descendant of Selborne. Very energetic. Wholly devoted to Parish. No fuss. Got excellent school, bad population.

39 **Waterstock, R.** Small endowment. Mr Jordan a quiet man, but talker – does little. 2 Miss Ashursts admirable curates. all in village.
Wheatley P C
Woodeaton R Small popn. Church good repair. Good House. No dissenters. Ballard of Cropredy.

38v John Ballard – Curate – only son. black. fond of field sports & worldly, not respectable. Married one of the Fanes of Wormsley.

38 **Yeffley** Rev.H Woolcombe. Active & good, lives at Exeter [College] but [?] cent[rally]

40 **Henley Deanery 1845**
Deanery of Henley Rev.F.K.Leighton
Bix 1 Church. Hor: Pechell R. Lady Caroline very amiable, excellent, so he also. But not clerk. All smallest measure. No pecul[iarity], kind. 53 or 54. Very estimable Gentleman. Church found in good repair. A small school supported by Mr Pechell. Lord Camoys the chief proprietor
NB a second service much <u>needed.</u>
Caversham P.C. £150. Joshua Bennett. Was in very neglected state. He been there 3 years, has built a house. Active and energetic. Sound Churchman valued in Parish. Brusque, rather [*in Greek letters*] agroikos. Good school at Caversham. One wanted in the higher up part near Shiplake

Mapledurham. He anxious to have one but failed. Yet undaunted & not self sparing. Not wealthy.

41 **Henley Deanery 1845**
Checkendon R W Crabtree. &c.
Crowmarsh Gifford Jno. Trollope, R. Not active. At South Stoke. Diss[ent] increased under him. No influence.
Goring, P.C. Hunter F Fell. A good man, rather bitter against Pus[eyites]. Macfarlane (x) lives a retired life, small means & weak health.
Harpsden Mr Hall principal proprietor of 4/5.... a peculiar Family. Now Church man – about 200 years. Sportsman. Not rel:[igious] man.

42 **Henley, R.** James King, R resident at Longfield Court, Gravesend. Quere ground of exemption.
F T Burlton, Curate – hard working, overworked – sound Churchman, not Pus:[eyite], married & large family. Mother lives & sister & blind brother.
J King promised the late Bishop a second Curate in 1845. Place overrun with Dissent. Mr Burlton unlicensed. Mr King left a Mr C F Fox – Pus:[eyite] Desiderata – 2nd Curate & Chapel at Greys.
T K Chittenden, Chaplain to the Henley Union. Respectable man without activity.
MapleDurham, V. Lord Augustus FitzClarence – very liberal & Kind. Sees no society. Married Miss Gordon.
G Hutchins – Quere is he licensed [NO] a very active painstaking parish Priest, rather noisy mannered, been about 8 years. Parish well in Hand.

43 **Henley Deanery 1845**
Mongewell, R. Dr Durell, 84 or 85. Mr Troloppe curate. Quere [*pencil* (by White)] licensed [NO]. Parish & Church in good condition.
Nuffield Rev. T Hopkins
Nettlebed Hazell a respectable & active man. Church enlarged & restored. Schools. [*Pencil note*: "Most have low standards" &c.]
Pishill cap [chapel] **to Rotherfield Greys** W.M Kinsey. Flag Admiral K. inaccessible. Dinnerer. Good Rectory. Mr Paxton C. Believed to be going. Son of the Oxford Surgeon. Very inefficient. No rel[igious] opin[ions]. Lives at Henley, supposed to take care of that part of Parish. Does not. NB Ask Archdeacon Clerke as to ordination.
Desiderata – Church at Henley. Curate & no K.

44 **Henley Deanery 1845**
[Rotherfield] **Peppard** Jesus NB. R. Prichard, very aged, quite past. Kindhearted, liberal. R Powys curate, not license. Too distant. Good many Independents.
NB No collection at Communion.

Shiplake D & C of Windsor. A Howman V. More than 80. Passee. Very small living – large parish with 2 or 3 Dissenting Chapels. Nice parish.
NB Mr Hockley Curate (28 or 30) very unpopular with poor – non–chalant & neglectful. Q. licensed. Dr Phillimore lives Here. Q His son might help. Mr Cotton, Son D[ea]n of Bangor was curate & good.
Ipsden R. T. Twopenny. painstaking , agriculture, eccl[esiastical] architecture, rather lo[w] than Pus[eyite]
North Stoke Mr Hurle curate. Good sort of man. Not very active.

45   **Henley Deanery 1845**
Newton Murren in Ipsden Chief endowment of Ipsden. NB Service once a month.
Church bad – & green
Stoke Row
South Stoke with Woodcote Philip Henry Nind… Good Churchman & not more.
Reyroux. Curate about 45…underbred. Farmer fellow. Great deal of Dissent. The yeomen diss[enter]s Independent & Baptist. Anglo–Saxon..
Swincombe Hon & Rev A H Napier – painstaking earnest zealous parish priest, full of prejudice against everything new, and so versus Mr K[eene] in terms of conversat[io]n , one pro the other opposing. (Mr Keene clerical squire here almost entire.)
Napier disappointed & proud & poor. [Faded as to margins]. Little dissent. Agricultural.
Mr Keene to be known. She a Sussex Shiffner Sir H's sister.

46 **Whitchurch** E Moore about 50, painstaking ... Churchman rather than Pus[eyite]. Was of B.N.C. of Lord Cottenham's [preferment]. NB Director of some London Waterworks. Par[ish] well attended to.

        Woodstock Deanery Rev Dr Richards RD Jan 1846
Aston North V Brown about 50 not resident, res[ident] at Kidlington.... because no House. There is a glebe… "Cracked Pitcher" – … Newspaper dabbler. Liberale. No work in him.
No seriousness. 12 miles off ..Very little there.
Begbroke R Ellis Ashton [*Pencil insertion*: Non resident – a very respectable man] There for six months. Richards lives in [rent] house. Son of R[ector] of Bath. Judicious...not energetic or devout. Of the High Church side. [*Pencil note:* Papists in Manor H[ouse].]
Bladon Suff[iciently] endowed 1or 2 miles from Woodstock & gets only a service between the Woodstock services. NB.
Woodstock [*pencil note*: NB] Dr Bowles. Character suspected. Funeral interpolated in service. Great coxcombe.

45v Quere? is the separate endowment of Woodstock enough to maintain

46v [rough inked-in map of parishes in Woodstock Deanery]

47   **Cassington** Small Ch Ch living. Forster Chaplain of New Coll: serves it from Oxford.. Sleeps one night in week. Respectable man. No great zeal or courage ...There is a decent House. Resp[ectable] no influence no courage or [spirit] or devot[io]n
[*pencil note*: A[rchdeaon] very poor no courage but a good man. Clever man & good]
Combe Long A[rchdeacon] Lincoln Coll. served by [*blank; presumably John Hannah*] clever man and good scholar. Pupils.
* Col. Bowles Patron talks of building house. Married a Montagu sister of Mrs Goulburn.
Aston North Browne, Robert. Nothing in his favour. Quere Radical. Low opinions. Poor benefice & no house – very ineff[icient] man. Resides at Kidlington – of a wine merchant's family.
Dunstew Malcolm ...temperate moderate man. (The Loftus case). Turned out of house for Col.[*replaced by* Sir] George Dashwood's Son (very zealous person – N Wilson) NB.
[*Pencilled note*: A[rchdeacon]: Nice little man. Timid. Nep[hew] of Sir Pulteney.[11] Father[12] a good parish priest in Worcestershire.]
Ensham Simcox Bricknell, presented by wife.... a lecturer at Carfax, low church, zealous.
Glympton .. small place. Old gentleman Nucella, a worthy man, primitive simplicity. Effic[ien]t Ord[inar]y church.
[*Pencilled note*: A[rchdeacon]: nice old man. Does his duty steadily.]

47v, 48 [*blank*]

49   **Handborough** Dr Wynter.
Mr Wright – respectable man, takes pupils, rather inclining to High Church.
[*Pencilled note*: A[rchdeacon]: A great cricketer, not low.]
Kiddington Browne. Good natured, hot headed, ultra low Church. The Ricardo case (– influential with his class), Hold [*sic*] clerical meeting at his house. Frank, unreserved.. earnest.
Kidlington Water Eaton (a domestic chapel) Dr. Richards ... Anstis. Satisfactory man from Menheniot – sober minded, sound judging, valued by Parishioners and Hardworking
South Leigh
Stanton Harcourt. 1 service on Sundays

[11] Admiral Sir Pulteney Maberton, 1768–1838.
[12] Gilbert Malcolm, Rector of Todenham, Gloucestershire.

49v [pencil]

Rousham A[rchdeacon] very amiable, ordinary, nothing at all amiss. Attends to his parish . Old fashioned, neither high nor low.

50

Rowsham [sic] Dandridge. Low Church, constitutionally indolent. Parish small –120 people....Cotterell Dormer squire, Miss Cotterell[13] his sister amongst poor & good Church Woman.
("quiet attentive P.P.". B of K)

50 **Sandford** House lately built. Mr Curme – private chapl[ain] to Duchess.[14] Low views as Evangelical. Man of piety. Devout. Pupils but tolerably active... Church nicely restored by him, which looks well. Anxiety about kneeling, getting up. Yet extreme in some way.
("xx" B of K "very nice person")
Shipton on Cherwell Small parish. Passand not clerical....wants gravity & sense. Companies with lower class of farmers &c. Sporting, yet overpowered with weight of his office....seems shy.....quere is he mad or <u>drinks</u>
Stanton Harcourt Walsh. Father late Rector. A house to be built. A pleasing young man, not impress you as having much mind or seriousness. Moderate views of his Church.

51 **Woodstock Deanery**
Steeple Aston Burrows about 60 – of the Old School. Church nicely restored by Parish – regularly sleepy (some pains taking). Browne of Kiddington .
[*Pencil note*]: A[rchdeacon] "D[itt]o" Long time fellow of Oriel. Obstinate withal.

50v [*Pencil*]

Steeple Barton – Wright

51

Steeple Barton – miserable thing. Oakley serves it from Enstone on stipend of £40. There is a non-resident vicar, pauper et ineps.

51 **Stonesfield** Robinson, son of Banker – rather inclining to Evan[gelicals] but moderate. Fairly good: nothing remarkable in activity, out of heart. "very useful man"– <u>B of K</u>.
[*pencil*]: A[rchdeacon]: Very good hardworking. I don't think low church. Associates with Brown[e] – Chieveley Br[other]. Best of 2.

---

[13] Presumably Elizabeth, half-sister by his father's first marriage of Charles Cotterell-Dormer, 1801–1874.
[14] Of Marlborough.

50v [*Pencil*]: 51

A[rchdeacon]: very earnest good man. Right minded. Quarrelled about Tithes

Tackley Sharpe...joins Mr Browne's clerical meeting. They complain of him as High Church. Nervous irritability – quarrel now with Turner about Baptisms. Anxious to do good. Devout. Conscientious, upright, well prin-cipled ("Was a Tractar: but is now open–eyed – remarks on Faber's letter as dishonest" B of K

Westcott Barton A[rchdeacon] Very undecided. Fond of smoking, plausible, talks well, unsatisfactory, Magistrate.

Westcott Barton Segrave....built house & resides. Sides rather with High Ch[urch], dry, frigid & unzealous. (Too fond of hunting for much past[oral] zeal. B of K) [*Seagrave.*]

52 **Woodstock Deanery**

Wilcot Very small, not 20. Served by curate of Handborough. 1 service on Sunday.

Wootton Lee. (New Coll. living) respectable, wealthy. House made too large. Not very zealous – rather high & dry – <u>did not know</u> if subscribe or not to S.P.G.

Yarnton Vaughan Thomas – a small house – high & dry. Above £300 a year.

Aston Deanery

Adwell Buckle R

Glandville (curate)

Aston Rowant Williams. Active man – respect[able] Good Clerk. Suggested as RD by Kerby.

Stoken Church Young, brother of Sir W.Young. Building a house. Doubt if means to live, & no exemption.

53 **Baldwin Brightwell R** Day. Respectable gent[lema]n. Active man. Married daught[er] of L Stone.

Q possible RD.

Brightwell Salome <u>Price</u> aged 92. Wonderful old man. Mr K remembers him looking much older. So very deaf.

Shute. Excellent nice young man.

Chalgrove Laurence Nephew of Arch[deacon] Lawrence[15].... Sensible, but odd. Married below himself. Keeps no company – needy; furniture seized. Interferes with [?Price].
Chinnor Musgrave. Brother of Sir J Musgrave of Bannersley in Glouces[tershi]re & probably successor. Very reserved. Gentlem[anl]y. Not particularly active as Clerk. More of farmer. Lord of Manor & has large farm & very fond of attending to it. Many Methodists & Dissenters in Parish – always so.

54 **Crowell** Beauchamp – very ill & thinks it does not agree with him – gone to the West for winter. Worthy good clerk, attentive to duty. R also of Shirbourne.
Q Licensed Curate – very respectable Gent[leman] Mr T G Dickinson for 6 months. Quarrel as to April or not. Brother to H W J Beauchamp of Monks Risborough.
Cuxham Rowden. Very respectable cl[e]r[k]: very attentive in parish.
Easington Fiddler (*sic*) (Very small thing, gift of Bp of Lincoln. £80 per annum. Very small House.) Very low origin – once missionary – "active man for serves all over the county when wanted".
Emmington held with Chinnor and served with it.

55 **Ewelme R** Dr Hampden...called on him as RD but never got admission, Though I have seen him all the time in his Study. Young Hulme curate of whom excellent character.
Ipstone R Belongs to Mr Rowden – always held with Cuxham. Merton Coll: a curate there.
[Morgan. Whether he has changed or not does not know. *crossed out, pencil note:* Mr Sewell]
Lewknor Dr Dean, holds with All Souls Fellowship. Paralytic. Attwood curate, worthy good kind of man but very odd. Welshman. Does not mix.
Ackhampstead Chapel tumbling down (Chancel at Lewknor pulled down & rebuilt without notice) College to be moved to rebuild it. Menzies once ('once' *replaced by* 'there')

56 **Aston Deanery**
Pyrton V Durell. Lives entirely. Very worthy good sort of man. Son of Old Dr Durell & to succeed him. "an elderly man rather the advantage of me". Most extensive parish, from near Hazeley to Henley.
Standhill Once a chapel. Only the remains of Tower in 1790. Q.
Shirbourne V Held by Beauchamp
Stoke Talmage R Kerby RD.

---

[15] Of Barbados.

55v
Violent ultra Calvinist. God did not intend the Redemption of the World. He never puts his children to bed in the dark.
F Scott's sorrow at death because he had been unfaithful to his light as to election. <u>Violent</u> & ignorant at Clewer meeting (F of C Dec 1849) Worthy peer of [#] as violent as ignorant.
Respected as worthy man in parish, really good & devout.

56 **Thame V** <u>Pec</u>[uliar] Prosser. Good kind of man. Act[ive] Clerk. Pretty well liked. #[16]

56 **Tetsworth** Peers. Worthy good kind of man very active & attentive to parish. Built a very nice House. Relative & to succeed, P of Chisselhurst [*sic*].

56v
LittleJohn. Less violent greatly than others of this trust. Has great arguments with Prosser at their clerical meeting

57 **Aston Deanery**
Sydenham W D Littlejohn. Hear a good character of him. Lady Wennman speaks well.

57 **Towersey** J Williams. Could not find any one who knows anything of him.
Weston South Queen's College. Just given up by Mr Gibson & no one else appointed.
Watlington Langford. Extremely respectable.
Wheatfield Glanville ... holds it for one of the family for [*gap*][17] Spencer of Ch. Ch.

57v **Witney Deanery**
1. Alvescott A Neate R. Clever man, about 46. Family living. Pretty well active. No party man. J Gwynne married heiress of Place will do. Baptists strong – in his father's time, who lax Squire – clerk. Ch[urch] in good repair.

---

[16] The symbol is used to avoid inserting a name: it is not obvious who is meant.
[17] Charles Vere Spencer, Vicar 1852.

57v

2. Asthall Pat. Eton Coll.
Rev. H Gregory V. lives at Witney.
the Grocers School, five or six.
"He serves Cogges & Asthall.
Cogges is part of Witney .. one
service at each. Cogges only £50
& no house. A very steady good
man & is meek."
Pop. 352

58

[*pencil*] Q A[rchdeacon] No
residence. Resides at Witney
serves Cogges. Rather a shuffler.
Wanted to hold Minster Lovell.
Bishop Bagot would not assent.

57v **3. Aston with Bampton**
I   Church. Mr Kerby 1st portion. 2nd portion Dacres Adams res-
         [ident]
III   Ralph Barnes (resides in Berks., proposed division & he will live
         at Aston)
Ardington. Not known. Will build at Aston.
I   Chapel Aston
II   Shifford old chapel
III   Lew
Curate Dr Giles resides in Kerby's house. Mr Whitehead in Lodgings in
Bampton.
Mr Barnes' House long unoccupied since Dr Winstanley's death.
Dacres Adams (suggested by Mr Lewis for RD) – a very excellent man.
Energetic. Magistrate. "Just right". Straightforward Churchman Priest,
Chairman of Witney Union. Will like good Parish, has done a great deal
to mend all ill.

58v Curates Dr Giles
Whitehead very good sort of man.
4. Black Bourton Ch Ch Rev J Lupton. House built lately. Attends to his
parish very well.
5. Brize Norton Ch Ch Rectory. Rev Pavitt Penson V. elderly man. Attends
to his duty. Not much looked up to, quiet inoffensive man. Rel: man.

58v

6. Broadwell 2 duties NB. T.W.
Goodlake July 1845. Whig.
<u>Vicarage House</u> not inhabited in
Filkins

l.d. C. Hollwell. Chapel and
house built by Mr Harvey
[Shelton Suckling *erased*].

59

6. Passionate, useful in neighbourhood. Very active. Church system

Nunn. (Going on well – not happy
in out of way spot 1849 Jan[ua]ry.
Serves Holwell)

l.d. C Kelmscott. Church served by Rector and Curate. <u>Curate</u> resides

58v **7. Broughton Pogis** James Joseph Goodenough D D. Family living. Just come. Good report. Kept school at Clifton. Church good repair, new pewed

59v **Witney Deanery**
8. Burford Pat[ron] <u>Bp of Oxford</u> Edward Philip Cooper – very good man – no pec[uliar] opinions, much liked

60

C. **Fulbrooke** [B.R. Stephens. <u>Sanders</u> 1848
Very good little man. Large Parish, ill-conditioned, no Squire.
all erased]

59v **9. Clanfield** Rev. P. Penson son of Mr Penson of Brize Norton. Quiet respectable man.
10. Cogges P.C.   Eton. Mr J Andrews. Non Resident. Q.
  H Gregory see <u>Asthall.</u>
11. Cokethorpe Ch[apel] of Ease to Ducklington, few houses. Ch in W Strickland's park. Man of fortune. Very respectable. Whig.

59v   60

12. Ducklington T Farley R. Very good man, done good deal & attends to Church Duties. Very straight.

[pencil] 12. A[rchdeacon]. Thorough Anglican – not discriminating between trifles & importance. Very conscientious, has been in hot water.

13. Hailey George Crabbe Rolfe. Was curate at Witney under Jerram. House built and he resides & chaplain of Union. Very good man.

[pencil] 13. A[rchdeacon]. Good man. Active & some reading.

60v   **Witney Deanery**
14. Kencott R Rev James Thorold. Very strange. Elderly. Once in navy. Nothing to point out, but negligent. Very rare at visitations – excuses. Does not attend to Parish. Family man. Don't think well of him
* Three bells broken for 35 years.

15. Minster Lovell V Rev Rob[ert] Erle non resident lives at Wateringbury Why? [*whole section erased:* Phil. W Copeman good character Short time. Things looking up. Great neglect of old. Pigeons kept by clerk in Belfry – dung in Church. House very small. Mr Copeman lives in Witney in lodgings. Quite young]
Eton Coll ½ Chancel, Par, Vic. ½ Sunday School held in Church – Ch Warden (Gillett) good man.

Bryan

16 Northmoor St John's Coll. Rev H Heming lately come, like him much, young man.

[*pencil*] 16.Unclerical in dress, tolerably well at St Giles. A little of the young St Johns jovial sporting school.

Witney Deanery
17. Shilton V with Alvescott above.
A Neate.
* 3 of the Bells cracked, & the chancel bad state.

18. Standlake R
Rev.T Biddulph non resd
F Burgess Curate. Young man of St John's Coll. A good deal in Oxford, does his duty well. Resides in the House. (Serves also Yelford, own farm)
19 Swinbrook Rev. W Raine P.C. Was before no House. One old man served 3 Churches, who had one son a carpenter and one a butcher. Lord Redesdale gave the land for House
Anon[ymou]s letter charging him with ploughing up Ch[urch]yard: all untrue. 2 acres &1/4 large.

[*pencil*] 18 A[rchdeacon]. Sportsman. Fond of hunting. Unclerical Dress. Adams speaks well of his influence in Parish. Leads fellows of St Johns jollification. "Goodwood races the day of the year"!
[*pencil*] A[rchdeacon]. Magistrate. Poorish old man, rather [shadowed future]

Just right in opinions. Active man but near sighted & low voiced, yet liked (see as to Widford End.)

61v **20. Taynton V** T Lewes[18] with Great Barrington on Lord Dynevor's property. Lives at Great Barrington. 81 years. She an aunt of D. of Buccleuch. A cottage at Great Barrington. Church at T in good repair. Centre aisle to be repaired since 1826

62v **Witney Deanery**
21. Westwell R Dr Gaisford's living – who never comes near it. Curate C Gaisford brother of the Dean. All Dissenters. He very inefficient. R of Chilton. Church Bad repair.
22. Witney R. C J Jerram, raised tone &c. S J Jerram. Church very good state.
23. Yelford Very small. Dr Foulkes.
24. Langford R Hodges. (Holds it for a young Vizard). An elderly respectable man, lives at [Great *deleted*] Little Barr[ington]. Mr Chute curate. Mild .. Low Church. [*pencil note:* Gone]

63 [*List in another hand*] Deanery of Witney

Alvescot R	Arthur Neate
Asthall V	Henry Gregory
Aston with Bampton	
Black Bourton V	Rev James Lupton
Brize Norton V	Revd. Pavitt Pearson
Broadwell V	Thos. W Goodlake
Broughton Pogges R	James Joseph Goodenough
Burford V	E P Cooper, R R Stephens Asst Curate
Clanfield V	P Penson Junr
Coggs P C	H Gregory, curate
Cokethorpe	T Farley, Chapel of Ease to
Ducklington R	T Farley
Fulbrook P C	E P Cooper
Hailey P C	George Crabb Rolf
Holwell under Broadwell	S Suckling curate
Kelmscott	do.
Kencott R	Revd James Thorold
Minster Lovell V	Philip W Copeman Curate
Northmore P C	Henry Heming
Shifford, Hamlet of Bampton	

---

[18] Inducted in 1819.

Shilton V   Arthur Neate
Standlake R   Frank Burgess Curate
Swinbrook P C   William Raine
Taynton V   Thomas Lewes
Westwell R   Charles Gaisford curate
Witney R   Charles Jerram (Maunder Curate, Jerram
                              asst Curate W Whitehead curate)
Yelford   Frank Burgess Cur.
Tew under Bampton

64. [*Notes in the hand of Justly Hill, Archdeacon of Buckingham*]

High Wycombe & Neighbourhood
The Rev Dr Almack of Fawley exc[ellent]
Piggott of Hughenden * R Dean
Youlden of Hedsor – Beaconsfield
Carter of Burnham * R.Dean
Shaw of Stoke Pogis

Amersham & Vicinity
The Rev Wm. Gleed Chalfont St Peters exc[ellent]
Lloyd of G[rea]t Hampden
Owen of St Leonards
Marsden of Gt. Missenden

Aylesbury & Vicinity
Rev W Harrison of Dinton* – R Dean
ExcReade of Stone
    Isham of Weston Turville * R Dean
    Hamilton of Ivinghoe
ExcWeighill of Chiddington
    Wroth of Edlesborough * R Dean
    Horne of Mursley * R Dean
    Alford of Aston Sandford * R Dean
    Young of Quainton
    The Rev Mr Ellis of Ickford

64v Buckingham & Neighbourhood
The Revd Mr Russell of Beachampton * R Dean
Mr Algernon Coote of Marsh Gibbon
Freemantle of Claydon
Cockerton of Turweston
exc – Drummond of Leckhampstead
exc – Adams of Gt. Horwood

Newport Pagnell & Neighbourhood
The Rev Mr Bull of Lathbury * R Dean
exc – Phillimore of Willen
exc – Athawes of Loughton
Broughton of Bletchley * R Dean
Talbot of Newton Blossomville
exc – Hughes of Newton Longeville
Whinfield of Filgrove * R Dean

NB Those marked <u>Exc</u> I think are admirably fitted for the office of Rural Deans. J Hill

65v **Bucks. Claydon Rural Deanery** Fremantle
Fleet Marston [*whole entry erased*: Jno Stevens, curate. Moderate, [clerk], knows his work, hopeful. Not decidedly pious[*erased*] man. Incumbent[19] insane]
Ludgershall Martyn. Very much improved. Very good sort of man. Of old school. More warm. Very sound. No extreme views.
(Claude Martyn son serving Edgcott conceited – Fremantle 1849)
Middle Claydon No curate
East Claydon Arden curate 50 years old. Worthy man of Gisborne school. Bottle.
Marston North Banbury
Oving Thelwall, brother of Black Patch – given by Lord Brougham on condition of supporting old Thelwald. Knew his young wife. Thelwall in <u>debt.</u> Not sequ[estrat]ed.
* Boyce. Good fellow. Working well…. <u>Stipend?</u>
Padbury, Hillesden Eyre. One service at each. Padbury<u> requires 2 services</u>: but small endowment – opinions just nothing. Mrs E valuable. Think very well… He light minded.

66 **Pitchcott** <u>Price.</u> Old Evang[elica]l Newton & Co. Contemporary of Romaine. Has been active. Very remarkable old man. 25 people.
Quainton <u>Young</u> ….. Brother of a Fellow New Coll. Incumbent of Q. 18 years. ..a very aggravated case of adultery 18 years ago. Now married, respectable, clever. No <u>appearance</u> of penitence in <u>high</u> sense. Perhaps 45.
Waddesdon Latimer….eccentric character. Great scandals about him… as to female living in the House. about 40. Son of Latimer Wine Merchant.. Too fearfully likely. Considerable ability. (Scandal about Clerk's wife 1847).
* <u>Lowry</u> has one medeity & lives away. No curate.

[19]   J Bull, instituted 1832.

Wootton Underwood Hill P C a nice fellow: quiet: very small place. about 40: no particular School. Moderate man, attends to parish.

66v **Addington** Scurr (see Shenley) his character very poor. Sporting man. Ford ...Tractarian. Young man... refused to come to Cl[erical] Meet[ing] We should deprave Liturgy – preached sermon on Confession. Agreeable man. Very taking.
Adstock Baynes One of oldest incumbents. I call him a very good man, of old school. Humble, right-minded man. Not <u>highly</u> spiritual: but a man to honour & love.
Claydon, Steeple Irwin. A zealous man.
Grandborough Whitfield. Odd – passed by by [?for] Archdeacon.

67   **Mursley Deanery** Rev T Horn
Cublington <u>Thompson</u> inc[umben]t Not much seen of him. Does his duty pretty fairly: not very zealous. No particular School, rather a man of the world. Fellow of Lincoln. Often at Oxford.
Drayton Parslow Old Shirley
C[urate] Heath worked well.
Dunton Cuckson, *corrected to* Cuxson curate... Well disposed. Pupils. Likely to be useful, been only a few months. Very small parish.
Edlesborough. <u>Wroth</u>. Energetic character as a magistrate. Don't know much about his parish working. NB his interest in the dilapidation question.
Hardwick Erle. Singular person – formidable attainments – resides but does not do much. Very charitable but not much ministerial zeal.
March, of New Coll[ege] Curate

67v **Hogston** Villar. No school. Good sort of man. Came late from Worcester Coll[ege] Not active: but kind man. Does not much preach. Mr <u>Kerr</u> from Winslow preaches – every Sunday. Mr Kerr has no duty – takes his brother's duty at <u>Tottenhoe</u>. His brother is licensed curate at Tottenhoe. No part[icula]r school.
Horwood Magna Adams. Very active man in parish. Between 30 & 40. Parish very well regulated. Observes Saints Days.... Strong Churchman & not extreme. No Rom[anisin]g. Fellow of New Coll[ege].
Stewkley Roberts incumbent. Resides. Elderly. Not efficient – perhaps age or mind. Quite competent to ordinary duty. Now unintelligible. No Curate. Place where Wesleyans great hold (no school) of old ... but much increased. <u>Not</u> zealous ... nothing against him, a widower, ch[ildren], grown up.

68 **Swanbourne** Collinson <u>Evangelical</u>. Very active and efficient – between 30 & 40 married. Good man in earnest. Parish well cared.
Sir T. Fremantle lives there.

Is very low Church. Has considerable powers in pulpit. Views on Sacraments very low. Much occupied with Pupils. Cantab. No lead amongst Clergy.
Tottenhoe Kerr curate. C. Lowndes non res[iden]t. One of brothers, of Whaddon Chase. No house.
Whaddon Meech. Can't speak favourably ... does some good. Goes about the Parish & visits. Habits such as cannot do good. Meech intemperate by common report. 40
+ Separated from wife. Once proctor at Oxford. Much shielded as New Coll[ege] man.
Whitchurch Turner. No extreme views. Active man struggling with Parish difficulties. Many dissenters. Raised the congregation. About to build a school. No strong bias. Preaches an accept[able]sermon. Sound.

Mursley

68v
69

1. Cheddington Weyghell [sic] Very active man. Very earnest good man. Rather evangel: school, not very extreme (Horn)

1. Trouble about his resignation of

2. Drayton Beauchamp

2. Kelk and family

3. Grove Mr Monins. Uncomfortable man. Sad early language. Ill behaved sons. Arguing with Wroth.

4. Ivinghoe Young Wroth curate. Hamilton

5. Linchlade [sic] Ouvry

6. Marsworth. Turner

7. Mentmore. North

8. Mursley Horn. Much respected.

9. Nettleden. Hamilton does duty one time here & once at Ashridge. Used to have service once

69v **Pitstone** Weighell
Slapton Burgess. Exceedingly good
Soulbury Hart (Service must be over by time for cows: second service should be here.)
Miss Lovett, (Lipscombe House)
Maj Joyce – rather too "ego". Complaining of farmers.
Wingrave with Rousham

70 **Buckingham Deanery** (see also 61 [= 144v])
Barton with Chetwode (a second service in Summer at Ch[etwode])
Smith – a good man ... not very strong health, a good deal of influence, about 30. Married. A new school. Evangelical in views, no extreme.
Buckingham Sylvester curate. Not efficient. Church badly attended. No zeal. Careless.
Gawcott Chapel of ease to Buckingham. Well attended. Field an active efficient man. No peculiar school. Evangel[ical].
Edgecott & Grendon Pigott. Uncle to R.D. 60 years old, a most inefficient man.
N. B. Service over in 1/4 of an hour. Teeth out. No zeal, no visiting. Wealthy? One service at each place
+ (Mr Marten 1848 resides at Ludgershall with Father)
Caversfield C. Marsham. Very ineffective. Well meaning.
Preston Bissett Sabin curate (son). I believe a good man. Not very effective. Sermons poor. Snare indolence but visits poor.

70v Father was extempore preacher. Was run after. A good man.
Radclive Coker curate
Tingewick J.Hill
Reade. I think pretty efficient. A great deal of good. Very active in schools. "Up to his light faithful". Amiable, in earnest. No particular opinions, quite in the mean. A devoted man. Thoroughly sincere.
Twyford Dr Radford once or twice.
Perkins – Married man. Can't say much for him. Never heard anything against character but worldliness. [Fancy] sort of man.
Water Stratford – don't know.

71 **Westbury** ! W M Gurdon.
Jno David Pigott 1849. Very successful tutor. Takes pains. Church well attended. Attends Rural Chapters with interest. Married, about 35.

71v, 72 [*blank*]

72v **Newport Deanery**
Bletchley
Bradwell W Drake. Lives at Moulsoe. Mr Bell
Haversham Mr Small. Embarrassment.
Hanslope Mr. Mayne. Corporation of Lincoln.
Castlethorpe Mr Williams [*corrected to:*] Hinde
Linford Great [*entry deleted:* Crole .... worldly, much away, wife so also. Confirmation preparation ill. Son of Lord E [?] She Miss Barker] Bakewell

Linford Little Wm Smyth (of Broughton) Lincolnshire squire, near Louth – Elkington. Phillimore: hunting Gentleman: not much more!!
Loughton Athawes. Very good man.

73 **Shenley**. Mr Scurr. (1849 Scandal about Woolverton.)
Stantonbury = Quartley
Stony Stratford Bond [*erased*] Bleamire. Son of Kendal attorney. Chose ministry of his own earnest choice. Doing well 1850.
Wolverton Quartley – Gentlemanlike
Wolverton New Church
Tyrringham

73v **Astwood** ..... Cumberledge. Calvinistic. Good, earnest. Brought no confirmation candidates because none converted, &c.
Brafield &c W. Tomkins. Walsh Tickell [*crossed out*]
Chicheley ..... Townshend = worldly = unclerical = hunting. Gentlemanlike, rather mad.
Clifton Reynes   .... Collins. 1850 going on well
Emberton Speke rather low [*crossed out*] Halton
Gayhurst (Trotman. Zealous good man)
Speck
Hardmead Talbot. Very worthy man.
Lathbury
Newport Pagnel Merley. Very earnest – always there. Odd. Very clerical. High minded [*Morley*]

74 **Newton Blossomville** (Talbot)
North Crawley C Lowndes Curate. (T. Lowndes[20] resides at Worthy in Hants) brought up at Whaddon. Good tempered man. Married to sister of Broughton. Few ideas except Horses & Hounds. 800 people. Neglected, wretchedly. Boswell Squire right-minded. Get School.
Olney Dr Langley. Man of Talent = not very low = pupils. Popular Talent.
Ravenstone Godfrey. Sound man.
Sherrington [*crossed out*: Williams. Good, conscientious. Rogers] Scher[?]. King good and well.
Newton Underwood Macnamara
Stoke Goldey [*Goldington*] Speck

74v   **Newport**
Brickhill Great Sir H Foulis. Worthy man & very attentive to duty

---

[20] Vicar of East Worldham 1823 and Curate of East Tisted, Hants, both some 20 miles from any of the Worthies.

Brickhill Little Jones. Old style.[21]
Brickhill Jackson. Man of property: Odd man. Qy if active.
Broughton W Smyth from Yorkshire. Irwin very excellent man..
Milton Keynes Jones. also [?old] style – sound.
Moulsoe Walter Drake – Lord C's pet chaplain. Gentlemanlike. <u>Much away</u>.
(Quarrel with Lord C 1850)
Newton Longueville Hughes. Excellent man, about best in the quarter. Chaplain to Bp Shuttleworth.

75 **Simpson** Hanmer (in poor condition) he been in debt, prison &c
Stoke Hammond Bouwens. Very excellent man. Gentlemanlike – in weak health.
Stratford Fenny
Walton
Wavendon
Willen Phillimore
Woolston Great Tatham Archn (Clarkson 1847 good man)
Woolston Little Dr Rose!
Wroughton Dr Rose. Odd man – magistrate. Little religion – shoots &c.

75v **Cheddington** Weighill Zealous man, high moral character. Not very low, but rather Yorkshire.
Drayton Beauchamp Kelk
Grove Matthews. V. nearly blind.
Morrice C[urate]. A sad blot – married his mother's maid.
Ivinghoe Hamilton C[urate]
Wroth Jun Cambridge
Linchlade Hart Chaplain in Union. Low man – not zealous. Relation (uncle) of Wing clerk. His Father a rich farmer. PC of Soulbury. Mortimer curate here – Poor creature.
Marsworth (Mr Smith of high character – son of [?] of Pitt Press. Zealous man, rather high. Takes much pains. Resigned 1847)
<u>I B Turner</u> high character from Bp of Lichfield – "Faithfulness, diligence & attendant Blessing."
Mentmore Wilson. Goes to every meeting. Curate of Leighton. Population of 5000[22]
NB with Grove.
Mursley Horn

---

[21] Instituted in 1813.
[22] The figure in *Clergy List* is 6053.

76 **Nettlesden** Rich resigned. Hamilton very good. No school of opinions – has been schoolmaster at Hampden.
Pightelsthorne or Pitston Hamilton does the duty. Bayley spoken well of by Weighell.
Slapton Bryant Burgess (tall rather thin gown [??])
Curate. A very good zealous good man rather high
Soulbury Hart. See above under Linchlade.
Wing Felix – indolent – proper
Wingrave Rousham J Dinton. Now going on well – has been drunkard.

76v, 77 [blank]

77v **Burnham continued from 230** [i.e. 142]
Wexham Kempe. Weak rather, wishing to have licence of non resid'e for economy 1848. Hedsor.
Wyrardisbury
Burnham Missenden

78v–88v [blank]

89 [omitted]

90 [Newspaper cutting, with names of clergymen underlined]

Game Lists, County of Berks 1847

List I – General Certificates of £4.0s.10d each

Barnes, Ralph	Hungerford
Birch, Thomas Frederick	Cookham, Maidenhead
Butler, John	Inkpen
Clementi, Vinct	Thatcham
Dundas, J .W.D.	Kintbury
Jenkins, Owen	Longworth
Kent, Charles	Watchfield
Nelson, J.	Sparsholt
Palmer, Richard	Sonning
Simonds, St J. Jn.`	Reading
Simmons, Thomas	Sonning
Sloper, Jno.	West Woodhay
St John, E.	Finchampstead
St John, H.	Finchampstead
St John, J.	Finchampstead

91
Deanery of Abingdon
3rd Division Hundred of Wantage
The Rev. Jno Nelson, Sparsholt House

Deanery of Wallingford
Hundred of Moreton

Rev. R. B. Fisher

Wantage P
Grove Chapel

(Aston Tirrold) P. Deanery of Abingdon
(Upton Ch)

Lockinge
Hendred East
Hendred West
Childrey
(Sparsholt
(Kingston Lisle Chapel
Letcombe Bassett
(Letcombe Regis
(Challow East Chapel
(Challow West Chapel
Denchworth
(Hanney
(Lyford Chapel

(Basildon
(Ashampstead Chapel
Brightwell
Cholsey
Moulsford
North Moreton
South Moreton
Streatley
(Wallingford St Leonard St Mary's

(Sotwell Chapel St Peter's
Blewbuury
Hagbourne
Didcot
Harwell

91v **Deanery of Abingdon**
1st Division
Hundreds of Ock & [? Hormer]

Rev. N Dodson

2 Division
Hundreds of Farringdon, Garfield, Shrivenham
Rev. Wm. Chambers
Archdeacon Berens

Abingdon St Helens
            St Nicholas
Drayton
Cumnor
Wytham
Hinksey, North
Hinksey South
Wootton

Astbury
Buscot
Coleshill
Eaton Hastings
(Faringdon
(Little Coxwell – Chapel
Littleworth
Gt. Coxwell

(Sunningwell
(Kennington Chapel
Radley (Donative)
Besselsleigh
Appleton
Tubney (not consecrated)
Marcham
Fyfield
(Sutton Courtenay
(Appleford Chapel
Lyford
Milton
Steventon
Long Wittenham
Little Wittenham

(Shrivenham
(Longcot Chapel
Compton Beauchamp
(Uffington
(Baulking Chapel
(Woolston Chapel
Buckland
Hinton
(Longworth
(Charney Chapel
Pusey
Halford
(Stanford
(Goosey Chapel
Shellingford

92   **Deanery of Newbury**

**1st Division Hundred of
Lambourn, Kintbury Eagle**

Rev. J. H. Majendie

2nd Division

Rev. T. Loveday, R of East Ilsley
[*deleted* : John Thomas Austin of Aldworth]

Lambourn
Lambourn Woodlands Chapel
East Garston
Shefford West
Shefford East
Welford
Wickham Chapel
Boxford
Beenham
Shaw
Woolhampton
Newbury
Aldermaston
(Speen
  (Speenhamland Chapel
  (Stock Cross Chapel
Hungerford P
Avington
Shalbourne P

East Ilsley
West Ilsley
Chilton
Farnborough
Cotmore
Peasemore
Beedon
Bright Waltham
Compton
Aldworth J.T.Austen
Hampstead Norris [*deleted*]
Hermitage Chapel [*deleted*]
Blewbury P [*deleted: Q to Wall*]
Chaddleworth
Hagbourne [*deleted: Q to Wall*]
Harwell [*deleted: to Wall*]
Didcot [*deleted: to Wall*]
Yattendon

Inkpen
Hampstead Norris
Hermitage Chapel
Kintbury
West Woodhay
Hampstead Marshall
Enborne
Brimpton
Wasing
(Chieveley
  (Winterborne
  (Oare
  (Leckhampstead
(Thatcham
  (Greenham
  (Midgham
(Bucklebury
  (Marlston Chapel

Frilsham
Stanford Dingley
Fawley

92v   **Deanery of Reading**

Rev Austen Leigh
Scarletts
The Knowle still Maidenhead
Reading St Marys
  Trinity Chapel
  St Lawrence
  St Giles
  St John's Church
  St Mary's Chapel – Caversham
Pangbourne – Mapledurham
Purley
Englefield (Eyre)
Tidmarsh Theale
Sulham Tilehurst
Bradfield
  Trinity Chapel
Burnham [*deleted: to Newbury 1 – yes*]
Woolhampton [*ditto*]
Aldermaston [*ditto*]
Padworth
Maiden Early

Astbury
Bray Mr Levett
Maidenhead
Cookham
Cookham Dean
Bisham
[*to Henley*] Hurley [*deleted*]
[*to Henley*] Remenham [*deleted*]
Shottesbrooke
White Waltham
Clewer
Trinity Chapel
Windsor New
Windsor Old
Winkfield
Sunninghill
[*Henley*] Wargrave [*deleted*]
Knoll Hill [*deleted*]
St Lawrence Waltham
Ruscombe P

Mortimer	Sunninghill Dale
Sulhampstead Abbotts	Maiden Earley [*deleted*] Ch
Burghfield Hurst Knoll House	Wokingham P
Ruscombe	Bracknell
Twyford	Sandhurst Pec[uliar]
(Shinfield	Binfield
(Swallowfield	East Hampstead
Arborfield	
Barkham	
Finchamstead	

93 We do hereby certify that we have examined the Glebe house of the Parish of Brimpton, in the County of Berks, & find it totally unfit for the residence of the Incumbent, by reason of its size being merely a Labourer's Cottage, and that to the best of our belief such unfitness has not been occasioned by the Reverend George Caffin the present Incumbent & that no house convenient for the residence of the said George Caffin can be obtained within the Parish.

          Dated 20 day of January 1846
             Samuel Slocock, Rector of Shaw
             & Miles Halton , Rector of Woolhampton

I certify that the above signatures are those of two Beneficed Clergymen in your Lordship's Diocese.
          Henry M Majendie, Rural Dean

To the Rt. Rev. the Bishop of Oxford

93v [*pencilled notes, on reverse of fol 93, written upside down*]
Tower fallen down
Chilton <u>Gaisford</u>. Dudley Curate. Incendiary fires. House miserable. <u>Why non resident</u>
Hagbourn
Small living. Zealous good man, rather loner. Whole time in profession. Jews Soc'y.
Whole heart in work
Harwell. New parsonage. Fletcher a new incumbent – respectable ze[*alous*]
Knight old servant exemplary 75.
Didcot. Incumbent lives in Suffolk. Old man. Curate lives at Didcote – House borne out arrangements by wh BNC £500 26 years ago.

94 [*blank*]

95v

Drayton properly a vicarage: the patronage was vested in Jerninghams by H VIII & they never presented a Clerk. It is now considered as a chapel to Abingdon and conveyed in Institution thereto.

Cumnor ... The most val[*uable*] man in the Diocese. Most val: par:[*ish*] priest.
Paralytic seizure last week (Jan 1846)

Wytham R Dr Bandinell. A great deal of good about him.

Hinksey N. G Tiddeman. Excellent good man...lives in Oxford

Hinksey S. Dr Ashurst

95v

Abingdon Deanery I Rev. N. Dodson

Sunningwell H Bowyer: ..a thoroughly pious excellent shy reserved not strong intellect man but excellent correct – <u>little</u> tendency to lo.

96 Archdeacon Berens Jan
Abingdon <u>St Helens</u>
Rev N Dodson. Energetic active man RD. Magistrate. Kind hearted. Perhaps a little overburdened with secular business but good & devout. St Nicholas. Lecturer from Trinity College. Short.

Drayton Chapel without endowment... served by curate of Dodson. The owner of the property pays £50 per annum to the curate

Cumnor Rev. W Slatter. Elderly, very excellent. Sensible practical man, devoted to his work.

Wytham Fred[eric]k Bertie R. Resides at Aldborough. Curate Dr Bandinell....active and earnest

Hinksey N. Rev G Tiddeman . Curate to E.G.Marsh. Simple. Earnest rather towards low.

Hinksey S with Wootton F. Bertie R.
J Ashurst DD fellow of All Souls, devoted, conscientious. £50 per annum and spends £500. Brother of Wm Ashurst. A vagabond only gave me 5/–

96

Sunningwell Rev. Henry Bowyer. Built a nice chapel at Kennington. Married awkwardly, keeps out of society. Much in earnest. No peculiar.

Radley Radcliffe. Many good points about him. Spent more always than gets. Not the man one would choose. Late Vice Princ[ipal] of St Mary Hall

Besselsleigh Dr Foulkes Curate: Brancker. A most valuable man. Well married

Appleton J Butler. New Incumbent – head scarce sound, rather tendency to low society. Ab[ou]t 36

Tubney

Marcham R H Randolph. Very weak, not quite sane. Mr Duffield now engages and pays Mr Elliston. Sincere good zealous man & gentleman

Radleigh [*sic*] Don. Rev. John Ratcliffe. Respect[ab]le scholar but not much anxiety about Parish

Besselsleigh President (*sic*) of Jesus Dr Foulkes ? licensed. Never a curate resident.

Appleton J Butler fellow of Magdalen recently Come

NB Tubney with above not opened

Marcham R Herbert Randolph about 52. New[]phew of old Bishop R <u>very</u> dry. No harm about him but entirely useless from great drought...and weakness. Thought crazy.

96v   97

Abingdon Deanery I Rev. N. Dodson

Fyfield PC under St John. Kitson useful in Parish Church & good man. Little too fond of field sports, hunting & shooting. Much liked. Does a great deal of good.

Sutton Courtenay Gregson – comes from Chester: was offered by Bp. preferment if he would stay. Fortune: lives in hired house. Curate in parsonage.

Lyford Chapel Williams. House build by Cotton. No complaints. Good man. Not quite a gentleman – "an excellent clergyman. It was terribly neglected but now the Church is crowded & the clergyman beloved exceedingly."

Fyfield PC of St Johns Francis Kitson fellow of St Johns a very good and amiable fellow, active. Waiting for better living to marry a cousin. Free from party.

Sutton Courtenay Ch[apter] of Windsor has great tithes. Has chapel at Appleford. Mr Gregson a very good man.

Lyford chapel (belongs to Hanney Rev H Baker vicar). <u>Non resident?</u> (Mr Sheard – unprepossessing manner. Not a very useful man – is to Hanney).
Mr Williams C[urate] of Lyford a <u>good man</u>

Milton Clerke. Not efficient in parish. Dissent growing.
Steventon W Vincent. very zealous very good, a little too low. (Works well with his cousin &c)
Long Wittenham. Clutterbuck away ill, consumptive. Harper Curate. Well spoken of by Clutterbuck who going to S of France Sept 1846

Milton C. Clerke

Steventon Wm. Vincent, a very good, humble man. very low church
Long Wittenham Rev. H Clutterbuck – good & intelligent man

97v

98

Wittenham Little F.S. Hilliard ...not "an immoral man much". All uncomfortable, much disliked in parish, happily very small. Most painful to give an account of. Not from very bad, kept back, but all unclerical.

Abingdon Deanery II

Ashbury W Chambers. Very zealous, very good, a thorough good man – rather too low views for me – ND

Buscott Hudson very good
A Brooke a very good man. Not a more valuable man in Diocese: humble minded good man
Coles Hill E Bouverie: as good as good can be

Wittenham Little F S Hilliard – good natured man, & tolerably active magistrate but very far from spiritual

Abingdon no 2 Deanery
Arch[deaco]n Berens

Ashbury Rev Wm Chambers. Well to do, but only boy of precocious talents; a very good man; lo[w] Church formerly RD to Bishop Burgess
Buscott Hudson non Resident: see Arch Berens's letter.
Rev.A Brooke, a very good man. Wid[owe]r?
Coles Hill Revd Ed[mu]nd Bouverie married Lady C's younger sister. Most active gentleman, spoils his parish. Old Fashioned Divinity. Mr Bertie Bouverie Father. Law – Serious Call.
Domestic tragedy – his sister's marrying Sir H Mildmay & Lord Rosebery, dead now.
('unspiritual' – Moore loq.) "Yes" Chambers

Eaton Hastings R Rice – a little puzzled – a good man & not without ability: but sure to get into a quarrel ... always so in Parish (Debt &c 1847)

Eaton Hastings Rev Rich[ard] Rice: a very respectable man with largish family. Rather dry as preacher. Built Parsonage. ("Unspiritual" Moore loq. Hunting)

98v **Abingdon Deanery II**
Farringdon

99 **Abingdon Deanery II**
Farringdon Pec[uliar] Pat[ron]s Simeons's Trustees.
Rev.W Hawkins. <u>ill N[on]R[esident]</u>
Rev <u>Vicesimus Lush</u> a very useful man & very acceptable man. Zealous – good preacher. No party man. Rather short-sighted, broken leg.
Coxwell Little (Chapel of ease) Same

Littleworth Chap[el] to Farringdon. Built by Oriel

Littleworth. Lately built. Pat[ron] Bish[o]p
(Mrs Barrington Price's son Robert Price curate & does remarkably well. Rev Jos[eph] Moore vicar of Buckland). Moore incumbent. Hooper curate

Coxwell Great– nothing better in Diocese – a very sound & very zealous & very good man.

Coxwell Great Jn Francis Cleaver (Son of Bishop). 1st class with Sir R.Peel. One of the most clear headed and best men. Three sisters live with him.
Well off & very liberal (Moore loq. very kind able and unspiritual) (Most highly esteemed clear headed charitable able man. Good lawyer, poor in sp[iritualit]y – Chambers)

Shrivenham

Shrivenham with Longcot
Archdeacon Berens

Compton Beauchamp [*entry later deleted*]
R Wintle (dead 1848)
Carter 1848, 9 (Purrier, a very excellent good man ... his views full high; a little deformed. Church well done.)
Price from Littleworth

Compton Beauchamp [*entry later deleted*] – about 20 houses R[ichar]d Wintle of Callum R. Has Henry S Purrier a very good man & clear headed & good scholar as curate who resides in Parsonage.
(Moore loq Hunting overbearing unspiritual)
[*pencil notes*: Harene Edw Alex Ford   R Price cur.]

99v **Abingdon Deanery**   100

Uffington. Incumbent Lord; bad health, never does duty. Dead Jan 1847

Uffington A very important Parish miserably off.
A pleasant & amiable & very clerical man & well informed in wretched health.
[*pencil note*: Ob. Tuffnall – earnest hope]

Baulking C. One full duty alternate Sundays 1/2 9
1st Sunday after Easter morning service and Communion. 200 pop[ulation] 20 commun[icants] regular at Chapel.
Woolstone Chap has been in very neglected state – seldom dutied. Moss grown.
A full duty regularly alternate Sundays at 1 1/2 2nd Sunday after Easter service. 300 Pop 20
1 ½ miles from Uffington

Baulking C Chap
Woolstone Chap [*pencil note:* Polson living in house bought of Mr Bishop]
Mr Garrard curate. Son of Brewer at Reading.
Fellow St John's Oxon
2 services & I Sermon each Sunday 11 & 3 sermon alternate morn[ing] & aft[ernoon]
Boys school endowed

Buckland J Moore. A very good kind of man, perfectly sound & always at his work.
(very anxious about Union Chapels 1847. Mrs M pleasing)

Buckland Rev Jos Moore – a very good man very intelligent & active in his Parish. House improved

Hinton G Evans. Does a good deal of good in parish. Getting heavy & infirm. Divine of 50 years ago rather than present day.

Hinton Rev. Geo[rge] Evans. Shrewd sensible man a good magistrate. Quite unblemished. Not part[icular]ly spiritual.

1 of nicest livings in Diocese. Ev[ans] about 59 one-legged
Longworth O Jenkins. One of Jesus livings.
Very kind in parish & attentive to poor. More of a fox hunter than one could wish. A nice living.
Charney Chapel J does it himself. The duty done by Mr Williams of Lyford
Pusey W Evans "12 children very little income & very little sense" Weak foolish man. Near 50.
Hatford James Hearn. Good kind of man. Nothing against him. Little low. Antiquarian.

[pencil note: H C Rhodes Second Master of Abingdon School curate]
Longworth Rev Owen Jenkins. A good man [I] believe

Charney. C served by Mr Williams ** who serves also Lyford & an almshouse. Church thronged.
Pusey Evans £50 a year respectable man with large family. Not part[icular]ly spiritual.
Hatford Very small parish. Very energetic not very
[?] man with Chap[lain]cy to Union.
Rev James Hearne, very low church [Hill] but he cannot quite trust. [ ] rather too ready.

100v   **Abingdon Deanery II**   101

Stanford in the Vale Saunders.
Odd: eccentric
Geare rather low

Stanford in the Vale with Goozey [sic] **Chapel**
Incumb[en]t Rev Sanders ... Spiritual Father to Bp Ryder – [Father] to Son. Very low church man. A good curate Rev E Geare: a low church & active in parish.
[ ]out by violence

Shillingford Mills 80 years, finishing a long fox-hunting life. Nothing more against him. Not likely to live.
(Mr Dennis from Farringdon serving it unlicensed : this to be for only 4 Sundays & then he to write to me June 2 1846)
[pencil note: Dupre]

Shillingford Good living ... Rev Wm Mills elderly man, very respectable secular man.
Failing

Abingdon Deanery III

Wantage. Dean of Windsor Button. A very valuable man (Correspondence with Bp Bagot of Goodlake as to increased salary)
Grove chapel

Lockinge Cottle. Duty exceedingly well done.
Church in very nice state.
Bastard family the property

101v

East Hendred Wapshire, race nearly run
Father in law to Mr Dodson
Parish very difficult one. Good signs.
(Young people seemingly well prepared for Confirm[atio]n 1847)

West Hendred Hearne. Good for nothing. Out of country, debts of great age. R[ectory] House unfinished, parts falling down.
<u>Curate</u> Collins lives at Lockinge ½ mile off. Clerk with some landed property. A very correct man. Youngish. (Pleasing and well spoken of 1847)

Abingdon 3 Wantage Deanery

Rev John Nelson, Sparsholt House
Wantage Deanery of Windsor R C Rev Button very like Button but a good useful & sober–viewed man

Grove chapel Lately built. Dr Cotton.
Simcox Bricknell (lately?) a very good man rather fond of newspaper. Strong anti Pus[eyite] not low church

Lockinge annexed to Warden[shi]p of All Souls.
A good curate who has been there long.
T. Cottle

102

East Hendred Mr Wapshare. Old man very respectable. Old fashioned. Steady.
A R.C.family in the parish who much annoy him.
A Mr Hussey who married a daughter lives with him and acts as curate
Salisbury Bish[op] Pat[ron] option

West Hendred Rev J B (Mr) Hearne. Corpus Out of sight for debt. A most grievous case. Curate charged used to leap ditches & escape sheriff's officers. A very old man.

Childrey Dr Whittingham. Very odd. Perfectly correct and sound in all views. So strange. Mixes with none...weakness of mind. Not deficient in attainment. Not aged 60.

Sparsholt Dodd. Just what one would say nothing about: neither favourable or unfavourable. Pains to a certain extent. (Duty to be double here and at K.L. He to write to me)

With Kingston Lisle Everett. Warm hearted kind useful man

Childrey Dr Whittingham....very much in earnest. Father a friend of J Wesley's, he good Churchman. Old Goodlake coarse magistrate – immoral &c.
Hope to see you often &c
Neither one nor other.

Sparsholt Dodd. Fellow of Queens.
Young man, simple minded, very respectable

Kingston Lisle Ch Curate Charles Everett, very anxious about par[ish] duties & very amiable Knew [? Bryant] for years.

102v **Abingdon Deanery III**
Letcombe Bassett W Firth. Not a sane man.
· Strange seclusion & weakness. Going into Idiotcy. Married twice. Threw himself once out of window, published his own banns first. Then married farmer's daughter.
No usefulness in parish. No care.
Letcombe Regis V Westcombe. [*Pencil:* Hunter]
C. B Morland. Respect[able] decent: very moderate powers. But lives amongst them & does his best in a very creditable way [*Pencil:* Gone to Shallington]
Challow E. Ch
Challow West Mr J Nelson
Many family afflictions. Good man, property, likes preaching
Denchworth (V. E Horton....late Cotton, knew nothing). Lewis

103 **Abingdon Deanery III**
Letcombe Bassett W Firth.
Amiable retiring man.
Corpus living. Mod[era]te low churchman, very anxious about his Parish.

Letcombe Regis Winton Cath[edra]l
Thomas Westcombe V
Benj[amin] Morland C very respectable, not v.active.

Challow East chapel with it.

Denchworth E Horton vicar, good man

Hanney Baker R, Sheard C done mischief by offending them with Club Sermon. Bad public houses. (MacDougall from Baldon School 1847)

Hanney R Mr Baker R Mr Sheard C very good

102v **Wallingford Deanery**

103 **Wallingford Deanery**
Hundred of Moreton
Rural Dean Rev. R.B. Fisher

Wallingford
Rev.R.B.Fisher
(This parish from Abingdon)
Aston Tirrold Hoskyns. Son of Sir Hungerford H: an excellent pious man; has formed arrang[emen]t for building a new Parsonage

Wallingford

Archdeacon Berens
Aston Tirrold Magd[alen]College
Told that a good man. New Incumbent
Hoskyns

103v **Wallingford** [Abingdon *crossed out*]
Deanery Rev. R. B. Fisher R. Dean
Basildon Very desirable to separate Ashampstead from B. Mr Benion de Beavoir & Mr W.Sykes Patron obj[ect] because of small endowment. Would be Ashampstead with commut £70 Glebe £15 = £85 (Rates £11.11.0) = £79.9.0. Ashampstead full of Dissent. Ashamp 400 Basildon 800
Brightwell He "fancies he can do not duty"
Dixon gives satisfaction

104 **Wallingford**

Basildon with Ashampstead Chapel which Fisher wishes to make independent.
R B Fisher

Brightwell Marmaduke Thompson. Good man, low churchmanship (Bp Winton)
Curate Mr Dixon a "popular preacher". Some of the Irish character features

Cholsey V Sound good man, about 30, overworking himself. Given by Lord Mex[borough] Moulsey just separated £30 per annum, i.e. £1000 £1000 to House by B.Morell & Mr Lloyd. £30 per annum from tithe.

Cholsey (Lord Chancellor) (with Moulsford)
H W Lloyd, a very zealous man: rather low church.
Comfortable House

Young Morell to be new incumb[en]t. The Church to be rebuilt by Mr B Morell.

Moreton North V H Taylor respectable, no fault to be found: rather think some good points. His neighbours speak well. Eccentric, nervous, very peculiar. Good scholar. Not much to do, not a very weak – a good scholar. Reads a good deal & is very intelligent. Morbid to insanity almost, very peculiar appearance; rel[igious]
July improving lives by himself on his £100 a year in a wretched parsonage.

Moreton South James Will[ia]m rather eccentric: cannot bear solitude & so much away. Bp Burgess forced him to reside at Wallingford & so did away with a resident curate. A very conscientious & benevolent: but not clear views on rel[igion]. Wishes to have a curate. Good man & (Fell). He tells Fell to give away 1sh a day & always in the day. James had lodgings at S.Moreton & Wallingford.

Moreton North R. Archdeacon Berens.
Vicar Henry Taylor – <u>very</u> weak man, but good well-meaning man. One of the weakest in the archd[eacon]ry

Moreton South* Wm. James predecessor to Jacobson at Magdalen Hall. Resides in Devonshire (and why?)
G Fell curate. Rector conscientious man.
NB Sep 1846 He write "too solitary to live". I reply that his license lasts till Dec 47. Then to be thought about. Meantime suggest the responsibilities of non: res: Mr Fisher thinks nothing would be gained by forcing him into residence

104v **Wallingford Deanery**
Rev R B Fisher RD
Streatley J Burgess. Very respectable & attentive to duties – – in rel[igious] feel[ings] his wife goes further than he does. But preaches well...a well conditioned Parish. New built Parsonage.
Mr Baker the Morrels' uncle cared during a long residence for morals

105 **Wallingford Deanery**
Archdn Berens
Streatley Rev Jas Burgess, great nephew of the Bishop. Good Heb[rew] Scholar & parish priest, retiring sort of man but anxious about his parish & think a really religious man

Wallingford St Mary's (Great Church) St Leonards & a chapelry of Sotwell
A good active useful man...not judicious always – not university educated & so not forbearing enough – irritable. Travels for Ch[urch] Miss[ionary] Soc[iety] not the man for it
Scratchley Quere if from London Diocese.
St Leonards worth enlarging
St Peters Dr Frith – respectable gentlemanlike man: nothing objectionable ... man of O & lives as the O is doing

\# Andrew Everard Parsons ordained to Sapcote Deacon March 1849: resigned curacy from ill health – fever intermittent, with old John Bickersteth seems quite right–minded – <u>quite</u> clear on baptism, wishes to raise the tone of churchmanship at Wallingford: right in all views after comes Jan 1856. God Bless him.

St Mary S W Yates, able man of business

Wallingford St Leonards & St Marys & Sotwell chapel
John Langley R. Very fluent, ready ... low Church & I should think active and useful. Low origin who married the widow of a captain with some money which set him up in the world.
Q NB Scratchley Curate Quere if licensed

St Peters Dr Frith. St Johns Oxford a straightforward old fashioned man – rather secular than spiritual

Reading Deanery no I
[Reading:]
St Mary S W Yates, a very excellent man, most courteous – very well off very much in earnest: very good preacher.
Curate [Mr Mereweather] [*rest illegible*]

105v **Reading no.1**
2. **St Lawrence** John Ball. Moderate

106 **Reading no.1**
St Lawrence John Ball. Great ability & Frankness, love of [? Joke? people] like him very much better

3. **St Giles** C Grainger, bad health, not objectionably but n.l.c

4. **St Mary Street Chapel** Goodhart
Curate C D Bell curate to be licensed Jan 1846
5. **St John's Chapel**
6. **Pangbourne** Church in dreadful state. Wants rebuilding. Mr Breedon Squire paup: Cartwright Dent lives there unhandsomely
7. **Purley** Mr.Palmer – In good order – bonus. Moderate, rather high

106v **Reading no 1**
8. **Tidmarsh** T Wintle. Very small parish
Hopkin squire – Elderly. good kind of man. There on Saturday & Sunday, resid[ent]
*NB <u>near St Johns</u>: has no license for non–residence
9. **Englefield**

10. **Sulham** J Wilder..Fellow of Eton ...
Gentlemanlike. All in order. Schools.
Does not reside in vicarage but in his nephew's house.
11. **Bradfield** T. Stevens, rather extreme laborious

Trinity Chapel

3. **St Giles** Cecil Grainger also very bad health for 2 or three years, rather less sense than preceding but pleasing & well behaved

4. **St Mary Street Chapel** Mr Goodheart. Good heart p.l. Built for Mr Cadogan

5. **St John's Chapel** F Trench
6. **Pangbourne**. Held by for short time, second son of Hulme. Very pleasing man but quite young

7. **Purleigh R** R Palmer. Easy man, active, good speaker, anxious about duties

107 **Reading I**
Tidmarsh Thomas Wintle of St Johns – very sensible pleasing man
Hopkins laid out much on Church

Englefield Arch[deaco]n Berens. Curate Francis Eyre. Married Haygarth's daughter. Good man anxious to be of use.
Sulham John Wilder. Would be Tractarian
(applies May 1846 that the Rev Lionel Carden tutor & sometimes parochial substitute may not be licensed)
Bradfield Thomas Stevens. amiable built a [?small house]
Trinity Chapel in Parish John [?Moor]the other d[eacon] by Win Dioc

12. Beenham W Bushnell...a good kind of little man...a young man. Grandpere Mr Sawyer's agent. A very worthy man. All in good order.
13. Wool Hampton "L M Halton ...a very good sort of man. Berens"
(Hunting, shooting, unclerical answered Maj. invite to Rural Synod 'lately as visitor went away 1847 without notifying who doing the duty, just before Confirmation. Mr Gill doing it
14. Aldermaston Bellairs. Excellent moderate active man. Queens Coll living

Beenham Wm Bushnell vicar – a good active well informed man.

Wool Hampton & Mr Halton vicar much fonder of Hunting

Aldermaston About £60 a year Septimus Bellairs
A very sensible amiable man

107 **Reading no 1 Mr Levett** 108
15. Padworth Dr Curtis... Nothing amiss...poorish house. elderly. No particular scope for activity
Mortimer Stratfield. H J C Harper.
Very active & excellent man... pupils but Parochial too
Sulhampstead Abbotts
R Coulthard

Banister

Padworth Dr G W Curtis. No great harm about him. Not much to [be] said about him.
Quarrels much with [*illegible*]
Mortimer Stratfield Mr H J C Harper, very excellent man. Many pupils & yet gives much time to p[arish]
Sulhampstead Abbotts
Queens Mr Robert Coulthard ....
Banister plain straightforward manly sort of man, no harm & no great zeal. About 50. 2 fellows before almost going mad
(1) Whitcock
(2) Briscoe
(Mortimer Thoyts Squire)

18 Ufton Nervet (Oriel Coll)
[*Following entry deleted:*
W Bishop. Everything in prime order, all excellent, worthy man, great ability, terribly nervous.

Getting old. Excellent Parish priest so beloved]
John Frederic Christie "no Romanizing views" March 27 1847.
Q about Church Militant. 2 full Services to be hereafter.

19 Burghfield H C Cherry. Very active man. Tractarian. Built in Lord Shrewsbury's parish... great dissent in getting it built. Antiq[uarian] lore....Private fortune. Very large family. Wants to buy the living. Very extreme views: does not give offence. No tendency to Rome.

Burghfield Henry Curtis Cherry. Energetic man. Rebuilt Church well. No party. Able. Published a book or two. 80.

108v **Reading no 1 Levett**   109

20 Shinfield M Fielde. Oldish but able to do all his duty Swallowfield

Shinfield V Swallowfield C
[*Entry deleted*: Gift of Hereford. Matthew Field. (Very small vicarage. Swallowfield should be separated. Field simple minded elderly man, very little energy, very bad health. great family afflictions. Ob 1847]
Bayfield

21. Arborfield Yeo

Arborfield. Good natured elderly man.
Pec[uliar] of Dean of Sarum
Sir John Conroy lives here

22. Theale Dr <u>Ellerton</u>. Very good parish priest
NB Some annoyance about license[23]

23. Tilehurst Dr Routh
C[urate] J H Worsley. A good report of him

---

[23] Dr Ellerton, a fellow of Magdalen, was also from 1825 to 1851 Perpetual Curate of Sevenhampton, Glos. His licence to the curacy of Theale appears to follow in 1846 from this note.

24. Barkham. E St John. Young, good natured.. inefficient. Sports-man. Nominally resides.. i e has fitted up a room in the house at Finchampstead – a resident curate at Barkham
Mr Roberts to reside at Wokingham with his Father, Mr St John to marry Roberts sister. More disposed than his Father to do the duty.
Mr Clive very valuable man
N.B. All to be seen

25. Finch Hampstead

Barkham Family living of St Johns.
Henry St John of late living out of parish ap[poin]t[e]d present Son Edward St John very stupid & bad resider. A small parsonage house, & he to be called into residence. Nearly worst Church in archdeaconry. Mr & Mrs Clive laymen residing there very useful, but St John wishes to do his duty

Finchamstead
Same patronage. Edward St John as above.

109v **Reading no 2 Rev.W Levett**

1. Bray. 400 acres. Chiefly under plough. Lets for £450 gross. 12 acres in hand. Surplice fees £25 in lieu of Vicarial Tithes.

2. Maidenhead Chapel PC – land estimated £120, £60 from pew rents guaranteed by corporation to present incumbent but no pew rents legal, i.e. at present incumbent's demise there would be no legal claim on pew-rents.
Holds barely 800 ... a good many free, perhaps ½ – & bound to free 200 more.

3. Cookham V G F Grantham ... infirm ... pauper, lo Church, large family, about 60. Attends to Cookham

110 **Reading no 2 Bray Deanery**
Rev Walter Levett
Bray Walter Levett amiable, sensible practical man
George Welford chaplain to an Alms House. Very low Churchman but good man – simple minded & manly. Very different tone from his Rector.

Maidenhead ½ Cookham, ½ Bray. Chapel. Jas. Knollis PC. Resides at Lord Howe's place in Bicester. James Birch Curate a very useful man.
Desireable to make the Chapel independent district but failed in efforts. Funerals &c go to Cookham.
Sawyer[?] [soldier] good man – speech maker.

Cookham V (Tom Whateley was here for years)
J Grantham. Know no harm. Seems a heavy man. Never ventured on him for Visitn Sermon. No curate.

4. Cookham Dean PC a very valuable man: G Hodson, Trin[ity] Coll fellow; a complete nest of dissenters. GH has done much good.

Cookham Dean A very pretty chapel.
Rev. George Hodson ….a very good man & not as low as Father

110v **Reading no.2 Rev W Levett**   111

5. Bisham Rev V. Thornton. Very delicate man, ..a little ultra in his leaning to Pus[eyism]: but not offensively so.

6. Hurley. F T Weatherhead.[24] Good kind of quiet man. No party. Son of Marlow Brewer. House and Church in good order.

7. Remenham (to be removed to Henley)

8. Shottesbrooke. 1 Duty. Dr Van[sittart]: first cousin of Mr Neale. Preb[endary] of <u>Carlisle</u>. Old School: too little of a reformer....miserable voice
cum White Waltham 2 duties

9. Clewer T T Carter. Son of Carter fellow of Eton. Able man, very zealous, strongish opinions but not so as to give offence

Bisham <u>Rev.V Thornton</u> – a very good man
C[urate] <u>Rev.H Pritchard</u> ord[ained] Dec 1845

Hurley F T Weatherhead. Manner not prepossessing, quite young man. I believe a good man.
Dr Mavor had it some time. Parish then much neglected.

Remenham Owen Briscoe Rector (just come)
[*pencil:* Coarse smoking Jesus fellow]

Shottesbrooke } (Col. Vansittart)
White Waltham }
Dr Vansittart, bit of Hebrew scholar. Good man & very dull preacher.
Very respectable. Canon of York [*pencil* Carlisle]
Old fashioned man

Clewer T T Carter, a very pleasing man, a very High Church man approaching Tractarianism.

111v **Reading 2 Rev W Levett**   112

10. Clewer Stephen Hawtrey
C. Henry Hawtrey
C

Clewer Chapel Stephen Hawtrey

---

[24] Actually F.J. Weatherhead.

11. New Windsor Rev. I Gosset …. Old school, good natured liberal
Gould. Very active, clever man Takes active part at Windsor & Eton Union. Valuable.

12 Old Windsor Jas. Steuart[25]

13. Wingfield C J Elliott, active little man
Nephew of Dean of Sarum. Same opinions.

14. Sunning Hill A M Wale. Know nothing. Church beautiful order

New Windsor Isaac Gossett. Good man. Deaf wife. He lives at Datchet. She a very excellent person.

Old Windsor Jas. Stewart R. *[Steuart]*

Wingfield Charles Jno Elliott. Nephew of Mrs Pearson. Low Church man but very able man. Spoke well & readily against Maynooth.

Sunning Hill (Pec). Alex. M Wale fellow of St John's Cambridge. Very heavy, but know no harm ... 'Foreign wife[26] De Devil, de Devil shd: there you make a clergyman's wife use bad words!' – TVF Aug 8

15. Wargrave to Henley Hitchings a very excellent man

Waldegrave [*corrected to* **Wargrave**]
James Hitchings, son of Hitchings the Tailor.
One of our best men. Lord Braybrooke gave him living. A very able & active Clerk.

112v

16. Knoll Hill Austen Leigh. To be centre of Reading No I.

113

Knowle [*corrected to* **Knoll**] **Hill Chapel** in Wargrave. <u>Austen Leigh</u> serves gratuitously.
Curate Austen Leigh living at Scarletts near Maidenhead. Great talent, zeal & energies. Quite right in opinions. I should have thought him low Church, but as right as can be... Good fortune: & very liberal.

---

[25] Actually C.A. Steuart.
[26] His 'foreign wife' was Caroline Ardrighetti, of Prato, Savoy.

17. Waltham St Lawrence. E J Parker, a very good quiet man, excellent Parish Priest. Holds the living for a young son of Lord Braybrook seven more years to come. No strong opinions. Much beloved. Very careful about singing in his Church – Aust. Leigh

18. Ruscombe Pec[uliar] L H Rudd

19. Hurst Cameron. Active; able.

20. Sonning Hugh Pearson

Waltham St Lawrence Edward James Parker <u>vicar</u>. Amiable gentlemanlike man, Fellow of Pembroke.
Very amiable, not very active but wishes to be of use. His [brother] was competitor for headship with Jeune.

Ruscombe (Pec[uliar]) C Chapel to Sonning

Sonning Hugh Pearson, a very good man & able. Very moderate in opinions.

113v

114

21. Maiden Early

22. Wokingham

23. Binfield Very good & able man...Relation of Lord Brougham. No part[icular] opinions. Able good Parish priest.

24. Easthampstead <u>Late Lord Downshire</u> wanted to exchange Patronage with Ch[rist] Ch[urch]. Mr Beddingfield ... acting as curate to Mr T. unlicensed for 1/2 a year Feb 1846 residing at Warfield House 4 miles off.

Maiden Early C New Chapel consecrated 2 years ago by Bp of Carlisle owing to Bp Bagot's fall. Difficulty as to finding a man.

Wokingham Pec. Morres. A schoolmaster & has been there long. Not efficient. Well meaning man.

Binfield Jas Randall. A clear headed sensible good man. Very active in Parish & in talent one of the ablest men we have. Large Parish, large Church & very good house.

East Hampstead Rev. A Boyle Townshend, ….bit of Irishman. Hot headed. Shrewd cleverish man. Kindly received by Lord Downshire at first at East Hampstead Park. Then quarrels about Roads & Pews. A Parsonage house standing handsomely pulled down to be rebuilt. Some purchase or exchange to be made & so 3 or 4 Bishops tried to make him build.

Phillimore & Marsh have tried to make him build.[27] A gentlemanlike man. Resides at Bracknell. Suffers from gout. When he can in temporal matters kind–hearted. Generally incapacitated from gout.

114v

115

25. Bracknell in Easthampstead Warfield and Binfield. A chapel wanted Elliott interested in this & also Randall

26. Sandhurst Pec.
[*pencil note*: Brazier in earnest in work, very good man (Randall)]

Sandhurst C Pec.

Newbury Deanery

(No. 1) Deanery of Newbury
Rural Dean Henry W Majendie

1. Lambourne E Thompson. Hard working...
Pauperitas & little Influence... a [curious] old Church wanting repairs. T wishes to do his duty.

Lambourne A most important parish. Will be enlarged to £190. E Thompson vicar.
Good painstaking man, right minded.

2. L Woodlands [Conventional] District
J Bacon. A very valuable & useful man.
Built & endowed by Miss Seymours: & House & Schools

Lambourne Woodlands C District
Built by Miss Seymours. J Bacon PC a good man.

3. East Garston [*Entry deleted in* pencil]
Rev. Martin Butt in confinement for lunacy.
R C Gaseley curate not a very clerical character incensed medical man at Newbury. Parish eaten up with Dissent.... a Mr Cornwall injudicious wild Irishman who upset all

East Garstone. Old. Like R Hooker in looks & lean. Martin Butt. But <u>mad.</u>
R C Gaseley curate good man. [*Entry deleted*]

C Smith passable. Field Sport. Arch[deacon]

---

[27] Townshend had been incumbent since 1826; when he died in 1860, the house was being built by Lord Downshire (see entry in second volume).

115v I Newbury Deanery 116

4. Great West Shefford Pop 886 people
Ashley. Old High & Dry – likes good dinners – does not buckle to work. Parish disorganised. Second service much needed. Excuse that one at Little Shefford. Church neat & tidy. A school

5. East Little Shefford
C.B. Coxe tottering on grave's edge ... irritable to a high degree. Quere is there more than an after-noon Duty. like the last.
[*Entry deleted. Pencil note: Stephen Brown*]

6. Welford with Wickham Chapel
... A very fine living ... next to Speen.
W. Nicholson (Irishman) admirable visitation sermon. Too much with Coxe &c dragged down ... property in Great Western Railway. Squabbling in paper as to lines. Kind to poor. Late Popham, now Eyre. Lives as Squire at Welford House. £1300 value. Only 2 services between the 2 Churches. Could a third service be got. A fine conditioned parish as to farmers & squires.

7. Boxford R G Wells... clever man, Son of a late Prebend[ar]y of Chichester & a brother sec[retar]y to ArchBishop. Does labour in Parish .. but occasional meet of the Hounds... "does it very quietly" say squires. Loss of money ... & [? Retracts] giving up Hunting.

West Great Shefford Ashley Gentlemanlike man. Friend of Lord Downshire. Wd be very much hurt if anyone thought him less than perfect. Very inefficient. Self indulgent old Bachelor, Interesting Church.
*NB only one duty. Plea is [*unfinished*]

East Shefford C B Cox. From ill health unable.. half paralytic. living of Avington extreme parish in county. Alderman curate (at Avington not here) good man.

Welford with Wickham Chapel
W Nicholson very earnest man. A visitation sermon shewed seriousness. Squires round dislike him – say he eats too much. He wants an active wife. Very well off besides his good living.

Boxford R. George Wells. Sensible intelligent man and active in his Parish ... right minded man. No very great zeal. Active & well meaning.

No extreme views. Acts as inspector of Schools. Old High so...

116v **I Newbury Deanery** 117

8. Shaw cum Donnington (a very nice Parish) gift of Dr. Penrose. S Slocock ... a good scholar ... Holds Wasing also. A steady Churchman of old school ... rather old & deaf & newspaper reading. A very respectable parish. John Hughes of Oriel lives at Don[ingto]n Priory, he secretary to Diocesan Schools.
[*Entry deleted; pencil note*: Ob 1847 Everett. Good report of successor from Herefordshire]

Shaw Samuel Slocock D D. A good driller – pompous sort of man, a great deal of good about him

9. Newbury Dr Binney. He never visits but Miss Bibby & other family females do.
Orders his curate Do this &c. Not the slightest parochial visit. *Licensed curate Andrewes. Sits at home all day ... preaches good sermons but so ill preached as to empty Church. Just ordained.... Dissent becoming rampant .... though Church feeling. People cowed by Him... He rules them with Rod of Iron.

Newbury Dr Binney. Shrewd clear-headed man – rough.

10. Speen Mr Pearson likely to leave.

Speenhamland Chapel

Speen. Henry Majendie got chapels. St Mary's Chapel Speenhamland
* Hardly possible to say enough. Frank manner
Meakin Good man – M
Stock Cross £500 spent on it
Incumbent Pearson –a good man

11. Hungerford
Mr Davis said to be serving other cure. Mr Majendie will enquire

Hungerford. Pec[uliar] of Sarum W Cookson out of sight in Cornwall for bad case of Fornication.
Curate * Mr Davis said to be good man

12. Avington
Mr Coxe [*deleted; replaced by*:] Gordon above. 2 or 3 houses. Served by a worthy curate, lives at Kintbury
2 miles off. Constantly there. Serves Mr Cherry's Chapel consecrated by Bishop Burgess in Kintbury. Mr C an admirable man.

Avington Mr Cox as above

13. Shalbourne [*pencil*: J Gore]

Shalbourne Pec of Dn of Sarum

117v   **I Newbury Deanery**   118

14. Inkpen Family living in family of Butler of Bishop Butler.
Rev J Butler does not live in the House but in his Father's – conceited foolish manner, attends to the duty.

Inkpen Rev J Butler Rector Good humoured but secular. Shows no harm but very fond of hunting & rather a secular man

15 Kintbury
Mr Lushington of Ch Ch. About 40. There temporarily.
Nothing satisfactory about poor D. Dancing at Balls &c. Done up his Church.
Lord Amesbury a 'ne'er do well parish'

Kintbury (painful case) large Parish.
Dundas son of Admiral Dundas married a lady who had had a child before marriage. D a little avoided good reader – rather coming back. Never followed it into Lords for his own conduct hindrance. Lord Denman tried it &c &c
(a family living Admiral Dundas)

16. West Woodhay.
Geo Sloper – one thinks a little mad, at daggers drawn with his uncle.
Par[ish] registers ill kept – pulled up at further meeting for not paying servants.
Happily a small parish & out of the way, but Vae! vae!

West Woodhay. G Sloper (worst case of all) lives at Boulogne. John Sloper (nephew) Patron Curate. Subject of enquiry about 7 years ago. Whitewashed for want of proof, but in Arch[deacon's] mind guilty of Fornication swearing. Married a respectable person since – a niece of Garter King [of Arms] (Miss Cockerill)

I Newbury Deanery

17. Hampstead Marshall C T Johnson Chairman of SPCK. An excellent man. About 58. He has been thinking of double duty – doubtful if desireable [*sic*]. He would be very ready to do all that right. Good pious man and Faithful clergyman.

[*Entry deleted in pencil*]
18 Brimpton V. G B Caffin (holding the living for a son of Mr Holton of Wool Hampton). A hunting, idle man, conceited, [*pencil ring around words:* Hallos etc.] 'GB Hasty intemperate. 28 or 30'

19. Wasing S Slocock died 1847 [*pencil note:* Cleminson now curate]
(Mr Mount steady Churchman. Worthy man & clever. Large fortune...attends Diocesan Board. Quere <u>value</u> ..... saying that £100 is given & no question) Cleminson

20. Chieveley A very large parish.
J Robinson son of Barker. Hardworking man, anxious to do his duty: <u>was</u> very low Churchman but rising to clearer & steadier views.
Valuable living ... 4 churches and only curate. Could he arrange with any neighbouring man. Perhaps Shefford.

Hampstead Marshall Enborne (pat[ron] Lord Craven) (where Dowager Lady Craven lives a nice place
Charles Thomas Johnson, a quiet sensible man – "one of the best men I have".

Brimpton V Geo B Caffin, a good man, a very small living. Not a man of much power or reading yet zealous & active.

Wasing where one of best laymen of the county, Mount. A strong sense of religion.
S. Slocock incumbent – curate Quere licensed.

Chieveley with 3 chapels –
Winterbourne C
Oare C
Leckhamsted C
John Robinson Student of Ch Ch, married younger daughter of [? Rowden] of High Wycombe. Very good & zealous rather low Church line but one of best men.
Hon & Rev Powys Curate. Married some one beneath him & poor in consequence

119v

21. Thatcham. John Hanbury V embarrassed as a younger man curate here. Came under trial for immorality – horrid kind Sod[omy] nothing more than impropriety appeared – treated kindly by Mr Mount & Mr Foulke.

Mr Clementi ... not paid for 3½ years. He an active man. Singular. He serves Mother Church.

Probably Hanbury mad. Mr Hanbury one service at Midgham & Mr Bowman C serves Greenham. Chaplain of House of Industry..... lives at Speen. Desirable to get Greenham C & Midgham as separate men. Mr Majendie to enquire & report.

22. Bucklebury Dr Williams ... an important Parish. Romans with schools & proselytizing a good deal. See p. for facts about Marlston.

Mr Price Curate married a Baker's daughter of Bath. Mrs Bunbury a she–epis. Miserable attendance at Church. [*entry on Price deleted*].

Mr Kyrke 1847. Welshman.

120

Thatcham with Greenham C & Midgham C
John Hanbury V. Father innkeeper in Staffordshire. Lowish man ... don't much fancy him. Does not pay Curate. Rev. Vincent Clementi very good man.

Very nice place. Mr Foulke purchased he perhaps would endow. No harm about Han[bury] or good.

Bucklebury Pretty parsonage, painful case. Incumbent gouty old man – a Cowleech – got into Orders Olim Chaplain of Gaol in Reading. Preached good Visitation Sermon. Past work, very slow in getting curates.
<u>Dr Williams.</u>
See P. <u>Marlston Chapel.</u> Mrs Bunbury squire's wife here always complaining of Dr Williams. He a well meaning man Mrs Bunbury "of the self–willed school", "one of his tenants"...."over–womaned" A friend of Whitaker Churton.[28]
Mr Price Curate

---

[28] H B Whitaker Churton, fellow of Brasenose, prebendary of Chichester and Vicar of Cheltenham.

Add Beenham, Woolhampton & Aldermaston to Newbury I

Newbury no II

1. East Ilsley Rev. T Loveday Low Church in opinions. Worthy man.

120v

2. Ilsley West. Hon & Rev E G Moore.
Canon of Windsor. Just come.

3. Chilton Mali ominis. Full of incendiary fires. Morland late Curate has purchased next advowson & will do all he can. Grasping farmers & discontented population.
Curate?

4. Farmborough W H P[rice] well spoken of by neighbouring clergy. All this district torn by Ranters & Mormonites (Wroughton of Woolley, clever man, good magistrate, Persiflage (May St Quentin))
W H Price said to be Tractarian.
T. Loveday.
Very attentive. Takes Union.
5. Fawley Don[ative]

2nd Division Newbury.
Rev T. Loveday

East Ilsley Magdalen
Very good man. Rather tending to the low Church. Married sister of Churton's who dead leaving one son & several daughters.
Large good house. He well to do.

121v

Ilsley West Hon & Rev. E G Moore, brother of Lord Mount Cashel – man of no power but straightforward man. In earnest I should think.

Chilton An unpleasant case. No clerical turn whatever – brother of Dean of Ch Ch when able used to hunt a good deal. C Gaisford new curate I think very well of. Son of attorney at Highworth. States [?Crowley] always non-resident in fact better he should.
[*Entry deleted in pencil; new entry:* 1847 called Gaisford into residence. Things said alike to me]

Farnborough Wm Price R. Non resident.
W H Price Curate, nephew. Good man

Fawley Don. Wm H Price above

6. Catmore & Peasemore.
Parish belongs to Mr Easton of Hendred RC.
T Houblon heavy mannered man (your boy would call him Donkey – a good D) brother of J Houblon of Essex & of C Eyre Esq. Of Welford. "very amiable man – very good man" – T Loveday (Peasemore) C Casey & they serve alternately. 2 full services in each. Parish well looked to....a bad spirit in Parish not yet overcome. Bad feeling to Church. Mr Tull calls himself a steady Churchman, & squire between yeoman & gentleman .... – a bouncing ..... Bp Grey a low churchman sowed seeds of dis[sent]. [*carried over to foot of 121v*] Then came Greville & Fiddler & Dissent rages.

Cattemore & Peasemore. A satisfactory cure. Thos Houblon rather High Church & brother of Eyre &c Very good man.
* In own patronage)

Charles Casey curate here.

121v   **Newbury Deanery II**   122

7. Beedon D R Murray V. Lives at Family Living Brampton Bryan[29] nr Ludlow. Married sister of Sir John Reade of Shipton Court. Does not accord with him.
Small living £130 per annum, allows £80.
Harwood newly come. Mr Majendie will look at the House.
all ill T Loveday

8. Bright Waltham
R Marter Lately come to it ... inactive No evidence of devoutness

Beedon Never had a resident incumbent.
D Rodney Murray
Curate.
Quere why non resident.

Bright Waltham called Brightlington
R Marter From bad health inefficient. Good man.

---

[29] The patron of Brampton Bryan was the Earl of Oxford, its value £300 compared with Beedon's £126.

J Day.³⁰ Trouble with Day 48 about Daughter
Mem. (Mr M's origin as given me by C Barter &c)

9. Compton P Jones V. <u>non resident</u> on living in Hereford.³¹ (Jumping Jones)
Mr Wasey squire: an attorney residing at Chieveley. Our Westminster tenant Priorspark ... Ill conditioned man. Forbids Tithe payment & Jones afraid of moving from the way he got living.
Mr Jones dying.
Erck was at Chaddleworth – disliked by Wroughton when curate there – "irk"some.

10. Aldworth J T Austen. Sen[io]r Wrangler married niece of Dr [Michel]
Shy man. Very good man: Moderate man.

J Day curate.
[Cox sen. fellow of Pembroke doing the duty very well & efficiently & bringing the people back 1848. q. not licensed]

Compton New vicar P Jones.
Erck curate for years: a disagreeable mannered man; but wishes to do his duty.

Aldworth. John Thomas Austen a very good man, retiring man, very able & clear headed.
Delabeech family monuments [Grants of Aldworth]
[Some allowances: does his duty. Good man (Loveday) Bullock[?]
She is impar to Austen: [rougher]

122v

11. Hampstead Norris. J Blizard. Pupils, a good mathematician. A son of Dr Locock's rather an indolent man in spirituals. (Constitutionally –Loveday) has not parish in hand. Very infirm health. (Very efficient preacher – Loveday)
an assistant curate author of book on different in world to come.

123

Hampstead Norris J Blizard. A very good man indeed – very low Churchman. Lord Downshire gave the living.
NB Application Jan 1846 towards help from Nat.Soc for School + existing School. 1 Sunday 27 boys 46 girls. One in Hamlet with 20 children. The new 90 children.

---

³⁰ Really George Day

³¹ Actually Chalsfield, Glos, to which he presented himself in 1816, value £351; he gained Compton, value £330, in 1829.

12. Hermitage Chapel district assigned & house built. W Sheppard. injudicious, unguarded tongue – rising. A brother-in-law of Dalby. About 32 ... married to judicious wife – improving man. (Not strong, good man, very active on School – T Loveday)

13. Blewbury Mcdonald. Forward disagreeable man, converted from R.C.s
2 Chapelries Upton C & Aston Upthorpe C

14. Chaddleworth R Milman. A very worthy man. Rather Pus[eyite]: exceedingly useful to Parish & to Mr Wroughton.... I hope would not run into extremes. The most far to that way of any we have: reading & thinking man.

15 Hagbourne V Meredith – good man & devoted to Par: pauper. T Loveday
Quere Abingdon or Wallingford

16. Harwell V Fletcher letting schools &c slip. A gentlemanlike man.
<u>Do. Mr Knight was for 40 years curate</u>

Hermitage Chapel Walter Sheppard. A very good man, low Church

Blewbury Well endowment. Pec of Sarum. Incumbent an oddish man. Bp Burgess gave him the living. Very low Church & unsatisfactory.

Chaddleworth R Milman an able good man, simple [?single] much liked in the Parish.
(Difference with B Wroughton about Societies meeting in School)

Hagbourne V A very good man but very low Church
R Meredith.

Harwell V. A new incumbent W. Fletcher. Great neglect of ArchD[eacon]'s injunctions and by Sir J Chetwode patron as to Chancel

123v   124

17. Didcote

Didcot J Hodgkinson from Bad Health inefficient for many years. Non resident. A sum of money put by for Parsonage House from Dilapidations in Arch's & Bishop of Chichester's hands.

18. Yattendon
A very good valuable man. Getting on in Churchmanship. Nice congregation

19. Frils[ham]

20. Stanford Dingley C Holloway.
A very good man, also rising & getting on in Churchmanship

Yattendon & Frilsham Distinct livings held together. Rev John Flory Howard. A very amiable man but a low Churchman. A painstaking & very liberal & anxious clergyman.
[*pencil note*: Tall (hook nosed) sleepy – good]

Stanford Dingley C Holloway a good man
Low Churchman but good man
[*pencil note*: Dark, spectacled, thin]

124v

125 **Bucks**

Mr Cartwright 1846 **Waddesdon Deanery A**
(had Rural Chapter May 1848)

Chearsley PC (not been to) Amos Hayton
Has also Thame Workhouse
Chilton PC (Do.) Chetwode!!
Crendon Long T Hayton
<u>Commission</u>
Pigott Alfred Chetwode
(Payne Smith finds himself uncomfortable. Hardworking. Quite young. Of Pembroke Coll. Oxford. Many dissenters.
Ilmer (not visited) Partridge. Married man
Kingsey (not visited) W Jackson ... abroad. Licence for wife's health (See Bp of Lincoln's note)
Mr Moody <u>for a season</u>
Marston Fleet J Bull m. J Stevens curate resides at Aylesbury 38 people in parish. [*crossed out*]

Churchyard wants enlarging 1849

Doing something to Church

Mr Springs 1848 Curate

Salisbury Humfrey

Marston North John Pigott of Hughenden PC. Church in dreadful state, praesertim Chancel. In the Patronage (Future) of Dean & C[hapter] of Windsor.
Bunbury <u>curate</u> active, useful. Parsonage in a bad state

Knights

125v **Waddesdon A** Mr Cartwright   126

Oving Thelwall, unpopular with farmers unma[rried] 40. No particular views not active (Freemantle)

Boyce doing well

Pitchcott Price....very old. 80[32] Pop 69 (Freemantle)

Quainton Young. aged 50 Moderate man. Magistrate not [worst] (Freemantle)

Winchendon Lower (not visited)

Shabbington 1849 Morland. Church in a bad state. Doing what he can.

126v   127

II Wendover Deanery. Rev. Harrison.

1. Aylesbury Pretyman

Edward Norman Coles Curate Sep 1850. From near Birmingham & then Thorley I of W. Pleasing earnest mannered man. Mannings Sermons but Churchman not more. Speaks strongly of Roman errors.

2. Holy Trinity [A Campbell *deleted*]
Pennyfather

Spring (now assisting Pennyfather)

---

[32] He had been the incumbent only since 1841. The value of the living was listed in 1845 at £310.

3. Bierton V Apthorpe. Non resident in consequence of an unfortunate marriage. Miss Wallis etc. Stevens curate respectable, High Church. Active. Brother of Stoke Mandeville curate.
  1. Buckland C served by
  2. Stoke Mandeville C   new school
4. Bledlow Stephens . A most excellent man. Sickly wife. Low Church. Active. Lives to himself (Dec 1849 sinking into dejection) Chapel of ease
5. Dinton Harrison. Mr Goodall a clerk. The Squire active & useful man and magistrate. Strong anti–Pus[eyite] Why?
6. Haddenham Wilks. Obliged to leave for immoral[it]y married common woman a year and ½ ago, a commission for drunkenness & immorality. He suspended for a year, now returned & promising.
Cuddington C Meeres an excellent man.
Moderate low.
Farley .... a valuable man given too much way to dissenters. Mod. Low.
Among the most important parishes in Bucks. Dissent

127v   128 *blank*

7. Hartwell Rich ... aged man. Non Resident Ch: Lowndes C[urate] lives at Hartwell.
Respectable Clerk. Rather High. Not too high.
Little Hampden 8 miles off served by Ch.Lowndes also. 1 Service a day in each.
8. Horsenden. D[uke] of Buck[ingha]m. Partridge. Little to do man. Respectable man. Moderate opinions
9. Hulcott Smith. Rather Low Church but good man [ ] SPG at Ayles[bury] Ability. Married man

10. Princes Risborough. D of B. Gray. Moderate opinions. Very respectable active man. Married daughter of Sir H.Compton. Important parish.
11. Lacey Green PC. Landon. <u>Rather</u> High but not objectionable. Active.

128v   129

Wendover I

12. Stone. Reade (43 ac) Low Church but sound. Advised Mr Campbell not to preside at Wesleyan meeting .... takes [pains] Clever & Scientific.

<u>Wendover II Rev Arthur Isham</u>

1. Aston Clinton Pat. Jesus Coll. Oxon. Rev. John George. Just 80. Non resident by exemption in Montgomeryshire
W J Burgess cur[ate] (small salaried) evangel: but lover of order. <u>Was</u> curate of Gt. Missenden. Active. Mr Chapman at Aston Park Churchman, not goer.
School wanted. Dissenters active. Baptists about building a larger Chapel.

2. Aston St Leonards. Pec[uliar]. <u>Don[ative]</u> Rev. E Owen ... has been pol: is coming right. Mainly this. Son – is lecturer at Gresham Coll: clever man.

3. Ellesborough W.H.England Rec[tor] eccentric man [*sic*] Offhand, not hard but little with others. Non devot[iona]l. Independent pol[itical] op[inions] Respectable
Sir R Frankland Russell. Good man. Lady Frankland sister of Bp of Roches[ter] built a schoolroom. Old School man. Bp Rochester's man.

[*pencil notes*]
England of Ellesborough.
No school, never visits
end of parish wholly given to Dissent
almost always in London
leaves his Duty to others
In smock frock
Trinity Sunday 1845 No service
Coal cart
Greatest happiness is to walk up & down in Regent Street.

4. Halton R. Pec. Arch[bishopri]c [*entry deleted*: Henry Dashwood, Son of Sir J Dashwood King, dying at 42. Sad case. Sir John old English Gent[leman] values earnestness & real religion. Above 80. Only one service] Dead.
E Owen.

Poor old woman sent did not come. Lord's Pr.

[*pencil notes*]
Brown, Little Kimble. Rheumatic gout. In bed all week, sees nothing of his people, does not do duty

129v, 130, 131, *blank*

131 **Wendover II**

5. Hampden Great Charles Lloyrd [*sic*] D Ways. Energetic & good. High Church, conciliating
[W Moody C *deleted* – now at Kingsey]
Kimble Great
6. Kimble Little Brown R (Brother to Sir G Beral) no part in school Churchman, inactive. Rheumatic gout disabling. 35 to 40 But undevout £120 per annum 177 Popn.
7. Lee PC Isaac King (incumbent also of Bradenham where resides) Changeable: once low Church; now Tractarian; injudicious.
Statter curate inefficient; bad enunciation; one afternoon duty/
No Parsonage.
Rupert Rowton, Curate of Wendover, officiates at Lee for a number of Wendover people who reside there ... Mr Dearney (Squire) would like to pull it down & rebuild in a more [medieval] character. Very desireable to build large enough for Wendover & Missenden people ... very impt to get it so. Mr D difficult man to approach; fortune; not religious, an architect by profession.
Ranters prevail much on these commons.

132 *blank*

Wendover II A Isham

8. Missenden Great V J B Marsden Health poor. Young Carrington man of High Principle

1849 Mrs & Miss Hornbuckles now residing here & doing a great deal of good. He old Cambs. tutor.

9. Little [Missenden] V Hanmer ("Tally ho H")
Rev T Pegus Curate. Excellent little man devoted to work. Very devotional. Most delightful character. Evangelical. Love of order. 40 to 50. There some years. Married.

10. Risborough Monks. H.T.Beauchamp. High Ch: Old School. Dissent rampant. He always there & wishes to do duty. Not devot[iona]l, quiet, inoffensive, about 50
(Brother to Beauchamp of [*blank, presumably W J Beauchamp of Crowell*] Oxon

11. Wendover Spencer Thornton. Very good man, a very successful ministry
Comm[union]s & Bapt[ism]s much cared for.
Rupert Rowton cur.

12. Weston Turville. A Isham. Agriculturalist.

Wycombe Deanery Rev Pigott

1. Bradenham Isaac King, was Evangel[ical], <u>is</u> good Churchman. Weak health, wishes to exchange

JWR I. King. Rheumatic gout, was very low, served at Teignmouth where drawn to high

2. Fawley Dr Almack (will go to Henley Deanery)

JWR Dr A – try & do his very best

3. Fingest Baker (gone away for 3 *or 4 months Nov 1845) Elderly man, sensible man. Embarrassed from money spec[ulation] at Bath.
Fingest, Turfield & Ibstone <u>all</u> with Single Duties.
Churchman

Believe temporal

4. Hambleden W H Ridley Menzies

5. Hitchenden or Hughenden
1400. Mr Pigott RD
Rev A Ormerod C[urate] Good hardworking man.
Brother of Archdeacon Ormerod

Pigott – very hard working – kill himself
Ormerod 'Likes Barrow – very good – very high distressing voice – good hard work

134v

135 [*pencil*]

6. Lane End Peers. Working man. Elderly, Low Church. Father of V[icar of] Tetsworth

7. Loudwater Arnold. Irishman, very low Church. Good man, working man about 45.
A chapel in the hands of Trustees. The old clerk of the parish was sole Trustee. Quere how these Trustees appointed &c.
Consecration Deed.
No District. No font.

8. Marlow Great Coxwell: very old man. One sermon. Nothing against him but the great sin of omission. All miserable.
No curate – one ought to be.

Marlow. Coxwell. Last Confirmation stuck on door when Conf to be & told them to prepare themselves for the last week

9. Marlow Little Dr Birch. Has a living in London, resides in Heigh resident curate respectable man

9. Dr Birch has gout – suffers nothing to be done, won't allow second sermon.
Fred C Bussell Curate hardworking famous [fellow] rather coarse – [bell] on Easter Sunday to see if more comm[unican]ts & 15 came. Very sensitive. Wife heiress Dr [?]

10. Medmenham Powys,. Excellent man – extreme opinions. Obstinate. Conscientious. Interest of his parish. Scott Murray's Parish & Townsends. Stone altar & monuments care. (ab 40)

10. P a hold on all in Parish by kindness or terror.

135v   136

11. Princes Risborough. Gray. Excellent man.
Good, sound, pleasing mannered
12. Penn Jas Knollis. Good sensible elderly man. Parish schools excellent.
13. Radnage. Symons. Lived much abroad. Widower. Fond of society. Good man.
Par[ish] not in best state. No school

Symons (Whig)

14. Saunderton Frank Faber. Bad health. Of Magd[alen] Just come. Nervous. 45...fancies himself dying.
Hughes

WHR Untidy. Green umbrella. Very high Church. Very good. Was to have married Eleanor Reade Hughes good soft working man.

15. Turville Dr [*erased*] Scobell. Young Scobell only 1 duty (very poor)
[*pencil note:* WHR conversation unsatisfactory unprofessional]
16. Woburn Dupre. Excellent man, sensible, good schools, 2 Services

136v [137 and 138 blank]
Claydon
Edgcott Marsham
Grendon Underwood Pigott curate: hurries through the service inaudibly.... Hunting

138v **Marston North** John Pigott incumbent
D[ean] & C[hapter] of Windsor
Curate very careless. Apathy

139v **Preston B[issett]**

140v **Burnham**
Beaconsfield Rev J Gould about 65 debts to {?Brandryth]
Married & 6 children. In gaol. No opinions.
All wretched. Eaton [*sic*] with dissent.
Colnbrook Butler curate. Letter to Champneys

BOOK ONE 79

Datchett
Dorney Palmer V working 1849 to return. Test Carter's Character &c
Bull C
Farnham Royal Grover R. Kewley. Active earnest sensible, School Inspector
Hedgerley Baylis. Young man R. Nervous, rightly disposed, weak.
Hicham [*sic*]

141v **Horton**
Iver
Stoke Pogis
Taplow
Upton cum Chalvey
For rest of Burnham see 38 [i.e. 77v]

142 [*blank*]

143 [*pencil notes:* The God of Hope fill you with Joy & peace Novr 5 / 46

143v "What are these which are arrayed in white robes? and whence come they?"
"Sir, Thou knowest."
"These are they who came out of great tribulation and have washed their robes & have made them white in the blood of the Lamb. Therefore are they before the throne of God ... and God shall wipe away all tears from their eyes."
Marlow Nov 1846]

144 [*blank*]

144 v See also 82 [= 151v] **(Buckingham Deanery)**
    Tingewick – Justly Hill, Rector
    Reade, Curate – valuable man, good fellow, hard working – High Church
    Barton Hartshorne Smith hardworking man
    & Chetwode united hear that Low Church
    Radclive
    Water Stratford Mr Coleman ... incumbent. Does not stand high – got the living from the Duke suspiciously for alleged political services to the Father. Took Archdeacon's glebe and let it to poor advantageous to himself – arch[deacon] [?wrathy]
Wife nice person. No part in religious opinions or anything. Small parish. She very kind.

145 **Woughton on the Green** [Cox Gt?] Dr Rose recently DD in Scotland to take precedence. Considerable ability – pushing forward – quickness about him. Active. Holds also Little Woolston.
Bradwell – Bell dresses unclerically "like Smith". Young man about 30. Hunts a good deal. His sister married to Mr Quartley of
Wolverton Woolverton: second wife. The son of Mr Quartley disgraced himself (*expelled) at St Bees. Case known to Mr Russell of Beachampton. Old Quartley trying to send him into Orders!!

145v **Biddlesden** H Rice
                H Smith Curate
Buckingham Silvester Curate works hard in Parish & liked but no liking to Church Societies – no head to the clergy
Turweston Cockerton
Westbury Pigott Curate (also Radstone in Northamptonshire of which incumbent see letter on // sends) low church, respected, has pupils, works pretty well non-residence worth ten of Guerdon.
2 services at Westbury & 1 at Radstone licence Guerdon not like a clerical man. Farmed his glebe and lived with the farmers his brother a very intemperate [man]
Shalstone Littlehales. very respectable man, well educated people, and very good congregations & beautiful little Church. Old Churchman aged about 65

146 **Loughton** Athawes. Curious case – an old man merchant in London wanted to find out man of same name, found nephew – educated him condition to go to bar. Trained by preference to Church. Property of £4000 a year land. Lives at Loughton a very good consistent man, active & good. Would not say that he was high or low, of a very sound mind, referee for almost every one in parish (aged about 45) married.
Calverton Charles Perceval. Very active in his parish, keeps to it. Quite right-minded, sober-minded – author of Plain Sermons to Country Cong[regation]s. Brother to Arthur, married Miss Knapp of [Shenley] died leaving one daughter (£50,000 settled on her) Married Devonshire Lady by whom 1 son. Very large fortune, built almshouses near Church & supports old people, health poor, mixes little in society. Church nicely filled up by C P.

146v **Buckingham Deanery**
Akeley Jno Risley fellow of New Coll brother of W C Risley. A very nice fellow & Thorough Gentleman & excellent parish priest: ranks high & not like too many clerks hereabouts very [conscientious] & not resident yet, but resides at Tingewick with his aged Father. has built the house at Akeley about 12 months ago ... a beautiful place. Risley coming to reside

in spring. 2 or 3 miles from Buckingham, views to Aylesbury. Duke says Risley just what Clergyman ought to be, goes about his duty & does it with no nonsense. "A leaning to the low Church, though I should call him a High Churchman. Very consistent" Cole. "A good shot & this evil: friend of Dukes & Tim T Sheppard. I think he will give it up" Russell
Stow Andrewes. Gloomy looking man aged 48. Know little of him. Through his wife Long's daughter of Maidsmoreton £30,000 & is to have Maids Moreton. Of no particular opinion. No leading part save as magistrate.
Lillingston Dayrell Littlehales Rector.
C Nothing in him "got along very quietly in his place & did not see why he should get into any excitement about Church Matters. The Living sold to Mr Reade of Tingewick. Seller dying before vacancy money lost.

147 [*blank*]

147v   **Buckingham Deanery**
Leckhampstead H Drummond – very active. Good clerk. Built a new House.
Addington Scurr (resides at Shenley). Sportsman. Character does not stand high (Athawes of Loughton) will not visit him "No ladies visit her – discreditable & he not [virtuous])
R R Ford Curate active parish priest – no particular views. "very high church – extreme" – Russell
Adstock Barnes. Old man. I believe a very good man. Rather low church. Very good in Parish. "Very good sort of man".
Barton Hartshorne Smith. Very excellent [parish priest]
see above [*144v*] Rather low church. "Excellent young man. Not very low" – Russ[ell]
Beachampton Russell. A very clever man, quite above ordinary class. Of valuable opinions. about 40, a very good man, very good [priest], good scholar – Fellow of Coll at Cambridge. No special school of rel[igio]n – a great education man. The best almost in Diocese. Has school almost a training school.

148 [*blank*]

148v **Biddlesden** – above
Buckingham – above. Crow non visit. Sylvester 'like the dissenters to get money for SPG' The people very well inclined
Gawcott – hamlet of Buckingham
Caversfield
Claydon
Edgcott

149 [*blank*]

149v **Foxcote** Mr Uthwatt, brother of Mr Andrews now of Maids Morton took name of Andrews. Much troubled – Bishop of Lincoln – by quarrels with brother. Rector resides [ ] at Maids Moreton.
Nothing one way or the other' delicate man. Good sort of man.
Hillesdon Very fine Church, sadly dilapidated. Eyre bears a high character – The best part of him is his wife. Raised £20 for SPG & a very good School. Correspond[ence] to Bishop of Lincoln that his wife would work him to death. She has worked wonders in him. Hillesdon in pretty good order.
Horwood Great Adams. Thought extreme, but is not; a pattern of a parish priest
Heart so it that worries to death, though of so different a school.
The most zealous man in neighbourhood.
Great friend of Mr Watkins.
Horwood Little
Leckhampstead Drummond. Can't have a better man. High Church school but not extreme – zealous parish priest. Married Lady E[li]z[abeth] Drummond & wealthy
Lillingston

150 [*blank*]

150v **Marsh Gibbon** I fear very low
Maids Moreton Andrews see above (Mr R offered the brother Uthwatt the living of Linford if he would give half the income. Uthwatt refused. Then quarrels and gave it to Lichfield. Appeal to Bp of Lincoln. He could do nothing.)
Padbury Eyre
Preston Bissett J E Sabine (Father) Curate J E Sabine Active young man, right–minded (Very low on ch. Started Aylesbury paper [*indecipherable.......*]
Took an active part about the Potato famine. Seemed to take a great interest in his parish.

150 [*blank*]

151v **Buckingham Deanery**

Radclive (Coker above)
C Curate residing at hamlet. Mrs Coker very active.
Shalstone C Littlehales (above) Mr [?] very good but old worn & rather inefficient.
Stowe Andrews (above). Duke pulled down the vicarage house & not rebuilt
Water Stratford C (Coleman above) p

Thornborough D Watkins. A very good man (Cockn)
"a very excellent man of Fremantle's school. Very poor, no vic[ara]ge house, a very good man" "a most excellent man – no great education. Welshman not[ ] altered his views, grown sound on Church.
Thornton C Risley (Father to Mr Risley)
Tingewick (see above)
Turweston
Twyford
Westbury (see above)

152 [*blank*]

152v [*in Bishop's own hand*]
      Oxford List 1847
  Rev J H Ashurst*
  Rev John Ballard (Wood Eaton)
  Rev W Bathurst New Coll
  Rev C Barter Sarsden*
  Hon & Rev F Bertie
  Rev Frank Burgess
  Rev J E Chaplin (Magdalen Coll)
  Rev John Coker New Coll
  Rev L G Dryden
  Rev Evan Evans   Pemb Coll
  Rev G D Faithful   Lower Heyford
  Rev John Fox DD   Queens
  Rev J L Goodenough (Broughton Poggs)
  Rev R Harrington DD   BNC
  Rev T Harris   Magd
  Rev Robt E Hughes   Shenington
  Rev Jos: Hunt   Queens
  Rev Francis Kelson   St Johns
  Rev Thomas Lewis   Taynton
  Rev C Marsham
  Rev Andrew Matthews (Jun)
  Rev Henry Matthews   Weston on the Green
  Rev C Meredith   Lincoln Coll
  Rev Rowland Micklestone   Worcester
  Rev Arthur Neate   Alvescot
  Rev J H Passand   Shipton
  Rev G W Pearse   Hanwell
  Rev F Pretyman Magd
  Rev C Rew

Rev H Reynolds   Jesus Coll
Samuel Rev T   Heythrop
Scott Rev E D   Queens
Smith Rev W   Magd
Wetherell Rev W   New Coll
White Rev G   Ewelme
Wilson Rev J   Stanton St John
Wintle Rev J   St John's Coll
Wyatt Rev F   Bletchingdon
Young Rev W B   New Coll

Press cutting inserted   Game-Hunting Missionaries
It will no doubt be of the very highest importance to the interests of humanity that we should give publicity to the fact, that the county of Buckingham can this year boast of having twenty-nine reverend and learned clergymen to wage war against the vermin which molest the farmer's crops. The names of these philanthropic worthies deserve to be handed down to futurity, seeing "their feet are beautiful upon the mountains" because they "publish peace" to the turnips. We therefore cannot do less than give their names in rank and file, having some difficulty to single out the best of them for the head of the list.

Rev W Andrews   Maids Moreton
Rev W Bell   Bradwell
Rev W Carter   Eton College
Rev F W Cartwright   Oakley
Rev E T Champneys   Slough
Rev A Chester   Chicheley Hill
Rev G Chetwode   Chilton
Rev G Coleman   Water Stratford
Rev E Coleridge   Eton College
Rev W Drake   Moulsoe
Rev G T Dupuis   Eton College
Rev C E Gray   Princes Risborough
Rev C A Hall   Denham Rectory
Rev T W Hanmer   Simpson
Rev T Hayton   Long Crendon
Rev E R Horwood   Aston Clinton
Rev M Kerr   Winslow
Rev C Lowndes   North Crawley
Rev J W Meech   Whaddon
Rev W E Partridge   Horsenden
Rev H R Quartley   Wolverton
Rev H J Quartley   Wolverton

155 The following clergymen have taken out Game Certificates for the ensuing year for 1851-1852
Revd C Barter   Sarsden
Revd Joseph Burrows   Steeple Aston
Revd F Burgess   St John's College
Honble & Revd F Bertie   Albury
Revd Thos Cookes   Chipping Norton
Revd John E Chaplin   Magd Coll
Revd John Coker   New Coll
Revd T H Deane   Magd Coll
Revd G D Faithful   Lower Heyford
Revd John Fisher   Magd Coll
Revd Godfrey Faussett   Magd Coll
Revd Thos Harris   Swerford
Revd H E Hughes   Shennington
Revd R Harrington D D   Brazenose
Revd F Kitson   St Johns Coll
Revd Thos Lewis   Taynton
Revd J Lockwood   Kingham
Revd F B Levy   Queens Coll
Revd A Matthews   Weston
Revd Junior Marshall   Sandford *[Jenner]*
Revd A Neate   Alvescott
Revd Chas Rew   St Johns Coll
Revd John Samuel   Heythrope
Revd Charles Shottoner   Jesus Coll
Revd H Smith   Magd Coll
Revd Glyd White   Ewelme
Revd Wm Wetherell   New Coll
Revd N B Young   New Coll

156 [*Pencil note in Bishop's hand*]
Diocesan Schools
Girls W H Risley – no work in House – all young ladies, no practice in schooling. What learned with Anstice good.
[*Press cutting of persons present at the Watlington Annual Ball*]
The company, to the number of 113, began to arrive about 10 o'clock, and dancing to the strains of Weippert's band was continued, with slight intermission, until 4 o'clock.
[*amongst the list of those present, the following names are underlined*:
Rev J Ballard and Mrs Ballard, Rev R Chetwode and party, Hon and Rev Edward Moore, Rev – Cartwright]

156v Curates
J Garrett Jnr. Curate of Aughton. Bulwith Selby. Irish. Ability. Tendency to self-suff[icie]ncy, safe opinions, vide letter RJW &c
Fell G
Schierz

157 Dissenters Nov 22 Reading opposition
    Francis Trench — Islip
    C J Goodheart [deleted]

W Vincent	V of Steventon
H J Lloyd	V of Cholsey * for 1 Reason
J Langley	V of Wallingford
W Thompson	R of Brightwell
F Hazel	Nettlebed
C Jerram	R of Witney
J J Grantham	Cookham
Gab. Valpy	Brickersley
J F Howard	Yattendon
J Prosser	Thame
J P Penson	Clanfield
J W Barnett	Towersey
J Peers	Lane End
J W Peers	Tetsworth
J Gore	Shalbourne 16

C J Goodheart	St Mary's
W J Springett	C of [ ]
J T Jerram	C of Witney
W Mills	C of Witney
W Ritwell	C of Witney
W C Bolton Powell	Minster Lovell
W G Cooke[r]sley	Eton
G R Bell	Cookham
R W Sheldon	Greenham
C Hole	C of St Mary's Reading
W H Madden	C of St Giles Reading
J B Honeywell	C of St John's Reading 12 [Honneywill]

J W Watts	Bicester	To Reason IV	Double Signer
W H Cox	Oxford	To Do.	Do.
T R Tyndale	Holton	To Do.	Do.
E Arnold	Loudwater	Simple	Double Signer
W Simcox Bricknell		Do.	Do.

157v [*Pencil notes*]
Hambleden & Medmenham / Ashampstead
Turville [*deleted*] / Fingest
Fingest – Turville, – Fyrstone – Fazeley – Lane End?

Dissenters Nov 22 1850
   G Arnold   Loudwater *[E]*
   A F Aylward Chesham
   E Bayley   Claydon
   R Bellis   Curate High Wycombe
   Ch: Blackman Chesham Bois
   W Simcox Bricknell Ensham
   C C Champneys Wendover
   G T Collinson *[George John]*
   R J Cockle   Algernon Coote
   W Haywood Cox
   Thos. Curme
   John Fry   Haslemere
   W R Fremantle
   Isaac Gilliam (Northleigh)
   R Cox Hales
   R Holt (Eton)
   J J Irwin
   John Jordan Enstone
   J B Marsden
   W W McCreight
   H Paddon
   W Pennyfather
   Wro: Russell
   Philip Derle
   E L Smith
   J Thomas
   W Watkins
   W Walton
   J C Whitehead
   J W Watts
   G Dundridge R of Rousham
   S W Jordan

26 Incumbents + 17 = 43
6 Curates + 12 = 18
32   61.

158 Private Memoranda [*from the Bishop of Lincoln on black-edged stationery*]

Burnham Deanery

Chesham (minister) Mr Stanhope claims exemption from residence, as Domestic Chaplain to the Earl of Chesterfield, tho' he resides in New Street, Spring Gardens. It cannot, however, be desirable to call him into residence. The curate, Mr Reynolds, is on the point of quitting Chesham, and is to be succeeded by Mr Woods, lately Curate of Latimer, a very excellent man; but there ought to be an Assistant Curate.

Colnbrook A plan is in agitation for assigning a District to Colnbrook Chapel out of the adjoining Parish.

Dorney Mr Palmer's Licence of Non-Residence has expired. He has sent me a Petitition [*sic*] which I enclose. I had promised to renew the Licence.

158v Hitcham Mr Grover will not apply for a renewal of his Licence.

Upton I have permitted Mr Champneys to delay the building of the House, until the Income of the Living, which is likely to be much increased by the letting of land on Building leases, is better ascertained; but the building of a House should not be lost sight of. Mr Champneys and his Curate Mr Knox [?] are not on good terms.

Wycombe Deanery

Hitchendon I consecrated a new Church at Haslemere in the Parish last Summer. A District is to be attached to it, formed out of part of the Parishes of Hitchendon. High Wycombe and Penn: and a clergyman of the name of Fry is nominated to it but not yet licensed.

Turville I have pressed upon Mr Scobell the propriety of having an Evening Service at Turville. The Churches of Turville

159 and Fingest are so near to each other that the Inhabitants, residing near to them, can with equal convenience attend either: but another Service is required for the convenience of out-lying Parishioners.

Stewkley Mr Roberts, when I confirmed at Stewkley in 1844, appeared to be imbecile.

Waddesdon Deanery

Long Crendon I was under the necessity of issuing a Commission of Enquiry into a charge of immorality against Mr Hayton: there was no legal evidence sufficient to sustain it: but

		there was room for grave suspicion. He afterwards applied for a Licence of Non-Residence on account of his Wife's Health, and I was too ready to grant it.
	Fleet Marston	Mr Bull is insane.
	Kingsey	Mr Jackson, I suspect, prefers a residence in Italy to one in Bucks: but I believe Mr Jackson has weak lungs.
159v	Worminghall	Lord Down's Trustees hold out the hope that a Parsonage House shall in due time be furnished.

Wendover Deanery

	Haddenham	I was under the necessity of suspending Mr Willis ex officio et beneficio for one year for immorality. He is now at Haddenham: and, if any trust is to be placed in the continuation of his present good intentions, he will not again offend.
	Aylesbury	A new Church was consecrated at Walcot, a Hamlet of Aylesbury: I had determined upon assigning the Hamlet as a District to it, but Instrument is not completed though in progress.
	Bierton	I shall be happy to explain to the Bishop the circumstances under which Mr Apthorp is non-resident if necessary.

Buckingham Deanery

	Akeley	Mr Risley is building a House which must be nearly finished.
160	Foscot	Mr Uthwatt has promised to put the House into a state fit for the occupation of a Clergyman.
	Maidsmorton	I am afraid that the Bishop will receive complaints respecting the extravagancies of Mr Long, who is very old, and yet will persist in performing the duty.
	Turweston	I conclude that the new House here is in progress towards completion.
	Westbury	I shall be happy to explain, if necessary, the circumstances under which Mr Guordon is non-resident.

Newport Deanery

	Chicheley	Mr [?]Townshend is now in residence.
	Great Linford	Mr Knipe has left Great Linford and a Curate is residing in the Rectory House: but he is not licensed, Mr Lichfield not having seen his Nomination.

162 [*Notes in the hand of Bishop Wilberforce*]
Curates – useful.
C Carey – a good man, would be well placed in a more polished place.
[*pencil*] Rev Z Nash late curate of Denham – Delicate. recommended by Mr Ettrick – moderate – moneyed – <u>good</u>]
Knox (of Upton, purse of between £50 and £60)
Scott – Bucks – some income
Cleaver of Coxwell useful for Abingdon R Dn 2 suggests Majendie

162v Facienda
Chieveley I Newbury another curate [*pencil note*: agreed to]
Thatcham Parish – Greenham and Midgham to be separated Newbury I
Marlston Chapel. At Bucklebury. Question whether a private Chapel or a chapel of ease. Dr Williams has the great tithes & says he need do no duty. Mr Barbury says he must.
Bucklebury Mr Price to be known about.
Aston North R   House (Woodstock). The incumbent Brown lives Kidlington.
Bladon W I service between the Woodstock services. Quere as Woodstock the daughter is this legal
Cassington W To have resident
Bracknell in Easthampstead A chapel wanted

163 Curates
Quere licensed   Wasing   Newbury <u>Payment</u>
                   Chieveley   Newbury
                   Bucklebury   Newbury
                   Chilton   Newbury 2
                   Bright Waltham   Newbury 2
                   Hampstead Norris
                   Beech Newbury II Salary only 80 Pop 334
                   Shottesbrooke & White Waltham
                   Saunderton – Hughes?
Asthall – Witney – <u>Unfit House</u> Eton Coll[eg]e

* Fewcot in Stoke Lyne & close to Ardley to be joined to it.
Stoke Lyne pop 500 no house. Mr Giles in Ireland proprietor
Newton Purcell & Shelswell to be united}
Hardwick & Tusmore   to be united} expence

* Aisle to Church £10 a year (Mr Lowe suggests) to seat = 60 – qu £20

* no land belonging to the Church near the CH:
* Has the House left by Joseph Bullock of Caversfield 1800 & 1810

163v Double duty – non Residence
Great Shefford   Ashley   D[ea]n[ery] of Newbury
Little Shefford   Coxe   do.
Welford & Wickham Chapel   do

Mr Price of Farnborough Newbury II Non Res: why?
D R Murray of Bierton   Do   Do   Do   Rector of
Brampton Bryan Herefordshire
Vicar of Steeple Barton?
Turville wants double

164   D & C of Windsor
Shiplake   Old incumbent. Small living. Much dissent. Mem. as to next incumbent
Bucks
Stow Parsonage. Pulled down by D[uke] of Buck[ingham]

164v   Bp of W
Licences of Curates. How enforce Double duty
Mr Cherry's chapel Dinford Kintbury Cons[ecrate]d by Bp Bagot
Marlston in Bucklebury
Nash Parish   Meech £500. Athawes Coker &c. Cavendish vicarage of Whaddon £700-£800 a year & New College. <u>Vicarage</u> land in Nash

165   Facienda &c
Mr Wintle   Tidmarsh. His Privy Council return
North End Foxfield Chapel
Swallowfield   Ought to be separated from Shinfield. Dean & Chapter of Hereford Patrons.
Little Hampden to be sep[arate]d from Hartwell
Great Hampden from Little Kimble
Little K & Great K & Litle H & Great H might be together
<u>Bishopston</u>. Church wanted in parish of Stone for it & <u>Marsh</u> population belonging to Great Kimble
<u>Prestwood Common</u> Mr Pigott £25 to pay on day of Consecration
Holwell & Kelmscott to be separated from Broadwell
Witney Deanery - Broadwell called Bradwell Vicarage house not inhabited
Loudwater   High Wycombe   – no district
Great [*deleted*] Little Tew Church?

165v   Steeple Barton / House
<u>Middle Barton</u> wants Church
<u>population</u>   Quere could it not be joined to Westcott Barton?

Brightwell Priors should be joined to Brit[wel]l Salome – one Church taken down other enlarged

Widford Church should be pulled down & an aisle added to Swinbrook Church: Lord Redesdale the principal proprietor. Widford Church in a very dilapidated condition Jan 1849

Horley & Hornton to be divided

Fawley Bucks quere Donative – income or what?

166 Quaerenda

Milcom [Milcombe] in Bloxham – served by Inc[umbent] of Wigginton

Loudwater <u>Trustees</u> Quere by whom appointed no <u>font</u> – no rates, how to be enforced

North Stoke & Nuneham Minor ought to be 1 & sep[arate]d from N[uneham Courtenay]
       Done

Great Marlow – one service Quere can I order a second?

Mursley Deanery & Mr Adams

Fawley in Newbury II claimed by Mr Wroughton –Church & Parish

Woodcote endowed School 1720 Woodcote School called School of Industry – Founded & supported by R Morrell for 30 girls. Kept in 5 years.

South Stoke School   Foundation by Dr Griffith Higgs 1670 Quere the Trust

Lyford Chapel in Hanney – Worcester will furnish £20 per annum. Quere how best to use it. 130 pop.

Curme Evensong

166v Index [*Bodleian pagination as followed in the transcript in brackets*]

Aston Deanery	24-26	[52-57]
Buckingham Deanery	35 & 79-83	[70, 145, 146]
Burnham Deanery	78-79	[140v - 142]
	88	[*actually 114*: 77v]
Brickhill	36-7	[74v] -

Broughton, Milton Keynes, Moulsoe, Newton Longueville, Simpson, Stoke Hammon, Fenny Stratford & Water, Wavendon, Wroughton, Willen, Woolstone

Claydon Deanery	32-33	[65v]
Mursley Deanery	33-34	[67]

Cublington, Drayton Pars[low], Dunton, Eddisboro, Hardwicke, Hogston, Horwood Mg & Parv, Stewkley, Swanbourne, Tattenhoe, Whaddon

Newport Deanery   35   [72v]
    Bletchley, Bradwell, Haversham, Hanslope, Leafield, S.Loughton, Shenley, Stantonbury (Stony Stratford), Woolverston, Tyrringham

Newport Deanery 2   36   [73v]
    Astwood, Brafield, Chicheley, Clifton Reynes, Emberton, Gayhurst, Hardmead, Lathbury, Newport Pagnell, Newton Blossomville, North Crawley, Olney, Ravenstone, Sherrington, Weston, Stoke Goldington

Witney Deanery   26   [*actually 78*: 57v]

167

Wycombe (Piggot)   76   [133v]

Waddesdon   71   [124v]
    (Oving, Pitchcott, Quainton, Winchendon, Shabbington)

Wendover (Harrison)   72   [126v]
    Aylesbury, Bierton, Bledlow, Dinton, Haddenham, Hartwell, Horsendon. Halton, Risborough, Stone

Wendover (Isham)   74   [128v]
    Aston Clinton – St Leonards, Ellesborough, Halton, Hampden, Kimble &c, Missenden

DIOCESE BOOK II 1854

ii   *Pasted to Flyleaf: Printed list of Churches in the Diocese of Oxford.*

iii   A LIST OF CHURCHES AND CHAPELS CONSECRATED FROM THE 1ST JANUARY 1845, TO THE PRESENT TIME

Date	Church or Chapel.	County.
1845		
May 15	Cookham Dean Church (Parish of Cookham)	Berks.
Octr 10	Broadwell Church	Oxford
1846		
April 22	Woodcot Chapel (Parish of Southstoke)	Do.
23	Bearwood Church (Hurst)	Berks.
Oct 20	Stoke Row Chapel (Ipsden)	Oxford
Oct 22	Seer Green (Farnham Royal)	Buckingham
Decr 3	Nettlebed Church	Oxford
1847		
Feby 11	Tubney Church	Berks.
May 26	Twyford Church (Hurst)	Do.
Augt 12	Crawley Chapel (Witney)	Oxford
"	Curbridge Chapel (Do.)	Do.
1848		
July 4	Bradfield Church	Berks.
	[Rotherfield Grays Church. Oxford *Damaged entry*]	
Sept. 29	Littlemore Church	Do. (Oxford)
1849		
May 1st.	Penn Church	Buckingham
June 15th.	Linslade Church	Do.
June 5	Hambledon Church	Do.
July 11	Woodgreen Church (Witney)	Oxford
Septr 11	Wavendon Church	Buckingham
Octr 19	Prestwood Church (Hughendon Parish)	Do.
Novr 22	Headington Quarry Church	Oxford
1850		
April 6	Winkfield Church	Berks.
April 16	Stubbings Church	Do.
August 5	St. Leonard, Wallingford (rebuilt)	Do.
Septr 18	Grazeley Church	Do.

Novr 30	St George The Martyr Chapel of Ease to St Mary Magdalen	Oxford
1851		
Feb/ry 26	Bracknell Church (Warfield)	Berks.
June 20	Milton Church (after repairs & alterations)	Do.
28	Cadmore End	Oxford
Decr 2	Upton cum Chalvey, Chapel of Ease	Buckingham
1852		
June 17	Colnbrook Chapel	Buckingham
June 25	Lamborne Woodlands Church (rebuilt)	Berks.
Decr 24	Kidmore End Church	Oxford
Aug/st 13	Holy Trinity Chapel of Ease Great Marlow.	Buckingham
Novr 10	Hedgerley Church (rebuilt)	Do.
1853		
February 7	Saint Paul Chapel of Ease, Banbury.	Oxford
February 19	South Banbury District Church	Oxford
April 12	Saint James Eastbury (Chapel of Ease)	Berks.
June 10	Clifton Chapel of Ease (Parish of Deddington)	Oxford
October 27	Little Tew Chapel of Ease to Great Tew Church	Do.

vii –xiv An Account of the mode of augmenting Livings by the Governors of Queen Anne's Bounty, to meet Benefactions, – and also (in conjunction with them) by –

I	THE TRUSTEES of	PYNCOMBE'S CHARITY	
II	"	"	HORNER'S	"
III	"	"	MARSHALL	"

xv–xvii Printed Copy of the Address to the Bishop of Oxford signed by the Archdeacons and Rural Deans, 1 March 1859, and the Bishop's Reply, 7 March 1859, in response to the pamphlet *Facts and Documents Showing the Alarming State of the Diocese of Oxford*

xix Continuation of the list of Churches opened

    Reopened Denchworth. March.1854
    St Michaels Oxford.   Do.

(Reopened) Henley 1854.
(Reopening) of Aylesbury Jan 17. 1856
(reopening) of Cheddington March 6 1856

567b *inserted letter*

Chichester

Nov: 21. 1907

Dear Lord Bishop

I am sending you a book by my brother in laws advice, which if you ever have time to look at it may be of interest as recording so much about the Diocese which was once the Writer's, & is now yours –

I am venturing to tell you that our second boy is to be Confirmed at Eton on Sat: & perhaps you will give him a special thought, for he has lost the very best & most devoted of Fathers –

Believe me dear Lord Bishop your sincere

Emily Wilberforce.

folio
1. **Abingdon Saint Helen. V. with Drayton Curacy**.
   Rev N Dodson. Confirmed here <u>again</u> March 13, a largish number though very small for the population.

   T H Hulme C[urate]. of Shippon. – Confirmed here again March 13. 63. Above 240 candidates (Marcham coming) & a pleasing confirm-[ation]

   Dodson has got near £400 more for Shippon

   Henry Joscelyne now C[urate] of Shippon O H Carey of Sandford

   Alex Goalen Chief Curate well spoken of

   E T H Harper Chaplain of Union

   T G Mortimer of Drayton.

2. **Abingdon Saint Nicholas. R**.

3. **Ackhamstead (See Lewknor) with Milton & Barford**

   Adderbury. V.
   Rev J Alcock – Rev W S Sanders Curate & doing well 12 March 1855. Confirmed here – for A, Bodicote (Wariner) Deddington (Brogden) Clifton (Risley) Lt.Worton & Hempton (Best) Barford (Hookins) Milton (Dr.L Hutchinson) –a pleasing confirmation. The infant School built through Sanders agency, which I inspect.

   <u>1 April 1856</u> Comes to consult me first whether to continue a habit

he had accidentally begun without knowing it was not the custom of collecting from all the congregation – I advise not to continue it, & he quite agrees. A case of conscience also as to a poor fallen woman.

Richard Ruding Stephens – comes Feb 20 1858 to be instituted. A right minded man not very efficient. He means to keep a Curate & to keep up the Services. The rents far too low, hopes after payments it will be £600 a year. The College helping by giving up copyhold to mend house. Confirm at Milton for March 11/58 a very nice confirm [ation]. Old [Hookins] & V Green acting as Curates.

*W S Sanders as Curate of A. well spoken of by the Goddards. NB.Confiirm March 21 61. Rather a nice confirmation. Nov 11 61 come here with Arch [deacon] Clerke & most hospitably received & open Little Barford Church of which the Vicar of A. is Rector – NB The desireable thing to unite the Barfords close together & raise endowment to £150 – Getting the college as well as Vicar to give.

R R Stephens – Confirm here March 1 1864 H D Gordon Curate See his letter to me Feb 64

* Now rec [ommende]d by me 1861 to Gosport.

4 **Addington. R.**
Rev T Scurr. Giving all sorts of trouble to good Hubbard July 1855 Yields in the course of the autumn & yields all Hubbard wishes D. G.
<u>Jun 7 1859</u> come here to Hubbards to consecrate church rebuilt by Hubbard. NB After Row.

5 **Adstock. R.**
Rev A Baynes. Only brings 6 girls to confirm [ation] Feb 1856. I hear that the Parish sadly neglected. He half blind old & magistrating – wrote to consult Fremantle. March 1856. Baynes writes back, deprecating having to preach a second sermon. I write back March 3, trying to stir him up to sense of duty & pressing Curate – Jan 1857. He proposes to me Plummer late of Roberts parish. Licensed. Sep.57. I urge monthly communion & preaching for Pastoral. He sends crusty reply; his curate will undertake the trouble of monthly communion so far, but too poor for Pastoral! Nov 26.59. Robert Matson writes from Devizes for leave to be licensed, highly commended by late Bishop of Antigua & I assent. License him in person at Oxford, & much pleased with him. He gets A.B. to agree to reading Comm [union] Office from Comm [union] Table monthly communion &c. Mr. Baynes dies June 27 1860 & on the 22nd of Dec [ember] – comes

to me at Cuddesdon John Hart for institution on his own Petition. **NB** His pledge in writing as to money for Church restoration to be Paid in 1864.

[Loose page inserted] Endowment of Adstock.

	£		£
300 acres= with Rectory & Fees	496 1	Deductions Land Tax. Interest of Money borrowed	18 16
Total Value	497 43 454	Poor & other rates about 1d =	9 43

Besides these deductions there are Repairs, Insurances, Agency & other incidental expenses, which I am unable to state until I hear from my Agent.

6 **Adwell. R.**

7 **Akeley. R. with Stockholt.**
J H Risley. R. 1854 A miserable old tumble down Church. Risley moving long for its redress – gets a poor plan from a Mr. [Tarring] 2[3] Charles Street Middx. hospital – but adopts improvements of G Streets – which amended plans Ap[ril] 24.54 I promise to support Consecrate the new Church July 30 1855 a pleasing building with faults – saved from being Horrible by Street – confirm here Feb 23 1856. Day beautiful & the confirmation a specially nice one in all respects. Nice attendance from the Parish at Maids Moreton March. 21/59.

8 **Albury. R.**

9a **Aldermaston. R.**
I B Burne. Confirmed here March 31 1857. Orderly & attentive but not much impressed apparently. Ordered again the Earth removed from the side of the Church. A poor Farmers orphan Sarah Keefe with a white swelling crippled. Excellent statement of parish accounts. March 15 – 1860 confirmed here. All pleasing – Edward Burne second son.

9b *Inserted printed document.*
1856.

ALDERMASTON PAROCHIAL CHARITIES.
ANNUAL SUBSCRIPTIONS.

	SCHOOL.	CLOTHING CLUB.
	£.	£.
Burr, Higford.Esq.	20. 0. 0.	5. 0. 0.
Burr, Mrs.	40. 0. 0.	3. 0. 0.
Burne, Rev.I.B.	5. 0. 0.	1. 0. 0.
Bush, Mr.	0. 5. 0.	0. 0. 0.
Fox, G. F., Esq.	1. 0. 0.	1. 0. 0.
Gilchrist, Mrs. [2 year's School Subscription]	4. 4. 0.	0. 10. 0.
Hicks, Mr.	1. 0. 0.	1. 0. 0.
Joplen, Mrs.	0. 10. 0.	0. 10. 0.
Keep, Mrs,	3. 0. 0.	2. 2. 0.
Mount, William Esq.	12. 0. 0.	3. 0. 0.
Phillips, Richard, Esq.	1. 0. 0.	1. 0. 0.
Soper, Mrs.	0. 10. 0.	0. 10. 0.
Strange, Mrs.	3. 3. 0.	3. 3. 0.
Tew, Mrs.	0. 10. 0.	0. 10. 0.
Vidler, Mrs.	0. 10. 0.	0. 10. 0.
Wimball, Mr.	0. 10. 0.	0. 10. 0.
	93. 2. 0	23. 5. 0.

DONATION

Oughton, Mrs., Broom Park, Canterbury, per Rev.I.B.Burne	1. 1. 0.	0. 0. 0.
	£94. 3. 0.	£23. 5. 0.

GRANTS FROM THE COMMITTEE OF COUNCIL ON EDUCATION IN SUPPORT OF THE NATIONAL SCHOOL.

	£	s.	d.
Capitation on account of twenty Boys and six Girls	7	10	0
Augmentation of Master's stipend	16	10	0
Gratuity to temporary Monitors (Dec.31,1855– May 31, 1856) including £2 1s.8d. to the Master for their instruction	6	5	0
To the Master, for industrial instruction of eleven children	1	7	6
	£31	12	6

It is proposed to send annually to an Industrial School, the girl who shall be considered most eligible to receive instruction as a Domestic Servant.

9c

RECEIPTS

NATIONAL SCHOOL

	£	s.	d.
Balance in the hands of the Manager from last account	18	17	8½
Children's payments	17	18	10
Subscriptions and Donations	94	3	0
Books and Stationery sold	0	8	10
Work sold	2	17	2½
Grants from Government	31	12	6
Night School receipts	0	11	3
Garden produce sold	2	9	8
	£168	19	0

CLOTHING CLUB

	£	s.	d.
Balance from last account	6	14	0
Depositor's payments and fines	55	12	9
Interest from Saving's Bank	0	6	8
Subscriptions	23	5	0
	£85	18	5

CHILDREN'S SHOE CLUB

	£	s.	d.
Depositors' payments	9	0	1
Subscriptions – Burr, Highford, Esq.	4	16	5
Burr, Mrs.	3	0	0
	£16	6	6

ALMS MONEY

	£	s.	d.
Balance from 1855			
Offertorial Collections at the Holy Communion	4	0	6
Offerings at Private Administrations	0	1	3
Alms gift – Miss Bennett, London	3	0	0
May 4 – Royal Berkshire Hospital – General Thanksgiving for Peace	3	0	10
June 29 – Society for Propagation of Gospel In Foreign Parts	4	15	1½
December 14 – Diocesan Board of Education	4	1	0
	11	16	11½
	26	9	0½

9d

EXPENDITURE.
NATIONAL SCHOOL

				£	s.	d.
Master's Salary				70	0	0
Management Expenses				1	8	2
Repairs and Apparatus				15	11	11
Books and Stationery				3	0	8
Materials for Work				8	10	6
Night school Expences				0	16	3½
Garden.	£	s.	d.			
Labour	1	1	5½			
Manure	0	7	0			
Seed, Potatoes, &c.	0	8	3			
				1	16	8½
Monitors				5	4	10
Gratuity to the Master– Government Grant				19	19	2
" to Children(Cloaks and Capes), do.				5	7	9½
Prizes given at Christmas (Cloaks, &c.)do.				1	2	9
Balance in the hands of the Manager				36	0	2½
				£168	19	0

CLOTHING CLUB

	£	s.	d.
Paid to Mr.Hannington, draper, Newbury, for goods supplied	73	14	6
Money returned to Depositors	1	18	2
Fines distributed among Depositors	0	14	1
Expenses at Sale	0	0	10
Balance on closing Michaelmas Account	9	10	10
	85	18	5

CHILDRENS SHOE CLUB

		£	s.	d.
Paid for Shoes supplied Mr. Tull, 22 Pairs		8	17	6
"	Mr. Stair, 14 Pairs	5	5	6
"	Mr. Bushell, 3 Pairs	1	1	6
"	Mr.Soper, for tipping 28 pairs	1	8	0
Money returned to Depositors		0	4	0
		£16	16	6

9e NUMBER OF CHILDREN AT THE NATIONAL SCHOOL IN JUNE, 1856.

Number of Children at the School aged under										over	Total No. on the Books
v years	vi	vii	viii	ix	x	xi	xii	xiii	xiv	xiv	
6	96	11	7	9	8	16	9	3	0	1	79

NUMBER OF CHILDREN WHO HAVE BEEN AT SCHOOL.

LESS THAN I YEAR	I YEAR OVER	II YEARS	III YEARS	IV YEARS	V YEARS AND OVER
29	18	11	6	6	9

Admitted in the last twelve months	29
Left in the last twelve months	30
Highest weekly average	65
Lowest weekly average	43
Average attendance for the past year	55
Present ordinary attendance	58

9d ALMS MONEY

	£	s.	d.
Distributed to the Poor at Aldermaston	7	9	1
May 8,– Transmitted to Mr.Wm.Dredge, Secretary, Royal Berkshire Hospital	£3	0	10
July 3.– Transmitted to Mr.Wm.Robt.King on Account of the Society for the Propagation of the Gospel in Foreign Parts	4	15	1½
Transmitted to Rev F.Menzies, Oxford, on Account of the Diocesan Board of Education	4	1	0
	11	16	11½
Balance in hands of the Incumbent.	7	3	0
	£26	9	0½

9e

THE HOLY COMMUNION WILL BE ADMINISTERED IN ALDERMASTON CHURCH UPON THE FOLLOWING SUNDAYS AND HOLIDAY DURING THE YEAR 1857.

IV. Sunday after the Epiphany	February 1
II. Sunday in Lent	March 8
Easter Sunday	April 12
Whit Sunday	May 31
III. Sunday after Trinity	June 28
VIII. "	August 2
XIII. "	Sept. 6
XIX. "	October 18
Advent Sunday	Nov. 29
Christmas Day	Dec. 26

January 1857.

I.B.BURNE,
Incumbent.

10   **Aldworth. V.**
George Bullock. May 48 succeeds good Austen. Dies of consumption Oct 1858!, & Dec 16, 1858 Francis Llewellyn Lloyd Senior Fellow of St Johns Cambridge comes for Institution. James Bp Ely D 1841 1842 P. has been curate to his Father Mr Lloyd grandson of Blick of Tamworth.
June 29. 1861 consecrate an addition to the Churchyard & preach for the rebuilding of the Tower.

11   **Alkerton. R.**
Robert Hughes. Comes with candidates March 11 to Horley.

12   **Alvescot. R.**
The Rev A Neate. At the Visitation Robert Killmaster one of the Churchwardens of Shilton (which see) – comes to Broughton cum Filkins March 19. 1858. See Shilton.
Edward B Welburn Curate. 1860.
I preach here Feb 14/64 at the time of the Mission to a very full & most attentive congregation on, We beseech you not to receive in vain. Hear about Poyntz from Sturges who thinks I might by writing to him get him to support Neate in Church restoration – Neate married grand daughter of old Goodenough of Kencote. Has done a little in the chancel. A great respect for me & will do anything.

13 **Ambrosden. V.**
   Rev L Dryden – [Comely's] Failure to whom Bp Lloyd leased the Episcopal property threw it into the hands of Carter dissenter & Brewer at Portsmouth, whose tenant also a dissenter preacher.

14 **Amersham. R.**
   Rev J T Drake – attended a meeting here for Diocesan Ch Building Dec 1854 very successful & seemed to move the place a good deal. <u>March 12 1856</u>, confirmed here again. The candidates too few especially the males. A good deal of Feeling in them – O Gordon who has worked well on the whole going in consequence of defective eyesight in September. Suggested to Drake to secure Travers. Luce going on better & more popular than he was. But still almost without pupils. <u>April 10/59</u> confirm here again the best I have had. E J Luce. <u>R H Kingdon</u> Curate seeming earnest. Poor Drake lost a son of 20 & much affected. <u>Aug 59</u>. Mr. Chedwin moving again towards church in Hamlet of Coleshill. Aug 8, 1859 Matter before Evetts. see letter. John Drake Dies, 25 June/60
   <u>Nov. 7</u>. <u>1861</u>. I consecrated the Chapel of Ease of All Souls to Amersham. [*marginal note:* At Coleshill] John Drake before his death had collected the money & <u>R H Kingdon</u>. holding the Living carried it on. J Drake leaving in his will that instead of a monument in the church at A. he wished an East Window put in Chapel. I at Shardiloes. All the Drake Family attending nice service. Curates Baynes from Essex well spoken of by L Owen. <u>Not</u> to me very prepossessing. Pember, poor. R H Kingdon doing very well. <u>March 24 62</u> Confirmed here. The most promising looking confirmation I ever had here. Pleased with Kingdon in conversation too.
   [*marginal note:* E F Luce Chaplain to the Union]

15 **Appleton. R**.
   <u>W J Butler</u>. applies June 19. 1856 for leave to be six months abroad at Naples from October next for health– Mr Smith of Magdalen Coll taking his place. I consent. <u>W J Butler</u> respectable. Was a self indulgent man at Magdalen.

16 **Appleford. V.**

17 **Arborfield. V.**
   <u>Sir John Warren Hayes</u>. The church in dreadful plight: poor Hayes cowering before Sir E Conroy & going to move. He comes with a very few candidates to Shinfield. April 3/57. Proposes Godfrey

Thring as Curate vice. A Pott gone to near his Fathers. A Pott being promoted to a benefice.

Alexander Buchanan comes June 28/58 to be licensed J Lichfield 53.54

Visited the Old Church & gave directions March 24/63 & looked generally at the New. June 19 1863 consecrated Arborfield New Church. Built by Sir W Browne Sir J Hayes &c.

Preached Rev X1X – worship.

18 **Ardington. V.**

Ralph Barnes. Reopened this church. When ?

19 **Ardley.R.**

John Lowe. March/58, attended confirmation with flock at Stoke Lyne. He once would have taken Fewcott if added with NB. only £10 a year to Ardley but now not up to it. aet 68.

Visit the church &c. March 9. 61, & approve of what Lowe, now 70 last Dec. going to do in it – Sophia C Barr, pleasing from Leeds at confirmation. March 5. 64 confirm here. The church now greatly improved. Chancel raised &c. North side rebuilt with Barbarous windows by old Mr Hurd 70 years ago. A very nice confirmation.

20 **Ascot under Wychwood. P.C.**

Rev G Lott – Confirmed here March 22.1855. A rough impressible set from here & [ ] some Leafield. Church a pretty small & easily restorable– old Harris & churchwarden B inclineable stirred them up to write to Lord Churchill. Street to survey. Mrs Marshall Hacher would help. April 1856– The vestry moving. Jan 1858 G Lott resigns appointed to Bampton. After much doubt I appoint Tarbutt. Open the Church which except the Chancel & stove well restored by Street & confirm here Sunday March 14.58.

Arthur Charles Tarbutt. comes May 27./ 58. Wishes to exchange some of the glebe for the government House & then to add to it – Pleased with first aspect of things – June 11. 1858, government offer to exchange their house there for land – & to give £200 towards 6 for making the House fit– I assent. Dec 1858. He full of dread about expense &c. Barter thinks him A C.T. almost insane hereon. Comes to me at Wells Oct 59. Wife ill at Bath gets allowance to go to Bath put in a brother of Tweedy's of Stratton Audley as Curate with probable succession I refusing more.

[*marginal note:* Robert Tweedy A of Exeter Coll. Priests orders Sarum 55.]

19b The Ascott Income from these

	£	s	
Grant from Ecclesiastical Commission	39	0	0
Annual Rent of Ascott Glebe	20	0	0
Charge on Shipton Tithes (at least paid to me by Col: Wood's Tenant)	19	6	8
Rent of Vicarage Cottage	3	0	0
Rent of field at Bourton on Water bought by Queen Anne's Bounty	20	0	0
	£101	6	8

——— Return (S.W.) ———

21 **Ashampstead. P.C.**
Rev Jno Holden [*sic*] I preach here April 19.1857. A very good & very attentive congregation. Holden good active & low. Says want of moral tone is the evil of the place. Much rel. knowledge. Ranters very strong here. Church restored 7 years back mainly by J Hopkins. All well except the seats in Chancel with back to Altar: New House & a nice one.

22 **Ashbury. V.**
W Chambers. Confirmed here Sunday afternoon March 22/57. Church crowded– a nice confirmation Mr Lee the Curate. Nervous has worked hard– Poor Chambers with his chancel walls spangled with the records of his grief Henry Lee Curate leaving March 1860. Well spoken of by W.C. W Chambers dies May 29. 60.& Aug 13 1860, I institute to it the * Rev H Miller– ordained by H Exeter 54.Deacon 55 Priest. Held a living near Banbury at Radway. Cousin to Miller near there.

*[*marginal note*: Henry Miller.]

Between pages 22 & 23 there are 2 newsprint cuttings from unidentified source.

A.D. 648. At Ashendon an agreement was made between Kenwalch, King of the West Saxons, and his brother's son, Cuthred (by whom he had been deposed), by which he was restored to that part of his kingdom which lay northward of the river Thames, – (Kennett.)

A.D.661, – Ashendon and the adjacent country pillaged by Wulphur, King of Mercia.
A.D.871. – At Ashendon, the Danes defeated by King Ethelred, and Alfred, his brother.

23 **Ashenden. P.C.**
Rev E Gardiner. Miserably poor preferment £60 a year paid by Lord Chandos on behalf of Christ Church, which has £700 every 7 years as a fine & £30 a year reserved rent. No house & always held with something. Lord Chandos going to try if he can do anything with Dean of Ch Ch. No school Feb 1856.
Oct 1857 Bickersteth preaches for SPG & describes the attention of all as extreme.

24 **Asthall. V.**
Rev Henry Gregory. Sep 1857, promises henceforth monthly communion.
March 19 1858– Brings his candidates fairly prepared to Witney.
March 22.58, at Witney consults me as to getting a Chapel built at Asthall Lye, where 150 souls, a mile & half from A. Of old the greater part of congregation thence: but of late the Ranters have made great way there. I encourage a Chapel. March 2/61 he reports it as ready by May.

25 **Aston Abbotts. V.**

(**Aston-in-Bampton** see page 36)
Rev J Thornton The Churchwardens claim Sep 1857 that he as Vicar should repair & clean Chancel. Refers to me. I advise him to require the special ground of such a claim in writing.
Mr Thornton I hear Oct 1857 scientific. Entomologist makes money by dissection of insects. His drawings excellent. Retiring, yet able.. great thing to get Beazley of whom Lady Miriam Alford speaks well to stand up for these parishes of Overstones.

26 **Aston Clinton. R.**
The Rev Eyton Confirmed here again Feb 10.1856, Isham &c. attending. The Chancel frightfully cold – I think slates laid on open woodwork from the feeling. A nice confirmation. Cust, Lloyd &c. there. Correspondence 1861.2. with Eyton as to keeping a regular curate. He promises he will & repeats it Aug/62 at Buckland.
Charles W W. BD Fellow, Jesus College, Oxford.

27 **Aston Saint Leonards [see Leonard Saint.]**

Aston North. V.
Rev C R Clifton. Confirmed at it March 12 1854 – The young people very nicely prepared. From Canon Clifton, Somerton, Campbell, Duns Tew, Cyril Wood, Fritwell.

The Church been improved since my last visit. Seats lowered & well restored, pillars & arches scraped. Col Bowles projects taking away a hideous Corinthian deformity by the Chancel Arch. Some fine old monuments. March 8. 58 Clifton comes with his candidates to Somerton nicely prepared.

March 7.61 to Steeple Aston. Col Bowles has just sold this. Examined Church &c July 26.63, to see if Mr Milliar had better move it – I think so. He doing much for the Parish, building cottages &c. March 3./64, I confirm here, & come after to F. Milliars to dine & sleep.

28 **Aston Rowant. V.**

Rev T Williams Confirmed in it Feb 24 1855– For Lewknor Sydenham Stokenchurch Adwell & [gap] a pleasing confirmation all seeming attentive – John Brown & Arthur B live at Kingston Lodge here– Kingston the most populous hamlet of A.R.

29 **Aston Sandford. R.**

R Monro– Dies [Dec] Nov 31 1857. May 27. 1858 comes for Inst. from Barnet George Alford whom I ordained in 1847 to the curacy.

He speaks very pleasantly of his ordination here. Of enlarged views of being right on regen[eratio]n &c. I hope a good & useful man.

Benjamin Hayward Huddleston Browne, from Claughtons neighbourhood see his & her letters. At first I refuse exchange. But he professing himself indeed a man of peace I consent – & he is instituted March 31 1862.

30 **Aston Steeple. R.**

Rev J Burrows. Dec 1855 complaint of non-visiting – I try to get him being rich[33] to keep a curate. He resents hotly – alas!

March 13 1855. Confirmed there. Nothing amiss. Heyford Upper (Gould) Heyford Lower (Faithful) Rousham (Dandridge). A curious altar cloth seeming to have been made from copes. The church restored a little too soon but well for its time. Cold . Everyone ready to complain of poor Burrows who now disposed to give a title. Gives a title Christmas 55–56 to Borrow who falls sick & obliged May 1856 to resign. I try to persuade Burrows to have intermediate curate he having chosen one who cannot be ordained till Sept or Christmas. March 7/61 confirm here. Church very full & they attentive.

*Mills Curate going away. & (blank) coming. Old Burrows failing Jan 27–1863 comes Henry Brookes to be instituted from whom I

---

[33] The income of the benefice in 1845 was £582, the population 580. The Bishop had already written to Burrows in December 1854.

hope everything good. First went to his father in Shropshire. Then to an uncle in Northamptonshire & holding also a small living. The squabble about the school alleged.

* [*marginal note:* J Burrows Ob Sep 1862.]

31   **Aston Tirrold. R.**

1852 Preach at reopening

Rev J L Hoskyns. I confirm here March 10.57. A very nice confirmation – sleep at Rectory. Confirming March 28 60 & sleep, & see about deanery. – July 25–63: come here for a re–opening after the building N Aisle & restoration of the Church. Wonderfully improved. & Hoskyns much admires Hymns Ancient & Mod. A procession in Surplices &c. & as earnest & devout & simple as ever.

32   **Aston Upthorpe [See Blewbury]**

Astwood. V.

Rev S F Cumberlege. Confirm his candidates March 26 1856 at Chicheley only 4 but they well prepared a great softening in his mind as to Extremes & he & she very pleasant at Mr Chesters after confirm/n. April 1856. The Duke of Bedford gives Cumberlege Woburn when E Bayley goes to Bloomsbury. The Lord Chancellor (on Lord Spencers, who on Lady Lytteltons, request) offers it to Thomas Burrows brother in law. He finds that it is only worth £126 net & is obliged to decline. Cumberlege applies for his nephew late of our College: I apply to Chancellor who says he gave the D of Bedford a promise after Lord Spencer. So I to D of Bedford who May 12/56 comes to me at Harts & assents to Cumberleges appointment. Charles Cumberlege– doing well. Much with Jeudwine, brings some well prepared candidates to Crawley March 16/59 – marries 1860 Miss Williams who will have £2,000 a year – He very anxious Nov/61 to restore the Church but Mrs Williams a sad opponent.

33a   **Avington. R.**

J James March 17 visited again Church nicely done. Candidates for confirmation at Kintbury nicely prepared. James liked Teste Majendie better than Gordon. Confirmed here. March 20.1860. A nice little company.

33b [*handwritten paper*]

Offertory Collections in a Parish (Avington) of 100 Inhabitants. A.D. 1867.
1. Jan/ry 27th. In aid of the Orange River Brotherhood – Canon Beckett. Prior.

2. March – In aid of the same.
3. May. In aid of the Oxford Diocesan Spiritual Help Fund.
4. July. In aid of S. Stephens Parochial Mission. New Brunswick. Edward Medley. Rector.
5. Nov/r In aid of the Oxford Diocesan Small Livings Endowment Fund.

---

6. Jan.5th.1868. In aid of the East London Distress Relief Fund.

33c N.B. These are in addition to the Collections. Annual. Quarterly. & Monthly. made in the same Parish in aid of the Church Miss/ry. Soc/ty. and of the Society for Propagating the Gospel in Foreign Parts.
The whole of the money so contributed by the Parish in question exceeding £20 and is little short of £25.

33d [*Copy of a Pastoral question from A Newdigate P*]
(For the Bishop only)
The chief impediments to the due exercise of my ministry from within have been a feeling of irksomeness & sloth in carrying out day by day the work of teaching in the schools and visiting – either too much study in preparation for sermons or dilatoriness in visiting them. At times fear of expressing fully to particular individuals my own convictions of the truth. The care for too many things. Those from without have been the difficulty of knowing nearly all the people under my charge even superficially – and still more of knowing their hearts in such a way as one ought to be their spiritual guide with spiritual confidence to direct individuals in their difficulties & temptations. The same difficulty prevents my praying for the special needs of so many individuals.

The want of submission to the will of God simply because it is His will, or His command prevents people from doing their duty when that is pointed out, & pressed upon them, unless they can see exactly how the performance of it will benefit them. This is especially the hindrance to persons becoming Communicants or candidates for Confirmation. – What applies to all respecting the want of literally fulfilling the precepts of God in Holy Scripture, applies still more generally to Churchmen not doing what the Church directs simply because it is commanded. The similar insubordination of the understanding to revelation & authority prevails and produces a subtle kind of infidelity even in the minds of many well meaning persons who little suspect it. Self satisfaction & spiritual pride nurtured by the teaching of sectarians, the prevalence of Dissent, deeply rooted Calvinism, the exclusion of objective truth makes the influence of that which is merely subjective, the bad example of some of these above the Poor, & of parents. Poverty & worldliness is inducing parents to send their children at a very early age, to work, and to a factory, for the sake of which they are kept from school, & at the Factory are exposed to the contagion of much vice. Above all the <u>immorality</u> of the town, and the light estimation in which the sin of unchastity is held; General apathy about a religious life, and the little fear exhibited as to the end of those who have led very ungodly lives, fostering the general indifference. The fact that many of the best young men of the parish belong to a Christian young man's association based upon the equality of all Christian sects, is a drawback to the influence of the Church. The inconsistency of conduct, & hypocrisy of a few attendants at Church or communicants. Most of these external impediments might be in a great measure overcome if it were possible for the Clergy to obtain greater influence over individuals, by pastoral visiting & intimate acquaintance, than can be effected by so few labourers among so many souls.

33h–j *A pamphlet giving information about the organisation of Mission Services, including 11 Confirmations, with prayers to be used, for Aylesbury and district, 1862*

Special Services for Aylesbury & The Neighbourhood, during the Lenten Ember Week, 1862.
Under the Authority and Personal Superintendence of the Lord Bishop of the Diocese

Holy Communion will be celebrated daily in Aylesbury Parish Church with an Address to the Communicants, at 8 o'clock a.m.; and also on Sunday March 9th, at 8 o'clock, and on Sunday, March 16th, at noon. Morning Prayer daily at 11 a.m., and on Sunday March 9th, at noon. Evening Prayer with Sermon daily at 7 p.m.
The Bishop will address Communicants only, at the St.John's School Room, Bierton Road, on Saturday, March 8th, at 7.30 p.m.. The Bishop will hold a conference in the Vestry, with the Clergy of Aylesbury and its neighbourhood, on Monday, March 10th at 12 0'clock, and on Sunday, March 16th, he will hold his Lent Ordination in St. Mary's Church, at 11 a.m.

Parishes and Churches in which Services are to be held

Aston Abbots	Cuddington	Mentmore	Waddesdon
Aylesbury	Haddenham	Nettleden	Wendover
Bierton	Hardwicke	Oving	Weston Turville
Buckland	Hulcot	Quainton	Whitchurch
Chearsley	Ivinghoe	Stewkley	Wingrave
Long Crendon	Great Kimble	Stoke Mandeville	Wing
Cublington	Linslade	Stone	

Preachers

The Lord Bishop of Oxford	Rev. M.W. Currie	Rev. Sir G. Prevost, Bart.
The Ven. Archdeacon Bickersteth	Rev. R.C. Dickerson	Rev. J.M. Price
The Ven. Archdeacon Randall	Rev. W.R. Freemantle	Rev. A. Redifer
The Rev. The Warden of All Souls	Rev. C.D. Goldie	Rev. G.G. Ross
Rev. R.H. Baines	Rev. J.R. Hughes	Rev. W.T. Sankey
Rev. R.B. Burge	Rev. A. Isham	Rev. C.H. Travers
Rev. W.J. Butler	Rev. H.P. Liddon	Rev. T.J. Williams
Rev. H.C. Calverley	Rev. L.G. Maine	Rev. J. Wood.
Rev. T.T. Carter	Rev.G.W. Pearse	Rev. J.R. Woodford

33m *Flysheet announcing the Mission Services, requesting prayers for their success, and requesting that all sittings should be considered free Prayers are recommended for the Preachers, for the Conversion of Sinners, together with the Collect for the Ember Weeks.*

34 **Aylesbury. V.**
 The Ven E Bickersteth.
 Feb.17.1856. Held my ordination morning & confirmation afternoon here. The church (at the opening of which for service I officiated on the 17th of June. & which has been beautifully restored under Scott) most appropriate & looked noble. J W Evans preached morn. Randall even/g a great confirmation. Thank God for the work doing here
 April 1/59 confirm here a delightful confirmation & all going on well.
 Sep 23 1860 I ordain here– having confirmed last night– a grand & beautiful service – inter alias John Daubeny Priest curate here & Hugh Scales Fullegar to be curate here & at Fleet Marston & Upper Winchendon. March 8.1862 addressed communicants at opening of Mission. March 9.Preached at Do & again 16th. Confirmed on March 10– ordained 16th all doing excellently well here. D.G.

Newspaper Cuttings.
A.D.571. – Aylesbury (as it is conjectured), taken from the Britons by Cuthwulph, brother of Gaulin, King of Wessex.

A.D.921.– Aylesbury and …… dered by the Danes. Elf ….. [this side of the cutting is torn away] Daughter of King Alfred, is suaded by her brother, Edw….. "Eldsbury."

35 **Aylesbury County Prison**.

36 **Aston. one portion of Bampton**
Rev R Barnes. The Rev [J.A] Greaves has been curate & done well amongst a rather ranting population – He going to Natal I recommend Hartley from Islip who almost too sensible. The church built some 20 years ago & then considered perfection is really horrible. I come & preach here April 13 1857 for a new School just built which we open a pouring wet day but church crowded. Collection of £80 on school building fund H Hippersley the chief proprietor giving £10!

37
38

39a **Baldon Marsh. R.**
H Willoughby. endless trouble about – Interviews with Wilde &c. Jan 1855 as to best mode of proceeding saw John Willoughby – sane & good Jan 55
Henry Samuel Musgrave Hubert. D. C. J. London. 1837/ P. 1838. comes for Institution March 19.1858 on Sir H Willoughbys presentation. I set strongly before him that he must take it on no contract or promise not to take the whole value of the living he assenting entirely & solemnly declaring himself at liberty to enforce its full value. C Lloyd & C Barter martyres. I suspecting evil apply to Arch/n Bouverie.

39b. Memd/m
Toot Baldon. Perpetual Curacy.
The annual sum of Five Guineas is charged upon the Rectory. – to be expended in repairing the Chancel of the Church, – & any surplus of the 5 Guineas in any year to belong to the Incumbent. –
The sum of £600.18.3 consols now stands in the names of the Bishop of Oxford. Mr Hobhouse & Mr Pott – (it having been augmented to that sum from £540.10.10. by half yearly investments of the Dividends,) – upon trust to apply the Dividends (in aid of the 5 guineas) to indemnify the impropriate Rector from expenses of repairing the Chancel; and, subject thereto to pay the Dividends to the Incumbent, as "an Endowment for all time to come." –
The surplus beyond the £540:10:10: might be sold out by the Trustees, & applied to the purposes of the Perpetual Curacy. – It was endeavoured to give like discretionary power to the Trustees as to the £540:10:10: but Mr Fry, who contributed it, would not allow of this. –

There is also the sum of £230 new 3 per cents, standing in the same names, as to which the Bishop alone has plenary control (for the benefit of the Perpetual Curacy.)

The Dividends on this last sum have at present been regularly paid to Mr Wheelwright, the Officiating Curate, – (The amount is £6.14 yearly.) –

J.M.Davenport.

Oxford March 26. 1858. –

[Footnote by S.W.] Sold out in 1860. towards House building realizes about £214.

39f *Newspaper cutting re Lambourne & a Presentation to the Rev.C.W. Barnett Clarke.*

40 **Baldon Toot. V.**

Rev T Fry V. C[urate] Wheelwright – Preach here Jan 1855. Long & intricate matter as to Patronage of &c. made over to me by Fry. Fry formally resigned Oct 1858 & I collated <u>Rev C W Barnett Clarke</u> – July 59, Clarke in consequence of losses wishes to resign – E Peel offers. Comes over to me Aug 25/59, long interview as to ways & means. He willing if they can be found. Peel raises £1,000 & offers it to Eccles comms who grant March 1860 £1000 to meet it. Also £200 from QAB. which to build a good House.

<u>Edmund Peel</u>. Collated. Oct. 18. 1860.

41 **Balking with Woolstone [see Woolstone]**
   Balscot C. [see Wroxton.]
   Bampton. 1st. portion V. with Aston and Cote, Lew, and Shefford.

C L Kerby. Oct 54. & March 55 – Poor Dr Giles affair ending in his imprisonment for a year.

Frederick Edwin Lott. Nov 17. 1857. Instituted. Told him I should require double duty = Church of Lew – J S Hartley Curate when I confirm at Bampton March 58.

<u>Jan 1864</u>. W W English at Shefford his troubles at my visit Nov 63 with <u>G Sandham Griffiths</u> the Curate.

At the Lent Mission Secretan, being come to preach. Mr Griffiths being there to read Prayers English preaches & appeals to the people <u>most improperly</u>.

Shifford. Visited the Church March 27.1855 – a miserably poor building standing just over the low ground of the Isis & one house & one or two cottages only near. J S Hartley Curate March 58.

Long communications Dec 58. with Barnes Adams Harcourt/ old G as [to] pulling down Church.

42   **Bampton 2nd. portion. V. [see 1st. portion]**
Rev D Adams. Confirmed in mother Church March 28 1855 – a fair confirm[ation] Vernon Blake, Newman – Black Bourton [Lupton], Brize Norton Penson [Kerby] many & well prepared. Clarified excuse from Penson. Order communion service to be read always from communion table –epistle & gospel from stalls north & south on entering chancel.
Confirm here again March 20 1858. A large confirmation – still as always something lacking. Adams moved into old Kerbys house.
Confirmed here March 4 1861
arrived here with Woodford & Arch Randall. Feb 13./64. Held confirmation. Opened the Mission by an address to comm[unican]ts.
Preached Sunday evening on refusing calls, & again at close of Mission Feb 21 on accepting calls.

Bampton 3rd. portion. V. [see 1st. portion].
Rev R Barnes

43a   **Banbury V. with St. Paul Chapel of Ease.**
      Neithrop
Rev W Wilson – applies Dec 10. 55 concerning the burial ground – The Board of Health constitute themselves a burial board & propose to buy our new churchyard & treat it as a cemetery ground.
March 1856. Applies through diminution of private means to have only one curate. I assent – hear from C Holbeck of the greatness of his work, his quietness under it & the good done by his monthly clergy meeting in his new room. March 31. Application for sub[script]n to School Funds. / I preach here twice Nov 15/57. For Wilson's plans for moving the organ... & good collection. The Free seats for the poor bare in morning. . many sit in pews … more go to Neithrop Church.
March 12.58. A confirm at South Banbury.. Curates John D Fish – W Best. W H Hewett. Attended Ch Miss meeting March 11.58.
Jan 7.59 I come & preach at opening of Chancel opened organ large congregation collection near £70 – very hearty gathering after at Vicarage. Dec 1859 ordain F Braithwaite from Wells for Wilsons curacy.
Henry Back. Collated by me after prayers & much enquiry March 28/60. Q.D. benedicat. – Come here for Mission Feb 19 61 preach Sunday 23. Confirm: Friday 21. A noble congregation Sunday night. Feb 29. 64. confirm again. H Back greatly improved.

43a *Insertion: Letter to The Times 16 September 1858 concerning omission of the Bishop & Clergy from the Loyal Toasts at the Oxfordshire Agricultural Society Dinner on 14th September.*
.... 'The British farmer gave a silent but convincing proof that he is not yet prepared to subject his wife and daughters to the filthy questions and insinuations of Cuddesdon neophytes or Anglican divines....'

43b *Printed notice of Mission Services in & around Banbury, Lent 1861.*

44 **Banbury South. P.C. [Christ Church.]**
The Rev C Forbes. – Confirmed here March 16.1855, for Banbury. N.S & Neithrop – a nice confirmation – Sir W Cope brought his daughter. The new Church looked very nice. Good Wilson consulting me on his troubles – he having "set F straight" twice by considerable sacrifice ought he to continue doing so. I advised him certainly not to do so. Confirmed Friday March 12 58. A nice confirmation.
Feb 6 1861. Complains of Back instructing some of his people. Sad jealousy between the two.
C F claiming to be "Vicar of South Banbury" I obliged to rule him P.C. of Ch. Ch.
Nov 12/61. Come to preach at opening of his schools £1.500 laid out £1.200 raised – I preach here in the day £50 – Sir C Douglas member there & speaks &c &c. &c. Forbes aged 46 in 62. Gross income £199, net £174. The deductions pay £10 a year on tithes & £15 on house – He is also poor law Chaplain with £57 Free accom. in the church 694, population 4.500 2 miles long 1 &1/2 broad. Services 3 full Sunday. Prayers 2/ce a week & holidays. From 6 to 700 congregation. A Curate kept between Addl Curates & Spiritual Help. Confirm March 1 64.
James C Fish Curate

45 **Barford Saint John. C. [see Adderbury].**
James Marshall acting as Curate, attends at Milton for confirma/tn March 11.58 – 1861. reopen the church Nov 11 after restoration.

46 **Barford Great [or Saint Michael.] P.C.**
P Hookins with his candidates at Milton confirm/tn March 11.58. Poor Hookins with all his goodness has made himself hated – rough words honestly meant to farmers very irritating – He offers to resign Lady Day 62 – Payne strongly advises me to accept. [see Hookins Letters. of 1860, for all particulars of Parish].
1863.4. Proposes to resign & take Claydon. Settled & W Risley to succeed. Then trouble about dilapidations. Hookins yields to me Feb 20 1864.

47   **Barkham. R.**
    Edw/d St John. Arth. Roberts, attended with candidates at Bear Wood confirm/tn April 3/57. The church rebuilt by Mrs Clive & opened by me March 15 – 1861 a very pleasing & hopeful day. – Mr St John Resigns Dec/62 & <u>Arthur Roberts</u> comes for institution to Cuddesdon March 3 1863. D. C.J. London Dec 22/39
    P. Do ————————40
    purchases the advowson of St John.

48   **Barton Hartshorn. P.C. with Chetwode. P.C.**

49   **Barton Steeple. V.**
    A Pakenham – who Irishman like on his poor brothers death suddenly abandons 1854 & writes to me to resign – Curme intrigues & gets Mr Hall Patron this turn to let L. Blandford appoint who Scott (see Woodstock) suggesting names poor Spring. I refuse to accept – & after struggle with Blandford he yields. – Then * it is offered to Green. Then conversation March 14 with Hall at Great Tew. He understands Curme & Bricknell "two worst in Diocese". At the reopening of Westcote Barton Jan 2/56 Green does not come because Lockyer had invited the clergy to attend in surplices though told that it was quite at his option to come in gown, but Greens two sons attend at Sandford March 9.58.
    *[*marginal note:* William Green.]

50   **Barton Westcot. R.**
    Edmund L Lockyer – March 1855 moving to restore Church, at estimated cost of £700 — £200 to be raised on Rates. Mr L. responsible for rest. I promise to help him & preach at opening.
    March 15. at Great Tew examine & sign the plans.
    <u>Jan 2 1856</u> go to the Reopening. Preached on Isaiah XXXVIII 18.19 Sir F Ousley H Drury & all my own clergy around except Curme & co attending – a very nice service. The Church exceedingly well restored – Lockyers house bearing marks of art – Last in it to administer the communion to poor Seagraves long invalid daughter since dead & he too attends with candidates at Sandford March 9/58.
    March 4/64 confirm here – a very pleasant confirmation except the face of Curme a mixture of self complacency & [verjuice].

51   **Basildon. V.**
    Rev R B Fisher. Sep 15 1858 William G Baxter comes to be licensed. Ord/ n. D. by Bp Llandaff. 50. P. 51. to Newport Mon. 2 years thence to Bagpath, Gl[oucestershire], 5 years. Spoken well of by G Prevost.

E J Sykes V succeeds R B Fisher who dies 1859. He applies Feb 12/61 for sanction for a service in schoolroom at Upper Basildon which I give.

52 **Baulking. P. C. [see Uffington.]**

Beachampton. R.
Rev R N Russell. Visited the Parish & confirmed March 14.59. Nash & Whaddon there – a nice confirmation – one Whaddon girl Mary Smith misbehaved ... The Church a pretty one but sorely wants restoring. Russell talks of doing it sometime or other when he can afford to do it well.

53 **Beaconsfield. R.**
John Gould. Rector. Nov 3 1855. Poor Mr Simon Edwin Major who had seemed likely to rescue all has fallen into debt & spent money belonging to the club. Bickersteths letter as to his going away – alas. March. 12. 1856. After confirmation at Penn, Mr Sheppard Mr Millais & Mr Major came. Old Gould quarrelling with Major because *quotha* he will not bow down to Hussey Gould – & threatening to stop even/g service. I tell them he cannot without my consent. They say Major has recovered the good will of Parish. D.G.
Nov/57 I write to Gould to say I wish him to keep Major & I will find for Ross another curacy.
June 1858 .... Mr Gould writes that wishes to part with Major .... I remonstrate – Gould asks an interview – He comes with Daughter Hussey who complains. Long winded complaint of ill–will, mischief. &c. Old Gould sitting by & reads my papers & ! ! She eloquent, & dealing the Hand –. Told Hussey – that I would enquire & if the charge [*incomplete*] July 10. Archdeacon reports. Favourably to Major & with much difficulty I re–arrange their relations amicably.
Dec 58 Churchwardens present that the Curate allowed no portion of [sac] alms. I interfere for him ... August 60 to Feb 61 perpetual attacks on [Major.]

54 **Bearwood. P.C. [Saint Catherine].**
R A Willmott – signs Horace Roberts Testimonials – & on Bishop of London through me remonstrating writes a pleasing letter of explanation –
April 3. 1857. I confirm again here. Rather a cold unimpressible set Hence & from Barkham.
J Walter has built a nice house near the Church in which he lets Willmott live: but does not make it over to Church – so about School & Diocesan Inspector: had not refused his inspection anybody might inspect it & welcome.

Henry F Burnaby Curate. Confirm here, March 5. 1860. Nice Walters eldest son & daughter. Inter alios.

1862. Willmott goes with quarrel. J Walter behaves very well – see pamphlet – He nominates W H E Welby whom I welcome with his nice wife second daughter of Bp of Llandaff – confirm here again. March 24/63. a nice confirmation. J Walters second son confirmed.

55 **Beckley. P.C.**

The Rev G T Cooke. Good & somewhat odd – of the High Church. Applies to me Oct 20 to be allowed to advertise me as approving of the industrial boys school under his sister &c. She very efficient & wise & I consent.

56 **Beedon. V.**

D.R Murray – March 1857. Find Thomas J Heard who succeeded Davis last August here & seemingly attentive.

March 1860. At the Chievely confirmation tells me all the wretchedness. I write & urge resignation on Murray: an affecting answer. In debt & raised money on it for sons & cannot, though conscience stirred –

* see Heards Letter March 60.

[*Unnumbered papers – inserted between 55 & 56*]

Copy.
Remarks.
School. there is no proper schoolroom – A Dames school is held in a Labourers Cottage – better school buildings are much needed.
Parsonage. There is nothing worthy of the name. The Curate in charge lives in a poor labouring-mans cottage, to which, in 1850. a bed-room & small sitting room were added, at the expense of Sir John Reade, the farmers of the parish, & some few of the neighbouring clergy. The present curate has, during the 3 years of which he has had charge of the parish, at his own expense, expended close upon a year's stipend, in repairs, absolutely necessary to keep the place barely habitable.

Copy
Letter.

Beedon. Newbury.
Jan/y 28th. 1860.

My dear Sir.
I beg to return the Form you sent me a few days since. I have given, in the manner you wished, all the information I am able to furnish.

I hope you will excuse my taking this opportunity of bringing under your notice the present disgraceful state of the Parsonage. It is totally unfit for the residence of a clergyman, & is constantly needing repairs.

I am the more justified in mentioning this, because I happen to know that the present Patron, Col/l Lindsey, is only prevented doing much for the good of the Parish, from the fact of the Incumbency not being vacated.

I am.
    Rev/d Sir.
    Yours very truly
    John G. King.

    Rev.d D.R.Murray.

57 **Beenham Vallance. V.**
Rev W Bushnell after long consumption dies in Guernsey Spring of 1855 – His mother the Patron appoints next brother of whom I hear well & who is Instituted.

T H Bushnell June 27. 1855. – comes March/57 to Bucklebury consults about a sad case of incest in Parish.

Nov 6 1859 Reopened the Church the whole nave of which has been well restored under Woodyer at a cost of £1160 which was all raised except £30 – & £28 was collected this morning. At the afternoon service I consecrated an additional Burial Ground & confirmed 24 who seemed to be well prepared. H.Majendie to preach in the evening. Some discontent on the part of Mr Gill &c. tenant to Col D.

Confirm here March 63..

58 **Begbrooke. R.**
C Fort Curate. Correspondence after Vis[itation] 1863 about Baptising

59 **Benson. P.C.**
S. Cooke – Vicar. Feb 1855. Held confirmation there – every appearance of utter inefficiency in C. Only two male candidates out of 1,300. The other parishes round the candidates poorly prepared. Ewelme Crowmarsh. Newington Berrick Salome. Ewelme under Gillam seem best.

March 24.57 hear from him touching Bell ringing: is it right to ring for elections? &c. had he done wrong in trying with his own hands to stop them. I say yes! –

Nov 23. 1861 open after the rebuilding of Chancel, removing West Gallery &c. A luncheon after Newton in the chair – all the Parish & great Harmony. J M Collyns through Gods mercy doing great things here. – March 14/64. confirmed & consecrated Church Yard all delightful – choir excellent – attention marked. Church Wardens at luncheon & as hearty as possible D.G. For the Hamlet of Roke W H Nottley Curate.

60 **Berrick Salome. R.**
Robert French Laurence. Is held with Chalgrove – Now <u>Jan. 1861</u> – served by <u>Wm Henry Young</u> – as Curate of Benson. 160 population mixed with Roke & Benson. The church ill place, & mixed up with Berrick Prior a district of Newington. Probably the best to have a new church for Roke & Berrick Salome, Berrick Prior being in fact the main population of <u>Newington</u>. This to be seen to at any vacancy of Chalgrove. Roke population very dissenting. Baptist & much influenced by Wallingford revival meetings of last year 1860.

61 **Besselsleigh. R.**
Dr Foulkes incumbent. Cleobury Curate retires 1855 & writes me a touching letter – Dr Foulkes dies Everett nominated.
<u>Charles Dundas Everett</u>

62 **Bicester. V.**
Rev M Watts. Confirmed there for the third time March 10 1855 – Wendlebury(Brown) Caversfield(C Marsham) Launston (*sic*)(H Blomfield) Piddington Hill (Brown), Ambrosden(Dryden) Price Curate Clerke Curate. A pleasing confirmation – Watts speaks of his Parish difficulties as past. Ferguson quiet Capt Styles friendly.= Curate Irish Aug 1857 whom he wishes to have he drops. Then obtains Mr Lingwood, whom he speaks of Sep 16/57 as perfection. He has been with Allan Cornwal, Estcourt & other leading Evan[angelicals] fine voice &c.
<u>March 5. 1858</u> confirmed here again having alas disappointed them yesterday. Not over pleased with Mr Lingwoods manner, but Watts as ever earnest. Says he never had so good a set. At Swifts house I hear [1] That Watts reads the service so low & indistinctly that scarcely audible & keeps all his voice for his sermon. [2] That hardly anyone sober at Bicester. Surgeons &c all drunken!----- Jan 30/59 – I preach here for the new Schools on which perhaps 1,600 laid out – a very good & very attentive congregat[io]n! C Coker there from Shalstone says Watts less violent & extreme & more influence – Watts speaks very highly of Blomfield / NB
March 1860 Watts on outbreak of Revival, plays into hands of Dissenters, is strangled by them. Vide Blomfields letter.
<u>Nov./60..</u> Trouble about Burial ground ... no way for public Path to

Dissenters ground. I reply I cannot give permission because illegal. Oxford Herald abuses me. Watts proposes to restore Church. Sir E Turner consents & Nov 3/60 gives £20 then, Jan 6, I preach for Schools. Great Trouble between Watts & Fowler. He Delates the sermons...[at last I interfere] Nov. 25/61. I consecrate the new burial ground. & preach. A meeting in vestry after where Paxton at first opposes but consents to borrow £500 on Rates if rest can be raised. See Page 613.

63   **Biddlesden. P.C.**

64   **Bierton, V. with Stoke Mandeville. C. (– 609)**
      Buckland. C. and Quarrendon. C.
Rev J. C. <u>Wharton.</u> Stapley Curate to Stoke & Buckland to Oct 1855 retiring
   I write as strong a letter as I can to Dean of Lincoln urging them to separate & add £40 to the £80 Wharton will give & on next vacancy let them have their own Tithe of £70 & £80 per annum.
   Feb 18. 1856.. I confirmed here for it Aston Abbots, Hulcote Cublington – a fair confirmation. The Church a great deal improved & a fine one. All through 1857, still urging on Lincoln Chapter the separation of Stoke Mandeville & Buckland.
   March 9. 62 confirmed here – all rising here.
   T Bristow from Cuddesdon Coll. Curate 1861–2
<u>Armstrong.</u> Instituted by me at Bicester March 7/64 I find he was ordained Deacon & Priest with me in /28 & /29.

65   **Binfield. R.**
Ven Arch Randall
   I confirm here again Feb.28. A <u>very</u> nice confirmation. Edmund Savory son in law & Curate — Aug 1. come here to preach for SPG Aug 2 & meeting. The Sunday congregation large & very attentive. Evident marks of Gods blessing on dear R's long & faithful ministry here. A most encouraging SPG meeting afterwards. <u>Arch R</u> resigns & E Savory succeeds, 1860. Confirm here March 9 1860 very pleasing.
   Dec.3.1861. Consecrate new Churchyard preach for SPG. Good collection. Luncheon after, & all most cordial. March 25/63 a very nice confirmation. The Church looking beautiful. Service very nice.

66   **Binsey. P.C.**
   <u>Professor Hussey</u> – dies suddenly 1856! of heart complaint. Prout succeeds. Deaf but good man.

67 **Bisham. V.**

Rev T.E. Powell – Feb 4 1854 went down to Bisham Abbey & spent Sunday there preaching for Culham College – collected £7.10.0 – £2.10.0 above average. Mr Williams of Temple opposes & prevents the completion of the goodly Church repair.

Nov 11/56. Here to preach SPG, sermon for Marlow anniversary & act at reopening of church at the same time. Church now admirably done throughout – Powell asks me for another G Herbert.

I confirm here again Feb 27, a very nice confirmation – I send him Porter our first college pupil from Cropredy. and in 1859 Richard Harvey who had been at Wantage.

March 29.63. Confirm again a very nice confirmation – Powell's choir beautiful & the whole service very delightful.

68 **Bix. R.**

H P Pechell. Correspondence with him Sep 1857, as to frequency of communion, Services &c. Only one sermon – no pastoral &c. He quite kind & civil but peculiarities of parish. Church far from people &c. No use pressing him. Tell him that unconvinced & leave it on his conscience – renew correspondence & insist on Full double duty from Easter to Michaelmas he most reluctantly assents to this ... Nov 17. 57. He writes to explain he meant not full double duty, but only afternoon prayers & teaching the children afterwards in the Church – I refuse this but allow the substitution of public catechizing for a sermon.

Nov 60. Troublesome about coming to visitation but retracts some "unusual & unreasonable demand" & I allow on allegation of Rheumatism.

69 **Blackbourton, or Burton Abbotts, V.**

J Lupton. Consults me March 58 as to actuaryship of Oxf Ass Co.

W Dry Curate comes March 20/58 to Bampton with a good company.

Jan 1864 E Davies Curate odd talking man would not join mission because "he need lent (*sic*) the Church Sconces". Nice new house built by Ch. Ch.

70 **Bladon. R. with Woodstock. C.**

[see below]

returned by Mr St John as worth net £350

Nov. 1857. I sound him on exchange. Jan/59. A nice new School erected by Duke. Duchess teaches on Sunday. I visit it Jan 31/59. Mr Steele Curate well spoken of & pleasing.

George Steele Curate. Preach here Feb 2 1862 – confirm March 11.64 nice. The two young ladies Cornelia & Clementina Churchill.
G W Browne Curate.

Woodstock.
St John [Incumbent]. Mr Scott Curate put in by L Blandford – from simple wish to do good. Scott an Irishman <u>quite</u>, recommends poor Spring to Lord B: for Steeple Barton – Spring mad & imbecile – I fight it off & succeed. Scott tells me in fact that Spring was residing at Woodstock & offering to help him & that he wanted to get rid of him! – He speaks truly of St John as desperately weak – The confirmation tolerably pleasing, a good man specially affected – 8 parishes [owing] to Yarnton parishes coming through Giles trial. Yarnton: Summertown – Begbroke: Bladon: Cassington. Wootton Handborough – W A Scott comes to me Feb 1857 about a scandal & with a confession. At his request I at last issue a commission to enquire. They report <u>no ground</u> on actual guilt: but E Coopers evidence shows attempt to seduce. E Reddell calls for new commission.– I advise Scott to retire & he assents in a pleasing letter. D of B, after consulting with me puts in E Geare <u>Oct & Nov 1859</u> E <u>Geare</u> very troublesome at going – correspondence D of Marlborough.

71 **Bletchingdon. R.**
Rev Thos Dand. March 1855. Walked over after confirmation at Stoney Middleton in consequence of Lord Valentines complaint of no 2 Sunday services & no Lent week day. His character of Lord V. till quite recently blaspheming & Lewd – will have Wednesday & Friday. 2 younger Miss Annesleys trying to do good – not judicious – Just [serves] Church.
Long contest about Lord V & communion.
March 5 1858. Speak to him again after confirmation at Kirtlington. An earnest nervous man, perfectly respectable, convinced that Lord V. "a very wicked man" <u>now</u> in consequence of this outbreak careful in the parish, but wicked at Oxford teste Williams late Curate. Favourably impressed with Dand.

72 **Bledlow. V.**
Rev W Stephens – Long trouble about Curate between him & Burgess they always finding bad men – happily settled by an ordination autumn 1854
<u>Grace</u> goes as Curate 1857.8. Ordained Priest at Henley Feb 1858, gives a very bad account of poor W.S's parish & utter lack of influence therein especially amongst the young men. Grace leaves for Fabers Curacy & gets the Union Chaplaincy.

W Stephens after much toil & leaving it in my hands gets <u>Bellingham Swan</u> from Peterborough Diocese Nov.59.

<u>James T May</u> Curate 1862 March 30 when I visit old W Stephens 82 years old & rather failing in health.

73 **Bletchley. R.**
<u>Thomas Delves Broughton</u>. Dies Aug 10 1859

William Rawson – comes Jan 20/60 for institution, to reside at Aylesbury. Mr Clarke is to reside in the Rectory, & have the full legal stipend. Wm.R. going often over: <u>March 27/</u>61 I accept his resignation & <u>Joseph Bennitt</u> comes to me for institution.

<u>Joseph Bennitt</u>.

74a

Rent of Farmers	706.	0.	0.
Landtax	80.	13.	4.
	625.	16.	8.
Dividends on Stock	18.	10.	0.
Income	643.	16.	8.
(*added by S.W.*)	250.		
Charges. —	£393.	16.	8
Tithe Rent Charge on [Brodies]. Insurance.			
Repairs etc	40		
Reading School	210		
	250	....	

77b Expenditure by the Schoolmaster

	£		
In 1852. – – – –	307		
„ 1853. – – – –	285		
„ 1854. – – – –	321		
„ 1855. – – – –	312		
„ 1856. – – – –	287		
[*pencil Additions by S.W.*]			
	393.	16.	8.
	287.	0.	0.
	£106.	16.	8 surplus.

74c & d *Blank.*

74e

Blewbury Vicarage.
March 7/57

My dear Mr Hoskins

I shall be happy to find that anything I can suggest would be likely to benefit the Schools in this Parish. Supposing it could be done it would be necessary to

1st revise the rules, regular times & Holidays.

2 – to have one uniform system in all the Schools

3 – the Infant or mixed School to be made competitive for admission into the Upper School.

74f 4 – the upper School being supplied with the most advanced scholars in the mixed School, higher branches of knowledge be taught

5 – An annual examination be appointed with rewards, & a School treat.

6 – Singing to be taught, that the children may be able to join the congregation in Divine Service with credit.

7 – The Schools to be opened to all the children in the Parish, including the Hamlets –

74g 8 – The object & design of the scholastic system be, to bring the mind into action that thought be elicited, Religious truths imbibed, & the moral affections cultivated.

The question arises, when can anything be done? I know the Bishop's mind upon the subject of education without speaking to his Lordship & so I do the Trustees, from what they have said, that they intend to wait for the decease of the Schoolmaster, whether they are obliged to do so I cannot say, perhaps it may be a freehold – he has a vote for M P arising from the School lands.

He is Treasurer appointed by the Trustees to my great surprise, in short he is the official manager of the whole at Blewbury. The Bishop will understand the case in point of law. The Incumbent ought to be ex:officio connected with the school. Here is the cause of the present evil

I can only add that I remain
most truly yours
J Macdonald.

74h Will you be so good as to give Confirmation cards to the two candidates that have attended your lectures. I cannot say that I have examined them you can include them with your other candidates under Aston. there could be no great objection I suppose to this.

PS. the Parish Churchwarden said one day the Schoolmasters situation was a freehold & he was glad they could not turn him out

74i [*Bishop's writing*]
210

£21 – each 10 boys at Reading

Reference to Charity Comms..
Mem. 42 boys formerly of whom we pay for only £10.. now only 30 but by the advise of Char Comms we pay the rate of 10 out of £42. now £21 a head but this will lessen as the expenses of building the new school are discharged.

74   **Blewbury. V. with Upton. C. and Aston Upthorpe. C.**
see 616

Rev Jacob Macdonald. – Dec 1853. Endeavouring to escape the maintenance of a Curate for the chapelries – provided for by Bp of Salisbury & Lessees. Sons of Clergy – but not actually insisted as a condition in the deed – very shabby. Vide Bp Salisburys letters.

Blewbury School. Meeting of Trustees at East Ilsley after the confirm-[ation] March 25/57 – Mr Brown, F Crowdy – Charles [Lanfear], W. []acle.. Thom Floyd. Mr John Sharpe. (absent). Long discussion. Settle that only Sat 1/2 holiday, & include Hamlets – & I to visit & suggest. Dr. Macdonald March 29. 1860. The Corporation of Sons of Clergy rent under Bishop great tithes & rectorial glebe on a lease for 3 lives. Worth about £1,100 a year – pay a reserved rent of £153 – of which £50 paid to V of Blewbury: £50 granted to the Curate. Dr Macdonald suggests severing As – Upthorpe, Pop. 150 & As/n Upton, Pop.350 joining West Hagbourne to them & making them into a new parish. He promises to give up the Rent charges of the Hamlet £88 a year. [Meredith] will add £25 – & Hoskyns undertakes to see what can be got from the neighbourhood. Aston Upthorpe chapel rebuilt & nice.

75   **Bloxham. V. with Milcombe. C.**
see after Burwescot

Rev James Hodgson. Confirmed here March 16 – 1855 – in a noble old Church, for Milcombe, Hookins. South Newington, Harrington S Sanders. Hewitt, Livingston, &c. here. Singing excellent. The confirmation in all respects pleasing. Kept in the Church till 8.30 about pew quarrels. [Coterill] Potter's &c. &c. Pews are the Devils

Freehold in a Church about which he can at any time stir up malice & hatred. <u>May 1856</u> troubles with Mr Hewett as to the attendance of his scholars at Church.

<u>March 12.58</u> attend for confirmation at South Newington. Few.

Feb 21/61 confirm here – & after at service Woodford preaching: a grand sermon. "redeeming the time" A hurricane raging.

<u>1859 P. Reginald Egerton</u> takes the School. Consults me May 23/60 on cousins marriage in a letter showing great goodness – 1863, arrange to lend him 1,500 without interest or repayment whilst The School a Church School. (From Langston Hubbard, D of Marl & others)

Feb.26 1864 confirm here, a pleasing confirmation.
Vernon Green Curate & good.

76   **Boarstall P.C.** [See Brill].

Bodicote C. [See Adderbury]. – 603

Bolney C. [No Church. See Harpsden.]

Boveney. [See Burnham].

Boyne Hill see page 106.

77   **Boxford. R.**

George Wells – come to Welford March 26 57. She energetic & excellent clergy woman.

78   **Bracknell** [See Winkfield] next page (80)]

Bradenham. R.

<u>Isaac King</u>. Confirmed here Sunday April 10 1859. A vast crowd. The Church miserable. King rather going back says Mr Graves from churchmanship.

<u>March 29. 1862</u> confirm here again, rather a poor confirmation. Staying at Grave's who wonderfully opens on acquaintance. Our common grief bringing us together & I trust our common hopes & joys. To try to arrange with King to give up the charge to him.

79a   **Bradfield. R. with Trinity Chapel of Ease, and Saint Simon and Saint Jude.**

T Stevens. March 1857. R P Manclarke Curate. I gently stimulate him to subscribe to Diocesan Charities & he kicks. Still more March/57 see my Letter. Confirm here again June 61.

Confirmed at the Church Dec. 9/62 B of Salisbury & Majendie – here – a very nice time – Slept at Marriotts.
J F Falwasser Curate March 17 63
John Robinson Chaplain of Union.

79b.   DISTRICT CHURCH BRACKNELL May 1859.
                    PROPOSED ADDITION.

        Plans and Appeals for Funds.

80   **Bradfield. Saint Andrew's College.**
[This title has been erased]
Bracknell.
Rev E Hood Linzee Jan 1855 – approve of noble plans for building a parsonage for £2,300 only £800 Linzee doing the rest & having provided Schools.
Confirm here April 6 1857. A nice confirmation & stay at Linzees. He now about an infant school. His curate inhabiting the Parsonage.
P B Collings. He to lay out gardens &c. Autumn 1859. Needful to enlarge Church. Oct 13/59 140 add[itiona]l. sittings to be obtained at cost of £535 – hope to begin next summer. I confirm here March 6. 1860, a pleasing confirm.
Nov 60. Reopen the church after the addition of new aisle.
Linzee resigns and mainly on G Hodsons commendations I present Herbert Taylor Howes to it. He offends Lady Mary Berkeley & others by alterations – I try to allay, & April (Good Friday) 1863 confirm here. A nice confirmation – a long talk with him about Miss Rickards he promises to recommend her to consult Goulburn.
Writes April 7 all but 5 of the confirmed communicated & one of these at Reading. Asks my aid again with Lady Mary B. C Flint speaks very strongly of his congregations &c.

81   **Bradwell. V. with Kelmscott**
      [Oxon.] P.C.
Thom W Goodlake. Confirmed here again March 29. 1855. A very nice confirmation. Broughton Pogges (Goodenough) Kencote Thorold. Alvescot & Shilton (Neate) (Halifax there) Langford (Leman). Church on the whole nice – proposal about Kencote. I proposed taking the part of Kencote near Bradwell & appending it.
Goodlake presses this. Mr Hammersley the Patron Kelmscott ought to be severed from Bradwell. "That Township of Bradwell be united to Kencote: That the Vicarage Farm of Bradwell £106 per annum go with it & Vicarage House. – That Kencote remain to

Vicar of Bradwell. That Mr Hammersley pay £2,400 for House & Endowment of Kelmscott" Mr G's suggestion. My idea had been to make Kelmscote take the place of Kencote as to endowment & make Kelmscote a separate living & Kencote cum Bradwell. Mr Woodman wishes Dec 1855 to buy Patronage of Kencote – unite two & separate Kelmscott – Mr Hammersley defers settlement till midsummer next.

F T Woodman Dec 10 1855 for institution. Mr Herveys letters of complaint 1857. That duties diminished at Bradwell. I speak to him at Broughton, March 20/58. At first he loses his Temper I pull him up, & he recovers. He has now full alternate duty at Kelmscott (where the farmers &c. all church people & Bradwell. Saints days &c. Willing if can get help to have a curate & further service. I hope I have arranged it with Neate but W. refuses. I promise to see if Hervey will give anything. Feb 20 brings only 4 for confirmation. Feb 22 I write a kind faithful letter.

82 **Bradwell. V.**
[Bucks.]

Bradwell New united with Stanton Bury.

83 **Bray. V.**
Rev J E Austen Leigh. I preach here 1856.
In January 57, W Hill Curate complains of Austen Leighs intended removal of him most unjustly. Confirm Feb 27, a goodly gathering.
* W Hill goes on worse & worse – Tries to foment division in the Parish. I at last remove him. Hear of his preaching out of Doors at Hurst.
Confirm here Feb 28
Feb 28/60 [*sic*]
The Chancel &c still restoring – June 22/61 preach here for SPG.
Hemming Robeson C[urate]. nice Fellow – Discussion about giving * part of Bray & Cookham to Spiritual charge of Maidenhead.
Dec 13 1862 Reopen the church – a nice Service preach on Renewal. March 30/63. Confirm. A large confirmation & pleasing. The Church Beautiful.
W B Turner. Curate has done specially well at Tutchen End, in influencing the young men of the Parish.
April 1863 Mrs Sewell; £1000 to be invested in my name Randalls & Austen Leighs to pay the interest to him & try to get Capital met by Commissioners.
* *W Hill NB*
* *(A Leighs Letter May 28–61)*

84 Brayfield Cold. C. [See Lavendon.]
Brickhill Bow. R.
<u>J Marshall Jackson.</u>

Parishioner comes over to me March 29 1856 at Mr Duncombes to complain that Jackson & the parish have appropriated land belonging to the poor &c. &c. I get Lloyd to write to Jackson for some explanation.

Sep 1857... correspond[ence] touching services no morn/g. Few communions to be increased.

<u>1862.</u> Give him licence of Non Res for his wifes ill health – She dies soon after – Corker comes as Curate & begins a great renewal of parish D.G.

Dec 63 Jan & Feb 64. Jackson having engaged to leave Corker – corresponding for return writes to me Feb 14/64 for licence to give the notice.

85 Brickhill Great. R.

Sir H Foulis. Confirm here again March 28 1856. The confirmation rather unquiet for a good while: the Church being a difficult one to keep all quiet, but got it so D.G. at last. A new churchyard much wanted. Mr Duncombe to give it & disposed to move in His church's restoration.

Rev Vesey Curate. Come here. April.12/62 intending to confirm. But taken so ill Sunday that in bed at Sir P Duncombes & most kindly kept till [*blank*]. On Thursday April 17 the Bishop Chapman confirms for me.

86 Brickhill Little. P.C.

E Jones. Died April 1. 1856 – having been just before at the confirmation, *NB on the 28th of March. After endeavouring to get the *endowment raised: which it seems cannot be till the 21 years of the Archbishops lease of tithes is out [grown].

<u>James Charles Lett Court</u> who has been Curate there since Jan 1852. he hears that some of the land has been abstracted. The House hardly habitable. Sep/57. Correspondence as to communion – which to be monthly.

<u>Thomas Pym Williamson</u> on the resignation of Court Licensed at Newport P. Nov 19 1860.

87 Brightwell. R.

Rev R Sumner appoints H Walmsley when first absent in 1855 who offends some of the farmers – who used to extreme low – appoints Leighton when he resolves on staying through the winter. Leighton dislikes the place & is scarcely civil to me. <u>March 58</u> Sumner wishes to resign Rural Deanery for health, nerves &c. After persuasion of Hoskyns to whom I offer it retains it. <u>Dec. 6 58</u>. I come to Brightwell, to reopen restored Church. The Archdeacon preaches aft/n. I morning, a nice gathering. Dear R Sumner very full of affection coming into my room the Tuesday morn/g Alas! next morning he seized in Head. W H Ridleys affecting account! Alas! Alas. He dies the following <u>Sunday</u>!

Robert Newman Milford. Instituted April 30. 1859.
I <u>confirm here March 1.1860</u>. all pleasing.

88 **Brightwell Baldwin. R.**
<u>G Day.</u> Confirmed here – Feb 23 1855. The people not stimulated at all but quiet & reverential .
<u>Sep/57.</u> Correspond with him as to frequent communion. Pastoral letter &c. Communion to be more frequent. A nasty dry tone rather about the man. Snarling at Culham.
<u>Feb 1858</u> comes with flock to Ewelme I stay at Squires, who cordial..

89 **Brill. P.C. with Boarstall. P.C.**
Rev J Baron. Confirmed here again Feb 19 1856 to please old J.B. a small confirmation – young people attentive. Snow on the ground. Poor Baron in a peck of trouble about harmonium. School master &c... Had "followed six children & their mother to the grave.

90 **Brimpton. V.**
<u>Edward Golding.</u> Comes with his Catechumens to Aldermaston confirm-[ation] March 31/57... Meeting at W Chatteris Nov. 12/57. & he sings Long Fellow's beautiful song of <u>Never & For ever,</u> at 2.a.m. Nov 18. He died having caught a Rheumatic fever by exposure to cold when heated on the 13th, leaving alas nine young children & a widow very slenderly provided for. I write to her.
<u>George Benjamin Caffin.</u> Formerly V. & patron comes April 24 58 for re-institution – giving up a living he has held of the ArchBp he was in 48 the V. & resigned by taking the living poor Golding was to have had.

91 **Britwell Prior. C. [See Newington].**
Britwell Salome. R.
Johnson. Long negotiations for uniting the 2 above. July/63 I get consent of Lord Lansdowne thereto.

92 **Brizenorton. V.**
Rev John Penson – Wrote to him Dec 27. 1853 to urge as mildly as I can the need of a Curate – I hear that all is going to ruin for want of one. He has Hallifax, who leaves from family outgrowing house 1857. Leaves it to my appointment. I offer it to numbers. Meanwhile his son serves it from his parish, Old man writes to me, imbecile. He dies, July 10/58. & Ch Ch. nominates to it G Fereman – ordained by me in 47/48. whom I institute Dec 19. 58.

G Fereman Visit the church July 24/63. In miserable state – G.F. has been planning restoration but the plans lost by Ch. Ch. In trouble about his Clerk – (he fears a bad man & his tenant) charged with immorality. He & D Adams examine but nothing proved & so he charged with privity.

Feb.64 Avoids mission for want of sconces. I fear it is a miserably poor inattentive ministry.

93 **Broadwell. [see Bradwell. Oxon.].**

Broughton. R. [Bucks.]
John William Irving. Brings his candidates well prepared March./59.

94 **Broughton. R. [Oxon.]**
C F Wyatt Rector – Falcon Curate of Queens intemperate at an archery meeting – on general testimony that no habit & unknown in parish I agree to his continuance waiting another year at least as D. Sep 25 1854. NB had got into something like it after degree at Oxford. See Thomsons letters.

March 18. 1855 Confirmed here. Sunday confirmation – a nice one. Some of Wroxton & Tadmarton came – a party with us at the Castle – Overstone. [illegible]J S Lefevre &c. Church going on towards a good restoration in the Hands of G. Scott – Lord Saye ready to help.

Feb 26 1864. Confirm here, staying at the Castle & most warmly received. The Church very nicely restored. Lord Saye's part at a cost of £150 to himself. C W Bradford the good Curate going on Goddards nomination to the living of his unhappy brother!

95 **Broughton Pogges. R. with Filkins see 617**
Rev Dr Goodenough. Visited it March 28. 1855 – after confirmation at Bradwell. Very poor Church & small congregation – This just united to Filkins, where a new church to be built & this left as a mere sepulch[ral] Chapel. Goodlake proposes taking this & selling the other.

T W Goodlake Sep 20 1855 – This done.

April 14. 1857. I consecrated the new Church at Filkins of the new united parishes. A good attendance & all apparently attentive.
March 19 – 58 I confirm in Filkins Church, a very interesting confirmation. T.W.G. nice letter to Guardian March 23/59
Confirm in Filkins church March 4./61. A nice confirm [*illegible*] scandal of Goodlake have been violent with servant.
<u>Goodlake</u> sells & retires & is replaced by (1861) <u>J M Farrar</u>. He finds that one formality omitted by Goodlake & determines the people with him on reopening Broughton & making Filkins a separate parish.
I preach at the Reopening of Broughton July 24. 1863.

95a–e

Special Services for the Working Classes in North Bucks.
During Lenten Week of 1859.

List of Parishes and Churches in which Services are to be held.

Buckingham.	Stony Stratford.
Fenny Stratford.	Stewkley.
Hanslope.	Shenley.
Linslade.	Tingewick.
Newport Pagnell.	Winslow.
Olney.	New Wolverton.

List of the Preachers.

Right Rev. Lord Bishop of Oxford.	Rev. A. B. Evans.
Ven. Archdeacon Bickersteth.	Rev. W. R. Freemantle.
Rev. C. Bayley.	Rev. J. A. Hussey.
Rev. J. W. Burgon.	Rev. J. Lawrell.
Rev. W.Butler.	Rev. C. Lloyd.
Rev. T. T.Carter.	Rev. J. W. Nisbett.
Rev. C. F.Champneys.	Rev. A. W. Thorold.
Rev. T. C.Claughton.	Rev. W. W. Watson.
Rev. F. Cox.	Rev. D. Watkins.

95f Days of Administration of the Holy Communion in the Parish Church of Buckingham in the year 1856 [*23 Occasions*]

Appropriation of Alms, signed by the Vicar and Churchwardens
[*Whit Sunday and Trinity Sunday for the Church Sunday School for Infants Ascension Day, the 5th, 9th, 13th, 16th, 22nd and 26th after Trinity, charges*

for bread and wine, surplices, and the remainder to be divided, half to pious uses within the parish, half to similar uses for the promotion of the Gospel at home and abroad
On the remaining occasions, to relief of the poor and sick parishioners]

95j   Vicarage of Buckingham. [Statement of income and Expenditure]

Endowments		Outgoings		
103 acres 3 rood 18p George Genge	114. 0. 0	Land Tax at Gawcott		3.18. 0
of land at Gawcott Thomas Miller	12. 5. 0			
Allotment	11. 7. 0			
5 acres 2 rood 7p of Rebecca pasture		Poor Rates at 4s.00 in the £		
in Prebend End Summerfield	18. 0. 0	Leaborough tythes £80. 0. 0		
Commuted Rent Charge on		Bourton tythe	95. 5. 0	
117 acres of land in gardens,		Borough tythe	18. 0. 0	
closes, &c	32.10. 0	Vicarage House	38. 0. 0	46. 5. 0
Do on lands in Leaborough	108. 0. 01	Poor Rates on allotments		
			6. 6. 9	1. 5. 6
Do on lands at Bourton	127. 0. 0	Highway rates on do.		10. 6
		Highway & lighting rates on Vicarage & tythe commuted annually		5. 0. 0
Annual sum due from the Great	6. 13. 4	Vicarage House:		
Tythes of Kings Sutton at Easter		Quit rent to Lord Chandos		11. 2
		House Tax		1. 7. 0
Augmentation from Dean Clarke's	30. 0. 0	Land Tax		6. 0
estates		Insurance for £300		14. 3
	10. 0. 0	Moeity of Loan to Queen		
Easter offerings and surplice fees		Anne's Bounty Office		12.10.
		Collection of Borough		0
		Tythe		2. 2. 0
	469.15.4			74. 9. 5

Gross Income	£469.	15.	4
Deduct Outgoings	74.	9.	5
Net Income	394.	5.	11

H Roundell
March 26th 1859

951 *Insert – Printed Invitation*

Buckingham,
March 14, 1859.

Dear sir,
We beg to invite your attendance at a Conference of Clergy and Laity, which will be held in the Latin School, at Buckingham, on Saturday next, 19th instant, under the Presidency of

THE BISHOP OF OXFORD.
SUBJECT, –
"THE CO–OPERATION OF THE LAITY
WITH THE CLERGY."

The conference will commence at
Twelve o'Clock, and conclude at Two o' Clock.

We are,
Your faithful Servants,

W.R.FREMANTLE,
R.N.RUSSELL,
H.ROUNDELL.

An early Answer is requested, addressed to
REV.H. ROUNDELL, BUCKINGHAM.
[*Hand – written*] Luncheon at 2 o'clock.

96 Buckingham. V.

Rev H Roundell. Held a confirmation here again Feb 22 1856.. a conv[ersation] after with HR – as to purchasing an advowson to change. He against when giving <u>notice</u> always reading whole addresses &c.

The church necessarily noisy from gallery &c. but much doing under good Roundell who great influence from wisdom. At Buckingham <u>May.14/56,</u> for opening School consecrating Burial ground.. Luncheon. Poor man's Dinner. An useful day, spero…

March 19/59 confirm here, a nice confirmation. Hold meeting of Clergy & Laity in Latin School. Preach March 18 59 to a great congregation of working men I stand at the Door & knock. Ordain here March 20.59.. Preach for SPG Nov 15/63 & find W Foxley Norris doing very well spero in all ways.

Nov 16, great yeoman &c dinner after confirmation.

97 Buckland. [Berks.] V.

Rev Jo Moore. Confirm again here in the well restored Chancel March 16 57… The Puritan squire still stands out because of cross in chancel.

Sir R Throckmorton given ground & cottages for new School which rising promisingly under Street as architect.

Pleasant Mrs Moore wishing me to bless her children.

Sep. 18./57, went from Wantage. Large gathering of Lay & clerics. Preached: coll £34 – & opened the Schools Mr Sotheby giving. Sir R Throckmorton present & kind & asking me to his House. Schools excellent. NB. Mrs Moores wish for him.

98   **Buckland. [Bucks.] C. [see Bierton].**

[*Marginal note*: Partington incumbent of Stoke Mandeville under B]
Letters from Curate Sep 1857 as to the miserably neglected condition of Buckland Common – He recommends union with Cholesbury – I had inclined to St Leonard's. Now an Iron Church served between St. Leonards & Buckland.

E Bonus Curate 1862 – I preach there for schools Aug 3/62. Crowded congregat[ion] £10 collected. – Sir A Rothschild very liberal as to money & support to Bonus in all ways. Built him a curate house in Aston Clinton.

99   **Bucklebury. V. with Marlestone. C.**

G Valpy – March 14 1854 He excusing himself from attending confirmation at Yattendon by a cold at Bath — & sending 7 females & 3 males from that large Parish! – Propose to Gabriel to change with <u>Campden.</u> He declines 1855 Jan[ua]ry. 30 March/57, a confirmation here, & nice. <u>She</u> marvellous as always. <u>Francis Tilney Bassett</u> Curate, consults me about a case of incest in parish uncle & niece in blood. I advise proceeding.

<u>Confirm</u> here March <u>16.</u> <u>1860</u> a moving confirmation. G Y Bradshaw Curate. March 63 seems pleasing. Mrs Bunbury complains that old Valpy almost foolish & will not let any curate preach drives good ones away. The living promised if Valpy dies in Hartley W's time to a low connection named Watts –

100   **Bucknell. R.**

<u>Wm Master.</u> At visitation 1857 shewed his reasons against a second sermon: unconvincing. But I talked March 5/58 to old Mr Lowe of Ardley about it & he thought it would be useless "Master no preacher. Shines in the sick room" so let it wait. Chancel very fine. NB to confirm here.

101   **Burford. V. With Fulbrook. P.C.**

G Joyce – V. who resigning to take Stratfield Saye at Ladyday 1855 I offer it to Goddard. Long at Warfield & centre of good there.

Confirmed here March 23 1855 – Fulbrook Sanders C. Teynton Lewis – Asthall – Swynbrook (Layton C). Not a nice confirmation – great many children in galleries &c to remove – The church too long & galleried up to be good for Purpose. Goddard here to meet me – A Testimonial given to Joyce – Allan Faulkner complained to C Barter of his sermons as long & wearisome. It would be excellent to increase endowment or separate Fulbrook from which comes most of income.

Daniel Ward Goddard, comes to Cuddesdon Dec 11 1855 & we have long discussion as to schools. (see a long letter of Joyce's thereon.) We decide that he should take Joyce's purchase for boys school & wait old Mr Faulkners death to settle about Wisdoms School – To do about Prices Tomb & Mr Cheakles improvements in Churchyard.. Confirm here & sleep at Vicarage March 19/58 ... Compton Reade Curate.

Ordain William Cotton Risley P. at Aylesbury Sep 23/60. Goddard resigning I collate John Hugh Burgess to it April 16/60. Confirm here March 2/60 all pleasant.

Feb. 18. 64. Confirm again. In spite of the Evil of the Church The confirmation promising H.S.N.Lenny Curate.

102 **Burghfield. R.**

H.Curtis Cherry. His troubles about his new wife 1856!! Brings Parishioners & 2 sons to be confirmed at Sulhampstead.

April 2/57 – Sep 57 correspondence with him touching sermon on communion days. Pastoral letter sermon &c. He promises improvement herein.

I License Wm Barker Drawbridge. Dec 7. 57 to the curacy at £100 a year. Drawbridge persecuted by some parishioners resigns. Cherry & his wife obtains verdict in Divorce court Dec 59 for restitution of conjugal rights.

Confirmed here again March 12– 1860. Not pleasing noisy &c.

103 **Burnham. V. With Boveney. C.**

Rev T Carter. Confirmed here again March 19.1856. The Rev Bent the Curate has done a good work here – Far more candidates than ever before & far better prepared. Old Carter failing.

Proposal of rearranging Burnham & Hitcham to be considered at next vacancy of Burnham.

[*Marginal note*: NB Letter of Prov. June 1861]

March 18.1862 confirmed again here – as always rather dead & cold. Henry Prentice Curate.

104 **Buscot. or Burwestcot. R.**
F A Dawson Rector.. attends at Faringdon with conf. March 25.60.
NB. Mr Campbell come & going to build.
Friend of W's favourably spoken of: Australian wealth. NB to confirm here if I live to /63. Alice C. 15 & 10 months confirmed at Kencote Feb 20/64.

105 Milcombe severed from Bloxham in 1854
Rev P Hookins   Mr Blagden proposes to give £600
                            Eton College £50
                            Jesus £15
                            Miss Holloway
Mr Hodgson & Mr Blagden come to Jan 21 1861.

106 **Boyne Hill. District Church constituted & consecrated 1857.**
William Gresley. came before me praying to be licensed hereto on the 6th of May 1858.. I having consecrated the church on the 1st of December 1857.
Dec 9. 1858 Confirm here. A nice confirmation. A memorial from A Leigh &c as to Gresleys Book.
H Bedford C 1859.
Alexander Chirol. March30 /63 brings his mother for a reconciliatory benedictus to Bray.

Inserted Newspaper cuttings re Boyne Hill from *The Times* 25 September 1858.
[*The Revd Richard Temple West, curate of Boyne Hill, was charged by the Revd John Shaw, vicar of Stoke Poges, for seeking to induce a pregnant woman to make confession to him. A Commission had been set up by the Bishop under the Church Discipline Act, consisting of V Gilliam, Archdeacon Randall, the Revd Austen Leigh as Rural Dean, Mr Charles Sawyer of Heywood Lodge, and Mr J Hibbert of Braywood Lodge*
The Commission met in Maidenhead Town Hall.

West was stated, during a sick visit to an expectant mother, to have systematically asked her whether she had broken any of the Ten Commandments; when the woman said she did not know the meaning of 'fornication' or 'adultery' he had carefully explained them to her. He denied telling her that if she did not confess her sins she would lose the child or that if she was not confirmed she could not go to heaven.

It was claimed that when Curate of Hemel Hempstead his license had been revoked because he refused to use a prayer ordered by the Privy Council unless it was ordered by the Bishop; he denied that afterwards the Bishop of Rochester had refused to sign his Testimonials.

His counsel, Coleridge, persuaded the Commission not to put to him a question designed to trap him into claiming support for the Roman practice of Confession.

Eventually, after a session lasting 11 hours, the Commission found that there was no case to answer.]

107   Blank

108   **Cadmore End. Saint Mary le Moor. P.C.**
   The Rev F Parry.* Going on excellently well loses his wife 1855. May 25 1856 I confirm here. A very pleasant confirmation, such simplicity & earnestness. Parry very pleasing.
   * [*Marginal note*: Frederick R Parry.]

109   **Calverton. R.**
   The Hon & Rev C.G.Perceval. Confirm here again March 25 1856, a nice confirmation. Perceval ill in bed. Travers acting for him. I have had curious correspondence with Perceval defending Sidney Herbert in re Old Wolverton appointment – It ends well. Perceval taken in the Tower into Church since I here last. I do not remember his having mentioned it to me.
   Wm Pitt Trevelyan: comes to me Jan 21/59. for institution for seven years certain with Wolverton. March 13.59 confirm here, a very nice confirm[atio]n. Church crowded orderly [adults] Candidates affected. Church beautiful. All full of impress of poor Perceval. Most kindly received by widow & [Mary]. Laugharne from the Buckingham School, Curate & residing at Stony S.

110   **Cassington. V.**
   Forster Trouble about residence house Dec 1858 – parish want resd[ident]! Examine & find so long as Forster here he legally exempt – Mem at vacancy Poor Forster Jan 1861, breaking his arm, W J Bristow prepares his candidates for conf[irmation].

111   **Castlethorpe. C. [see Hanslope]**

   Catmere. R.
   T.G.Onslow. Has just lost his wife. March 1857. 13 days after her confinement.

   Newspaper Cutting.
   A.D.290 – At Caversfield, Bishop Kennett states that Carausius, Emperor of Britain, was slain in battle by the treachery of Alectus: and that from that action the place was called "Carausfield".
   Brown Willis derives the name from "Cafer". an inclosure.

112 **Caversfield. V.**
Rev C Marsham. Long strife with Warden of Merton as to uniting this with Stoke Lyne – rather advised by Percy Barrington who living much in neighbourhood a fair judge.

113 **Caversham. P.C.**
Rev Josh. Bennett. A conscientious man & wishing to do his duty, but cold & dry: & very little real spiritual work in the place.
Confirm here, Feb 22.58 & the place visited ahead of mc by
Fremantle – Woodford – Claughton Bickersteth & Butler during Henley Mission.

114 **Chaddleworth. V.**
Rev E Thompson. Consecrated a new burial ground Oct 1854 & preached –Came to Woolley [Park] March 23.57 for confirmation tomorrow – March 24 confirmed for Fawley, Farnborough – Bright Waltham. A nice confirmation. Wroughtons chancel coming well out. Poor Bart Wroughton dies May 22/58 – from fall from horse!! Confirm here March 22/60. A nice confirmation. Mary M & L going to [? Bonham[34]] came here Oct 30/60

115 **Chadlington.** [See Charlbury.]

Chalfont Saint Giles. R.
Rev.G.Pretyman,
Curate Rev Clarke.. A talk with him after confirmation at [(next)] March 13/56. He brought the best number & best prepared. But they seemed a very rough lot. The parish in a very bad state. Farmers exceedingly dissatisfied at Pretyman's non – residence. No helping Squire – all wrong & out of joint. Oh the lifelong mischief this miserable plurality system has done as it has fattened Pretyman for the day of Slaughter. Vae, Vae.
Rev C Lloyd Presented by me on Pretymans death (July 1859) gets the parsonage right – 1860. The school which I open, from the [Vache]. Allan getting right with Lloyd. I visit it Nov 7/61 The chancel very nicely restored – Confirmed here March 22.1862. Very promising improvement already. Movement for Church restoration going creepingly on. Mrs Lloyd broke her arm – <u>June 7 1863</u> Sunday. came for re–opening Services. The Church very nice – East & West windows &c. Miss Brown playing. I preached 2ce & Arch

---

[34] The identification is conjectural, based on the fact that in 1870 Mary Anne Wroughton, niece of Bartholomew Wroughton, married the son of the late Revd John Bonham, of Co.Kildare.

Bickersteth even/g. Dear Lloyd depressed about defection of some builders through not having been employed in the church.
[*Marginal note*: Best Curate.]

116 **Chalfont Saint Peter. V.**
Rev G Gleed Rev Fenner (Curate) Confirmed here March 13.1856. One of the least pleasing confirmations this time – The young people so unimpressible. Scarcely any males. Talked fully to Fenner & a little to old Gleed as to my disatisfaction*(sic)*. Old G. Failing in body a good deal & not likely to be long here.
March 22 1862 a confirmation & then talk with old Gleed who consents to a second curate – Fenner not efficient.
Just after 12 on the night of Friday June 5 1863 Gleed dies of Bronchitis after a few days illness.

117 **Chalgrove. V. with Berrick Salome.**
Rev G Laurence Great troubles between him & his parishioners. 1854 – April 1855. Mr Stephenson the Ch[urch] Warden came to me April 13.55 – to say that he had been cutting down the hedge of the churchyard.. & Mr L. had been to Eyre & sent him a lawyers letter – & Mr S had been to Mr Perry of Stadhampton who from law book said he was right = April & May 1856 Laurence having obtained possibility of an exchange I apply to Dean to get Chapters leave which refused on ground of their rule! Alas!

118 **Challow East and Challow West. P.C.**
Rev G Purdue. Correspondence with Mr E Butler & Purdue touching site of Parsonage &c. May 1856.
April 1. 1858. Butler's letter about a false scandal as to Purdue.
West Challow Church opened by me after restoration Friday in Trinity Week 1858. March 1860 scandal again Mr Roe: writing to Butler on charge of departed servant made, charging him with concubinage with Miss Bennets ? his house keeper. Butler disbelieves – Confirmation here very pleasing March 27 1860.
Pearson Curate.

119 **Charlbury. V. with Shorthampton. C.**
   Chadlington. C. and Finstock. C. (see next to Curbridge)
Rev W W Stoddard *(sic)* Confirmed here again & after preached March 21. The Fast day. Finstock attending – & the Churchill family. A full Church, Whipping &c. The candidates with less marks of care than most – Fordyce just gone has been Curate at Finstock. Stoddard so feeble & sleepy that I could have thought him asleep in many of the

prayers. Conversation March 29 with F Burgess about Chadlington – He proposes: Stoddart to give £60 per annum. College £1000. QA£200 Lectureship £20 – if Langston will build a house. College to keep Patronage. To see Langston thereon.

<u>Jan 10 1856</u>. Mr Stoddart applies from ill health for a years license of non–residence. I apply for more curates and July 14.1856 meet <u>Mr Davis</u> not licensed but resident Curate. He very popular in the parish & moving toward a Church restoration. Advised him to get a good general plan from Street & then do well whatever part of it his money will reach. Poor Stoddart dies Dec 1856 = The Rev George Davis Curate comes to me Jan 17/57 to complain that the Church Warden has given him notice to quit – Mrs Stothart's last letter making all up. Her first letter quite wrong about Cotterill & poor.

<u>Samuel Henry Russell</u>. Comes May 7.1857 – for Institution. Friend of [Binney's] seems right minded.

Confirmed here March 19.1857. Quite a pleasing confirmation – & the young of this parish well prepared. The church at the re–opening of which I preached last year looking well. <u>John Cross</u> Curate at Finstock going to marry Russells sister – Finstock in consequence I hope really to be separated. At Chadlington, T H Griffith much improved since married to very taking little Miss Whitmore.

Oct 10.59 Russell writes that he has proposed to Eccl Comm plan for separation of Finstock. Confirm here March 1/61 pleasant. Confirm again Feb 16/64, a nice confirmation SHR says all not satisfactory yet.

[*Marginal note*: <u>George Carpenter 1864</u> Curate at Chadlington in Langston's house.]

120 **Charlton on Otmoor. R.**

Rev G Higgs (*sic*)[35] – confirmed here Feb 28 – 1855 – for Oddington – none. Islip & S [*gap*] & Beckley all poor & cold here. But Higgs very grateful for my coming & seeming really moved. Oct.1855.

<u>Rev H Gough</u>. Comes at Buckingham for institution Feb 22.1856 a long letter consulting me on various plans for school &c.. June 1856. Dies. <u>T W Falcon</u> succeeds. Bearded & rather conceited but active. Sister living with him. I confirm & consecrate add/l burial ground March 8 64.

---

[35] Should be Riggs, but both entries read Higgs.

119b [*inserted letter*]

Charlton upon Otmoor,
Sep. 23nd.1857

My Lord,

I beg to acknowledge your Lordship's communication respecting the more frequent administration of the Sacrament. It is a subject upon which I have thought a good deal, & upon my first coming my impression was immediately to increase the number of times. On second thoughts, it seemed best to wait & see what the condition of the Parish was before making any change, and at the expiration of a year, and with such experience as I have gained by a tolerably free intercourse with the body of the people, I feel assured that an alteration to the extent proposed by your Lordship wd not be beneficial. The offer of privileges, for which people are in no sense prepared, wd, I fear, tend to defeat the object proposed. At the same time I feel it a most [*illegible*] duty to endeavour to create a feeling and a longing for additional sacraments, & I hope gradually to come up to your Lordship's measure. If we had a nucleus, however small, of faithful Churchmen, I shd be delighted to take any steps to promote their growth in grace; but what with drunkenness, indifference, & dissent, the condition of the Parish, spiritually considered, is most lamentable. I do not believe there is more than one person – if one there be – by whom a monthly Sacrament wd be hailed as a boon, while I fear the great majority of regular communicants would absent themselves as a matter of course. Such a state of things is not to be spoken of without sorrow. But I trust some reformation may take place hereafter.

I have the honour to remain. my Lord,
Your Lordship's most obedient
H Gough

121 **Charney. [See Longworth].**

Chastleton. R.

Horatio Westmacott. M.A. Attends again at Chip[ping] Norton with his candidates March 16/58.

G.H.Nutting on Wesmacotts death: instituted by me. Came from Sherfield – resigned because Piggotts tenant bullied him.

Newspaper Cutting.
A.D. – At Chearsley, the Britons defeated by the Saxons, under Cerdic (whence the name) and Cynric. Camden notices the prevalent opinion, but assigns this action to Charford, in Hampshire.

122 **Chearsley. P.C.**
Rev A Hayton writes Feb 1856 to say that Lady Wiseman wishes for double duty in her chapel & so he wishes to be let to give a title & have a curate at small salary say £56 at C. I assent if satisfied with man.

123 **Checkendon. R.**
W. Crabtree. R. Write Sep 1857 to curate as to future monthly communion which he promises. Confirmed here again March 15 1864!
Edward Hensley Curate. Saw several of the old people Amie Whitfield Hannah Wynter – &c. Went over our rooms. A good account of E Hensley.

Cheddington. R.
Rev A P Cust – visited it Nov 23 – 1854 with Cust from Ashridge – all undergoing a complete work of restoration – a new school – The Parsonage being made a very nice House – grounds &c. & the church – to have its restoration & I trust the spiritual temple rising.

March 6 1856. Came down for confirmation & reopening of the restored Church. At the confirmation, Ivinghoe, Ellesborough, Slapton, Marsworth, Mentmore, Pitstone. The church very nicely done. The confirmation candidates well prepared, all encouraging. The House very nice – & its inmates charming. One small sweet voiced boy – all rising. D.G.

Feb 8 1862. Here for confirmation & presiding at Custs taking leave – a very affecting & touching sight in all ways from great affection of people to him.

125 **Chenies. R.**
Lord Wriothesley Russell Talk at Chesham March 13 1856, he very friendly & communicative – never candidates so promising – dissenter with hat on in church &c. &c. Poor Matthews Curate here applies March 1856 to me for a living. I obliged to tell him that no chance.

126 **Chesham. V. Consisting of Chesham Woburn and Leicester.**
Rev F Aylward Correspondence about separating outlying hamlet & giving it to Hawridge: 1854 – 1855 – Duke of Bedford at last consents & will not pay expences then Mr Ducane patron of Hawridge refuses. –
Confirm here again March 13 1856. A most marked improvement D.G. since I was last here. More devotion in the congregation as well as the candidates. These from Aylwards account had quite passed through a persecution. Hooted at &c Mrs Lowndes says Aylward much improved, less with very low &c. suggest to him getting leave

for subscribers to new Church to let him lay out the £800 raised in a thorough restoration of the old church first as best mode of getting the new.
Oct. 28 1857 Mr Lowndes having complained of the Railfull administration of Holy Com/n, I require F.A. to abandon it as contrary to Rubric ——
Consecrated Cemetary & chapel & preached Dec 21/58.
* March 23/62 confirmed in aft[ernoon], preached in eve/ng. Great congregations both times. Aylward I think improving in all ways. D.G.

* [*Marginal note:* G Lowndes[36] confirmed.]

127 **Chesham Bois. R.**
Rev Charles Blackman I preached & consecrated New Burial ground added to churchyard, with large concourse of people Aug. 5 1860, coming from Ashridge.

128 **Chesterton. V.**
Rev W F. Fortescue. Church restored 1855. I object to a good deal of the plans when Mr F. sends them to me for my assent & at last it appears that the work was already done, when he sent them. See letters.
March 5 1858. Confirm here. A very nice confirmation. The Church done with good taste & as far as completed very well done. Also a nice parsonage built & the grounds well laid out.
1863 Fortescue abroad for his wifes health. His Curate's wife dies suddenly Nov/63 P A. De Tessier comes as locum tenens.

Letter from W.F.F. to the Bishop

Chesterton Vicarage

My dear Lord Bishop
I beg to acknowledge your note on the subject, of administering the Holy Communion monthly, – and of preaching for the Societies advocated by your Lordship.
　In both these matters I am glad to receive your express directions – as I now am able to make these necessary changes in our Parish Customs, on better Authority than my own. I remain,
　　　　　　　　　　　My D[ear] Lord Bishop
　　　　　　　　　　　Your obl. faithful Servant
　　　　　　　　　　　　　William F. Fortescue.

---

[36] Second son of William Lowndes, by his second marriage. Born 13 August 1846.

129 **Chetwode. P.C. [See Barton Hartshorn]**
E L Smith. Confirmed here Monday March 21.59. A confirmation where many seemed earnest.

130 **Chicheley. V.**
The Rev Partridge. V. 50–59.[37]
After all the Tragedy as to late vicar Townshend Mr Chester[38] puts in Partridge. Sep 26 1855. I visit at Chicheley – Church some what improved – pews lowered – reading desk 3 decker removed &c.
Poor Partridge ill – They fear with softening of brain. Too nervous to do the duty. Mr C[hester], asks for his absence for a year & I to find curate to have furnished house & stipend. Whole value £113 – & Mr P. that & interest of £4000 to live on.
Chester writes Oct. 21/1855, that Mr Jeudwine formerly for three years curate takes it at £50 & House furnished Rents & taxes paid. I assent subject to testimonials.
Rev W Jeudwine as Curate & well. He seems sound useful active spiritual man. Confirm here March 26 1856 again a <u>very</u> interesting confirmation from earnestness sobriety &c. Astwood & North Crawley here.
<u>Visit</u> again as Chesters guest Nov 12/58. On the 10th of December by some sudden bursting of vessel dear Chester dies! What a loss! March 16 59 pass house going to N Crawley with Hatchment for my kind warm hearted friend.

131a **Chieveley. V. With Oare. C. Winterbourne. C. and Leckhampstead. C.**
<u>The Rev J E Robinson</u> about building a school for service at Leckhampstead.
Always in trouble with Curates – Curate after Curate. Appoints 1856 T G Butterfield. Arch[deaco]n Thorpe writes me word that he has been intemperate & irregular. I write March 30 to stop his officiating till he has answered the charge to my satisfaction. He comes up & solemnly denies it. Meanwhile I learn that he has been inebriated at Chieveley & * Robinson asks leave to withdraw his nomination. I write again & expostulate with B[utterfield] & forbid his offic[iatin]g in the Diocese.
Mrs Stackpoole builds 1856 a school at Curridge which I license for Service,
J Hilton Jephson Curate there.

---

[37] Actually from 1851 to 1859.
[38] The Revd Anthony Chester, 1800–1858, of Chicheley Hall.

March 25 1857. Confirm here. As always the confirmation here unquiet & with a very unspiritual look. He quarrelling with farmers. I fear an inefficient ministry of a good man.
Edward Salter new Curate at Winterbourne. Going soon.
March/58. Mr Robinson proposes to build a chapel at Leckhampstead by Teulin – I consent –.
Jan 1860 The Rev T Carey now curate complains of JER. that having offered house rent free & £100 a year he now wants to charge £6.10.0 for the house to re–imburse him. I hear both sides & decide against JER. & counsel liberality. JER. describes himself to TC as "Evangelical in the right (not party) sense of the word combining sound churchmanship quite free from tractarianism & inclination to Dissent & am what is called a via media man. my age 61. of Ch Ch !!" Confirm here again March 17.1860. A nice confirmation.
Leckhampstead consecrated Oct 30/60. A nice day, with churchwardens very active. Poor J H Jephson gets intoxicated at the dinner & exposes himself in trying to read se[cond] lesson & at night &c. I make him resign.
* [*Marginal note*: T G Butterfield impudently uses my name in Staffordshire 1857. Nearly takes M.C Flint Do].

131b–c [*Inserted page, blank.*]

131d Leckhampstead Church Account. – 1859.60 –

	£ =	s =	d
Subscriptions			
The Vicar & His Friends –	673 =	6 =	0.
Residents in The Tything –	50 =	2 =	0.
Offertory on the Day of Consecration	184 =	5 =	6.
Grants from the two C. Building Societies	200 =	0 =	0.
Raised by Loan, borrowed upon the Security of Rate	400 =	0 =	0.
Total Receipt –	£1507=	13 =	6.

131   Expenditure

	£ =	s =	d
Total Cost of Fabric	1449 =	0 =	0
Architects Fees &c.	92 =	5 =	0
Law expences rendered necessary thro' the Bankruptcy of First Contractor	70 =	18 =	6
Re-purchase of materials left by him on site	15 =	0 =	0
Conveyance of Glebe	8 =	8 =	0
Necessary Furniture for new Church. e.g. Altar Cloth. Flagon &c. &c.	26 =	3 =	6
	£1661 =	15 =	6
Receipts	£1507 =	13 =	6
Balance still to be made up	£154 =	1 =	6
by	J.Ellill. R----		

131f–g

Chieveley Vicarage
February 15

My dear Lord

I have not been unmindful of your kind wish to be told exactly the state of my Church finances & the extent of my remaining liabilities – but until yesterday could not get in the lawyer's account: whose interference was made necessary by the battle I had to fight with the assignees under the Bankruptcy of the first contractor & for which you will see I have had to pay pretty dearly but it could not be helped. I now send it with many apologies for the delay, for which I hope I have satisfactorily accounted.

I have not been able as yet to engage with a Curate in Mr Jephson's place, from the difficulty of finding a sufficient residence. Miss Wasey having foolishly let the house which he occupied.

Mrs. Robinson, whose health I am thankful to say, is quite re–established, begs her best respects & regards to Yr. Lordship –

Believe me to be
Yr. very faithful & obedient serv/t.
J.Ellill Robinson.

131h. *Insert*: Leckhampsteads proposed new chapel. Estimate £1200. J Ellill R—

132 **Childrey. R.**
Rev Sam C Whittingham Butler tells me March 17./57. that poor W. satisfactory but Ranters mowing down his people. March 19/57 confirm here. At first an air of irreverence amongst many of the candidates but after a time I caught their attention & was I trust able to impress them. Old Whittinghams strange preaching reading ! He says he is 74 – rejected the notion of a curate.
March 27. 1860 Dr Whittingham asks about Litany in aft[ernoon]. I assent.

133 **Chilton. R. [Berks.]**
C Gaisford – March 25/57 comes with a most scanty & rough company to E[ast] Ilsley confir[mation]. Seems very tottering himself. Poor Gaisford dies /57.& Dec 1857. *Edward Morland Chaplin MA nephew to Morland comes. He seems to be actively inclined. May God bless his coming to this unhappy parish. He means to restore the Church next year & wait till the year after for parsonage. The School very wretched. All depends on Mr Morland, who owns 1000 acres of the 1,500
Communion only 2ce hitherto Mr C proposes monthly at once & at chief Fest[ival]s. & hereafter 14night [ly]– Talks of night schools. He & his wife working it & also the day school.
Confirm here &c. Friday in Trinity week 1858...
Oct 1860 great trouble between him & Smith of Harwell about visiting Mr Robey with difficulty but at last appeased.
[*Marginal note:* Edward Morland Chaplin.
D. H Ex.54.
P. H.Ex.55.]

134 **Chilton. P.C. [Bucks.]**
Rev G Chetwode. Confirm here again Feb 19 1856. Mr C's guest who as always most Hospitable. Mr C. about £5000 a year says Mr Barnard – & his son to inherit Sir T Chetwodes fortune. Chetwodes reading of the service fearfully slow & pompous.

135 **Chinnor. R.**
Rev W Musgrave. Confirmed here (for second time) Feb 25 1855 Sunday only 16. The Church sadly empty but the congregation much larger than usual. A good deal of talk with A Latter the Curate & with Halton Mr Turners tenant & chief Farmer. Both attributed the whole Evil state of C[hinnor] to poor Musg[rave]: all the religious poor

are dissenters. Musg[rave]. a gentleman & with no vice wholly I fear unreligious. Seen working in his garden & minding his farm on Sunday after service. His voice &c. in church are as bad as possible & the people wholly lost – at Emmington sometimes only him & his clerk. One of the confirmed threatened for it with loss of place by His master at Oakley a dissenting Hamlet of Chinnor. With Mr M. live Mr & Mrs Wickham.

Oct 1855. Latter going back to Henley – I appoint after much enquiry & search Buttenshaw mainly on Arch[deacon] Bicksteths recommendation. He seems to me a little shallow. He goes awkwardly to Musgrave. I try to smooth matters. Dec/58 awkwardness about organ erection with Church Warden. NB I notice Sir W Musgrave that I cannot renew his farming notice it having been granted on plea of need.

Jan 23 1860 I preach at the opening of the School – Bishop of St Davids with me.

136 **Chippingnorton. V. with Overnorton.**

Rev A Whishaw Confirmed here again for the (4th ?) time March 20 1855, & baptised W's new born Helen = Anne = Lily – Whishaws whole heart in his work & has been labouring with manifest fruit for this confirmation – converts – & others – an entire individual care & knowledge evident. He chanted the Litany beautifully – Curate [gap] now going on well with him – soon to be married.

March 16.1858. Confirmed here again. Again an encouraging confirmation. J Edwards now Curate with Whishaw. Leaves him [gap] on W's suspecting him of Roman taint which I think not unfounded. Goes to Liddell.

Come to opening of his new schools Jan 3 1861 which excellent. Preach & attend meeting in Town Hall. Full & cordial. Confirm here Feb 25.61 a nice confirmation. A Whishaw talking of leaving. Income insufficient for him.

Wm Cuthbert Barwis Curate & excellent. John H [?Rainby] came from Birkenhead where 16 years. The informant of Arch Allen as to Baylee's offer to Cud[desdon] men. He is said to be truthful. Mr Dawkins sent £10 for an altar cloth.

Confirm here Feb 23.64.

137 **Chislehampton. P.C. with Stadhampton. P.C.**

138 **Cholesbury. P.C.**

Rev Henry P Jeston. Nov 24 visited this with A P Cust – Found Bandinel sermonizing. Examined Church wherein nothing remarkable. – again & again. Jeston residing at Tours Nov 59 James Hodges leaves for Lane End <u>Nisbett J M</u> makes attempt to get in. Ticket of leave [forger] – Hodge a good man from Sarum Diocese proposed.

March <u>23–1862</u> Confirmed here. A wet Sunday & snow on ground. Church full & all seeming very hearty. Jeston again in residence & his new work a great comfort to him.

139 **Cholsey. V.**

<u>H W Lloyd</u> good man. Led alas! to join in the Gresley wickedness. In long interview with him at Warden of [Wadham's] His spirit & temper quite different from the ruck of assailants.

140 **Churchill. V. [See Sarsden].**

Rev C Barter – E Holmes C. Confirmed again for I think 4th time here – The young people as always well nurtured & prepared. Great marks of the Miss B's influence in the young women – Cornwell (Marah C) –Sarsden CB. & Kingham Lockwood attended – All the candidates with plain marks of care – July 13 1856 preached here. <u>March 14.58</u> Confirmed here again a very nice confirm[atio]n bearing out Bellairs that best girls school anywhere.

Confirm here March 2/61 a very pleasant confirm. Preach for dear Barter June 28/63. <u>Feb 22/1864.</u> I confirm here again a very nice confirmation.

141 **Clanfield. V.**

<u>John Pavitt Penson</u> comes March 20 to Burford anxious that I should find curate for Brize Norton &c. He declines to have his parish included in Mission Feb 1864 – Because if the trumpet gives an uncertain sound.

Claydon East. V. [See Claydon Steeple].

143 **Claydon with Mollington. P.C.**

<u>The Rev Tait.</u> Visited Cl[aydon] Church March 31, with Rev C Holbech. Mr Hammond & Mr Curtis Church Wardens there – in a wretched state internally – rather picturesque out. Pewed quite up to communion rails & all sordid – The cottages with every stamp of neglect & wretchedness.

March 7 1861. Reopened the church after its restoration – very nicely done & the church very pretty. All the population at church half standing for lack of room & most deeply attentive.

144 **Claydon Middle. R.**

<u>Rev W Fremantle</u>. Came here again with Arch Randall Feb.20 1856. for confirmation tomorrow – examined churchyard monument &c. March 25/59.

145 **Claydon Steeple. V. with East Claydon. V.**
W Fremantle. see. Weston Turville. Dec 1853.
Feb 21.1856 Confirmation for the Claydons. Twyford, Marsh Gibbon, Padbury, Hillesden &c. The young people manifestly much laboured with. The four women a nice set the men roughish. All speaks of activity earnestness zeal, with too puritan a tone.
March 24–26/59 halt here. F & Mrs particularly cordial. The confirmation a nice one A M Preston. [gap] Burgess & Lloyd curates.

146 **Clewer. R.**
T T Carter – Confirm here Feb 27 1857. The Chancel has been well restored since I was last here. Reopen the Church. All well done
Nov 30 1861. Opening services at the opening the New Aisle – & Infant School. Collection £100 – the deficiency needed – all most happy. The Laity with Carter heartily – I preached.

147 **Clewer. House of Mercy.**
Preached again at anniversary July 7/63: Thrust out a little from land. Tudor Greaves & O'Brien – Carter kept abroad.

148 **Clifton Hampden. P.C.**
Jos Gibbs – Officiated Dec 1854 Le Geyt Curate. Fanshaw takes his place – L. G. getting too much as Gibbs thinks under Huntingfords influence.
Oct 27.60. Come here for very pleasant visit. Wesley Henry Gibbs the young Squire & others – preach Oct.28. for Spiritual Help. Opening of new organ which at cost of £150. H Gibbs has given. Parish giving clothes to children. Collect £24–10–0.
Confirm March 13/64. A nice confir/n ArchB[ishop] of Armagh with me. J L Hallward Curate.

149 **Clifton Reynes. R.**
H A Small – Applies Sep 1854 to be allowed to reside here instead of Haversham – refuse. Jan 1855 – Bull rather advises me to accede – Henry Burgess Curate comes to Olney Mar 17 59
C A Jenkins Curate in 1861 – as temporary – Bull says a vulgar poor man.

150 **Cogges. P.C.**
Thos. Andrewes. Dec 1855 correspondence about the Duty. The in-cumbent old & nearly imbecile: to be two services on Sunday after Easter. ——
– candidates for confirmation 1855 few & ill prepared. – The College of Eton till the present lease expires. NB in about 10 years have only

£100 a year of which they give a large proportion to augment the P.C. The living lapses 1856 to me: I allow the college to appoint & they take my recommendation & appoint James Bandinell.

Feb 1858 begs to be let to postpone confirmation till Parish riper. Sends one candidate to Ducklington.

March 58 Brings a fair number to Witney. I visit church which really a nice one – only alas some 20 years ago pewed up to the eyes. Income only £90, 900 inhabitants, no house. Harcourt & Eton principal proprietors, to try if possible to mend endowment.

Dec 58 proposes to Eton to do much if they will make over Farm & House. I see Provost who favourable. Feb 23.59 Saw Harcourt & urged him to give to Bandinells scheme to which I promise £10 – Eton College consent – Autumn of 1862 resigns taking Living of Elmley in Yorkshire & Jan 14 1863 Henry A H Nourse* comes to Cuddesdon & is by me licensed to the Cure. having been curate of Standlake & very well spoken of by all. D.G.

[*Marginal note:* * Ordained by Bp of Llandaff]

151 **Coleshill. V.**

Coleshill Chapel of Ease. Amersham.

E Bouverie – At the confirmation at Great Coxwell March 21/57 tells me that his right eye is beginning to lose its power – ordered not to use it: asking me if I can help him to assist[ant] Curate. I recommend at least temporarily Jacob – Trench recommended. He takes Allsop from Arch[deacon] Berens & is well pleased.

R. W. Allsop Jan/59 Allsop comes. & Lord Radnor writes complaining of Romish innovations. Being (1) cardboard crosses on marks in Prayerbook, (2) most moderate Christmas decorations in body of Church, 3. candlesticks Iron standards near Comm/n rails. I rejoin defending Bouverie.

March 25./60. Confirm here again Sunday morning. Great fruit of All-sopps ministry – a deeply impressed people. Poor Bouverie evidently failing. A rumour from Augusta Barrington that next pres[entation] sold. dubito.

152 **Colnbrook. Consolidated Chapelry.**

Rev C D Goldie. P.C. Confirmed here the afternoon of Good Friday March 21 1856 having preached in the morning.. The church full morning. Crowded aft/n. A very pleasing confir/n. Goldie well supported by Havilland his Curate. He speaks with great affection of the people & place – Many earnest in serving God. A man of a good deal of power – The endowment miserable. Mainly dependant on a Pembroke

College lectureship. Indeed nothing else but the House & ground. Goldie some idea of hereafter getting an endowment.

I think a very successful appointment. Haviland excellent Curate takes leave with tears April 24/58, going to a Sussex P.C. near Hurstmonceaux.

Sorely tried March.1860 loses daughter by Scarlet fever. Wife very dangerously ill there from.

March 18. 1862. Confirm here all life as usual.

153 **Coombe Long. P.C.**

J Hoskyns Abrahall officiating here March 1861. As yet without license. I speak to him & he to come for license – Licensed. Unsatisfactory March 64.

154 **Compton. V.** [in Bishop's hand] Parva.

John Spearman Wasey. March 25/57, when I confirm at E Ilsley comes with his people. Few. Complains of great prevalence of Dissent. Wishes to take children baptized by Diss[enters] to grave & not to church. I leave him free.

Compton Beauchamp. R.

155b Inserted printed leaflet

THE
PARISH CHURCH of the HOLY TRINITY,
COOKHAM, WILL BE REOPENED (D.V.)
ON MONDAY. DECEMBER 24th. 1860

There will be Morning Service and Holy Communion at 11.45 and Afternoon Service at 4.30. The Sermon in the Morning will be preached by the LORD BISHOP OF OXFORD, and that in the Afternoon by the REV. H. J. ELLISON, Vicar of Windsor.

A Collection will be made after each Service in aid of the fund for the restoration of the Church.

The Clergy are requested to attend in gowns and to meet at the Vicarage.

Sermons will also be preached on Thursday Evening the 27th by the REV. FRANCIS CRUSE, Incumbent of St. Jude's, Southwark, on Sunday Morning, December 30th, by the REV. J. E. AUSTEN LEIGH, Vicar of Bray, and on Thursday Evening, January 3rd, 1861, by the REV. J. H. GURNEY, Rector of St. Mary's, Marylebone.

The Service on Thursday will begin at 7 o'clock.

156 **Cookham. V.**
Rev J Grantham Dec 1853 – writes wishing to get rid of Simon Sendall Curate for getting into debt &c– I write for S's account of matter.
March 1855 complaints sent me through Davenport as to the state of the parish. – wrote to Grantham who spoke of languishing. Find Jonathan Akroyd assisting him for some time past, write by return March 27 1855 to inhibit him: sending it to Grantham to deliver to him. Point out to Grantham why such trouble about curates.
Rev G Welford[39] June 28.1855 – The Rev G Welford comes for Institution, says he is willing to co–operate in endowing both Maidenhead & the Boyne Hill district. G Welford resigns again at once & Sep 4/57 J T Brown is by me Instituted July 5 1857 went over unexpectedly from Clivedon a wet night & yet found a very fair congregation – preached on the character of Saul – Brown quite cordial.
December 4.1860 I preach & celebrate at the re–opening of the restored church.
C Baber Curate March 18 1860
June 22./61. preach for SPG. March 30 1863 a very nice confirmation here, afterwards at Lady Youngs. Brown had just heard from J Rogers wishing to place Reginald R – here. Brown proposes to resign at the end of June. How sad!
G E D De Vitre Curate – His Father living in the larger Formoys House. Edward Hussey also here & helping. Confirmed his second daughter & son.

157 **Cookham Dean. P.C.**
George Hodson. Done a great work here. Herbert Taylor Howes his Curate – wants an independent post – much commended by GH. A trifle too much leaning to Ultra High.

158 **Cornwell. R.**
C Barter R. E Holmes Curate. – Comes March 14.58 to Kingham confirm/n Poor old Miss Penniston getting blind her notions of great responsibility as to souls of her tenants.

159 **Cottisford. R.**
C. S Harrison – Building a parsonage – signed papers March 1855. All sadly neglected before his time – Finds it very lonely after Eton. Cottisford house nice to be had – rent £120 with little land.
Jan 7 1856. He is moving for a schoolroom. gets an estimate for £60

---

[39] Actually G. Wellford.

[sic] – collects £50 – Eton £20 & sends through me an application to Nat Society.

Brings March 6 1858 a few well prepared candidates

March 9.61 brings to Hethe a careful looking set – moving for restoring his church – Oct 11 1861. I preached &c at the re-opening. whole deficiency £20, collected £26. He very pleasing. I stayed at Mr Rousby's & hospitably received.

160 **Cowley. P.C.**

Rev Benson. Proceeded against March 1856 for marrying without banns or license & convicted by Registrar, acquitted without going to jury by Baron Alderson.

161 **Coxwell Great. V.**

J F Cleaver – Confirmed here March 21/57, for this & Coleshill – The people seemed to me dull & inapprehensive but not ill prepared. The Miss Cleavers & he a deep interest in it. "This day will never be forgotten here" &c. The church Horrible, 2 vile galleries, & with them insufficient in accommodation. Lord Radnor the Rector & he will suffer nothing to be done as to Rector's Chancel.... Lord R. has suffered a great displeasing Waggon entrance to be made into the great historical barn.

March 25 – 1860. Confirmed here Sunday afternoon. All disheartening. Only a few candidates quite unimpressible. The congregation slouching & utterly undevout – School children laughing in the Chancel. Curious talk with JFC. after – never would touch the church. Could not believe that the Apostolical blessing had anything but merely outward effects or The Eunuch would not have been a perfect Churchman. The veriest dry of high. Yet a thoroughly good man. How mysterious.

Henry Skinner Templer. From Thornton collated May 2 1861 a long [*unfinished*]

162 **Coxwell Little. C. [See Farringdon]**

Cranbourne | Saint Peter | P.C.

Conyngham Ellis – [Cran] – poor C E's troubles Nov & Dec/54 & Jan 55 ! all made up D.G 1856. – Troubles about Irvingism.

May 58 yielded – May 21. I confirm again here, a very nice confirmation. Feb 18.1859. I come to re–open the church.. staying at Fern Hill with Mr. Gilliatt, a very pleasant visit. The church greatly improved.. a friendly difference between Elliott & C Ellis leads Aug/59, to the discovery that C Ellis was never properly made the

Incumbent. He comes to me at Ascot place Aug 13 59 for license, & receives it. Questions continuing till March 1860 as to different rights of Elliott in district.

March 26.1863. Come to Winkfield confirmation. Edward B Ainger. Curate now for a year – to be licensed at once.

163 **Crawley** [See Hurley]
250
Crawley North. R.

Thomas Lowndes Rector resigned, I accepting resignation Dec 19 1855 –

Jan 21 1856 Charles Selby Lowndes comes for Institution. He says the afternoon congregation good. The morning mending. Holy Communion to be henceforth monthly, has quite given up hunting. By his grandfathers will the Patronage of this turn has come to him & now goes to his cousin W Selby Lowndes of Whaddon.

March 26 1856 brings his candidates fairly prepared to Chicheley. Hear of Mrs Williams Bosworths sister as settled here on property, said to be Presbyterian & very religious. Talked with Lowndes as to trying to gain not alienate her – Lowndes seeing more in him DG.

March 16/59 .. confirm at C. a nice conf'm & visited Mrs Williams after. Lowndes promises to get rid of 2 square high pews & put chancel–wise seats. NB.

164 **Crendon Long. P.C.**

T. Hayton applying Nov 57 & Feb 58 to Spiritual Aid for curate from failing sight. T. Parr employed for a time as Curate a mad Irishman whom T.Hayton obliged to get me to send away Jan 1859.

165 **Creslow. R. [No Church]**

Cropredy. V.

Rev A Noel. Confirmed here for the third time March 16 1855. The Cropredy & Mollington people well prepared. The Wardington fairly – but not so well. Church looking very handsome – Noel now in good health. The people respectful & well to do. The living worth only about £230.

Dec 1855 Porter who comes up for his ordination as Priest says that the Bourton people have no room in the Parish Church & therefore do not go to it. Would if they could, – need of making the Bourton Chapel really effectual. Quere how? The Trustees of it grumbling at small rent.

March 6/57. A.N. comes about a Bourton trouble. Wanting to leave as place disagrees &c. Confirm here again March 11/58 a nice confirmation. C.Knipe Curate – Knipe leaving, I ordain at Aylesbury Joseph Mason Austen of BNC & Cuddesdon Sep 24/60 for him. J.M.A. very highly spoken of & seeming to be very pleasing.

Philip Hoste. Exchanges 1860 with A.Noel.. Trouble about a memorial Font. Hoste wishes at first to yield. & I get Noels consent: to quiet a Mr Eagles. Knowing the parish better Hoste finds Eagles to be a would be Westerton & resists (Letter June 61) Nov 18 – 1863 I consecrate Great Bourton church – a good restoration of the old Chapel. Feb 29.64 confirm here.

C Dent Curate.

166 **Crowell. R.**

Rev J. Beauchamp. Confirmed & preached in it Feb 25 1855, G. 89 1 B. who <u>seemed impressed</u>. A good congregation mainly I believe from Kingston a hamlet of Aston – Long talk afterwards with Mr. Beauchamp as to his duties trying to make him feel that the duty is the <u>first</u> thing the property the second. At his reckoning Crowell worth gross £220 is worth net about £150 – agreed at last that he should through this summer give one duty at Crowell himself his curate also giving one & that at Michaelmas he should provide a second curate. Mrs B. a sister of late Sir G. Beaumont pleasing & well spoken of.

<u>Rev J Beauchamp</u> comes Jan 15/56 to wheedle me into agreeing to single duty. He charges Mr. Jonah Brickness with having made the presentment from spite – & he desires that before Conybeare's Church is open – I would reconsider my requirement that there be double duty. Wyatt (from the College) takes his curacy Christmas 1855, & comes to me Jan/56 to complain of Beauchamp lowering his salary. &c. &c. Beauchamp states to Wyatt that Mrs Beauchamp writes his sermons.

167 **Crowmarsh Gifford. R.**

Rev John Trollope – comes to Nuffield Feb 1855 about Blackstone cutting down Church yard trees. Correspondence thereupon with Blackstone.

168 **Cublington. R.**

169a **Cuddesdon. V.**

<u>A.Pott</u>. Vacating it 1858 for East Hendred: on the 6th of May 1859 Henry Hutchinson Swinney collated by me – which may God accept & bless

<u>Edward King</u> …. collated by me March.1863. Q.D.O.B.

169b *Memoranda as to the Income of the Vicarage & College at Cuddesdon.*

The Vicarage Tithe at the present rate amounts to about		250.	0.	0.
But from this you must deduct				
Curates stipend	50			
Parish Charities	25			
Repayment to Queen Anne's Bounty	65			
		140.	0.	0.
Leaving a net Balance of		110.	0.	0.
The College in a good year produces to the Principal about		240.	0.	0.
Total		£350.	0.	0.

Upon the above it is to be remarked
1. That the Curate's stipend is rendered almost essential, as the Parish work cannot be discharged satisfactorily without such help.
2. The Parish charities cannot be well reduced below the sum named. In most years they have greatly exceeded it.
3. I have placed the College receipts fully as high as they can be safely counted on. The finances need continual watching to produce so much.

170 Cuddington. P.C.
(Culham. V. see next page.)
<u>Rev. James Mansel Price.</u> This Hamlet after years of labour separated from Haddenham & given by Rochester Chapter to JMP. who builds house & sets about restoring church: which with aid of Morrell &c. is done & on the 9th of October 1857 I preach administer &c. &c. at its opening. A very gratifying service – great attendance – & 500 of the Parishoners &c dine afterwards in tent.
The Morrell Family – see Fred J Ms letter Jan 8.59 give £1000 Stock in augmentation.
Nov 9 1863 come here with Archdeacon to open School & Organ. I preach on Eccles.xi. A very happy day. Price's influence excellent. All his Farmers communicants.

171 **Culham. Oxford Diocesan Training College.**
[This title is crossed out & replaced by **Vicarage**.]
R Walker. Declines signing the Cuddesdon address & writes me a letter about my having spoken of the fears he had as to Cuddesdon College as "weak" in an unintentionally insulting tone an essentially vulgar man.....Confirmed here for Nuneham Clifton Hampden & Cul[ham]: March 3/58 an essentially cold confirmation.
March 1860. Dodson loud in his complaints of Walkers tiffy mismanagement of James Morrell. Confirmed March 3/64, nice.
3 Painted windows to J Morrell to be put in – J Phillipps promises to rebuild the chancel in two years.
[*Marginal note*: T Henry Gillam]

172 **Cumnor. V.**
Hon & Rev Charles Frederick Octavius Spencer. – I confirm here again March 14 1857 a nice confirmation. Confirmed here again April 2 1860, specially pleasing. Attended by Besselsleigh Wootton N Hinksey. March 19.1861 at Baldon comes Francis George Henley for Institution – a good account of him in his work from the Jas Ashursts & laborious beyond most – Willing to go out night after night to Night School with a few. Ordained by Bp of Lincoln D March 51. P March 52. Held on bond of res[ignation] for Albert & [*gap*]Bertie.

173 **Curbridge [see Witney** erased].

Cuxham. R.

174 **Curbridge.**

175 **Chadlington.**
Rev [...*gap*] Griffith. Curate here under Stoddard – married to a cousin, a pleasing pretty young woman. Both related to ArchB[ishop] of Canterbury's wife – from whom expectations. Very poor. He not very wise but painstaking & pleasing – good draughtsman & gets from his sketches money for his parish.

176

177a **Datchet. V.**
Rev H Hall – Appointed by Lord Wrio[thesley Russell], having been curate to Vaughan at Brighton – about rebuilding the church 1855–6. March 17 1856 brings his candidates to Horton for confirmation. Scarcely any males. Mrs Hall tall puritan sour looking person & very uncourteous in discourse.

BOOK TWO   163

177b *Insert: Cutting from The Banbury Guardian. Thursday. 6 October 1859 re the departure from Deddington of the Rev.J.H.Burgess, who had served as locum tenens during the third sequestration of the benefice.*

178 **Deddington. V. with Saint James**
     Chapel of Ease at
     Clifton. & Hempton.
   Rev J Brogden. 1856. March His difficulties increasing. He says he must speedily send his wife into union &c. that I resolved if possible to starve him out of this miserably abused vicarage &c. March 10/58 confirm here – at first a miserable confirm from children in aisle & after they gone all mended. John H Burgess Cave & Egerton curates. A good deal of opposition but from bad people – a move for restoring the church.
   W C Risley – serving Clifton & H T. Harrington Hempton.
   Jan 19.59 sequestration withdrawn (Curme, Field & [*illegible*] & in 6 months Brogden back) Oct 11.61 W C Risley tells me that yesterday poor Brogden taken up Drunk by Policeman on the Road had got £5 from a grave spent it in Brandy & drunk. He to enquire & settle with Payne if it can be brought home to him.
   Ash Wednesday 1864. Poor Brogden after service ordered by me drank himself drunk at Public & in aft. is struck down senseless with apoplexy & never recovers ! ! I try to get living for W C Risley.
   Confirm at Clifton March 3/64. a nice confirmation. Hempton now served by E. Marshall. Clifton Risley, He & his son Deddington.
   James Turner – instituted by me April 21 1864 he has been helping Hall at Datchet.

179 **Denchworth. V.**
   Rev. E. Horton – Rev W Eaton curate – with Butlers aid has got the Church excellently restored & I reopened it Feb 21 1854. A rumour as to – nothing quite sober – to be watched.
   Rev. H. Tripp – Instituted him Oct 27 1855 on poor Hortons final resignation. The Parish having latterly suffered much by change of curates. March 17/57 I confirm here a small confirmation in numbers but nice toned = he is meditating a new school. I hear all good of him. Land lets ordinarily at £2 an acre in the parish.
   T. S. F. Rawlins – obliged March 60 to give up confirming here & bring them to Challow.

180 **Denford Chapelry. P.C.**
   F C Alderman March 27/57 candidates from at Kintbury .
   NB Complains that not in Confirmation letter.

181 **Denham. R.**
Rev Hall. Sir H Dukinfield writes Feb 1856 has been visiting here. Dissatisfaction with Halls inactivity – squire wishes Church restored &c. March 13.1856 after confirmation at Chalfont St. Peters where he attended a talk with Hall, he allows moderate inactivity, seems willing to have a curate. I recommend Travers. Fears being overridden by a Curate.– Wishes to see Church restored. But Ben Way horse racer &c would oppose & he fears Mortimer Drummond not aid. I write again to Dukinfield.

I confirm here <u>Lent 1859.</u> & stay at Drummonds. Young Way Babe born son of Ben Way now squire & after a little while will help materially in restoring the church. NB

Corresponded <u>Hall</u> <u>April 59.</u>

<u>March 21 1862</u> – reopened the restored church, which done very nicely with sermon & confirmation.

182 **Didcot. R.**
<u>John A Ashworth</u> seen of none, has restored privately his Church – only obtaining my consent &c to plans – no opening service &c. <u>July 1863</u>, gone to examine at Wellington college but I hear Aston Tirrold & pleasing. A very shy man: hardly seeing anything of any neighbours.

183 **Dinton. V.** With Upton.
J. Harrison – see Weston Turville 1853 – loses his second daughter April 1855 sends John Smith Hill for license Sep 17/58 rather loud but old from Lichfield Diocese.

Upton Hamlet of under charge of Rev R M Boultbee.

184 **Dorchester. P.C.**
<u>Rev W Fountaine Addison</u> Confirmed here March 5 – 1855 – a [?hearty] confirmation for numbers & preparation – Nuneham Drayton Clifton Hampden Wittenham Long & Little – Mem. disorderly scene at Public House ev[ening] out of the Town.

Poor Addisons trouble about Harcourts Letter. The church excellently restored – 2 of good Hannams daughters & one son here confirmed.

<u>Jan 24 1856</u> Mr Mangin of St Matthias the brother in law of Addison, comes over. Sad tale. Poor Addison before he came to this Diocese building a Wood Church with Lord Falmouth at Truro. This cost him £1000 or so: & he foolishly borrowed of Sylvester Thompson & Co Oxford at 20 per cent &c. & the £700 laid out on the church. £2 or £300 to Monro – £600 responsible for Radley. Liabilities amounting to £6000 – Assigned everything on Monday – gone. Writes me a

most touching letter, his property entailed about £600 a year. Nixson excellent: taking the duty gratuitously & working very hard. Poor Addison tenders resignation.

W. C. MacFarlane P.C. Addison hereupon resigns & Burrows gives it to W. C. MacFarlane who comes April 8 for license. March. confirmed March 2 1858 intensely cold. a nice confirmation. MacFarlanes house nice. <u>Dec 7.58</u> Attended to open the restored N Aisle & preached. Collected between £60 & £70, a noble gathering after in the Town. <u>Oct 28/60</u> preach for Spiritual help. Great gather[ing] . Collect £16.10.0.

<u>Oct 1861</u> Blackstone troubling MacFarlane. See Letters & Phillimore

185 **Dorney. V.**

<u>Rev Henry Palmer.</u> I keep him out by refusing to let him remove his Curate. He appeals to ArchB. who confirms my decision. In 1855 Mr Hor. C. Palmer comes to me at Lavington – They are keeping a Sister of Charity there & want to keep poor Bull on – Bull & the Deanery of Down! Palmer says Jan 1856 he will resign if I will nominate a Mr Gardner. I assent.

Resigns & on the 22nd I institute at Shinfield Lambert Campbell Edwards, a friend of Daltons.

186 **Dorton. P.C. [See Ashendon]**

Drayton [Berks.] C. Saint Helen. [See Abingdon]
[The MS is rather confused here. The entry seems to relate to Dorton]

Rev E Gardiner: <u>Dorton</u> miserable poor Ch Ch. having great tithes. No school – Lord Chandos trying to get mended.

187 **Drayton. R. [near Banbury. Oxon.]**

<u>Wm Lloyd</u>. Loses his wife after 14 nights illness from [*in Greek letters*] pneumonia

March/58 I see her daughters, he much affected. Poor Lloyd. died <u>Oct 20 1861</u> & on the 13 of Jan 1862 Richard MacDonald Caunter instituted by me, then in bed, from Trachitis at Cuddesdon – 1864 has made the House good.

188 **Drayton. P.C. [near Wallingford. Berks.]**

<u>Coley</u> – charge of immorality – giving notice in church that there would be no more School because I enforced second sermon &c commission– prima facie – reprimanded.

<u>Jan 5 1855</u>. Rode over & examined the church – All most wretched a square tomb just in front of porch made a privy by children – A

cottage in the Churchyard said to belong to Lord Abingdon – Heard that poor Coley dying – a respectable farmer owning a pew wished to see all open seats &c.

J M Collyns. July 6 1855 – comes for Institution having been since I ordained him Priest at Kirkham with Husseys nephew & done very well there. Dec 11.1855. He comes over on the affairs of Parish. The Parish claim possession of the Church, Churchyard & Houses as being in the hands of Trustees. The churchyard is let from year to year & the Houses & some other bits of land which by their rents save a church rate – Deeds go back 200 years & are in Mr. Hedges office Wallingford but no original deed. No trustees – Mr Collyns has collected £70 without colleges for building a School. Lord Abingdon refuses land unless all denomination scheme ! & even the appeal to the Bishop taken away. Promised to hold a confirmation after Easter. Rather recommended him to build in lieu of the School House – on the corner of the Great Churchyard with the materials of the existing houses which for this purpose the parish would demolish. The church now quite full. April 4 I ride over with Em[ily] & Bas[il] & inspect all. The old Parish School house is to be kept & turned into the new School. Feb 13 1860 re-opened the Church after a good restoration – A J Williams now P.C. Collyns at Dorchester. 1860. Apply to Queen Anne to augment.

189 **Drayton Beauchamp. R.**
W. H. Kelke July 1855 find him employing Skeffington Armstrong against whom warning from ArchB & Bishop Lincoln & Rochester for immorality.

Sep 59 consults me whether bound in honour to resign for young [Jenner]. I decide not. Resigns Aug. 60 called H H Crewe on by Mrs [blank] & I institute H H Crew[sic] Aug 29 1860.

190 **Drayton Parslow. R.**
Rev. Spurrell confirmed here for second time Feb 24 1856, going with C Lloyd – Newton Longville & Mursley. Hughes & Holt curate attending. Church crowded & very attentive – day beautiful & situation very pleasant. Communion rails badly [balanced].

191 **Ducklington. R. With Cokethorpe.**
Rev Dr.Farley Thomas Farley His quarrel with Strickland Dec 1853. I try to mediate. F. has behaved with great want of forbearance & exacts too much from S. being set against S. as a low Churchman foe to the University &c. S. willing if F. retracts charge of "falsehood" improperly brought to be friends & to pay for sitting in Cokethorpe chancel but not to pay rent charge.

Feb 1854 Brought the quarrel to a peaceful termination & received F's thanks.

March 27 1855 A confirmation here & a very nice one for Northmoor (Heming) Standlake (Burgess) Stanton Harcourt with Southleigh (Walsh) The church a very nice one. Two Hideous square pews of fine solid oak put up with a screen in 1826 by present Rector. Mem. to urge removal if a change. Mrs Strickland very kind to poor (see about their family under Standlake).Cleaver doing well here. Urged monthly communion on old F. he will increase times & approximate.

March 18.57 F. Daubeny now Curate, Cleaver having left for violent illness. Writes to ask recommendation to Nat[ional] Soc[iety] for a Nat[ional] school now building. 21.March 58. Confirm here on Sunday, a nice confirmation.. candidates seeming cared for. Urge old F. to move pews.. find that in consequence of them he reads communion office from Reading Pew. I tell him he must give up doing so & read myself from altar. G.E.Watts here. Hardwick a hamlet here seeming populous where Cokethorpe Chapel should stand. March 1860 – he falls out with new Curate* for being engaged to his daughter – wants another. I propose more services he consents thro' winter. Ordain at Aylesbury Sep 23/60 Edward Odell Vincent to be curate £100.

March 4.61 confirm here.. rather a nice confirmation.

Feb.16/64 confirm again. a pleasing confirmation. Richard Yorke Curate. Reads well, but too slow & "[*illegible*]"

[*Marginal note:* Welburn.]

192 **Dunstew. V.**

Archibald Malcolm Brings his candidates nicely spero prepared to Somerton March/58. March 61. Comes 7th to Steeple Aston with candidates. The Church being restored by H Dashwood..1 March 1862 I re-opened it preaching on "give ye them to eat" – a very interesting congregation. The work excellently done at a cost of above £2000.

July 26. 1863. I come here for a small confirmation to take Sir H D's daughters – & Preach morning on gospel. Doing the Will &c. – again struck with the congregation. The church beautiful – Sir H D. going to leave for Kirtlington & having let the place to Mr. Hall. The family going to put in a nice East Window by Hardman. – Sir H going to improve Malcolms house to receive a sister: his Mother just dead. Sir H receives sudden news of his brothers death & goes off to London at once.

193 **Dunton. R.**
Rev E Q Ashby *Rector – Divorced from former wife after much opposition in H[ouse] of Lords. In June 1855 elopes with daughter of Rev E H Hoare & marries her the next day in London. See letters of Mr. Hoare & Mr. Watts. She dies. He on ill health gets dispensation for non residence Her brother E Hoare Curate, Arch/d Bick: tells me 1856 that he getting into idleness & discredit. [*Illeg.*] ill health Bick[ersteth]: intercedes for Hoare, & March 18/57 on a new certificate of unfit health I consent to Ashby being another year absent & tell him & through him Hoare that it is for 1 year only.
Hoare comes with a few candidates very rough to Hoggeston Sunday March 27/59.

*[*Marginal note*: writes from Oriental Club, Hanover Square]

194

195 **Earley. P.C.**
Rev W Manley Hawker – Writes April 9 1856 to give notice of the resignation of his cure – succeeding to a living bought for him.
Horne Feb 24/58 I confirm here during Henley Mission & Woodford & G Prevost preach.

196 **Earley. P.C. [see Sonning].**

Easington. R.
Isaac Fidler – 1854. Quarrel with Mr [Lay] Farmer mutual recriminations &c – see letters Sep 1854. Writes March 29 [56] that he has convicted his farmer of Perjury & Stealing & wishes him put out of Churchwardens office therefore & he to serve for himself there being no other in parish – Reply April 9.1856 that a clergyman cannot be his own churchwarden or the existing warden be removed but by due process of Law.

197 **Easthampstead. R.**
Rev. A B Townsend R. Takes Horace Roberts for Curate – a very discreditable man: Hires a manor & takes in disreputable Boarders for the Shooting. Quarrels & behaves abominably with & to E.H. [Lindzee] yet a popular preacher. Quarrels with A B Townsend 1855 & I gladly give him leave to notice to quit. Oct 55.write to Squire as to future intended arrangements,
A.H Pearse. From Cuddesdon College 1856. Going on well in all ways, March 57.. Nov 57 writes that about to marry a woman his inferior in birth & education & so resigns. I put in Sturgis who bitterly complained of by Lord Downshire Jan 1858 Mad. I replace

him by young W.F.Adams 1860. Feb. poor Townsend dies. After discussion Osborne Gordon resolves to take it. I confirm here March 9.1860. W F.Adams doing well. Church horrible. Lord Downshire building a good House but saying he does not see what amiss with Church! O.G. Instituted July 1 1860. Keeping Adams for a year whilst he looks around House &c. Nov 10/ 60 O.G. wishes to replace 2 Chancel pews by 4 seats parrallel[sic] & looking East. Hopes to see the Church in a few years rebuilt – delay of builders lost the year for building.

198 Eaton Hastings. R.

Richard Rice <u>Rector.</u> Applies for aid to Friends of Clergy Dec 1854. Four children – formerly of Merton – Income of living assigned to Creditors. £120 allowed him by Trustees & £100 last year from a relative & £20 from Sons of Clergy. Education of children the ground. Unwearied begging – I referred to 1854, 1855 by countless persons in consequence of his begging letters. I suppose having canvassed for Friends of Clergy this the natural result! Attends March 24.60 Far[ingdon] confirm/n.

199 Eddlesborough. V.

Rev W B Wroth Visited it Nov 23 1854 with A P Cust from Ashridge. A miserable village. The Parsonage house dirty & forlorn to the uttermost – A fine Church rather – Strawplaiting everything in the School – A large hamlet <u>Dagnells</u> where according to Wroth Lord B had provided money for a church which abstracted by Mr Attey. Q.
Nov 26.1854. Preached in it Nov 26 1854 aft[ernoon]. A very large & attentive but unquiet & somewhat undevout congregation. All the Ashridge party there – <u>March 1856</u> The confirmation candidates who came to Cheddington few & not well prepared. Loses his wife March 1859. Sad story about his daughters intimacy with a low young man. 1861–2. Charles B. Wroth Curate helping his Father Dies <u>1863.</u>
Augustus Frederic Birch comes Sep 30 1863 for institution.
Alexander Douglas. Curate for the year – finds it all in a sad state, people pigging in Hovels unbaptised children &c. &c. but in good heart.

200 Edgcot. R.

<u>The Rev D E Dewar.</u> Instituted July/52. To begin to build in 3 years. In bad health & I allow him to take other duty & have a curate 1854. In fact I then think him not likely to live – He better /55. & Sep 55 – I write to Warden of Merton & him about building – A bad account from Fremantle of Claude Martyns inefficiency.

Oct 24 59. Engages to pay £100 a year to Curate – I to find one.
Resigns Aug 1860 & comes to me at Cuddesdon Sep 21.1860 Cloudesley Dewar Bullock Marsham for Institution – Has served there for 15 months under Mr Leonard at Newbottle – He to build next spring – borrowing in my name 4 years income.

201 **Ellesborough.R.**

Rev England [*erased entry*: A magisterial ministry. A good deal of pain about the] Blagden Curate. His trouble with Lady Frankland Russell. Mainly caused by his own great want of Tact. She inexorabilis acer – Poor England! having lost another daughter goes abroad for change & dies of Fever at Milan!! Oct 1858. March 26./59 comes to me Joseph Bancroft Reade – at Whitchurch for Institution.
John Sumner. I collate at London by Exchange Feb 1864.

202 **Elsfield. V.**

Rev R Gordon. Confirmed here, 28 Feb 1855, for Headington, Marston, Noke, Wood Eaton – an encouraging demeanour amongst candidates. High pews &c. RG writes to me about non signing the Arch/d & RDs address & hurt at my answer March 1859 offers resignation. I reassure him & he replies lovingly & well & resumes.

203 **Emberton. R.**

Rev T Fry Rector – Rev C G Hulton Confirmed here March 26 1856, a nice confirmation as to quietness – But the people hard as though Hulton's ministry were rather hard: which I fear it is & in some sense shallow. Plans now afloat for rest[or]ing the church at considerable expence – I advise thereabout. Hulton says baldly in reply to Lloyds offer of help about SPG the ground here quite preoccupied. We do all we can for Ch[urch] Miss[ionary Society] &c.
March 17./59 comes to Olney with Catechumens.

* Campbell Grey Hulton. (D. J B Chester 37, P 38) Comes May Seven 1860 for Institution. His complaint & irritation at my visitation, 1860 about Davenports fees for his institution – thought I did not enough respect him &c. & behaved vulgarly & ill.
Dec 17.60. Complaint from his Church Wardens of his indecorous manner in Church at Service – I believing him in the main right manage to quiet matters for him.
* [*Marginal note*: See Denson's letter.]

204 **Emmington. R.**

205 **Enborne. R.**

C A Johnson March 28/57 – Luncheon here & tried to stir him up to begin the restoration of his small but very interesting Church.

206 **Englefield. R.**

Francis John Eyre. The Church nicely restored Confirmed here March 13.1860. A very nice confirmation. Confirmed here Sunday March 22.1863. Charles Anderston James from Bradfield & [*gap*] Phillimore amongst . A very nice confirmation. Poor Eyre – lost eldest son – Has a daughter now March 63 at Torquay dying of consumption – His wife subject to such depressions that sits & cries all day. Said he could not dare preach before me so Archd[eacon] preaches.

207 **Enstone.R.**

W S Bricknell – From Nov 1854 to March 1855 corresponding with Bandinel to try to bring him to terms of Christian concord – alas in vain. See Eynsham.

Rev J Jordan. Confirmed here March.14.1855, for Kiddington (Browne) – Sandford (Curme.) Nucella not able to come for Glympton – confirmation fair. Great want of reverence amongst all – Curme's countenance simply shocking from its arrogant self righteous complacent inflation. Jordan kindly: but looking to me insane. Defeated by his own people in trying to repair church. A Church trust abused to lower poor rates. He appealed to Charity Commissioners.

July 14 1856. I preached at the reopening. The church well done on the whole. Jordan grateful for my coming & cordial. Brown in surplice. Mr [?*] gave £200 towards the Fund – Lord Dillon very friendly.

March 9 1858 attends confir/n at Sandford with a good many.

* [*illegible: might be Revd Edward Marshall of the Manor House, Sandford St Martin, the Revd Jenner Marshall of Westcott Barton, or Robert Bullock Marsham, Warden of Merton College*]

208 **Epwell [See Swalcliffe].**

Eton. R.

Provost Dr Hawtry. I consecrated the new Church here with the Bishops of New Zealand (who preached for me) & Bangor. Licensed H.S.Eyre as additional Conduct Dec 1855. Confirmed in it 1856. Confirm in college chapel Dec 9/10 1859. Dec 6. preach & celebrate in Do [Eton chapel] Dec 11 striking attendance

Charles K Paul Conduct T H Roper greatly liked.

March 19.62. Confirmed here again. A large number of candidates. Well cared for Paul just going to a Salisbury Diocese living.

Henry S. Eyre.

209 **Ewelme. R.**
Dr. Jacobson. H T Gillam Curate. Confirmed March 2 1858. Very cold. No churchwardens here I suppose from the old Hampden offence of the Franklins kept alive doubtless by Jacobsons timidity – March 1864 William A Plumptre Curate brings remarkably few candidates for ordination.[*sic*]

209b *Printed Handbill*:

£100 REWARD ! ! !

Will be paid by me, the undersigned, to any person who will produce a Vicar free from the vices below, named and possessing the qualities herein required, and who can at once take possession of a nice house and income, in a large and respectable village near Oxford.

" He must not quarrel with the parishioners, nor cause Generals, Captains, and Privates to be apprehended by warrants obtained from magistrates out of the district, for no other cause than that of administering wholesome correction when at fault. Must not illegally interfere with the Trustees of the various Charities, or attempt to remove a person's nose, or strike a person in a place not allowed by the rules of the Prize Ring. In his walks he must not be accompanied by an offensive Bull Dog in pursuit of swans, or allow such a dog to gnaw the people's "Hams".

He must not prosecute persons for selling a farthing's worth of lollipops on a Sunday. Must pay his share of Parochial rates without litigation. Must not distribute stones in lieu of Coals to the Poor. Must not be ambitious for, or possess the Queen's Commission of the peace. Must not prosecute the School Master when acting in the discharge of his duties; or vex, annoy, or disturb the feelings of all well disposed persons in the Parish. Must not act as Parish Constable. When in want of mutton for his Sunday's dinner, he must not go to the Grave-yard for it. He must not refuse to perform Christian burial on a Sunday; or refuse to administer the Sacrament to persons of known good characters. Must not attempt to disturb the true course of the Water-Springs.

His Sermons must be perfectly free (on all occasions) from tallow, grease and treacle. He will be required to abstain from making Brickbats, Tiles, and Lime. Must pay what he may promise to the burial or other funds. Must drink Porter in moderation; and must assist in distributing the Coals impartially to the Poor, and not to House and Landowners. The Sacrament money must be given away, and not retained by him. Must have a good and clean surplice, (the washing of which he must pay for,) and if he should borrow one, he must return it in due course, or forfeit £10 to the Churchwardens. He must *once* in his life time visit the Parishioners. He must keep going the Organ Grinder and Bell Ringer. When Chairman at

Vestry's, must do the duties of the Chair, and not attempt to bolt out of the room with the minute Book under his fore-leg." For further particulars. and the reward, apply to

N. SNEKE,
BRICK BAT HOUSE,
ASSAULT DOWN ROAD,
HAINTSHAM.

August 1865.

209c *Newspaper cutting*:

The Eynsham Enquiry.
TO THE EDITOR OF THE TIMES

Sir, – As you noticed the issue, by the Bishop of Oxford, of a commission of inquiry into certain charges brought against the Rev. William Simcox Bricknell, you may, perhaps, be glad to insert the letter which the Bishop has sent to me for transmission to Mr.Bricknell, containing his Lordship's decision upon the reporting the commissioners.

I have the honour to be, Sir, your obedient servant,

JOHN M.DAVENPORT.

Oxford, Oct.17.
Secretary to the Lord Bishop.

"Near Henley, Oct.15/59.

"Rev. Sir, – I have received the report of the commissioners who acted at the inquiry at Eynsham.

"It gives me great satisfaction to receive their report, stating,—

"1. That your not reading the service from the reading-desk was a temporary practice, and *Bona fide* caused by the still remaining dampness of the wall; and,

"2. That the bricks, as to which complaints had been made, were inserted *bona fide* with a view to drying the wall by the safe use of a chafing-dish, though the commissioners condemn, in my judgment rightly, the non–removal by the churchwardens of the bricks during the intermission of the use of the chafing-dish.

"On the subject, then, of these charges – on which you are substantially acquitted, – I need only say that I strongly advise the adoption of the Archdeacon's recommendation, that the reading–desk be advanced further from the wall, the dampness of which has prevented your using the desk.

"As to the remaining charges, I am glad to find that on the Sundays on which the Lord's Supper is actually administered, the whole Communion service is read from the appointed place; and further, from your own evidence that this has been your ordinary custom since your ordination, only interrupted at Eynsham, from your wish to be made perfectly audible.

"After the examination of the whole matter by four able and impartial commissioners, and with their conclusion that there is in the conformation of your church no sufficient reason to neglect the rubrical injunction, you will, I trust, see it to be your duty to give to give a full and fair trial of your power of making yourself audible from the communion table every Sunday. Should your parishioners generally find, upon the trial, that the great object of their hearing the service is defeated, you will find me ready to leave you, as in very special cases I have left others, to use your own discretion in the matter.

"I am. rev. Sir, faithfully yours, "S.Oxon.
"To the Rev. William Simcox Bricknell."

209d Reprint from the Oxford Chronicle, 16 October 1858
Mr Joseph Druce and Eynsham Charity Property.

Letter from James Gibbons, Vicar's Churchwarden. Eynsham, accusing Mr Druce (a) of securing a farm at too low a rent from the Churchwardens; (b) of charging the Charity too high a price for coal to be distributed to the poor; (c) of charging the poor excessive rents for allotments rented from the parish.

209 h–f

Cutting from the Oxford Chronicle concerning charges laid before the Bishop by Joseph Druce accusing Bricknell of having changed service times and shortened services in order to get into Oxford to preach as a Lecturer at Carfax. Gibbons defends Bricknell's conduct and countercharges Druce with abuse of parish charities.

210 **Eynsham. V.**

W S Bricknell see entry by mistake under Enstone.

1855 He wishes to dismiss Mr Cranmer. I refuse to allow it, & appoint Mr Cranmer his full salary. He appeals to the ArchBishop.. who decides against him. Complaint from Druce Churchwarden July/57 that WSB has moved the communion table – I enquire & find it so. Summon him – case heard by Phillimore & he condemned in costs & ordered to restore it. He gives notice of appeal to Arches – But lets the day pass & Sept the monition issues requiring him to restore it. Record attacks.

Nov 14 57. At Oxford visitation, he did not communicate – Presented by Churchwarden – Heard the case with assessor & made order. He reads all service including sadly communion from pulpit ... rather brought down I thought.

At length 1859 issue commission. Druce fails in his charges, & I acquit B. Write to B immediately after about Grove – He does not reply. Nov stir him up again he writes Nov 7 in excuse. March 3.58 Ensham [sic] farmers apply to Wesleyans to come. Letter of Bandinel. May 27.58. He grants a warrant * to open a coffin charged to contain a sheep. See Dav[enport']s letter.

Commission of enquiry 1859 on Druces' charges which break down.

* [*Marginal note*: Letter from Gloucester Oct 20/59].

211

212

213a **Faringdon. V. With Little Coxwell. C.**
Rev H Barne – A good & earnest man – though a low churchman. Busy about getting his church cleared of Galleries & Pews. In great hopes of success when I was with him at the confirmation 1854 – But again opposed at Easter by Goodlake & co & the rate for it refused.

The church going on. Sep 1854 Mr Bennett applies for my permission for a step of encaustic tiles he has put for communion table. Mr Barne objecting – consented. March.21/57. Confirmed here, a nice confirmation. The church beautiful: large attendance: young people most att[entive]. I most hospitably received, with Fosbery for the night &c. at Mr Bennetts (Dan). Conversation with Mr Barne about sermons for Diocesan objects I hope: he willing to concur *= Oct 59, asks to have Mr Hayward a new Curate allowed to reside in lodgings his old Curate & family Mr Thompson living in Vicarage. – I assent – Dec/59 I go to Faringdon for SPG. He does not appear, or call at Mr Bennetts but writes letter to Far[ingdon] Guardian abusing SPG next week !

March 24.1860 confirm here. Numbers rather scanty especially men – But seem carefully prepared .

Henry Hayward C of Little Coxwell. Feb 1861. Correspondence between a Mr Lovell in Faringdon Paper !

*[*Marginal Note*: Correspondence 1859 –60.]

213b *Insert.*

Salisbury,
Nov/r 11.1851

My dear Bishop,
I have today countersigned testimonials for the Rev H. Barne presented by Simeon's Trustees to Faringdon. In writing to him on the subject the other day I referred to the regret I felt that he had appeared to me of late disposed to be forward in what I called "unwise agitation", and I advised him in going into your Diocese to place confidence in you, & to endeavour to act with you, not against you.

I think it may be satisfactory to you to see his reply, which I therefore send you, requesting you to return it. I think it indicates a good spirit: for I felt quite doubtful how he would take my letter.. He is a man of some ability – a fluent speaker; and has of late been put forward rather as a leader at meetings for mixed associations of Churchmen & dissenters.

How have you got through your Visitation? The Chronicle, I see, has honoured you with a column; but in a nasty spirit. Its whole tone is, I think mischievous.

Will you recollect that you promised to send me the names of some books for a lending library:–

Ever yours
E. Sarum.

214 **Faringdon Little. C. [See Langford].**

Faringdon Union Workhouse Chapel.
H Hooper. Presented March 21./57 some boys of 14 saying they meant to be comm/s.

215a **Farnborough. R.**

W H Price. W W Price Curate to his Father. B. says toadies Wroughton. He breaks his leg 1856. Has E.S. Williams as his assistant meanwhile & speaks well of him.

W. W. Price March 1860, here with pleasing wife. Sep 21.1860 W H Price – comes to be Instituted holding it for 12 months for his cousin Edmund Price & A Pott – He says E Price now serving near Clifton. Diocese of Gloucester, in every way unfit for such a post.

Edmund Price instituted May 15 – 1862.

215b *Press cutting*;

THE BISHOP OF OXFORD

At the dinner which followed the annual meeting of the Royal South Bucks Agricultural Society, which took place a few days ago at Slather, near

Windsor, a somewhat extraordinary scene occurred in connection with a toast usually drunk at the agricultural meetings, "The Bishop and Clergy of the Diocese."

Mr. WANKLYN, a county magistrate, in proposing the toast, said, that since they had last assembled in that room, circumstances had occurred in that neighbourhood which had given it a world-wide importance. In consequence of these circumstances his toast was invested with a more than common interest. Public attention throughout the county had been directed to these circumstances principally through the instrumentality of the amiable and excellent Vicar of Stoke, Mr Shaw.

(Here applause of a most rapturously enthusiastic character broke forth, which prevented the speaker from proceeding for some moments.) He trusted that the proceedings which had taken place would have the effect of checking and rooting out of the Church those practices which were abhorrent to the feelings of every true Christian. The system to which he alluded he unhesitatingly described as anti-Protestant and un-English, as anti Christian and unscriptural. To use the language of the Bishop of Oxford in a document published a few days since – "God forbid that our clergy should administer such a system, or that our wives and daughters should be subjected to it." He would add a prayer – May God grant that both bishop and clergy and laity may hold the faith in unity of spirit, in the bond of peace, and in the righteousness of life. It was because he believed that the bishop was sincere in the utterance of these sentiments – (loud cries of "No, no" and continued interruption) – that he was a sincere – (No, no mingled with an occasional "Yes, yes") – that he was an exemplary and faithful – (loud noise and discordant yells) – bishop, that he begged to propose "The Bishop and Clergy of the Diocese." (cries of "No bishop," "Mr Shaw and the clergy," followed by loud cheers.)

The great majority of the company drank the toast, at the same time calling out "Mr Shaw and the clergy." It should be observed that the Vicar of Stoke was not present. After some degree of tranquillity had been restored.

The Rev.S.F.MARSHALL, vicar of Farnham, Royal, responded, amidst considerable interruption.

A pencil note by Wilberforce at the end of the above states "go at once to Rome."

216 **Farnham Royal. R.**
Rev S Marshall. The candidates who came March 14 1856 to Stoke for confirmation appeared to me well & carefully prepared.

217 **Fawley. D. [Berks.]**
W H Price W W Price acts as Curate to his Father. Tells me March 24/57 That the Fawley people were too low church to bear his Curate Williams so he has to go to them & send Williams to Farnborough.
H R. Hayward March 1860, trying in vain to get P Wroughton to <u>endow</u>.

218 **Fawley. R. [Bucks.]**
<u>Rev Dr.Almack</u>. The confirmandi come to Hambledon. March 10 1856. They appear carefully prepared. Feb 58. Carter preaches in Henley Mission. Dr A Aug 4/59, objects to being moved from Morrells into Ridleys Deanery.

219a **Fifield. P.C.**
<u>Mayow Talmage</u>. March 18 1858 attended again at Confirmation at Milton... his long dissatisfaction as to endowment. I believe I satisfied him today.

219b *Copy of map (to scale) of Fifield & environs.*

220 **Filgrove. [see Tyringham] Filkins** see p 617

Finchampstead. R.
Rev E St John. In 1854 strove much when here to stir up Mr S John to restore – February & March 1855 he moving in this – has got subscription & applying to incorporated Society.
<u>April 5 1857.</u> Confirm here. Sunday afternoon a large & very attentive congregation. Samuel Slocock from Cuddesdon College Curate here & doing I trust good though a little egotistic – The Church has come out really <u>very</u> well – The Meeting said to be empty now – Fine view from Church tower: Hindhead &c. Mozley's house nearly ready. March/63 St John comes with his people & J Pickford Curate March 24 to Shinfield confirm[ation].

221 **Fingest cum Ibstone. R.**

222 **Finmere. R.**
Rev Francis J Walker – succeeded good W Palmer – at first unwilling to take the living because the Presentation had been bought for him by his Father – going on well March 1855 – But poor.
<u>March 7:58</u> brings his candidates nicely prepared to Mixbury. Moving for the improvement of his Church, the good Palmers having largely contributed.
<u>Nov 15/58</u> I preach & celebrate at the re–opening of the church. A delightful attendance & all the parish after at luncheon &c. & most hearty.

Confirmed here March 10.61 a nice confirmation the Church crowded with a most attentive congregation – March 6.64. Confirmed again & all as before.
Fleet Marston. p.

223 **Finstock** [See Charlbury 619]

Foresthill. P.C.
Rev [...*gap*] Wyatt. Confirmed here. Feb 27.1855. for Wheatley Stanton St John (Headington– *erased*) Headington Quarry – a nice confirmation.

224 **Foxcote. R.**
E. A. Uthwatt – Came to Maids Morton with more than before March 22.59. At peace with brother.

225 **Frilsham. R.**
John Flory Howard. Attends at Bucklebury March 30/57. Cordial.

226 **Fringford. R.**
Rev Henry Jerome De Salis R. Confirmed here for second time March 10 1855 – Shelswell & Newton Purcell (Meade) Cottisford (Harrison) Goddington (Perkins) attending – The most attentive set perhaps of any: & here as occasionally this time the males most numerous.
March 7.1858. Confirmed again, & a nice set. A Sunday & most of the Parish present. A great deal been done to the Church £600 laid out South Aisle rebuilt &c. Miss Roundell giving half. Many wet eyes when I spoke of Roundell & her. Palmer gives a very good account of De Salis work: he unpopular & amongst gentry. E.G.Pierpont. Comes to Hethe with candidates March 61.
Confirm here March 5 1864. A nice confirmation very. Follett Curate ill: found him on sofa in drawing room. Cared for.

227a **Fritwell. V.**
*

March 8 1858 Edward Gordon comes with his candidates to Somerton. Pleasing in appearance. Poor Rawlins dies Sep 1862 – I hope his great weakness of intellect one main cause of his useless life. & sins.
– Jan 1863 comes Samuel Yorke to be Instituted – Well spoken of from Peterborough & Worcester Dioceses – where Bp offered him a living. The advowson purchased for him by friends I fear beneficio vacante – I consult the Chancellor about him: on whose answer I institute Jan 12/63.
April & April 6.63.[*sic*] S.Y. writes to ask if he may occupy the Manor House. I demur. He objects that the M.H. would be too large

for successors. I ask if he will give me a plan of restored Vicarage to be carried out in say five years if I assent to his wish as to the Manor House.

* [*Marginal* note: J Rawlins.]

227b   *Inserted Letter*

5 Arlington Street
LONDON
S.W.
Sunday Jan:11.1863

My dear Bishop

I have seen Mr Yorke and read to him the oath as to Simony – –
He says he can conscientiously take it – that he has neither paid or promised money for the Presentation – nor will hereafter pay any. Nor has he promised directly or indirectly any money to be paid by others for this Presentation. So far therefore he is free from any taint of Simony.

It is clear however that an advowson sold during vacancy of the living, does not carry with it the next presentation. – In this case the old Patron presenting, but if he has received directly or indirectly more money for the advowson, sold during the vacancy, on account of the next presentation, and is the agent of the Purchaser a difficult question might arise at any time whether Mr Yorke tho' innocent himself would not be <u>Simonise promotes</u> and his institution void. I do not know however that you are <u>bound</u> to enquire as the old patrons presents – The presumption would be that the next presentation was not sold with the advowson – –

But I cannot say that the case is free from doubt – and there is the further difficulty that you appear to have enquired and not to have taken the old Patrons presentation as a matter of course.

I am afraid I can say no more

Ever affect[ionately]
RP

228   **Fulbrook [see Burford].**

    Fulmer. R.
Confirmed here March 21 1862 – High pews. Poor Butterfield &c. all cold & sad –

229   **Fyfield. P.C.**
F. Burgess – who has built 16 March 1857 when I confirm here for first time a new & nice parsonage. Means to move after a year for the restoration of the Church. The College will give him £1000 – has got it to build Model Cottages.

230

231

232 **Garford. V.**

233 **Garsington. R.**
Dr Wilson V. Macdougall Cur[ate]. Preach here Jan 1855. Jan 25 1856 consecrate new burial ground Dr Wilson present. I preach on the occasion.

234 **Garston East. V.**
Leveson Randolph. April 1859. Randolph gets into correspondence with Elijah Bew about refusing to bury a dissenting child on the ground of its being a non Parishioner. I condemn him privately to himself. But shelter him. Milmans letter April 21/59. Wishing to exchange to a warmer spot.

235 **Gawcott. P.C. [In the Parish of Buckingham].**
Thomas C. Whitehead. Away from confirmation March/59, for ill health. Well spoken of.

236 **Gayhurst. R. With Stoke Goldington. R.**
Trotman   E W Pears Curate March 1857. Not very pleasing.

Gerrards Cross. see 611

237 **Glympton. R.**
Nucella. Call on him March 14,1855, to persuade him to have a curate. Mr Barnett Jun/r saying they if not old Barnett would help to provide one. The old man now 83 refuses saying he never was more up to all his duties &c.
C. M. Bartholomew. Succeeds on his death. Pleasing but shy & rather shrinking from work. After much trouble takes the School Inspectorship. I confirm here March 9 1858, a very nice confirmation.
Came here March 10.64, dine & sleep. Confirm March 11. Bartholomew promises to set about a real restoration of Church. If he raises £350 the Barnetts will do the rest.

238 **Goddington. R.**
William Perkins officially minister. Comes with a few March 6 to Launton confirm[ation]. Wishes much for one at G. next year.

239a **Goosey. [See Stanford in the Vale.]**

Goring. P. C.
The Rev W H Stokes.
  Confirmed here April 2 1855 – a very small company. The Parish cold & unreligious – Eaten up with Dissent & Stokes a well meaning bad mannered man utterly incompetent to deal with it.
  Feb 25/58. I confirm here during Henley Mission. Rather a nice confir/m. But find Goring lads & girls in [garden] romp as I ride home – [praesertim] one Smith.

239b *An Address to the Home Secretary, Lord Palmerston, from John BULL, comparing the excellent sanitary conditions in Moulsford with the appalling state of South Stoke, and the excellent conditions in Goring around the Temple with the terrible conditions in the village. It is implied that this is chiefly due to the poverty of the curate of South Stoke, compared with the wealth of the rector of Moulsford. The curate "speaks only with the authority of his calling, and not with that of his purse", whilst "the farmers know that he has another Master besides Christ, an absentee Rector...."*

240 **Goring Heath Almshouses. Chaplaincy.**
R T Powys. Dull – but laborious & conscientious.

241 **Grafton. [See Langford.]**

Granborough. V.
John Wheeler Hayward.. Instituted on Mr Whitfields death in 1855,& in October I allow him a license of non–residence to minister to the army in the Crimea & then at Aldershott, & Dec.1855, license G.O.Corbett to the curacy.

241b *Inserted Letter*

Highlands. Nr. Reading
2nd Feb.1861.

My dear Lord,
However much I must regret being unable to fulfil a wish of yours so kindly expressed, it is quite out of my power to undertake the work proposed in your note forwarded to me by Mr.Goldie.
  My hands are too full already & I am now plunging into the extra labor of building a new District School to belong to Grazeley Church & which I am told will cost me from £800 to £1000.
  My contribution in aid of small livings will be as I think I once mentioned to you, £5000 to April – The Endowment of Grazeley Church, & as a man who scored 68 last birthday may fairly hope to be not far from

the Home of a Christian journey of life, the new Endowment may not be long waited for.

>I have the honour to be
>Your Lordships
>very faithfully,
>W Merry

The Lord Bishop of Oxford.

242 **Grazeley. P.C.** otherwise Lambswood Hill to which Mr Merry objects.
Saulez. nominated by me as first incumbent. Not successful. He resigns & I nominated Freeman H. Bishop married to Evan Nepeans daughter & brother to Lady East. He goes on well. Brings his candidates April 3/57 to Shinfield. – In the allotment of the district Grazeley proper is excluded. Merry remonstrates. I instruct Davenport to remedy this. He assures me Nov/57 it shall be done out of hand – Merry. Feb 61. going to lay out from £800 to £1000 on the schools & meaning to give £5000 hereafter for Endowment.

G W Stuart Menteath. instituted by me on Bishops promotion 1861.

243 **Greenham.** [See Thatcham next page but 2 (246) (erased)]

Grendon Underwood. R.

W J Marshall – nominated by Mr Pigott from knowledge of him under Walton at Fleet Marston – He comes to me to Lavington for Institution late on the 30th of August 1855 – Holds it for a nephew of Patron. It has been sadly neglected by late curate Claude Martyn.

March 59. Fremantles speak very highly of Marshall. Oct 10.59. He writes me a cordial letter & gives good account of his progress. Blessing in last confirmation. Resigns in Oct 1862 in order that Dear Pigotts son

Randolph Henry Pigott may take possession. Whom I institute at Cuddesdon Nov 21 1862. Quod Deus Benedicet.

244 **Grove. [Berks.] P.C.**

W S Bricknell – PC – always in Hot water with & about his Curates – specially 1855 as to Cranmer: denies validity of License which I establish – applies Sep 55 for leave to give Cranmer 6 months notice of going which I refuse. I by letters thro' Dav[enpor]t, give him leave. Oct 20 1859. Write myself to Bricknell, offering to remove Cranmer & take off sequestration on his appointing another.

Nov 5 No answer, bid Dav[enport] enquire why. At length I revoke Cranmers License Aug 1860. Bricknell leaves Church unserved. But Oct 20./60 Dav/t sees him & he promises future services.

March/63. Charles Ashfield Joy Curate. Seems to have taken pains as to confirm. I urge Bricknell to put in a more efficient C. He wishes to wait for his son.

245 **Grove. [Bucks] R.**

246 Charles Whittle – Greenham [In Bishop's hand – additional entry] comes for a Test/ml. for the sinecure rectory in Wilts Dr Giles bothering about. brings a few nice looking candidates for confir/n March 28 1857 at Newbury.
Archibald Robert Hamilton comes Aug 11.59, for license as first incumbent. Dr Rose purchased the advowson for £300 & got H to give him £1000 for it. The Bp of Bath & Wells speaks very highly in all ways of Mr H..seems a very pleasant person & well minded. Greenham worth £130 gross rent charge about £30 a year. H. hopes to build.. ordained D. by Arch Armagh/54. P. by Derry for Armagh 55.
March 1860 going on well. Very hearty & Irish.

247 Cuddington = Preached in it Nov 19 1854. A very attentive congregation. Pleasant shell of parish Church though greatly injured by M & needing judicious restoration.
March 1862 I hear all good of Price's ministry here.

248 **Haddenham. V. with Cuddington. C.**
Rev J Willis(ob 1855)
The Rev H Meeres (D.41 P.42 J P London[40]) Comes to be instituted Nov 3 1855 having been curate of Cuddington of old. Feb.16. A confirmation here. First this tour, on my way to Aylesbury to confirm. The third I have held here. First since Meeres Vicar – There was still amongst some of the people an air of fearful irreverence but the general tone greatly improved since my first visit.
I agree to receive Jas Skerett Baird, at £30 per annum. He fails at the first. Is ordained Jan 57. Gets into debt I fear disgracefully & I accept his resignation of his License – H Meeres writes Oct 57. Gets cottages for Nat School & fits them for it Hopes to open it Nov.2. £50 debt remaining.
March 14 1862. I preach here during Aylesbury Mission to overwhelming & very attentive congregation.

---

[40] This should be C.J. London.

249a **Hagborne. V.**
Richard E Meredith. 1860. About his church. Proposes to sever West Hagborne – with £25 per annum for new consolidated chapel, with Upton.

249b [*The start of this petition is "stuck" down and the first lines illegible*]
the Inhabitants of West Hagbourn held June 9th 1860 it was unanimously agreed to memorialize the Lord Bishop of Oxford, and request him not to make any alterations in parochial matters with West Hagbourn.

Upton is a distance of half a mile from here, and a very bad foot path to get to it, while Hagbourne is only a few furlongs further, with a much better road, beside there are many parochial charities belonging to Hagbourne which we should lose by being severed from it, and most of us have departed friends buried there, and we should like to [be] buried beside them, therefore we request your Lordship to let us remain as we are.

We have likewise requested the Revd R. Meredith not to sanction the proposed alteration.

John Bullock Chairman	Diana Essex
Isaac Dearlove	Kezia Powell
Jacob Woodley X	Martha Ann Dearlove
Joseph Lousley	Hannah Woodley
George Bavis	Sarah Day
Alfred Dearlove	Harriot Powell
William Woodley	Harriaut Powell
Moses Bavis	X John Broad
Arthur Andrews	X Letitia Beavis
Ezra Dearlove	X Daniel Dearlove
X Abraham Woodley	X Naomi Norris
X William Day	X John Fidler
X William Bishop	X Jane Bond
X Harriot Beckenham	X Thomas Powell
James Powell	X Thomas Broad
X Mary Woodley	Isaac Redwood
X William Essex	X Thomas Beckenham
Emma Dearlove	X Thomas Norice
X John Andrews	X James Norris
X William Broad	X William Thatcher
X George Woodley	John Woodley
X Thomas Woodley	Sarah Woodley
X John Dearlove	Francis Woodley
X Igal Woodley	X Maryan Bishop
X William Woodley	X James Bishop

X William Dearlove   X Edmund Yates
X Jane Dearlove
X Martha Andrews
X Hannah Dearlove
X Hannah Fidler
X Eliza Broad
X Sarah Powell
X Caroline Fidler   These are the voluntary signatures of almost
X Hannah Dearlove   the whole of the adult population of West
X William Powell   Hagbourne.
X Amos Woodley   John Bullock Chairman
X Amos Fidler
X Abraham Woodley
X Ephraim Woodley
Edwin Woodley

250 **Hailey. P.C. with Crawley.**
G.C Rolfe 1857. Trying to exchange with Leeds man. At last it falls through. Comes March 22 58 with candidates to Witney. – 1864 I hear of Barne invading this parish amid poor Rolfes [screeches].

251 **Halton. R.**
Rev E Owen (Jun/r) No glebe: but great suspicion of foul play thereanent Nov 1854 Old Mr Owen undertook to investigate. The Curate Mr Sandwith living up at St Leonards because no house. If old Owen makes nothing out then I to try Sir Anthony Rothschild – for a site on which to build by borrowing 4 years income.
George Appleby Cuxson* presented by Baron Lionel Nathan Rothschild Nov 6 1857. The Baron originally held out hopes that he would give a site. The B[aron] & Sir Lionel & Fined it – They proposed that the Manor House of Weston Turville with 8 acres formerly let at £80 should be rented at £50 – Tithe comm £344.12.0. Yet Owen says he never got more than £250.0.0. from some puzzle as to Rating. Mr C. to keep his Chaplaincy of Goal, for 3 years. John Browne, from Stert Devizes to reside meanwhile in Manor house spoken well of by B[isho]p of Salisbury &c. Mr Browne an old friend of Henrys licensed Nov 6 57.
[*Marginal note*: Instituted at Aylesbury Nov 6/57

252 **Hambledon. R.**
[see also Lane End]
Rev W H Ridley Come here again for a confirmation March 10. 1856 – most kindly welcomed a very nice confirmation the most striking this

time – many deeply affected & my spirit greatly drawn out towards them. All evidence of a well worked Parish. C Powys here as Curate but going to Maple Durham. Ridley wanting to build a school at Skirmetts & have it licensed. I assent. W B Ridley rather growing deaf. Feb 1858. Ridley away for a year for ill health. Thomas Cox principal Curate seems a very valuable man. Randall &c preach there in Henley Mission & report well. Claughton specially speaks most highly of Frieth congregation. Money collecting for church in R's absence. Cox reports ante nuptial Fornication almost universal. Visited in mission by J Lawrell, Randall, R Milman, W Butler
Oct 11.1859. Reopen the Church – beautifully restored at cost of £2.800 & all raised. Gathering of whole parish in school & all most animating. Ordain Sep 23/60 Duncombe Herbert Sawyer to be Curate. Risley going to Burford. Confirm again* March 28 – 1862. Very nice confirm/n. Preach night to young men. Let both grow &c. Sawyer & Pooley Curates – both pleasing.

* NB Ella Frances Ridley

253 Hampden Great. With Great Kimble
(near Wendover)

Rev C Lloyd – His candidates at Prestwood March 7/56 marked. His own eldest son amongst them. What marks of labour with them & Prayer. His correspondence with poor Paddon – who likening himself & me to our Lord & the Evil Spirits. God forgive him: I hope he is mad – Aug 9/57 I preach here for Spiritual Aid Society.

April 10/59 Confirm here. As usual a very interesting confirm/n & preach at night on " looking diligently lest &c." Amongst others confirmed Lloyds niece Emma Frances [Jun.]. – I appoint Lloyd to Chalfont St Giles.[Great Kimble *is crossed out*] & Ashpitel's brother begs the next presentation for him & July 27.1859 I institute Francis Ashpitel here to..

254 Hampden Little. [See Hartwell.]

Hamstead Marshall. R.

Rev Blissard – Cambridge schoolmaster Evan[gelical] clergyman – fluent speaker. See next page.

C.A Johnson[41] Confirmed here March 28/57 Few but attentive. Curate B.G.Goodrich – Tried to stir up Johnson to restore this & Enborne.

---

[41] Is this really C.T. Johnson, instituted 1811?

255 **Hampstead Norris. V.**
John Blissard At the confirmation at Yattendon only 8 males (1854) & 13 Females from his large parish – Comes again March 30.57, to Bucklebury, brings a pleasing daughter his youngest – 5 males & 12 F = 17. Kind in manner – I having helped him about a son lately. People seemed to me remarkably prepared for confir/n Lent/60

256 **Hampton Gay. P.C.**
F C Hingeston. To be ordained P to it March 59 at Buckingham & licensed March 20 1859 – <u>Dec.</u> 5 <u>1859</u> He has managed to get old Venables who has just disgraced himself by an incestuous alliance with his wifes niece to let him restore the church which has cost him £165 – all but £38 raised & £25.10 this mornings collection nearly done. A family Willoughby cousins of Willoughby of R[ousham] have tried the [*illegible*] & House. Old Venables property much [most aged]

257 **Hampton Poyle. R.**
Rev. Joseph Dodd. Dealings with him (1857) to move him to a more important post. He would move to Woodstock., I propose to St John.
<u>Dec 5, 1859</u> Visited the Church..some beautiful specimens of old work, but the Church shamefully in want of renewal. Parsonage comfortable.

Hanborough. R.
Rev. Dr. Higgs. Visited it Aug 17 1860 with D[uke] & D[uche]ss of Marlborough under repair by bad architect Seckham I not having been at first consulted – settled to keep screen and curious old work over side aisles they wanted to demolish
<u>Open the Church</u> with a very nice Service, 1860. Confirm here, March 4.61, a very satisfactory confirmation.

259a **Hanney. V.**
The Rev James Macdougall. V. Writes to me Jan 1856 about building a chapel for an outlying population. Dean & C[hapter] of Salisbury as Patrons at first refuse assent. I advise him to apply again saying I so feel need that I shall license it when built. Feb 1856 they assent.
July 31.1857. I go to lay the first stone of the Church & address at length the Farmers labourers &c. present on the day & their duties to each other.
March 31st – April 2/58 fixed for opening of the new church.
Oct 27 1859 Long trouble between him & Goalen.* G. [in enquiry] & stirring up parish against him. Miss <u>Heading</u> rules. Go[alen] having married her niece.
After corresp[ondence]. MacDou[gall] gives up choristers surplices &c. & the trouble is hushed.

March 14.63 I confirm here a nice confir/m.
A. H Cunningham Curate of E Hanney, March 63 & doing well.
[*Marginal note*: *Goalen Alex]

259b [*Inserted Letter*]

Hanslope
Stony Stratford
Feb/y 16 – 1860

My Lord,
Under present circumstances I am decidedly of opinion that Castlethorpe is better as it is under the Vicar & the Curate.

If a separation were to ensue I suppose the population would be numerically according to the census returns of each Parish – for except ecclesiastically they are 2 distinct Parishes.

I cannot think your Lordship is serious in asking me what portion of income I could sacrifice to be let free from the charge of Castlethorpe.

As to your 3rd query I repeat that the Corporation pays the Vicar £70 – Glebe £30 per ann: e i total endowment £100 besides occasional fees.

I wish to know your Lordships mind respecting Cottage Lectures for I have sometimes thought a Lecture at the extremities of the Hanslope Parish occasionally given might be of benefit.

   I am my Lord
   very sincerely
   M A Nicholson
The Bishop of Oxford.

259d [*Inserted leaflet*][42]

Harvest Thanksgiving Services
Sunday. Oct.4.1863.

———

Proper Psalms.
Mattins,–Psalms lxv, lxxxi, ciii.
Evensong,–Psalms cxliv, cxlv, cxlvii.
Proper Lessons.
Mattins First Lesson – Deut.xxviii,1 to 15.
Second Lesson – St.John vi, 26 to 59.
Evensong First lesson – Hosea ii, 6 to the end.
Second lesson – 2 Cor.ix.
Epistle– St.James v 7, to the end.
Gospel – St.Matt. xiii, 36 to 44.

---

[42] The text of the leaflet is reproduced since Harvest Festivals were then relatively new. This example indicates the care taken to conform as far as possible to Biblical and Prayer Book formats.

COLLECT

Ps.lxv 8.9. O Thou that makest the out–goings of the morning and evening to Praise Thee,

Mat.iii, 10. Who visitest the earth and blessest it and makest it very plenteous: Open the

Ps.cx.3 window of Heaven and pour us out a blessing, that there shall not be room

Ps.xcii 13 enough to receive it: That we being refreshed with the dew of our youth, may bring forth more fruit in our ages: through Jesus Christ our Lord. Amen.

HYMN I
[Tune – TROYTE OR ST.AUSTELL]
" They joy before Thee, according to the joy in Harvest" Isaiah ix,3.

Earth below is teeming,
   Heaven is bright above,
Every brow is beaming
   In the light of Love.
Every eye rejoices
   Every thought is praise,
Happy hearts and voices
   Gladden nights and days.
O Almighty Giver!
   Bountiful and free!
As the joy in Harvest
   Joy we before Thee!

Every youth and maiden
   On the Harvest plain
Round the waggons laden
   With their golden grain,
Swell the happy chorus
   On the evening air,
Unto Him that o'er us
   Bends with constant care.
Refrain

For the sun and showers,
   For the rain and dew,
For the happy hours
   Spring and summer knew;

For the golden Autumn
   And its precious stores,
For the Love that brought them
   Teeming to our doors:
     Refrain

Earth's broad Harvest whitens
   In a brighter Sun,
Than the orb that lightens
   All we tread upon;
Send out labourer's Father!
   Where fields ripening wave,
All the Nations gather
   Gather in and save.
O Almighty Giver!
   Bountiful and free!
Then as joy in Harvest
   We shall joy in Thee!

Hymns of Love and Praise.

259f

HYMN II
[TUNE – ST GEORGE'S.]
" Thou crownest the year with Thy Goodness."
Ps. lxv. 12.

Come ye thankful people come. [*the version still currently in use*]
    Dean Alford.

259g

HYMN III
[TUNE – JERUSALEM THE GOLDEN.]
"He reserveth unto us the appointed weeks of the Harvest." Jer.v.,24.
   Sing to the Lord of Harvest
     Sing songs of Love and Praise!
   With joyful hearts and voices
     Your Hallelujahs raise:
   By Him the rolling seasons
     In joyful order move;
   Sing to the Lord of Harvest
     A song of Happy Love!

By Him the clouds drop fatness
    The deserts bloom and spring,
The hills leap up in gladness,
    The valleys laugh and sing:
He filleth with His fulness
    All things with large increase,
He crowns the year with goodness,
    With Plenty and with Peace.

Heap on the sacred Altar
    The gifts His Goodness gave;
The golden sheaves of Harvest,
    The souls He died to save;
Your hearts lay down before Him
    When at His feet ye fall.
And with your lives adore Him
    Who have His life for all.

To God the gracious Father
    Who made us "very good",
To Christ! Who when we wandered
    Restored us with His blood,
And to the Holy Spirit!
    Who doth upon us pour
His blessed dews and sunshine
    Be Praise for evermore

J. S. B. M[onsell]

260   **Hanslope. V. and R. with Castlethorpe C.**
M A Nicholson V. Complaint against him Sep 1854 from Mr Shower Church Warden & others that he had from the pulpit recommended the parishioners to send their children to a Wesleyan School, The Church School being unsupported – His defence very poor & lame. Complaint of the Town Clerk of Lincoln Dec 19 1855 as to his taking legal proceedings against the Corporation unless his dues paid on the day they are due – March 15 1859 come here to Hanslope Park occupied by Mr & Mrs Walpole. He have married her the widow of young Watts who died in /53, & guardian to boy who heir to property 3000 acres about £5000 a year, the boy been at Eton but delicate.
I confirm here afternoon = preach evening – mount the tower – but the day thick. Nicholson deaf & querulous complaining of parishioners &c. I preach at night Lent Mission sermon on Mat.vi.i. A large & very attentive congregation & interested. God grant a blessing. Some idea

of getting advowson.. At Newport March 16 Mr Bull of Castlethorpe all anxious about a *curate will find a lodging — To get the Patronage & add to Endowment. Oct/61. Here[sic] of poor Nicholson having a personal collision with his C[hurch] Warden Checkley about a pond. Call each other "Mark" & "George".[remainder illegible]
[Marginal note: *NB]

261 **Hanwell. R.**
Pearse – Resident at his other living.[43] March 11 1858 Richard McDonald Caunter comes to Horley with candidates for confirm[ation] moderately pleasing.
Vincent Pearse Instituted by me – Nov 1861.

262 **Hardmead. R.**
Bartlett Goodrich – R – dies 1855 – & on the 18th of January 1856 Bartlett George Goodrich comes for Institution.. On the presentation of William George Shedden of Lime Street Square.. The Sheddens owning Hardmead – Mr Goodrich holds under Bond of £3000 to resign in favour of one of 2 nephews William Hawthorne of [...gap] Coll[ege] Cambridge: or William Galloway just entered at [...gap] Coll. Oxford.. There is to be three years income borrowed on the living – & the Sheddens are to make up the deficiency & so build, on a new site. He to be non resident till the House is built, not being able to get one nearer than Newport Pagnell 5 miles distant. The building of the House to be begun at once.
March 16/59. Brings candidates seemingly well prepared & carefully obtained to N.Crawley.
Nov 26 1861. Preached & celebrated at the Reopening of the church, & planted Wellingtonia[44] – Rev E Shedden attending for self & two brothers who now the Squires & have helped greatly in the good work. Also school built & Parsonage finished. Mr Tarry the Churchwarden (Clerk Wait & other Ch Warden Linger!!) capital man. All seeming on the rise here D.G.

263 **Hardwick. R. [Bucks.]**
Christopher Erle His kindliness March 1859 in sending sherry to the poor turners for Luncheon. H Rich Curate & not very pleasing manner in his candidates.

---

[43] Assuming this is W Pearse, instituted to Hanwell in 1816, he had also been Perpetual Curate of Shaugh, Devon, since 1803.
[44] Then a novelty.

March 15/62 Confirm here. Poor Erle seems to me to be breaking fast. His Curate R Mayo son of Dr M. I hope well of.

264 **Hardwick. R. With Tusmore.**
[Oxon.]
Thomas Prater – Vacates by taking another living June 1856 and on the 19th of June comes for Institution Charles Montague Styles, to it & Tusmore. Ordained Deacon & Priest by me. A good deal of eccentricity of character & manner about him. He comes for both — comes with a few candidates to Stoke Lyne March 6/58 I fear nothing satisfactory here.

265 **Harpsden cum Bolney. R.**
F K Leighton Confirmed here Feb.21.1855. A very cheering confirmation in the beautiful Church, with a manifestly well prepared People. Lady Barrow here with sailor son.
Dear Leighton loses his Frank Aug 1855 miserere Domine.
Feb 23/58 I confirm here. A delightful confirmation, & preach after on I stand at door. Feb 26 I open new school. Leighton in very interesting speech explaining how it was got – Fremantle Bickersteth, Butler, Claughton Burgon all address or Preach in Henley Mission. Leightons girl very ill.

266 **Hartwell. R. With Little Hampden. C.**
John Rush – Old & incompetent dies 1855 – When the Astronomical Society nominates Charles Lowndes who comes for institution Sep 20 1855.
C Lowndes. Sees no way of mending the arrangements. Population & income very small. His people at Little Hampden go in the evening to Coblers Hill where Champneys has a service from his Curate – C L. has for 13 years ridden the distance missing only once – & once in snow having no congregation.

267 **Harwell. V.**
Visited it in Oct.1854. In sad need of restoration. Some talked of. John Smith[45] writing his name with obliterating scratch: said to be a very sporting man. I confirm here March 29.1860. All the parish turning out to receive me: banners &c. Luncheon for candidates in the School – a great many confirmed. But Pott sure that Dissent spreading from his pastoral carelessness. He has plans for restoring the church. Is a moneyed man & may carry them out.

---

[45] According to *Crockford* the vicar was Samuel Mountjoy Smith.

268 **Haseley Great. R.**
   Rev W Birkett. Confirmed here Feb 27 – 1855. Albury Great Milton Little Milton attending – a satisfactory confirmation. Morning. 3 decker pulpit & reading desk March 1860.
   Confirmed here March 14.61. A nice confir/m.
   [*In Bishop's hand at foot of page*: Hazelmeer].

269 **Hatford. R.**
   Rev J Hearne – Rather mad. Brings a candidate March 1856 to Stanford in the Vale. His affecting & very kind speech after Luncheon at Dr Wordsworths. Called on him March 18.1857 … a good old man of the low church school, full of antiquarian susceptibilities about his parish which should be Headford – The ford of the Head a stream running into Stanford Stream & so into the Ock. Dies 1864.
   C B Smith[46] – Comes for Institution April 20.64. He brings a strong letter of recommendation from Canon Dale & professes non–party.

270 **Haversham. R.**
   Rev H A Small. Rev Josiah Rogers complains March 25 1856 of Small not yet NB evacuating the house though now long possessed of Clifton Reynes. Rev Arthur Bruce Frazer comes to be instituted June 7 1856 to it – Small having sold. Frazer well spoken of by North & others of Brighton: seems right minded & sober with Drummond & wishes to maintain sound church views & to save his peoples souls D.G.
   March 15 1854 Come here from Wolverton to confirm = a specially nice confirmation – a striking church. Frazer very hearty & good & deep in Parish Welfare & his wife charming.. Mr Greaves chief proprietor whose daughter Small incestuously married, a good churchman. The prop of the church. All looking up here.
   Oct 17 1861 Came to Frazers whose wifes father a Mr King a Brewer ? at Brighton dead & left her £70,000. Most kindly received. 18th opened the schools – very nice ones & laity & clergy all pleasant. Frazer thoroughly liked & his little wife pleasing. All well DG here.

271 **Hawridge. R.**
   Rev A Codd. Rode to it from Ashridge Nov 24 1854. A miserable church in most wretched repair. The Parsonage newly restored & not uncomfortable on a cold & bleak spot. Mrs Codd in sad health – a school opened tried to see Mr Field to make peace but he out.
   Jan 1855 – Tried to get a portion of Chesham attached to Hawridge

---

[46] George Burder James was instituted in 1864.

– D[uke] of Bedford at last consents & then Mr Ducane Codds Father in Law & patron declines. March 13 1856. Codd brought 7 candidates down for confirmation. Mr Field still obdurate. He would not come to dine & eat a Turtle when Codd hoping to win him invited. The church new built 1856 & opened with consecration – Codds humour illustrated as to roof – also as to refusing in /56 to preach the Pastoral. Angular & unpleasant – In 1857 he at last arranges for an exchange after many efforts with the Rev Alfred Cornelius Richings from Beaminster Dorset – in delicate health & needing a bracing air. Well spoken of by B[isho]p Sarum but no great energy.

272 **Hazelgrove. P.C.**
George Allan Incumbent Much trouble Oct 1860 about the district.
1862 Hugh Allan Curate.

273 **Headington. V.**
Rev J Pring Dec 1855 A miserable account of the neglect of nearly all things since Golightly left. Preach here, Jan 27. 1856 for Dioc'n Ch Board. Curate Rev I Rogers. Moving Oct/59, with some effect for restoration of the Church.

274 **Headington Quarry. P.C.**
Rev J. Brown – Presented by me on James resignation & mainly on his recommendation. I fear a total failure. James goes over Dec 1855 & finds all going to ruin. The people unvisited &c. &c. He came to me at Cuddesdon The anniversary & tendered his resignation which I accepted.
On Thursday Jun 10 The Rev Samuel Waring Mangin came to me. I asked him have you absolutely arranged for accepting what will vacate St Matthias "I have" "I have accepted Timsbury near Romsey" "Then your leaving is settled" "It is." Then I feel at liberty to ask if you will take H.Q. He went down the same day – came up June 11 & was Licensed there to – which may God bless. Writes to me March 62 that accepted one of the Haggerston districts.

275 **Hedgerley. R.**
Rev Baylis. I come again to Rice Claytons for confirmation tomorrow March 13 1856. The disagreement between Rector & Squire still unhealed V.Q. Confirmation here March 14 1856. The candidates seem to me well prepared & attentive. After went to Rectory to try to heal matters – Poor Baylis very stupid & mulish. His mother advised yielding, his sister the demon stirring him up. Got him at last to write a letter which I hope I got Clayton afterwards to accept & so

the quarrel may be healed. NB The stones on the North side of the church shivering dreadfully. to write to [Ferrey].

276 **Hedsor. R.**
Rev A Youlden[47] – Growing extremely blind – March 1856 applies to have Mr Wordsworth aid him. I enquire about W[ordsworth.] Poor old Lord Boston said to be dying.
July 5 1857 I preach here afternoon to a small Rural Population Gladstone with me. Youlden much worse. The curate seeming rather conceited, a poor congregation – & he complaining that they go to meeting Gladstone overhearing a poor woman – "I don't know who he be that preacht but hes a good un".
Poor Youlden Dies Nov 13.60
<u>James Reynolds Williams</u>: Mr Neales protegee nominated by Lord Boston this & next turn being his & he comes to me for institution at Cuddesdon. Dec 20./60. Hoping for Lord Bostons help both in getting the church restored & 2 little cottages now the glebe house made habitable.

277 **Hendred East. R.**
C Wapshare – Confirm here March 10.57. Poor Hussey in great nervous excitement sad sin of churchwarden Roby having come out in the preparation for confir/m. Wapshare very feeble in bed. Husseys Eldest daughter confirmed invalid. Dies 1859 & I give it to Pott*. Visit it March 1860. House reformed & school.
March 16/63. Confirm here again, a nice confirm. George S Robertson Curate. Well spoken of & his wife too but Barbatus.
*Alfred Pott

278 **Hendred West. V.**
John Tucker. One of the bitterest councillors of strife 1859. Personally rude, refusing to open a private letter unless he had liberty to publish his answer. Writing Credo in Lon[don] Observer
I confirm here 26.March 1860. The only man in the Archdeaconry who refused the apparitors Fee. A very cold confirmation. Less interest in the Parish than almost anywhere.

279a **Henley on Thames. R.**
T B Morrell. Preached at the reopening 1854.
Preached on Ash Wednesday evening 1855 – Confirmed April 2 1855 – A very noble sight & many present.

---

[47] Should be Youldon (instituted 1841).

Feb[10]58 Curates Henry Benson & [*gap*] Fixsen, poor Fixsen from accident unable to stand exam & sadly distressed Dec 57. & Feb 58. Here all the week from Feb 21 to March 1 on Mission. Confirmed 22nd Ordained 28th preached 4 times.. Nov 16/60 Henry Benson stirs up dissenters by intemperate treatment. On receiving on his own request my advice heals matters. D.G.

Dec 1861 – Confirmed here Sunday aft[ernoon], preached in the even/g & Dec 2. at the schools & SPG meeting at St Marys Hall, purchased by T B Morrell & repaired at near £500 –

H Benson most highly spoken of by Powell of Bisham March 63.

279b–i *Notices concerning the Henley Mission 1858*

280 **Hermitage. P.C.**
Philip A Longmore. P.C. Comes to Chieveley confir/m March 25/57 His candidates <u>seeming</u> more prepared than any others at this confirm/n. Oct 29/.60 Preach at the consecration of additional burial ground.

281 **Hethe. R.**
Rev F Salter Lately come (March 11.1855 –) by Exchange with Shurlock from Devon. The church miserable – utterly too small for the Population, & in most miserable order altogether – Tried to stir him up to seek to rebuild or enlarge it. He despairing: could not raise above £25 in the Parish. Only one wealthy man lives in it Webb: a tenant of Harrison of Shelswell a brewer. Wrote to Lady Louisa H. & D G Webb.

Nov 4. 1855 G H Palmer sends me £120 he has collected for it. I send it to be invested in funds in my name, Arch Clerkes & J C Blomfields: 1858 March. <u>been</u> ill. The sub/n rather standing still. £450 or £500 raised £700 needed, tried to give him a stir. March 9.61 Confirm here. a very pleasing confirm/n. NB opened the restored Church. March 21 – 59 & preached &c.

282 **Heyford Lower. R.**
G D Faithful. Loses his son in Indian Service Spring 1858. Comes March 8 with his to Rousham confirmation &c. Rather a wild lot in appearance.

March 7.61. His son* comes with candidates to Steeple Aston. He almost past. Son worthy good man. March 4.64. A good account of young F. The old man fast sinking.
*Charles H Faithful

283 **Heyford Upper. R. or Warren.**
Rev J Baker. Sad old man. grows bed-ridden 1855 – I require a curate & Dec.1855, I license Thomas Browne to the curacy: complaints about him. Rather an odd man. Comes March 8 with candidates to Rousham.
William Wetherell. Comes April 2 1859 to be instituted at Aylesbury, strange hand shaking. Rheumatic gout – Formerly served Aston Tirrold. Of late has helped Stonhouse at Stanton St Johns. D.42.P.43 R Oxford. Speaks of people as civil &c. Going to reside, & chancel & House to be restored.

284 **Heythrop. R.**
Rev J Samuel – Called on him after Visitation 1854 to have double duty – He asks time to arrange – serving at Lord Dillons in afternoon – Comes to me May 15 in Pall Mall thereon. Willing to give 60 guineas & furnished lodgings for an assistant, Lord Dillon paying – recommended Bates at Cuddesdon. Brings few candidates March.16 58 to Chipping Norton.

285 **Hillesden. P.C.**

286 **Hinksey North. P.C.**
R.P.G Tiddeman a good man – overworked & underpaid –

287 **Hinksey South. P.C. With Wootton.**
Bertie W Morrison Curate – March 1860 comes to Sunningwell. Seems in earnest.

288 **Hinton Waldrist. R.**
W Jephson – a good & zealous man [registered] March 57 for school inspector – Consults me about moving some memorials to Simmonds family at East End in way of windows &c.

289 **Hitcham. R.**

290 **Hitchendon [See Hughendon.]**

Hogston. R.
J.G Villars. Confirmed here on Sunday March 27.1854. Mr Villars reading wonderful, starting with almost a snarling Hallo & then running down into a deep growl. The congregation utterly without devotion in manner. The church terrible. The chancel almost gone – immense pews! A very rough set to be confirmed. With great difficulty caught their attention: but I believe did so at last. All

the parish belongs to Lord Stanhope – about 1400 acres The living between £4 & £50048 –

291 **Hogshaw. Curacy. [The Church which is now desecrated was dedicated to Saint John the Baptist.]** see 316

Holton. R.
T. G. Tyndale. The good old rector resigns – and Nov 8.1856 Henry Annesley Tyndale having been ordained 14 years ago by my predecessor to Baldon comes for Institution.

292 **Holwell. P.C.**
(T Astley). Resigns Aug 1854 on promotion in Kent. Nominates Rev F Couch to be his temporary curate – whom I inhibit – Mr Couch at Wallingford formerly & lately at Midhurst having acted as a lunatic – in spite of which Bayley of Midhurst gives him Testimonials.

Mr Harvey offers it to Mr Bowden – he accepts but his wife very dangerously ill is less there before institution than Mr H approves & once goes back to her Sunday ev/ng, Mr H withdraws offer – He comes to me I advise re–offer – made but Mr Bowden refuses in consequence of Lay dictatorship. Nov 1854 <u>C Boothby</u>, takes it. – March 19 1858 Boothby comes with his candidates to Burford. He looking very ill, & old Harvey breaking. Not able to receive me– Boothby shortly after dies of cancer, & I institute <u>Daniel Ward Goddard</u>. Confirm here at Sunday morning service March 3/61 a nice set – The church built in 1842 by Harvey: a fancy church. Nice parsonage in which Goddard nicely ensconced.

293 **Hooknorton. P.C.**
John Richard Rushton – Troublesome at Visitation 57. at Chipping Norton about Diocese. Confirm here again March 13 1858. A nice confirmation old Rushton creaky. Got a nice school built mainly by Miss Davies of Swerford Park.

Confirm here again Feb 23 1864. The church fine but not quite rightly restored – all good owing to C Barter – Rushton wishes to reglaze the windows & put in a stone. I promise to subscribe

294 **Horley. V. With Hornton. V.**
Rev W O Pinwell. Confirmed here March 17. 1855. Hanwell, Pearse Jun/r, Wroxton T Murray, Drayton Lloyd. A very interesting confirmation from the deep attention of the People. Miss Stuart Rev E Stuarts

---

48 According to the *Clergy List* the value was only £280.

sister going to restore the chancel. Mr Hitchman churchwarden (occasionally insane) good man – said "but we have not yet got one curate" settled with Pinwell that to give £50 & title at September ordination. His heart in his work & in restoring &c. but pressed by large Family. Confirm here again March 11.58 a rough set – write same day to E Stuart about the restoration of the Chancel. Thomas Russell formerly with Chamberlain Curate. One boy sulking & sent away.

Dr Moulsey. Soi–disant Curate in Oct 1861. Not licensed & ousted.

Mr [blank] of Home Office writes kindly to warn.

Confirm here Sunday aft[ernoon] Feb 28/64. Pleasant enough.

C J Knapp Curate.

Hornton [See Horley.]

295 **Horsendon. R.**
Rev W E Partridge He has been with Mrs Partridges plans busy in reseating & restoring his little Church. I attended Sep 25 1855 & preached & administered at its re–opening to a very attentive congregation – preached on Ps 37.7.

Nov/57. I apply to <u>her</u> trustees on C Lloyds suggestion to allow of Land being given at [blank] for church &c.

296 **Horsepath. P.C.**
Henry Harris – Vacating this by taking the Living of Winterbourne Bassett. Charles Humphrey Cholmley is licensed to it on the nomination of his college. He provides <u>Rev W T Read</u> from September as locum tenens, till end of Jan/ry.

Temperley House. Mr Read has been scholastic at Huddersfield & brings good testimonials. He calls on me Jan 10/59.

297 **Horton. R.**
<u>Rev R Gorges Foot</u>. Rector. Instituted by me.1855. Confirmed here March 17 1856 for this Parish, Wyrardisbury & Datchet. The Church quiet & for an old restored church rather nice. New East Window with painted glass put in by Mr Tyrrell. He & a farmer torments Mr Foot. Foot not strong but pleasing in all ways.

<u>March 56</u> Foot consults me about signing lease to Williams for the glebe farm. He signed agreement <u>after</u> the living was bought but before he was instituted to let the farm to Col Williams at a fixed rent. I charged him at institution not to let it below its value as that would be Simonaical. He supposed this fixed price was its value. But finds now it is little more than half. He consults me what to do

& J Phillimore who doubts whether the original contract was not Simon'l but is clear he must not let it below its real value. Nov/57. at the Visitation Pollen claiming to be Church Warden presents that bread given at West End of church & not as should be in vestry. Said P. not yet churchwarden so presentation dismissed. On my advising him on such a matter not to irritate parishioners he explains that it is all Tyrrells,. Col Williams opposition which he is getting under & will subdue if I stand by him. P e contra says all leaving church !! Oct 1860 [? Goldie] having enquired at my request & reported Foot attacks his report as unfair.

298 **Horwood Great. R.**
Rev J Adams Confirm here for second time Feb 23 1856. Urge Adams to alter communion rails. A very promising confirm/n. Nice old Churchwardens. Candidates good. Adams said he had been at some of them for 12 years.

299 **Horwood Little. V.**
T B Holt Dauncey comes to me at Cuddesdon April 25 – 1865 – a charge of grossly lewd behaviour to a young girl.

300 **Hughendon. V.**
Clubbe complaint of Donkey in churchyard. I warn Mr C. not lawful. 1857.

301 **Hulcot. R.**
Rev W Morgan. June 26.1855. contains 700 acres. 4 farmers. The Rector & 160 poor: farm labourers, Straw plaiters & lacemakers, no resident gentlemen. School just beginning by old Morgan actively raising £244 £30 promised for its annual support.
*Nov 1857 The poor old man has married again. Had a Paralytic Stroke & applies to me to give him another living. – The curate whom next present/n. bought then applies to be let to serve it from Aylesbury which I refuse.
Frederick G Hughes. Afterwards disappointed of the presentation.
Godfrey Richard Ferris. presented to me Sep 58 by Francis Wells Esq. of Cradles Lodge, Warnham, Sussex.
I confirm here Lent 1859, & pleased with all. DG.
**March 62 He speaks very sensibly & right mindedly at Aylesbury conference.
May 15. 1862.Mr Ferris comes with Mr James representing Baron Rothschild as to exchange of glebe.
*Hunt curate "respectable, well disposed. Father low."
** Patron Dr Kelly Halifax

301b *Inserted correspondence*

Hulcott. May 13th.1862.

My Lord.

The attention of your Lordship is asked to the following:

The Rev G.R.Ferris was instituted by your Lordship to the Rectory of Hulcott in 1858. At that time The Rectory House was in a most dilapidated ruinous state, & it became necessary to remove & rebuild one half of it. The cost of this was met –½ by Mortgage to Queen Anne's Bounty – ½ out of Rector's private means.

The remaining half of the house has now become so dilapidated that it will be necessary shortly to remove it also.

An <u>Exchange</u> of part of the glebe lands has already taken place with the Lord of the Manor, the effect of which is most beneficial to the living. It has increased the annual Income by about £20 besides enabling the Rector to restore both <u>Chancel</u> & Church in a very complete manner.

A further exchange of the remainder of the glebe – except one close – is now proposed.

The terms offered are: I To give lands in the immediate neighbourhood, in exchange equal to the full value of this part of the glebe – 48s per acre.

The effect of this part of the Exchange – together with that which has already taken place – will be to raise the Net Income of the living from <u>£195</u> to about <u>£270</u>. II To place the Rectory House & buildings in a state of complete repair. III To remove the present School House which is almost rendered useless as a school by reason of its great distance from the village, down to the village green.

The only objection which appears to offer itself is – That by parting with his glebe the Rector might be thought likely to lose influence in the parish.

Against this must be set,

I.(i) the great increase to the Net value of the living: (2), the repair of the house & buildings in such a way as to render any further outlay for the purpose unnecessary for years to come.

II. That, from the situation of the glebe, it is impossible to make more than one holding of it, whereas by having two or more holdings in the immediate neighbourhood, an indirect source of influence is created by offering facilities for the farmers in the parish to obtain their farms for their sons.&c.

Your Lordship is asked kindly to consent to & support with your influence the above scheme before the Commissioners.

    I am My Lord
        Your Lordship's obedient servant
         G.R.Ferris.
         Rector of Hulcott.

The Right Rev
Lord Bishop of Oxford.

Denford, Hungerford
2 Decr 1858

My Dear Sir,

I hope to find you at home this afternoon, for the enclosed plan will not be of much use to you without a commentary, & I cannot make one at all like sufficiency in a letter.

You will see that if the claims for Church accommodation of our Edington village, taken irrespectively of Hungerford town, be contrasted with those of Hungerford Newtown, there is nearly an equality between them: Edington has rather the larger population, Newtown is at a greater distance from the Mother Church. The loss to Newtown of the service in Barron's Schoolroom will be considerable; one of my tenants used to attend there, and thinks that about 50 persons frequented it for the service; one of Barron's supporters in Hungerford sets the attendance at 70 but he must be somewhat over the mark, for the room could hardly hold so many.

The opinion which I gave you, and still hold, of the greater propriety of building at Edington than at Newtown rested on the wish to relieve Hungerford Town. I understand that nothing is likely to be done in the Church there, & I think that a Church situate at Edington capable of accommodating 200 or 300 persons would be very convenient for residents in Hungerford Proper and in Edington and not much out of the way for those at Newtown.

If I miss you today and this note is unsatisfactory I will come over to Speen at your bidding. I am disengaged for the afternoon of Saturday next and the morning and afternoon of Tuesday.

  Very truly yours
  George C Cheney

Sketch map of the parish of Hungerford, with note that in the 1851 census the population of the Parish was 3072, living in 609 houses, whilst that of Hungerford Town was 2255, living in 424 houses

302 **Hungerford. V.**

W Cookson. He gives £200 – towards 2 curates of my appointing.

 The Union Workhouse is £50 per annum held by one – Mr Pease, had the House, takes paid & £130 clear payment with fees... *Mr Baron is licensed at £70 – & Mr Pease being <u>licensed</u> chaplain pays Baron the £50 – Baron has had a subscription of about £10– a year for the New Town service & Mr Pease £25 last year for Fees – this year about £20 –

 <u>George Clifford</u> Pease – leaves for a living in Yorkshire July 1856.

March 27 1857. Confirm here for this & Shalbourne. A better appearance about the candidates than before. R Chilton manifestly doing better as head curate than his predecessors. After the confirmation a long discussion as to the church. The last annuitant being dead & R Phillimore giving his opinion that the acts had exhausted their uses & the church returned to the normal condition of a Parish Church. Much warmth of feeling between the parties. Willes angry at having been turned out of Ch wardenship by Pease. I advised going for new seating &c. to see Hall new Ch Warden again April 11 – a warm letter from J Hall & wrote to him, & to Chilton

April 14.58 talk of Chapel at Edington: all seems most promising when prevented by quarrel between Michell & Chilton! Jan 1859.

[*Marginal note:**William Joseph Baron]

303 **Hurley. V.**

F Wethered Vicar. Church nicely restored. I preach &c. at opening – Feb 28 1860. I again confirmed here a nice confir/m. March 29/63. Confirmed here. a Sunday confirmation – very pleasing. Lady Clayton East & Lady Gilbert East there with her three sons. sad story about Sir Gilbert – adulterous & evil to her.

304 **Hurst. P.C. With Twyford. C.**

Rev Archibald Allen Cameron – A good man – Restores in 1855 the chancel & chancel aisle of his church, the reopening of which I attend Dec 17 1855 a goodly gathering & service well performed.

Jan 1856. J Walter writes to me about dissatisfaction musical services &c. – memorial threatened on curtain at East End. Surpliced choir, Chanting. Heard all & got Randall to go to Barker of Standlake[49] &c. to enquire. It appears that the hostile demonstration merely "got up" by Mrs Garth &c. reported that I approved of no change – Cameron being grateful but moderate.

March 9. J Walter writes having made enquiries amongst high & low & satisfied that it is a matter of mere Garth Pique – April & May 1856. The trouble raging J Leveson Gower writing foolish & insolent letters at length I offer to meet the dis–satisfied gentry in London with R Palmer & see if we can arrange. They decline by J L Gower.

Jan 9 & Feb 57 at Walters advice a meeting of gentry who will come who advise certain concessions which Cameron me suadente

---

[49] George Barker of Stanlake Park, Twyford, High Sheriff for Berkshire 1856.

makes.. serving only to put the Garths more wrong – all as bad as can be Conroy suspected of keeping it up to find opportunity of at least Flirtation with Pen: Garth. old R Palmer a rock –

April 1857, all as bad as ever. Mrs G. Forbidding her tenants to come to confirmation – Feb 21 & 28 during mission at Henley H C Moberley & W Chambers preach.

Newspaper cuttings concerning the disputes at Hurst inserted between pp 303 and 304

305 **Ibstone**

Rev J.Baker.[50] Confirmed here on Sunday afternoon March 9. 1856 only 4 – but the Church crowded with a most attentive population. After Church walked to look at site of new Parsonage – hope to live to see it & new Church, which greatly wanted.

Ibstone [See Fingest] *deleted.*

306 **Ickford. R.**

Rev Rich/d.Townsend. Writes Oct 1857 to ask to be excused attendance at Visit/tn, by reason of illness. Brings candidates April 4/59 to Brill. Said to be very delicate. Hardly any candidates. W May Ellis – married a Miss Townsend – became Patron – Left it alternately to daughter with a presentation to Stephen Hemsted. – Sep 25 at Lavington John Hemsted came for institution.. I hear all good of him.

Newspaper Cutting.
A.D.907. – AT ICKFORD (? Itchenford, in Hampshire, – [Camden.]), a treaty signed between King Edward and the Danes.

307 **Idbury. P.C.**

308 **Iffley. P.C. Otherwise Yeftley, Yefley, or Eyfley.**

Rev Warburton – Confirmed here for second time Monday March 5 1855, for Sandford, Cowley.(Littlemore) A very nice confirmation Church beautiful.

1856 April & May. The Parishioners moving to complete the restoration of their Church which done in 1843 ? under Hussey without a particle of real ecclesiastical taste & hideous in parts. They wish to remove his hideous W Gallery – restore west circular window remove heavy row of Poppy heads in Tower seats &c. Old

---

[50] Should be G Baker.

John Parsons objects & threatens to oppose faculty. I go over May 23 1856 & meet J Parsons & committee. Warburton Parker Underhill Walsh & Slatter & after much discussing all parties agree to refer it to Street to settle (1) if architecturally safe (2) If it will give as many seats as at present. All agreeing that these are essentials.

309 **Ilmer. V.**
W E Partridge. Dec 1859 proposes next Feb/y to restore Ilmer Church & Aug 30 1860 I re-open it. [Tuesday] before Mrs Partridges child born.

310 **Ilsley East. R.**
T Loveday Confirmed here March 25/57. As always here a cold service. Decent highly but a sad want of visible life –
Jan 29.59. Mr L. wishes to have Rev W N Turner of Pannall as Curate – formerly at Chichester Coll[ege].

311 **Ilsley West. R.**
Hon. & Rev Moore. Confirmed for this place at E I. March 25/57 W Spraggett Curate. No male & only 5 females. He said he could not think why: none would come. I fear the parish is in a most dead state NB to enquire further. – He in 1858 ill – heart complaint applies for a non resident license & appoints on my permission Thomas Cox who comes to Thatcham Oct 5/58, to be licensed.
Confirm here Wednesday March/60 a nice confirmation – Morland speaks most highly of Cox's work. –
Henry J Morant. Curate on my presenting Cox to Mollington – Strange uncomfortable man – debt – asks me to take charge of parish he wanting to go out. Moore notices him to leave in 6 months March 1863.

312 **Inkpen. R.**
J Butler. Visited the Church which in miserable state in all ways. A good new School built 1856.
March 1857. Well prepared confirmees came to Kintbury. Jan 29.59. March 19.1860. I confirm here. After luncheon with good old Mr Butler – Church wanting restoration sadly – air of rather staring ignorance about the candidates – Great view from Inkpen Hill Coombe Hill.

313 **Ipsden. V. [See Northstoke].**

Islip. R.
F Trench. Dec 13/61 I preach at the reopening of the restored Church on which nearly £2000 spent mainly through the liberality of J Parsons. The Dean Trench preaches afternoon. March 8.64 confirm here a very nice confirmation F & G Trench's daughters.

313b *Permission Card, signed by Francis Trench, for Mary Eliza Trench, aged 16 years, to present herself for Confirmation 8 March 1864*

314b *Copy of a hymn used for a wedding in Iver Church 11 February 1862*

314 **Iver. P. C.**
  Rev W S Ward. At March 15 1856 – met Edward Tompson Esq of Dromina Uxbridge. He disposed to help in building a Church for a new district in Iver parish. Ward says that the division of new district should be from Langley Park South of the Poor House by Banger's Farm, Galley Hill north of Delaford to River Colne – Mr Ts' inclination from a district following line of road from Crooked Billet to Uxbridge so striking off the population & making it rather a personal accom/n. T. a solicitor in Stone Buildings, now owns Dromina & Round House – quarrels between him & brother & Mrs Pegus sister.
  March 16 A conversation with Mr Tompson hereon. He agreed to the larger partition of the Parish & will give 2 acres of ground & £1000 for endowment & £100 to start the subscription for the Church. H Kingscote has promised to get subscriptions & Tower is to set him about it. Mr Meaken has purchased Richings & the advowson of Iver. A very low churchman.
  March 16 1856. A most marked improvement in the behaviour of the general congregation as well as candidates & children: at the confirmation service today DG. Quite a new appearance of devotion & quietness.
  P. D. Bland. Comes 1856 – & July 1/57 Ward comes to complain of him. So haughty that doing great harm. Nov 20/57 writes to ask legal license to give him notice to quit. I write to Bland to enquire if any answer. Gets rid of Bland. /59. Trouble about Housman & long correspondence. I keep Housman, Tower & at last Ward desiring it. Nov 14.59. Housman asks to be let go to Wolverhampton & I assent – Williams a good second curate come. Ward * really busy about church on Iver heath. Confirm March 26 62 – A nice confirmation. Beatrice Tower amongst them.
  Iver Heath Church. see page. Consecrated after par[ish] trouble. March 12.62
  J. E. Longlimbs Curate.
  [*Marginal note*: Curate /58 Rev. Phipps]

For Iver continued see 614. [*In fact the page is empty after the heading*]

315 **Ivinghoe. V.**
   Rev Hamilton. A sleepy & ineffectual ministry. March 1856 when candidates come to Cheddington for confirmation. Those who came seemingly ill prepared & not one male. I fear that <u>here</u> dissent quite prevails over poor Ham[ilton].
   Nov 1857. He fights hard against a sermon on communion Sundays which at last I compel.
   March 13/62 Confirmed here. A nicer confirmation than before.

316 Hogshaw. [Extra entry in Bishop's hand]
   Examined the foundations March 26 1859, with Fremantle.

   Insert:Newspaper cutting relating to a commission enquiring into Tithes at Hogshawe.[Recent dry weather had revealed the foundations of the Chapel, ruined since 1650, which at one time had been a separate parish. Fremantle was seeking to recover for the benefit of East Claydon, where the six Hogshaw households currently worshipped, an endowment for the maintenance of a Chaplain. The Commission eventually agreed on an apportionment of the tithes as follows:
   James Du Pre MP 273 acres valued at 5s.6d per acre
   Bernard Fountain 164 acres at 3s.6d per acre
   Sir Harry Verney, Bart, MP 93 acres at 8s.9d per acre]

317 **Kelmscott. [See Bradwell.]**
   Oxon.

   Kencot. R.
   Rev J Thorold. I consent Nov 3/55 to allow Mr Halifax Curate of Brize Norton to assist T. by giving an afternoon service at 2.30 during the winter.
   <u>Edward Sturges</u>. Presented by Hammersley to hold it 1857. March 20/58 He comes with flock to Broughton confirm[ation]. The parsonage very well restored. He is about to rebuild the Chancel. State of Church, a grievous hindrance to Godliness.
   Church re-opened.
   Feb 20.64 confirmed here – a very nice confirmation his young people specially well prepared.

318 **Kennington.**
   Rev Sawyer – Lee placed here by Sawyer – on Dr Peter Morriss going. Lee here 1855–6. Writes me word passim that <u>all</u> going on most favourably. I remove him in fact his demonstrativeness doing harm: & recommend Julius Henderson, nephew of Henderson of Messing.

He had given offence by a sermon at Isleworth which I heard & which was really unobjectionable. He comes to me Dec 16.1856, having been 1st at Messing 2nd at Hadleigh (till Espin). Then went to Julius Shadwell in Lancashire left him for ill health = Then went to Leigh under Fred Murray on his presentation – there became acquainted with my wife. Symptoms of consumption & medical man said she must marry or die. Married. Only 2 people who speak well of Lee – one a labourers wife one a publican. Most think him a Romanist in disguise: wishes for a hymnbook & proposes J H Parkers Hymnal which I assent to. Consult as to school, recommend night school through winter & then other.

319 **Kiddington. R.**

Rev J G Browne. In multitude of quarrels with his poor Squire Ricardo who appeals always to me – Mrs Ricardo dies after confinement 1855, & He advertizes the place for sale. Bought by <u>Gaskell</u>, pleasing right minded man. Old Browne remarries 1858 poor Springs widow Hill's daughter with many children. Comes to confirmation at Glympton with scarce any company. I invite explanation. Says none to give.

320 **Kidlington. V. With Water Eaton**
Curacy

Rev Dr Lightfoot – Whitehead Curate – Confirmed here March 29 a very nice confirmation – Rectors' daughter inter alias. The Church nicely done & now the Parsonage much improved.
Visit <u>Water Eaton Church</u> April 18/63.
Confirm[ation]. March 12 64. Very nice Lightfoot Arch Lower (Henry) & G J Thomas ordained by me at Bampton Curates.

321 **Kidmore End. P.C.**
(District Church.)

Compton resigns & after offering it to several I give it to Fleming, who for the year appoints Gooch Curate.
Visited in Henley Mission 23.25.27. of Feb/y by Fremantle, Butler & Woodford. Gooch & Fleming succeeding well. D.G. The parsonage rising. Built & I twice preaching. – Poor Flemyngs (*sic*) health fails. 1861.Risley takes his place. Then negotiation 1862 as to Risley succeeding. Ends in his refusing & I offer it to <u>John Wolstenholme Cobb</u> Sir J Seymours Curate who after demur accepts & whom Feb 19/63 I license.

Insert: – "Historical Memoranda".
AD 43 At Little Kimble the Romans, under Aulus Plautus, defeated Caractacus and Togodumnus, sons of Cunobeline. Togodumnus was slain.

To Cunobeline (the Cymbeline of Shakespeare) is popularly ascribed the name of "Kimble", and likewise the square camp at the north–west corner of Pulip–wood, with deep ditches to the east and south,. Kimble abounds in entrenchments, and remains of Roman occupation are found here in great quantities. (See "Records of Buckinghamshire, p.140)

322 **Kimble Great. V.**
For Kimble Little. R. see after Lyford 360
Separated by C Lloyd & resigned 1859 in order that by Cameron John Ormond may be presented. He to hold with it Little Kimble first by Dispensation & with the view of their being hereafter united into one benefice.
John Ormond 1861. Ormond ill & away. John Whateley taking the temporary duty brings young men in some numbers & seeming well prepared to Princes Risborough confirmation March 1862.

323 **Kingham. R.**
Rev John William Lockwood – Sunday July 13 1856 preached here & consecrated additional Burial ground. An excellent congregation & seemingly well cared for parish.
Confirmed here March 14.58. A very nice confirmation.
March.2/61 he & his come to Churchill.

324 **Kingsey. V.**

325 **Kingston Bagpuze. R.**
J. F. Jowett. Rector. I thought rather ageing March 1860. Here young Blandy Jenkins – & his mother with much good about them – March 13/63 went to them & March 14 confirmed there. B.J. & his pleasing young wife seem well disposed.

326 **Kingston Lisle** (3 pages on)

Kintbury. V.
James Deans Dundas. Confirmed here again March 27/57. A nice confirmation on the whole & the church full of parishioners.
I go there Dec.13.58, & find great works going on in the church of which no notice whatever had been sent me. Write to JDD. He replies Dec 18./58, lamely. Confirmed again March 20 1860. Tolerably nice. The church a good deal improved. Femmetts 3 unicorns settled about 1672 – Then heiress married a Raymond, Raymond a Wittley. Then Dundass when to these Deans Dundas.

327 **Kirtlington. V.** JG. anonymous letter.
Rev J Guillemard – Applies & I press his application to be allowed to borrow under the Gilbert Act for enlarging his House according to the need of his <u>family.</u> Refused by St Johns Coll[ege].
March 9 1855. Confirm here, for Bletchingdon, Weston on the Green, Hampton Poyle. A nice confirmation – especially for here & Weston. Turton here now & doing exceedingly well. Guillemard away for ill health.
The Church except Chancel very well restored. Tower built & bells mounted. I move Turton 1855 (Guillemard reluctant) temporarily to Wycombe & put in from helping Perry.
Turton from Wycombe by the return of Paddon & given Great Milton by me – Guillemard talked of removing his Furniture in <u>May.</u>/57. The stipend would be £135 – 3 acres of glebe – say £6 – & use of Furniture £40 – morning service – & on communion Sundays no Litany. Litany <u>always</u> afternoon – with collecting – & even/g service.
<u>Dec 1856</u> <u>Mr Atkinson, Curate,</u> has set up a cricket club, which answers under Dashwood. <u>March 5 1858</u> confirmed here. A nice confirmation. J.Augustus Atkinson's Child Walter Chetwode A. Baptised by me. Mr Dashwood suggests a travelling lecturer for our villages, &c..
Poor Guillemard dies Jan 11./58, & June 6, comes for Institution the Rev <u>Thos Knapp Chittenden</u> ordained by my Predecessor D. May/42 P. June/43 wishes not to come into residence till Xmas, whilst the House is prepared = Confirm here. March 7.61. A nice confir/m. He wanting "to stop Ch/yard Path. (Choir improved by Lady Dashwood March 64.)

328 **Knowle Hill. P.C.**
S. Sturges. H J Ellison & R Milman preach during Henley Mission 1858.
<u>R Aldridge</u> succeeds S Sturges in 1859. – Confirmation 1860 very few Knowle Hill people. I write fully to Aldridge who replies pleasingly – But I fear from what I am told that not an efficient ministry.
<u>Arthur B Wrey</u>. Licensed by me March 27/63, late Curate of Buckingham.

329 **Kingston Lisle.**
Rev H Dodd V. Chapelry to Sparsholt. Rev R Z Walker Curate, when March 19 1857 I come here on confirmation tour & hospitably welcomed by Atkins. Had intended to confirm <u>here,</u> but church unfit. Wish to urge him to fit it up. He has had much expense with his House.

330 **Lacey Green. [See Risborough]**

Lamborne. V. With Saint James the Greater

Chapel of Ease at Eastbury.
Robert Milman. Preach here Sunday March 22/57 coming from Lord Cravens for Diocesan Board collect £12 – 0/d. Curates Hayward, Clarke. Parish well worked. Milman after troubles greatly respected. I confirm here March 23. About 160 & a very striking confirmation in all ways. After at new Schools of M's where tea for candidates.
Confirm here again March 22.60 all very encouraging, numbers. – choir – appearance.
W Monteford Bramston Curate – Oct 17.1860 preach for School, & open School at Eastbury & consecrate a churchyard addition at Lamborne proper.
Oct 15.1861. Preached & celebrated morning at opening of Chancel Aft. Luncheon in School. Evening preached again. Grand choir. Milman greatly beloved. Most highly spoken of by Lady Craven &c. Shakespeare now here as Curate –
Henry Barter 1862. I moving Milman to Marlow. HB. going on excellently. Dec 7. I here at H Hippisleys. Preach morning & evening. Collect £43– for School maintenance. All right between HB & H's = as Curates Majendie & Shakespeare. S. going & young Luxmoore coming. Treaty still pending as to getting the Rectory house for Living: Hughes slippery about it. HB. Chanted Litany beautifully. Dear old Charles Barter here & preached at at [sic] Eastbury.

331 **Lamborne Woodlands. P.C. (Saint Mary's)**
John Bacon P.C. – March 1855
Applies as to dismissing Parish clerk for obstinate Wesleyan meeting going. I advise carefulness not to make him a martyr – comes to Lambourne confirm[ation] March 25/57 as to Curate. Nov 57. Writes anxious to begin short sermon before communion..dismiss after offertory &c. I advise consult squire.
H W Stillingfleet goes as Curate Oct/57.

332 **Lane End. P.C.**
March 1855 old Peers dies – Ridley thinking of Latter: offers it to C.Flint & then to J H Worsley – Taken by Ashpitel* – Church as far as it can be restored & opened by me after the works. June 30.57. Preach on prayer. Blessed to C Lloyd.
Sep 23/60 Ordain at Aylesbury William George Nottley from Cuddesdon as Curate. £50 –

James Hodges 1860. I confirm here July 1861. (Jan 1861 he applies to open a room for services at Wheelers End I assent.)
[*Marginal note*: Francis Ashpital]

333 **Langford. V. With Little Faringdon.**
Francis G.Lemann. Discussion when he presented as to Vizards removing right of Patronage, made out to be his. Leman [*sic*] – low – but I hope good. Appoints James Whytt as Curate who attends with him at confirmation at Broughton. March 58. Dissent still violent. Tenant of Eccles Comm[issioners] would not allow his labourers to come to be confirmed unless they gave up day's wages: March.4.61 They come to Filkins for conf/n. Lemann says a real work of revival going on in the Parish. Feb.18/64 I confirm here during Mission Week. Lemann covenanting to have none but Bishop & Fremantle. On to Lord de Manleys – now settled here. Lady de Manley speaks of Lemanns narrowness. Preaching only to one set as having life &c. *Tilbury of the same school but as younger not a full crop of these absurdities – no Church Services but revival meetings with Dissenters of evening
[*Marginal note:* R Tilbury, C]

334 **Langley Marsh. V. [see also Wyrardisbury]**
[Lathbury. P.C. see for end page 3]
Dec 1.1855.
The living of Langley in process of separation from Wyrardisbury legally lapses to me. Matter referred to Dr Addams who in fact gives the legal question in my favour putting it however on the question of whether the lapse was caused by me. I have no doubt that legally it was not but I think the Chapter have in this view an equitable right to consideration in as much as my advice led to the separation which led to the lapse & therefore greatly as I desire to put Nash in I refrain from interfering with the Chapter's rights – The Chapter had shown the greatest forbearance & consideration in the whole matter – But I grieve for Langley – March 14 1856 at Stoke Park Mr Scoones comes for institution. Rather pleasing in manner & appearance. May 31 1856. I go to Mr Harveys & next morning June 1, confirm during Sunday Service. Mr Scoones reads 1/2 morn/g service with an isochronous & monotonous drone. H Swabey now residing in the Parish to attend on his paralytic Father reads half the service well. The confirmation a nice one The young Harveys both very pleasing. Mr Harvey silent as ever Mrs H seemingly in a consumption.

335 **Latimer. R.** Claims to be a Donative.
Samuel King. ob. Dec 13 1856.. The Patron Charles Compton Cavendish. MP. presents Bryan Burgess who has been acting as Curate to it. He comes April 9/57 for license to it as P.C.

336 **Launton. R.**
James Charles Blomfield. I come & preach for him Spring of 1852. 6 March 1858 I come here for a confirmation. He has done the Church up nicely. The people quiet but seemed un–impressible.
His distress during Revivals from poor Watts folly March 60.

337a **Lavendon. V. with Brayfield.**
The Rev W Tomkins.. Preached for his School Sep 26 1855 – going over from Chicheley as many as 16 clergy present many of them borderers from the next 2 Dioceses. Poor & pressed by family. His Church Tower very old – probably Saxon.
March 17./59 comes with his people to Olney & shews me plans of church restor[ation]: by Butterfield. Would not have ventured to begin but for Chester. B: said it would be £800 –
Reopening Nov 4.59 preach. All I understand raised except £120 – Mr Huggins curious account of him. Had come to his door for umbrellas to mend. Father a dissenting tradesman in Olney. He sent to school much through exertion of old Fry.. Did well, & does well Farms his own glebe & succeeds. Has money. Has just NB – bought advowson of Lord Gainsborough. Now about severing Brayfield. The church work excellently done. A cordial gathering in the School. Nov 16/60 "Church filled for last year" I consent to Title to Mr Shewen.

337c

LAVENDON CHURCH RESTORATION.

ON FRIDAY, NOVEMBER the 4th, 1859,
SERMONS
WILL BE PREACHED IN LAVENDON CHURCH,
In the Morning by The Right Reverend
THE LORD BISHOP OF OXFORD,
Divine Service will begin at Eleven O'Clock.
AND IN THE AFTERNOON BY THE
VENERABLE EDWARD BICKERSTETH
Archdeacon of Buckinghamshire

Service will begin at Three O'Clock. Collections in aid of the Restoration Fund will be made after each Service. Luncheon will be provided between the Services in the School Room.

Also, on the Evening of the same Day,
A SERMON
WILL BE PREACHED IN THE PARISH CHURCH, TURVEY,
BY THE RIGHT REVEREND
THE LORD BISHOP OF OXFORD.

Divine Service will commence at Half–past Six O'Clock.

By the kind permission of the Rector, Contributions will
be received at the Doors, after the Sermon, in aid of the funds
FOR THE RESTORATION OF LAVENDON CHURCH.

337c *Photograph of ? Lavendon Church, apparently undergoing restoration*

338 **Leafield Chapelry. P.C. with Wychwood**
Rev S Lott Visited March 23, with Barter & good Carter to see about joining new Parish &c. Determined that best to get old Harris' ground adjoining for burial ground & future church uniting new parish to Leafield which will be the real seat of population & have endowment hereafter from Shipton Estate. Lott good & rather rough.
John Henry Worsley. Instituted Dec. 7 1857. To build D.G. House & Church – after many troubles correspondence &c. Lott having given this up on his nomination to Bampton. March 15.58 confirmed here after the Eclipse a most affecting confirmation.
By order in Council 31st July 1858 Leafield united to the new Parish of Wychwood. A new Church & Parsonage built. The St Michaels Church consecrated Oct.19.1860. A beautiful Church & Spire. I preach.
Feb.22 1864. I confirm here. The congregation markedly devout & attentive. Buckle holding the new Royal Farm & losing on it supporting Worsley. Glebe of 26 acres now: & now worth about £127. To have £200 a year from the Shipton Estate on the falling of the Wood lives.

339 **Leckhampstead. R. [Bucks.]**
Rev H Drummond. The candidates confirmed at Akeley March 1856 singularly attentive & promising. March 59, at Maids Morton. Do. Miss D[rummond]. confirmed by me at Cuddesdon full of feeling Sunday March 20/59.

340 **Leckhampstead. C. [Berks.] [See Chievely].**

Lee. P.C.
Stephen Spicer Crutch. Miserable place – Few inhabitants – wretched endowment poor incumbent – Tried to stir up life in him. March /62. To move for adding Lee Common rebuilding church &c.

341a **Leonard Saint. D.C. [In the Parish of Aston Clinton].**
Rev E Owen Jun incumbent He resides in a house bought by the Suttons mother to […] for them, with his Father now a widower – a tidy little parsonage near. The church small & [?anglicised] internally in the worst taste at the expense of Lady Frankland. NB A district & cure of souls to be appended some day to this – Mr Lowndes & T Drake chief Trustees consent readily. Rev H Sandwith Curate up to October 1855 a respectable moderate Evan[gelical], wishes to retire: I reprove him mildly for not asking leave before taking another curacy. Lowndes promised Dec/58 at once to get the district assigned & to proceed as to the building a parsonage.

Robert Sutton Incumbent..gets grant for Buckland Common & ordain at Aylesbury Sep 23/60 Frederick Pember to be Curate £70. Day/ R Sutton resigning to go to Chichester Diocese appointed 1861. After much trouble Oct 10 1861 I preach here for opening of very nice Schools, which inaugurated by R Sutton & now completed by Day. Day rather rough with the people in manner. W Lowndes says that surplice &c. offends Miss Sutton thinks not.. I ordain Sep 61 Thomas Hancock as a Literate as his Curate. Hear well of him March 62.

342a **Letcombe Bassett. R.**
W Firth. Old, mad = Dies 1856, & the college nominates Charles Francis Willis ordained by me in fifty three & fifty four, whom I institute Jan 15 1857. The living worth near upon £300 a year.. House dilapidated & Firth having left separate provision for his wife dies nearly intestate having given his money to his brother I suspect roguery.
Dec 10 1858. I come here to open new schools – cost about £350. Willis a poor man, & has done a great work in getting these schools up. Now looking on to the possibility of church restoration.
March 27. 1860. His candidates at Letcombe Regis well prepared, & numerous. Nov 1. 1862 The Church re-opened after a very nice restoration at which I preach. I am told that Willis & his wife both rough tempered.
March 15-63 I confirm here, a very encouraging confirmation.

343a **Letcombe Regis. V.**
Rev Edward Stanley James. Anxious to build a parsonage at small cost. At last Jan 1854 I agree to certain plans which he thinks may be carried out for £600 – I fear not –
Poor foolish Stanley writes me a stupid letter about not preaching for Dioces[an] Soc[iety] March 57, & I reprove him. Spoke to him after the confirmation at Childrey March 20/57, when for the time he yielded entirely. Afraid of "Wantage ways". "Mr Tucker thought

&c." Tucker the real opposer hereabout of all Diocesan Unity. Dec 10/58 visited James in his new House. Cordial. March 27.60 I confirm here, cold rather. James & his wife cordial. Speaks of Butlers great success – Poor James loses his wife – & marries again with[in] the year.

344a **Lew. [See Bampton].**

Lewknor. V. with Ackhamstead.
Hon W Byron Instituted Dec 1855 on Dean's vacancy resigns on being appointed by Lord Macclesfield to Stoke Talmage, & Dec 15/57 William Henry Fremantle comes for Institution thereto. Takes B[ishop] of London's resident chaplaincy.

345a **Lillingstone Dayrell. R.**
William Bell. Who 1859 quarrels with Maul[51] &c of Newport first offended by saying that "troublesome little beggar" complains to Sec/y of State &c. Cut by other magistrates &c. Confirm here March 20/59 after ordination at Buckingham.

346a **Lillingstone Lovell. R.**
Wm Lloyd – Visit this after confirmation at L Dayrell March 20.59. Interesting little church. chancel mauled. 2 daughters who had been confirmed at Maids Moreton &c.

348a **Linford Great. R.**
Litchfield 1852. 1853. Great Troubles with his Curate Mr. [... *gap*] who was to succeed: about terms of curacy ending in his going. John M Webb Curate. Litchfield makes him promise to make no alterations in service. I at last forced to order second sermon – He brings some nice candidates especially Maria Clode to confir/m at Haversham March 15.59.

349a **Linford Little. P.C.**
L Spencer Incumbent, J William Irving Curate. He brings some very strikingly prepared candidates to Haversham confirmation March 15 1859, daughters of Knapp.

350a **Linslade. P.C.**
W E Richardson writes for £5 promised by me to Parsonage in 52 which he says never paid – I doubt but pay.. Bickersteth thinks him factious & troublesome. Cust Oct/57 speaks well of him. Not a gentleman but laborious & effective.

---

[51] Possibly John Compton Maul, J.P., of The Green, Newport Pagnell.

Nov 23.59. He asks aid for his school. <u>She</u> Mr Gibson of the [? Locks] daughter for Do for a girls Industrial both which I promise. Jan 30.60. Give £5 – to her industrial Home.

351a Littlemore. P.C.

Rev G. W. Huntingford. Great trouble with his Churchwarden who presents services having got brother churchwarden to sign without knowing what – He put up to it by the Chaplain & Chaplains wife at the Lunatic Asylum. Long correspondence. <u>Oct/58</u>. Complaint as to moving a childs body. Nov/58. Mr Thompsons complaint about circulating a Tract inter alia inculcating the necessity of private absolution on confession. I remonstrate – long correspondence.q.v.

352a Littlemore Pauper Lunatic Asylum.

353a Littleworth. P.C.

I open the School & preach in the Church for it <u>Dec 1859</u>. negotiations with Clarke as to taking it & building. Joseph Budd. Curate – Attend at Faringdon confirm[ation] March–25–60.

March 8.60. Provost writes offering glebe house site & to raise it from £82–100 to £156 if I will give up Patronage.

354a Lockinge East. R.

Sneyd dying My dear Friend F K Leighton succeeds, has plans for the Parish – *Col[onel] Lloyd-Lindsay[52] too building in it 1860. Fernando Collyns not very satisfactory Curate.

Confirm here & consecrate new piece of Burial Ground Sunday March 15. Both services delightful. Curate James Stuart – good & […]. But rather lacking in common sense.

* *Marginal Note. 1859.*

355a Longcote. P.C.

<u>John Hughes</u> Confirmed here March 21 1857. A very nice confirmation for Shrivenham & this. The church slightly Berensed but not otherwise than a great farm. Income £270 net nominal £300. I instigated Hughes about a church at Fernham. Street coming down about Watchfield tomorrow & he to see him, quod D O M. The First stone of the Fernham Church laid Sep.14.58. Finished & day fixed for consec[ration] Nov.59, when found that ground not conveyed through [*illegible*] delays.

---

[52] MP for Berkshire 1865.

356a **Longworth. R. With Charney. C.**

Rev Owen Jenkins. Mr James Hissey...Farmer...first writes & then Oct 29/57 comes to me at Clifton & charges Jenkins with adultery with his wife: now penitent & distracted: a child born & buried: he suspects foul play. I write Oct 30 to Jenkins to inform him of the charge. H[issey], declares he is a well known profligate with other women.. Sep 17. I wrote a letter telling him I must proceed & before it is sent Davenport informs me that Major Blandy tells him Jenkins is mad & they have been obliged to remove him: Dec/58 Kersey writes that he has compromised action for adultery. I having licensed Currie, on Blandy's assurance, write that he must resign or I proceed by commission: I find (1) that the offence more than 2 years ago so cannot prove (2) that Jenkins as testified by medical advice in extreme illness so most reluctantly let it sleep.

April 2.1860 Confirmed here – a very cheering confirmation. P R Atkinson doing well in all ways. Young Mr Edmonds son of Ch[urch] Warden, aiding in all ways. Confirmed.

Mrs Blandy Jenkins lives at New House ... she is mother of B.J. whom I met at Marcham who comes of age speedily. Mr Dew has been so alienated by Jenkins that he has built a chapel & school Eheu! Gives largely & might have been ours ! !

356b *Insert: Davenport's Reports.*

My dear Lord –

Banbury Burial Board.

I last week heard from the Clerk &, by return, sent him an outline plan of a Chapel shewing Communion Table &c: & I said that your Lordship would be very particular as to the Plan. –

I inclose a copy of the Plan which has been sent for approval. –

Shall I send it back saying your Lordship requires it to be amended according to the standard Plan I sent? –

Do you think you can object to the fact of it being under part of the same Roof as the unconsecrated chapel?

Longworth

Mr Robinson has, I am sure, exhausted the inquiries which can be made in the Parish & neighbourhood, – & I can report nothing beyond this that all believe that he has lived on familiar terms, & had intercourse with Servants in succession, & also with Mrs Hissey : but there is no proof of it.

I subjoin his address, & would submit to your Lordship to write to him to resign his Living, because he never can return to the Parish to do good or to regain respect : – only so framing your letter as you would do to a man who, it is believed, is in a precarious state of health. –

356d

     The Rev Owen Jenkins
     at W.Wayne Esq's
      Aberdare
     Glamorgan:

    Mr Pearse, Rural Dean.
  Be pleased to sign & forward the appointment.

    Stoke Mandeville & Buckland.
Please to sign the Representation where I have pencilled a X at p.3 & last page but one: & return it to me. –

     Mr. Carter.
  I am sure I have not the Testimonial.

     Advowson,
  I have made every inquiry & cannot at present hear of one. –

The day of sale of Mr Blackstones Advowson is coming on, but not fixed. – I will inform your Lordship. –

I am greatly vexed with Mr. Burton. – He has made excuses & not paid the Fine. – I have written two or three times. – I have written strongly by the present post.

Mr Morrell is entirely sensible of your Lordship's kind willingness to have been one of his Guests if it had been possible.
     Cuddesdon College.
The sum in the Deed is £820.7.11. Consols.–

I have the honor to be
  Yr. Lordship's very faithful
    servt. J. M Davenport
To the Lord Bishop of Oxford.

356h *Rough Draft.*

I have received from more quarters than one earnest applications to move as to the suspicions which are afloat in your neighbourhood as to your moral character.

Charges not only of Mrs H but female servants: see not how I shall be able to withhold a commission of enquiry.

May be false & then his painful duty to meet them openly – but there may be some substantial truth in them –

If there be, I most earnestly beseech you in Gods name, not to add to your fault in His sight by a false defence nor to add to the great scandal which must attach to such an enquiry but to place in my hand resignation.
         Rev O. J.

356f

Rev/d. Owen Jenkins.
17 Sept/r. 1858 –

Rev/d. Sir,
I wrote to you on 13 July last a Letter relating to certain scandalous Reports concerning you, & I required an answer to the Alternative I then proposed to you of either resigning your Living, or abiding the Effect of a Commission to be issued by me to enquire into this case – To this letter I have received from you no answer. I must now require you to give me within 14 Days – a direct answer or to abide the consequences of your neglecting to do so.

My address will be Lavington House. Petworth, Sussex
[*This is a copy of a rough draft – the deletions are not included.*]

357a Loudwater. P.C.

Edward Arnold – A mere licensed, calvinistic dissenter – no district – no cure of souls – no font – very little Christianity 1856, as I fear – 1862. He applies for leave of Non Res[idence]. I assent if satisfied as to locum tenens –

Tries to get the Curate of Ashley [... *gap*] trouble about – Then nominates [.... *gap*] Woolcombe, of whom I can learn little but seeming respectable I admit him.

358a Loughton. R.

<u>John Athawes</u> Brought son & daughter & some nice candidates to Shenley March 14.59. <u>Nov 16.62.</u> I preach morning for their choir a very good congregation & collection. J.A. kind good man of old school. The son who has been at Cuddesdon seems quite to bring new blood in. D.G. I choked at luncheon.

359a Ludgershall. R.

T Martyn – a good old man. A touching letter from him March 21 1856 as to the good effects of the Wotton confirmation – Baptists seeking Baptism &c. D.G. Came at a moment of extreme depression.

360a Lyford. P.C.

William Williams. Suffers from paralysis & resigns 1857. & Nov 25 1857 comes for License Walter George Wilkinson. Seeming a modest rather nervous man. Duty to be henceforth double: the income at present £20 a year from Worcester & the chaplainship of a workhouse in the Parish gives £40 a year – hopes from Dean & Chapter of Worcester which has property in the Parish.

361a **Little Kimble. V. & Rectory**
Henry Browne – Long disabled offers his resignation early in 1857 & accepted by me to enable J Ormond to take it.
John Ormond Instituted April 22 1857. July 1859. Ormond writes to me that he finds it impossible satisfactorily to discharge the duties of both Parishes & wishes to resign. After consulting with C Lloyd &c. I assent to receive his resignation that the Rev Adam Newman Beamish may take possession of it: he having purchased the advowson & praying for his own institution, which he comes for Aug 3 1859.
Adam Newman Beamish came in 1848 to England: Odcombe near Yeovil for 8 years, then 2 years with Mr. Moore at Romsey.. a year Studleigh & then 2 months at Tylers Green – been 20 years in orders. Very Irish. Nephew to Beamish. "a lover of the Ch[urch] of England" & "a man of peace".
Oct 26/60. Proposes to exchange with Mr Saunders of Stowmarket, suadente Mr Ormerod. I assent.

362a

363a **Maidenhead. P.C.**
Jas Knollis P.C.
J Lindfield Roberts C. March 1860.
Edward Owen. Presented by Mrs Fuller Maitland, & licensed by me, Aug 29/60. – 1861. Movement about giving cure of souls resigns 1861, for a living in Suffolk from Lord Chan[cellor].
Thomas John Lingwood. Formerly Curate of Bicester & since of Alton Hants. Presented by Fuller Maitland.[53] Jacob speaks well of him. Rather dull as a preacher but a good man. // Only brings March 30/63 1 male & 15 females to the Confirmation.

364a **Maids Morton. R.**
Rev Andrewes Uthwatt. On Travers leaving him for Wolverton 1855, he takes F Bathurst as Curate – Bathurst getting on well. But U. very hostile to vitality – allowed an Ash Wednesday service to B's entreaty but made his own labourers work all churchtime! The young people confirmed at Akeley well prepared by FB.
Matthew Watkin Davies. Licensed by me Dec 7/57. He coming from Yorkshire. Confirmed here March 22.57. A very nice confirmation. Davies read the service particularly well. Uthwatt more cordial. Church in good Church Warden order & warmed with Hot Water.

---

[53] E.F.Maitland or Thomas Fuller Maitland J.P., who lived at Wargrave.

365b *Insert: Correspondence re Mapledurham and the residency of Dr Hawtrey, from Berkshire Chronicle, 31st August 1858.*

365a **Mapledurham. V.**
The Rev E C Hawtrey.
Confirmed here April 1.1855. Caversham (Bennett) & Kidmore End Compton attending – The Church crowded. Mr Blounts[54] aisle opened for us – Not worth stirring the question of that aisle – but recommended throwing in with proper arches the present vestry. Church deal fitted with low seats – mean & poor ! – Feb 22/58 I confirm here at an evening service during Henley Mission. J W Burgon & G Prevost preach.. A second curate to be appointed & paid by Powys.
Edward Coleridge Nov 1863. The Church opened by him after a thorough restoration. Brings his candidates earnestly prepared, March/64 to Whitchurch.

366a **Marcham. V.**
Rev H J Randolph. Rev F F Fixsen wishing to leave Oct/55 for ill health has been a respectable Curate there. I write to Randolph as to appointment of Successor – // Confirm here March 13–57. T J Williams Curate taking pains & doing well. I stay as guest with C Duffield. An ugly new Church built by late Mr Duffield. Oct 57. Randolph sends no answer to my Visit[ation] queries. Williams a sad one as to Parish – consults Nov 57 as to removing clerk whom Randolph protects & will never allow W. to do any more duty if he is proceeded against. I come here March 31 to April 2.1860. Confirm on Sunday. Poor Randolph more eccentric than ever. Place Oldfield here from Newbury. C Elwes pleasing. Alas! March 10.60, I settle Oldfield to leave – after great difficulties place Sidebotham here.

367a **Marlow Great. V. With Holy Trinity Chapel of Ease**
Rev F Bussell Went Feb 5 1854 to preach for Culham College – the Church said to contain 1,200 most cold & unchurch like – preached on Sons of Sceva[55] – The people attentive promised collection to be £10 – was about £23 – 120 at communion more in common.
March 11.1856. Confirmed in the new Church. A beautiful one for

---

[54] ? William Blount, barrister and JP, had residences at Ludlow and at Chalfont St Peter.

[55] Acts xix 13–17. These were seven sons of a Jewish chief priest who attempted exorcism in the name of 'Jesus whom Paul preacheth' but who were set upon by an evil spirit who said ,'Jesus I know, and Paul I know, but who are ye?'

a confirmation – a very pleasing confirm/n. I trust that Bussell has indeed been enabled to do much here. He often low & over burdened = endeavoured to comfort & encourage him.

Dec 8.58. Staying with Mr Wethered for SPG meeting at night & preaching next morning. – Poor Bussell dies after attack of influenza & Fever. We collect for his widow a considerable sum.

R Milman accepts. Instituted –

I confirm here March 27.62, a pleasant confirmation.

P Henry Boissier. Curate I hear that he & Bussell did not agree.

Nov 19.1862. I come for SPG meeting, with B[isho]p Chapman. A good meeting. Next day preach for organ & Parish gathering in Schools. Milman very successful. I move them for new Vicarage, Chancel pulpit &c

Owen Wethered good man dead since I here last. A great loss ... Milmans Curates

Jan 29 1864 I come to open district chapel at Handy Cross, & confirm. Lee Hayward. Lear (of Cuddesdon) going on very well. Horne a nice little man, too artistic but not a good parish Priest. Thoughtful & able not very audible. The Vicar wonderfully won confidence.

368a **Marlow Little. V.**

Rev W Milton resident Curate. The candidates March 11 1856 at Great Marlow seeming well prepared. Reports a Church wanted on Hackwell [*sic*]Heath, also Schools. The poor Richard Cattermole dies 1858 & March 3/59 John Baines (from Haverstock Hill) comes for institution– a very promising addition to Diocese. Confirmed April 9.1860 a pleasant confirmation & tried to stir up Ch[urch] Warden &c. to restore the Church – Jan 1861. Baines writes "Trustees of Mr Ellames promise to bear half the expense of building a School for this parish if such half does not exceed £300"

NB & Q Flackwell's Heath. Baines proposals for School or other chapel. Letter Jan 3./60.

369a **Marsh Gibbon. R.**

Rev A Coote – Wants to exchange Dec 1854 with Mr Roberts of Foots Cray whose wife has eloped from him – I refuse. He & His Father &c. angry going on to March 1855 – Tell him in answer to a very reproachful letter that I must fall back on general rule of no exchange.

Feb 1856. Fremantle says thinks going on well with new curate. Coote again applies to exchange with Plumtres' incumbent. I beg him not to re–open the exchange question. After long negotiation I arrange that Thomas Huntley Greene should come to Marsh G[ibbon], Mr Enraght going to Leominster[56] & T H G. comes to me to Lavington Aug 12 1856 for Collation.

March 25 1859. Confirm here – Gardner acting as Curate. Poor Greene away at Malta for throat affection. Fear he never will stand the damp of this place. Marked out new churchyard with Ch[urch] Wardens & stopping of churchyard paths.

Oct 3 1859, he nominates Thomas Little to curacy. Late of Uxbridge highly commended. – March/60. Greene writes, good work going on. – A move in the parish – Prayer meeting at which good Farmer Michael Parker leads prayer. Q. effect. This synchronizing with the neighbouring "revivals" & giving I hope a calmed tone to them here.

370a Marston. V.

Rev R Gordon – March 1855 – His fearful account of its utter demoralization – a perfect Sodom for wickedness – alas ! Its neighbourhood to Oxford.

Golightly undertakes the curacy. Oct 57. He & Golightly think 6 times a year enough celebrations of Holy Commun[ion]!

371a Marston Fleet. R.

S. [M] Humphreys ob. April 15 1855 July 4. 1855. Hibbert Wanklyn comes for institution He about having borrowed money to build an house. comes from Clewer. Sep 58. A sad account of him from Arch[deacon] Bick[ersteth]. In pecuniary difficulties & was certainly more or less drunk – The living to be sequestration for his debt & then a curate to be appointed to work also in Aylesbury. George H Turner purchases the advowson, & resigns.

William Wilson King. Nominated by Mr Turner. April 23/62. W W King has been Curate Evans St Mary Le Strand. Ordained by Bp of Lichfield. P & D 49 High churchman. Sacramental system means to act with Archdeacon Bickersteth.

372a Marston North. P.C.

Rev R Knight – I get Dean of Windsor to nominate him &c. Confirm here Feb 20 1856. The Church crowded – gazers – The chancel restored by the Queen as memorial to "Butcher" Niel. Gaudy & incomplete – Hear a poor account of Knights ministry. Fremantle says the dissenters have quite upper hand & always will have against Knight.

---

[56] Leominster appears to be an alternative spelling for Lyminster, Arundel, Sussex.

He has never got over nor ever will a quarrel with the people at first about some allotment ground – has now just been quarrelling with his Ringers & they cutting down the trees that he had planted in churchyard. He asked Sir T Fremantle to subscribe to a communion cloth Sir T answered they had done well in Bucks ever since the Ref[ormation] without !

Brings candidates March 26/59 to Whitchurch Fremantles say that when Sir Thomas bought the property he asked K[night], to tell him of really deserving objects for his charity. Knight "was not going to be the Squires relieving officer" & [*entry ends.*]

373a **Marsworth. V. –**
Turner. C Lloyd gives good account of poor Turner Feb 1856.

374a **Medmenham. V.**
Rev Dr Wright – Endless trouble about him with Parishioners – & then with curate – never paying Harris. Dies suddenly Autumn 1854. Harris to succeed – March 10 1856. The Medmenham people confirmed at Hambledon & apparently well prepared. March 28/62 Do.

375a **Mentmore. V.**
The Rev John North Ouvry North ... Feb 18. 1856 – A question as to the constitution of the School which Baron Rothschild wishes to have British – Shall North start an opposition. I advise not. Where service to be while Church restoring. I assent to Wesl[eyan] meeting if it can be hired out & out. Going April/59 to resign. Living offered to Maynard Currie who leaves it to me to say if he shall take it. I advise yes. – North resigning in 1859. Aug 18/1859 comes to me Maynard Wodehouse Currie at Aylesbury. Gives a good account. The Baroness kind, paying for Redhead coming over to teach the children to chant. March 14/62 confirm here. A nice confirmation – Rothschilds supporting Currie in all things

376a **Merton. V.**
Rev Tudor Curate to poor Stupart. Gave a fair account of his work. March 1855 when I met him for Confirm/n, at Charlton. Sep.58, Stuparts strange forgery of a Mr Sinclairs signature professing to be an old Fellow of Exeter Coll[ege]. Stuparts debts all but paid – saw the Rector of Ex[eter] about it – The college voluntarily give to make up the living something like £100 a year. I urge that whilst he is under suspension a Beneficio he should not have it. At last in 1863, he resigns, & with all hope I institute W M Wollaston of Exeter – Find him putting things in order March 1864.

377a **Middleton Stoney. R.**
Rev R Pretyman. Confirmed there March 9 1855 – rather a nice confirmation Ardley – Tusmore & Hardwicke – Bucknell, Chesterton. The Tower unsafe & to be rebuilt. Chancel to be restored by Pretyman. Write to him & Lord Jersey that must see plans. March 10 1855. The young people at the confirmation at Chesterton March 58 seemed attentive. Confirm here March. 8/61… Few & Cold. The Church ill done. No vestry. Living tithes £400 – & 100 acres of glebe farmed by Pretyman.

378a **Midgham. C.** [See 352].

Milcombe. C. [See Bloxham. 373].
Milton under Wychwood
600. see after Yelford.

Milton. R. [Berks.]
Ven Arch Clerke. I consecrate an addition to the churchyard 1856. Friday March 30.1860 I confirm here a nice confirmation. W H Hewett now Curate here. 1862–3
T Francis Curate. A nice confirmation here March 13 63.

379a **Milton Great. V.**
Rev H M Turton Appointed by me on Mr Ashursts[57] resignation 1856 [Micklemas(*sic*)]. Jan 11 1857. I confirm 26 there. Jan 18.1857. Preach on the marriage of Cana in Galilee.. Confirmed here again Dec 26 1858.. A nice confirmation. Services well attended. The poor greatly gained. The Farmers rather aloof. Progress in various matters as by annexed paper. A

379b *Insert*:

From Advent 1855.	From Advent 1856.	From Advent 1857.
To Advent 1856	To Advent 1857.	To Advent 1858.
Celebrations. 11.	Celebrations. 20.	Celebrations. 57.
Communicants. 629.	Communicants 1207.	Communicants. 1408.
Alms – £20.15.9.	Alms. £36.15.7.	Alms – £57.13.7½.
	India. £8.6.5½.	Dio: Ch.Bls. £5.3.3.

---

[57] Given in *Crockford* as Ashhurst.

S.P.G.	Schools
1856.subs: 5. £4.19.0	1856 {24.B. in attendance
	{42.G.
1857. – 15. £13.11.9	1857 {42.B. —
	{51.G.
1858. – 51. £17.10.6½	1858 {42.B. —
	{53.G.

Milton Little. P.C.

Rev H Shute. Presented by me on J Ashursts avoidance – We get the Parsonage House built by Eccles[iastical] Commis/rs. Shute very much improves in 1854 the internal arrangements of the Church & buys a plot of land between Parsonage & Church.

William George Sawyer comes Jan 13/60 to be licensed after good & true service at Wantage.

380b *Insert*:

File No. 4690
Little Milton St James P.C.

The property vested in the Commissioners upon which this living has a local claim consists of a Tithe Rent Charge of £316. arising in the parish of Little Milton formerly belonging to the Prebend of Milton ecclesia, which became vested in the Commissioners upon the vacancy of the Prebend in 1840, subject (with other property not applicable to this local claim) to a lease for 3 lives; now aged (if living) 80, 77 & 31 years.[58] Reserved Rent now payable to Commissioners: £40 per annum.

The Commissioners are also in receipt of the fee farm Rents, amounting to £124 which are charged under a private act of Parliament upon an Estate in the Parishes of Great & Little Milton formerly belonging to the Prebend of Milton Manor cum Binbrooke, and are not of a nature applicable to local claims

The only sum available for this local claim is therefore a proportion of the above mentioned Reserved Rent of £40; which may be estimated at £11 per annum.

The Commissioners however made a Grant of £95. per annum in 1845; and have subsequently erected a Parsonage House for the Living, at a cost exceeding £1900.

---

[58] This method of granting leases for the duration of three named lives was the normal method in the nineteenth century; the selection of names involved a high degree of guesswork over life expectancies, and was open to renegotiation, for a fine, at any time.

Great Milton V

The property vested in the Commissioners upon which this Living has a local claim consists of Tithe Rent Charges amounting to £559.2.6. subject to the before mentioned Lease.

The proportion of the Reserved Rent of £40. applicable to this local claim may be estimated at £15. A grant of £36 was, however, made thereto in 1842.

It will be seen therefore that the Grants made by the Commissioners to these Livings are considerably in excess of the amount at present available for this augmentation, as local claims; & that, until the Lease, under which the Tithes are held shall have expired; the Commissioners will not be in a position to make any further Grants in respect thereof.

initialled *25 Oct 1859.*

381a **Milton Keynes. R.**
Rev E Jones Rector Very old & infirm 1855. Loses his sight. His son quits curacy. A J Morris comes but knocks up with walking from Newport Pagnell & calls for sudden resignation. They apply to me to license Irving of Broughton – I object Dec 19 that he cannot give the Broughton & Milton services.
March 27 1856. Confirm here again a much more attentive congregation than the last but the people rather rough. Sat with old Jones who 85 turned – Blind & quite done up but sound in mind. The parish some years since had a religious [?resurgence] of Methodists – All belongs to Finch, who never visits it to their offence. Instituted Rev Dalton at Newport Pagnell Nov 5 1857.

382a **Minster Lovell. V.**
[*no name given*] Curate. Sep.1857. A plan for buying the old F[??] Hall for Chapel –Seems energetic. March.22 58 James Slade Curate comes with candidates to Witney.
R Earle. Comes to me May/59, asking me to receive his son, instead of Mr Slade, who has fits. Young Earle in Ripon Diocese, at Dent. In Deacons orders,. A good account of him from Mrs Sedgwick. Robert H Earle Curate brings his candidates to Witney March 4.61.

383a **Missenden Great. V.**
Rev Josh. Greaves. Applies Jan 1856 for me to subscribe to new parsonage I refuse because of the Patronage being in dissenting trustees.[59]

---

[59] Trustees of the late J.O.Oldham, Esq, *Clergy List* 1845.

March 24 1862. Confirm here. Gallery full of disorderly children. Very few male candidates some nice female. Mr Carrington talks of when [matters] in order setting about restoring Church.

384a **Missenden Little. V.**

Rev Hanmer. V. Sequestrated. Lord Howe puts Bickersteth here. When I move him to Aylesbury, wishes to have a curate under new Penn Street incumbent. I allow & he places Moreton, who gets afterwards into row with Cuffe. March 13 1856 tried at Assizes. Moreton gets 1/4 damage on one count & £50 on another.
Rev T Staples Pepper Curate.

385a **Mixbury. R.**

Rev G Horsley Palmer. Come to him March 10 1855 – R Cecil there – House very nicely furnished good copies of best Raphaels &c. He says bad cottages The Great Evil of Place. In hands of one proprietor resident in Cambridgeshire, old & helpless.
March 6 58. Come here again, & March 7.58 a very nice afternoon confirmation. Great attention amongst all. G P. very pleasant. The Hunts, J Talbot &c. here. G P. has just written a very good letter to poor Gol[ight]ly, as to his mischievous move. G P. proposes leaving £1000 to better this small living. I advised his offering it to Eccles[iastical] Comm/s for grant to make it £1,600.
Sat Nov 13 58 at SPG meeting in school with B Nelson Lord R Cecil & on Sunday 14 preached & celebrated morning & catechized afternoon.
Sat March 19.61. Come here again. J Talbot &c.. Sund[ay] 10. Celebrate early, & confirm morning. Also some young men from Brackley with F B Falkner. A delightful service.
March 6 64. Come here. R Palmer &c. Confirmed Sunday morning March 6. A nice confirmation.

386a **Mollington**. [See Claydon.]

Rev T H Tait. Went up & examined the new House. Which ugly outside but comfortable in & very well situated. Mrs Tait looked sadly delicate with 3 great children. He gone to Cropredy trying to raise money for Church.
April 1.1856. Came for opening, after Tait had restored the Church. A very pleasant service: I preached on "They that are Christ's", & spoke to C Holbech afterwards & offered take my proper share of restoring the chancel if

NB the Trustees will do the rest. He to speak to Loveday & to act for his Father.

March 11/58 comes to Cropredy with candidates.
March/59. Writes again about Chancel. Old Loveday obstinate. Holbech obstante
*Confirm here [March. *altered to* Feb] 22.61. All very encouraging. Church nice.

387a **Mongewell. R.**
Durell. Thinks Nov 57 that there are peculiar circumstances making the expediency of a second sermon doubtful. Wishes to talk over it with me.

388a **Moreton North. V.**
Henry Taylor – Dec 1854 wish him to have two full services every Sunday. He pleads age infirmity & poverty & after consulting with R Sumner I forbear to press it. He is looking for a living which does not fall. Accepts another living in 1855 – & the Archdeacon presents the Rev. Richard Edward Hollinsed who comes for institution Sep 21 1855.

Richard E Hollinsed. Means at present 1855 to pin it up & build a room.. Hollinsed died March.1858. & Arch/d nominates

Albert Barff – Who comes for Institution June 17 1858. Thursday 11 Nov 1858. I preached & celebrated at the reopening. Trouble about the Reredos. Sumner & Hoskyns objecting. I censure B[arff], for having without leave erected it. But retain it as legal. The Restoration a beautiful work. All the Parish hearty. A most satisfactory gathering after in barn.. March 12.63 a very nice confirmation here! the new parsonage almost ready – all still most hearty & Barff succeeding well. D.G.

389a **Moreton South. R.**
Wm James. Ob. Dec 1855 –
Richard Michell comes Feb 15 1856 to be instituted I tell him I shall after due time for building a house require residence.[60]
James Frith Curate still: March 1860.

390a **Moulsford. P.C.**
G K Morrell. Confirm here March 2.1860. A very nice confirmation. July 25–63. I hear privately that Mary Morrell shaken, Romeward.

391a **Moulsoe. R.**
Rev Walter Drake. Neither attended confirmation at Milton or asked to be excused March 29 1856. I sent him a letter of reproof. W. T England Curate 1859. W.D very poorly.

---

[60] According to the *DNB* he never resided at South Moreton.

392a **Mursley. R.**
> A Holt Curate. Feb 24 1856: Mr Holt complained that the Parsonage getting greatly out of repair & Rector will not answer him when he writes.

Poor Harris dies suddenly 1859. Holt hopes for living.
> Nov 1859 see G.V T Selby Lowndes, who says it is in the hands of his trustees. The day before the lapse <u>John Cross,</u> <u>named</u> to me son of a Winslow Tradesman after full enquiry appears to be no simony & May 19/60 I institute him after full explanations. Teste T V Fosbery.

393a **Pishill. P.C.**
> Prince. Separated by C E R Keene after great discussion 1854 from Nettlebed & very nicely rebuilt under Ferrey's auspices. Visited it Oct 1854 with Mr Prince.

394a **Nash see Thornton.**

Nettleden

Visited it Nov 23 1854 from Ashridge with A P Cust. The Church a sad restoration of Lord Bridgewaters before the restoration of taste. – Now to be separated from Pitstone – a parsonage house just planned. Mr Cautley lives there.

<u>George Spencer Cautley</u> Licensed Nov 6 1857. Excellent good man Preached a capital sermon in the Chapel at Ashridge. The house finished. March 13/62. Confirmed here. A most affecting confirm[ation], from deep interest of all candidates.

395a **Nettlebed. D. With Pishill. P.C.** (Separated 1854 see Pishill back overleaf.)
Jas Hazel – Candidates confirmed at Nuffield Feb 22 1855 & seeming least prepared of that set– NB. No service on Ash Wednesday Mrs [Ripon] loud in complaint – to write to him about it. Wrote to him March 1855. To have two Sunday duties & at least Christmas Good Friday Ash Wednesday Ascension – Correspondence, he says "it is downright cruelty to get more duty out of an incumbent of only £130." I try to wake him to the blessedness of Gods service for little or much.

396a See <u>last</u> page.
Nettleden. P.C. [See Pightlesthorne.]

Newbury. R.
<u>H Binney</u> DD. Confirmed again, miserably few for the number in Newbury, 5 males only! The Dr. very feeble looking to me death struck & very unusually gentle.

H T White Curate Leslie Randall. Dec.12.58. I preach morning & confirm afternoon all D.G. altered.
Went over House with L R Dec 14. Churchyard still refusing the field close to Rectory. – – Feb.16. O. comes to me & confesses sin.. loose life whilst an undergraduate. Then doubts as to ordination – hoped to overcome. Then 3 falls in 6 1/2 years, last lately. From Rugby delay 3 hours, dine &c. Knew not & not known. Saw him 2cl. full talk think that he should retire for a year of prayer & reading &c. Rather recommend Cumbrae. He has told Norris. I say I must see N. before I finally decide – he to come to me Sun[da]y. Confirm here, March 17.1860 a great confirmation & all well behaved. Preach for L R's schools March 18.
Nov 7 1863 Come here from Reading. Open chancel beautifully restored, with service, communion & preach. Rev xxii.3/2 & 4. Also on the afternoon of Nov 8. Both full congregations. Collect 7th £125 – 8th aft[ernoon] £17 – Leslie Randall DG greatly succeeding.

397a **Newington. R With Britwell Prior. C.**
Septimus Cotes Applies Nov 4.59 to separate Britwell 6 miles from mother Church & join it to Britwell Salome: which years back I had wished but Lord Carrington would not. He has now sold the Patronage to L[ord] Lansdowne who will. I agree.

398a **Newington South. V.**
H D Harington Confirmed here 18 [blank] consecrated Burial Ground. Confirmed again, March 13.1858. A nice confirmation.

399a **Newnham Courtney. R.**
H Pennant Cooke. March/64 – Moving for a new Chapel. Mrs Harcourt held out hopes of that & burial ground between Harcourt Arms & Rectory.
Houses of poor in bad order.

400a **Newnham Murren. V. [See Northstoke].**

Newnton Longville. R.
see Weston Turville Dec 1853.
R J R Hughes. Confirmation to be at Feb 1856, but I obliged to move it to Drayton Parslow to get down to Torquay.[61] Mr Hughes & Ch[urch] Wardens much wish it next time here. Two meetings – one Primitive Methodist opened recently.

---

[61] The Bishop's son, a naval officer, was dying there of consumption.

341b[62] **Newport Pagnell. V.**

Rev G Morley. Confirmed here 3 times – man strange beyond measure. Held a meeting for the Diocesan Church Building in School room Sep 26 1855. Advertised on his Church door but he absent! Will not visit the girls School because it is indecent nor will he suffer his wife to do so because her place is in the nursery!

Preached for the new intended girls school Nov 13 58. A good attendance. The chancel wonderfully improved. SPG meeting on 12th also good.

<u>March 16 59</u>. Confirmed here. Very few Newport candidates especially male. Preached at night to a very large congregation & very attentive. Talk of getting M a curate.

342b **Newton Blossomville. R.**

<u>James H Talbot</u> comes to me at Olney at March 17.59, with some tolerably prepared candidates.

343b **Newton Purcell cum Shelswell. R.**

<u>The Rev John Meade</u>. Nearly deaf. A few of his people come to the confirmation at Fringford March 7.1858.

344b **Noke. R.**

Mr Carlyle dies, 1863, Dec.

<u>Brisco Morland Gane</u> Comes April 18 1864 for institution. Ordained by B[isho]p of Exeter/42 ... Comes from Rochester (Stanford le Hope) in which Diocese since/36 [?56]. Known to Canon Blomfield, seems sound & moderate.

345b **Northleigh. V.**

<u>Isaac Gillam</u> – After for many years emptying the Church gets an exchange with Mr Morrall, who professes orthodoxy – see his letters of 1856, & comes for Institution Nov 8.1856. His testimonials signed by Cecil Wray J B Monk & C H Barter.

<u>Cyrus Morrall</u>. From Liverpool = March 1857. He writes word Church full & all going well. D.G. Remarried in 1860, woman of Fortune – wishes to resign. Attempt Nov 15/60 to get an exchange with Cecil Wray Liverpool. The Lord Chancellor refuses.

<u>Robert W Fiske</u> gets it by exchange. I confirm here March 12 1864. Great improvement & at luncheon got the Churchwardens to agree to borrow on rates what needful for restoration of Church.

---

[62] The pagination changes here, reverting to 341b.

346b **Northmoor. P.C.**
 Rev. Heming – Just going to another living. Visited it March 27 1855. Mr Parker Churchwarden & college tenant – A fine old Church with a good many fine features. Recently warmed with Hot Water by Heming. Moved him & the Churchwarden & wrote to remove a hideous west gallery needless & blocking up some very picturesque work. The Church wants reseating strangely – The monuments some of them curious. What desirable is, that the college should add to the endowment build an house & make it a living. They have the great tithes now it is virtually served from Oxford. A hideous little stone altar put in long ago by Dr Silver.

 Talked afterwards with F Burgess about it. He proposes to wait the death of Miss Nalder about the House – But at once to propose & he hopes carry "passing down" the offer, whereby Junior Fellows may take it St Giles &c. & marry on them. Hunter would have done so on St Giles but was bound in honour to resign if he married that it might be held by a senior with Fellowship.

 Arthur Starkey. March 22. 58, I confirm here, a pleasing conf[irmation]. The Church might be made very nice by restoration. I try to stir Starkey up thereto: leases running out &c.

 Edward Coupland. I explain to him that if he takes the living he must reside. Ordained D by J Lichfield 51 by H Worcester P/53 Curate of Bishops Itchington to old Lee of Tadmarton: comes March 4/61 with his cand[idate]s to Ducklington.

 Feb/64 something pleasing about his manner with candidates.

347b **Northstoke. V. With Newnham Murren. V. and Ipsden. V.**
 N Denton Newnham Murreen. [*sic*]

 Ipsden Rev R Twopenny In 1855 after long preparations Mr T. sets about preparing to restore the Church. I hear from G Street Aug. 7.55 that the plans most objectionable. Write same day to Twopenny.

348b **Nuffield. R.**
 W T Hopkins. Confirmed here, Feb 22.1855. All with impress of care & wisdom. The parishes too which met here except Nettlebed seemingly cared for. A very cheering confirmation.

 Confirmed here March [1] 58. Another very cheering confirmation the young men specially affected. Snow, as ever.

 March 14 64 confirmed here. A nice confirmation. Visited Sarah Besswell. The fruits of Hopkins wise 38 years ministry in altered parish.

349b

350b **Oakley. V.**
F W Cartwright. Waltons complaint of his galloping over service which he denies. Brings candidates to Brill April 4/59. Kindly & cordial. Confirmed here March 6.62. Rather wretched.

351b **Oare. C.** [See Chieveley.]

352b **Oddington. R.**
Searle – A grumbling ill conditioned indolent old undogmatical & I fear rather sceptical priest.
Dies March 31 1857.
George Petch. (See my ordination book). Fellow of Trinity comes to me June 26 in London for Institution.. Going into residence as soon as he can get in. Feb 64 wishes only to have one sermon &c. I consult with Gordon & say 2.

353b **Olney. V.**
Rev Dr Langley. Confirmed here again March 26.1856. A most marked & blessed improvement in the whole bearing of the people congregation &c. The Church too has been greatly improved. The chancel reseated by Scott – pews cut down. Three decker abated &c. Mrs Langley NB very anxious for full restoration & I promised to back it up with Lord Dartmouth. They are going at once for demolition of galleries &c. On the whole the tone certainly rising here abouts. DG.
March 17/59 Confirm here. A nice confirmation. Women prepared by J P Langley now here, & men by Edward S Wilson Curate. I preached here at night to a large & very attentive congregation on Lukewarmness.
Feb 15.59 Got a grant from Sp[iritual] Aid of £80 & £20 from Lord Dartmouth for a second curate. A Mr Mawgan coming well spoken of by men of whom Arch/n Moore speaks well.

354b **Oving. R.**
J H Thelwall. Curate H Le Grand Boyce. Good Friday 1857 Miss Butler comes with a strange story, produces a book written as she says by Mrs Boyce the heads of charges she Miss B. late governess in the family is to make against B. to me under promise of secresy. These violence, cruelty. Throwing stool, knocking her down with Poker, violence to children. Great cunning &c. Miss B. adds nine months ago when she first came attempts on her. Sent 2 maids out & her dress being thin tore it almost all off in his assaults of an unchaste kind. Promised to provide for her. Doubt the truth of all. Quere whether Miss Butler is mad or bad. She professes to be daughter of

the Chichester Architect & to have been governess in Laprimdayes family at Graffham. I fear by communication from Mrs B. that all true. He brings candidates to Whitchurch March/59 & argues very unbecomingly in favour of 14 as common age for confirmation. George Gould Ross Curate on Boyce leaving 1861.62.

355b **Oxford, Saint Aldate. R.**

Rev H Swabey. Nov 4 1855 Preached here for Dioce/n Church Building & met the Church Wardens Cozens & Mallam after at Luncheon to try & win them over to S's plans as to setting apart the S.Aisle for the poor – They afraid of alarming parishioners. "Room not wanted" &c. &c. March 28 Swabey sends me a sermon on Parish difficulties to be Circulated on Easter Tuesday, he to be absent 3 months and if no help comes means to resign.

May 1856 after many doubts. His Fathers paralytic stroke leads Swabey finally to resign, and on Nov 8 1856 his successor Thomas Charles Litchfield Layton comes to me for Institution. [ordained by me see Vol.1.page 74], has given up I am sorry to say mwk [midweek] prayer. I advised him to retain. The usual low church view hinders private & family prayers &c .Wishes to keep Mr Bussell at present being in poor health – applies to have evening service at 6.30 instead of 3, so as to set the aft.free for school teaching Catechising &c. Assented on his assurance that the parishioners would not dislike & gave leave for Litany thereat.

Jan 26.1857 St A shares much of the most degraded population…a great many beggars, one or two bad Houses, schools inefficient.
Francis Hannan curate in the interval–Irish.

Alfred Millard William Christopher comes Aug 27/59 for Institution.. has been head of La Martinere Calcutta. 6 years at St Johns Richmond (Hales Church) very highly spoken of by Bp Wilson of Calcutta, & Bp of Winton (Sumner) & by Swinney. Seems a good & mild & loving man of Evangel School. Living having been sold by June scarcely fairly it is said to Simeon Trust, nominally Samuel Hanson of Epsom. Jan 12/60. Good done by prohibition of supper parties at Ch.Ch. some years ago. Not in favour of early age confirmation, approve of present. Nov 1861. Christopher wishes to build galleries. I object & he yields. June 14/63– Preach for his repair fund having been kept by illness from him on opening day.

356 **Oxford. All Saints. P.C.**

Rev W.W West – a clever man. Strong head & not apparently religious or a pleasant man. Not at meeting Jan 57. Asked too late. Feb 7.60

- applies to give title to Cornish. Son of H H Cornish. Stipend £35. Whole income of Living being £100. I assent. Wests vote given at Election for [ga*p in script*] & the Reason [commonly being *unfinished entry*].

357 **Oxford. Holywell. P.C.**
Rev W Walton.[63] Confirmed here Nov 4 1855 at afternoon service.

Jan 26.1857 Little shopkeepers very irreligious – very few poor & those demoralised by the number of gifts & charities from the colleges. Many religious persons, not the poor here – lodging keepers..College servants a most unsatisfactory set of men. Imitate those above them, extravagant eaters & drinkers. Live in better houses & take lodgers. Their lads & girls dressy & spoilt. Some few really religious. The recognized plunder destroys them, & absence from Church. Servants of certain colleges better. The upper the best. Care taken of them & better examples the cause.

Dec 4.1858. A memorial presented to me signed by many parishioners complaining of "Innovations gradually introduced. Lighted candles in the day. Strange vestments, intoning. Piscena & supercilla, extreme decoration of the chancel, *at last DG allayed. Jan 12/60. Thinks the religious state improved since 57. More interest in religion both outwardly & inward. The Poor most improved. College servants least. Not fit after work for church. Consider themselves absolved. . . They come to Evening services. Attempt by Vice Chancellor NB. & Mayor to provide for younger college servants during Long Vacat[ion]. Most difficult to deal NB. with the young men, dissipated, out at night, even the well disposed. The homes not attractive – & they get to public House. Another scheme just beginning for Miss[ionary] organization, mainly paying Miss Coll[ector]s through offertory & getting persons to circulate intelligence. Believes great object to get children confirmed younger. .number of communicants & frequency of attendance. Thinks the early communion & frequent have been most blessed of all other means – A greatly increased interest in the services of the Church. Wishes for earlier age at confirmation. New school for middleclass very promising . . children pay 6£ a year. Confirm here April 15/63.

[*Marginal Note*: * I there Dec/59 preaching & all at peace.]

---

[63] The initials given here are as printed, but later are found as W.W.Walton, and in the inserted letters as H.B.Walton.

357b *Insert*: (Copy)

>20. Inverness Terrace.
>London W
>Feb.5.1858.

Rev.d Sir

I have carefully considered the questions submitted to me in the Memorial of May 16.1857, together with the further questions proposed for my determination in Reply of the Memorialists to the Rector's answer dated the 31st of July, 1857.

I have also taken the opinion of competent assessors on the points of Ecclesiastical and Statute law raised therein.

I hereby decide as follows:

1. That the Churches of All Saints and St Michael's are and have been from the issue of the order in Council of the 27th of August 1846, under the jurisdiction of the Bishop of Oxford, within the meaning of the Statutes of the College.

2. That the Chaplains of the said Churches are at liberty to marry without thereby vacating their fellowships, subject to the conditions laid down in Statute II.

3. That the right of amotion given to the Rector for the time being, by Bishop Fleming, and by the original character of the College and recognized in Bishop Rotheram's Statutes, is preserved to the present Rector during his Incumbency.

I have the honour to be
>Your faithful Servant
>John Lincoln
>Visitor.

The Reverend
Octavius Ogle.

Draft Letter

Gentlemen,

On receiving a memorial to which your names are attached touching the services in Holywell Church, I put myself into immediate communication with the Vicar. I have from him a letter which (I enclose) & which will I hope allay all the disquiet and annoyance in the Parish. The Vicar at once expressed to me his regret that he had been induced [against his better judgement *erased* Is better judgement to be omitted or qualified by perhaps?] [*inserted:* in the course of architectural alteration] to place the Stone Slab with Stone legs instead of the old [*changed to* Former] Holy Table in the Church, & his readiness to replace it by a proper wooden table. This I shall direct him at once to do. His letter shows his readiness to meet as far as possible the wishes of the parish as to the mode of conducting Divine Service, & I hope that this will be duly appreciated by the Parishioners.

As to what the memorial speaks of as the "extreme ornaments in the decoration of the chancel", I requested the Archdeacon of Oxford to inspect it & report to me concerning it. He reports that 'the floor & fittings in the Chancel are very Handsome, the execution of the work shews that great pains have been bestowed upon it. The walls are elaborately coloured but there is nothing in the designs or patterns to which I see reason to call your Lordships....

My dear Sir,
I trust that your letter of Dec 9 when read by your parishioners will go far to restore amongst them the peace and harmony for which you pray. The only order I need make is that the stone erection which without my privity has been placed in your Church instead of the Holy Table should be removed, & that a new Holy Table should be placed in its stead.

I approve of your proposed arrangement of the services for the next six months and earnestly pray God to prosper your ministry to His Glory in the salvation and edification of many Souls

I am your faithful friend and brother
S Oxon.

Christ Church, Oxford
December 7 1858

My dear Lord
According to your request I visited the parish Church of Holywell yesterday, where I met the Churchwarden and Mr Walton.

The Churchwarden informed me that many of the Parishioners had objected to the Decorations of the Chancel, to the fixing a Stone Altar in it, to placing a Superaltar on it, and to ornamenting it with flowers. All these things are I believe amongst the items of a Memorial which has lately been addressed to you.

The walls of the Chancel are very elaborately coloured but there is nothing in the designs or patterns to which I see reason to call your Lordship's attention; no objection (as far as I have heard) was made to them at the time when the works were in progress, and I believe that nothing new has been introduced since your Lordship was last in the Church.

The construction of the Table is to be altered.

I conceive that a Superaltar cannot reasonably be objected to.

There were no flowers or vases on the Communion Table when I saw it but the Churchwarden informed me that they were in use and that the Memorialists objected to the practice.

There were small ornamental shields on the candles which are to be removed.

The floor and fittings of the Chancel are very handsome and the execution of the work shows that great pains have been bestowed upon it.

    I am very sincerely
      Charles C Clerke

I enclose a letter to you just delivered at my house. I was very sorry to find this morning that it was out of my power to appear at Dorchester this morning.

Private   Merton College
                                 Dec. 15

My dear Lord Bishop

Nothing, as far as I can see, could be added or suggested otherwise. And I return the draft, and the Archdeacon's letter with many thanks for your Lordship's extreme kindness and consideration.

It seems to me that your Lordship's manner of dealing with the case ought to prove most conducive to the Ends of Peace and Truth – these I shall myself most earnestly keep in view.

As verbal suggestions, I have ventured upon a few points in your letter to the Churchwardens, but they involve what is, for the most part, quite immaterial perhaps.

1) "been induced (partly?)against the better judgment" might possibly be qualified by "perhaps partly"

2) "instead of the <u>old</u> Holy Table". This was not <u>really</u> (as described by Memorialists) an 'ancient' Table but a mean inappropriate structure dating from about 1842–3: "previous" or "existing" might save the meaning: yet this is perhaps not necessary.

3) I have suggested an alteration to the 'work of architectural restoration': as possibly qualifying the substitution of one Table for another. The act might then seem more to involve questions of taste and archaeology, than of controversial <u>doctrine</u>: in which light it is naturally interpreted, when viewed by itself.

4) Does 'alledged' extreme ornament &c seem to cast too strong a reflection on the views entertained by the Memorialists?

5) The words "I enclose" wd perhaps involve an inconvenient <u>delay</u> in getting my Letter out, for it wd have to reach your Lordship in its corrected shape – <u>then</u> the churchwarden <u>privately</u>, before I was at liberty to circulate it with the others. Such words as 'I have requested him to send you' or 'which is to reach you' &c might meet what I proposed.

On receiving your Lordship's Reply to me, I shall understand that the Churchwardens have at <u>the same time received theirs</u>. A proper interval will then elapse while I am finishing the printing. <u>If possible</u> it wd be desirable to have them sent some time tomorrow (Thursday) for delivery by private hand.

I must beg the favour of an authentic <u>Copy</u> of the Letter to the Churchwardens: unless you request them to furnish me with the <u>original</u> for printing. But this latter wd involve greater delay here.

I could not <u>at all rely</u> on due publicity without what I suggest being done.

As regards <u>Flowers</u>, they were actually used by Dr Goulburn, & by me ever since being at the Church. The objection <u>now</u> is vexatious: and I must not <u>promise</u> to discontinue them <u>finally</u>. But I certainly will discontinue flowers for some while until our minds are more composed.

The <u>White Stole</u> shall be <u>entirely</u> discontinued: unless indeed I may at some future time first apprise your Lordship of any other course.

I will send your Lordship a copy of my Letter when printed off. Excepting verbal corrections it will appear identical with the Proofs already submitted.

With many thanks for your Lordship's great kindness & confidence

I remain, my Lord,

Yours most faithfully & obliged

H B Walton

358b Oxford. Clement Saint. R.

Rev N Moody 1855/[or 6]. No religious feelings, nor as to church. Rather tendency to attach themselves to their minister. About 100 householders of the shopkeeping class. 2 Roman Cath[olic]s. 8 Dissenters, a lingering Baptist meeting. A few earnestly religious Tradesmen. Moody attempts to get men of this class to work for others...6 or 7 Tradesmen as a committee work with him in the night school, – as to the lads & daughters of the Tradesmen. To these the Dissenters chiefly address themselves by Bible Classes &c, services for them. Moody has a Bible Class for this class & lads from 9.30 to 10.30 at the vestry – 8 to 10 attend it, going through St Mark =catechetical lecture – mainly taught by a senior undergraduate ....For the girls, M. takes a bible class of about 20, *aged about 13 to 20. <u>Not</u> mingled with the Sunday school at School or Church. 3rd rate shopkeepers he classes with poor. Not much professed immorality. No positive houses of ill fame but light girls residing with parents who do not like to drive them out. Spirit & beer drinking the great evil of the Poor. A simple spirit of religion in an undefined way amongst the poor. Yet more amongst the tradesmen than them. . Most useful 2 lectures one on Thursday & one on Sunday in School from 7 to 8.30. Persons by 20s come... collects & expounds. Night school for working men 18 & upwards, useful, for evenings in week from 7 to 8 30. One tradesman teaches & is paid. They pay 1d a week towards books. 70 on books. 35 average. It is worked in classes, reading writing & arth/m & the better readers read Bible with M[oody] or some representative. Many amongst the Poor & 3rd class of tradesmen, strongly disposed to Holyoake's secularisation. The main evil of the University in [ ]. Lower class of college servants irreligious. Magdalen servants best from <u>Rigaud's </u>influence.

Preach here for Ch[urch] Miss[ionary] Feb 15/57, collect £17, more by £5 than last year. Congr[egation] large. . largest Moody has seen & devout, as he in manner &c.

<u>Rev E A Litton.</u> Much the same state now. The small NB. tradesmen worst infidels, <u>especially shoemakers</u>. NB. Many college servants, Colleges to blame. The <u>Sunday breakfasts of young men</u> & this kept up by Tutors &c. giving breakfasts. Girls maybe earlier confirmed. Approves of rules.

Marginal *Note:* *N.B Like old Sunday School.

358c *Insert*: Rectory of St. Clement, Oxford.

	£	s	d
Tithe Rent Charge	74	0	0
Glebe Land –	15	0	0
Forest Shares –	3	0	0
Surplice Fees			
average about	18	0	0
Queen Anne's Bounty	20	0	0
Easter Dues –			
average about	16	0	0
Augmentation office	17	0	0
	£163	0	0

359b **Oxford. Ebbe Saint. R.**

<u>Rev G D Cameron</u> <u>Jan 26/57.</u> Few but the smaller tradesmen. The higher few good men. 8 professed <u>Infidels</u>. Tailors &c.(Deists) 3 mormonite (2) women *(1) carpenter – 89 Dissenters heads of families men & women. Men who make no profession of relig[ion] 118, women 98. Men who <u>occasionally</u> attend church 102 – women 126.. Men who <u>regularly </u>heads 40. women 62. – much real religion amongst the Dissenters especially Wesleyans. Bulteel left a large dissenting

body. Pews a great practical evil on this Parish, reason for absenting. . Tried a Scripture Reader .. & thought him during 3 months very useful. He went from House to House as C's agent [Sharpe].
March/60. I put in Griffith. John Taylor writes remonstrating Davenports letter March 60 "wretched cottage rent ill paid " Samuel Griffith comes June 26.1861. The Parish anxious to reseat the Church.

Population between 2 & 3000

360b Oxford. Saint Giles. V.

Preach here for Diocesan Church building Jan 27.1856. After at F Morrells rather too warm an argument with poor Vicar as for Miss Nightingale. F Morrell the strength of all good in the Parish.

Rev. G. F. Bullock. Jan 26/57.. The mass of shopkeepers are attached to the Church as a respectable profession. No earnestness. The female members valuably aid in District visiting &c. & many more pious. The lower tradesmen very loose as to Church hardly attend except aft[ernoon].. Many pious poor. Much good from Miss Hughes & the other Sisters visiting. The poor attached to Church. A great many of the poor go nowhere. Drinking the chief sin amongst the poor, especially am[on]g women.

Feb 1857 I preach here morn[in]g & confirm afternoon – all striking. Mr Bullock shews me his plan for new Church, but March 16/57 Burgess says the College wont agree because near parks & not near their building land. He Burgess will set up a temporary Iron Church for the poor.

Jan 12.60 Coll[ege] servants, difficulties. If breakfast parties were reduced in number, & allows confirmation by classes formed at once to prepare them for Communion.

GFB Approves of present age for conf/n congregations communions & alms increased, much owing to frequent confirmations. Lower middle classes being won back by an open seat evening Sunday service. Labouring classes still difficulty. District visitors sending out girls through alms.

361b Oxford. Saint John. P.C.

H W Sargent. Jan 26./57 – Chiefly college servants. An unsatisfactory set, bad church goers &c. Jan 1860. Mostly consists of college servants. Evils of Sunday employments unless early chapel be enforced on the men, so as to let the rooms be done. Unless the rooms are cleared no good is done. Thinks 16 a difficult age as to confirmation. Earlier [and/or] later – rule works well.

Choirs do they lead to growing indevotion. <u>Hackman</u> is afraid of daily service. <u>Chamberlain,</u> thinks it a great means of educating the mind. [<u>Paley</u>] fears the effect. [Mainly] men, good but <u>Bullock, Sunday</u> attend Wottons, 3 times a week. Effect very good, on boys, men very good. <u>Sargents </u>choir Sundays & Saints days good effect so long as watched. Very good effect on the men. Brought 2 from dissent & led in all to devotional nothing particular, but that weekly communion & offertories, which he thinks have been a great blessing to the more pious & to good undergraduates. I confirm here Nov.3.1861 & preach for his choir in the evening.

Preach in ante chapel April 19/63 & confirm in choirs in evening.

362b Oxford. Saint Martin. R.

<u>Rev R C Hales</u>. Jan 26.57. Scarcely any poor. 6 heads of House more or less Dissenters – one joined the Parish Choir. None active in Dissent. Church accommodation for 1000. Pop[ulation] 450. Mor[nin]g parishioners attend well.. Even[in]g mixed.. Some really pious men. Late Hodges.. corporation.. improved. Scarcely any poor. Nixsons school for Freemen now *an efficient & improving school.

Jan. 60 ... No college servants. Approves of present age at confirmation.. much the same. Comm[unicant]s increasing. Corporation still improving. Had all [few] churchwds [*sic*] to dine, & this works well. Parish choir a great help in getting hold of young men. A few years back Church Rate raised by casting vote. Last year no seconder to proposer of no rate. Hales resigns & Nov 27. 1860

Benjamin Charles Caffin comes to Ch Ch. to be instituted.

<u>Samuel Joseph Hulme</u>. Instituted, March 3.1863, on the resignation of Caffin.. Ordained D SO. Xmas 48.
       P–H Worcester June 3 55.

[*Marginal Note:*] * <u>Freeman's School Trustees</u>.

362c *Insert*:

THE OXFORD CITY LECTURESHIPS

A copy of a letter dated 6th August 1856, to the Rt. Worshipful the Mayor of Oxford, from W. Simcox Bricknell raising questions about the formal and informal attendance of the Mayor, and the responsibility for conducting the service and for preaching when the Corporation was not present for the evening service at Carfax. He claims that the City Lectureships are attached to the Corporation, not to the Church of St Martins – and could be given in any church in the diocese, subject to the incumbent's permission: otherwise Mr Hales would have a sinecure

363b Oxford. Saint Mary Magdalene. V.
with Saint George Chapel of Ease.

Jacob Ley. Attends Jan 26 1857 with Marshall & Macray; a considerable number of the lowest class in gutter &c. Number who beg, & no improvement to be looked for in those who have once learned to beg. The class <u>utterly</u> demoralised, promiscuous giving. Petition receiving the most injurious ... The small citizens from 24 to 30 a week. Men, great assertions of independence, & irreligion & vice. Not got any hold upon them – few dissenters. 4 publican feeling in Ch & St. a great deal of religion amongst quite the poor. Conscience towards God – but little distinctive attachment to the Church. He takes May/58 Bulls Living & on the 11th of June 1858 Richard St John Tyrwhitt comes to me for Institution. He speaks very pleasantly of following in such a track as Jacob Ley's. Going to be married to Miss Spencer Stanhope of Yorkshire.

Jan 12/60 Rev Macray. Few college servants except the highest & they very respectable. 1/4 past 1 opening of Butteries would, eg. for <u>Buttery of Exeter.</u> Balliol Sunday breakfasts. – Approves of present age. Parish much as it was in /57, at peace & much good. Working men not well got in hand. Asks about giving of alms. Great evil now from promiscuous giving. 10 or 12 [wd feel] afternoon service for them. Choir at St Georges very effective.

364b Oxford. Saint Mary the Virgin. V.

Rev C Marriott. Vicar. After His Paralysis, C Marriott asked me to advise his resignation I did so & he resigns & I accept it Dec 1855.

The Rev Drummond Percy Chase comes May 16. 1856 for Institution. The [living] have gone through the College. He takes it on the new condition (1) that he is not to vacate if he vacates his fellowship. (2) that so long as he retains it he may take any other College preferment which falls. (3) with an augmentation of income. He is arranging with Hobhouse so as to secure double daily duty between the two churches instead of separately in both. He means to keep the early communion except on the days when it is later administered. St Mary's Church declared unsafe & the University migrating Jan 20/57 to Ch Ch. // Only 3 actual Dissenters, 2 strong, one old man [hostile] <u>Marshall</u> – pours out that serving as ChurchWardens has improved the character. <u>Scarcely</u> any poor – trying now to get the servants sent for an hour. The evil of college servants from the long vacation, & from their hanging on with hope of becoming servants & so living on plunder.

<u>Jan 12. 1860.</u> <u>Only</u> 2 college servants regular. Opinion for present age &

rule. The opposite of Mr Wests – 2 poor people & 2 poor children & a Curate to [dumb].
<u>Nov 10</u> 1861. Preach at even[in]g service. Great attention. Collect £30 for SPG.

364 d – e *Insert*: List of Clergy participating in Oxford Mission. Lent. 1860 at St.Mary's and St.Giles'.

The Bishop of Oxford.	Dean of Westminster.	Rev.T.L.Claughton.
Rev. J. R. Woodford.	The Bishop of London.	Canon Stanley.
Rev. J. Lawrell.	Rev. W.C.Magee.	Rev.C.P.Eden.
The Warden of All Souls.	Rev. J.Mackarness.	The Dean of Canterbury.
Archdeacon Randall.	Rev. T.T.Carter.	Rev.H.P.Liddon.
Rev.Dr.Pusey.	Rev. D.Moore.	Rev.H.Drury.
The Provost of Queen's.	Rev. A.W.Thorold.	Rev.H.W.Burrows.
Rev. Alfred Blomfield.	Rev. W. J.Butler.	Archdeacon Bickersteth.

365b Oxford. Saint Michael. P.C.
<u>Rev F Metcalfe</u> Chaplain. Re Opened the Church, March 16.1854. Street architect. Trouble about the step on which Comm[unio]n Table. Mr Metcalfe being afraid of being called Puseyite. Happily arranged all & luncheon of amity at Lincoln. FM: excitable ungoverned speech. He comes over to Cuddesdon Dec 28 1855, as to the Rector's refusal to call a meeting of the College to consider now the Cures. I recommend him to the Bishop of Lincoln.
<u>April 9 1856</u>. An anonymous female parishioner writes to complain of the dropping of weekday services. I send her letter to Metcalfe with enquiry. His reply unsatisfactory, that attendance small &c.
<u>Jan 26. 57</u>. Many of the shopkeepers of highest class Dissenters. They are active in Business & throng into Cornmarket Street. None attend daily service. Very few poor ... comm[unican]ts 63 on Xmas day. 14 public Houses & a dancing saloon next to the Church: open on Monday from 9 to 12 kept by Mr Wart ... one R Cath[olic], 2 Jews. Few comparatively after confir/n become comm/ts.

366b Oxford. Saint Paul. P.C.
Rev A Hackman Jan 26 1857. Venables & Trinder. The upper most class morning churchers. The next tradesmen class 1/2 & 1/2. From past neglect, often personally religious, not many.
The class (2) is about to be attacked ... Out Parishioners fill the seats at church & keep out parishioners. Great preponderance of women in congregat[ation], & comm[unican]ts. A Sunday School for girls & boys of Tradesmen's class. Well attended. Some conversions

from Prostitutes. Full of interest. Sent up last year £50 to SPG, from poor.

In this Parish, the Great Blue School draws away 300 of the best boys from Parochial Schools and so withdraws them from all parochial influences. Jan 12/60 – Mr Hackman few college servants.

On the whole approves of present age of confirm/n. Rather leans to earlier. Main difference that has instituted communicant classes with great effect: 2 nights before the men, 1 night before the women.

367b Oxford. Saint Peter in the East. V.

Rev E Hobhouse aided by <u>Codrington</u> Jan 26.57. The effect of the Papal aggression still seen in disaffection in the parish. Between 3 & 400 artizans &c. in parish. All perhaps in communion with Church. Indifference to public worship a worst sign. Church services do not lay hold of them. All regularly visited by ladies of parish for temporal wants. <u>C.Cure.</u> Jan 12.60. Thinks college servants as a class better than domestic.. Thinks <u>hot</u> breakfasts <u>the</u> evil at Ch Ch only days they are allowed if the tutors set example numbers restricted to 4 or 6. But plan to represent to <u>Dean</u> S as to the Evil.

I preach here, Nov 5, at Hobhouse memorial meeting.

368b Oxford. Saint Peter le Bailey. R.

Rev R C Hales <u>Curate.</u> Quarrel between Mr Turrell Curate & him. July 1854 – sent Turrell away. Churchwardens take his side. Rate refused. They complain. Letter Sep 1854. I try to maintain R C Hales.

Henry Linton. Instituted Nov 8.1856, rather underbred ["Grad Painful"] allowed him to reside with large family at Rose Hill. He has taken a small house in the Parish for receiving persons. The Bishop of Ely regrets his leaving, had been 29 years in his late (first) parish, a pop[ulation] of 230... about £170 a year: less his present. Proposed if Ecc[lesiastical] Comm[issioners] would give £2000 he would give £1000 for endowment insuring his life for £1000 & so guarding against loss.

at the gathering <u>Jan 26.57</u>. The Thirst for Education so strong that the caste feeling does not prevent their going on week days. But for Sundays & religious teaching they must be separated. The smaller trades [being] people. <u>Begging</u> one great evil. Distinction between systematic begging & seeking relief in special cases. A great many college servants in this parish. The luncheon at 1, makes attendance on morning Church impossible. Small number of comm[unican]ts, pop[ulation] 1,500. Yesterday 38 only, devout & chiefly from the poorest. <u>None</u> of the small tradesmen.

H Linton. Jan 12/60. Great evil from luncheons as to servants. Exeter College best. Thinks Confirm <u>Rule</u> best, fears childish impression, classes for communicants. Agrees as to present rule of age as to confirmation. <u>Hobhouse's</u> plan of alms. The early communion alms at the years end to Church Societies. Later – given to Ch[urch] Warden given by Vicar & Churchwardens regularly to poor & sick. <u>Never</u> given to casual mendicants or evil lived people.

369b **Oxford. Saint Thomas. P.C.**

Rev T Chamberlain. In 1854 all trouble about Rewley School. Scott correspondence &c. In Feb 1855 Dr Macbride writes full account of one of his undergraduates deterred from Reading Scripture by Chamberlains sermon & prays me to communicate with him. This I do & also as to my connexion with His boys School & Robert's account of Postures at communion.

Attends with Fish Smythe [*gap*] Jan 12 1857.

<u>Lower class</u> of tradesmen, shaken as to dissent... not very religious. Considerable improvement in mechanic class. An annual confirmation bringing <u>all</u> under observation a great instrument. Many of the lower class really religious, & attached to the Church. The very bad improved. Only one man Lawrence Wyatt a retired publican who allows his house to be brothels. Numbers absolutely degraded in scale of society, no regular work. The habit of begging a great demoralizer, destroys truth, self respect & honesty. Before a confirmation, Public Teaching by Chamb[erlain]. Then everyone put under someone (well educated & religious persons), who undertakes to instruct them. The whole children almost all of the Parish under education. Only one family (he knows) goes to Dissenting Schools. Some to St Peter le Bailey Schools. – Sunday School teacher & district visitors knowing little of distinctive doctrine a cause of poor being alienated. J H Blunt resigns June 58 because <u>T Chamberlain</u> cannot sympathise with Sisterhood &c.

Jan 12/60 no college servants: would like more put on spiritual preparation than age at confirmation, by trying the <u>whole </u>church system not particular parts, such as Bible Classes. Found Saints Day services very useful with frequent confirmation & vigorous preparation. Early communions & to bring people after & <u>not </u>to make all weekly comm/ts especially Festival Service.

go on to 610

610 **St Thomas Oxford**.

Broughton.

<u>Rev T Chamberlain</u>. I preach for Schools & celebrate Feb 2/62 Purification. The communion table seeming arranged to make me consecrate in front but I went to the N Side. Still too much prostration at receiving. C. & Curate keep the cup in their own hands always, &c.

370b **Oxford. Holy Trinity. P.C.**
Rev Jos. West. Jan 1860. His aristocracy did consist of college servants. They were most irreligious mainly attributable to their seeing clergymen in their undress motives. This leads to want of religious Family life. This the great bad. Schools have tended to declining sense of parental obligations. Also evening services, which came in with Dissenters. Then taken up by Cecil, so family catechizing &c. go out & Family religion declines. 11 o'clock & 3 PM the good old times. Want of sense of responsibility. Then see the evil increasing: dissipation within keeps pace with increased means without. Approves of present age for confirm/n. Many Beer shops & want of Parental responsibility. Preaching chief object. If I did more I should be in my grave..Cannot go to Houses. As large an amount of spiritual life as any in Oxford.

371b **Oxford. Summertown. P.C.**
John Sanson. Vacated 1855. The Rev E Palin (see ordin[atio]n Vol 2, p.63) nominated to it. He comes to speak to me about it Dec 10/55 – – Population increasing rapidly, Nov./55/1300.. The Schools in bad order, one only used by School mistress. Palin anxious to enlarge & mend Church by Chancel building &c. The College would probably with [*here there is an erased entry by the Bishop*] for the sake of amending the living. Perhaps Ryman might buy it & endow. Palin anxious for good.

Edward Palin. Comes Jan 24 1856 to be licensed to the P.C.

Jan.12.60. No college servants in his parish. The college servants gain too much from breakfast. Approves of present confirm rules. Thinks Earlier cases or very late generally best... ... Migratory character of the Parish one difficulty. Go on into St Pauls &c. United: increased alms.. Frequent confirmations have done a great deal. 1/2 yearly preparations – night schools – effective. Fears effect of choir unless watched produces deadness as to Public worship..

Francis Arthur Powys comes to me April 6 1861 to be licensed to it.

372b **Oxford County Prison**.

373b **Milcombe**. Severed from Bloxham.
Rev P Hookins. Visited it March 13 1858, nearly falling down. Hookins a good plan for its restoration: & has got one chief proprietor to agree to double or treble the rate. I see Miss Holloway about it at Hook Norton & write to Provost of Eton as to restoring Chancel. They both D.G. consent & the work goes on.

Nov 1860. Hookins resigns & Hodgson for his second nomination names H C B, who comes for license.

Henry Charles Blagden Nov 27./60 & is to build a house &c. there. Difficulty about site. I to write to Miss Holloway. Confirmed here Feb 25 1864. The little Church beautiful & the candidates even unusually attentive. Heavy snow falling.

374b

375b **Padbury. V.**
G Eyre.[64] Has inflammation. Richard Leak temporary curate brings candidates March 20 to Buckingham /59 –
Aug 3/59. Engages Rev H Robson.

376b **Padworth. R.**
Rev G W Curtis. Complaint Sep 1854 from Mr Griffith (Disley) of his alteration of Chancel roof &c. Sent it to Wilder: whose report rather unsatisfactory. Sent the case to Street. A most unchristian letter from Curtis to Wilder refusing to meet Griffith. Comes with a very few young people March 31/57 to Aldermaston confirmation.
Francis H Curtis Curate March 60, & the young people more cared for.

377b **Pangbourn. R.**
Rev H Breedon NB. Heard from Hobhouse that B. had offered to let the Parsonage on a lease of 5 (?) years to his mother – Q.
Poor Breedon dies Jan 14 1857. I hear that the next presentation sold after his death by his brother to pay his debts. J. Hopkins[65] says he had it from the solicitor but I may not quote him. Mr Hall the solicitor of Hungerford, told him that sold to Wade of Ryde but he could not raise the money. Young B Candy told him Do. Told as Creditor that his being paid would depend on the sale. After much communication Cap[tain] Breedon assures me on his honour as a gentleman that having intended unknowing of the pact to sell he had on leasing it given it freely to Mr Finch. Mr Finch after enquiry amongst relatives who might have covenanted to buy solemnly asserts the freedom of the gift. Mr Hopkins' of Tidmarsh letter of May 22 says no more can be done but Institute so May 23 1857 Institute Robert Finch from Can[terbur]y Diocese. Spoken well of by Arch[bishop]. Ordainer.
   Test[imonials from]Nares
   R.Warrener
   R Smith.

---

[64] According to 1845 *Clergy List* the incumbent was W.T. Eyre, instituted 1830. He died in 1868.
[65] Robert John Hopkins of Tidmarsh Manor?

June 28 young Hopkins writes to complain that Cap/t Breedon has removed the Credence & Stole. I write to Church Wardens to ask. Archdeacon goes over to settle it. Nov/57. R Hopkins renews complaints & I see Finch with Archdeacon & he <u>very</u> mulish. I refuse to advise about a letter in Union unless he consents to act on my advice, which he refuses to do. (Aug & Sep 59 his trouble as to refusing to take a corpse into Church because the man had been irregular in attending.)

<u>Aug 62</u> complaints of omitting Athan[asian] Creed on St Bartholomews. Write. He snarly. I reply see copied letters. <u>March 63</u> he comes to me at Englefield, very anxious to clear himself of supposed low Churchmanship.. Says he will set about restoring the Church, seems to feel the importance of it. I am more hopeful here. <u>Some</u> signs of life. Bad accounts of R Hopkins, supposed to beat his wife to live immorally very ill this Spring nearly lost sight. <u>Nov</u> 63 R Hopkins complaining of All Saints collect &c. missed. Finch will not promise to alter. See letterbook Nov 10/67.

378b **Peasemore. R.**

Thos. A Houblon. Confirmed here March 24 1857. I confirmed here before in 1851 on the same day. The birthday of Houblons eldest girl. A nice confirmation. 2 Eldest of H's girls confirmed here today. A nice School close to Church & parsonage.

379b **Penn. V**

Rev J Knollis. <u>Confirmed here March 12.1856..</u> Penn Street.. Tylers Green: Beaconsfield attending. A nice confirmation. Old Knollis much affected. Fine view from windows of Parsonage. Penn Wood destroyed! – T.O Hall, Curate April 10 1859 brings candidates to [*Illeg.*]

<u>Grainger.</u> Nominated on J Knollis death. A mathematics master at Eton. I confirm here March 25 1862. The Church greatly needing restoration. Mr Grainger fears Mrs Knollis will oppose & prevent L[ord] Howe giving. Mr G. very anxious that Tylers Green should not as Lord Howe seems to wish held with Penn. Mrs Grainger a daughter of Fells. They very kind & pleasant.

380d(ult.) **Penn Street. Trinity Church. P.C.**

Rev A S Butler. Lord Howe filling it on Bickersteths departure with Low Churchman. He Dec 1854 trying to upset local SPG. Correspondence with Lord Howe. Brings his candidates April 10/59 to Prestwood. <u>Thomas Bayley.</u> Ordained by me 1846 & May 47 (vide vol 1.83) comes Sep 21 for licensing. Has been 1st at Worthing then in Rochester Diocese near to C Pearson, seems humble & Pleasing.

381c *insert*
　　Piddington Church Accts. from Xmas
　　1857 to Xmas 1858 inclusive.

	£	s	d
185 Communicants. Sacramental Alms.	4	11	2½
Oct. 10 Sermon for Diocesan Church Bldg Society	1	0	2½
Nov. 16 Sermon for New Schools	14	8	..
Subscriptions from parishioners	71	3	..
Clothing Club for the Year from the poor	23	6	6
By Subscription from the Farmers	6	12	6
11 Baptisms			
9 Deaths			
5 Marriages			
	£121	1	5

381e, g *Inserts*:
　　Cuttings from *Jackson's Oxford Journal*. June 25 and 25 September 1853.

　　　　　　Election to Piddington Perpetual Curacy

[*The patronage of the living was in the hands of the householders, some 83 in number. The Bishop had prohibited the preaching of trial sermons, but it was felt that the clergyman serving the parish in the vacancy either had a better claim or else an unfair advantage over the other candidate. The newspaper described in graphic detail the slow progress of the counts on each of the two days. On the first, each candidate secured 40 votes, and Davenport declared the election void. Charles Hill won the second election by 42 votes to 38.*]

381b **Piddington. P.C.**
　　Rev Charles Hills (*sic*). Doing well – rough candidates for confirm March 1855 but seeming to have been cared for. Setting the Church to rights July 1855, pretty well by an Oxford Builder. Street makes some suggestions Aug 7 1855 which I write to Incumbent & Wardens.
　　Nov 3 1855. The Church having been nicely restored I opened it for Divine Service this Day preaching on Acts III, & administering. Present 10 clergy & nearly all the Parish. Mrs Hills pleasing with the children born May 54, 55 June. Married 53/ April 19 57 poor Hills Father in law writes that he brain fever & asks me to provide <u>cheap</u> curate, Deacon &c. Mr Whitaker Curate of Bicester at parish & Mrs Hills desires licensed. Aug 57. Evident he aiming at succession. Mr Hills recovers, asks for leave to dismiss him which I give.

Poor Hills creditors still troubling him. 1857 I persuade him to retire. He takes a curacy in Isle of Man[66] & I license William Gilbert.
1859 W Gilbert sets about getting a School. Builds a nice one. I preach there for it, going with L[ord] Carlisle. Total cost £581.13.8. Raised by Dec/59 £538.16.2. The rest raised in the year.

[382b] *Unnumbered page*
Pightlesthorne or Pitstone. P.C.
with Nettleden. P.C.
Vacant 1853 by death of Mr Weighell, with whom of old very painful correspondence touching his honourable obligation to resign it that Lady Bridgewater might build at it a residence & secure a resident clergyman. All this set aside by Lady B's death & now he dies just before the decision in favour of Lady M Alford. She corresponds with me Dec 1853 as to her duty with regard to it: & Jan 1854 proposes to build a house & present Mr Robinson to it.
Visited it with P Cust from Ashridge Nov 23 1854. Good yeoman layman there Mr Proctor who has mainly restored the Church internally. Preach there Nov.26.1854. Harmonium played by Miss Proctor & all promising.
March 1855 Mr Robertson declining it Mr Hutchinson who has been serving as Curate to be presented. He busy at this time applying for Bounty aid for building.
Charles R Hutchinson. Instituted. Oct 1857 writes arguing against sermon on communion days. I insist.

383b **Pishill. P.C.**
Autumn of 1853 C E Keene after years of delay obtains separation from Nettlebed & in altering Church had it fall down.
March 1858 Prince, appointed by Keene & giving him no satisfaction. P. comes to me, to consult what he is to do because his vestry vote that they cannot afford to put up a bracket for the elements I advise him to put one up at his own cost. Sep/59 Mr Webb of Stones Farm writes that Prince charges 2/6 for Baptism. Prince says for registering – I tell him illegal & require dropped.
John Haydon Cardew. D.Dec 19/47 R B & Wells. P.Dec 48. S.Bests Curate & well spoken of instituted July 25/60 by whom commended to Keene.

---

[66] Charles Hill retained the incumbency until his death in 1878.

384b **Pitchcott. R.**
W. Noble. Away for ill health March 1859 when I again visit the Parish. G.Gould Ross acting as temporary curate & well spoken of. Oct.59. He writes to resign having committed simony &c &c. Then letter from wife & from T D Fidler Whitehaven. MD saying he mad. I advise WN. to put himself for a time under medical care.

385b **Pitstone. [See Pightlesthorne.]**

Preston Bissett. R.
J E Sabin Rector. His son comes to me 1858. His Father insolvent, & with very little allowed out of the living for his support. His Father nearly imbecile, wants all kinds of impossible arrangements, getting some efficient man to reside in Parsonage at no cost, &c. &c. I say I will do all I can for the poor man but the duty must be properly done as a first matter. Young Sabin comes at Chetwode with P.B. candidates & an old nearly helpless not over respectable looking Mr Russell, who with Smith of Chetwode has been preparing the candidates. I repeat that I must have a due arrangement. Young Sabin to write.

386b **Prestwood. P.C**.
Rev T Evetts. Visited this again March 7. 1856. Always an encouraging place. So much manifestly done since the Church built in 1849.
A very large congregation & very attentive at the confirmation. I brought the Missenden people up here this time. A far more comfortable confirmation than there where all cold & unfeeling. Confirm again here April 10/59 a deeply interesting confirmation. Stay afterwards with good Evetts who doing very well. Some nice new glass in windows.

387b **Purley. R.**
Richard Palmer Wished to be included in Reading Miss[io]n 1860 & Leighton preached good attendance &c. Mr & Mrs Store (She daughter of John Willoubey) come to reside (when poor Popham died.)
March 1864 Mr Store anxious for restoring & remodelling. Says the Rector quite asleep. Old Clerk waiting for the Bishop to move something.

388b **Pusey. R.**
W Evans. March 1857 A poor account of Parish from Miss Pusey through Miss Hughes. Evans dies. Feb 1860 R H Hooper applies. Long

trouble as to Dean Liddells brother. Then Romanis.. Offer it to A Noel who *cannot afford. Then to Atkinson who accepts & whom I collate at Longworth April 2 – 1860.
> [*Marginal note*: Herbert Waddington C.
> P.R.Atkinson.

389b **Pyrton. V.**
Rev. C Conybeare The Church being in terrible state of dilapidation Conybeare sets manfully about restoration, & College & Lord Macclesfield being won by him to aid. The Church is set about 1855 & finished 1856 May, & on May 24 I consecrate it. Preaching on Ezek 14. Large congregat: & all very attentive. All working men & their wives as well as Farmers present. Afterwards at Hammersleys to meet the farmers all amicable.
George Marshall Tutor at Ch Ch. Comes July 1/1857 for Institution on Conybeares going to Itchenstoke. Letters of orders R Oxf. 43. 44.

390b

391b

392b **Quainton. R.**
Rev E Young. Walton complains 1856 that after my last confirmation here disgraceful public House entertainments. At my advice he speaks to Young who seems helpless... Negotiations 1858 for his leaving through Archdeacon. Confirm here March 26/59 & all depressed & miserable in the highest degree. 1861, & 62. Alfred Redifer Curate in residence & sole charge. E Young away.

393b **Quarrendon. C. [See Bierton.]**

394b

395b P.C. Ramsden separated Nov 30 – 1861 from Shipton.
Robert Lowbridge Baker. Licensed to it Jan 24 1863.. to hold with Wilcote. The holding Finstock with it being by him Abandoned. It is worth now £19.10.0.
The House cost £2.300. – £1000 from Comm/n £200. Publicly. Rest made up by Baker.

396b **Radcliffe or Radclive. R.**
John Coker. Rector. Comes with candidates to confirm at Buck. March/59. Mr Paulets eulogy of exposition in this Church. Quere were they J.C's.

397b **Radley. D.**

Robert Gibbings. I confirm here March 14. A nice service. Much talk afterwards about Kennington & letter written for Sawyer to Bowyer about it. Confirm here, March 31/60 pleasant confirm. Gibbings account of Bowyer's jealousy. No Bishop even admitted. I give to Dav[enpor]t to search into the rights of case.

397c *insert on black–edged paper*: Names of those confirmed by the Bishop at St Peter's College, Radley, on Trinity Monday June 8th 1857

Arthur Sewell, Dawson J. Greene, W.S. Greene, H.C.B.Bazeley, R.J.Raikes, Edward A.Gilbert, Edward Molloy, Alexander Grant, Alexander Bell, W.E.Knollys, Lewis G.Fenwick, C.J. Hill, R.M. Jennings, C.E. Salkeld, Nugent C. Wade, H.B. Griffiths, R.S. Godfrey, C.A.W.Troyte

398b **Radnage. R.**

George Phillimore. With a very nice wife ne Prescott, comes with candidates April 10/59 to Bradenham. Cordial now. March 30–62, confirm at Radnage. Crowded & very attentive, an interesting congregation. Amy Phillimore inter alias.

399b **Ramsden. C.** [See 395. * Shipton *has been deleted.*]

Ravenstone. V.

Wm Godfrey. March 17.59, comes over to Olney June 1 to confer & stays to service. Just married to a young woman rather looked down on by old Mrs Langley &c but said by Lloyd to be pleasing. He wants to exchange. I object.

400b **Reading. Saint Giles. V.**

Cecil Grainger. March 57, very ill with stone & nervous depression. Dies soon after – & after thought & prayer I offer it to T.V Fosbery, who accepts & which may God bless.. Nov 17/57 I visit him there. Meet clergy. Great SPG meeting in Town Hall. Next morning early go round the parish. Whitley Hill – where by pond Church wanted. Silver Street – His St Giles. Its courts, Ragged schools. Great intent. Question as to District of St Johns. Mr Blandy promises me more information.

Oct.1858 Dr Cowan stirs up strife about Ridleys book on Holy Communion. See all correspondence in Guardian of Nov 24.1858. – April 1859, J H Armstrong comes keeping a small living in Taunton. Bicknoller. Confirm here in connexion with Reading Mission March 3.1860.

NB – Curates W F Wilberforce, J H Armstrong, W.Fountaine Addison.
[Goulding] subscription for him March 1860. Feb 8. 1860 I lecture for Fosb. Address presented to thank me for Mission, from three parishes April 10/60.
July 12./63. Preached for his new Church, on Women at Sepulchre.
Nov 1.63. Preach for SPG. morning. Attend 2 SPG meetings in his rooms Nov 6.63

For Ch Ch see p 645

401a **Reading. Saint John. P.C.**
Rev F. Trench. Resigns Jan/57 & appoints his late Curate Will/m Payne, who seems disposed to be friendly agrees to preach March 57 on Arch/d Letter for Diocesan Board.
Declines to take part in Mission 1860. Evidently to his & Blenkins regret but they fear their party!
Fred B Blenkin applies for leave to have afternoon communion service Feb/60. Well behaved on my refusal.

401b *Insert*: From The Reading Mercury, 19 January 1856.

DEATH OF THE REV. SPEDDING CURWEN, OF READING:

We have to announce the death of the Rev Spedding Curwen, the respected minister of the Congregational Chapel, Castle Street, Reading, at the age of 66.
At the close of the service, the corpse was removed to the hearse, and the funeral cortege proceeded to the Cemetery, on entering which the whole line of carriages halted, and the following was the order of procession to the grave: –

The Undertakers,
Messrs, Atkins and Todman.

Pall Bearers.	Pall Bearers.
Rev. G.I.Tubbs, Incumbent St. Mary's Chapel.	Rev. J.C.Grainger, Vicar of St Giles's.
J. Rowland, Henley.*	Rev.F.Trench, Incumbent of St John's.

THE CORPSE

Rev S. Lepine, Abingdon*   Rev.W.Fairbrother,* of Maidenhead.

Chief Mourners:
Rev. J. Curwen, and Mr. T.T. Curwen.
Relatives of the deceased.

Mr. E.Brown, Jun. and <u>Rev. – Matthews, Vicar of Shalford.</u>
Deacons of Castle Street Congregational Chapel.
Revs. J. Aldis, W. Garrett, and J.Tyndall.
Revs. T. Welsh, and I. Caterer.
Revs. E. Davis, and W. Woolley.
Deacons of Broad Street Chapel.
Deacons of Trinity Chapel, Queen's Road.
Deacons of the Baptist Chapel, King's Road.
Members of the late Mr.Curwen's congregation.

Near the vault, the corpse was placed on tressels, and the funeral service, adopted by Dissenters, was read by the Rev. W.Legg: a pause was made, during which the coffin was lowered to its final resting place, and then the remainder of the service was gone through in a most impressive manner. The scene altogether was one of solemn interest, and demonstrated most fully the general respect entertained for the memory of the deceased gentleman.

The members and personal friends of the late Mr.Curwen, at the close of the service returned to Castle–Street, and the rest of the procession broke up on leaving the Cemetery.

[*Names of "Dissenters" marked by the Bishop.
The underlining is also in the Bishop's hand].

402a **Reading. Saint Lawrence. V.**

Rev J Ball. Who very fussy kind & pleased at my confirming here as well as at St Marys, March 12/57. Nov/57 he at once obeys as to Elements at communion. Comes Dec to a discussion with other Reading clergy as to a Mission at Reading this Lent. J Ball speech which Blenkin would not for any money have spoken. Vital difference between us &c. Vile suggestion that waited for Graingers death &c. Confirm here March 5 1860, a nice confirmation. J Balls sad speech to his Churchwarden. March 23/63 confirmed here, a really nice confirmation & J Ball very cordial.

402b – 402e *Insert : Programme of Reading Mission.*

Lenten Ember Week, Sunday February 26th–March 4th.

Parishes & churches in which Services to be held

Arborfield	Hurley	Reading (St. Mary's, St. Giles)	Tidmarsh
Bradfield	Hurst	Sandhurst	Tilehurst
Bray	Kidmore End	Sonning	Ufton
Brightwell	Lambwood Hill	South Stoke	Wallington
Caversham	Mapledurham	Stratfield Mortimer	Waltham St Lawrence
Earley	Moulsford	Streatley	Wargrave
Englefield	Pangbourne	Swallowfield	Windsor (New)
Harpsden	Purley	Theale	Wokingham.

Clergy participating in The Reading Mission. 1860

The Lord Bishop of Oxford	Rev. J.S. Blunt	Rev. D. Moore.
The Lord Bishop of London	Rev. H.W. Burrows	Rev. H. Pearson.
The Lord Bishop of Lincoln	Rev. W. Butler	Rev. Sir G. Prevost, Bart.
The Dean of Westminster	Rev. H.C. Calverley	Rev. J. Riddell.
Archdeacon Bickersteth	Rev. T.T. Carter	Rev. W. Romanis.
Archdeacon Randall	Rev. T.L. Claughton	Rev. H. H. Swinny
The Warden of All Souls'	Rev. C.J.P. Eyre	Rev. A. W. Thorold.
Rev Canon Stanley	Rev. T.V. Fosbery	Rev. F. Trench
Rev Dr Vaughan	Rev. A. Hackman.	Rev. C. Warner
Rev J H Armstrong	Rev. J. Horne	Rev. W. F. Wilberforce
Rev W F Addison	Rev. H. Lanphier	Rev. J. R. Woodford
Rev J E Austen Leigh	Rev. J. Lawrell	
Rev A Blomfield	Rev. R. Milman	

402f – 402g *Insert*: Correspondence concerning Dr Ridley's book, from the Reading Mercury. November 6 1858
[*Ridley was accused of publishing Romanising doctrine on the Holy Communion in a pastoral booklet which T V Fosbery's curates were circulating with his permission in Reading. A detailed list of objectionable statements was provided.*

The writers referred the matter to the Bishop, who on 22 October replied that to require withdrawal of the booklet would be 'a very strong measure for a Bishop to take. I have never, during the thirteen years I have held this See, so far interfered with the liberty and discretion vested in the parish priest. Nor can I conceive this to be an occasion for taking such a step. Mr Fosbery's courteous, wise and Christian letter shews, I think, with what entire safety such a discretion may be left to him, and will, I earnestly hope, when you have thoroughly weighed it, remove all your apprehensions.'

The agitators not professing themselves satisfied, the Bishop again wrote on 30 October, agreeing that some of the language in the booklet might be open to misinterpretation, so that Fosbery had ceased to circulate it, and Ridley had been advised to revise it.

On 4 November, the Bishop urged Cowan, the chief protestor, to publish the whole of the correspondence if he were intent on publishing any of it].

403   Reading. Saint Mary. V.

S W Yates. Lecture here staying at dear Levetts Nov 56. Confirm in this Church March 12 57. Levett gives an excellent report of Curate Calverley, good preacher. Yates I fear poor as a parish priest &c. 1860 poor Yates Paralytic seizure. I see him March 60. He intends next year to resign. Wishes now to be away. I assent. He is to have a third curate besides Calverley & William Romanis. (Aclands Letter), & I suggest Swayne. Confirm & preach here as opposite[67] in Reading Mission 1860.

<u>A P Cust</u>. Appointed by me, 1862.

I preach for Diocesan poor boys, Nov 2/62. Great congregation & good coll[ection]. D.G. March 19/63. I confirm here, large number & nicest confirmation ever had here.

Curates J H Jenkinson William Seth Few William Powys & W Romanis Oct 31.1863 Nov 1.63. Preach for SPG. Lay first stone of All Saints Church.

[404] Reading. Trinity Church. P.C.

<u>W W Phelps</u>. Nice look about candidates March 1860. Declines Mission 1860.

405   Reading. Saint Mary's Chapel, Castle Street.

G I. Tubbs. A good deal done that was nice in look of his candidates March 5 1860. He celebrates evening communion after I write to him my objections: Declines Mission 60.

Drops evening celebration with a snarl.

---

[67] i.e. as in the schedule of services inserted in the book opposite this entry.

[406] **Reading. County Prison.**
J H Colvill.

407 **Remenham. R.**
Brisco Owen. Comes with his flock to Wargrave. A poor account of him, little out, save with incumbent of Peppard.

[408] **Risborough Monks. R.**
Rev Beauchamp R. Confirmed here for the first time Feb 16 1856 a very pleasing confirmation. The young people gathered under a hot fire from the Baptists. The Church a very fine specimen of common country Church.
G S Finden Curate 1861 marries the daughter. His account of the Parish most disheartening. Scarcely any congregation all in the hands of dissenters. A mere handful come 62, to P[rinces] Risb[orough] to be confirmed.

409a **Risborough Prince's. P.C.**
C E Gray. Incumbent. Goes abroad for his wife's health 1853. Wishes to get a curate cheap. Rather troublesome. 1854 comes back & very troublesome about curate. Writes an improper letter Sep 5. 1854. – Objects 1860 to Partridge building a School for outlying hamlet. – March 17.62, confirm here. All most depressing. Church dirty & uncared for. Candidates Do. No males to mention, alas! alas!

409b
Princes Risborough.

	£	
Brook Farm Rent Charges,	56.	-----
Glebe 77a. 3r. 13p rental,	85.	-----
Allotment Field.	10.	-----
Gross value	£151.	-----
Net ditto,	£145.	-----

[*No indication of origin of this account.*]

Risborough. Saint John's. Lacey Green. P.C.
March 9/60. Tilbrook Curate. "Eccentric almost to aberration." Bick-[ersteth].

[410] **Rollright Great. V.**
[Rev T Brookes]. Dies by sudden Fall at his brewhouse on the Moselle Feb 1855. Alas!
Confirmed here March 19 1855. The Church well restored & School

built at a cost of £800 raised by C Flint. The aspect of the candidates very good.

Rev H Rendall. Comes for Institution June 27.1855. Comes with his candidates March 13/58 to Hooknorton. He & his wife dine at Barter's March 15.58. Some special talk with her & very much pleased with both. D.G. Feb 25 1861 confirmed here & baptised Rendall's child. He just having lost sadly his girl.

411 **Rollright Little. R.**
W. E. Stevens. Attends with candidates at Ch[ipping] Norton March 16.1858.

[412] **Rotherfield Greys. R.**
Joseph Smith. Go here with Arch/d Randall & Warden Sunday Oct 16.59, to consecrate High Moor Church. Built at Smiths sole expence who building Parsonage & giving endowment at cost of between £3 & £4000. Greatly pleased with day here & preached at Greys afternoon.
Horace George. Rev H.Monro, who I license Jan 14.60. NB His talk with [*illegible*] baptizing with sand &c & Eliz. Symons wonderfully high character of him.
North Pinder comes Aug.3 1860 at Davenports & is Instituted.

413 **Rotherfield Greys. Trinity Church. P.C.**

[414] **Rotherfield Peppard. R.**
Rev H Reynolds. A miserable attendance at my confirmation 1858 & March 7.58 I write to expostulate & beg him to appoint a curate.

415 **Rousham. R.**
George Dandridge. His Father R. before him. Confirm here March 8 1858, & lunch meeting most of the neighbourhood. Church quite unrestored, high pulpit &c. &c. The confirmation a little wild. Isobel Atkins Bowyer amongst them. The Cotterill Dormers all very kind.
Charles S Peel. Succeeded. Comes to Steeple Barton March 7/61. I confirm here March 4/64, all markedly improving. The Church poor & hopeless. Someday I hope maybe rebuilt. Could not apparently rouse the candidates. A grand attendance of Church Wardens, Way of Steeple Aston presiding.

[416] **Ruscombe. P.C.**
Leonard H Rudd serves it with Twyford. The wonderful nasality of his reading the service at my confirmation April 4.1857. George Parker Esq, gives an organ to the Church Nov.60. & seeks permission for its erection.

417

[418]

419a **Salford. R.**
> W E Stevens, R. 1854. Charged with intemperance &c. Allows the charge, after much enquiry, &c. as to Dawkins &c. Resolved that if he would sign a paper pledging himself if within 2 years he offended or frequented Cricket matches &c. he would submit to my sentence for the past I would remit it for the present. C Barter strongly advising. This discussing Aug & Sep 1854.
>
> 1863. Falls again into all evil & after a long correspondence agrees to leave for good & let me nominate Curate. R L Baker of Ramsden finds Delisle Dobree whom I license Feb 1864 meet him at Chipping Norton I hear a good report of him.

419b–d *Insert*:

Salford. Oct:14th,
1863.

> My Lord.
> In reply to your last letter I beg to say that having consulted with my family I am now prepared to assent to your Lordship's proposal that I should retire into non–residence upon your Lordship's licence & I shall be ready to do it on the 6th of November leaving it in your Lordship's power to appoint a Curate in my place – and I also undertake not to resume the duties of my parishes (during your Lordship's Episcopacy) without your consent.
> I remain my Lord
your faithful servant
W E Stevens.

[420] **Sandford [Dry] V.** (not 608)
> Rev T Curme. <u>Dec 1853</u> Complaint of Mr Burrows V of Steeple Aston that Mr C visited his parishioners. Mr C. in letter stated he always would do so. I wrote on being referred to by Burrows with Chancellors opinion &c. – He Jan 1854, charges the Chancellor with "Lying", & me with uttering a lie. Writes a most contumelious reply to my letter. God forgive him & teach me how to deal with such gainsayers. March 8 dine here at Dr Guests, & next mor/ng confirm, a really nice confirmation. Though Curmes reading of the hymn was slow & pompously conceited [*illeg.*] to a marvel. A long talk with him after breakfast & I hope restored friendly relations. I am sure I simply tried. Guest speaks well of his work in the parish but says he is sadly

excitable. He wrote a bitter letter against me in the Oxford Journal about 14 night back.

March 61, does not come with candidates, daughter ill. I condole.

421b Letter from T Curme: "The Convocation", *applauding the rejection by Lord Chancellor Westbury of the Bishops' assertion of the right of Convocation to meet and act, predicting a revival of persecution if Convocation were ever permitted to pass votes of condemnation for heresy.*

421d *Insert*: Editorial in *The Clerical Journal* March 22. 1858.
Defections to Rome
The writer argues that High Church clergy are driven by problems in the Church of England over some aspects of the development of the Liturgy, over the denial of Convocation, and over erastian appointments, to ignore the darker side of the Church of Rome. At the same time, Low Church persecution drives many Romeward.

421a **Sandford. [Wet]. Donative.**
Rev J Slatter. Bought by Hussey Sep 1853 with 2 farms for 16,000. Wanting School &c. Hussey wishing Slatter not to attend visitation in 1854.

[422]**Sandhurst. P.C.**
The Rev H Parsons. Feb 8 1856 comes to me: Mr Gibson having now given notice That he will on the 11th take possession of the School which he built & professed to give to the Parish but now in his anger resumes. Charges Parsons with Romanizing because he holds The Communion to be a means of Grace. All the neighbour[hood] with Parsons. Gibson hard up for money. The question is what to do about the Furniture. I advise Parsons doing nothing. Leaving all the furniture attending till he is thrust out. His daughters too so as to put G. if violent most completely in the wrong.

Gibson trespassing on glebe & taking bit of it. I advise letter proposing arbitration & if refused an action.

March 4.57. Come here with Arch & Mrs Randall. Sunday morning walk off with Arch to Gibsons to try & make Peace. After much prayer, a long struggle ending in his letting me bring good Parsons up to shake hands. This after a very nice confirmation in the very pretty Church we do.

March 10 – 1860 confirm again here.

423 **Sarsden. R. cum Churchill. V.**
Charles Barter R. Edward Holmes Curate March 1858.

[424] **Saunderton. R.**

F A Faber Rector. From the peculiar shape of the Parish I have allowed one duty. His Curate [Mr Batey Cauntle] comes Dec 1855, to aid Blagden at Little Kimble alternately with Fabers Saunderton Duty Faber paying £60 & Bl[agden]£30per annum to him.

Herbert J Phillips <u>leaves</u> Oct/59 in debt, trouble about his Testimonials. O.J. Grace Curate here.

<u>March 30 1862</u> Confirm here Sunday, quite a nice confirmation. Faber's daughter Edith [Curtis] inter alias. Visited him in his room. How stately looking asked aff[ectionate]ly after Henry.

425 **Seer Green. P.C.**

Rev Cockle. <u>March 13 1856</u> Mr Cockle again brings no male candidate for confirmation: this time to Chalfont St Peters. He assures me he has worked &c. but Miss Duprees oppose &c. I try to rouse him seeing that he is manifestly all asleep. Dies 1858, & Feb 25 1858 at Sonning I institute Rev Henry Herbert to it. Bishop of Capetown gives a good account of H. Sound, laborious & gains the affections of his people. Had been at Worcester Coll. got into debt. Left without degree went out to Cape & recovered himself..

Jan 31/59 he sends me plans for a School, for 50 children population of District 315. Only a Cottage School now kept by a Baptist wife of Carpenter. 2d a week. Proposed that 1d weekly be paid. Cost £150, raised 30. 3 Farmers no res/d gentry. A very nice opening by Archd[eaco]n I not being able to attend /59.

[426] **Shabbington. V.**

427a **Shalbourne. V.**

<u>Rev John Gore.</u> Jan 1859. J L <u>Ross</u>(see his letters) writes to complain of Mr Gore coming to lecture on Romanism in his Parish against his protest. I write to Gore, Oct 59. Rev T P Michell + <u>writes</u> that Built a School room at Bagshot 1 1/2 to 2 miles from Church 30 houses, 200 people & wishes Sunday service I consent.

427b –c

Insert: Letters to the Editor of the *Devizes Gazette. (Jan 1859) from John Lockhart Ross, Vicar of Avebury and Monkton, Wilts, complaining of the proposal that the Revd Mr Gore, vicar of Shalbourne, should lecture on Romanism in his parish on the invitation of a dissenting farmer, Mr Pinnegar. The lecture was not permitted to take place in either parish school room, and eventually was given in a schoolroom attached to the "Free Church" before about 200 people. Mr Pinnegar, however, was dissatisfied with Mr Gore for not attacking Rome strongly enough*

[428] **Shalston or Shaldestone. R.**
The Rev C Coker. Visited the Fitzgeralds here Feb 21.22.1856. Saw the Church with its affecting memorial of their son & daughter Geraldine. Each aged 10 years
The Church wretchedly restored about 1829 on plans of Miss Littledale I urged a real restoration which I hope will be carried out. Visited School, a nice new one built by the Fitzger/ds. Who have also built new cottages for the Poor.
Nov 19.1857. Coker writes that Mr & Mrs Fitzgerald will new seat the Church & send plans on which up to Street. I sent remarks assent, & suggest faculty. Brought some nice candidates March 24/59 to Westbury.
May 30. 1861. Mrs Fitzgerald wishes to add a South Aisle to the Church in memory of her children. I assent.
Nov 15./63. Spend Sunday here & preach aft[ernoon].

429 **Shaw. R. with Donnington.**
G F Everett. Confirmed here March 29 1857, a specially pleasing confirmation. Church within power of voice. Catechumens intelligent & affected. Ever: improved on acquaintance.

[430] **Shefford Little [or East.] R.**
Stephen Brown. March 27.57. A poorish creature of the Typhous low church school. Brings one or two to Welford for confirmation March 27 57. I understand he is chiefly occupied in digging his garden.

431 **Shefford Great [or West.] R.**
T.T Churton March 27/57 he comes with a good number to Welford chilled in Church so that I missed him after the service, low & wandering. March.1860. Randolph assures me that Churton subscribes to a dissenting meeting. Put up the dissenting teacher to pray in his presence & when a young woman asked for a book about confirm/n, gave her Spurgeons ridiculing it.

[432] **Shellingford. R.**
Henry R Dupre. Visited it again with Dr. Wordsworth March 18.57, rejoiced to find all going on apparently well. Here the Chancel had been a step below the rest of the Church. A seat for common people behind the communion table. Windows blocked up by monuments. Square pews &c. Now all as it should be Mr DuPre supported by his farmers. Wednesday Morn/s & Friday even/g service attended by them all. D.G.
Confirm here March 24 1860. A very interesting confirmation & all seemingly going on well. D.G.

433 **Shelswell. [see Newton Purcell.]**

Shenley. R. [Erased].
At Shelswell House, Mr Harrison parvenue wealthy. Close – Lady Louisa – Lord Clonmells daughter. Both there for Hunting People – a son & daughter– about 55.
[1855] Money made by an uncle originally a porter: after in Russia trade. Ecclesia Destructa – did not send son to Oxford after Eton because "cheaper to hunt from home".

Shenley. R.
Rev W Scurr. Visited the parish & confirmed in for it Loughton & Bradwell March 14 1859. A nice confirmation on the whole Loughton most Bradwell least feeling. The Church a fine old Fabric but much dishonoured W Scurr very hospitable. Mrs Scurr very fond of birds & a great number & many rare water in pond well wired in. Spoke very hardly of Knapp the squire living at Linford.

[434] **Sherrington. R.**
Rev A. King. Call on him with C Lloyd March 26 after the confirmation at Emberton. He pleased, & after stout discussion says he will give £500 towards carrying out Streets plans for restoring the Church & will apply to societies & set himself to the work. NB Bickersteth to attend a parish meeting.
March/58 asks Lloyd what did I say to the Bishop about repairing. "That I would set about it at once & give £500" "No did I say quite as much as that" "Yes if my ears could hear, very plainly".
March 17/59. Confirm again, for here & Tyringham, a nice confirm. But the Church not begun, gave him one more dig. He "hopes to see it begun &c".

Shifford. [*Bishop's writing: no entry.*]

435 **Shilton. V.**
Arthur Neate. At my visitation 1857, R Killmaster one of the Churchwardens presents the needing more Service. I write to Neate who replies kindly Nov 5. I consult D Adams & write again Nov 20, urging a curate for Shilton. Neate fully weighs the matter but decides that with the expenses of Schools &c he cannot afford a curate. After confirmation March 19 58 at Broughton much talk with him & he [willing] at once to have one with Woodman. Woodman refuses!
March 1.61. Comes to confir/m at Filkins with curate Edward B Welburn for Alvescot.

[436] **Shinfield. V. with Swallowfield. P.C.** [*Swallowfield is erased*] see Slough.
Consecrated an additional burial ground Nov 1854 & Preached. Rev B Bayfield. Preached & administered at the reopening of the Church after a very good internal restoration March 22 1856 Easter even[ing].
A good Parish congregation. The restoration Scotts work & very well done. Money in a great degree furnished by Hulmes i.e. they gave £800, towards it. W Hulme complains that too much spent in repairs the Parish ought to have done & so less remained for beautifying. Mrs Bayfield pleasing & they both seem right minded with an appreciation of Arch of York. But I fear no warmth of spirit.
He rather learned & his sermons too studied. April 3/57,Confirmed here. The Church very nice. An interesting set of candidates.
<u>Confirm</u> again Sunday March 11./60 again a nice confirmation. Confirm here again March 24/63, more in number & very nice.

437 **Shiplake. V.**
Rev Rawnsley. He communicating with me 1855, & early 56 about building a School for service in a distant hamlet. I press chapel instead <u>if possible,</u> but if not, assent to School. – 23 Feb/58 I confirm here, a nice confirmation. Nov 4.59, asks to nominate R Carden on £50 as assistant I agree & ordain him Dec 59. Then Sturges applies that R C may visit Wargrave. I assent.

[438] **Shipton under Wychwood. V. With Saint James, Ramsden. C.** 620.
<u>W D Carter</u> going for Church restoration March 1858 & all looking well.
<u>Feb 22 1859</u> I go down from London & take part in re–opening the Church which is <u>very</u> well done. A delightful day. C Barter the Warden 30 clergy & all heartily affectionate: a parish luncheon *[illegible]*. D.G.
<u>George Carpenter licensed by me to Ramsden</u> Dec 7/57. Confirm here March 1/61. Confirm Feb.16/64 a choice confirmation. Inter alias Ellen Elizabeth Carter.

439 **Shipton on Cherwell. R.**
Passand. Absent on sick leave. March 1864 A H Birkett Curate absent at confirmation.

[440] **Shirburn. V.**
Rev J Beauchamp. Feb 24 1855, confirmation here: for Watlington Pyrton not a very encouraging confir/m. – "Jesse Beauchamp". Curate H Martin fair in work but vulgar & forward. After next autumn to have two duties here. Wyatt from the college goes Dec & Jan 1855,56, & acts very foolishly. Knocks up in June 1856, & I release him.

441 **Shorthampton. C. [See Charlbury].**

Shottesbrooke. V. With White Waltham. V.
C Vansittart. All his family miseries. His wife turns Romanist. He resigns & Mr W W Yonge is nominated. His father having purchased the next presentation. W W Y, highly recommended by Pinder.

Wm Wellington Yonge. Instituted Jan 22 1857, seems in Earnest. Son of a R.D. of Winchester Diocese, of Rockburne // Confirm here Feb 28.57 a small confirmation but a nice one. Sawyer writes about intended chanting of communion responses March 57, which Yonge denies. It turns out a mistake.

Sawyer Blunderous. Yonge peppery & sensitive see letter March/57. Naunton Shuldam Curate resigns in 1860 to go to St Giles Oxford he wants another but only gives £80.

March 27.63. Confirm here, a very nice confirmation. Yonge ill in bed. His cousin curate. Luncheon Hazelwood who giving up the House. Denys W Yonge Curate.

Showell. C. [See Swerford.]

[442] **Shrivenham. V.**
Edward Berens. Jan 1857 he writes to me about rebuilding capella destructa at Watchfield, 2 miles from Shrivenham. Correspondence Feb 57. The trust deed executed by good Arch[deacon] for making this money over to Education, not forthcoming &c.

March 21. Street coming down tomorrow to see about it. Lord Radnor will subscribe if not too medieval. March 21 – 1857. Visit it. The Archdeacon much altered. Very full of rebuilding Watchfield Church. Street there today. I promised £10 & to consecrate wherever [restored.]. March 3.,1858, came to reopen Watchfield Chapel.

The Archdeacon greatly altered in the year, many infirmities of age on him.

Living worth £540.

George William Murray. From Welton le Wold Lincolnshire instituted by me May 26 1859, seems a nice fellow right minded & good. A friend of Lord Chelmsfords.

1859 writes Nov 16 to consult about Fairthorne, farmer of Lord Barringtons married uncles widow. Confirmed there March 23/60. All much improved. Vicar been ill, but better. [Flemyng's] health failing. H Suckling's work most highly spoken of by Murray.. He getting on with Church at Bourton. Alfred Lush licensed Oct 29/60 brother of V Lush late of Faringdon. March 7. 63 I confirm Bp Morrell helping, a very nice confirm. Poor Murray ill.

443 **Shutford. [see Swalcliffe].**

Sibford Gower. P.C.
Rev S Miller. Confirmed here March 17.1855. Church well attended though the day very wet. Miller presented several very young but in his choir &c. & probable communicants under his eye. Epwell attended & Mr Fielding, & good Payne.

Miller resigns – & 27th November 1860 at Ch Ch comes Edward Eliot, for Licence ordained by me 53 & 54. Vacates early in 64.

444 **Simpson. R.**
Rev T W Hanmer. He applies to me again by letter March 27 1856 to get him an allowance from sequestrators. I call & offer if he will have Mr Pearse of Walton as curate I will allow £75 to him he to pay Hanmer £38 of it. Hanmer almost promises to agree. To see Pearse & to try to get his cousin Col[onel] Hanmer to engage to recommend it to him. He refuses & I write to say I hope he will reconsider since if he finally refuses I must issue Commi/n 1853 April.

June 26.1856 I send the Commission to Bickersteth, Broughton, Binney, Hill.– appoint Pearse on finding of Commission. H will not let him officiate. Withstands all confirmation preparation. I inform him March/59 I shall not receive his Tickets for confirmation in consequence of hearing that he gives without any examn. Nov 58 Col Hanmer corresponds at last acquiesces. I appoint F G Wilson Curate. Hanmer very violent. I consult Chancellor

445a **Slapton. R.**
Rev Ludlow. Visited it Nov 23 1854 with A P Cust from Ashridge. A nice Church only wanting restoration. But a most vile Ch.Ch. 1816 built chancel. The Church damp hideous ditches round churchyard & sheep in it. Oct 1857 I hear from Cust that very unpopular in parish. A sharp petulant manner which offends, inefficient too in [pulpit]! Jan 7./59. Hear from Cust that charged with immorality with servant girl, & confessed bulk of charge, which well known. He submits & is suspended & the living sequestered & curate found by Cust appointed.

Sep 1859 applies to have sequestration & suspension taken off that he may marry & return. I refuse this but take it off on condition of his not returning without my sanction. See letters with Cust & Davenport files in registry. His letter promising not to return.

April 1860 write formally to remind him of this.

April 17.62 applications from Digby Walsh as to Ludlow on a quite false statement of Case by L

> Aug 1862 Little moving to Marsh Gibbon & the Brownlow Trustees agree to C F Porter as his successor. Porter about to marry Bickersteths niece.

445b (*Copies*.)

Oct.24th.1859. –

My Lord,
I engage not to attempt to return to Slapton without your Lordship's approval – and in no way to interfere with Mr Baker or any future Curate whom you may appoint – and as to the spiritual affairs of the Parish to communicate with your Lordship or Mr Cust – and as to the temporal with Mr Cust and acquiesce in your Lordship's retaining £150 per annum for the Curate —
  I am My Lord
  Your obed/t Servant
   T.B. Ludlow
The Lord Bishop of Oxford.

445c

Oxford 12th. Nov: 1859

Dear Sir,
It is my welcome duty to inform you that the Sequestration
upon your Benefice of Slapton is withdrawn upon the understanding conveyed in your recent Letter to the Bishop of Oxford, dated 24th ultimo –

Your suspension is also withdrawn on the same understanding. –
I have sent Mr [? Punter's] agreement to Mr Cust, who will
most kindly manage the affairs –
  I am &c
  J M Davenport.
The Rev/d T B Ludlow
Cheltenham.

[456] **Slough.**

In the Parishes of Stoke Poges and Upton cum Chalvey, Bucks.

Swallowfield
[*In the Bishop's hand*] separated from Shinfield.

457 **Somerton. R.**
The Rev R.C. Canon Clifton. Walked over from North Aston with Randall, March 12 1855. A wet & blowing walk. Examined the Church, a curious Crucifixion on the North Side of the Tower under the window, a very good D Screen – late – a curious Stone Reredos

representing the last supper as from Leonardo Da Vincis Fresco. Canon Clifton has restored last year the chancel arch, & repaired chancel & cut down pews: much still to do, pews to root out a hideous gallery & to open Tower. The Fermor now Ramsay family have a burial aisle.

March 8. 1858. A confirmation here & a very hopeful one. Many young men moved visibly. DG

John Aldworth Curate & I hope doing well. March 61, going to be married to a Miss Smith who has nothing & he only £100 a year.

W W Price. Poor Clifton dies 1861, & Nov 61 Price applies for institution on the nomination of the Trustees having bought advowson. I lay the case before the Chancellor & only institute on his written opinion that the act of Simony had been avoided. See Letter.

Oct 17.64 Custs Letter with Addisons charge. Phillimores &c. letters unsatisfactory termination.

[458] **Sonning. V. With All Saints, Eye and Dunsden. C. and Saint Peters. Earley. C.**

Rev H Pearson. Confirm here again Sunday March 1/57. A crowded Church & most interesting confirmation. Church quite beautiful since restoration.

Feb 24.58 I preach here during the Henley Mission & sleep. Pearson low mother *lately dead. Confirm 25th both very nice services. Lawrell, Bickersteth, Woodford & Carter preach here. Feb 1.63, with [ ] Reg[ular] communion. Dear P charming. July 12 preached & addressed candidates whom Bp. Morrell had confirmed in March. Capital congregation preached for School receive not Grace in vain.

* [*Marginal Note*] Curates Rev E F Clayton & H E Hulton.

459 **Sotwell. C. [See Wallingford].**

Soulbury. P.C.

John Hart. Vacates by presenting himself to Adstock. The whole income is £100 a year, paid by Capt Lovet. Mr Hart gives me a letter from W White solicitor to Robert Lovet, in which he speaks of a bequest from D.Verney Lovet, towards the close of last century. See book. There is one acre & ½ lying between Stewkley & Soulbury occupied by John Cotechings of Southcot in Linslade. Yields 2 guineas – given by [?Tarbox]

Thomas William Sandes Colles licensed by me Dec 13/61 at Islip. He recommended by Arch Bickersteth. Sets vigorously to work.

April 62 busy about restoring Church. Gets his parish to borrow £800 on rates & Squire Lovett to repair chancel. April 18/63 I attend at the opening, a good day. Between 30 & 40 clergy. The work well Done. Duncombes, Hanmers &c, here. Preach on Door Shut
Nov 14.63. Preach on opening of Schools, very nice Schools but the service, loud, highly gregarious & too rigidly demonstrative in ritual. Spoke a little to Colles. Troubles with his squire; A very good Yorkshireman Barton now come to Lipscombe.

[460] **Souldern. R.**
Rev L Stephenson. Offered to confirm here March 11 1855 but Dr Stephenson thought better not on account of the Typhus Fever which is raging like a plague. The medical man on the 12th prevented the candidates coming to Adderbury for fear of spreading the disease there. March 8/58. Comes to Somerton, reports his Church restored. Visit it June/63, very poor small work done in it. But he rising in frequency of communions &c

461 **Southleigh [See Stanton Harcourt.]**

Southstoke. V. With Woodcote.
Rev P Nind. Moving about Church restoration 1857
*Tuesday after Easter Week 1858. I preach at its re–opening.
John Ashby Stafford Hilliard appears before me at Cuddesdon Dec.17/57 to be licensed. Church has been well restored. J A S Hilliard very earnest & good. Swinney here in Lent Mission /60 & much pleased. March 26. 1861. I confirm here, & find Hilliards candidates well prepared. He just leaving for his own living of Little Wittenham. He speaks strongly of the good done by the restoration of the Church. George Carpenter who formerly was curate to Carter at Shipton comes instead of Hilliard & I license him March.26.61.
R Ibbetson Porter Curate. Great difficulties of past March 1864.
* [*Marginal Note*:] C[hurch] restored at cost of about £900.

[462] **Sparsholt. V. With Kingston Lisle. Curacy.**
Henry A Dodd consults me 1856 about indecency in Church porch.
Brings candidates March 27/60 to W Challow. Feb 8/61. Dodd nearly Dying, gets T Jenkyns formerly at Rhyll as curate. He not sober. I get rid of him. A low fellow too as to money I fear.

463 **Speen. V.**
H Majendie. Confirmed here again March 29.57. A large confirmation Church Crowded, all attentive. Robert Gordon Curate. Tried all I

could to [press] dear HM to begin restoration of his Church. He shrinks from fear of odium. But at night at Mr Chatteris's I succeed & it will be done. It is done <u>Nov 8</u>. Preach morning for Majendie, Heb xi.

DG a grand [*entry ends*]

[464] **Speenhamland. Saint Mary's. P.C.**

<u>J. A. D. Meakin</u> attended at Speen Church with catech: for confirm March 29.1857. March 60 Francis W Harnett second curate.

Spelsbury. V.
Rev J Williams.

Rev C Carey <u>Curate.</u> Confirmed here & preached to a most crowded Church March 21.1855 The Fastday. I much interested by their apparently great attention Chadlington & Chilton attended with Griffiths of whom Barter speaks well. All their candidates had manifestly been greatly laboured with. The old Vicar having come into a fortune talks of resigning. I tell Carey I shall remonstrate & try to get him to give some of the profit of his wealth to the Parish first.

Thomas Childe Barker of Ch.Ch. writes 1855 to say the living offered to him (I having after a struggle agreed to accept the Rev John Williams resignation. C Carey leaves) & he wishes to accept if I will allow a years non-residence to fulfil a present Tutorial engagement with Mr Talbot M P for Glamorganshire.

I agree & he proposes to Carey to return who on my advice accepts. On the 11th of Jan 1856 Mr Barker comes to me for institution – pleasing thin & black.He was ordained deacon by me in 1851 & I was pleased with him. By Bishop of Lichfield P in 1852.. July 14.1856, called with Barter & Lord Dillon to inspect the reseating. Done by Carey very well & cheaply. The Parsonage in a very dilapidated state requiring rebuilding. March 19 1858 brings his candidates seemingly well prepared to Charlbury. Married to a very pleasing wife formerly Governess as he Tutor in Welsh Talbots family. <u>Feb 1864</u> Barker away for ill health.

<u>T H Cookes</u> Curate. Friend of Lord Dillons brother of Gloucestershire Bar/t well spoken of.

[466] **Stadhampton. P.C.**

467 **Standlake. R.**

Rev H Biddulph R. Rev F Burgess Curate. Visited it March 27.1855, a roomy handsome Church hideously bepewed. The monuments to

Stricklands & Westerns from whom the property came to Stricklands having been bought by Westerns of Harcourts first Lord having built the House on what seems to have been an old park. A new School here. F Burgess gong to Fyfield. Great evils from always non Resident incumbent. Burgess encouraging & defending to me Sunday Cricket: presiding himself, as against drinking &c.–

Write to H Biddulph March 28 1855 about paying new curate full salary. Finding one &c.

Licensed Oct 27/55 Cecil Jarvis Clarke to the curacy a pleasing young man professing sound church views.

March 22.58. A H Nourse now Curate has had chest attacks, in respirator &c. Seems a nice & earnest man. Candidates brought to Northmoor well prepared.

Mr Davis from St Asaph Diocese who refused the comm/n &c. helping him pro-tem: comes March 4./61 with candidates to Ducklington.

Q what is Brighthampton whence some candidates come?

1864 I recommend James Pooley from Hambledon who NB. he cannot [*illeg.*].

[468] **Stanford Dingley. R**.

Holloway. Non resident at his other living in 1856. T W Cockell, Curate comes with flock to Bucklebury confirmation March 20/57. He succeeded Fosbery in his curacy of Etchel Hampton & spoke warmly, also as to this confirmation.

Daughters looked like Church woman he low.

T W Cockell Curate 1859 – 60

469 **Stanford in the Vale. V. With Goosey Curacy.**

Rev Dr Wordsworth. Confirmation March 1854 Sunday service very well done. Candidates well prepared. The Church very well restored & an excellent Parish Church. Visited Goosey chapel which also well done.

March 17 1856. I come down here to be ready for a confirmation tomorrow morn/g. Only Dr Wordsworths family. All but the eldest son & Miss Frere who now settled in the village & a good curate. A charming family. Oh if St Peters Westminster could send many such men into the Diocese. March 18 confirmation for Stanford & Goosey well attended, & a sprinkling from many neighbouring parishes. All attentive & promising. The East End painted window not yet up. Poor Mr Stephens grave close to Wordsworth door. He getting on well, but now too lonely. // Come here again March 16

1857 for confirmation tomorrow = As always very delightful. March 17 I confirm here: a most encouraging confirmation. Farmers &c. at a plain hospitable luncheon afterwards.

Confirm here again May 22/58 .. A very nice confirmation. Mary Wordsworth &c. 48 Females 26 Males (74.) Again all most pleasant.

Dr Camilleri Curate March 1860.

Confirm again <u>Jan 25 – 1862</u>. Again a very nice confirm. 49 confirmed.

469b *Insert*: Copy of Churchwardens Accounts for Stanford in the Vale. 1553, *containing a detailed inventory of all the Church goods*

469d *Insert*: Extract from sermon preached at Goosey, !6th Sunday after Trinity, October 1857.

- 1 Unbaptized aged 14 – Preparing to be Baptized.
- 10 who are still not confirmed and who have not yet yielded to the teaching of Christ's Church on that holy rite.
- 54 who have been confirmed, but who have as yet refused to partake of the sacrament of the Lord's supper putting it off as they think to a more convenient season or quieting their conscience, with various kinds of excuses.
- 19 houses of the <u>37</u> where there is no family prayer morning or evening Sunday or weekday <u>4</u> houses out of the remaining <u>18</u> where family prayer is <u>sometimes</u> used but not <u>regularly.</u>

We have also

- 11 grown up persons who have not entered the Church of their forefathers, nor once come here <u>to pray</u> during the past three years.

On the other hand there is much to be thankful for.

- 41 persons have been admitted to the holy rite of confirmation.
- 15 have become communicants who were not communicants before, and many it is to be hoped have been gradually growing in the faith of Christ, gradually becoming more & more fond of and devoted to the religion of Jesus, more & more earnest in their private & public prayers, in their acts of alms giving, in their love to God & man.

The true growth of the spirit of man in holiness cannot of course be estimated by figures, nor indeed seen by man except superficially and to a very limited extent. The Father the Son & the Spirit know of & take notice of this. The Holy Angels also look upon it.

[470] **Stantonbury. V.**
Rev R Quartley. Resigns 1855.6. Lord Spencer agrees to my suggestion to make it if possible supply aid for New Bradwell. In the course of 1856 it is served by poor Jos Rogers & the plan of union goes on.
Feb. 4.1857. Lord Spencer having presented Henry Brancker, found by Russell & friend of Swinney whose letter see in 1856, he comes for Institution. The company going to aid us as to Schools. Mr Duncan of Bradwell objects to the union as unfair to Bradwell. The Directors instigated by a relative of Branckers declare him a Tractarian & will give no aid. After a long business with Russell Trevelyan &c. it is agreed on all sides that he had better resign & a new man be appointed. He takes Thursley & so vacates & Russell finds a curate in Canterbury, (Hadlow.)
Charles Purcell Cotter whom I recommend to Lord Spencer & institute July 7.57. Seems a sound man of Evangelical School. D. Bishop of Cloyne/49. P.E Sarum.50. Brings his candidates to Wolverton March 18/59. I hear that he not managing very well & this the reason of hitch as to funds. Oct 59. R N Russell, very feverish as to Funds. I write to Dugdale &c. Second appeal of Lord Chandos & Russell to 1,6000[sic] subscribers only bringing in £291. They bound for 1,200.

471 **Stanton Harcourt. V. With Southleigh. Curacy.**
Rev W P Walsh. Heard from G Harcourt 1855, that old Walsh promised £500 towards a parsonage if his son appointed. Apply through Davenport for it. He allows but says that conditional on others producing £500 which they did not. Apply back to G Harcourt who offers erecting House worth more than his gift & Confirm here March 21 58. 73 candidates and a crowded & very attentive Church. An interesting service.
W P Walsh. Comes to me at Burford to say That £500 was paid Sep /58 by late Mr Walsh to B.Board to get £200. This never done because of alleged informality as to Bishops signature & attestation. Davenport written to repeatedly, & promises but does not.
The exec/s about to file a will in Chancery. I speak to Da[venport].

[472] **Stanton Saint John. R.**
Stonehouse. E Payne 1857 – Speaks highly of his former tenderness of conscience. I believe was mad during his latter years or so nearly mad with jealousy &c as to be scarcely responsible.
Dies 1859. To try to use the vacancy to get bound[ary] of Forest Hill & Cuddesdon better adjusted.
John Murray Holland. MA. R. Oxford 41.D. 42.P.
[*Marginal note*: NB R Gordon's Letter Dec 6/59]

473 **Steventon. V.**
Will/m Harley. Confirm here March 13.57, having reopened the Church after complete & good restoration 1856. <u>March 1860</u> His candidates marked in their good conduct & I hear all good of his doings in the Parish.
<u>Jan 1861.</u> Applies after Bronchitis for 6 months exchange with Rev J L Shephard of Abdon Salop, granted.
Gross value £260 with 2 or 3 acres of Land (62) deducting £90 on deed of mortgage on house so net £170. Harley moved to Turweston 1862.Jan, & the living offered by Dean to 5, & then to me. I offer it to <u>Herbert Waddington</u> who accepts.

[474a] **Stewkley. V.**
Rev Roberts Vicar & Swayne Curate. Obliged 1856 to put off intended confirmation here to go to Torquay. The candidates came to Wing March 6 1856, numerous & seeming to me to shew marks of preparation. NB. Mrs Fremantles statement from some Stewkley people that S's sermons jejune & gospelless. That diligent but thinking souls could be saved by Music &c. <u>To enquire.</u>
Roberts dies March /59. I offer it to G Phillimore, who reports that £2000 wanted for House draining &c. when it would be greatly improved. Then I offer it to Travers, who most gratefully accepts.
A delightful opening of his new School Nov 1860. All the Parish as one man. I preach.
Bishop Chapman confirms for me April 17 62 Consultation with Travers & agree to restore existing Church & hereafter try to get a chapel at South End.
<u>Nov 17/63</u> I attend, preach & celebrate at re–opening of restored Church. Well Done. D.G. & the parish gathers lovingly round T. in School.

476 *Insert*:

Stewkley Feb y 28th

My Lord Bishop,
In reply to your Lordship's questions respecting the value of this Living, I subjoin a statement wh. you will not find far from correct –

Rent of Land	£	353		
Value of Closes about		20		
Interest of £100		3		
Fees about		4		
Gross Total		380		
Deduct				
Land Tax		21	11	6
Rates about		5		
Net value	£	353	8	6

477a *Insert*:
And now My Lord, I must say a few words about myself I trust that in the disposal of this Living, my claims, such as they are will not be overlooked by Your Lordship. One claim I have to wh. I may refer without being guilty of self praise the claim arising from length of services, I have now been almost Twenty – two years in Holy Orders.

It is now about nine years since your Lordship invited me into your Diocese.

It is almost nine years since I took by your Lordship's desire & appoinment the spiritual charge of this Parish, & from that time I have had the sole charge of it. Although, I cannot flatter myself that I have so done my duty while here, as to attract your Lordship's special notice, yet I think I have, under no very favourable circumstances, & not without a measure of success, fairly done my duty.

Asking your Lordship's kind consideration of these points.
  I have the honour to be
  your Lordship's faithful servant
    James Swaine

The Bishop of Oxford.

475 **Stockcross. [Saint John's]. P.C.**
Thos W Burridge. P.C. Attended with Charlotte Owen wife & child at confirm at Speen March 29/57. Wishes for it next time at Stock Cross. Consulted with Majendie about it. He has endowed with £1,500 & now proposes to buy land with 7 or £800 more.

Feb 1858 at Henley Burridge resigning to take his Fathers living.

May 22.1858 John Adams from Exeter Diocese, (Grampound Curacy) comes on H Majendies nomination to be licensed. A somewhat heavy eyed man but well reported of. I hear that J.A has dropped the daily service. Majendie advised he has Wednesday & Friday prayers with catechising & will prefer daily service when in his own house near the Church. Seems quite high minded.

Consecrated the Church after the addition to the Chancel: preached &c. Nov 1 1864.

478] **Stokenchurch. P.C.**

Stoke Goldington. R.

[480a] **Stoke Hammond. R.**

[480b] *Insert*:

Stoke Hamond,
Bletchley,
March 26 – 59

My dear Lord,
I have much pleasure in sending you the subjoined statement of the gross & net value of the Rectory of Stoke Hamond.
I remain
Yr Lordship's
Ob[edien]t [humble] Ser[van]t
T Bouwens.

	£	s	d
Gross Income	304	0	0 [68]
Net	280	0	0

481 **Stoke Lyne. V.**
Charles Marsham. A kindly inefficient man. Resides with Admiral Styles at Bicester but constant in visiting the parish: which a bad one & he not revered. The children call out " here comes old Charley". Sir H Peyton March 1858 anxious to have something done. I talk to C.M. who agrees to support a movement for building a school. Says he would subscribe for restoring Church NB. This to be done hereafter. I consent reluctantly to its union with Caversham on condition of the future parsonage being built at Stoke Lyne. I press a curate on C.M. He says he cannot afford it. NB/ At hamlet of Fewcott a population quite Heathen & dissent.
NB H Kingscote interested in this parish. Confirm here March 8.61. A much nicer conf. than last time. Hear that C Marsham is active in the parish. Fewcott greatly needing some relief. The best to join it to Ardley. Build an aisle & give some NB endowment to Ardley. March 5 1864. Henry Joscelyne Curate brings a good many candidates to Fringford Church.

[482a] **Stoke Mandeville C. [See Bierton]**

Stoke Poges. V.
Rev J Shaw. Confirmed here March 14 1856. The Church miserably pewed up & very difficult to get the candidates well before me. From Farnham Royal & some from Stoke had manifestly been well prepared. Dec.16.1856. Mr Shaw came to me, to consult as to going for 5 years to Cape as miss[iona]ry retaining living. I told

---

[68] According to the 1845 *Clergy List* the gross value was only £249.

him I would not forbid but did not approve & undertook to consult the ArchB. Who decides against.

<u>Confirm</u> here April 10.60. Lord A Leveson Gower. <u>Confirm</u> again, March 27.62. Staying at Laboucheres. A nice confirmation. The Church has been very greatly restored, yet not quite right. No architect &c.

482d–482g. *Newspaper reports about the Boyne Hill affair.*

A hostile editorial published in The Times 18 August 1858, and correspondence printed in the Windsor and Eton Express June–August 1858, largely duplicating material annexed to the entry on Boyne Hill

483   **Stoke Row. Consolidated Chapelry. P.C.**
Arrowsmith first incumbent. Good & painstaking.

[484a]   **Stoke Talmage. R.**
Mr Kerby. Apply to Mr Kerby through Mr Brown Nov 1854 to get a resident curate. All happily settled & Mr Pigou a cousin of Goldwin Smith ordained to it Lent 1855.
<u>May 1856</u>... Mr Pigou asks to go with Bp Spencer to Paris. I offer it to Mr Hayter who has been at Kirtlington who accepts.
Jan 18. Confirmed here 26. <u>13 M 13 F.</u> A nice confirm[ation].
<u>W Byron</u>. Presented by L[ord] Macclesfield <u>Nov 9 1861</u>. I reopen the Church after rebuilding of nave. On the whole a most satisfactory change from what it was. Though not quite what it might have been had Byron dared. A<u> black</u> collection of clergy.

485   **Stone. V.**
Rev J. B. Reade. 1854 & March 1855 Trouble resulting from Mr Reades [ink] speculation, & Mr Lowndes of Chesham sequestration of the living. June 1855 Mr L. having written vehemently against Reade. On the 27th of June Mr Reade comes about his affairs: he has offered if they allowed Saunders Farm of £80 per annum: if they would restore him his £1000 policy = & he would give them a policy for £3.000 to be secured on the living.
<u>1856 May.</u> He writes that he cannot live longer all the income being taken from him. He writes <u>June</u> that he is going away at once; W Lowndes having failed in arranging the matter. Mr Reade came to me June 13 1856 to make his statement. I agree to write to W Lowndes to point out that if he maintains Reade will go: & I must appoint a curate. I to propose that they should retain enough to pay the policies £165 per annum & pay the rest £55 a year making the

living £220 to poor Reade. Reade presented by Lady Frankland to Ellesborough on poor Englands death. On the 26th of May 1859 Dr James Booth instituted, a Philosopher " more that than a Divine". C W R, seems a straight forward with a N Country accent corpulent & 50. Ordained by H Ex & JB Ches.

Nov 1861 Dr Booth candidate for lecturership here.

Jan 61. He writes "I have converted my coach house & stable into an excellent school. I have expend £700 on the House & offices & propose to borrow £200 from the land com[mission].

486 **Stonesfield. R.**

Rev F Robinson. Confirmed here March 24 1855, for Combe... (Barrett.) They seemed well prepared. Robinson's daughter confirmed. The Church quite detestable. A vast Pulpit raised almost to the ceiling & then curtained against chancel still higher. Curtained pews &c. Galleries all round in one front of which two ill behaving young women whom I reproved &c. One had withdrawn after first lecture on confirm. One been refused at last. I fear hardened in [impudence]. R's ministry I fear a weak & inefficient one.

March 14.58 brings a few candidates to Charlbury.

March 6/61 do to Wootton. The Church about to be much improved by his son.

487 **Stowe. V.**

The Rev Wm. Uthwatt. Residing at Maids Morton, inefficient & I fear a mere worldly man under wifes influence hostile to all church movement.

Oct 57. I write to him touching a second Sunday Service, he refuses the distance of the population from Church, darkness of Church &c. make it undesirable.

Proceedings in court begun for moving Church.. I write Nov 20 to know if the progress of these cannot be promoted.

[483] **Stratfield Mortimer. V.**

H C Harper V. Correspondence Feb/ry & March 1855 with Mr R Benyon: & Harper touching the offer of B. to build Chapel; House; & endow if met by Eton College as Patrons for outlying Hamlet – disagreement with Eton. Who offer little & disgust Benyon. At Harpers desire I consent to his building a chapel to be at present licensed for a curate to Harper. Dr Harper consecrated Bp of Ch Ch Aug 10/56 by ArchB of Cant. Bishops, Winton [Chichester] Oxon.

Aug 13.1856. John Alexander Clarke comes Aug 13 to Lavington with presentation & after demur & telling him I do not believe the

living vacant I institute him to [it]. Clarke formerly with Lee at Wootton.
[Feb/57] The Lord Chancellor nominates Mr Field of Reading Goal I reply that the benefice is full. Whereupon legal proceedings begin. 1856 I open the new Church at West End built by Mr Benyon. A very nice Church & parsonage to which A.L White formerly at Arborfield is licensed. Confirm at Stratfield Mortimer April 2/57, a nice confirmation. 1859 Poor Clarkes head affected. R J Gould takes the duty gratuitously. But *Nov.1859, I require at least £20 for a new 1/2 year to be paid him. Letters with Mr C. & Gould. 1860 Clarke Dies & Gould succeeds. Quere about not paying for Randalls Fly at Mission. Confirm here Sunday March 11.1860.

*[*Marginal Note*]: See letter Ap 28.59.

484 **Stratford Fenny. P.C**.
Steward ob 1855
    Population at census of 1850. 860.
    Income of the living £100 per annum.

annual rent of farm	£78		
Do of cottage & yard	10		
Queen Annes Bount.	2	11	4
Accountant General	8	1	0
Surplice Fees say	4	10	0
	£103	2	4

March 28 1856. Licensed Rev H Williamson to the curacy he being under bond of resignation to a son of Mr Bennett the new owner a very wealthy Iron Master & who has bought it & is disposed says Broughton to do something for it. Great dissatisfaction at the inhabitants of Sympson who form one half of the street & pay no rates &c. Having parishioners priviledges. T H Williamson propose to NB put them into the parish. If so Sympson should contribute to the Endowment.
June 1856 Mr Williamson applies for one of Lady Conynghams Lectureships. A very proper man for one. G R Scobell proposes to give up curacy here Jan 1860 for one of double value. St Pauls. Bickersteth says fond of the aesthetic part but very deficient in visiting. He Thinks Williamsons usefulness much over & that his resignation would be a blessing.
Charles William Barnett Clarke. Licensed Nov. 19. 1860, at Newport Pagnell.

[490]
See 622

Stratford Stony. P.C.

Rev C.M.Christie agreed March 13.1856 to plans sent by Mr Worley for cemetery chapel, with one or two suggestions for their improvement.

Joseph Boord Ansted is allowed by me after much doubt to exchange from St Simon Zelotes Bethnal Green with Christie & I license him Dec 23/57. He is highly commended by Swainson of Chichester Harvey Goodwin &c, & I trust if it please God may succeed. Ordained D. June 43. P. June 44 by The late Bp of London to curacy of Champneys at Whitechapel. He seems to me a sound & moderate Man. Preached here Dec 3 58 The first week in Advent, to a most attentive congregation.. Many attacks on Ansted, anonymous at length Mrs Smith well spoken of complains bitterly.

I confirm here March 13./59. The candidates few but seeming well prepared. Preach after for Spir. Help collecting about 52£.

Talk with Worley and Ansted & Lloyd much with Miss A. who at bottom of all trouble. Some gossip about Miss Smith & Christie stirred I suppose Mrs A's jealousy who venomous & [illeg.]: & she refused her teaching. Hear all stir & trouble in parish! Mr Trevelyans plan for new Church March. 59. Called & saw Ansteds having seen Smiths & proposed amnesty on oblivion of past. Mrs A. Furious. Preached to a full congregation in Stratford Ch. March 14.59.

William Thompson Sankey. After much negotiation Ansted gone to Longdon Staffordshire. Majendie to Cocking & I license W T Sankey to Stoney Stratford June 28 1859. Which may God Bless.

Nov 8/59. Sankey moving cautiously for rebuilding the Church. See letter.

Anon letter of Thanks Dec/59 for his appointment. Nov 15.62. I there. !6th address Commun morning. Preach even/g. Adjust difference between good Trevelyans & S about T's new Church. Sankey not quite a gentleman & grasping. Presses for Henley.

491 Stratford Water. R.

Rev Coleman. A new churchyard wall Feb 1856. Mr Coleman dies suddenly May 1858, & there is presented to me Joseph Bosworth D.D. now Anglo Saxon.

John H Goffin a friend to keep residence until March 1859, when Dr Bosworth *comes from Send & Wickham Hants. Dr B. comes Dec 4/58 for institution. Said to be sound & moderate.

John H Goffin well commended, Curate, comes with Dr Bosworth to Chetwode confirm March.59. Rather pleasing.
* *Marginal Note*: Recommended by [*illegible*]

[492] **Stratton Audley. P.C.**
E Clayton. Excellent, Got Church & churchyard &c. done. Resigns Spring of 1857 to go to S Africa. May 12 1857 came to me
John Edward Tweed. Ord/n deacon by Bp Bagot / May 45 by me P. June 46. Chaplain of Ch [Ch] for 7 years then Master of Northern C of E School. He has been in ill health. March 58. Comes to Launton with small Flock, dejected about his parish, which a difficult one & he pupils: inevitable from poverty but ruin. Reopen the Church nicely restored 1864 3? March 7/64 confirm here. A very nice confirm/n. Tweeds family all here &c.

493 **Streatley. V.**
Rev J. R. Burgess. I confirmed here March 3/57, & slept at Mr Stones where most hospitably received. The Church old fears its decay.
1859. He is dangerously ill. A Testimonial of regard between £1 & £200 given him. Applies Oct 59 for leave to let Rev J Bussell brother of Great Marlow help him. I assent.
Confirm here, March 12 1860. Sad account of poor Burgess succession of Epileptic fits almost deprive of reason. In great poverty. Living about £200.
June 1861. Poor Burgess dies & I offer the V. to J Slatter (The Stones Pressing for J Bussell). Visit the House with him June 29 & agree to his purposed improvements. He accepts & July 1, I collate him.
March 16/63. I confirm here & stay the night. Church far too small for population, difficulty of moving from Stones. J S. thinks he is in difficulty. The Parish dreadfully improved. Old Wetherall seduces the House Maid at Kensington Palace & keeps her at Streatley. Burgess marries one of the Bastards for her money, & has no influence. Old Stone (Father) a profligate. I Believe Mrs Stone alone kept anything straight.

[494] **Stubbings. [Saint James] P.C.**
[in Bisham Parish]
W H Skrine
Studley Chapel. [Extra = Episcopal.]

495 **Sulham. R.**
John Wilder. Wrote to him June 25 on the sudden death of his wife. Visited the parish & modern Church March 2.57.
H W Wilder Curate March 64.

[496] **Sulhampstead Abbots. R.**
Robert Coulthard. Confirmed here April 2/57 for These Parishes Burghfield & Upton. Coulthard has put the chancel in order & would greatly like to have the rest of the Church restored but Mr Thwaites is unwilling. I spoke to him about it today & he did not seem quite unwilling. Wife died Feb 1860.

497 **Sulhampstead Banister. R.**
[See Sulhampstead Abbots.]
Summertown. [See Oxford].
Sunninghill. V.
A.M. Wale. All in a very helpless state April 1857 Eheu! Wale a good Greek scholar.
Aug 16/59. Found him early out visiting his parish & reading Pilgrims Progress to them. Preached Sunday aft[ernoon] April 12/63.

[498] **Sunningwell. R.**
The Rev G Sawyer. Rev F Lee Curate Jacob charges with having altered chancel &c. Confirm here March 31 1860. A small but pleasing confirmation. Poor Sawyer evidently doing all his best. He attempts his life Jan 63. I agree to his non residence &c. & put in as resident curate W H Young who has done well at Benson.

499 **Sunningdale. P.C**.
T V Fosbery. Curate A.Carey. I confirm here April. 7/57 a very nice confirmation. Visit School next day which excellent. Fosbery vacates on my Donation of St. Giles, Reading. I offer it to & he accepts C R Flint (C R Winton 43 & 44) & comes Aug 3. 1857 to Binfield for license. Which may God Bless.
Confirm here April 1.1863, & preach April 12/63.

500a **Sutton Courtney. V.**
Rev J Gregson. Good man very & very odd. His quarrel with Norris the Papermaker & unfortunate publications. Resigns alas Oct [illeg.] Theobald wishes for Ashwell. I discourage. Norris [illeg.] Geare. I reply D & C Patrons not T. Rev Howard Rice. Nominated & instituted by me Dec 28 1855. Married to Miss Irby, young Llewel/n Irbys account at Bray: but denied by Lord Alwyne Compton
see letter Dec 26.1855.
Trouble between him & Gregson touching delapidations. Hoard claims for him £182, including Gregson says claim for cottage pulled down with consent by Bounty Board. I pray them to stay law & advise arbitration. Gregson offers £80 & fixtures valued at £25 by

him at £21 by Hoard. I advise him to pay £85 & fixtures & Rice to take it. After considerable difficulty the matter so arranged.
Dec 1859 troubles with Mr Norris touching Pew doors.
March 1860 Dodson gives a very poor account. Rice so great a fool!! HR, Longing to change. James Evans Riadore Curate but going & Rice wanting another with small salary!

500b, c, d, e Sutton Courtney and the *Morning Chronicle*
Correspondence sent by John Thomas Norris, with the endorsement of a parish meeting, to The Morning Chronicle 18 January 1850 and to The Reading Mercury, 2 February 1850
The Rural Correspondent of the Morning Chronicle had accused Sutton Courtney of universal immorality, to the extent which led to its exclusion from the Abingdon Poor Law Union. The women were accused of having families by several men, naming the children after the various fathers; marriage was never considered before pregnancy was established. The young were accused of habitual drunkenness.
Though the vicar had involved some of the unruly young in churchgoing, the older men shamelessly played quoits before the Church door on Sunday mornings.
As a main employer of labour in his paper mills, Norris protests against these generalised imputations. The parish had become a Union before 1834. Despite the clergyman's determination to use police powers, no complaints had been recorded against the public houses. Quoits had never been seen until supplied by the present Vicar, who himself provided the equipment for the villagers to pay cricket. Many attended chapels in Abingdon, as many more attend Church. "There is not only no open and gross violation of the laws, moral or divine, on the Sabbath Day, but there is evidence of a decent and orderly regard for Christian duties prevailing amongst us."
Considering "how virtuous poverty has in sickness and old age the Union for its sole reward, and vice is offered a dietary in a gaol superior even to that obtained by honest labour" he wonders why their crimes are so limited, and he must "admire the moral principles which enable them to pursue the even tenor of their way in honesty and contentment."

501 **Swalcliffe. V. With Shutford Curacy:**
and Epwell Curacy.
Rev E Payne.. Confirmed here March 18.1855. Shutford attending. (Mr Salmon). A very pleasant confirmation from the number of Friends present & the deep attention. The Church very Nice.
* The Norris's there & youngest Mary Eliz/th confirmed. Gave her & Albinia a Euchardia & good Mrs Norris sent to Broughton to ask for

one for elder sister Annie which to send. Confirm here Feb 20.1861 <u>very</u> nice Again 1 Feb 26 1864 a wet day again. The confirmation on the whole pleasant one young woman from Epwell light to whom I spoke after the service in the Aisle.

Marginal Notes: * Epwell G Montagu Curate 1864.
** Shutford D W Teape from H Allen

502a Swallowfield. [see Shinfield [erased]] 4 pages on

Swanbourne. V.

The Rev Niven. Came here again Feb 23 1856 to spend Sunday Sir T F. coming down to receive me. Confirmation moved hence into Winslow. Nov 9 1863. Came here again with Arch Bickersteth & preached at the re-opening of the Church after a rebuilding of the Chancel & good restoration of all under Mr Wilkinson. Preached on Luke vi. 49 Arch[deacon] after[noon] Collections.

502b Swanbourne.

Mr Groves Statement			
21 May 1863	869.	7	
Architects expenses	100.		
Mr Nivens estimate of furniture	15.		
	984.	7	
Subscriptions to this date as Furnished by Mr Niven	865.	19.	6
Deficiency to this date	£118.	7.	6
Estimate for further works Porch (&c) omitted from the contract	72.		
	190.	7.	6
Expected contribution from the Incorporated Society	30		
9 Nov 1863 Total deficiency	£160.	7.	6

Contract for the Chancel after deducting for the old Lead £380. Architects & other expenses to be added. Chargeable to Lord of the Manor.

502e Financial Statement for the Bishop of the Diocese.

9 Nov. 1863

503 **Swerford. R. With Showell. C.**
Rev T. Harris. Confirmed here March 15 1855, for this & Hook Norton Rushton attending. The Church in good Parochial order. A good confirmation. Harris married to one of the Whitmores of Chasledon who very pleasing. The Study utterly cold. Attended March 13.58 with candidates at Sherrington.
Sunday June 28/63. Preach here on Death &c & consecrate addition to churchyard sad slopping by Belfry.

[504] **Swinbrook. P.C.**
W Raine wishing Feb 1855 to be non–resident for age. Proposes J Mason as Curate. I hear from C Mount of his & her hunting tendencies & make non-sporting a condition of Licensing. Mr Mason Feb 27, very huffy – not unnaturally. Mr Mason finds the house strangely haunted. Suspicion falling on old servant & on the Postman but never discovered. Mr Raine dies autumn of 1857. Lord Redesdale gives it to Rev Turner Layton.
Joseph Halifax meanwhile acting as curate, respectably. Comes March 19 with candidates to Burford...
G D T Layton comes April 29 to me at 26 Pall Mall for License to this & Widford Feb 1864. Poor Layton gone abroad in search of most needed relaxation & health.
J A Fenton allowed by me as old missionary[69]

505 **Swyncombe. R.**
Napier. March 1 1858, confirmed here for it & Pishill. Napier & Keene[70] on better terms but Napier will not allow the enlargement of the Church.

[506] **Sydenham. V.**
The Rev Wm Douglas Littlejohn. I go on the 9th of April 1856 to reopen his Church in the body of which he has carried out a very creditable work of restoration. A nice attendance. Peers & Prosser reading the lessons Conybeare & C Lloyd as my Chaplain from Cuddesdon celebrating with me.

507

[508] **Swallowfield**
John Kitcat. P.C. Separated from Shinfield... Kitcat brings candidates to Shinfield April 3./57.

---

[69] Fenton was in New Zealand until 1865.
[70] The Revd Charles Edmund Ruck–Keene, JP for Oxfordshire and Cambridge.

509 **Tackley. R.**

L.A Sharpe resigns in 1856 Inspectorship of Schools. Sensitive fanciful man. March 5 1858. Mr Dashwood says his School inspection very useless. He brings candidates carefully prepared in appearance to Kidlington March/58.. Poor Evetts widow & daughter confirmed.

[510] **Tadmarton. R.**

Rev Lea. Visited the Church March 18.1855. Has been sadly mauled. Found white wash hand bason for baptisms, concerning which wrote to Payne. Feb 1864 Herbert Linton[71] Curate well spoken of.

511 **Taplow. R.**

C Whateley. July 5 1857. I go from Cliveden & preach. Whateley abroad in [Salty Kammergut] Mr Birch temporarily doing the duty. The Church really horrid, & the empty pews dreadful. A very poor congregation of the upper class hardly any poor. The poor complain that in the end of the Church where they are they can hear nothing & so have become quite alienated. This is a bad case Domine Miserere. 1863 Whateley makes divers alterations at Taplow without leave, for which I pull him up. Feb 1864 Whateley going to build a real Chancel.

[512] **Tattenhoe. D.**

Vacant & S[72] Randolph applies March 1856 to hold it with the Curacy of Bradwell. After consulting with Arch & R Dean I consent April 10 1856.

John Randolph. Instituted by me July 2 1856 all the old people about say it worth £80 but JR. can only make out that it is £40 ord.n by Bishop of Chichester D./45,P.46. A nice hearty fellow.. Eldest son of Saunderstead.

513 **Taynton. V.**

Thomas Lewes inducted in 1818. Younger than Barter. Much respected for kindness attention & all secondaries well done. Not high toned in actual spiritualities.

Miss Rices quite admirable. 6 Sisters of Charity & very wise. Comes with candidates (& to dine) March 19 1858 to Burford.

---

[71] Really Hewett Linton junior.

[72] In the margin the name Samuel has been erased and replaced by John. He had been Curate of Bradwell since 1850 and became Rector of Saunderstead in 1866.

[514] **Tetsworth. V.**
Rev J Peers. Consecrate new Church built after such sad distresses autumn 1855. Mrs Peers all the day thought to be dying but recovers.

515 **Tew Great. V. With Little Tew**
    Chapel of Ease.
Rev J J Campbell Confirmed here <u>again,</u> March 14 1855. For <u>Westcote Barton</u> Lockyer With Worton Nether & Upper. F Wilson & Best. A cold confirmation but nothing wrong... B. doubts as to personality of H S, &c & not come to church whilst not clear as to all doctrine.
Rev J Hewitt C Comes March 9 58 to Sandford with confirm. <u>March 13 1858 for Little Tew</u>. attends conf at S Newington
Jan 12 - 61, applies for absence for a year for his daughters sake I assent.
<u>Confirm</u> here Feb 25 1864. Mr Campbell with his new wife, &c.

Tew Little [Chapel of Ease to Great Tew].
Henry Tudor Curate March 9/58 see Page 531.
N.B. William Henry Hewitt Curate 1854–1857.

[516] **Thame. V.**
James Prosser V. Confirmation (3rd) Feb 26 1855. about 70, & JP. says satisfactory. I should say fairly so, but the Church unquiet & a meeting house want of reverence common. The Churchyard to be enlarged: they hope by purchase or gift of meadow by Lord Abingdon. JP very anxious to move Lord William's monument. I undertake to negotiate with Lady Wenman: & succeed: But after few days she writes about memorial against from Thame. I ask for & she sends it leading Churchmen deprecate alteration. Can hear perfectly &c. = <u>1857</u> he proposes a curate for ordination whom I am forced to refuse because after several interviews he formally & dogmatically denies the remission of original sin in Baptism. I license Nathan Challis from Leicester April 58. Confirm there March 58. "Few of the confirmed communicate it had not been pressed on them". N.C.

Insert:
517b On referring to the several Clauses of the Act of Parliament and more particularly to the Clauses at p11 and to the general saving Clause at p37 I am of the opinion that the Justices and Commissioners had power to make the reservation contained in the Order and consequently that the reservation is not a nullity, nor the order bad on account of it. I am also

of opinion that the view taken by Mr Frankam in his letter of the 25th of March last is perfectly correct and that the reservation does not apply to one road in particular but overrides the whole of them

7. One obvious reason against the limited application of this Clause, is, that the last description of Road which is set out and to which if it is to be restricted at all it would properly be confined, is a Bridle way, and yet the reservation is a free way not only for persons and horses but also for carriages to the Chapel. It appears that by the case that Mrs Gill has been seriously inconvenienced in going to and fro on her attendance at Divine Service – Such inconvenience would upon the principle established in Greasly & Codling 2 Bingh *263 enable her to maintain an action upon the case against any party obstructing the way in question. And I am of opinion that this mode of proceeding would be the most advisable, and the most likely to lead to an amicable – or at least to a final adjustment of the dispute.

   Fred Thesiger
  (copy) Temple 3rd May 1850

*on referring to the report of this case I find the note to be "Any (the least) special damage is sufficient to enable the party injured to maintain his action against the obstruction of a public Highway" – F. T.

517c Copy of Sir Frederic Thesigers opinion
   May 3rd 1850

[517e] Words of the Reservation and the Justices order are these: & those in the [Guard] precisely the same –
   " Reserving nevertheless a free passage for all persons, Horses, and Carriages at all times hereafter to Midgham Chapel."

517d " Midgham A Register of the Christenings
   beginning in the year of our Lord 1622 Alice Lambe the daughter of Edward Lambe was baptized the 24th day of August in the same year " –

  Copied from an old Book of Midgham Registers.

517e Copy of Midgham Register
   1622

517 **Thatcham. V. With Greenham Curacy;** 601.
    and Midgham, Curacy 532
  For Greenham see p 601. after Yattendon
    Confirmation in it March 27 1854. The Church a fine old one greatly

mauled. Chancel restored by Mount of Wasing alledged that he takes rent for all chancel seats. The side aisle stopped out by glass & even the [squints] with dull plate.

The Rev H Hanbury Vicar, & long painful work with him. He always resting under the vilest imputations & in 1853 (?) being charged so that he absconded: promising *resignation – which effected only so late as Aug 1855, when Mr Milner presented. He comes highly commended by Birch of Prestwich & Dean of Rochester: for institution Sep 20.55. In opinions holds the doctrine of Baptismal Regeneration in its full vigour. Consulted me as to the three services.

**I confirm here March 30 1857, & all pleasing. Plans for restoring the Church & a considerable part of the money needed already raised. Evan Yorke Nepean acting as Curate & serving Midgham & Crookham.

Aug 1862 J H Milner resigns from alledged ill health & disagreement of the Place with him, & Sep 6 1862 comes to Lav[ingto]n Richard Edward Rains for institution. Comes with Tes[timonials] signed by W Pusey, who speaks very well of him. Only rather wanting in energy. Ordained D.52. P54 by Arch of Cant. R E R speaks well wishing for Curate. His mother & aunt have bought the advowson meaning it ultimately for him.

Marginal Notes: * John Henry Milner
** Henry B Stevens Cur. 59.60.

[518] **Theale. [See *Tilehurst.]** next page. *Erased.

Thornborough. V.
Rev D Watkins. Writes Nov.16/57, that has introduced the placing the elements on the Lord's table rubrically & will next year monthly communion. Fears lest the offertory collection should make people fear that it is made more numerous to get their money.

519 **Theale**.
T Butler. Confirm here March 12 1860. Rather A nice confirm. Butler odd. A good congregation for Mission preach 1860.

520a **Thornton. R.**
H S Templer. Todo about destroying Churchyard wall &c. Letter from Ashurst. Cavendish's denial forwarded to H Barton who will contradict, 1854. Went July 1855 to Inspect the site of Nash Church &c with Templer Cavendish Bick/th & Adams. Templers temper alas! Street reports in favour of new site & he agrees. Commee. appointed. He writes Oct 55 a troubled bleating letter about the

amount paid with my sanction to Risley during vacancy! Feb 1856. I see all the correspondence & speak plainly to him about it. He having consulted Sir G Rose, who says I cannot be touched, but on T's saying have damnified him. He touched at my expostulation. His distrust of Mrs Cavendish. Story from Russell & Perceval of her cheating her cousin Miss Lowndes about property.

Sir T Fremantle denies, only house left to Miss L. & that on condition of her living in it. Accounts as to new house. Church Schools &c. March 26.1856. Templer tells me that after interview with me at Whaddon he had it all out with Mr Cavendish & came to full reconciliation. D.G. The Church likely to be completed.

March 31.1856. New letters from Mr Cavendish & T. touching his encouragement of Tyrrel's claim to Mrs C's property. The Cavendish's view this.

March 57. Templer applies to retire to Curacy C. says he cannot get rid of tenant for 2 years. Mrs C. speaks out will not sign anything or help anything while T. is there. March 21. R.C. writes that will do nothing he can help to conclude matters for Nash whilst Templer there... I resolve to write & tell T.

Mrs Cavendish dies /58. After much trouble Templer & he reconciled

Chancel built & consecrated. Church to be sometime or other money slowly collecting. March 59

March/60. Correspondence with Templer as to paying Wyatt.

520b *inserted leaf in continuation*

R H Hooper comes June 6.1861 for Institution he has collected some £300 – for new Church. Templer giving trouble about dilapidations.

520c

520d

520e

521 **Tidmarsh, R.**

W Hulme = Hopkins[73] offers him the Rectory. First with conditions then refused. Then with none, but disagreements.

Hulme comes to me for Institution & resolves not to take it. Then off[er] to J H Worsley, he doubts, he & she come to Cuddesdon, resolves to accept if Hopkins yields about House. H refuses & so

---

[73] Robert John Hopkins, J.P., of Tidmarsh Manor.

ultimately H re-offers it to Hulme & he takes. They coming together to Cuddesdon for interview Oct 1854.

H H Woods. Having been ordained by Bp Winton 1829.1830, to Mr Hodgson's curacy at Wood Hay, & curate to Dodgson at Buttermere comes for Institution Sep 22 1855. Charged him to continue matters as heretofore conducted by W Hulme. He seems a highly respectable. Write to him Oct/55 specially to name his putting the Elements on the table rubrically. Young Hopkins have written privately to me as to this.

March 3.57.. Confirmed here. Visited farmers wife from Checkendon. Spoke to Woods about placing Elements on as ordered in rubric & monthly communion. Hopkins has quarrelled with him for building the new parsonage a few yards nearer the road than he wished! –//

Preached here April 1857 afternoon to a good & very attentive congregation. March 1860 included in Reading Mission Prevost preaching. Woods at Englefield professes warm desire for full reconciliation with squire. March 23.63 confirm here, a very nice confirmation. Hopkins will give £1.000 & let me nominate if only he can get rid of Woods.

[522] **Tilehurst. R. and V. With Theale Curacy.**

Rev John Wm Routh. The Church beautifully restored, re–opened by me. A confirmation here March 2.57. Cold but decent. In Reading Mission Lent 60 & well attended. Confirmed again March 19.63. Still a lack of earnestness in appearance.

523 **Tingewick. R.**

John Marsh. Succeeds old Justly Hill to whom G V Reed had been curate, in 1853 ... & dies in 1855 having praeter spem set himself well to the work.

John Coker whom I ordained P at my first ordination Dec 1845 with good hopes.

1856. Feb 21. A confirmation here for itself & parishes round. The young people not showing any great signs of life. The parsonage building is a magnificent House. Too good, poor Marsh laid out a large sum on it & it will cost Coker £2000.

The Church greatly wants restoring well, bearing frightful marks of poor Hills unfortunate activity in spoiling a good old Church. I begged Coker who speaks of a Thorough restoration when House built to move at once the com/n rails. I hear that JC. is not any great thing.. March/59, meet him again & think him cold & unclerical as to earnest [discourse.]

[524] **Towersey. V.**

Tubney. R.
W James Butler of Appleton, of which this is a hamlet. I consecrated the Church 1846.. March 1860 Francis Kewley Curate.

[526] **Turville. R.**
Rev E Scobell. Confirmed here March 10 1856. Some of the young women attentive. Only one male from the Parish.. No School in the Parish. The farmer Rixon at Luncheon said he would give £100 to Church on Heath. I trying to stir up Scobell. He agrees if a district Church for NorthEnd. Mem.

1859. He gets a Mr Wood, who drinks & I dismiss. Then deals for one or two. At length settles with Rev Arthur Maitland Sugden from St Georges Hanover Square with £60 & Furnished house. Dies 1860.

John Fitz-richard Hinde.. B.A. Instituted Aug 31.1860.
D. G Peterborough June 22 45.
June 46.

Comes from Norwich Diocese.. Mr Richardson settled at Turville Heath/60. Useful layman. Hinde moves 60.61 for Chapel on Heath: resisted by Mr Overy 1 of Patrons. Letter June 61.

Hinde, presented to living, June 61, proposes from Richardson aiding to build a schoolroom & begin service.. North End in deplorable state. See Letters.

Jan 19/61: from Ridley H Quits for another living.

July 1861 Overy as Patron finally refuses to consent to new Church or School as burdening the living. Presents J.H. Deane Chaplain of Bedford Workhouse. Well commended by H Ross &c. But seems to me a poor underbred helpless man. Confirmed there March 28 1862. The Church &c. very poor & the people not seeming well in hand. Rode up to Mr Richardson at Turville Park. I incline to one Church on the Heath.

* *Marginal Note*: Quere Christian name aged 50 in 60.

J A Wood NB

527b–f *Leaflet, with* Present State, and Plan of Restored Turweston Church, With invitation to subscribe to the cost. Plan of Turweston Village. [Hand drawn.]

527 **Turweston. R.**
Rev Jas Cockerton.
Candidates confirmed Feb 1856 at Shalleston [*i.e. Shalstone*] & seem carefully prepared Cockerton much affected by his brothers death.

Mrs Fitzgerald says he is much mistaken, i.e. tender heart under rough exterior. March 10/56 I receive an address of condolence from his Rural Chapter. 1858 after long forbearance, I urge him privately to resign his R Deanery. He will not answer a letter & after writing many & he dodging me when I was at Mixbury I revoke his commission. Hear from Stratton March 23 at Westbury that he will not answer him. Standing shooting *Barringtons coursed hares on the glebe. Almost cut now by all the Gentry round. Strange – does nothing in Parish. To enquire about the commission for exchanging of glebe. March 24.59. Comes with candidates to Westbury. I talk freely with him, he not angry. Recommends Whitehead as inspector. A heart complaint. Thinks he answered my letter! Has got a copy of his answer. Manifestly not sure that he sent it. Says that Strattons temper has so altered since he married Miss Wills. Will very soon be in his House, in a few months. Has had great expenses from his brothers death. Speaks fair.

Poor Cockerton dies, & William Harley from Steventon put in on [? Cureton's] nomination. Long trouble about the money paid by the nominee for the House. Stratton taken the Church restoration really in hand & Dec 21.1863 I come for reopening. The work very nicely done. Consecrate the churchyard Early service on morning of Dec 22 & address the people.

The Church restored at a cost of £1,200. Preach afterwards, Abraham & the [?vultures]. = Reopened the Church Dec.22/63 after a very nice restoration costing not much less than £2,000.

[528] **Tusmore [See Hardwicke.]**

Twyford. R. [Bucks.]

529 **Twyford. [Berks.]**
A.A. Cameron Curate resident & officiating Leonard H Rudd. I confirm here April 4/57, a very promising confirmation. L H Rudd very queer, declining March 1860 to being included in Mission. July 1863 an endowment of £100 a year for a curate here added to Hurst for this I try to get Cameron to use it as a happy occasion for getting rid of Rudd of whose uselessness I hear on all sides.

[530] **Tyringham. R. With Filgrove. R.**
Rev Jos. Tarver. March 26 1856 at the confirmation at Emberton consults me as to School room to be licensed for service at Filgrove. I agree if separated chancel. He assures that a Chapel impossible.... Brought over candidates to Sherrington, & nicely prepared, March 17/59.

Tylers Green 536.

531 **Tew Little.**
After much trouble to fill it Burgon finds & highly commends Charles Foster Garratt a cousin of the Wilsons as ready to take it. He comes for Institution April 23/58. is a very pleasing man, quod D.O.M.Ben[edicat]
Oct 1858 £875 raised for house original estimate £783 –5 –0. After Garretts *add/n £1.109.16.0.
<u>Sat June 27.63</u> attend here for Festivities for Princes marriage, consecrate Churchyard open School & Alm's Houses Built by Garrett as memorial of mother & preach.
* *Marginal Note*: Letter of <u>C F Garrett.</u>

532 Midgham P.C. separated from <u>Thatcham</u>.[in Bishop's hand}
<u>Thomas Barton..</u> From Manchester sent by Mr Wood whose niece he is about to marry.<u> An odd man,</u> trying to reconcile. Afraid of speaking about Baptism but avows holding the truth. Vulgar & unpleasing. Long contest with him 1859 as to double duty which he tried to avoid giving: only yielding to the legal notice of a commission.
<u>Call on him</u> at Newbury March 1860 I almost doubt his sanity. Wrote after to Churchwardens to know if they would maintain their charges before a commission.

533 **Uffington or Offington.**
Roger Bird. Having changed with Mr Tuffnell changes again with Henry Peter Gurney who comes for Institution Oct 27 1855. A pleasing young man. Friend of Trinders. Not extreme. Vast Church & seeming<u> hearty</u> in the same March 21.1857. Confirmed here. Gurney poor in health a cough &c. & the Church too large. Suggested to him Hawridge. His wife delicate. Said that not above 70 came to Church on a Sunday. Came from Tregony, here. The confirmation on the whole pleasing. He proposed moving the pulpit to the <u>West</u> End & shutting up the transepts, & [Quere] the history of Church deterioration. <u>March 23 1860</u>. Confirm here. Not satisfactory, cold. Few. Not seeming well prepared. Gurney wanting to get the 2 hamlets <u>restored</u> to Uffington.

534a **Ufton Nervet. R.**
<u>John F Christie.</u> I call here March/57. April 2/57 he comes with his candidates to Sulhampstead confirmation.
In Reading Mission Lent/60 & well attended.
<u>James Fraser.</u> Comes Dec 20.1860. The question of Church rebuilding going. <u>Nov 2/62</u> Reopen Church & preach & celebrate. Prov[ost] of Oriel in morning. A very nice work. J F doing excellently.

535a **Upton. V.   With Chalvey. C.**
Saint Lawrence Chapel of Ease.

Rev E Champnes 1854 very unsatisfactory person. Great trouble about curates House. April 1854 correspondence as to House building renewed.

Rev T H Tooke Curate. March 16.1856. Confirmed at St Lawrence Chapel, a very striking confirmation. A crowded but attentive & devout congregation & much feeling evinced by the candidates.

NB. Champnes threatening to oppose Tooke in the nomination of a Churchwarden.

Rev Louis Heurtley has been four years from his ordination to it with Mr Tooke at £70 a year, for the sake of work with Tooke & his work has been very efficient. Leaving now June 1856 for a College Living. 2/3rds of Mr Tookes own classes became communicants. – Tooke goes on well. – *1858 BP Sarum gives him living at Salisbury. I appoint Mr Cree on Arch Bickersteths recommendation from Dover, & Lovekin, on Woodalls. Jan 59. Tooke writes to me Lovekin drunk. (I write to Woodall.) & I fear unchaste.

1861 consecrate new Church at Chalvey. Cree doing very well DG. March.18/62 confirm at the old Church, an unusually interesting confirmation.

H R Whelpton Curate under Cree & doing well.

A G Begbie.

*Marginal Note: John Adams Cree.

536a Tylers Green. St.Margarets served from
Wycombe Haslemere & Penn. [*in Bishop's hand*]
Walter Gibbs. First incumbent dies Nov.1861. On April 23/62 at the Warden of All Souls John Power comes for license. Has been employed as missionary from Ryde in chapel to Merchant Ships chiefly.

539a **Waddesdon. First Portion. R.**
Rev Latimer.

Rev W Walton Curate. Confirmed here again Feb 20 1856, a nice confirmation. The place most markedly different from what it was when I visited it at my first Bucks confirmation in 1847. When poor Latimer confessed to me the truth of scandal against him & went into non-residence. Walton active zealous devoted to his work & I believe much beloved has refused a living of £400 a year says Mrs Fremantle because he will not forsake it. Oh how I wish he was not so vehemently a party man. Dies almost suddenly of Typhus Sep 1859 just as about to be presented to living. D of Marlborough communicates plans for future. Letters Oct 59. He nominates Burgess, Fremantles curate.

[540a] **Waddesdon. Second Portion. R.**
R B Burgess.. Presented by D of Marlborough to —

541a **Waddesdon. Third Portion. R.**
The 3rd Portion. He writes Feb 28–60, that through D of M. a School built at Wescott where 300 people for Schools & even/g Church on Sund/y. March 15–62. Confirm here. Things seem greatly mending. Burgess's a much quieter & I believe deeper ministry than poor Waltons. April 8 1863. I reopen the Church after a good substantial restoration. D of Marlb.& D & D of Buckingham Disraeli's Fremantle attending, & nice meeting after in School.

[542a] **Wallingford. Saint Leonard. R. With Sotwell**
                                                          Curacy.
John B Coles. Curate 1863.

543a **Wallingford. Saint Mary the More. R.**
Rev John Langley. Confirmed here again March 3rd an attentive congregation. The Church now restored well fitted for it. A new curate an Englishman. Confirm here, March 1.1860, a nice confirmation Langley said by Hoskyns to be a good deal softened. 1862 Langleys Paralytic Stroke, given over: but struggled back to life. March 12 1863. Confirmed here & a nice confirmation. J Baly recommended by me curate here.

[544a] **Wallingford. Saint Peter. R.**
W.C. Frith. Died after Paralysis in 1855, & the new incumbent W Hazel comes to me for institution at Lavington Sep 12/55. He is brother to Hazel of Nettlebed & brother in law to Trollope of Crowmarsh. He has been 25 at Portsmouth in the Grammar School, only taken occasional duty. His wife & himself Wallingford people.

545a **Waltham Bright. R.**
R Marter. He ill March/57, with Erysipelas in Head. His wife very ill with diarrhoea, his daughter very ill with kidneys &c. NB. Mr Duncan says nephritic complaints abound in this chalk country. The water contains 16 grains of lime to the gallon. Says it possible solution. W Heslop a fat man has for 2 years his assistant curate here.
March 60. Gerard Moultrie Curate seems to have done much: brought many to confirmation & seeming moved. Poor Mrs Marter dies April 1860. – 1863. Frederic L Currie Curate on Martyrs [sic]

going into non residence. Not I fear much in him. Son of Sir F Currie. <u>Aug 3 1863</u> I come to consecrate the new Church. (Streets his best) begun by P Wroughton & finished by his wife. His 2 sons confirmed in the evening, a touching & interesting set of services.

[546a] **Waltham Saint Lawrence. V.**

<u>Edwin Parker</u> V. Remarried to Rich Widow. Edward Garnier Curate. Confirmed here Feb 27.1860. Quite a nice confirmation. A few to dinner after. Mrs A E Garnier.

March 27/63 very much affected just lost a child. Wants March/63 an additional curate for house & small salary.

547a **Waltham White. V. [See Shottesbrooke]**

Walton [near Fenny Stratford] R.

<u>Rev G W Pearse.</u> Called & examined the Church & P's intended improvements. Might be made a nice simple Church of one halve. Pearse a good fellow altogether. His house very poor & mean but gentleman like in fittings up. He willing to take any work. License him to Sympson. 1859 – 60 poor him (unwell mad about Lady of Manor & harassing him with charges & me with letters. May &c. 60 Miss Fanny [ ] Pinfold hinderings.

The Church <u>re-opened</u> by me snowy day but capital congregat. 186. June 25 & 26 <u>63</u>. I conduct here a retreat of clergy.

[548a] **Walton [near Aylesbury.] P.C.**

W M Beresford resigns autumn 1857, & on the sixth of February there comes to me

Frederick Young to be licensed. The young man complained of for a sermon a very weak one at Phelps Church against all Church observances. Ordained to Trinity Church Reading & there for 5 1/2 years. Then to St Pauls Balls pond Islington. Then association secretary at Cambridge for Jews. Ordained by me at Cuddesdon 48, & 50. He is married to Mr Payne's sister of St Johns Reading.

Nov 8/60. Consulted me as to ev/g communion which he had begun & gave up on my advice.

549a **Wantage. V.**

Rev W Butler. Feb 21 1854. A confirmation here. All very striking the number 130 the manifest preparation, the proportion of <u>young men</u> showing the fruit of Butler's ministry.

Admitted Sister Harriet (Day) to the office of Supervisor of the Home. Confirmed 1856. A very notable confirmation.

Came here March 18 1857, all work prospering. The Church advancing in the material building & spiritual. School excellent: remarkable geographico– historical lesson by Blackbourton boy. Mr Trevylians home. The Home all visited & prospers.

July.30. 1857. I go there to reopen the now restored Church. Preach &c. A most happy day. The parish all of one mind. 1000 in Church. More than 200 comm/ts £227 raised for a def/c of £300. 600 dine in Tent & Butler seems repaid for his long service. He presses Mackonochie for Reading.

Sep 17/57. Come here for Ordination – services &c in the Chapel at Mrs Trevilyans. The ordination on Sunday 20th a noble sight. A little too much of ritual for my own taste but hardly any. Mor/g sermon very striking by Mackonochie. I preached evening.

Dec 10.58 Confirm here in Home & at Parish Church, having preceding night opened the Schools & preached at Charlton. Oct.16.60 I preach at the opening of the organ. Grand luncheon &c. Confirm, Feb 19.61.. Dec 2.61 confirmation Overstone. Confirm June 25/62 all as usual. W B. lived down opposition. The Farmers all speaking most highly of him. D.G.

Marginal Note: Curates 1857.
   Mackonochie
   Sawyer
   Harvey
   Porter
   Schoolmaster Palmer.

[550a] **Warborough. P.C.**
Herbert White. I fear March 64 things in a sad state of self contented neglect here – !

551a **Wardington. P.C**
Rev Charles Walters. Walked up March 16.1855 after confirmation at Cropredy & examined Church, & parsonage. The taking away of the gallery a great gain: the House too small in its rooms &c. & the money too much laid out on small ornaments but a wonderful gain to have got a resident clergyman. The Living worth £140. Comes March 11/58 with candidates to Cropredy.

[552a] **Warfield. V.**
C J.Furlong. Leslie Randall Curate Jan 1857 a movement to get parsonage & res/t Vicar. Interview with Mr King ? after confirm at Bracknell: I advise to get Mrs Webbs assent to a public appointment before Furlong recalled.

I am applied to Nov 59, to get him either to return or resign. I correspond with him & he resigns.

April 3. 1860. The new incumbent collated.

Francis Turner Gill. The next presentation purchased by Lady Sutherland for Mr G. Says £500... about 1858. Mr Gill going to build. I urge on him strongly residing in Parish till his House is ready, he assents. But strikes me as unsatisfactory.

Gets off on excuse. I hear that she says she never will live here. March 63 William Andrews appointed Curate Christmas 63 for 6 months when F G (*sic*) Gill to come into residence.

553a **Wargrave. V.**
Rev J H Swinney

Instituted by me 1855 on poor E Peels resignation. I come here March 18, & March 19 confirm, a nice confirmation service for Wednesday in Easter Week. Evening, meeting to form association for SPG. Ch.Miss Jews. I advise dividing into 5. 3 SPG 1 other. Much talk with S. whose heart all in his parish. Anxious to put Pigotts School on a better footing. £6000 odd left in 1796 for 20 boys. He wishes to unite it & Nat. Sch: making the P. scholars in it a reward class.. Also to build on Crases' Hill. the N E limb of the Parish a School room with recessed chancel for prayers. Cheales his Curate working well.

March 19, confirm at his Church mainly for his own parish with sprinkling from neighbours. On the whole an encouraging confirmation. Sep 22 1857 Swinney comes to me at Lavington.

Feb 25 – 58 I preach here, & 26 address comm/s & confirm.. All very promising Swinney's confidential communication [Lion]! Bickersteth Burgon Butler Lawrell Barne preach during Mission. On the 4th of June comes for Institution, good Simon Sturges for Swinney's vacancy.. Feb 1860 he applies to me to allow evening communions. I refuse. John Monkhouse left by Swinney here as Curate still. I confirm here Feb 27.1860. A very nice confirmation.

Sep 23/60 I ordain Henderson Fairbairn from E.Coll Camb to curacy Monkhouse going. Confirm March. 27.63. A very nice confirmation. Open the Schools. 62 Lord Braybrooke here, a good day. Confirm here 63. July 6.63 attend SPG in Schoolroom.

534b[74] **Warpsgrove. R. [No Church].**

---

[74] The pagination is as in the original, the alphabetical order of parishes being preserved despite the confusions.

535b **Wasing. R.**
W Cleminson. Rector. Struck by Paralysis & after long suffering dies 1857. Feb Mr Mount nominates the acting curate*: who comes for institution after the confirmation at Aldermaston bringing with him some pupils seeming well prepared.
Marginal Note: George Samuel Rees March 31 57.

536b **Water Eaton [See Kidlington]**

Waterperry V

537b **Waterstock. R**

[538b] **Watlington. V.**
Rev W Longford. = all troubles about Church &c.
  Jan 1857. Memorial from Lord Macclesfield..Hammersley &c. send for W L. who comes Jan 31.57.... He states his Case. He found no Girls School, & very anxious for one, got the site from Sister, & money from Nat Soc. Dioc Soc. £265 cost– £100 –£75 himself. C Baring promised £20, but it not being finished in his time he declined paying it. Hesters Charity of £28 a year – given ½ to boys ½ to girls. Schools &c cost him £8 or £9 a year. Jan/55. The vestry decided (Orvetto movente) that Hesters Charity not to be given to girls School. April 1856. Longford consented to a Board on condition of nothing being done but what he wished as to any allocation of its management.
Longford complains that Hammersley entrapped him into appointing a comm[itt]ee & at last he agrees to a letter I read to him in answer to Memorial.
Peel: whom I saw shortly at North Moreton (my letter) Nov 10, Nov 11/58 comes over Dec 15 – 59... Charge.. 1845 first movement for restoring Church of which public notice given 1845... Estimate £1,200.. £629.1.0 being promised matter dropped. Of this £99.9.6 was paid to Vicar. This he held...... [*illegible*] unquestioned.. till May/52... On being appointed Parish Ch Warden (56) Peel asked for account... "Would furnish one" which he never did... Through /56/57. – Parish meeting held in 1858 probably May...10 attended. Res[olved] such course far from usual & unfit. To appoint. comm[itt]ee equal, for 5.. Res. May 5.57: that no money obtained for purposes, than for enlargement &c " unsatisfactory". Mr Carter claims Chancel poor.
Arthur Rikey Horan. Ordained Deacon 56 by C Glos. & Bris. 1857 Priest Auckland Ba & Wells (for Montr) since in Dorset. Says he is

mid-way between extremes. In bad health I fear but promises well.

*Marginal Note: <u>Langford alleges</u>
  say £6.3.0. advertisement
  Architects Fees
  Pews in chancel £40

539b **Wavendon. R.**
The Rev H Burney. Confirmed here for the 3rd time March 28 1856. Rev Mayor Curate. A very encouraging confirmation. The Church full. The candidates numerous & devout. A well worked Parish. Discussion about Woburn Sands Church with Burney & Moore of Apsley Guise. Agreed that it should be built. That if present endowment could be got from D of Bedford at once should be a district Church. Agreed to recommend the patronage in Bishops of Ely & Oxford alternate. That if endowment could not be got then opened by license as Chapel of Ease to Wavendon until the £5000 to be left by Mr Moore should be forthcoming & that then it should be made a district. All which Mr Moore is if possible to arrange with Duke.
<u>March 3 59</u> Burney very strongly recommends his curate Mayor for Stewkley or other preferment on 11 years service

[540b] **Welford. R. With Wickham Curacy.**
William Nicholson. March 26./57. Confirm here having come overnight to Mr Eyres, where most hospitably received. W R Dickson an Irishman Curate of Wickham. A nice confirmation in all respects. The Church advancing to completion. Chancel still walled off. Tower & spire rebuilt. A nice School just built which I informally opened, cost £1000. Nicholson £100 Eyre £150, in proportion to whole expense. Confirm here March 21./60. A nice confirmation. Church incomplete whereat the Eyres annoyed .. <u>W L Lewis</u> married to a Herbert has been curate. Fell out* with Nicholson who rather difficult with curates & going.
 * 1860

541b **Wendlebury. R.**
<u>W.L. Brown.</u> Writes to me 1858 as to grounds on which to put confirm[ation]. Stumbles at Example of Apostles. I bid him to Cuddesdon & took talk much pleased with him.. See him again March 5/58 at Chesterton after confirmation & point out serious omissions in his Eucharist tract which he received well. Mr Lowe says very good, has done much in parish. <u>He</u> describes a religious

earnestness in it & most of his candidates coming to communion, inter alias 2 Daughters of his own of about 12. <u>Jan 27 1862</u> poor Brown dies in apoplectic fit having not a year outlived his wife.

<u>John R Armistead</u> succeeds. Try to get him to rebuild or restore Church. Parishioners ready to contribute for monument to Brown. A. suddenly holding back for fear of personal expence; going on Fathers death to Cheshire living. March 7 64 he promises me to try hard to get Church restored.

[542b] **Wendover. V.**

Rev Champneys. Visited it again for confirmation March 7 1856. The aspect of things the same. A <u>familiar</u> earnestness about some members of the congregation, unconcern about many. The lads confirmed as always here <u>very</u> few. Mr C. attributed it to Dissenting opposition. But in my Judgement this when properly met helps us. Arch Bick/h says that it is an earnest ministry only greatly wanting in distinctiveness. Consecrated an additional Burial Ground here.. Confirmed here March 9 & preached during Aylesbury Mission March 11. As always a marked want of devotion & reverence about the congregation.

543b **Westbury. V.**

Rev C Thompson Curate. Confirmed here Feb 22.1856 & examined Barringtons site of new House. Consecrated new burial ground.

<u>March 24 59.</u> Confirmed again, a nice confirmation amongst others Wm. Aug. Curzon Barrington & Richard Purefroy Fitzgerald.

Thompson going to be married again to I hear a nice person & with money. Oct 27/63. I re-open the Church & preach after a nice restoration. Arch Bickersteth preaches Evening. A nice gathering.

[544b] **Weston on the Green. V.**

<u>W.L. Dry</u> comes with candidates seeming well prepared to Kirtlington March 5 1858.

545b **Weston South. R.**

Rev Charles Lowry resigned in 1855. [Jan 13 *inserted over* "in"]. C L Roberts being Curate.

T Bagley Levy, a fellow of Queens takes it to hold with his fellowship & intending to reside. An odd married man & of some years. Mr Roberts comes wishing to stay a little longer. Mr Levy wishing him to go at short notice. NB. Roberts out hunting with Gar[sington Hunt].

June 1856. Mr Levy vacated by accepting Knights Enham Nr Andover & June 26 1856 I instituted The Rev G Hayton with good hopes. He does very well, as R & School Inspector. He takes 1858 the living of Niton on Southey's rejection by Bp of Winton & Feb 28 1859 comes T Nowell Twopenny.. from Little Casterton Peterboro for institution. Professes sound church, free–from–extremes views & speaks accordingly. The advowson has been sold by Queens Coll to Mr Birch of Henley Park & the sale not being quite complete when Hayton resigns the College present his nominee & Friend of his nephew Reynardson.

Reopened the restored Church & preached, 1861. March 62. He resolves to resign & try his fortune in Australia. Mr Reynardson presents H.L.Fanshawe whom I institute April 30 1862.

[546b] Weston Turville. R.

The Rev A Isham. NB his former troublesome correspondence about his preaching in the Scotch Schismatical meetings. Ever since which he has been as troublesome as he could be. Dec 15 1853, sends me signed by himself Fremantle & Harrison & Hughes a fishing letter as to "dis-satisfaction" about curates not licensed on acct. of Bap[tismal] regen[eration] views. This being really stirred up by the Records statement of the resignation of Rural Deans &c. and I fear greatly by Fremantles manifest disappointment & Bickersteths being appointed Archdeacon. Tried to reply with firmness & reproof & still a tone of kindness. May God give us Peace. Jan 6 1854. Their answer to my reply. Satisfaction &c. Writes to Post Feb/58 dissatisfied as to Cuddesdon Coll[ege] from Gol[ightly]. Publishes letter against me in Oxford Journal very insulting March 59. May God forgive him.

Dec 9.59 writes to ask my aid in reseating Church &c. Which I promise. The Church re-opened Dec 18/60. I unable to be present from being ill at Bath. Gave as promised £10. March.11.1862. Confirmed here. Really a nice confirmation & they very cordial.

547b Weston Underwood. P.C.

[548b] Westwell. R.

Rev T.G.Bode writes 1857 to ask to have dry communion service even/g of Passion Week. I object & recommend [?Evensong] with gospel as text. 1858. On Lord Derbys coming in asks me to recommend him for Canterbury Canonry. I write him a letter to send to Lord D. Brings his people March 19 to confirm/n at Burford

& dines. Pleasant & unassuming.. Gets living from Governors of CharterHouse 1860.

<u>Wilfred Fisher</u> instituted March 2.1861. Chancel nicely restored by Bode. A very nice congregation. Pretty little coombe with old Elms, rooks: good looking Manor & farmhouse, & a nice clean fresh stream. Feb 64 W F is not well & Winchester people [*remainder illegible*].

[Marginal note: W.S.Miller occasional]

549b **Wexham. R.**

Rev A A Kempe. An unhappy man in hot water with his Parishioners. Major Bent & others &c. I obliged to approve of their complaints against him as valid. Then sadly in debt. I allow him to appoint a curate (Fawkes) at a small stipend let the parsonage house & try to get a curacy. He takes the benefit of the Insolvents Act. The living sequestrated. Oct/55. Mr Fawkes comes to me to allow him by being paid actually £80 instead of the £65 he had consented to take to be paid up a £20 due before sequestration. I assent.

Poor Kempe always in trouble. <u>Nov 16.60</u> on complaint of Fawkes & after correspondence sequestrators to let <u>F F Fawkes</u> have the curacy for 3 years at £60 per annum 50.guineas stipend 6.13.4 /16.8 to repay arrears.

March 1864 troublesome correspondence March 13 I sent ultimatum to reside in Glebe House or be permanently non resident.

[550b] **Whaddon. V.**

W Pigott. Ill. <u>W J Baker Curate</u>. March 14/59 brings some rough candidates over to Beachampton. One very rough one.

551b **Wheatfield or Whitfield. R.**

552b **Wheatley. P.C.**

Rev E Elton. Lay the first stone of new Church, Jan 22.1856. Consecrate it June 10/57. Bishop of Kentucky &c. there preached with unusual interest on worship. Oct. Nov 1860. Poor Elton very savage with Swinney &c. about charge of neglecting parish, because they thought there was no case for Curates Aid grant. Confirm here March 19/61.

553b **Whitchurch. R. [Oxon.]**

The Rev E Moore <u>V</u>. Confirmed here April 1.1855. Church fitted up in the George III rd style well. Moore reads well, but too dramatically has little hold over the Parish. Eheu! <u>Nov 4 1858</u> Reopened this

Church. Preaching & catechising after a noble work of restoration. A great congregation. <u>March 1863.</u> Dry rot found everywhere through Woodgers neglect of providing any ventilation, when the Church restored. All in a terrible condition. <u>March 15 1864</u> confirmed in the now beautifully restored Church & all most pleasing.

554b **Whitchurch. V. [Bucks.]**
<u>Alfred Turner</u>. Confirm here again March 26.1859. A good deal done to the Church. But since T. had to resist Mr Butcher much opposition. Dissenters have got up a School & got most of the children. We no School. Turner moving for one & I promised £5. Difficulties about site. Poor Turner hopes of preferment from Lord Chelmsford. He depressed by poverty, says a man with £500 a year might do a great deal. A poor man downtrodden.

555 **Wickham. C. [See Welford.]**

Widford. R.
On the Death of Mr Raine Lord Redesdale presents G D T Layton to this & Swinbrook & I institute him to it April 29.1858.

[556] **Wiggington. R.**
<u>J Williams</u>. Attends at S Newington with candidates March 13.1858.

557 **Wilcot. R.**
Bush. Dies April 1860. Mr Pickering for his aunt offers it to W E D Carter.. who declines. After much settling it is not to be united with Ramsden but held with it.
<u>Robert Lowbridge Baker</u>, who had done so well at Slapton comes to Clerkes Oct 11.1860 for institution & is instituted. It is worth £75 per annum.

[558] **Willen. V.**
John Benthall. Good man but crotchety, does not like to preach Dioces. Past. Let. Sermon. Brings a few well prepared March 18.59 to Great Wolston. Sep/60 moving about Chancel. Wretched plans. Gambier pavings impossible &c. Visited the Church Nov.60.

559 **Winchendon Nether. P.C.**
Rev T Hayton. Preached in it Nov 19.1854. Mr Barnard having in some degree restored it. Rather a nice Church. The plan now on foot for uniting it with Cuddington in patronage or alternate Patronage of the Bishop of the Diocese.

[560] **Winchendon Upper. P.C.**
Rev F Cox. Visited it Nov 20 1854. A nice old Church wanting restoration round the communion table along the walls the old seats of the Puritan communicants still left. I get him to appoint curate. Weddell, Walton's assistant takes it working also with Walton at Waddesdon. Brings candidates to [*gap*]

1861 J Hilton Jephson, tried here again as curate after suspension private for drinking too much at Chieveley: his good brother at Hinton Waldrish testifying to his amendment.

561 **Windsor New. V.**
The Rev I Gossett. Dies 1855 & Mr Ellison instituted 1855. June 1856 I confirm during afternoon service inter alias. Aug J Miller candidates from Baptist Chapel for ordination a vast attendance & I think more sign of life than in poor Goulds days. Ellison reads the service remarkably well. Feb 29.1860. Confirm here. Confirm again March 30/63.

[562] **Windsor New. Holy Trinity. P.C.**
Rev H Hawtrey. Confirm here again Feb 26 1857, as always here a very striking confirmation from number of men & attention. Confirm again for soldiers &c. March 16.1860 good John D Jenkins has been labouring nobly with them. Francis Sterry too but he going. Ordain at Aylesbury Sep 23/60, Wm Thomas Image Curate Sal[ary] of £50. Francis Sterry Curate resigns [ ] of health. H.Hawtrey writes Feb 16.61 "To our very great sorrow my much valued & beloved curate &c. A more earnest real & devoted man I never &.

William T Image & Henry T Simcox Curates March 26 1863 when I again confirm here a very interesting confirmation amongst others Lord March.

563 **Windsor Old. V. With Chapel Royal. D.**
       Windsor Park.
Rev A A Cornish. March 1856. Cornish without consulting me stands for Chaplaincy of Union vacated by death of Rev A Hopkins but is beaten by 1 vote by the Rev Grainger assistant maths master at Eton, of whom I approve.

James St John Blunt. Instituted at Fosberys, Nov 12 1860. Confirmed here, Good Friday 1863. Pleasant confirm. Mary Blunt here, April 13.63.
Nov 3 [Oct.30 erased]/63 I consecrate the Chapel in the Park, & preach on Heb xi.

[564] **Wing. V.**
Rev Peter Ouvry. Confirmed here March.6.1856. Dunton Cublington Stewkley Grove Linslade attending. The Church crowded, but rather with gazers than prayers. The Stewkley seemed prepared. An air of indevotion about the Wing people which appeared habitual. I fear this is the tendency of Ouvry's ministry to intellectual excitement but no devotion.

March 14 62 confirm here again, on the whole pleasing. A want of apparent spirituality about O & his work.

565 **Wingrave. V.**
John Molesworth Butt. V. Feb 1856 after the confirmation at Bierton, said matters mending. One farmer given a good organ &c. £130 Lucas also a Brewer at Reading small Proprietors, strong dissent. He mending under influence of Lady M.Alford.. Met him at Askridge Oct 9/57. The farmer <u>Lucas</u>.. Beazley might do much. He speaks in all respects pleasingly. The dissenters proposed to poor Denton to give them up <u>the Chancel</u> for their meeting <u>as he never used it.</u>

N.B. Crockfords entry name John Martin Butt.

[566] **Winkfield.** & School.
<u>Feb 13.1858</u> Elliott proposes The Rev Sam/l B James to be Master of <u>Cranborne School</u>. Endowment £70 & House...with opportunity of private day pupils or others. The Curacy to be £140 a year. He of Evangelical School but apparently moderate holds regeneration in Baptism & separates from Conversion.

567a **Winkfield.** [Bracknell. Comprising parts of the Parishes of Warfield and Winkfield– this heading is erased.]
C J Elliott. Confirm here again April 6 1857. A tolerably nice confirmation. In vestry after look at plans: & agree to an alteration Elliott wishes for the Economy in them as prepared by Street. Reopen restored Church [1859] Jan 58 ? or 9.

<u>S B James</u>. Mr James late curate of St Nicholas, Warwick elected Master at Lord Ranelaghs School Cranborne. Elliott to allow him £40 to appoint deputy in School. Elliott anxious about Ellis district &c. & 1859. 1860.

Confirm here March 8.1860. Pleasing. Confirm March 26.63 a tolerable confirmation but <u>very</u> few males. Amongst others Mary Roma Ferguson & Florence May Elliott my Godchild, aged 16, & Gertrude Harriet Lyttledale 14.

[568] **Winslow. V.**
Rev W.W. McCreight. Confirmation here again Feb 24 1856. Large number of people but orderly, & the young people affected. Far too few males for the population. White Curate His Resignation &c. 1863, & (entry ends)

569 Winterbourne. [See Chievely.]

Witney. V. and R. With Hailey
　　with Crawley. Curacy;
　　and Curbridge Curacy.

Rev R Sankey. A confirmation in Woodgreen Chapel here March 26 1855, for W: Ensham, Bricknell Cogges Gregory Minster Lov: (Whitaker) North Leigh (Gillam) Hailey Rolfe. This Church too small for confirmation yet better than Mother Church, with its high pews. The pulpit moved in this which a great advantage. Stirred S. against pulpit. S: complained of no visits from Gillam Bricknell &c. &c. The character of people so unlike Farnham &c. Jerram had so symbolised Schools &c.that they think him a Tractarian [ ].
*The Ensham people seemed to me well prepared: do Witney. The Cogges & Northleigh entirely neglected. March 22 1858 confirmed at Woodgreen Church again. The number small. The congregation indevout but many especially of the Females seeming much affected. Sankey complains of the utter irreverence of the place. Bandinel says, "S. preaches excellently but is very unpopular. The Church people of the Place have always been above their teachers in church truth. Jerram lowered the tone of Church feeling by symbolising with dissent. He was personally popular. The trades class he conciliated by social intercourse, the poor by charity. S. has wholly withdrawn from first & is severe as to charity even at Union with last. Harrison unpopular. Mills popular. He does not think Mills very Low" Watts of Ducklington lodges with Mills, says Mills is lower than Harrison. Crickland says that Sankey never mixes, keeps no [company &c.] He seems to me utterly depressed.
Sep 1858 Sankey sends account of 57, having invested for account £150, & meaning to do £50 more. July 5 61 opened the Union Chapel with service & sermon. Feb.[16] 64 confirmed again at Woodgreen. Instituted F M Cunningham before the people.
Continued at Page 618.
　F M C. A little too much about money! Hear that he is starting very low Church. "Gospel coming again"
　W A Harrison, who has been the only strength here & memorialised

for by Parish dismissed as too high. W Mills from Curbridge weak & inefficient probably also going. F.M C professes much to me.
E Norman Curate since summer going too.

> *Marginal Note: C.Wm Mills
> C.W A Harrison.*

[570] **Wittenham Little. R.**
Rev J Hilliard. Has an apoplectic or Paraly/: seizure 1855 & goes abroad. A W Morrison strongly recommended by Lord Nelson comes in as his represent. He has a quarrel April 1856 with young J.Hilliard which I make up. He gives a miserable account of the state of the Parish. The dying out of Spiritual life not to be re-awakened. No dissent but no life, alas! The fruit of poor Hilliards wretched ministry. Dec 23.56, young Hilliard comes over to me, disagreement as to Morrison & as to Nixson also. Son came. […] of Dingford squire & does little. C.C.Egerton Curate 1859.
John Ashby Stafford Hilliard: instituted by me March. 26/61, having done excellent work at South Stoke. June 13.14. here, & preached. Church very nicely rebuilt, at large cost.

571 **Wittenham Long. V.**
J Clutterbuck. Confirm here for the first time March 9.1857. Confirm again March 30.1860. Clutterbucks interesting account of old man seemingly converted under my sermon at re–opening the Church D.G. Brought him to me & the old man loud in gratitude. Dodson says Clutterbuck very poor.

[572] **Wokingham. P.C.** St Pauls 621
Thos Morres. Jan 1854, moving for a Church parsonage & Schools near Crooked Billet here. Confirmed here April 4.57. A set of young people bearing little outward mark of previous pastoral care. All I fear very ill here. Confirm here on their special request March 6.1860 still all seems dead.. May 3 1861. J Walters comes he will build & endow a Church at the West End of Wokingham for 4, or 500. Have a district & the Patronage. I assent. Preached celebrated & consecrated St Sebastians Church Dec 10.64. Mr Morres promises daily double duty Adams to undertake it. Mr M against making it a separate district.

573a **Wolverton. V.**
Rev H R Quartley. V. A bad subject I fear. 1855 deep in debt & away. Agrees at length to be permanently non resident. The Radcliffe Trustees allowing him £[blank] per annum: all the rest to go to His

Curate whom I appoint Oct 20 1855 being The Rev C H Travers. <u>Resigns 1856.</u> I accept, hoping to get it for Travers find promised to Mr Trevelyan Mrs Percivals brother. Travers behaves <u>exceedingly well.</u> Mr Williamsons & others sorrow. March 25.1856. His candidates come to New Wolverton confirmation evidently excellently prepared. <u>William Pitt Trevelyan.</u> Comes to me April 10 1856, day of meeting of Rural Deans for Institution. Much pleased with all I see of him.

573e [*insert*] Farewell to Wolverton.
On Sunday last the Rev.– Travers preached his farewell sermon to a numerous congregation in the Parish Church. It was a pretty sight to behold the people wending their way from different quarters up the hill to the house of God. Though the Rev. Gentleman has been so short a time in the place, he appears to have gained the confidence and heartfelt respect of his people. We saw the tears trickle down manly cheeks, as well as those of softer and more susceptible portion of the congregation. We are not going to criticise the probable motive to tears which we observed, but rather rejoice at the most charitable spirit of the pastor, and the evident affection of the flock. The sermon was lucid, terse, and to the point. There was no effeminate weakness on the part of the preacher. He felt, and keenly too, parting from friends with whom he had hoped to have laboured long, exhibiting manly vigour united with dignified sorrow. We felt, while listening to his excellent discourse, what power there is in real religion, what sympathy, what charity, what resignation dwells in the bosom of the genuine Christian. We felt, too, the infinite folly of religious bigotry. Here was a man preaching who believes some things which from my soul I respected him. I felt, too, there must be something wrong, desperately wrong in that church government which drags from the pulpit and the hearts of people the man whom they desire to retain, and who desired to "spend and be spent amongst them", and thrusts upon them another, perhaps a stranger, an altogether different man. Were congregations allowed to choose their own pastors Mr T. would not have left Parting sorrow. He begged those prayers of his hearers and while he begged: those prayers ascended to heaven on his behalf. We are sure the blessings of the people will follow him, and as the world is God's vineyard, he will not want for work nor lose his reward.

ADELPHOS.

The Bishop notes "This is written by a Dissenter".

[574] Wolverton. Saint George the Martyr. P.C. [The Railway Station Church]
The Rev G Weight. Confirmed here March 24 1856, a nice confirmation. The Wolverton men more intellectually intelligent than seemingly devout,

yet devotion in them. Heard that W. had at first preached. That the Bishop ordered him to preach on confirmation & so he did it though he could easily have found more interesting subjects. Yet he seems to have really taken pains with his people, undertaking the spiritual charge of those at New Bradwell. 2 Rooms fitted there for service.
March. 13/59. Preach here in the Lent Mission to a most affecting congregation from size attention &c. Weight has been very ill, looks old & shakey.
March 18.59 confirm here far too few but visibly affected. Poor Weight dies.
Francis William Harnett. Licensed to the P.C. Aug 13.1860.

575 **Wooburn. V**

Rev F B Ashley. Comes Feb.17./59, asks about evening communion. I cannot approve. Comes about a lad to be confirmed who behaved ill in Cookham Church, 7 years back. F Dacres Curate well spoken of except as to work amongst poor. F.D. rather looking for some educational work. A Takes up my defence warmly March 59. The Union Catechism being sent about as approved by me &c ! Oct 1859 gets Mr Cadwallader as Curate from Prevosts neighbourhood who testifies to him as good efficient sound moderate churchmanship.
Frederick Davis. Curate. May 1859, quarrels with Ashley, & gives him great trouble. But Oct.59 gets another curacy & goes.
July 61. Letter from Ashley proposing addition to Churchyard. I approve. March.17/62. Confirm here. Great appearance of care as to candidates but an air of depression on all.

Insert:

Sketch of Hamlet Chapel.
Contributions for the Wooburn Hamlet Chapel –
will be rec/d by Messrs Currie & Co.
29 Cornhill.
Messrs R. & J. Wheeler & Co.
Wycombe Bank.
and Rev/d F.B.Ashley.
Wooburn.
Beaconsfield, Bucks.

Insert: Letter.

My Lord,
In this Extensive Parish there are various populous Hamlets at a great distance from the church. Cottage Lectures have been held in them: these

have been useful, but the rooms are very small & inconvenient. It is therefore proposed to build a comely Room, which shall be moveable, of material which shall be adapted for the purpose.

This can be set up in each Hamlet successively, & suitable services regularly held in it. This additional means of grace will be brought within the reach of those divisions of such; & it is hoped with God's blessing some hitherto neglectful may be led so to value joining in Prayer & hearing the Word, that when the Prayer-Room is removed to the next Hamlet, they will make the effort necessary to come to church. About every twelvemonth the little chapel will come round again to the same group of cottages, & then others may by the grace of the Holy Spirit, be reformed & become worshippers in the House of God.

During the day, where a suitable person can be found in the Hamlet, the younger children would be assembled at the Room for Education in the first principles of knowledge & religion, & thus these outlying temporary gatherings for instruction would also form feeders for the central National & Infant Schools.

The estimated cost is £160. The proposition is cordially approved by the Lord Bishop of the Diocese.

The Parish is extremely poor, & there has been much distress owing to 5 of the mills having been standing still, so we are obliged to look for help from a distance.

Any kind of aid you may be inclined to afford will be thankfully acknowledged by

       Yours Faithfully
       F B Ashley.
Oct/60   Vicar of Wooburn.
       Nr Beaconsfield, Bucks. (P.T.O.)

[576] **Wood Eaton. R.**
March 1859. In V[icar]'s absence I having appointed C Gooch from Kidmore End Weylands complaint about mixing water with wine. I censured C Gooch. He active & diligent but not wise. Goes hence to Edgcote & does well, fussy & troublesome. Thence to Charlton [ ]. Thomas Daubeney, ordained May/56 to Ducklington Instituted May 29/64 See ordination book.

577 **Woodcot [See Southstoke.]**

Woodhay West. R.

G.A Moullin succeeds Sloper sen/r Sloper later Curate thinks he has right & continually writes [ ] Threatening 1856. [ ]. Moullin very nervous & shy hardly to be tempted out anywhere, brings his candidates to

Hampstead Marshall <u>March 28/57.</u> / Sep 1861, poor Moullin loses his senses I put in curate from Welford.

[578] **Woodlands [See Lambourne].**
  next to Wytham (595)

Woodstock. [See Blaydon]. Blaydon erased.

Woolhampton. R.
<u>L Miles Halton.</u> R. He writes March 31/57 asking to be excused attending with His candidates at Aldermaston sending them by his curate Dugald Campbell Gill, who signs all the tithes. Halton going on the nomination of his nephew W Sclater from North Hants.
<u>C W Everett</u> ordained by Bp Sarum to Uffington. /32./33. was curate of Kingston Lisle 43.48. Brings the advowson. Considers himself old orthodox. Instituted March 12.59. March 1860 hear that new squire Bligh going to restore Church.

579 **Woolstone Great. R.**
<u>The Rev E Hill.</u> This now united to next.
  At visitation 1857 his absurd anger because I had suggested to him sitting on pulpit steps. Clergy touchy! But he comes round at once on a kind letter. March/58 asks if he may allow parents to be sponsors has refused for 8 years. I advise his consenting with the reason.
  March 18.59. Confirm here. A nice confirmation Church full. Dear Hill greatly affected. Oct 16 1861 he opens his new School, asks me to attend too late.

Insert: (letters underlined are printed in red)
Wolston, Bletchley.
It is intended to <u>D</u>edicate The New School
Buildings at Wolston on <u>W</u>ednesday,
<u>O</u>ctober <u>16.</u>
<u>M</u>atins and <u>H</u>oly <u>C</u>ommunion at <u>8.</u>
Litany, <u>S</u>ermon, <u>O</u>ffertory at <u>11.30.</u>
Preacher the <u>V</u>en: The <u>A</u>rchdeacon.
Luncheon at <u>1</u>
<u>E</u>vensong at <u>6.30</u>
The honour of The Bishop's
presence and an
answer are requested.

Rectory. Sept.30. 1861.

The Bishop indicated at the top of the invitation "answered"

[580] **Woolstone Little. R.**
The Rev E Hill. Instituted by me Sep 26 1855 at Chicheley. Little Woolstone being now united to Great Woolstone

581 **Woolstone. P.C. [Parish of Uffington].**
With Balking.
The Rev F Rose. A long talk with Dr R... nearly 6 miles apart very desirable to part them. Woolstone would provide a site for a parsonage if they could be severed.

[582] **Woolvercot. P.C.**
S Edwardes proposes Nov.60, to get from Merton Coll. an offer of rent charge to raise Ecc Comm Fund paid..

583 **Wotton. P.C. [Berks.]**
Rev A Robarts. *I confirm here again, Feb 19 1856. A nice confirmation Lord & Lady Chandos. I sit some time with Robarts, who seems to me on his death bed from consumption. * This entry belongs to Wootton Underwood two pages on. *[Correction written by the Bishop.]*

[584] **Wootton. R. [Oxon.]**
Rev W Blackstone Lee. Lost his wife March 1856, writes a very feeling letter in reply to me. Confirm here March 6.61. A really nice confirmation. J C Hurst Curate for Old Woodstock March.64.

585 **Wootton Underwood. P.C.**
Rev A Robarts. See two pages back.
He dies Ap[ril] ? 1856 of consumption & Nov.8 1856 comes John Cramer Addison for institution he having been curate to Walton at Waddesdon & recommended himself during R's illness. I hope a good man but forward & vulgar.
April 1863. [ ] grown. "Not so active as when curate of Waddesdon" D of Buck[ingham.]

[586] **Worminghall. V.**
J Statter. Vicar 1854. After giving me much anxiety on the Romanising side, communicates to me confidentially by letter which see that convinced of the Faith of Irvingism & that this had removed all his Romanistic tendencies. Told him that I did not feel bound to enquire into his speculative opinions so long as in teaching & acting he was thoroughly & simply true to Church of E[ngland]. To this he most solemnly pledged himself. I told him I could give him no sort of permission to be an Irvingite but that I should not enquire into

what I could not prove: at the same time warned him against the spiritual Dilemma. The Church had been Romanly ornamented by his curate Oxenham whom I most doubtfully ordained to keep from Rome & Statter at once removed all. Oxenham behaving extremely ill & ungratefully to me, see letters . May God keep & save him: but he must fall. <u>Jan 20 1856.</u> I spend the day here, preaching mor/n & administering & confirming. Confirmed here March 7.62. Statter laid up by fall from Horse. A nice confirmation. Ickford now cared for by Hemsted.

587 **Worton Nether. P.C.**
<u>Francis Garratt Wilson.</u> Throat better but still weak comes March/58 with candidates to Sandford.

[588] **Worton Over. R.**
<u>Lancaster</u> Incumbent Dr W Wilson Curate March 58
W.Wilson. <u>Oct.1860.</u> Dr Wilson comes with W Wilson jun/r for institution to O.W. Jan 13/60. Full of poor Franks disappearance. Francis Garratt Wilson instituted by me at Haddenham March 31 62. He to reside still at Sympson. Oram acting as curate. Dr Wilson in the Rectory helping as he can.

589 **Woughton on the Green. R.**
<u>Maurice Farrell</u> Brings a few who look carefully prepared for confirm March 17/57.

590a **Wroxton. V. With Balscot Curacy.**
Rev J Murray. March 17 1855. His deep emotion at Horley as to his confirmation candidates whom he had felt obliged to refuse. Wish to provide a resident curate at Balscot this greatly wanted.. Nov 14. I come to Wroxton, talk with him. He has seen in old deed that H[enry] VIII grants Wroxton to Ch Ch, with proviso that it shall provide 2 sufficient priests. This to be seen to at once /58 March 10 & 11 Murray dining at the Abbey being careful about his confirm/n cases.
Feb 23/61 confirm here a nice confirm.
<u>Nov</u> 1862 poor Murray opens his Troubles. North a real obstructive see papers opposite. Resigns & Sep 25 1863 <u>Alfred Hooke</u> from Peterboro' diocese comes to Lav/n to be instituted. Feb 28, confirm here at Sunday morning service. Preach at night Josephs Brethren.

590b–i *Insert: The papers referred to in 590.*
        1. Curate at Balscott.
        2. Parsonage house at Wroxton.

3. Restoration of Balscott Church.
4. Rebuilding of Balscott School.
5. Increase of Income.

I.

Appealed to Col. North & Cht. Ch. meanwhile I have added a service at Wroxton.

II.

Subscriptions promised.
Christ Church ...	£100.	"	"
& an acre of land........			
Trinity College	100.	"	"
& an acre of land valued at	110.	"	"
The Bursar of Trinity..	50.	"	"

I have offered this site & £500 to the Ecclesiastical Commissioners.

III.

I have procured plans from Mr. Street, & had to pay for them myself.

IV.

Subscriptions promised
Christ Church.
National Society.
Trinity College..	25.	"	"
H Norris Esq...	20.	"	"
Brasenose College..	5.	"	"
Rev.d J.A. Gould...	5.	"	"

590d

I have procured the plans.			
The estimate is	£340.	–	–
The ground is given by Trinity Coll:			

V.
Nothing done.

Deanery of Deddington
27 Parishes.

IV. Schools

1. Adderbury.
2. Cropredy.
3. Deddington.
4. Hempton.
5. Nth. Newington.
6.*Swalcliffe.
7. Sth. Banbury.
8.*Great Tew.
9. Little Tew (purchased).
10. Wiggington.

[*The above Schools are bracketed as "built new."*]

11. Bloxham.
12. Wardington.

[*These are "in progress."*]

13. Sth Newington. repaired & fitted up.

Jan: 9th.1863 John Murray.

590f Paper given me by poor Murray to shew what done round whilst Balscot &c still 1862.

I.

Adderbury
    with a curate at Milton.

Bodicote
Little Barford } separated.

---

2 Banbury
    with a curate at Neithrop.
    x Sth Banbury. separated.

---

3 <u>Broughton</u>
  x with a curate at <u>Nth Newington.</u>

4 <u>Cropredy.</u>
  x <u>Wardington</u>
  x <u>Mollington</u>
  <u>Claydon</u>.} separated
  about to have a curate at <u>Bourton</u>

5 <u>Deddington.</u>
  curate at <u>Clifton.</u>
  Do. at <u>Hempton.</u>

6 <u>Milcomb.</u>
  separated from Bloxham
  & Wigginton.

7 <u>Swalcliffe.</u>
  x <u>Sibford</u> separated
  x curate at <u>Shutford.</u>
  Do. at <u>Epwell.</u>

8 <u>Great Tew.</u>
  <u>Little Tew</u>. Separated.

590h

			II. Parsonages.
	1	Adderbury.	repaired & enlarged.
	2	Banbury.	"
	3	Bloxham.	"
	4	Barford.	rebuilt.
	5 x	Wardington.	"
	6	Sibford	purchased.
	7	Sth Banbury	"
	8	Bodicote	quite new
	9	Milcomb.	"
	10 x	Mollington	"
	11	Little Tew	"
	12	Claydon	in process.
	13	Drayton	"
	14	Hanwell	"

590i
  III.   Churches.
      1   Clifton.   quite new
      2 x   Sth Banbury   "
      3   Hempton.   "
      4 x   Neithrop.   "
      5   Milton.   "
      6   Little Tew   "
      7   Claydon.   thoroughly restored.
      8   Barford.   "
      9   Milcomb.   "
      10   Mollington.   "
      11   Swalcliffe.   "
      12   Shutford.   "
      13   Worton.   "
      14   Broughton.   restoration nearly complete.
      15   Deddington.   "
      16   Tadmarton.   "

591 **Wycombe**   See also Loudwater and
    High. V.   Hazelmere.
    H. Paddon. 1854 continued trouble about his curates, requires Paul to preach particular redemption & Dinsdale not to preach against.
        "Wanted a Man if such you know
        Neither very high, or very low
        Neither bent towards Geneva nor going to Rome
        But willing to work in High Wycombe
        In a good old quiet easy way
        Such as moderates like in the present day
        If the Path of Duty he steadily walks on
        He'll have the Help of mighty Oxon
        And for his secular Health and Cheer
        He'll be paid per quarter a £100 a Year
        The Vicar being absent, Head he'll have none
        So the curate must bring a Head of his own
        But he'll have as <u>Cojustor</u> a moderate low
        So send us dear Todd the best Man that you know"
        [*apparently copied in by another hand*]
    1855 Paddon refuses to return into residence. After due notices &c I sequester & Sep & Oct appoint & license H Rice & Turton to the curacies. Applies & I consent Oct to his giving them six months

notice he meaning to return. They getting on D.G. well W Rose applies for help to school deficiency sent Oct 20 £5 as second gift.

March 11 1856 I confirm here, all different since Rice & Turton some 120 confirmation candidates instead of 30. D.G. But what when poor Paddon returns? May 25 1856. I go there to preach (on woman of Samaria) striving to wind up & point their [ministry]. Reynolds & others have offered Paddon £100 a year if he will stay away & let me nominate curates. He declines. They to go after next Sunday, a grand congregation: May 25 1856 complaints as to P's interpolating a hymn in the service & not giving the notices. I enforce the rubric. He then drops all notices & puts them on the Church door (go on at p. 606 after Earley)

606 Rev H Paddon Wycombe High continued from P.[591]

1856 This complained of Ap[ril] 57. I obliged to say that no power save matters in the rubric. 1856 7 He quarrels with the Com/mee of Nat[ional] School & goes to British School instead. I license Curate & enjoin on him attendance.

Aug 9.57 the committee apply to me he refusing a sermon & after trying everything to bring him to a better mind I go & preach myself & collect £20. At the same time persuade the commee to give him a key of the School, the withholding which the alleged offence. Paddon goes to Rugby for the day. Nov 7./57. I visit at Wycombe. Paddon reads prayers. Changes lesson. "Thought he had a right to" "Would not do it again" Would not communicate you must excuse me. I try as in Gods sight to win the poor man over: but all in vain. Touched in money his one weakest point & perfectly irreconcillable. He wrote me a bitter denunciatory letter. Bishop Shuttleworth was cut down for opposing him. His Church Wardens presented him. I tried to make peace. March 1858. He proposes to do away the Clerk: have a choir & clerk in Orders. I assent to all. 1858, at last I heal the quarrel between the School commee. Dec 58 He quarrels with his new curate Johnson: he leaving the parish absolutely to him. This continuing Jan 59. Feb & March P. applies to be allowed to dismiss him. March 16 writes that I cruel. All/59 This continues. At length Johnson gets another curacy & then long correspondence as to his being paid till the end of his License. In Nov 59 at last P. pays.

*2 Oct 11 1861 Hear that Paddon gone out for 3 months leaving all in charge of a deacon! Complains Dec 61, as to the doctrine of R Covey Curate as antinomian.

Marginal Notes: *1 Ellice.
                   *2 Richard Covey.

612a **Wycombe High**. continued from 606

H Paddon 62 Confirm here March 29 62. Better number than last time Paddon giving my health at Luncheon. Begging more frequent confirmations. Lamenting the prevalence of dissent. No chance of amendment till the Church restored & wished for Street plans &c &c.
R Covey –Welford
Return of Paddon of value of Wycombe March 1863.

Tithe Rent Charge of £246 =	275.	18.	9.
Vicarage house & gardens –	50.		
Glebe lands	61.	—	
Surplice fees	37.	9.	11.
Easter offerings	13.	17.	2.
[ ]	438.	6.	6.
Disbursements	148.	7.	2.
Net	289.	19.	4.

for year 1861.

Newspaper cutting:
'The Church in High Wycombe'
Buckinghamshire Herald. Uxbridge Advertiser.
Windsor & Eton Journal.
Saturday, December 2. 1865.

[592] **Wycombe West. V.**

Rev George Broadhead. Come here March 7 1856 to Sir G. Dashwood very kindly welcomed. On the 8th confirmed at the \\church. Very few from the parish. Poor Broadhead read the service miserably. Bradenham, Radnage attended also. April 10/59 Broadhead brings a very scanty number for confirmation at Bradenham. Says that Dissenters & ague have thinned them!

Dec 1859. Applies for license of non residence in consequence of great offence he has given by a low marriage I assent on condition of non-interference. £130 income, non-return without my assent. I offer curate to Milton* now at Newbury.

I place Edward King moves Sep/60, for a chapel at W Wycombe. See letter of Lloyds.

[*Marginal Note*: *Late of Little Marlow]

593 **Wyrardisbury or Wraysbury. V. with Langley Marsh Curacy**.
[*in Bishop's hand*: see 3 pages on.]
The separation of this from Langley accomplished Jan 1856.
Neville Seymour comes for institution March 21 1856.

[594] **Wytham. R.**
Hon & Rev F Bertie. Dr Bandinel Curate. After 46 years service as he desires Oct 55 to resign, Bertie proposes to appoint H O Coxe.

595 [Heading in Bishop's hand] **Woodstock Chapelry.**
Rev G W St John. Rev W A Scott Curate paid by Lord Blandford. Dec 24 1855 Mr St John complains that Mr Scott lectures in the schoolroom without his sanction & denies his authority. I write to Mr Scott. Rev W S. comes to me about a rumour false in letter. <u>Alas</u> true in great measure really by his confession of sin in June/55. March 21.57, receive report of commission issued at his desire. E Coopers evidence plain as to <u>repeated</u> efforts at seduction, but finding that no carnal intercourse, she having rejected him. I write to Lord Blandford to know his mind. <u>Poor Man!!</u> He leaves under sad cloud, suspicion of other cases!! Geare comes. Chosen by Lord B. I giving a doubtful recommendation, specially pointing to <u>her</u>. Jan 30 1859. I here & preach in the Chapel of Blenheim Palace to all the great Household on Family religion – Kingscote Vanes Ld Vamberley, Whateley &c here. The Duke wishing Browne to have a separate curacy & have service of Curate. NB. ——
1860 Jan. Geare goes out with a smell of Brimstone raising a [party] against the Duke &c. &c. & Jan 26 Rev H Munn 5 years curate under Part of Mother Church of Edmonton comes for licence. The D[uke] giving him £150 per annum.
1861 March 6. Comes with candidates to Wootton. They seem well prepared.
<u>Oct 30/63</u>. I consecrate the Poor House Chapel & the new cemetery. March 11 64 confirm here. Evident that pains had been taken yet the Woodstock Palsy on all. G.Steele now Curate & good. W.Sanders Union Chaplain.

[596] [Heading in Bishop's hand] **Langley Marsh.**
Separated Jan. 1856 from Wyrardisbury. Long doubts & discussion whether I should act upon its lapse to me & present Nash. At last determined not to do so the lapse having arisen from the Chapter acting on my advice & separating the parish from Wyrardisbury.

597 **Yarnton. V.**
Vaughan Thomas Dies 1858.
& <u>Peter Maurice</u> D D is presented by All Souls College. He comes Dec 4/58. First applies to know if he must reside. I tell him that he must.. He proposes to get the House improved. Jan 27. D. Bangor Oct 27 B. (Majendie).

[598] **Yattendon. R.**
>Rev Jno F Howard. March 14. Confirmation Here. All the marks of a good man & a remarkably inefficient ministry. The Parish is overrun by Ranters who all come also to church. Very few at the confirm/n. The Church utterly uncared for. Damp green walls. The carpet at the communion <u>rotted</u> through under the Hassock &c &c. She a sister of <u>Hansell.</u>[75] Comes March 30/ 57 with flock to Bucklebury. Confirm here March.17/63. A very nice confirmation. The Church has been nicely restored by him. Though a poor man with many trials. 2 idiot sons. A very high minded man, divided the inheritance with his brother. The whole property now for sale.

599 **Yelford. R.**
><u>George Hough</u> presented by Mr Lenthall. (He had been near 34 years at the Cape) March 16 1858. Proposes at present to let Mr Burgess go on. There being only 10 people in the parish. He was curate of St Peters in the East when commended by Howley ArchB to L[or]d Bathurst.

[*From this point all page headings are in the Bishop's hand, the office headings having come to an end.*]

Milton under Wychwood.
><u>Willm Stoddart</u> <u>Curate</u> at present. Confirmed here March 23 1855 a most comforting confirmation. Life in the Waste, Milton Carter, & dependencies attending. <u>Stoddart</u> doing well. <u>March 18.58</u>, another most moving one from Shipton Lyneham Idbury & Fifield.

601 **<u>Greenham.</u>** It is proposed to me Sep 29 55 in a letter from C Whittle that he should at six weeks from this time act as curate of Greenham until the separation & then take the incumbency, to reside till he can get a house in Greenham in Donnington Square Newbury distant 1 mile from thickest population.
[*Here there are 2 lines of the entry erased.*]
>Separated & First Incumbent & owner of advowson He wishes to make it over to Lee. Difficulty about the Mortmain laws. Solves by making it over to <u>me</u> personally & I by codicil to will leave it to my successor praying him to do the same by his successor.

[602]　　　　3. Lathbury

---

[75] Probably Edward Halifax Hansell, Fellow of Magdalen, Rector of East Ilsley 1866.

603/4 **P.C. Bodicote.**
> J <u>Aubrey Gould</u>. Comes to be licensed to the first incumbency at Mollington April 1 1856. Two full services, Saints Days &c. Income, £150 net from Rectorial Land. The Warden personally gave £250, for the increase c[irca] £7 in funds. Vicar of Adderbury gives £50 net in money glebe 22 acres equal to £50.

[604] **<u>All Saints Sonning.</u>**
> April 1856 at present a curacy to Sonning. Old R Palmer objects strongly to its being made independent, as severing it from him & his; he gives £50 per annum to the curate. Nov Pearson wishes to get from Eccles Comm/n £25 to meet £75 from Palmer & have a separate curate there. The good Horne [*entry ends*]

605 **Earley in Sonning. P.C**.
> John Manley Hawker First Incumbent Severed from Sonning. Worth £100 a year, by an endowment of Q Annes Bounty & £60 from Eccles Com/n. A good house.
> Horne who tormented by Farmer 1859.

[606] see High Wycombe.

607 **Milton in Adderbury.**
> Consecrated the new Church here Nov 16/57. A striking gathering & beautiful Church. Good Hookins at present to serve it with Barford &c.

[608] **<u>Dry</u> Sandford**.
> Hamlet in Abingdon. Church Built & consecrated Cost say £1300. Confirm here Dec 20/58 & long talk after with Dodson as to making it independent. Write to Phipps about P[rince] of Wales aid. Confirm Jan 26/62 from Radley, a very nice confirmation. J A Pickard has done a great deal here. 27 confirmed 15F 12M.

609 **Stoke Mandeville with Buckland.**
> Constituted a separate benefice, Sep 21 1858, and the Chapter appoint Partington to it at my recommendation.
> 1859. Moving for funds for House, & planning great things for Church. —— Buckland <u>Common</u> undertaken Nov/59 by R Sutton from St Leonards with grant from Sp[iritual] Aid for curate.
> Edward Bonus 1861 acting as Curate at Buckland & I hear well of him.

610 See **St Thomas. Oxford**. [p.369b]

611 **Gerrards Cross**.
  Consecrated Aug.30 1859. Built by the Miss Redes.. & endowed with £1.000 & they offered £1.000 and got £1000 from Eccles Comm . (Teste. *Sic*)
  *1861. The District Gazetted, April 1861 & May 16 1861, the first incumbent comes for admission which I then grant.
[*Marginal Note:* William Joseph Bramley Moore.]

Bicester P.2 continued
  Dec 1860. Mr Fowlers attacks on Mr Watts calming & Defence of Parish. See Letter under B. – Then movement for restoring church. I able to try Fowler & Watts at one meeting in church & we carry a restoration. Watts collects vigorously. Plans Beasley a pupil of Scotts – March 27 63 I go with Clerke to F Hibberts – most kindly received. Sep 28 – we reopen the church. Communion Clergy surpliced. Watts delighted speaking most aff/ly at luncheon in School. Cost near £3000, collected nearly £200 in Morning. Bickersteth to preach Aft.
  Held visitation here Nov/63 & all friendly & pleasing. Confirmed March 7/64 not a pleasant confirmation. Unimpressible & rather inattentive. Poor Watts opened to me afterwards his poverty. Wifes West Indian property came to naught, Somersetshire living lost through voting against Harcourt, £60 a year lost by Cemetery

613b *Inserted Letter*:

The Vicarage of Bicester, Oxon
Dec: 24: 1861.

My dear Lord,
May I ask you now kindly to write me such a letter as I can append to my circulars of appeal for help in restoring my Church, pointing out the real necessity of heartily commending the work.

  We have gone thro' sad scenes with the dissenters who mustered in a strong body with Mr Richards their minister as their leader.

  My enclosed letter which I issued on the occasion will furnish you with the particulars.

  The poll was taken on Saturday last, & I send you the result. Mr Richards publicly states that he will throw every obstruction in our way that he can. He is a man of a bad spirit.

  I must appeal for not less than three thousand pounds, including the 500£ voted by the Parish. Would you also kindly tell me what societies I can apply to for aid.

  Will you allow me sincerely to wish you my dear Lord a happy Xmas,

blended with my poor imperfect prayers that all Blessings in Xt Jesus may be yours!
    Believe me with affect regard & esteem, ever
        my dear Lord
                Yrs very faithfully
                John Wm. Watts.

613f TO THE PARISHIONERS OF BICESTER

Bicester Vicarage. Dec 17th, 1861

My Beloved People,

Will you allow me to place before you in a spirit of Christian love, a few plain, simple facts relative to the matter now an issue in this parish.

    I am sorry that anything should occur to interrupt in any way the calmness which generally prevails among us. My great desire is peace and unity, and over a long vicariate of nineteen years, my conscience testifies that I have ever sought to promote this desirable end; and if I now intrude myself more especially upon you, it is for the purpose of rightly informing you on matters of which I fear many of you are ignorant. It is well then that I should tell you that our Parish Church is in a most defective state of repair. It has been found, on minute examination by a practical surveyor, that many timbers of the roof are in a dilapidated condition through the lapse of time, while the entire floorings are decidedly in a very sad state. In truth the whole of the interior needs substantial repair. To this my own attention has long been drawn, and I have privately consulted my Diocesan on the matter. At my suggestion he very kindly, on the 25th ultimo, met some of my more influential parishioners, and exhorted them to co–operate with myself and Churchwardens in carrying out so praiseworthy an undertaking as to the restoration of our Church, and after some amicable discussion, it was agreed that the Parish should be asked to vote the sum of £500, on the security of the Church Rates, spread over twenty years, on the proviso that I would by grants from societies and subscriptions find the sum of £1500, and this, under God's blessing, I pledge myself to do without any fear as to the result, fully believing that it is for God's glory that the house in which we assemble to worship Him should not remain in its present mean condition.

    On Saturday last, pursuant to due notice, a parish meeting was convened, and had it rested with church people only, the proposal moved by Mr.Paxton, and seconded by Mr.Fowler, would have been carried, as in fact it was, viz., that £500 should be given by the Parish, contingent on my raising the remainder of the sum required, and thus all would have been arranged in a peaceful and amicable spirit; but this was stoutly resisted by the Nonconformists, who mustered in a strong body, stating that they would throw every obstacle in our way. On a show of hands being taken, there were for the proposed plan 25, dissentients, 18, the latter being, if I mistake not, entirely Dissenters. On this, Mr.Richards, Minister of the Chapel in Water–lane, demanded a poll, which is fixed for Saturday next, and will commence at 10 o'clock, closing at 4.

I am deeply grieved at this, conscious that such a proceeding tends to create feelings of strife and animosity utterly repugnant to all real Christian feeling. But since a poll has been demanded, and there is no remedy, I now ask you, my beloved people, to come forward on Saturday next, and in a quiet spirit to record your votes in favour of the proposed plan. I appeal to you, as Churchmen, not to abandon your principles on this occasion. I ask you to come forward, and help in the restoration of your Parish Church, consecrated by the hallowed remembrance that beneath its roof you yourselves have received inestimable blessings, and beneath which roof, when you are mouldering in the dust, your children's children will be worshipping the Lord of Hosts.

I love the Church of England with increasing love. I believe her to be the best and greatest blessing of our land. I admire her incomparable liturgy and her scriptural articles of Christian truth; and if ever there was a time when there was less excuse for dissent from her communion, that time is the present, for the Church of England is putting forth her best powers and energies to meet the wants of the population. She is extending her arms far and wide to embrace all within her reach. Her ministers have all the license they could reasonably expect in carrying out her ministrations, and I have no sympathy with those whose cry is "Down with her, down with her, even to the ground," yet, such I fear, is too much the spirit of dissent in the present day, though I am rejoiced to acknowledge that there are many honourable exceptions.

Once again, then, I ask you as my parishioners, I appeal to you as Churchmen, to record your vote in favour of the Church on Saturday next. Let us strive for peace, but let it be peace based on solid principles, and let the votes recorded on Saturday give a plain and decided proof that we will not allow ourselves or our plans to be defeated by a body whose efforts, it is to be feared, are concentrated for the purpose of seeking to overthrow our Church Establishment.

Should you through culpable supineness or inactivity fail in this great Christian duty, and allow dissentient body to obtain the victory, then as long as Bicester remains a parish, I foresee nothing in the future but difficulty. Let us then unitedly with one heart and mind arise and restore the House of our God. "The work is great, the palace is not for man, but for the Lord God". I am willing to undertake the ponderous task, but I must look for your hearty co–operation and affectionate help, and then I have no fear as to the issue.

May the Lord guide and direct you, and show you the path wherein you should walk, is the fervent prayer, my beloved people, of your
Affectionate Friend and Pastor,

J.W. Watts.

613h

BICESTER
CHURCH RATES
CLOSE OF THE POLL
SATURDAY, December 21st, 1861

	Votes	Persons	Rental		
Church –	165	111	£5154	12s	6d
Dissent –	25	25	383	15s	0d
Majority	140	86	£4770	17s	6d

The Vicar and Churchwardens beg to return their best thanks to those Inhabitants who have so kindly come forward to support them in the performance of their duty, and to congratulate the Town on their well-timed attachment to the Interests of the Church.

JOHN WILLIAM WATTS. Vicar
SAMUEL BURROW
CHARLES FOWLER Churchwardens.

614 **Iver continued**. March [no further entry.]

615 **The District Church of Ch Ch Whitley, Reading. Perpetual Curacy** constituted 1862.
William Fountaine Addison, first incumbent.
   Licensed. March 3 1863

616 **Upton with Aston UpThorpe. P.C.**
   Separated from Blewbury in 1863. The first Incumbent Richard Hooper. June 15–63 I preached at the opening of Schools. Great gathering there, all promising. 1861 I consecrated Churchyard. Now Church to be rebuilt & Parsonage.

617 **Filkins**
After Farrars coming to Broughton he determined on getting rid of Filkins & Goodlake having left some legal act unfinished does – at length. He proposes to endow it with its own Tithes & fees about £35 a year & vest Patronage in See. An order in Council for these purposes.
Jany 64. Mr Smith gives house with near £600, & I offer it £100 from Diocesan Fund to commissioner.
Offer the cure to good <u>Robert Morgan Price,</u> who at Buscot as Curate.

618 See Witney no 569

619 **Finstock.**
Separated by order in Council from Charlbury, 1862–3. Feb 1864. Alfred Redifer incumbent going to build out of £1,100 we raised last year by subscription. £550, met from Eccles Comm/n. Redifer from Quainton seeming to do well here

620 **Ramsden**.
<u>R Lowbridge Baker.</u> Instituted to this & Wilcote.

621 **St Pauls, Wokingham**
<u>Edward John Selwyn.</u> Comes to me for institution on the 17th of April 1864. Going to take charge of the district before the Church is ready.

622 **Stony Stratford** continued from 490
Here Nov 20, 1864. Spent Sunday. Preached and confirmed Congregations good. Church much improved & Sankey seeming quieter.

622b *Insert*: England and Wales.

<u>ABSTRACT of the Return from the Diocese of Oxford for 1861</u>

INCUMBENTS RESIDENT. In the Glebe House	428
In a Licensed House	1
In the Parish	28
Virtually <u>Resident</u>	9
Total number Resident	466
INCUMBENTS NON–RESIDENT. By Exemption	33
By License	74
Without License or <u>Exemption</u>	4
Total number Non–Resident	111

MISCELLANEOUS. Vacancies and Recent Institutions 26
Sequestrations and Suspension 3
No returns "

Total Miscellaneous Cases. 29

Total number of Benefices 606

N.B. Of the <u>110</u> Non-Resident <u>58</u> were performing the Duties.
Number of Glebe Houses <u>494</u>

Annual Value of Benefices held by Non–Resident Incumbents.

Annual Value of Benefits... Returned 124
Do. do. ...... Not Returned —

<u>124</u>

Curates of Benefices where the Incumbent is Non–Resident.

Annual Stipends...... Returned 52
Do. do. Not Returned —

Number of Curates <u>52</u>

Of whom are Licensed..... 52
Resident 40

Curates Assistant to Resident Incumbents.

Annual Stipends...... Returned.–. 199
Do. do. ...... Not Returned.. 5
Nominal Stipends.... 2

Number of Curates <u>206</u>

Of whom are Licensed ...206

Services in Churches, Chapels, &c.

Vacant 22
Number of Services Weekly...Returned... 669
Number of Services   Not Returned .. <u>.. 1</u>
<u>692</u>

622d *Insert* MY DEAR PARISHIONERS AND BRETHREN IN CHRIST,

You have heard that the Bishop is coming among us, with a select band of Clergymen, and that we are to have more Services than usual in our Parish Church, and that some of the occasional rites and ordinances of the Church are to be administered here; you may therefore, expect from me some explanation of the objects which we have in view, and the motives which have led me to desire, and the Bishop to carry out, these Lenten Services.

The great object of all is the good of the souls who are entrusted to our care. We are most anxious that you should all increase in Godliness, that you should be drawn more and more towards our Saviour Christ in love, and that God the Holy Ghost may direct and guide your hearts.

We feel that it is impossible to do too much for your spiritual welfare; and the preaching of earnest and eloquent men, guided, as we believe, by the Holy Spirit, must be effectual to touch the heart. I am sure, then, that both the Clergy and the People require to be roused and stirred up to greater zeal and love – that there is great danger of spiritual sloth and indolence creeping over us all, lest we become like a stagnant pool, "settled on our lees," without life or freshness. There are many, I rejoice to think, in this Parish, who are really striving to serve God and to give themselves to His will, who yet feel the great difficulty of their warfare, and how hard it is to gain the kingdom of heaven, who seek for encouragement and guidance " to run with patience the race that is set before them." You will find that much needed strength and encouragement, if you try to profit by means of grace offered to you in the numerous Services to be held in the Church. Most especially I exhort you all, and urge you in every loving way that I can adopt, to prepare your selves to receive Holy Communion, which, in the early Services will be celebrated daily, with addresses from the Bishop and other Clergymen well qualified to offer them.

But there are others, I grieve to say, who are careless and indifferent, with but little concern for their souls, whose lives are unholy, and their thoughts "earthly, sensual, devilish". May the all–powerful Spirit of God touch the hearts of such, and enable them at this time to break the chains which bind them to sin and unbelief. I do most lovingly entreat them to make good use of this great opportunity now offered them, and avoid the awful sin of neglecting God's calls to repentance, and therefore of shutting themselves out from eternal life, remembering that the Word of God is " a savour of death unto death" in them that reject it. I do then, most earnestly desire and exhort you, one and all, to be diligent in attending these Services, and opening your hearts to the Spirit of Grace.

You will find annexed a list of the Preachers and the hours at which the church will be opened; Lay aside for once, your work or your amusement, or whatever else would hinder you from using such an opportunity which may never return. The old saying is true – "Where there is a will there is a way." I shall not cease to pray for you all, that the labours of the Bishop and his companions among you may be sanctified to your eternal benefit; that the Holy Ghost may dwell in your hearts; and that your whole body, soul, and spirit may be preserved blameless unto the coming of our Lord Jesus Christ.

Brethren, pray for us

YOUR AFFECTIONATE FRIEND AND PASTOR,
DACRES ADAMS.

The Vicarage, Bampton, February 1st, 1864.
I am sure I may confidently ask you to allow the seats in the Church to be open for all comers during these special Services.

622e

Three prayers follow this letter "to be added to daily devotions daily throughout the week":
    1. For the Bishop and Clergy
    2. For all those who shall join in the Special Services
    3. For the Conversion of Sinners

622f

List of Services in the Parish Church of Bampton, Saturday 13 to Sunday 21 February 1864

Names of Clergy participating

The Bishop of Oxford	Rev J. Mansel Price
Rev. A. Blomfield	Rev. J. Lawrell
Archdeacon Randall	Rev. J. Moorehouse
Rev. J. R. Woodford	Rev. L. G. Mayne
Rev. H. Lamphier	Rev. H. W. Barrows (*sic*)
Rev. Leslie Randall	Rev. W Fremantle
Rev. J. Williams	Rev. W. Williams
Rev. R Gregory	Rev. P.R. Atkinson
Rev. C. D. Goldie	Rev. P. G. Medd
Rev. T. Chamberlain	Rev. James Skinner
Rev. W. J. Butler	Archdeacon Bickersteth
Rev. R. Millman (*sic*)	Warden of All Souls'
Rev. J. M. Price	Rev. D. Moore
Rev. J. Erskine Clarke	Rev. C. F. Secretan
Rev. T. V. Fosbery	Rev. R. H. Baynes
Rev. A. K. Ashwell	Rev. J. S. Skinner
Rev. C. H. Travers	Rev. J. H. Iles
Rev. L. Rivington	Rev. H. Shute

Rev. C. Warner
Rev. J. W. Burgon
Rev. K. Randall

Rev. R. M. Benson
Rev. Sir G. Prevost

622h–i *Announcement of the Special Services for Bampton and Neighbourhood, 1864, with letters from the Bishop and from Dacres Adams, R.D. Further copy of the three prayers set out in 622e.*

623-641 *Blank*

642 *Newspaper cutting: a remonstrance, signed by 82 persons, addressed to the Bishop and to the Archdeacons and 24 Rural Deans who on 1 March 1859 had addressed him on matters of ritualism in the Diocese. It is claimed that the assurances given to the Bishop were contradicted in the following respects:*

  Stone altars existed at St Thomas, Oxford, Binsey, Wolvercote, Littlemore, Sandford St James, Radley, Wantage and the three cemetery chapels of ease in Oxford;

  The Chapel of Cuddesdon College was improperly decorated, and contained an altar shelf with a metal cross, altar coverings, a piscina, and a service book called Hours of Prayer; the defection of students to the Roman Church, and the association of a former student with the Directorium Anglicanum are also mentioned.

  Processions had taken place at Addington and at Cuddesdon College.

646 *Fragment of a letter marked "Bromley College", signed by H. C. Adams, 23 August 1860, claiming in strict confidence that the support of the Archbishop and of the Bishop of Rochester was essential to the success of any candidate for election.*

BIOGRAPHICAL APPENDIX

In this section of the document an effort has been made to trace all the clergy who are mentioned in the Diocese Books. Their university records and the dates and places of ordination as Deacon and Priest (D. and P. respectively) their curacies (C.) and other offices in order of date are provided for the great majority. It should however be remembered that the sources used made for many gaps and errors, since the men concerned were often expected to supply the information themselves, and no attempt has been made to correct what the sources provided. The question marks indicate the many places where information could not be gleaned from these sources. Foster's *Alumni Oxonienses* ended in 1886, the year prior to its publication. Unless otherwise stated, the university is Oxford; where similar College names exist at Oxford and Cambridge, to avoid confusion with more recent institutions, the name of the university is supplied.

Adams, Dacres, 1807–1871, Christ Church, 1824, BA 1827, MA 1833; D. 1829, P.1839; V. Bampton 1837–71; R.D. Witney 1846.

Adams, John, 1822–1877, Magdalen Hall, 1844, BA 1848, MA 1851; D. 1849, Exeter, P. 1850, Exeter; C. Creed, Grampound, Cornwall 1849–58; R. Stockcross 1858–77.

Adams, Simon Thomas, 1807–? New College, 1827, BA 1831, MA 1835, Fellow, 1832; D. 1832, Oxford, P.1833, Oxford; C. Combroke, Northants.? C. Compton Verney, Northants, R.Great Horwood 1839–?89; R.D.Mursley 1851. In *Crockford* 1880.

Adams, William Fulford, 1834–? Exeter, Oxford, 1852, BA 1856, MA 1857; D.1857, Worcester, P.1858, Worcester; C. Bromsgrove, Worcs. 1857–59; C. Easthampstead 1859–61; C. Wokingham 1861–64; V. Little Faringdon 1864-? Eldest son of Dacres Adams.

Addison, William Fountaine, 1818–? Wadham, 1835, BA 1840; V. Dorchester 1850–56; V.Christ Church, Reading,1863–69; Chaplain Gibraltar 1869–77, V. Ossett,Yorks.1877–?

Alderman, Francis Charles, 1803–? Exeter,Oxford, 1821, BA 1826, MA 1828; Incumbent, District Chapel of Denford, Kintbury, 1839–?

Aldworth, John, 1834–1870, Worcester,Oxford, 1853, BA 1856, MA 1859; D. 1857,Oxford, P. 1858,Oxford; C. Somerton, ? C. Haigh, nr. Wigan, 1863–70.

Alford, George, 1823–? Queen's, Oxford, 1842, BA 1846, MA 1849; D. 1846, Oxford, P. 1847, Oxford; C. Aston Sandford 1846–49; C. Holy Trinity, Tewkesbury, 1849–52; C. Holy Trinity, St.Pancras, London 1852; P.C. Arkley, Barnet 1856–58; R. Aston Sandford 1858–62; P.C. Cookley, Worcs. 1862–66; C. Mangotsfield, Bristol, 1866–72; V. St.Paul's, Bristol 1872–81; V. Mangotsfield, Bristol 1881–? Chaplain, Girl's Orphan Asylum, Hook Mills, Bristol 1875–81. In *Crockford* 1889.

Almack, Henry, 1806–1884, St.John's,Cambridge,1824, BA 1828, MA 1831, BD 1835, DD 1844, Fellow; D. 1830, Lincoln & Coventry, P. 1831,Chichester; R.All Saints, Southampton 1842–44; R. Aberdaron w Llanfaerrhys P.C. Dio. Bangor, 1843–84; R. Fawley 1846–84.

Ansted, Joseph Boord, 1821–1914, Christ's, Cambridge, 1839, BA 1843, MA 1846; D. 1843, London, P. 1844, London; C. Whitechapel, London 1843–47; P.C. St.Simon Zelotes, London 1847–57; P.C. Stony Stratford 1857–59; V. Longdon, Staffs 1859–61; R. Morborne, Dio. Peterborough 1861–90.

Armistead, John, 1801–?1865, Trinity, Oxford, 1819, BA 1823, MA 1827; D. 1824, P. 1825; V. Sandbach 1828–65. Father of the next entry.

Armistead, John Richard, 1829–? Christ Church, 1848, BA 1852, MA 1855, Student. C. Sandbach; R. Wendlebury 1862–65; V. Sandbach, Dio. Chester 1865–?

Armstrong, John Hopkins, Trinity, Dublin, BA 1843, MA 1856; D. 1843, Dublin, P. 1844, Dublin; C. St.Stephen,Dublin; V. Bicknoller, Somerset,? C. St.Giles, Reading? Chaplain, Alnut's Hospital, Goring Heath 1864–69; C. St.Mary's, Reading 1869–73; V. Staines, Dio. London 1873–?

Arnold, Edward, Trinity, Dublin, BA 1827, MA 1841; D. 1831, Clogher, P. 1831, Raphoe; Incumbent Loudwater, 1841–?65 Not in *Crockford* 1870.

Arrowsmith, James, 1825–1890, St.Edmund Hall, BA 1845, MA 1848; D. 1845, Lichfield, P. 1846, Ripon; V. Stoke Row 1850–90.

Ashley, Thomas, 1772–1851, Brasenose, 1791, BA 1794, MA 1797, BD 1810; D. 1798, Oxford, P. 1798, Oxford; R. West Shefford 1818–51.

Ashpital, Francis, 1828–? Brasenose, 1846, BA 1849, MA 1852; D. 1851, London, P. 1852, London; C. St.John, Hampstead, London 1851–52; C. Chipping Norton 1853–55; P.C. Lane End 1855–59; R. Great Hampden 1859–80; V. Flitwick 1880–?

Ashton, Ellis, 1789–1869, Brasenose, 1807, BA 1811, MA 1813, BD 1821, Fellow, D. 1813, Oxford, P. 1813, York; V. Hayton, Preston, Lancs. 1813–1869; R. Begbrooke 1821–1869; R.D. Prescot 1845; Sometime Chaplain to the Archbishop of Canterbury.

Astley, Charles Tamberlane,1826–? Jesus, Oxford, 1843, BA 1847, MA 1849; D. 1849, Oxford, P. 1850, Oxford; Evening Lecturer, Bideford, Devon 1849; P.C. Holywell, Oxford 1850–54; V. Margate, Kent 1854–64; R. Brasted, Sevenoaks, Kent 1864–76; V. Gillingham, Kent 1876–?

Atkinson, Peter Righton, 1829–1888, Trinity, Cambridge, 1852, BA 1855, MA 1865; D. 1855, Rochester, P. 1857, Rochester; C. Stisted, Essex 1855–57, C. Longworth 1859; R. Pusey 1860–68; R. East Hendred 1868–75; V. Dorking, Surrey 1875–85; V. Frensham, Surrey, 1885–88. R.D., Surrogate, Canon of Winchester, Archdeacon of Surrey, 1880–88.

Aylward, Adolphus Frederick, 1822–1871, St.Edmund Hall, 1841, BA 1844, MA 1858; D. 1844, P. 1845; V. Chesham 1847–71.

Back, Henry, 1824–1891, Trinity, Cambridge, 1843, BA 1847, MA 1850; D. 1850, London, P. 1851, London; C. St.George's, Hanover Square, London, C. Grosvenor Chapel, South Audley St, in 1859; V. Banbury w St.Paul Neithrop 1860–81; R.D. Deddington 1875–81, Surrogate.

Bacon, John, 1809–1871, Corpus Christi, Cambridge, 1827, BA 1831, MA 1834; D. 1834, Exeter, P. 1835, Exeter; C. Culstock, Cornwall 1835–37; P.C. Lambourne Woodlands 1837–63; V. Wymondham, Leics. 1863–71.

Baird, James Skerell, Trinity, Dublin, BA 1835, MA 1838; D. 1857,Oxford; C. Haddenham, about 1856; C. Almondsbury, Bristol, about 1860.

Baker, George Augustus, 1788–1866, St.John's, Cambridge, 1806, BA 1811, MA 1815; D. 1811, Bath & Wells, P. 1812, Bath & Wells; P.C. Godney Meere, Somerset 1835–41; R. Ibstone-cum-Fingest 1841–66.

Baker, James, New College, 1807, BA 1811, MA 1815, Lincoln's Inn 1811; R. Nuneham Courtney 1825–?55; R.Wheatfield 1831– 35; Chancellor of the Diocese of Durham 1818–?

Baker, Robert Lowbridge,1831–1904, Peterhouse, Cambridge, 1849, BA 1854, MA 1857; D. 1856, Lichfield, P. 1857, Lichfield; C. West Felton, Salop 1856–60; R. Wilcote 1860–99; V. Ramsden 1864–99.

Baker, William Innes, 1780–1859, New College, 1799, BCL 1807; R. Upper Heyford 1820–1859.

Baker, William John, 1830–1868, St.John's, Cambridge, 1849, BA 1853, MA 1856; D. 1856, Lichfield, P. 1857, Lichfield; C. Whaddon, Bucks. 1860–66.

Ball, John, 1800–1865, St.John's, Oxford, 1818, BA 1822, MA 1825, BD 1835, Fellow; D. 1822,Oxford, P. 1828; C. St.Giles', Oxford; V. St.Lawrence, Reading 1834–65.

Ballard, John 1782-? St John's, Oxford 1800, BCL from New College 1809; R. Cropredy 1811, and of Woodeaton 1823 (*Clergy List* 1845)

Ballard, John, 1815–1875, Trinity, Oxford, 1832, BA 1836, MA 1839; D. 1837, P. 1838, C. Woodeaton 1838.

Bandinel, James, 1815–?81 Wadham, 1833, BA 1836, MA 1844; D.1840, London, P. 1841, London; C. St.John the Evangelist, Westminster 1840–47; C. Marshwood, Dorset 1847–56; P.C. Cogges 1856–62; R. Elmley, Dio. Ripon 1862–81. Hon. Sec. Assoc. for the Reform of Convocation. In *Crockford* 1889.

Barker, Thomas Childe, 1827–? Christ Church, 1846, BA 1850, MA 1853, Student; D. 1851,Oxford, P. 1852, Lichfield; V. Spelsbury 1856–? Chaplain Rome 1874–75; R. Carleton-by-Skipton 1885–?

Barnes, Ralph, 1811–1884, Christ Church, 1829, BA 1833, MA 1835, Student; D. 1836, Oxford, P.1838, Oxford; V.Ardington 1839–84; V. Bampton (3rd Portion) 1833–84; V. Bampton Aston w Old & New Shifford, Aston Cote, Brighthampton & Chimney 1857–84.

Barnett-Clarke, Charles William, 1831–? Worcester,Oxford, 1848, BA 1850, MA 1855; D. 1854, Oxford, P. 1855,Oxford; C. Lamborne 1854–58; V. Toot-Baldon 1858–60; P.C. Fenny Stratford 1860–64; V. Cadmore End 1868–71; Dean of Capetown, 1871–?

Barrett, William, 1821–? Worcester, Oxford, 1840, BA from Lincoln College 1844, MA 1846; D. 1847, Oxford, P. 1848, Oxford; C. Ellesborough 1850; Chaplain to the Donative of Combe Longa 1851–?

Barter, Charles, 1786–1868, Balliol, 1803, BA 1807, MA 1812, Fellow; D. 1812, Oxford, P.1813, Oxford; C. Islip 1812–13; R. Sarsden w Churchill 1817–1868; R. Cornwell 1829–1868.

Bartholomew, Charles Willyams Marsh, 1826–1897, Exeter, Oxford, 1844, BA 1848; D. 1848, Exeter, P. 1850, Exeter; C. Morchard Bishop, Devon 1849–51; C. St.Mark's, N. Audley St., London ? C. St.Stephen, Westminster 1851–53; R. Glympton 1856–?

Barton, Henry Jonas,1797–1872, Brasenose, 1814, BA 1818, MA 1820; D. 1822, Worcester, P. 1823, Worcester; V. Latton w Eyrey, Wiltshire; R. Wicken, nr Stoney Stratford 1838–72; R.D. of Preston; Hon. Canon Peterborough 1854.

Barton, Thomas, 1814–1894, St.John's, Cambridge, 1832, Migrated to Queens', 1835, BA 1836, MB 1839; D. 1839, Peterborough, P. 1840, Peterborough; C. Kettering 1839; P.C. Midgham 1858–66. No other Cures recorded after 1866. Residing in Newbury.

Barwis, William Cuthbert,1824–1889, Trinity, Cambridge,1844, BA 1847, MA 1850; D. 1848, Ripon, P. 1849, Ripon; C. St.James, Leeds 1848–51; P.C. Christ Church, Leeds 1851–55; C. Chipping Norton 1858–66; C. Hoyland, Yorks. 1866–69; P.C. Hoyland Swaine,Yorks. 1869–79; C. Northallerton,Yorks. 1879–89.

Bathurst, William Duncan Mackenzie, 1821–1880, New College, BA 1841, MA 1846, Fellow: D. 1842, P. 1843; C. Hollesley, Suffolk 1843; V. Stradsett, Norfolk 1846–47; C. Marcham 1849–50; R. Stoke Abbas, Dorset 1861–62; V. Heckfield, Hants. 1862–80.

Baty, Thomas Jack, 1831–1869, Sidney Sussex, Cambridge, 1851, BA 1853, MA 1858, Fellow; D. 1855, Oxford; C. Saunderton 1855–58; C. Putney, London 1858–60.

Bayfield, Benjamin, 1814–1866, St.Catherine's, Cambridge, 1832, BA 1836, MA 1839; D. 1836, Canterbury, P. 1837, Ripon; P.C. Ripponden, Dio. Ripon 1840–47; V. Shinfield 1847–66.

Baylee, Joseph, T.C.D. BA 1834, MA 1848, BD & DD 1852; St.Aidan's; P.C. Holy Trinity, Birkenhead, 1842–? Principal, St.Aidan's College.

Bayley [post Laurie], John Robert Laurie Emilius, 1823–1917, Trinity, Cambridge, Transferred to the "Ten year List" 1847, Matric. 1861, BD 1862; D. 1846, Oxford, P. 1847, Oxford; C. East Claydon, about 1852; V. Wheatley, Notts. 1847–49; V. Woburn, Beds. 1853–56; R. St.George's, Bloomsbury, London 1856–67; V. St.John's, Paddington 1867–88; Select Preacher, Cambridge 1881.

Bayley, Thomas, 1819–1886, St.Edmund Hall, 1842, BA 1845, MA 1848; D. 1845, Oxford, P. 1846, Oxford; C. Ayot St.Lawrence, Herts; V. Penn 1860–1886.

Baylis, Edward, 1815–1888, St.John's, Cambridge, 1834, BA 1839, MA 1842; R. Hedgerley 1845–88.

Beauchamp, Henry William Johnson,1794–1868, Worcester,Oxford, 1811, BA 1815, MA 1819; D. 1816, Hereford, P. 1817, Hereford; V.Latton w Eisey, Dio. G & B, 1819–26; V. Whiteladies, Aston, Worcs. 1829–39; R. Monks Risborough 1839–68.

Beauchamp, James, 1804–1891, Clare, Cambridge, 1818, BA 1828; D. 1829,Oxford, P. 1830, Oxford; R. Crowell 1830–74; V. Shirburne 1832–74.

Bedingfield, Richard King, 1802–1884, Pembroke, Cambridge, 1830, Migrated to Queens',Cambridge, BA 1833; D. 1833, Salisbury, P. 1834, Salisbury; C. Elvetham, Hants.? C. Trowbridge, Wilts. 1864–70; Second Master, Trowbridge Grammar School 1864–70; C. Wingfield 1870–84.

Begbie, Alexander George, 1835–? St.Mary Hall, 1853, BA 1857, MA 1880 [Queen's College]; D. 1860, Salisbury, P. 1861,Salisbury; C. Beaminster, Dorset 1860–62; C. Upton w Chalvey and Chaplain to the Eton Union 1864–69; C. Swindon, Wiltshire 1869–72; C. St.Matthias, Stoke Newington, Dio. London 1872–76; C. Settrington,Yorkshire 1876–77; C. Manea, Dio. Ely 1877–? Sub-Warden and Tutor, Southwark Missionary College 1883–85.

Bellas, Septimus, 1804–1875, Queen's, Oxford, 1822, BA 1826, MA 1829, Fellow; D. 1827, Salisbury, P. 1828, Salisbury; V. Monk's Sherborne w Priory Church [Pamber], Basingstoke 1848–75.

Bellis, Richard, King's, London, Theo.Ass. D.1848, London, P. 1849, London; C. St.Pauls', Lisson Grove, London 1848–49; C. High Wycombe 1849–53; Incumbent. St.James, St.Helier, Jersey 1853–1870; V. All Saints, Jersey 1870. In *Crockford* 1889.

Benson, Henry, 1830–1890, Trinity, Cambridge,1848, BA 1852, MA 1855; D.1853, Exeter, P. 1854, Exeter: C. St.Mary's Church w Coffin, Devon 1853–56; C. Henley-on-Thames 1856–63; P.C. Weald, Dio. Cant. 1863–77; V. Horsell, Surrey 1878–81; R. Farncombe, Surrey 1881–90.

Berens, Edward, 1777–1859, Christ Church, 1795, BA 1798, MA 1801; D. 1801, Oxford, P. 1802, Oxford; V. Shrivenham 1804–1853; Prebendary of Sarum 1829–1853; Archdeacon of Berkshire 1832–1859.

Beresford, William Montgomery, Trinity, Dublin, BA 1840; D. 1840, Ripon, P. 1841, Dublin; P.C. Walton, nr Aylesbury 1853–57; Chaplain, Aylesbury Union 1853–?

Best, William,1825–1901, Trinity, Cambridge, 1845, BA 1849, MA 1869; D. 1849, Oxford, P. 1850, Oxford; C. Dinton, Bucks. 1849–55; C. Over Worton w Hempton 1855–57; C. Banbury 1857–60; C. Astley-bridge, Lancs.1860–61; R. Astley-bridge, Lancs. 1864–70; C. Ashley, Cambs. 1870–73; V. Holme w Langford, Notts.1873–74; V. Duns Tew, 1874–1901.

Bickersteth, Edward, 1814-1892 Sidney Sussex, Cambridge BA 1836, MA 1839; DD 1864; Select Preacher, Cambridge, 1861, 64, 73, 78; Select Preacher, Oxford, 1875; D 1837 Hereford, P 1839 Hereford; C Chetton, Hereford, 1838; C Shrewsbury Abbey, 1839; PC Penn Street 1849-53; RD Amersham 1849; V Aylesbury, Archdeacon of Buckingham 1852-75; Dean of Lichfield 1875-92; Prolocutor, Convocation of Canterbury, 1864, 66, 69, 74-80; Member of the New Testament Revision Committee.

Biddulph, Henry, 1796–1867, Magdalen, Oxford, 1813, BA 1817, MA 1820, BD 1830, Fellow,1820–33; D. 1819, Oxford, P. 1820, Oxford; R. Birdingbury, Warws.1826–67; R. Standlake 1832–67.

Birch, Samuel, 1781–1848, St.John's, Cambridge, 1799, BA 1802, MA 1805, DD 1828, Fellow, 1804–09; D. 1803, Lincoln, P. 1805, Lincoln; C. Stranground, Hunts. 1803; C. Ibstock, Lincs. 1805; R. St.Mary Woolchurch w St.Mary, Woolnooth, London, 1808–48; V. Little Marlow 1833–48; Preb. St.Paul's Cathedral 1819–48; Chaplain to the Lord Mayor of London 1808, 1809, 1814–15; Geometry Lecturer, Gresham College, 1808.

Birch, Thomas Richardson, Chaplain, Eton Union 1863.

Bird, Roger, 1800–? Magdalen, Oxford, 1816, BA 1820, MA 1823, BD 1827, Fellow; D. 1822, Oxford, P. 1823, Oxford; R. Lanteglos w Advent, Camelford, Cornwall 1842–? R. Donnington, nr Ledbury, 1843–? V. Uffington,1852–55; C. Ightham, Dio. Canterbury 1855–57; R. Ightham 1857–?

Birkett, William, 1794–1875, Brasenose, 1811, BA 1814, MA 1818; D. 1817, Chester, P. 1818, Chester; Preb. & V. Wolverhampton; R. Great Haseley 1846–75; Domestic Chaplain to the Earl of Buckingham.

Bishop, Freeman Heathcote, 1811–1876, Trinity, Oxford, 1830, BA 1835, MA 1847; D. 1836, P.1837; C. Littleton, Middx; Chaplain to the Earl of Lanesborough; P.C. Lambswood Hill, nr. Reading 1854–61; V. Bassingborough, Dio. Ely 1861–76.

Bishop,William, 1776–1847, Wadham, 1793, BA 1797, MA 1801[Oriel]; R. Ufton Nervet 1819–47. *Foster.*

Blackman, Charles (Ob.1868), D. 1829, P. 1830; R. Chesham Bois.

Blagden, Henry Charles,1831–? Queen's, Oxford, 1849, BA 1853, MA 1855; Wells Theological Coll; D. 1854, Norwich, P. 1855, Worcester; C. Shipmeadow, Beccles 1854; C. Frankley, Dio. Worcester 1855–57; C. Trysull, Dio. Lichfield 1858–59; C. Aldridge, Dio. Lichfield 1859–60; V. Milcombe 1860–75; R. Newton-Longville 1875–1903.

Blake, Vernon, 1828–1902, Wadham, 1846, BA 1850, MA 1857; D. 1851, Oxford, P. 1852, Oxford; C. Beedon 1851; C. Lambourne 1851; C. Banbury 1851–54; C. Bampton 1854–57; C. Stonehouse, Gloucs. 1858–62; V. Shiplake 1863–66; V. Stoke Poges 1866–? Domestic Chaplain to the Duke of Leeds 1882.

Bleamire [Bleaymire], Thomas, 1816–1851, Trinity, Cambridge, 1834, BA 1838; P.C. Stony Stratford, 1849–51; Chaplain to the House of Correction, Notts.

Blenkin[s], Frederick Beatson, 1825–1901, Caius, Cambridge, 1844, BA 1848, MA 1851; D. 1849, Lincoln, P. 1850, Peterborough; C. St.Martin's, Leicester, 1849–56; C. St.John's, Reading, 1857–62;V. St.Nicholas w St.John, Lincoln, 1863–1901; Chaplain to the Forces, Lincoln Regimental Depot & to the Lincoln Volunteers, 1878–1901; Preb. Lincoln Cathedral,1884–1901.

Blissard, John, 1804–1876, St.John's, Cambridge,1822, BA 1826; D. 1827, Lincoln, P. 1828, Lincoln; C. Hampstead-Norreys, V. Hampstead-Norreys, 1843–76.

Blunt, James St.John, 1828–? Balliol,Oxford, 1846, BA 1850, MA 1851; D. 1851, P. 1852; Chaplain, H.R.H.The Prince Consort; Hon. Chaplain to the Queen, 1872–75; V. Old Windsor, 1860–78; V. New Windsor, 1875–78; Chaplain in Ordinary to the Queen, 1875–? Master, St.Katherine's Hospital, London,1878–? In *Crockford* 1889.

Bode, John Ernest, 1816–1874, Christ Church, 1833, BA 1837, MA 1840, Student 1841–47; D. 1841,Oxford, P. 1843,Oxford; R. Westwell,1847–60; R. Castle Camps, Cambridge, 1860–? Select Preacher, 1849; Bampton Lecturer, 1855.

Booth, James (*Ob*. 1878), Trinity, Dublin, BA 1835, MA 1842, Ll.D. 1842, F.R.S., F.R.A.S. D. 1842, Exeter, P. 1842, Canterbury; Minister St.Anne's, Wandsworth, London; Domestic Chaplain to the Marquis of Lansdowne; V. Stone, 1859–78.

Boothby, Cunningham, 1819–1860, Trinity Hall, Cambridge, 1842, BA 1846, MA 1849; D. 1847, Rochester, P. 1848, Rochester; C. Little Chishall, Essex, 1849–52; P.C. Holwell w Bradwell Grove, 1856–60.

Bosworth, Joseph, 1789–1876, Aberdeen University, MA & LL D, a "Ten Year Man",Trinity, Cambridge, 1832, BD 1834, DD 1839; F.R.S. 1829, F.S.A.; D. 1814, P. 1815; C. Bunny, Notts; V. Horwood Parva, 1817–29; Chaplain, Amsterdam, 1829–32; Chaplain, Rotterdam, 1832–40; V. Waith, Lincs. 1841–45 and again 1848–58; R. Water Stratford, 1858–75; Professor of Anglo Saxon, Oxford University, 1858–76.

Boulthee, Richard Moore, 1794–1874, Merton, 1811, BA 1815, MA 1818, BD 1825; D. 1817,Oxford; C. St.Peter in the East, Oxford,1817; R. Barnwell, Northants, 1829–60; Chaplain to Lord Montagu (Patron of the Living); Sometime at Dinton.

Bouwens, Theodore, 1799–1869, Merton, 1817, BA 1820, MA 1823

Bowman, John, BA, C. Speenhamland, 1838; P.C. St.Paul's, Buttershaw, Bradford, Yorks, 1842; C. Greenham, 1844; Lecturer, Speenhamland, about 1845.

Boyce, Henry le Grand, 1813–1880, Worcester, Oxford, 1831, BA 1834, MA 1840; D. 1838, P. 1839; C. Oving ? V. Aslacton, Dio. Norwich, 1875–1880.

Braithwaite, Francis Gretton Coleridge, 1834–? Balliol, 1853, BA 1858, MA 1865; D. 1859, Oxford, P. 1860, Oxford; in Onslow, Dio. Montreal, Canada about 1870.

Brancker, Henry, 1818–? Wadham, 1836, BA 1839, MA 1841; D. 1840, Chester, P. 1841, Chester; C. Warrington, 1840; P.C. Padgate, 1841; P.C. Bishopsworth, 1847; C. Mortlake, 1854; C. Stantonbury, 1856; P.C. Thursley, Surrey, 1857–86.

Brazier, John Henry (*Ob*. 1850) P.C. Sandhurst, 1832–1850.

Breedon, Henry, 1791–1857, Balliol, 1810, BA 1814, MA 1817; R. Pangbourne, 1817–57.

Bricknell, William Simcox, 1806–1888, Worcester, Oxford, 1822, BA 1827, MA 1829; D. 1828, Gloucester, P. 1829, Gloucester; V. Grove, 1836–1888; V. Eynsham, 1845–1888.

Brookes [Brooks], Thomas William Dell, 1828–? Christ Church, 1847, BA 1851, MA 1854; D. 1852, Oxford, P. 1853, Oxford; C. Cropredy, 1851–53; C. Marston St.Lawrence, North, 1853–55; V. Flitwick, Dio. Ely, 1855–; R. Great Hampden, 1880–96.

Brooks, Joseph Heathcote, 1812–1855, Brasenose, 1831, BA 1835, MA 1836, Fellow; D. 1838, Oxford, P.1839, Oxford; Incumbent St.Philip's, Stephney, Middx. 1844–? R. Great Rollright, 1848–55.

Broughton, Thomas Delves,1802–? Brasenose, 1819; R. Bletchley, ? –1859,

Brown, Stephen, 1816–1873, Jesus, Cambridge, 1834, BA 1838, MA 1841; D. 1842, Exeter, P. 1843, Exeter; C. North Molton, Devon, 1842–44; C. Shipton-le-Moyne, Bristol, 1844–46; R. Little Shefford, 1846–72.

Brown, Walter Lucas, 1805–1862, Christ Church, 1824, BA 1828, MA 1831; D. 1828, Oxford, P. 1829, Oxford; R. Wendlebury, 1839–62.

Browne, Henry, MA, R. Little Kimble, 1838–1857.

Browne, Thomas Cooper, 1814–1888, Trinity,Cambridge, 1832, BA 1836, MA 1839; D. 1837, P. 1838; Reader, Christ Church, Newgate St., London, 1849; P.C. Headington Quarry, 1852–58. Afterwards resided in Oxford.

Buckle, William Lewis, 1791–? Lincoln, Oxford, 1808, BA 1811, MA 1812; D. 1813, P. 1814; C. Stoke Talmage, 1813; C. Crowell, 1821; R. Adwell,1817–? R. Easington,1819–? V. Shirburn, 1823–32; V. Banstead, Surrey, 1832–?65.

Bull, Henry, 1798–1889, Christ Church, 1815, BA 1819, MA 1821; D. 1819, P. 1820; V. St.Mary Magdalen, Oxford, 1834–? P.C. Lathbury, 1838–89 R.D. Newport Pagnell, Hon. Canon, Christ Church, Oxford, 1877. In *Crockford* 1880.

Bull, Israel, 1771–? Oriel, 1789, BA 1793, MA 1797; Fleet Marston, 1851–52.

Burges, Frank, 1813–1875, St.John's, Oxford, 1831, BA 1835, MA 1839, BD 1844, Fellow, 1831–61; D. 1835, Oxford, P. 1837, Oxford; C. Standlake, about 1855; P.C. Fyfield, 1854–63; R. Winterbourne, Dio. Gloucester & Bristol, 1863–75.

Burges, John Hugh, D 1856, Oxford; P 1857, Oxford; C Cuddesdon 1856-57; C Deddington 1857-60; V Burford with Fulbrook 1860-71; V Blewbury 1871- ?

Burgess, Bryant, 1821–1889, Exeter, Oxford, 1838, BA 1841, MA 1845; D. 1843, Lincoln, P. 1844, Lincoln; C. Slapton, 1843–50; C. Flaunden w Latimer, 1850–57; R. Latimer, 1857–89; R.D. Amersham, 1876, Surrogate Dio. Oxford.

Burgess, James Robert, 1808–1861, Oriel, 1827, BA 1832, MA 1833; D. 1833, P. 1833; V. Streatley, 1833–61.

Bu[i]rkett, William, 1794–1875, Brasenose, 1811, BA 1814, MA 1818; D. 1817, Chester, P. 1818, Chester; R. Great Haseley, 1846–75; Preb. Colllegiate Church, Wolverhampton; V. Wolverhampton [dates not known]; Domestic Chaplain to the Duke of Buckingham.

Burney, Henry, 1814–1893, Exeter, Oxford, 1831, BA 1835, MA 1836; D. 1839, Bath & Wells, P. 1840, Bath & Wells; R. Wavendon, 1847–93 ; R.D. Bletchley, 1866.

Burridge, Thomas Waters, 1819–1888, Magdalen Hall, Oxford, 1843, BA 1848, MA 1850; D. 1848, Oxford, P. 1849, Oxford; C. Speen & Lecturer, Speenhamland, 1848–49; V. Stockcross, 1849–58; V. Bradford, Somerset, 1858–61; Chaplain to the Forces, 1861, Retired List, 1867; C. St.Michael, Folkestone, 1867–72; R. Catmore, 1872–?85; V. Eastbury, 1885–88.

Bushnell, William, 1818–1855, University, Oxford, 1836, BA 1840, MA 1845; V. Beenham Valence, 1842–55. [information in *Foster* only]

Bussell, Frederick, 1819–? Worcester, Oxford, 1839, BA 1848, MA 1857; D. 1843, P. 1844; C. Little Marlow about 1845; V. Great Marlow, 1851–?81

Butler, Alfred Stokes, St.Bees, 1846; D. 1847, Peterborough, P. 1849, Peterborough; P.C. Penn, 1853–60; R. Markfield, nr Leicester, 1860–?

Butler, John, 1818–? Trinity, Oxford, 1832, BA 1836; R. & Patron, Inkpen, 1850–?95 (in *Crockford* 1889)

Butler, Thomas, 1812–1887, Magdalen, Oxford, 1830, BA 1834, MA 1836, BD 1845, Fellow, 1842–46; D. 1835, Oxford, P. 1836, Oxford; R. Theale, 1855–1887.

Butler, William James, 1802–1877, Magdalen, Oxford, 1820, BA 1824, MA 1827, BD 1838, Fellow; V. Aston Tirrold, 1843–44; R. Tubney & Appleton, 1844–77.

Butler, William John, 1818–1894, Trinity, Cambridge, 1836, BA 1840, MA 1844, Hon. DD 1885; D. 1841, Winchester, P. 1842, Winchester; C. Dogmersfield, Hants. 1841–43; C. Puttenham, Surrey, 1843–44; P.C. Wareside, Herts. 1844–46; V. Wantage, 1846–81; Dio. Inspector of Schools, 1849–80; R.D.; Founder and Warden of the Penitentiary Sisterhood of St.Mary's, Wantage, 1850; Hon. Canon, Christ Church, Oxford, 1872; Canon of Worcester 1881–85; Dean of Lincoln, 1885–94.

Butt, John Martin, 1774–1853, Christ Church, 1792, BA 1796, MA 1799; V. East Garston 1802–1846.

Butt, John Martin, 1807–? Magdalen Hall, 1824, BA 1828, MA 1831; V. Wingrave 1850–84.

Buttanshaw, Francis, 1829–? University, Oxford, 1847, BA 1851, MA 1854; D. 1851, London, P. 1852, London; C. Harmondsworth, Middx., 1851–53; C. Foving, Essex, 1854–55; C. Chinnor 1855–72; C. St.Giles, Camberwell, London, 1872–78; C. Sunbury on Thames, Dio. London, 1878; R. Smeeton, Westerby, Leics.1879–?

Butterfield, Henry, 1801–1875, Christ's, Cambridge, 1821, BA 1824, MA 1837; D. 1825, Chichester, P. 1826, Chichester; R. Brockdish, Norfolk, 1826–42; Minor Canon, Windsor, 1828–67; R. Fulmer, 1842–75.

Byron [The Hon.], William, 1831–? Balliol, 1849, BA 1852, MA 1857; Fellow of All Souls, 1852–57; D. 1854, Oxford, P. 1855, Oxford; V. Lewknor 1855–57; R. Stoke Talmage 1857–74; R. Stow Langtoft, Suffolk, 1874–78.

Caffin, George Benjamin,1809–1878, St.John's, Oxford, 1828, BA 1832; C. Wasing, 1836; V. Brimpton 1840–50; V. Chiselet, Canterbury, 1855–58; V. Brimpton 1858–1878.

Calverley, Henry Calverley,1826–? Corpus Christi, Oxford, 1844, BA 1848, MA 1851, Fellow about 1848; D. 1853, Oxford, P. 1854, Oxford; C. St.Mary, Reading, 1853–61; C. Aylesbury 1861–67; C. Ashcott, nr. Glastonbury, 1873–75; R. Bassingham, Dio. Lincoln, 1875–79; R. Church Brampton, Northants, 1879–?

Cameron, Archibald Allen, 1810–1880, Pembroke, Oxford, 1827, BA 1831, MA 1833; D. 1832, Oxford, P. 1833, Oxford; C. St.Giles, Reading, 1832–33; V. Twyford, Berks, 1833–76; P.C. Hurst, nr Reading, 1833–80.

Camilleri, Michel Angelo, Malta Theological College 1834, DD 1838; D. 1836, Malta, P. 1836, Malta; Chaplain, S.P.G., Capetown, 1848–54; C. Goosey w Stanford in the Vale 1858–63; P.C. Lyford 1863–97; Chaplain Lyford Almshouses, 1863–? Translated the Bible & Prayer Book into Maltese.

Carden, Robert Augustus, 1836–1873, Exeter, Oxford, 1854, BA 1859, MA 1862; D. 1859, Oxford, P. 1860, Oxford; C. Shiplake 1859–61; Chaplain, Missions to Seamen, Sunderland; C. St.Peter's, Plymouth,1868–?

Cardew, John Haydon, 1824–? Exeter, Oxford, 1842, BA 1847; D. 1847, Bath & Wells, P. 1848, Bath & Wells; C. Currey-Mallet, Somerset; C. Belton, Leics; C. Cleeve Prior, Worcs; C. St.Paul, Forest of Dean; C. Abbot's Ann, Andover, Hants; P.C. Pishill 1857–65; Chaplain, General Hospital, Cheltenham, ?–1887; Chaplain, Union Workhouse, Cheltenham, ?–1887; R.Winkfield, Trowbridge,Wilts.1887–?

Cardew, Lionel, 1817–? University, Oxford, 1837, BA 1841, MA 1844. *Foster* only.
Carey, Charles, 1816 – ? Oriel, 1834, BA 1838, MA 1841; D. 1840, Oxford, P. 1841, Oxford; C. Greinton, Somerset, ? C. Spelsbury ?–1855; R. Kingweston, Dio. Bath & Wells, 1859– Dio. Inspector of Schools [Castle Cary], 1863; R.D. Castle Cary, 1875.
Carlyle, John, D. 1817, P. 1818; R. Noke 1840–?
Carpenter, George, 1828–? Christ Church, 1847, BA 1851, MA 1861 D.1852, Rochester, P. 1853, Rochester; C. Great Berkhamsted 1852–55; C. Ramsden 1857–60; C. South Stoke 1861–62; C. Chadlington 1863–? In *Crockford* 1880.
Chamberlain, Thomas, 1810–1892, Christ Church, 1828, BA 1831, MA 1834, Student,1828–92, D. 1832, Oxford, P. 1833, Oxford; V. Cowley,Oxford, 1837–42: V. St.Thomas, Oxford, 1842–92; Sec. Dioc. Board of Education, 1839, 1844; Hon. Canon of Christ Church, 1882.
Champnes[s], Edward Thomas,1806–? Trinity, Cambridge, 1824, BA 1828; Succeeded his father as V. Upton w Chalvey, 1844–67. Disappears from *Crockford* 1876.
Champneys, Charles Francis, St.Bees', D. 1846, P. 1847; V. Wendover 1850–67.
Chaplin, Edward Morland, 1832–? Magdalen Hall, 1850, BA 1854, MA 1856; D. 1854, Exeter, P. 1856, Exeter; C. Haberton, Devon, 1854–55; V. Buckfastleigh, Devon,1855–57; R. Chilton, Berks. 1858–?98.
Cheales, Alan Benjamin, 1828–1911, Christ's,Cambridge, 1846, BA 1850, MA 1853: D. 1853, Gloucester & Bristol, P. 1855, Oxford; Travelling Batchelor of Cambridge University 1850–53; C. Lechlade 1853–54; C. Shiplake 1855; C. Wargave 1855–59; V. Brockham, Dio. Winchester, 1859–92; Chaplain to Lord Dynevor, 1870–78.
Cherry, Henry Curtis, 1798–1864, Clare Hall,Cambridge, 1817, BA 1821, MA 1824; D. 1821, Norwich, P. 1823, Norwich; C. Horningsheath, Suffolk; R. Burghfield, 1827–64; Domestic Chaplain to Lord Saumarez in 1847.
Chester, Anthony, 1801–? Merton, 1818, BA 1821, MA 1826; D. 1823,Carlisle, P. 1824, London; J.P. Resided at Chicheley Hall.
Chetwode, George, 1792–1870, Brasenose, 1809, BA 1814, MA 1815; R. Ashton under Lyne, Dio. Manchester, 1816–70; P.C. Chilton, Bucks. 1829–70.
Cholmeley, Charles Humphrey, 1829–1896, Magdalen, 1846, BA 1851, MA 1853, Fellow 1855–69; D. 1857, Oxford, P. 1858, Oxford; P.C. Horspath 1858–64; R. Sherborne St.John, Hants. 1864–65; V. Dinton w Teffont Magna, Wilts. 1868–?85; Prebendary, Salisbury Cathedral, 1882–? R. Beaconsfield,1886–96.
Christie, Campbell Manning, St.Bees, D. 1841,Chester, P. 1842, Chester; C. St.Nicholas, Whitehaven, Carlisle, 1841–44; P.C. Thornthwaite, Cumberland, 1844–51; P.C. Stony Stratford, 1851–57; V. St.Simon Zelotes, Dio. London, 1857–77; V. Compton Dando, Dio. Bath & Wells, 1877–?
Christie, John Frederick, 1807–1868, Oriel, 1824,BA 1829, MA 1832, Fellow 1829–48; D. 1834, Oxford, P. 1835, Oxford; V. Badgeworth, Gloucs. 1836–? R.Ufton Nervet,1847–68.
Churton, Thomas Townson, 1799–1866, Brasenose, 1817, BA 1820, MA 1823, Fellow 1821–52; R. Great Shefford 1851–66.
Clarke, Cecil Jarvis, Trinity, Dublin, BA 1852, MA 1860; D.1853, Chester, P. 1854,Chester; C. Newton in Mackerfield, Chester, 1853–55; C. Standlake 1855; C. The Abbey,Shrewsbury, ? C. Tisbury, Wilts.1866–68; C. Freshwater, Isle of Wight, 1868–70; C. Newland, Gloucs. 1870–71; C. St.John's, Broughton, Manchester? V. Christ Church, Mold Green, Huddersfield, 1864–?

Clark[e], Elisha Lorenzo, 1804–? Trinity, Cambridge, 1831, BA 1835, MA 1839; C. St.John's, Reading 1841–54; C. Bicester 1854; C. Ashby, Westmorland,1867–69; C. Wollaston, 1870–75. *Venn*; *Clergy List 1845*.

Clarke, John Alexander, 1815–1860, Trinity, Oxford, 1833, BA 1837, MA 1841; D. 1839, Lincoln, P. 1840, Exeter; C. Odcombe, Somerset ? C. Morville & Aston, Salop? C. Wootton 1852; V. Stratfield Saye 1856–60.

Clayton, Edward, 1817–? Christ Church, 1835, BA 1839, MA 1842, Student, 1855–59; D. 1841, Oxford, P. 1842, Ely; C. Withyham, Sussex ? P.C. Stratton Audley, 1846–57; Missionary to Kaffirs, South Africa, 1853–54; R. Astbury, Dio. Chester, 1858–78; R.D. Hon. Canon, Christ Church, Oxford, 1870; V. Iffley, 1878–1885.

Clayton, Edward Ffrarington, 1830–1907, St.John's, Cambridge, 1849, BA 1853, MA 1856; D. 1854, Gloucester & Bristol, P. 1855, Gloucester & Bristol; C. Stapleton, Gloucs.1854–56; C. Putney, London ? C. Sonning 1862; C. Winwick, Warrington, Lancs. about 1860; C. Stoke ? R. Ludlow, Dio. Hereford, 1867–1907; Surrogate, Dio. Hereford, 1867–1907; R.D. Ludlow 1873–1907; Preb. Hereford Cathedral 1880–1907; Proctor, Dio. Hereford, 1880, 1885 & 86.

Cleaver, John Francis, 1788–1861, Christ Church, 1805, BA 1809, MA 1811, Student 1813; D. 1812, P.1812; Sinecure R. Corwen. Dio. St.Asaph,1812; V. Great Coxwell 1815–61; Canon, St.Asaph Cathedral. Son of William, Bishop of Bangor.

Clementi, Vincent, 1814–1899, St.John's, Cambridge, 1832, Migrated to Trinity 1834, BA 1837; D. 1837, London [Canterbury], P. 1837, Canterbury; C. Chislet, Kent, 1837; C. Thatcham 1841–48. Lived in Canada for many years, where he died.

Cleminson, William, 1798–1857, Queen's, Oxford, 1817, BA 1821; D. 1821, London, P. 1822, Oxford; C. Chalgrove 1822; C. Wasing 1846; R. Wasing,1847–1857; P.C. Tranmere, Cheshire.?.

Clifton, Charles Rede, 1819–1902, Merton, 1837, BA 1841, MA 1848; C. Somerton 1846–48; V. North Aston 1848–1902.

Clifton, Robert Cox, 1810–1861, Worcester, Oxford, 1827, BA 1831, MA 1834, Fellow 1833; D. 1833, Oxford, P. 1834,Oxford; R. Somerton, 1831–61; R.D; Canon, Manchester Cathedral,1843–61.

Clutterbuck, James Charles, 1801–1885, Exeter, Oxford, 1820, BA 1826, MA 1829, Fellow 1822–31; D. 1825, Oxford, P, 1825,Oxford; C. Watford, Herts; V. Long Wittendon 1830–85; R.D. Abingdon, 1869.

Cockell, Thomas Whitehead, 1795–1870, Wadham, 1813, BA 1816, MA 1823; D. 1817, Bath & Wells, P. 1818, Salisbury; C. All Cannings, Devizes, Wilts,? C. Stanford Dingley 1856; C. Stanford in the Vale 1860.

Cockerton, James (Ob.1861), Trinity, Dublin; incorporated at Queens',Cambridge, BA 1830; D. 1830, Winchester, P. 1831, Lincoln; R. Turweston, 1843–61.

Cockle, Richard Tarn, 1822–1858, St.John's, Cambridge, 1839, BA 1845, MA 1846; P.C. Seer Green, 1848–58.

Codd, Alfred, 1825–1896, St.John's, Cambridge, 1845, BA 1849, MA 1860; D. 1850, Rochester, P. 1851, Rochester; C. Witham, Essex, 1850–53; R. Hawridge 1853–57; P.C. Beaminster, Dorset, 1857–90; R.D, Bridport, Dorset,1871–90; R. Stockton, Wilts. 1890–93.

Coker, Cadwaller, 1824–1894, New College, 1844, BA 1848, MA 1852, Fellow 1844–53; D. 1848, P. 1849; R. Shalstone 1854–72; R.D.; R. Fringford 1873–94.

Coker, John, 1793–1864, New College, 1811, BCL 1816, Fellow until 1816; D. 1819, Oxford, P. 1820, Oxford; R. Radcliffe 1825–1864; R.D.; Prebendary of Lincoln 1843–?

Coker, John, 1822–1901, New College, 1839, BA 1842, MA 1847, Fellow, 1839–56; D. 1844, Oxford, P. 1845, Oxford; R. Tingewick, 1855–1901.

Coleman, George, 1803–1858, Christ's, Cambridge, 1825, BA 1829, MA 1848; D. 1828, Lincoln, P. 1830, Lincoln; C. Tingewick until 1839; R. Water Stratford 1839–58; C. Maids Moreton 1846; Surrogate, Dio. Oxford; District Secretary, S.P.C.K.

Coles, Edward Norman, 1826–? St.John's, Oxford, 1844; D. 1848, Worcester, P. 1849. Worcester; C. Holy Trinity, Bordesley, nr Birmingham, 1848–52; C. Aylesbury 1850–52; C. Madron, Truro, 1852–54; C. Hardwick w Weedon,? R. Battlesden w Pettesgrove, Dio. Ely, 1858–?

Coley, Joseph Boughton, 1787–1855, Christ Church, 1805, BA 1809, MA 1812; D. 1810, Oxford, P. 1811, Oxford; C. Dorchester 1813; Chaplain Christ Church 1818; P.C. Drayton 1814–55.

Collis, Thomas William Sandes, Trinity, Dublin, BA 1859; D.1860, Cashel, P.1861,Ely; V. Soulbury 1861–64; C. St.Paul's, Brighton, 1864–68; C. St.Paul's, Knightsbridge, 1868–74; C. St.Paul's, Brighton, 1879–81; V. St.Bartholomew's, Brighton, 1881–?

Collinson, George John, 1813–1865, Trinity, Cambridge, 1836, BA 1840, MA 1858; D. 1840, Salisbury, P. 1841,Chichester; C. Witchampton, Dorset, 1840–42; V. Swanborne 1843–52; R. Compton Abbas, Dorset, 1852–53; P.C. St.James', Clapham, Middx. 1853–65; Secr. British & Foreign Bible Society 1852.

Collyns, John Martyn, 1827–? Christ Church, 1844, BA 1848, MA 1854, Student, 1846–68; D. 1850, Oxford, P. 1851, Oxford; C. Kirkham, Manchester, 1852–55; P.C. St.Leonard's, Drayton, 1855–58; P.C. Bensington, 1858–67; R. Daventry, Northants. 1867–? R.D. Weedon 1875, Chaplain Daventry Union 1877; Hon. Canon Peterborough 1885.

Colvill, John Burleigh, Trinity, Dublin, BA 1847, MA 1869; D. 1847, Chester, P. 1848, Bath & Wells; C. St.Mary's, Reading, 1854–58; Chaplain Berkshire Hospital, Reading, 1861; Chaplain Berkshire County Goal,Reading, 1861–72.

Conybeare, Charles Rankin, 1821–1885, Christ Church, 1839, BA 1843, MA 1846, Student, 1839–53; D. 1844,Oxford, P. 1851, Oxford; V. Pyrton 1852–57; V. Itchenstoke w Abbotstone, Hants. 1857–1885.

Cooke[r]sley, William Gifford, 1802–1880, King's, Cambridge, 1821, BA 1825, MA 1827, Fellow 1824–31; D. 1827, Ely, P. 1835, Rochester; Assistant Master Eton College 1829–54; C. St.Peter's, Ipswich,1855; C. St.John's, Fitzroy Sq. London, 1856–57; V. Hayton, Yorkshire, 1857–60; V. St.Peter's, Hammersmith, 1860–68; R. Tempsford, Beds. 1868–80.

Cookes, Thomas Horace, 1822–? Worcester, Oxford, 1840, BA 1844, MA 1847, Fellow, 1849–67; D. 1847, Oxford, P. 1848, Oxford; C. Wigginton 1847; C. Spelsbury 1864; R. Tadmarton 1867–83; R. Newton Purcell 1883–97.

Cookson,William, 1792–1866, Brasenose, 1811, BA 1814, MA 1817; D. 1816, Salisbury, P. 1817, Salisbury; V. Hungerford 1818–66; V. Broadhinton, Wilts. 1835–66; Domestic Chaplain to the Dowager Countess of Antrim 1834.

Corbett, Griffith Owen, D. 1852, Rupertsland, P. 1853, Rupertsland; Min. Holy Trinity, Assiniboia, 1853–55; C. Granborough 1855–57; Min. Holy Trinity, Assiniboia,1857–62; C. Egloskerry w Tremaine, Cork, 1868–69; C. St.Mary, March, Cambs. 1875–76.

Cornish, Arthur Athelstan, 1816–? Exeter, Oxford, 1834, BA 1838, MA 1840; D. 1839, P. 1840; C. Churchill w Sarsden; C. Old Windsor 1850; V. Old Windsor 1854–?

Cornwell, Thomas Charles Brand, 1827–1893, Emmanuel, Cambridge, 1846, BA 1849, MA 1852; D. 1851, P. 1852; C. Stanwick, Northants. 1851–53; C. Stanford in the Vale ? C. Geddington, Northants. 1856–61; V. Geddington 1861–85; R. Scaldwell, 1885–93.

Cotter, Charles Purcell, ob. 1891, Trinity, Dublin, BA 1845, MA 1860; D. 1849, Cork, P. 1850, Salisbury; C. Donoughmore, Cloyne, 1849–50; C. Tincleton, Dorset, 1850–53; C. Hadlow, Kent, 1853–57; V. Stantonbury w New Bradwell 1857–1891.

Coulthard, Robert, 1797–1868, Queen's, Oxford, 1816, BA 1820, MA 1823, Fellow 1829–45; D. 1823, P. 1823; R. Sulhamstead Abbotts 1845–1868.

Cox, Frederick, 1796–1879, Lincoln, Oxford, 1813, BA 1818, MA 1819; D. 1819, Canterbury, P. 1820, Canterbury; V. Upper Winchendon 1821–1879; Headmaster Aylesbury Free Grammar School 1840; C. Fleet Marston 1851.

Cox, William Hayward, 1804–1871, Pembroke, Oxford, 1821, BA 1825, MA 1829, BD 1841, Fellow, Queen's Coll. 1828–33; Vice-Princ. St.Mary Hall, Oxford 1836–? D. 1826, Cashel, P. 1827, Oxford; R. St.Martin's, Carfax, Oxford 1839–53; City Lecturer, Carfax, 1849–58; R.Tenby, Pembrokeshire, 1852–54; R. Eaton Bishop, dio. Hereford, 1854–71; R.D.; Examining Chaplain to the Bishop of Hereford 1848; Preb. Hereford 1848, 1854; Proctor in Convocation, Dio. St.David's, 1853–55.

Coxe, Charles Batson, 1780–1846, Merton, 1798, BA 1802, MA 1810; V. East (Little) Shefford 1804–46; R. Avington 1810–46.

Coxwell, Thomas Tracey, 1779–1855, Worcester, Oxford, 1796, BA 1799 [Pembroke], MA 1803; V. Great Marlow 1811–50; C. Westwell 1814; P.C. Eastleach-Turville, Gloucs, 1814–51; R. Horton 1830–55.

Crabtree, William, 1785–1864, University, Oxford, 1803, BA 1807, MA 1810, Fellow until 1821; R. Checkendon 1820–64.

Cranmer, James Stewart Gordon, 1800–? St.John's, Cambridge, 1842, BD 1846, DD 1869; D. 1842, Chester, P. 1843, Chester; C. Ancote, Lancs. 1842–44; C. Bradford,Yorks. 1844–48; C. Haworth, Yorks. 1848–51; C. Oakham, Rutland, 1853; C. Grove, 1853–60; C. North & South Brewham, Bath & Wells, 1875–81.

Cree, John Adams, 1825–? University, Oxford, 1843, BA 1847, MA 1849, BD 1856, Fellow of Magdalen 1852–58; D. 1848, Winchester, P. 1849, Winchester; C. St.Leonard's, Streatham, 1848–52; C. St.Mary's, Dover, 1852–58; C. Upton w Chalvey 1858–67; V. Great Marlow 1867–81; V. Sunningdale 1884–1903.

Cross, John, Kings, London, ob.1885, D. 1853, Ripon, P. 1854, Ripon; C. Chipping Norton ? C. Finstock.? R. Mursley 1860–85.

Cunningham, Albert Henry, 1835–? Queen's, Oxford, 1856, BA 1860; D. 1861, Oxford, P. 1862, Oxford; C. Hanney 1861–63; C. Combe St.Nicholas, Somerset, 1863–66; C. Basing, Hants, 1866–70; C. Henfield, Sussex, 1870–73; C. Chislehurst, Kent, 1866–?75; C. Minehead, Somerset,1875–?

Cunningham, Francis Macauley,1816–1899, Trinity, Cambridge, 1834; BA 1838, MA 1841; D. 1839, Norwich, P. 1840, Norwich; C. Lowestoft, Suffolk, 1845–? R. East Tisted, Hants. 1851–64; R. Witney 1864–79; R.D. Witney 1872–79; R. Brightwell w Sotwell 1879–99; J.P. for Oxfordshire.

Curme, Thomas, 1806–1884, Worcester, Oxford, 1824, BA 1828; V. Sandford St.Martin 1841–84; Domestic Chaplain to the Duke of Marlborough.

Currie, Sir Frederick Larkins, Bart. 1823–1900; Christ's, Cambridge, 1842, BA 1846, MA 1849; a "Cricket Blue" 1845; D. 1848, Norwich, P. 1849, Norwich; C. Clenchwarton, Norfolk, 1848–55; C. Bright Waltham 1861–72; C. Petersfield, Hants. 1872–85; R.D. Exton, Hants. 1885–86; R. Old Alresford, Hants. 1886–94.

Curtis, Francis Henry, 1829–1886, Merton, 1848, BA 1853, MA 1856; P. 1859, Oxford; C. Padworth 1859; Sub-Master, King Edward V1's Grammar School, Norwich; Master, King Edward's School, Birmingham; Master, Upper School, Liverpool Dio. College.

Curtis, George William, 1788–1865, St.John's, Cambridge, 1807, BA 1810, MA 1814; D. 1811, P. 1811; V. Leominster, Hereford, 1819–23; R. Padworth 1823–65; R. Wennington, Essex, 1826–65.

Cust, Arthur Perceval Purey,1828–? Brasenose, 1846, BA 1850, MA [All Souls] 1854, BD 1880, DD 1880, Fellow of All Souls 1850–54; D. 1851, Oxford, P. 1852, Rochester; C. Northchurch, St.Albans, 1851–53; R. Cheddington 1853–61; R.D. Mursley 1858–62; V. St.Mary,Reading, 1862–75; R.D. Reading 1868–75; Hon. Can. Christ Church, 1874; V. Aylesbury 1875–76; Archdeacon of Buckingham 1875; Dean of York 1880–?

Cuxson, George Appleby, 1814–? Magdalen Hall, 1835, BA 1842, MA 1843; D. 1843, Peterborough, P. 1844, Peterborough; C. East Carlton, Rockingham, Northants.1845; C. Dunton 1846; Chaplain, Aylesbury Union, 1850; R. Halton, Bucks. 1857–65; R. Dinton 1865–69; R. St.James'Chapel, Hampstead, 1872–74; C. Girton, Dio. Ely, 1874–?

Dand, Thomas, 1811–1868, Queen's, Oxford, 1828, BA 1832, MA 1836, Fellow 1845–46; C. Broughton ?, R. Blechingon 1846–68.

Dandridge, George, 1800–1858, Worcester, Oxford, 1818, BA 1822, MA 1825; R. Rousham 1841–58.

Davies, A.E., C. Hungerford about 1852.

Davis, George, C. Kirtlington 1856

Deane, Richard Wallace, 1821–? Exeter, Oxford, 1837, BA 1841, MA 1846; D. 1843, Ely, P. 1844, Ely; C. St.Cuthbert's, Bedford about 1852; Chaplain to the Bedford Infirmary and Union 1852–61; V. Turville 1861–74.

De Salis, Henry John Augustus Fane, 1829–? Exeter, Oxford, 1847, BA 1850, MA 1853; D. 1850, P. 1852; R. Fringford 1852–72.

Dickson, Richard James, 1827–? Trinity, Oxford, 1845, BA 1850, MA 1851; D. 1850, P. 1851; C. Churchstoke, Hereford, 1850–52; C. Welford 1854–64; V. Woodlands St.Mary 1864–?

Dobree, De Lisle De Beauvoir, 1828–? St.Peter's, Cambridge, 1846, BA 1850; D. 1850, P. 1851; C. Paulton, Somerset, 1852; C. Alderney w St.Matthew's, Guernsey, 1853–54; C. Herriard, Hants. 1856–58; P.C. St.Matthew's, Guernsey, 1858–63; C. Ashmore, nr Salisbury, 1863–68; C. Salford w Little Rollright, 1868–72. Disappears from *Crockford* 1874.

Dodd, Henry Alison, 1799–1869, Queen's, Oxford, 1815, BA 1819, MA 1822, Fellow 1829–42, Chaplain; D. 1825, P. 1826; V. Sparsholt w Kingston Lisle 1841–69.

Dry, William John, 1822–77, Wadham, 1839, BA 1844, MA 1848; D. 1844, P. 1851; V. Weston-on-the-Green 1854–77; Surrogate.

Dudley, William Charles, 1816–? Queens', Cambridge, 1834, BA 1838, MA 1851; D. 1838, Chester, P. 1839, Chester; C. Wharton, Cheshire 1838–40; P.C. Holy Trinity, Sheerness, 1840–41; Missionary, New Zealand 1841–55; C. Henley on Thames 1850–51 [while on home leave]; C. Clifton Reynes, 1855–57; C. Over, Cheshire 1857–63; V. Ashton Hayes 1857; C. Weaverham 1863–66; C. Penistone, Yorks. 1866–80. Disappears from *Crockford* 1881.

Dundas, James Whitley Deans, 1812–1872, Magdalene, Cambridge, 1830, BA 1834, MA 1837; D.1835, Norwich, P. 1836, Norwich; V. Ramsbury,Wilts. 1839–40; V. Kintbury 1840–72.

Dupre, Henry Ramus, 1810–1887, Exeter, Oxford, 1828, BA 1840; D. 1841,Chichester, P. 1842,Chichester; C. Forest Row, Sussex, 1841–48; R. Shellingford 1848–87.

Dupuis, Henry, 1808–1867, King's, Cambridge, 1827, BA 1831, MA 1834, BD 1849 [Oxford], Fellow 1830–52; D. 1842, P. 1843; Assistant Master, Eton College 1836–52; V. Richmond, Surrey 1852–67; R.D. 1858–67, Surrogate.

Durrell, Thomas Vavasor, 1800–1879, Christ Church, 1818, BA 1821, MA 1824, Student 1820–33; D. 1822, P. 1823; C. Checkendon 1823; V. Pyrton 1832–? R. Mongewell 1852–79.

Edwards, John, 1832–? Trinity, Oxford, 1850, BA 1856, MA 1857; D. 1856, Lincoln, P. 1857,Oxford; C. Harlaston, Staffs. 1856–58; C. Chipping Norton 1857–58; C. St.Paul's, Knightsbridge, 1858–60; V. Prestbury, Bath & Wells, 1860–?85; C. St.Paul's, Brighton, 1885–? Took name of Baghot de la Bere 1879.

Eliott, Edward,1827–? New College, 1845, SCL 1848, BCL 1853, Fellow 1847–61; D. 1853, Oxford, P. 1854, Oxford; C. Tredington, Worcs. 1853–56; C. Norton Bavant,Wilts. 1856–57; C. Sutton-under-Brailes, Gloucester & Bristol, 1858–59; C. Tredington 1859–61; P.C. Sibford Gower 1860–64; V. Norton Bavant, Wilts.1864–?

Ellerton, Edward, 1771–1851, University, Oxford, 1787, BA 1792, MA 1795, BD 1805, DD 1815, Fellow of Magdalen 1803–51;C. Islip 1797; P.C. Horspath 1814–41; P.C. Sevenhampton, Gloucs, 1825–51; C. Theale 1831–51; C. Tilehurst 1831–51.

Elliott, Charles John, 1818–1881, St.Catherine's, Cambridge, 1836, BA 1840, MA 1843; D. 1843, London, P. 1843, London; C. St.John's, Holloway, London, 1842–44; V. Winkfield 1844–81; Surrogate 1872; Hon. Canon Christ Church 1873; Cambridge University Select Preacher 1877; Member of the Old Testament Revision Committee.

Ellis, William May, 1804–1846, Christ Church, 1821, BA 1825, MA 1829; C. Great Milton 1828; R. Ickford 1838–46.

Ellison, Henry John, 1813–1899, Trinity, Cambridge, 1831, BA 1835, MA 1838; D. 1838, Ely [for Norwich], P. 1840, Norwich; C. Chelmondiston, Suffolk, 1838–40; P.C. All Saints, Brighton, 1840–42; V. Edensor, Derbyshire, 1845–55; R.D. Bakewell 1852–55; V. New Windsor 1855–95; Hon. Canon of Christ Church 1872–94, R. Great Hasely, 1875–94; R.D. Cuddesdon 1884–90; Chaplain in Ordinary to Queen Victoria 1879–90. Hon. Canon Canterbury 1894–99. Founded the Church of England & Ireland Temperance Society 1862.

Elton, Edward, 1817–1898, Balliol, 1834, BA 1837, MA 1841; D. 1839, Exeter, P. 1841, Salisbury; C. Erchfont, Wilts. 1839–47; C. Stanton St.Bernard, Wilts. 1839–47; C. Bierton w Buckland 1847–51; C. Stoke Mandeville 1847–51; V. Wheatley 1849–84; R. Sherington 1884–98.

England, William Henry, 1800–1858, Pembroke, Oxford, 1819, BA 1824, MA 1828; R. Ellesborough 1832–58.

Erle, Christopher, 1790–1870, New College, 1808, BA 1812, MA 1815; D. 1818, P. 1819; R. Hardwick 1833–70.

Evans, William, 1802–1860, Trinity, Oxford, 1820, BA 1827, MA 1838; R. Pusey 1827–1860.

Everett, George Frederick, 1794–1872, Balliol, 1810, BA 1813, MA 1818; D. 1816, Salisbury, P. 1817, Salisbury; R. Shaw cum Donnington 1847–1872.

Evetts, Thomas, 1821–1898, Corpus Christi, Oxford, 1838, BA 1842, MA 1844; D. 1843, Lincoln, P. 1844, Lincoln; C. Clifton Reynes 1843–48; P.C. Prestwood 1849–63 (*Oldfield* 1852); R.D. Amersham 1853–63; R. Monks Risborough 1863–98; R.D. Aylesbury 1863–87; Hon. Canon Christ Church 1880.

Eyre, Francis John, 1811–1878, Trinity, Cambridge, 1830, BA 1834; D. 1835, P. 1836; C. Englefield 1841; R. Englefield 1855–68.

Eyre, William Thomas, 1795–1868, Brasenose, 1812, BA 1816, MA 1819; D. 1818, P. 1819; V. Padbury 1830–68; P.C. Hillesdon 1830–68.

Faber, Francis Atkinson, 1805–1876, University, Oxford, 1822, BA 1826, MA, 1828, BD 1836, Fellow of Magdalen Coll 1836–45, Select Preacher 1834; D.1827, Durham, P.1828,York; R. Saunderton 1844–76.

Fairbairn, Adam Henderson, 1836–1888, Trinity, Cambridge, 1855, BA 1859, MA 1862, Rowing Blue 1858 & 60; D. 1860, Oxford, P. 1861, Oxford; C. Wargave 1860–63; C. Wilton, Wilts. 1863–64; P.C. Knowl Hill 1864–73; V. Waltham St.Lawrence 1873–85; R. Fawley, Bucks. 1885–88.

Faithful, George David, 1786–1866, Corpus Christi, Oxford, 1803, BA 1807, MA 1810, BD 1818, Fellow 1812–30; R. Gunby, nr Spilsby, Lincs, 1830–66; R. Heyford 1839–66.

Falcon, Thomas William, 1832–1883, Queen's, Oxford, 1849, BA 1853, MA 1856, Fellow 1855–63; D. 1854, Oxford, P. 1862, Oxford; R. Charlton-upon-Otmoor 1862–83.

Fanshawe, Henry Leighton, 1833–? New College 1850, BA 1853, MA 1857, Fellow; D. 1855, Oxford, P. 1856, Oxford; C. Shipton-under-Wychwood 1855–57; C. Clifton Hampden 1858; R. Adwell w South Weston 1866–1900.

Feild[e], Matthew, 1779–1846, Trinity, Cambridge, 1795, migrated to Pembroke 1796, BA 1800; V. Lancing, Sussex, 1800–?34; V. Shinfield w Swallowfield 1823–46.

Few, William Jebb, 1835–1879, Christ Church, 1853, BA 1857, MA 1860; D. 1858, Oxford, P. 1859, Oxford; C. Henley on Thames 1858–60; C. Alverstoke, Hants, 1860–61; C. St.Mary's, Reading, 1862–72; V. St.Luke's, Southampton 1867–75; R. St.Nicholas', Guildford, 1875–79.

Field, John, 1813–1884, Magdalen Hall, 1831, BA 1834, MA 1837; D.1836, Worcester, P. 1827, Llandaff for Worcester; C. St.Clement's, Worcester, 1836–39; C. Chipping Norton 1839–40; Chaplain, County Goal, Reading, 1840–58; R. West Rounton, Yorks, 1858–84.

Finch, Robert, 1829–1910, Trinity, Cambridge, 1847, BA 1851, MA 1854; D. 1852, Canterbury, P. 1853, Canterbury; C. Newchurch, Kent, 1852; C. Wittershaw w Brenzett 1853–57; R. Pangbourne 1857–96.

Finden, George Sketchley, King's, London, AKC 1859; D. 1860, Oxford, P. 1861, Oxford; C. Monks Risborough 1860; C. Newport Pagnell 1861–62; C. Moulsoe 1863–69.

Fish, John David, 1828–68, Caius, Cambridge, 1846, BA 1853, MA 1853; D. 1851, Lichfield, P. 1852, Lichfield; C. Brereton, nr. Rugeley, 1852–53; C. Banbury 1857–60; C. South Banbury 1862; without cure 1861–68; C. St. Sepulchres, Northampton, 1868.

Fisher, Wilfred, 1833–? Christ Church, BA 1855, MA 1858, Student 1853–62; D. 1857, Oxford, P. 1861, Oxford; R. Westwell 1861–80.

Fitzclarence, Lord Augustus, 1805–1854, 5th son of William IV by Mrs. Jordan Venn, Brasenose, Oxford, to Trinity, Cambridge, 1826, LL B 1832, Hon. LL D 1835; Chaplain to Queen Adelaide; V. Mapledurham 1829–54.

Fixsen, John Frederick, 1830–1909, Trinity, Cambridge, 1848, BA 1852, MA 1855; D. 1853, Oxford, P. 1858, Oxford; C. Marcham 1853–56; C. Henley-on-Thames 1856–61; C. Peasemore, Shipton on Cherwell,1861–63; P.C. Merton, Surrey,1863–69; V. Ugborough, dio. Exeter, 1869–85; V. Bucknell w Buckton, Salop, 1885–1909.

Fletcher, William, 1802–? admitted to St.John's,Cambridge,1821, but did not matriculate; D. 1824, Norwich, P. 1826, Norwich; P.C. Charsfield, Suffolk, 1829–?33; V. Stone 1832–?39; R. Foxcote 1839–43; Chaplain to the Duke of Buckingham 1843–52; V. Harwell 1843–52.
Disappears 1853 from the *Clergy List*. Information only in *Venn*.

Flint, William Charles Raffles, 1819–1884, Trinity Hall, Cambridge, 1837, BA 1841, MA 1844; D. 1843,Winchester, P. 1844, Winchester; C. Idsworth, Hants. 1843–44; C. Morden, Surrey, 1845–50; Great Rollright 1851–55; V. Sunningdale, 1857–1884.

Forbes, Charles (Ob. 1869), University of Edinburgh, MA 1839; D. 1840, Durham, P. 1841, Durham; Domestic Chaplain to Earl Grey 1840; V. South Banbury 1846–69; Chaplain, Banbury Gaol 1849; Chaplain, Banbury Union 1855.

Fordyse, Arthur Thomas Dingwall, 1821–1860, St.John's, Oxford, 1840, BA 1847, MA 1851; D. 1849, P.1850; C. St.Giles', Oxford,1849; C. Finstock w Charlbury, about 1856; C. Kirtlington, ? *Foster* only.

Fortescue, William Fraine,1809–? Exeter, Oxford, 1827, BA 1831, MA 1835, Fellow of New College, 1828–50; D. 1832, Oxford, P. 1838, Oxford; V. Chesterton 1849–89.

Fosbery, Thomes Vincent, 1807–1875, Trinity, Dublin, BA 1830, MA 1847; D. 1831, Salisbury, P. 1832, Salisbury; P.C. Sunningdale 1847–57; V. St.Giles, Reading, 1857–70.

Fraser, James, 1818–1885, Lincoln, 1836, BA 1840, MA 1842, DD 1870, Fellow 1840–60, Hon. Fellow 1870, Select Preacher at Oxford 1851, 61, 71, 77 & 1885[no sermon preached]. D. 1846, Oxford, P. 1847, Oxford; R. Cholderton 1847–60; Chancellor of Salisbury Cathedral 1858–60; R. Ufton Nervet 1860–70, Preb. of Salisbury Cathedral 1861–70; Diocesan Inspector of Schools, Oxford; Chaplain to Bp Hamilton of Salisbury; Bishop of Manchester 1870–85.

Frazer, Arthur Bruce, 1826–1895, Trinity, Cambridge, 1843, BA 1847, MA 1851; D. 1851, Chichester, P. 1852, Chichester; C. St.John's, Brighton, 1851–54; R. [& Patron] Haversham 1856–89.

Frith, William Cokayne, 1786–1855, St.John's, Oxford, 1802, BCL 1808, DCL 1814, Fellow 1802–18; D. 1808, Oxford, P. 1809,Oxford; R. Chilfrome, Dorset, 1824–55; R. St.Peter's,Wallingford 1828–55.

Fry, Thomas, 1775–1860, Oriel, 1792, BA 1796, MA 1798 [Lincoln Coll.], P. 1798, Oxford; R. Emberton 1804–1860; V. Toot Baldon 1858–?

Furlong, Charles Joseph, 1803–? Sidney Sussex, Cambridge, 1819, BA 1824, MA 1843; D. 1828, Salisbury, P. 1831, Bath. & Wells; V. Warfield 1834–59; English Chaplain at Versailles 1843; Min. Trinity British Episcopal Church, Boulogne-sur-Mer, 1847–68. Disappears from *Crockford* 1874.

Gaisford, Charles, 1782–1857, Caius, Cambridge, 1801, BA 1805, MA 1809; D. 1805, Salisbury, P. 1806,Canterbury; C. Devizes, Wilts. 1805; R. Chilton 1808–57.

Gaisford, Thomas, 1780–1855, Christ Church, 1797, BA 1801, MA 1804, BD & DD 1831; D. 1809, Oxford, P. 1810, Oxford; Regius Professor of Greek 1811–35; Preb. Worcester 1825–28; Preb. St.Paul's Cathedral 1833–? Preb. Llandaff,1833–? R. Westwell 1815–47; Canon of Durham 1829–31; Dean of Christ Church 1831–55.

Garratt, Charles Foster, 1833–? Oriel, 1851, BA 1856, MA 1857; D.1855, York, P. 1856, York; C. Ledshaw-cum-Fairburn, Yorks. 1855–58; V. Little Tew 1858–80.

Garrett, John, C. Garsington 1850. *Clergy List* 1852.

Gazeley, Robert Court, 1813–1900, Christ's, Cambridge, 1833, BA 1837, MA 1841; D. 1837, Oxford, P. 1838, Oxford; C. Caversham 1837–43; C. East Garston 1843–50; C. West Shefford 1847; C. Beedon 1852; C. Compton 1852; R. Wayford, Somerset, 1857–80; Lic. Preacher, Bath & Wells, 1891–1900.

George, John, 1763–1847, Jesus, Oxford, 1780, BA 1794, MA 1787, BD 1795; P. 1786,Oxford; R. Aston Clinton 1799–1847; R. Gromont, Monmouth, 1799–1847.

Gibbings, Robert, Trinity, Dublin, BA 1841, MA 1853; D. 1842, Killaloe, P. 1843, Killaloe; C. Peasmore 1847; V. Radley 1852–?

Gibbs, Walter Charles, (Ob. 1861,) Trinity, Dublin, BA 1829; P.C. Halliwell in Dean, Lancs. 1840–? P.C. Tylers Green 1854–61.

Gilbert, William, St.Aidan's, Liverpool; D. 1852, Chester, P. 1853, Chester; C. Blackburn ? C. Piddington 1857 & 59; C. St.George, Wigan; V. Chearsley 1867–72; C. Ashendon & Dorton 1868; C. Frampton, nr Boston, Lincoln, 1875–78; V. Holland-Fen, nr Boston, 1875–88; V. Aston Magna, dio. Worc. 1888–1900.

Giles, John Allen, 1808–1884, Corpus Christi, Oxford, 1824; BA 1828, MA 1831, Fellow 1832–33, D.C.L. 1838; D. 1835, Winchester, P. 1835, Winchester; Headmaster, Camberwell College School 1834–36; Headmaster, City of London School 1836–40; C. Bampton 1845–54; C. (in charge) Perivale, dio. London, 1857–61; R. Sutton, Surrey, 1867–84.

Gill, Francis Turner, 1830–1888, Downing, Cambridge,1848, BA 1852, MA 1857; D. 1854, Worcester, P. 1855, Worcester; C. St.James-the-Great, Stratford-on-Avon, 1856; P.C. Bishopton, Stratford-on-Avon, 1856–59; C. Warfield 1859; V. Warfield 1860–88.

Gillam, Thomas Henry,1821–? Pembroke, Oxford,1840, BA 1844, MA 1847; D. 1844, Lichfield, P. 1845, Lichfield; C. Blewbury 1847; C. Ewelme 1850–62; V. Culham 1862–75; Chaplain to the Bishop of Chester,1865–84; V. Weaverham, Cheshire,1875–? Surrogate, Oxford & Berks.

Goalen, Alexander, 1835–1872, Brasenose, 1853, BA 1857, MA 1863; D. 1858, Oxford, P. 1859, Oxford; C. Hanney 1859; C. Culham; C. Abingdon; C. Brompton, London; Hon. Chaplain Central Diocesan School, Thame. Sometime Lecturer in Natural Science, New Inn Hall, Oxford.

Goddard, Daniel Ward, 1812–1884, Exeter, Oxford, 1829, BA 1833, MA 1835; D. 1834, P. 1835; C. Warfield 1843; V. Burford & P.C. Fulbrook 1855–60; R. Holwell, 1860–84.

Godfrey, William, 1802–? Queens', Cambridge, 1820, BA 1824, MA 1828; D. 1823, P. 1823; V. Ravenstone 1823–61; P.C. Weston Underwood 1827–60; V. Studley, Warws, 1860–72.

Goffin, John Henry, King's, London; D. 1856, Lichfield, P. 1857, Lichfield; C. Wolstanton, Staffs; C. Wickham, Hants; C. Water Stratford 1860; C. Horley w Horton 1875–?

Goodhart, Charles Joseph, 1803–1892, Trinity, Cambridge,1822, BA 1826, MA 1831; D. 1827,Gloucester & Bristol, P. 1828, Gloucester & Bristol; C. Hazelbury Bryan, Dorset, 1827–30; C. Broad Chalke, Wilts, 1830–36; Minister, St.Mary's Chapel, Reading 1837–52; Chaplain, Poor House, Reading 1843; Minister, Park Chapel, Chelsea 1852–68; Clerical Secretary, London Society for promoting Christianity amongst the Jews 1863–68.

Goodlake, Thomas William, 1811–1875, Pembroke, Oxford, 1829, BA 1834, MA 1836, Fellow 1838–46; MA (Cantab.) 1843; D. 1834, Oxford, P. 1835, Oxford; C. Bampton 1845; V. Bradwell, Gloucs. 1845–55; R. Broughton Pogges w Filkens 1855–61; Surrogate; Dio. Inspector of Schools 1847–61; R. Swindon, Wilts. 1861–75.

Goodrich, Bartlett, 1790–1855, Oriel 1808, BA 1812, MA 1815; R. Hardmead 1817–55; V. Great Jaling, Essex,1817–55.

Goodrich, Bartlett George, 1832–? University, Oxford, 1845, BA 1848;
D. 1849, Winchester, P.1850, Winchester; C. East Woodhay w Ashmansworth 1849–52; C. Ebbourne w Hampstead Marshall 1852–58; R. Hardmead 1856–? (In *Crockford* 1903)

Gordon, Edward, 1828–1916, Corpus Christi, Cambridge, 1849, BA 1853; D. 1850, York, P. 1852, Carlisle; C. Kilnwick w Aike, Yorkshire; C. Fritwell 1856; R. Kildale, Yorkshire, 1860–67; V. Atwick, 1867–96.

Gordon, Osborne, 1813-1883 Christ Church 1833, BA 1836, MA 1839, BD 1847; Student, Censor 1846; D 1839, P 1840; R Easthampstead 1861-83.

Gordon, Robert, 1830–1914, Christ's, Cambridge, 1850, BA 1854, MA 1857; D. 1854, Lichfield, P. 1856, Lichfield; C. Norton, Staffs 1854–55; C. Longdon 1855–56; C. Speen & Lecturer, Speenhamland 1856–58; R. Hammerwich, dio. Lichfield 1858–90.

Gordon, Robert Augustus, 1815–1895, Trinity, Cambridge, 1833, BA 1837, MA 1840 [degrees from Pembroke College]; D. 1839, Canterbury, P. 1840, Canterbury; C. Charing, Kent 1839–40; C. Sundridge,Kent 1840–46; R. Avington, Berks 1846–53; R. Barley, Herts.1853–90; R.D. Buntingford 1854–82.

Gore, John,1800–1871, Caius, Cambridge,1820, BA 1824; D.1828, Lincoln, P. 1829, Lincoln; V. Shalbourne 1842–71.

Gossett, Isaac, 1783–1855, Exeter, Oxford,1800, BA 1804, MA 1807;V. Datchet, Bucks.1814–52; V. New Windsor, 1821–55; Chaplain (to 4 sovereigns) Windsor Castle.

Gough, Henry, 1812–1862, Queen's, Oxford, 1830, BA 1834, MA 1838, Fellow 1846–56; D. 1837, Oxford, P. 1840, Exeter; R. Enham-Knights, Hampshire,1855–56; R. Charlton-upon-Otmoor 1856–62.

Gould, John ob. 1866, Magdalen, Oxford, BA 1802, MA 1805, BD 1814, Fellow 1808-1819; D 1806 Oxford, P 1812 Oxford; ?V New Shoreham, Chichester 1816-56; R Beaconsfield 1818-66.

Gould, Robert John,1803–1880, Wadham,1824, BA 1828, MA 1833; D.1833,Lincoln, P. 1834, Lincoln; C. Clewer 1841; C. New Windsor 1844–54; P.C. Trull, Somerset, 1857–58; V. Stratfield Mortimer 1860–80.

Gowering, George James,1823–? Magdalen Hall, Oxford, 1847, BA 1850, MA 1852; D. 1851, Oxford, P.1852, Oxford; C. Ellesborough 1851;C.Banbury 1853; Headmaster Ilminster Grammar School, Somerset, 1859–75; V. Kingston, Bath & Wells, 1859–75; V. White Lackington, Ilminster, 1875; Chaplain to Viscount Bridport; R.D. Crewkerne, 1876; Assisant Dio. Inspector of Schools, Bath &Wells, 1877; Prebendary of.Wells 1880.

Grace, Oliver James, 1834–? Jesus, Cambridge, 1853, BA 1856, MA 1859;
D.1856, Oxford, P. 1858, Oxford; C. Bledlow 1856–59; C. Saunderton 1859–76; Chaplain to the Wycombe Union 1859; R. Saunderton 1876–1905. Disappears from *Crockford* 1918.

Grainger, John, 1818–1899, Caius, Cambridge, 1844, BA 1848, MA 1851; D. 1848, London, P. 1849, London; Tutor, Church Missionary College Islington, London, 1848–51; Assistant Master Eton College 1851–60; Chaplain, Windsor Union Workhouse; V. Penn 1860–98.

Grainger, John Cecil, 1801–1857, Downing, Cambridge, 1820, BA 1827; D. 1827, Salisbury, P. 1827, Salisbury; P.C. Burcombe, Wilts, 1827–57; V. St.Giles, Reading, 1834–57.

Grantham, John Foyster, 1786–1855, Exeter, Oxford, 1803, BA 1807; V. Cookham 1837–55.

Gray, Charles Edward,1813–? Brasenose, 1833, BA 1837, MA 1840; C. Chearsley ? C. Great Gaddesdon, Herts.? C. Rickmansworth, Herts.? P.C. Princes Risborough 1845–63; V. Skipwith, Selby, Yorks,1863–?

Gregory, Henry, 1803–1882, Christ Church, 1819, BA 1822, MA 1834; D. 1825, Oxford, P. 1826, Oxford; C. Cogges w Minster Lovell 1825–34; V. Asthall 1834–82; Headmaster, Witney Grammar School, 1834–76.

Gregson, John, 1817–? Brasenose, 1834, BA 1838, MA 1841; V. Sutton Courtney w Appleford 1845–1855; J.P.

Griffith, Thomas Llewellen, 1828–? University, Oxford, 1846, BA 1850, MA 1852; D. 1851, Llandaff, P. 1852, Llandaff; C. St.John's, Cardiff, 1851–53; C. Chadlington & Shorthampton 1854–62; R. Deal, Kent, 1862–? In *Crockford* 1880.

Grover, Henry Montague, 1791–1866, Peterhouse, Cambridge, 1824, LL B 1830; D. 1828, London for York; R. Hitchham 1833–66. Previously a London Solicitor, "owing to great bodily infirmity lived in seclusion." *Venn*.

Gunner, Edward, 1822–1885, Trinity, Oxford, 1841, BA 1846, MA 1847;
D. 1846, York, P. 1847, Ripon; C. Whiston, Yorkshire, 1846–49; C. Hambledon, Hampshire, 1849–51; C. Sparsholt, Winchester; C. Batheaston, Somerset; C. Waltham St.Lawrence 1858–65; R. Cheverel Magna, Dio. Salisbury,1865–85.

Gurdon, William, 1792–1876, Lincoln, Oxford,1811, BA 1814; V. Westbury 1817–1867. *Foster* & 1860 *Crockford*

Gurney, Henry Peter,1827–1909, St.John's, Cambridge,1845, BA 1848;
D.1850, Exeter, P. 1850, Exeter; C. Kilkhampton, Cornwall, 1850–51;
R. Tregony w Cuby, Cornwall,1851–56; V. Uffington 1855–1909.

Haigh, Daniel, 1812–1875, St.Catharine's, Cambridge, 1830, BA 1835, MA 1838; D. 1836, P. 1837; C. St.Mary Woolnooth, London; C. Little Marlow 1841–45; V. Holy Trinity, Halifax,1845–50; V. Buckden, Hunts. 1850–75, Surrogate, 1850–75.

Halifax, Joseph, 1829–1882, Queen's, Oxford,1847, BA 1851, MA 1854; D. 1852, Oxford, P.1853, Oxford; C. Bradwell 1852; C. Brize Norton 1854–55; R. Kirkbride, Cumberland, 1855–59; R. Breane, Axbridge, Somerset, 1859–82.

Hall, Charles Antill, 1821–1877, St.John's, Cambridge, 1840, BA 1844, MA 1863; R.(& Patron) Denham, 1845–77.

Hall, Thomas Owen, 1830–? Lincoln, Oxford, 1848, BA 1852; D. 1853, Winchester, P. 1854, Winchester; C. Hawkley, Hants, 1853–56; C. Penn 1856–60; C. Bringhurst w Great Easton, Leics. 1860–64; C. East Carlton, dio. Peterborough, 1864–74; R. Ashley, dio. Peterborough, 1874–1882; R. Tretton 1883–?

Halton, Lancton Miles, 1802–? St.John's, Cambridge, 1820, BA 1824; R. Woolhampton 1827–59; R. Thruxton, Hants. 1832–73. Disappears from *Crockford* 1876.

Hamilton, Archibald Robert (ob 1869), Trinity, Dublin, BA 1850, MA 1854;
D. 1854, Armagh, P.1855, Derry & Raphoe; P.C. Greenham Common, 1859–69.

Hamilton, William Jennings, 1804–1874, Pembroke, Oxford, 1821, BA 1825, MA 1828; D. 1826, Lincoln, P. 1827, Lincoln; P.C. Nettleden 1834–57; V. Ivinghoe 1845–74.

Hanbury, John, 1799–? Peterhouse, Cambridge, 1817, BA 1821, MA 1826; D. 1822, P. 1823; V. Thatcham w Greenham (C) w Midgham (C) 1842–55.

Hanmer, Thomas Waldon, 1780–1871, Brasenose, 1799, BA 1803, MA 1807; D. 1804, Oxford, P. 1804, Oxford; C. North Aston w Fritwell 1804; R. Simpson 1807–71; V. Little Missenden 1810–71.

Harington, Henry Duke, 1808–1875, Exeter, Oxford, 1824, BA 1827, MA 1830, Fellow 1826–36; D. 1830, Oxford, P. 1831, Oxford; C. Kidlington 1834; V. South Newington 1836–64; R. Knossington, dio. Peterborough, 1864–75.

Harington, Richard, 1800–1853, Christ Church, 1818, BA 1821, MA 1824, BD 1842, DD 1842; Fellow of Brasenose 1822–34; Principal 1842; D. 1829, Oxford, P. 1830, Oxford.

Harley, William, 1825–1870, Magdalene, Cambridge, 1844, BA 1848, MA 1851; D. 1848, P. 1849; C. Middleton-Scriven, Salop, 1851; V. Steventon 1851–61; R. Turweston 1861–70. A "Burgess" of Shrewsbury 1865.

Harnett, Francis William, ob 1894, King's, London, BA 1848, AKC 1851, MA 1856; D. 1851, Lichfield, P. 1853, Lichfield; C. Audley, Staffs, 1851–53; C. Walton in Aylesbury 1854–55; C. Watford 1855–58; C. Speenhamland 1858–60; V. St.George the Martyr, Wolverton, 1860–94.

Harper, John Chitty, 1804–? Queen's, Oxford, 1822, BA 1826, MA 1840, DD 1856; D. 1831, Rochester, P. 1832, Lincoln; Conduct of Eton 1832–40; V. Stratfield Mortimer 1840–56; Bishop of Christ Church, New Zealand, 1856–? Metropolitan of New Zealand, 1869.

Harris, Henry, 1818–? Magdalen, Oxford, 1837, BA 1841, MA 1843, BD 1853, Fellow 1850–58; D. 1842, P. 1853; P.C. Horspath, 1853–58; R.Winterbourne Bassett, Swindon,1858–?

Harris, Thomas, 1812–1895, Magdalen, Oxford, 1829, BA 1833, MA 1835, BD 1846, Fellow 1835–50; D. 1835, Oxford, P. 1836, Oxford; P.C. Horspath 1844; R. Swerford 1849–1895.

Harrison, John, 1787–1865, St.John's, Cambridge, 1806, BA 1809, MA 1812; D. 1811, London, P. 1812, Norwich; V. Dinton 1833–65. Chaplain to the Duke of Sussex; R.D ; J.P.

Harrison, William Anthony, 1828–1892, Caius, Cambridge, 1852, BA 1856, MA 1863; D. 1856, Oxford, P. 1857, Oxford; C. Witney 1856–64; C. St.Mary the Less, Lambeth, 1864–67; V. St.Anne, Lambeth,1867–91; R. Barnes, Surrey, 1891–92.

Hart, John, 1806–1867, Exeter, Oxford, 1824, BA 1828; C. Mentmore? C. Linslade, Gloucester.? P.C. Soulbury 1845–67; R. Adstock, 1860–67.

Haverfield, Thomas Tunstall, 1788–1866, Corpus Christi, Oxford, 1800, BA 1803, MA 1807, BD 1818; D. 1810, Durham, P. 1811, Chester; R. Goddington 1826–66.

Harvey, Richard, 1827–? St.Johns, Oxford, 1845 DA 1849, MA 1852; D. 1850, Oxford, P. 1851, Oxford; C. Wantage 1853; C. Bisham 1859; V. Sarisbury, dio. Worcester, 1863–?

Hawtry, Henry Courtenay, 1820–1906, Emmanuel, Cambridge, 1839, BA 1844, MA 1846: D. 1844, P. 1845; R. Holy Trinity, New Windsor, 1852–1873; Chaplain to H.M. Forces, Windsor, 1852–1873; R. Nursling, Hants. 1873–1879.

Hayes, Sir John Warren, Bart. 1799–1880, Wadham, 1817, BA 1821, MA 1824; D. 1822, P. 1823; R. Arborfield 1839–79.

Hayter, Charles Frederick,1827–? Magdalen Hall, 1847, BA 1852, MA 1858; D. 1853, Worcester, P. 1854, Guiana; C. Clatworthy, dio Bath & Wells, 1853–54; C. Stiffkey w Morston, Norfolk, 1854–55; C. Kirtlington 1855–56; C. Stoke Talmage 1856–57; R. East Mersea, dio. Rochester, 1857–71; V. Claybrooke w Wibtoft & Little Wilston, dio. Peterborough, 1871–? In *Crockford* 1880.

Hayton, Amos, 1809–1866, Queen's,Oxford, 1828, BA 1833; D. 1834, P. 1836; Domestic Chaplain to Baroness Wenman, Thame, 1834; P.C. Chearsley 1840–66; Chaplain, Thame Union, 1855.

Hayton, George, 1831–? Queen's, Oxford, BA 1853, MA 1856, Fellow 1855–58; D. 1855, Oxford, P. 1856, Oxford; R. South Weston 1856–58; R. Niton, IOW,1858–84; R. Charlton-on-Otmoor 1884–95.

Hayton, Thomas, 1794–1887, Queen's, Oxford, 1815, BA 1819; D. 1818, P. 1820; V. Long Crendon 1821–87; Incumbent Lower Winchendon 1832–7

Hayward, John Wheeler, 1825–1886, Trinity, Cambridge, 1843, BA 1847, MA 1850; D. 1849, Oxford, P. 1851, Oxford; C. Wantage 1849; Chaplain to the Forces, Crimea & The Curragh Camp, Ireland, 1853–57; V. Granborough 1855–71; V. Flintham, dio. Lincoln, 1871–86.

Hazel, William, 1804–1867, Christ Church, 1821, BA 1825, MA 1828; D. 1826, Oxford, P. 1827, Oxford; Headmaster, Portsmouth Grammar School, 1830–55; R. St.Peter's,Wallingford, 1855–67; Surrogate.

Hearne, James, 1785–1864, St.John's, Cambridge, 1807, BA 1810; D. 1809, Exeter, P. 1809, Norwich; R. Hatford 1836–64; Chaplain, Faringdon Union, 1843.

Heath, Christopher, BA , C. Drayton Parslow 1846

Hensley, Edward, 1834–1921, Christ's, Cambridge, 1853, BA 1857, MA 1860; D. 1858, Chichester, P. 1859, Chichester; C. Ore, Hastings, 1858–61; C. Checkendon 1861–64; R. Parkham, dio. Exeter, 1864–89.

Herbert, Henry,1825–? Worcester, Oxford, 1843; D. 1849, Capetown, P. 1850, Capetown; Fellow, Bishop's College, Capetown, 1849; C. Harkstead, Suffolk,1857; P.C. Seer Green 1858–67; R. Hemingford Abbots, dio. Ely, 1867–? R.D. Huntingdon,1874.

Heurtley, Charles Abel, 1806–1895, Corpus Christi, Oxford, 1823, BA 1827, MA 1827, BD 1838, DD 1853, Fellow, 1832–41; D. 1831, Oxford, P. 1832, Oxford; C. Wardington w Claydon 1831–40; R. Fenny Compton, Warws. 1840–72; Bampton Lecturer 1848; Hon. Canon Worcester 1848–53; Lady Margaret Professor of Divinity and Canon of Christ Church 1853–95; Select Preacher 1834, 1838 & 1851; Member of the Hebdominal Council 1864–72.

Hewett, John William, 1824–1886, Trinity, Cambridge, 1845, BA 1849, MA 1852; D. 1849, Chichester, P. 1850, Chichester; Fellow/Tutor, St.Nicholas College, Shoreham 1849–52; C. Bloxham 1852–56; Headmaster, Bloxham Grammar School 1853–56; C. St.George's, Whitwick, Leics.1857–66; C. Scropton, Derbyshire 1866–70; C. All Saints, South Hampstead, London 1870; C. St.John's, Clerkenwell 1871; C. St.Paul's, Finsbury 1872; C. St.Saviour's, Hoxton 1873; C. St.Mary's, Primrose Hill 1874–75; Senior Classical Master, North London Collegiate School 1874–78.

Hewett, William Henry, 1820–? Magdalen Hall, Oxford, 1850, BA 1854, MA 1856; D. 1854, P. 1856; C. Little Tew 1854–57; C. Banbury 1857–59; C. Milton, Berks. 1860–61; Minor Canon & Precentor, Carlisle Cathedral, 1861–63; R. Yarborough, dio. Lincoln, 1863–71; V. Scarle, Notts.1871–?

Hill, Benjamin, Trinity, Dublin, BA 1835; D. 1835, Lincoln, P. 1836, Lincoln; C. Ashendon w Dorton 1835–38; P.C. Wootton Underwood 1838–52; Chaplain at Valparaiso 1852–59; V. Norton w Presteign 1860–74; V. Chaldon-Herring, dio. Sarum, 1874–?

Hill, Charles, 1821–1878, Lincoln, Oxford, 1840, BA 1843, MA 1847; D. 1844, Peterborough, P. 1846, Peterborough; C. Thenford, Northants, 1844–46; C. Gt. Rollright 1847; C. Staverton, Northants,1848–53; V. Piddington 1853–1878; P.C. St.James, Dalby, I of Man, 1858–65; C. Dymock, nr Gloucester, 1865–67; C. St.Mary, Walthamstow 1867–69.

Hill, Justly, 1783–1853, New College, 1800, BA 1805, MA 1808, Fellow until 1820; R. Shanklin & Bonchurch, Isle of Wight, 1809–53; R. Tingewick 1819–53; Archdeacon of Buckingham 1825–53.

Hilliard, Frederic Joseph, 1797–1861, Matriculated Worcester College, Oxford, 1815, Peterhouse, Cambridge, 1818, BA 1821; D. 1820, London, P. 1821, London; R. (& Patron) Little Wittenham 1821–61.

Hilliard, John Ashby Stafford, 1830–? St.John's,Oxford,1848, BA 1852; D. 1854, Peterborough, P. 1855, Peterborough; C. Preston, Rutland, 1854–57; C. in charge Southstoke 1857–61; R. Little Wittenham, 1861–84; V. Tidenham, Glos.1884–96.

Hinde, John Fitz-Richard, 1818–1882, St.John's, Cambridge, 1840, BA 1844: D. 1845, Peterborough, P. 1846, Peterborough; C. Twyford, Leics. 1845–47; C. Fetwell, Norfolk,1848–61; R. Turville 1860–61; V. Dalby-Parva, Melton Mowbray,1861–1882.

Hodgkinson, Joseph, 1774–1851, Brasenose, 1792, BA 1796, MA 1798, BD 1811, Fellow until 1819: V. Didcot 1812–51.

Hodgson, Francis, 1781–1852, King's, Cambridge, 1800, BA 1804, MA 1807, BD 1840, Fellow 1803–15; P. 1814, Norwich; Assistant Master, Eton College 1807; C. Bradden, Northants. 1815; V. Bakewell, Derbyshire, 1816–36; Archdeacon of Derby 1836–40; V. Edensor w Bakewell 1838–40; Provost of Eton 1840–52; R. Cottisford 1842–52.

Hodson, George Hewitt, 1817–1904, Trinity, Cambridge, 1836, BA 1840, MA 1843, Fellow; D. & P. 1843, Gloucester & Bristol; Incumbent Cookham Dean 1843–69; V. Enfield, Midx, 1870–1904; R.D. Enfield 1882–1904; Preb. St.Paul's Cathedral 1883–1904.

Hogan, Arthur Ricky, ob 1880, Trinity, Dublin, BA 1855, MA 1858, MA Oxon 1860: D. 1856, Bath & Wells, P. 1857, Gloucester & Bristol; C. Corsham, Wilts. 1856–58; Domestic Chaplain, Earl of Normanton, 1859; C. Puddletown, Dorset, 1860–63; V. Watlington 1864–80.

Hole, Charles, 1824–1906, Trinity,Cambridge, 1842, BA 1846; D. 1846, Oxford, P. 1847, Oxford; C. St.Mary's, Reading 1846–52; Chaplain Reading Union 1855–58; C. Shanklin, IoW, 1858–68; R. Loxbeare, Devon, 1868–76; Lecturer in Ecclesiastical History, Kings College London 1870–1906; Fellow, Kings College, London, 1904–06.

Holland, John Murray, 1818–1877, New College, 1837; BA 1841, MA 1845, Fellow 1838–61; D. 1841, Oxford, P. 1842, Oxford; C. Bapchild, Kent, 1843–54; R. Stanton St.John 1860–77.

Hollinsed, Richard Edward, 1821–1858,Queen's, Oxford, 1841; V. North Moreton 1855–58.

Holloway, Charles, 1804–1864, Queens', Cambridge, 1822, BA 1826; D. 1826, Lincoln, P. 1827, Norwich; R. St.Simon & St.Jude, Norwich, 1830–61; R. Stanford Dingley 1830–64.

Holmes, Edward Molloy, Trinity, Dublin, BA 1851, LL.B.1865;
D. 1853,Winchester, P. 1854,Winchester; C. Brown w Chilton Candover, Hants, 1853–57; C. Churchill w Cornwell 1857–58; R. Cornwell 1859–69; C. Daylesford 1868–69; R. Marsh Gibbon 1869–93; R.D. Claydon 1876.

Holt, Robert,1823–1903, St.John's, Cambridge, 1842, BA 1846, MA 1850, MA Oxon (Christ Church) 1870: D. 1846, Oxford, P. 1847,Oxford; C. Soulbury 1846–48; C. Wardington 1849–51; C. Mursley 1852–60; C. Adstock 1861–68; V. Hillesden 1868–1903.

Honneywill, John Blake, 1825–83, Wadham 1842; St.John's, Cambridge, 1844, BA 1847; D. 1848, Worcester, P. 1849, Worcester; C. Whichford, Warws. 1848–49; C. St.John's, Reading 1850–51; C. Christ Church, Worthing, 1852–53; C. Bowden, Cheshire, 1854–55; P.C. Altringham, dio. Chester, 1865–59; C. St.Margaret's, Lee, Kent, 1860–62; V. Somting, Sussex,1863–83.

Hooper, Richard Hope, 1820–1899, Lincoln, Oxford, 1841, BA 1845, MA 1848; D. 1845, Exeter, P. 1846, Oxford; C. Littleworth 1846; Chaplain to the Faringdon Union 1848; C. Coleshill 1854–61; R. Thornton w Nash 1861–77; V. Great Coxwell 1877–99.

Hopkins, George Adollphus, 1802–1856, St.John's, Cambridge, 1824, BA 1828, MA 1831; D. 1828, Lincoln, P. 1828, Lincoln; C. Wraysbury 1828–56; Chaplain, Windsor Union Workhouse 1843; Master, Stroode Charity School, Egham, Surrey.

Horn, Thomas, 1800–1874, St.Edmund Hall 1822, BA 1826, MA 1827; D. 1826, Peterborough, P. 1827, Peterborough; R. Mursley 1833–51; R.D. Mursley 1833; R. St.Thomas, Haverfordwest, 1851–66.

Horwood, Edward Russell, 1821–? Brasenose 1839, BA 1843, MA 1846; D. 1844, Lincoln, P. 1845, Lincoln; C. Tring 1844–? C. Trinity, Gray's Inn Rd, London, 1845–47; Assistant Chaplain, Royal Free Hospital 1845–47; C. Christ Church, Marylebourne 1847–50; V. All Saints w St.Peter, Maldon, 1850–? Surrogate. J.P. for Essex & Maldon..

Hoskyns, Sir John Leigh, Bart, 1817–? Balliol 1835, Magdalen, BA 1839, MA 1841, Fellow 1843–45; D. 1840, Oxford, P. 1842, Hereford; C. Dunchurch, Worcs.1840–41; C. Lugwardine, Heref. 1841–45; R. Aston Tirrold,1845–1911; Hon. Canon, Christ Church, 1880 [Father of Sir Edwyn, 1851–1925, Bishop of Southwell 1904–25].

Houblon, Thomas Archer,1808–1874, Oriel, 1826, BA 1830, MA 1834; D. 1832, Salisbury, P. 1833, Salisbury; R. Peasemore 1836–74; R. Catmore 1837–48.

Howard, John Flory, 1801–1873, Trinity, Oxford, 1818, BA 1822, MA 1824, BCL 1829; D. 1823, Salisbury, P. 1824, Salisbury; R. Frilsham 1828–73; R. Yattendon 1829–73.

Howman, Arthur Edward, 1764–1849, Queens', Cambridge, 1782, BA 1786, MA 1789; D. 1787, Norwich; C. Gissing, Norfolk, 1787; V. Shiplake 1799–1849; R. Burstow, Surrey, 1800–1848; Preb. of Salisbury 1810–48; Minor Canon, Windsor 1823–27; Master, St.Nicholas Hospital, Salisbury 1819.

Hughes, James Roydon, 1810–? New College, 1827, BA 1831, MA 1837, Fellow 1827–43; D. 1837, P. 1838; P.C. Dorchester 1840–41; Prebendary of Chichester 1841; Examining Chaplain to the Bishop of Chichester 1841–43; R. Newton Longville 1843–75; R. Long Ditton 1874–? Select Preacher 1845–46. In *Crockford* 1880.

Hughes, Robert Edward, 1811–1869, New Inn Hall,Oxford, 1833, BA 1835, MA 1838; D. 1836, Worcester, P. 1838,Worcester; C. St.Mary's, Bungay, Suffolk; C. Tadmarton 1840; R. Alkerton w Shenington 1846–69.
Hulme, George, 1787–1845, Balliol, 1805, BA 1809, MA 1813; D.1838, Oxford P. 1839, Oxford; Incumbent, Holy Trinity, Reading, ?–1845.
Hulme, William, 1817–? Balliol, 1835, BA 1839, MA 1842; D. 1840, Oxford, P. 1841,Oxford; C. Arborfield 1840–42; C. South Moreton 1842–44; C. Ewelme 1844–45; R. Pangbourne 1845–47; C. Gatcombe, IoW, 1847–48; C. Weobley, Herefordshire, 1848–52; C. Hemyock, Devon, 1852–53; V. Corfe, Somerset, 1853–54; R. Tidmarsh 1854–55; R. Brampton Abbots, Hereford 1855–?
Hulton, Henry Edward, 1840–? Trinity, Oxford, 1838, BA 1862, MA 1864;
D. 1863,Oxford, P. 1865,Oxford; C. Sonning 1863–76; V. Great Waltham, dio. Rochester, 1875–? R.D. Chelmsford, 1886.
Hutchins, George, 1805–? Corpus Christi, Cambridge, 1823, BA 1827; D. 1827, Lichfield & Coventry, P. 1828, Norwich; C. Mapledurham 1838–56; R. Great Blakenham, Suffolk,1871–77; R. Telscombe w Piddington, Sussex, 1877–80. Disappears from *Crockford* 1888.
Hutchinson, Charles Ring, 1827–1884, Brasenose, 1845, BA 1849; D. 1851, London, P. 1852, London; C. Sunbury, Middx, 1851–54; C. Pitstone 1854; V. Pitstone 1855–81; V. Edlesborough 1880–84.
Image, William Thomas, 1831–1893, Trinity Hall, Cambridge,1850,BA 1854, MA 1857; D. 1860, Oxford, P. 1861, Oxford; C. St.John, Windsor, 1860–61; C. Holy Trinity, Windsor, 1861–66; V. Wickham Market, dio. Norwich, 1866–89.
Irwin, John James, Trinity, Dublin, BA 1832, MA 1843, BD 1863, DD 1863;
D. 1835, Derry & Raphoe, P. 1836, Derry & Raphoe; C. Melksham, Wilts. 1837–41; C. Steeple Claydon 1844–55; Chaplain, Hong Kong 1855–67; C. West Wycombe 1869; V. Thornton, dio. York. In *Crockford* 1889.
Isham, Arthur, 1810–1876, Christ Church, 1828, BA 1832, MA 1835, Fellow of All Souls 1833–37; D. 1833, Oxford, P. 1834, Oxford; C. Adderbury 1834; C. Westcote Barton 1836; R. Weston Turville 1837–76; R.D. Wendover 1838–76.
Jackson, William Nelson, 0b 1876, Trinity, Dublin; V. Kingsey 1833–76.
James, John, 1806–1886, Queen's, Oxford, 1824, BA 1828, MA 1831; D. 1830, Lichfield & Coventry, P. 1831, London; R. Rowmarsh, Yorks. 1831–43; V. Pinhoe, Devon, 1844; P.C. Tor Mohun & Cockington, Devon, 1844–48; P.C. Headington Quarry 1851–53; R. Avington, Oxon, 1853–79; Surrogate 1855.
James, Samuel Benjamin, Trinity, Dublin, BA 1853, MA 1864, BD 1882, DD 1882; D. 1855,York, P. 1856,York; C. Cottingham w Skidby, Yorks,1855–56; C. St.Nicholas, Worcester, 1856–58; C. Winkfield 1858–69; V. North Marston 1869–? Founder & 1st Warden of Schorne's College, Bucks. 1876. In *Crockford* 1889.
Jenkins, John David, 1828–1876, Jesus, Oxford, 1846, BA 1850, MA 1852, BD 1859, DD 1871, Fellow 1849–1876; D. 1851, Oxford, P. 1852, Oxford; C. St.Paul's, Oxford 1851–1852; R. Aberdare 1870–1876; Canon of Maritzburg.
Jenkinson, John Henry, 1823–? Christ Church, 1841, BA 1844, MA 1861; D. 1862, Oxford, P. 1863, Oxford; C. St.Mary, Reading, 1863.
Jephson, John Hilton, 1829–? Hertford, Oxford, 1847, BA 1851, MA 1876; D. 1852, Ripon, P. 1853, Ripon; C. Stanley, Wakefield, 1852–53; C. Chieveley 1853–56; C. Curridge 1857–60; C. Chieveley 1861–75; C. Hagbourne 1875–78.

Jephson, William, 1819–1905, Corpus Christi, Cambridge, 1837, BA 1841, MA 1844; D. 1843, London, P. 1843, London; Assistant Master Harrow School, ? C. St.John the Evangelist, Westminster, 1844–53; R. Hinton Waldrist 1853–80; Inspector of Schools, Dio. Oxford, 1856–76 ; R.D. Vale of White Horse, 1876–77; Chaplain, Geneva, 1877–81.

Jeston, Henry Playsted, 1797–1889, Worcester, Oxford, 1817, BA 1821, MA 1824; D. 1821, Lichfield, P. 1822, Chester; West Indies with Bishop Coleridge 1824; Domestic Chaplain to Sir Ralph Woodford, Trinidad, 1825; P.C. Cholesbury 1830–89; P.C. Wiggington, Herts. 1841–47; Chaplain, Kissengen, 1854–61. J.P. for Bucks.& Herts.

Jeudwine, William, 1814–1888, St.John's, Cambridge, 1832, BA 1836, MA 1842; D. 1839,York for Lichfield, P. 1840, Lichfield; P.C. Clive, Salop, 1844–56; C. Chicheley 1856–60; V. Chicheley 1860–81.

Johnson, Charles Augustus, 1821–1892, Brasenose, 1839, BA 1841, MA 1843; D. 1848, Oxford, P. 1850, Oxford; C. Enborne w Hamstead Marshall 1848; R. Enborne 1850–92; R. Hamstead Marshall 1850–92.

Jordan, John, 1804–1874, Clare, Cambridge, 1823; BA 1826; D. 1827, Gloucester, P. 1830, Oxford; C. Little Dean, Gloucs. 1827–30; C. Handborough 1830–36; C. Somerton 1836–40; V. Enstone 1840–74.

Joscelyne, Henry, 1826–? New Inn Hall, Oxford, 1859, BA 1862, MA 1877; D. 1857, Oxford, P. 1861, Oxford; C. & Schoolmaster, Holywell 1857–61; Chaplain Oxford City Gaol 1861–66; C. Shippon 1861–63; C. Stoke Lyne 1864–66; C. Caversfield 1866–68; C. Fewcott 1866–78; C. Ardley 1866–70; C. Hardwicke w Fingest 1868–75; R. Ibstone 1878; R. Fingest 1879–1906.

Joy, Charles Ashfield, King's College, London, AKC; D. 1853, P. 1854, Lichfield; C. Tunstall, Staffs.1854–60; C. Grove 1861–64; C. East & West Hanney 1864–68; C. Charney-Basset 1868–70.

Kelk, William Hastings,1803–1865, Jesus, Cambridge, 1824, BA 1828; D. 1831, Lincoln, P. 1833, Lincoln; R. Osgathorpe, Leics. 1836–?40; R. Drayton Beauchamp 1840–60. *Venn.*

Kempe, Alfred Arrow, 1814–1909, Trinity, Cambridge, 1833, migrated to Clare College, Oct. 1833, to Trinity Hall, Dec. 1833, to Magdalene, matric. Oct. 1834, BA 1838; D. 1838, P. 1839; C. Wittersham & Brewzett, Kent; C. St.Peters, Walworth, Surrey; C. Dinton; R. Wexham 1846–1909.

Kerby, Cranley Launcelot, 1765–1857, New College, 1784, BCL 1791; D. 1787, Oxford, P. 1788, Oxford; C. Chinnor 1790; R. Wheatfield 1807; R. Chinnor 1810–16; R. Stoke Talmage 1820–57; V. Bampton 1824–57.

Kerr, Charles William John, 1801–1869, Trinity, Cambridge, 1819, BA 1820, MA 1821; D. 1823, York, P. 1824, York; C. Tottenhoe; C. Bradwell 1845; C. Hoggeston 1847.

Kewley, Francis, 1826–1890, St.John's, Cambridge,1845, Jesus, Oxford, 1850, BA 1852, MA 1854, Fellow, 1852–67; D. 1859, Oxford, P. 1860, Oxford; C. Tubney 1859–63; V. St.Peter, Malvern Wells, Worcs.1869–72; R. Remenham 1878–90.

King, Alexander, 1825–1884, Oriel, 1843, BA 1846, MA 1849; D. 1847, Worcester, P. 1848, Ely; C. Broadway, Worcester, 1847–49; R. Sherrington 1849–84.

King, Isaac, 1804–1865, Christ Church, 1822, BA 1827, MA 1830; D. 1827, P. 1828; P.C. Lee 1832–52; R. Bradenham 1832–65.

Kitcat, John, 1821–? Oriel, 1838, BA 1841, MA 1851; D. 1844,Chichester, P. 1845, Chichester; C. Burpham, Sussex, 1844–46; C. Puttenham, Surrey, 1846–47; C. St.Mary, Reading, 1848–51; C. Llanigan, Hay-on-Wye, 1851–53; C. Harpsden 1854–55; P.C. Swallowfield 1855–75; C. St.Stephen, Windsor 1875–84; R. St.Benedict, Ardwick, Manchester,1884–?

Kitson, Francis John, 1811–? St.John's, Oxford, 1829, BA 1838, MA 1843, BD 1843, Fellow 1829–54; D. 1834, P. 1835; C. Fifield 1840; P.C. Fifield 1840–54; R. Heymock w Culm Davy Chapelry, dio. Exeter, 1854–72; R. Chilton Foliatt, dio. Sarum, 1872–? In *Crockford* 1889.

Knapp, Charles Tyrell,1835–? Exeter, Oxford, 1856; St.Aidan's, Birkenhead; D. 1860, Lichfield, P. 1861, Lichfield; C. Wellington, Salop, 1860–62; C. Horley w Horton 1863–64; C. Wells-next-the-Sea, Norfolk, 1864–68; C. Chard, Somerset, 1868–69; C. Wellington, dio. Bath & Wells 1869; C. Evenlode, Worcs. 1869–70; C. St.Agnes, dio. Truro, 1871–?

Knight, George, 1780–1855, St.Edmund Hall, 1799, BA 1799, MA 1805; C. Harwell? *Foster.*

Knipe, John, 1819–? Pembroke, Cambridge, 1838, BA 1842; D. 1843, P. 1844; C. Great Linford 1843–46; C. Wellesbourne 1846–67. Disappears from *Crockford* 1868.

Knollis, James, 1776–1860, Lincoln, Oxford,1794, BA 1798, MA 1801, BD 1809, Fellow, 1798–1815; P. 1800, Oxford; P.C. St.Mary's, Maidenhead 1819–1860; V. Penn 1823–1860.

Knox, Henry, C. Upton, Bucks. 1845. *Clergy List.*

Kyrke, Richard, 1820–? Queen's, Oxford, 1839, BA 1843, MA 1846; D. 1844, St.Asaph, P. 1845, Bangor; C. Bucklebury 1847; C. Whiston, Lancs. 1853–? C. Cassington 1866; C. Badby-cum-Newnham, Northants. 1867–72; C. Faringdon 1872; C. Stoke-Bruerne, Towcester, 1872–75; C. in charge, Maids Moreton, 1875–78; C. Haughton,Staffs. 1878–79; C. Braabridge, Lincoln, 1879–?

Lambert, Richard Umfraville, 1829–1905, Trinity, Cambridge, 1848, BA 1852, MA 1855; D. 1853, Oxford, P.1854, Oxford; C. Bensington 1854–56; C. Devizes w Holt, Wilts. 1856–58; C. Burbage, Wilts. 1859–67; Inspector of Schools, dio. Rochester 1868–73; C. Leytonstone 1872–73; V. Christ Church, Bradford-on-Avon, Wilts. 1873–1905.

Langford, William Watson James Augustus, 1800–1865, Trinity, Cambridge, 1822, BA 1826; D. 1826, Oxford, P. 1827, Oxford; C. Watlington 1826; C. Crowmarsh Mongewell 1826; V. Watlington 1841–64. Surrogate.

Langley, John, 1800–75, Magdalen Hall, Oxford, 1818, BA 1823, MA 1826; R. Wallingford St.Leonard 1829–72; V. St.Mary the More, Wallingford 1829–72. Surrogate.

Latimer, Edward William Forty, 1804–1881, Lincoln, Oxford, 1822, BA 1827, MA 1828; D. 1827, Oxford, P. 1828, Oxford; C. St.Aldate, Oxford, 1827; C. Sandford 1831; P.C. Sandford 1831; R. Waddesdon 1st Portion, 1829–1881; R. Waddesdon 2nd Portion, 1830–1881.

Latter, Arthur Simon, 1823–? Queen's, Oxford, 1846, BA 1850, MA 1852; D. 1850, Oxford, P. 1851, Oxford; C. Wiggington 1850–52; C. Henley on Thames 1852–54; C. Chinnor 1854–55; C. All Saints, Fulham, London 1855–64; V. North Mimms, Herts 1864–80; R. Downham Market, Norfolk 1882–?

Layton, George Dawson Turner, King's College, London; D. 1852, Oxford, P. 1853, Oxford; C. Swinbrook 1852; P.C. Swinbrook 1858–66; R. Widford w Wedford 1858–66.

Lea, Thomas, 1791–1866, Trinity, Oxford, 1811, BA 1815, MA 1820; V. Bishop's Itchington w Chadshunt C. & Gaydon C. dio. Worcester 1820–66; R. Tadmarton 1824–66.
Lee, Frederick George, 1832–1902 St.Edmund Hall, Oxford, 1851, SCL 1854, Hon DCL 1864; D. 1854, Oxford, P. 1856, Oxford; C. Sunningwell w Kennington 1854–56; Domestic Chaplain to the Duke of Leeds 1858–60; Incumbent St.John's Episcopal Church, Aberdeen 1860–64; V. All Saints, Lambeth 1867–99 Hon. Sec. A.P.U.C. 1857–69.
Lee, William Blackstone, 1795–1874, New College, 1812, BA 1816, MA 1820, Fellow, 1812–1836; D. 1817, P. 1818; R. Wootton 1836–74.
Leighton, Francis Knyvett, 1807–1881, Magdalen, Oxford, 1823, BA 1828, MA 1831, DD 1858, Fellow of All Souls' 1830–41; Warden, All Souls' 1858–81; D. 1830, Oxford, P. 1831, Oxford; R. Cardiston, Salop? V. St.Chad's, Shrewsbury ? R. Harpsden 1841–58; R.D. Henley 1841–58; R. East Lockinge 1858–81; R.D. Oxford 1858–70; Canon Residentary, Westminster 1868. Proctor in Convocation [Dio. Oxford], 1857–74.
Levett, Walter, 1784–1860, Christ Church, 1802, BA 1806, MA 1808, Student until 1817; D. 1807, Oxford, P. 1807, Oxford; P.C. Drayton 1808; R. Drayton 1810; V. Casleton,Yorks. 1816–49; V. Bray, 1823–25 and 1826; Sub-Dean of York 1827.
Levy, Thomas Bayley [Bailey], 1812–1872, Exeter, Oxford, 1830, BA 1834 [from Queen's], MA 1838 [from Queen's], Fellow of Queen's 1846–72; D. 1835, Oxford, P. 1836, Oxford; C. Sparsholt, Berks. 1836; C. Kirby Thore, Westmoreland 1838; Chaplain, Queen's College, 1843; R. South Weston 1855–56; R. Knight's Enham, Hants. 1856–72.
Lewes, Thomas,1794–1873, Brasenose, 1811, BA 1815, MA 1817; V. Taynton 1819–73;V. Great Barrington, dio. Bath & Wells 1820–73.
Linton, Hewett, St.Aidan's; D. 1861, Winchester, P. 1862, Winchester; C. St.Paul's, Bermondsey 1861–63; C. Tadmarton 1863–66 ; Chaplain, East Indian Railway, Allahabad 1866–71; C. Trysull, Wolverhampton 1871–72; C. Coseley, Lichfield 1877–78; P.C. Abraham, Wigan 1878–?
Litchfield, Francis, 1792–1876, Merton, 1811, BA 1815, MA 1818; D. 1817, Peterborough, P. 1817, Peterborough; R. Eltham, Kent 1830–76; R. Farthington, Peterborough 1836–1876; R. Great Linford 1836–76.
Little, Thomas, ob 1877, Trinity, Dublin, BA 1855, MA 1858; D. 1856, London, P. 1857, London; C. Uxbridge 1856; C. Marsh Gibbon 1859–62; C. Slapton 1861; R. Princes Risborough 1864–77; Diocesan Insp. Schools; Chaplain to the Wycombe Union.
Littlejohn, William Douglas, 1807–1891, Corpus Christi, Cambridge, 1833, BA 1837; D. 1837, Chichester, P. 1838, Chichester; C. Easebourne, Sussex 1837–40; C. Yeldon, Beds.1841–44; V. Sydenham 1844–79.
Livingston, Thomas Gott, 1830–? Magdalen Hall, 1848, BA 1852, MA 1854; D. 1853, Oxford, P. 1854, Oxford; C. Bloxham 1853–55; Precentor, Carlisle Cathedral 1855–58; Minor Canon, Carlisle Cathedral 1855–73; V. Addingham, Cumberland 1873–?
Lloyd, Charles, 1809–1883, Christ Church, 1827, BA 1831; D. 1833, P. 1834; V. Great Kimble 1840–57; R. Great Hampden 1840–59; Chaplain, Bishop of Oxford 1855; R. Chalfont St.Giles 1859–83; Hon. Canon, Christ Church 1868.
Lockwood, John William,1800–1879, Christ Church, 1816, BA 1821, MA 1828, Student 1816–38; D. 1825, Oxford, P. 1826, Oxford; R. Chelsea 1836–? R. Kingham 1836–79.

Long, James L. ob. 1847. Ll.B. R. Maidsmoreton, 1790–1847.
Longland, Charles Pitman, St.Bees' Theological College, 1845; D. 1846, Chichester, P. 1847, Chichester; C. Mayfield, Sussex 1846–50; C. Upper Norwood 1850–53; C. Holy Trinity, Rotherfield Greys, 1853–70; Chaplain to the Henley Union 1853–70; V. Headington Quarry 1870–91.
Longmore, Philip Alexander, 1825–1902, Emmanuel, Cambridge, 1843, BA 1847, MA 1850; D. 1848, Rochester, P. 1849, Rochester; C. Bygrave, Herts.1849–52; P.C. Hermitage 1852–1902.
Loveday, Thomas, 1789–1873, Madgalen, Oxford, 1806, BA 1810, MA 1813, BD 1823, Fellow 1818–31; D. 1813, P. 1814; C. Finmere 1815; C. Elsfield 1819; R. East Ilsley 1831–65.
Lowe, John, 1791–1874, Lincoln, Oxford, 1809, BA 1813, MA 1839; D. 1813, York, P. 1814, York; P.C. Swinton, Yorkshire 1814–15; R. Ardley 1815–73; Afternoon Lecturer, Wath-upon-Dearne for 30 years.
Lowndes, Charles, 1809–1892, Trinity, Cambridge, 1827, BA 1831, MA 1835; D. 1833, Lichfield & Coventry, P. 1834, Lichfield & Coventry; R. Hartwell w Little Hampden 1855–92; Chaplain, Bucks. Lunatic Asylum 1871.
Lowry, Charles Henry, MA, Headmaster of Carlisle Grammar School 1852; R. South Weston 1854–55.
Lowry, John, 1794–1859, Magdalene, Cambridge, admitted 1822, a "Ten Year Man"; D. 1817, P. 1818; R. Waddesdon, 3rd Portion, 1823–59; V. Burgh by Sands, Cumberland 1838.
Ludlow, Thomas Binfield, 1822–? Christ Church, 1841, BA 1845, MA 1848; D. 1845, Oxford, P. 1846, Oxford; Chaplain,Christ Church 1845–53; C. Hinksey 1851; R. Slapton 1853–74; V. St.Wendron, dio. Exeter 1874–83; R. Blyborough, Lincolnshire, 1883–?
Lupton, James, 1800–73, Christ Church, 1819, BA 1825, MA 1825; D. 1823, Oxford, P. 1824, Oxford; Chaplain,Christ Church 1823–27; Chaplain, New College 1823–29; C. St.Martin's, Oxford City 1828; V. Blackbourton 1827–73; Minor Canon, St.Paul's Cathedral 1829–73; Minor Canon, Westminster Abbey 1829–73; R. St.Michael Queenhithe w Holy Trinity 1832–73.
Lush, Alfred, 1826–1886, Corpus Christi, Cambridge, 1845, BA 1849, MA 1852; D. 1849, Winchester, P. 1850, Winchester; C. Odiham w Greywell Hants. 1849–58; C. Kibworth, Leics. 1858–60; C. Shrivenham 1860–62; C. Beaminster, Dorset 1862–68; C. Metherington, Lincs. 1868–72; C. St.Mary's, Marlborough, Wilts. 1872–74; C.Witney 1874 –76; V. Lee, nr.Ilfracombe, 1877–86.
Lush, Vicesimus, 1817–1882, Corpus Christi, Cambridge, 1838, BA 1842, MA 1847; D. 1842, Chester, P. 1843, Chester; C. Over Darwen, Lancs. 1842–44; C. Faringdon, Berks. 1844–49; C. St.John's, Hoxton, Middlesex 1849–50; Incumbent Howick, New Zealand 1850–68; Incumbent St.George's, Thames Goldfields 1868–82; V. St.Peter's, Hamilton, New Zealand; Archdeacon of Waikato, N.Z.
Lushington, Charles, 1805–? Christ Church, 1822, BA 1829, MA 1830; D. 1830, Oxford, P. 1831, Oxford; C. Kintbury; V. Walton-on-Thames, Surrey, ?1851–64.
MacDougall, James, 1813–? Brasenose, 1830, BA 1834, MA 1842; D. 1835, Lichfield & Coventry, P. 1836, Lichfield & Coventry; C. Marsh Baldon 1845; C. Hanney 1846; V. Hanney 1849–92.

Mackonochie, Alexander Heriot, 1826–1887, Wadham, 1844, BA 1848, MA 1851; D. 1849, Salisbury, P. 1850, Salisbury; C. Westbury, Wilts. 1849–52; C. Wantage 1852–58; C. St.George in the East, London 1858–62; P.C. St.Alban's, Gray's Inn, London 1862–82; Chaplain to the Rt. Hon. Baron Eliot 1870; V. St.Peter's, London Docks 1882–83.

Madden, Wyndham Monsom, 1823–1897, St.John's, Cambridge, 1845, BA 1845, MA 1875; D. 1846, P. 1847; C. St.Giles, Reading 1846; P.C. Holy Trinity,Wakefield 1853–91; Hon. Canon, Wakefield Cathedral 1853–91.

Majendie, Henry William, 1791–1869, Trinity, Cambridge, 1808, BA 1812, MA 1816; D. 1814, P. 1815; V. Speen 1819–69; R.D. 1827; Prebendary of Bangor 1818–69; Prebendary of Salisbury 1824–69.

Mallard, Charles Edward, 1827–? Trinity, Oxford, 1846, BA 1850, MA 1853; D. 1854, P. 1855; C. Forest Hill 1854; Chaplain, H.M.S. *Royal Albert* and H.M.S. *Princess Royal*

Mangin, Samuel Waring, 1819–? Wadham, 1838, BA 1843; D. 1844, Gloucester & Bristol, P. 1845, Bath & Wells; P.C. St.Matthias, Stoke Newington 1854–58; P.C. Headington Quarry 1858–63; P.C. St.Columba's, Haggerston 1863–73; R. St.Martin's, Salisbury 1873–79; C. Dilton Marsh, Wilts. 1879–?81; V. Bramshaw, Hants. 1881–?

Marriott, John,1809–1881, Oriel, 1826, BA 1830, MA 1833; D. 1832, Salisbury, P. 1833, Salisbury; C. Buckland 1832–34; C. Bradfield 1834–63; V. St.John's, Hythe, Southampton 1863–78.

Marsden, John Buxton, 1803–1870, St.John's, Cambridge, 1823, BA 1827, MA 1830; D. 1827, Lichfield, P. 1828, Lichfield; C. Burslem, Staffs. 1827; C. Harrow, Middx.; R. Lower Tooting, Surrey 1833–44; V. Great Missenden 1844–52; P.C. St.Peter's, Dale End, Birmingham 1852–70.

Marsh, John, 1820–55, New College, 1838, BCL 1844, Fellow 1838–54; D.1843, Oxford, P. 1844, Oxford; C. Hardwick 1846; R. Tingewick 1853–55.

Marshall, George, 1818–? Christ Church, 1836, BA 1840, MA 1842, Student 1837–58; D. 1843, Oxford, P. 1844, Oxford; V. Pyrton 1857–75; R.D. Aston 1860–75; R. Milton 1875–97.

Marshall, Jenner, 1817–? Worcester, Oxford, 1835, BA 1839, MA 1843; D. 1841, Oxford, P. 1842, Oxford; C. Barford St.Michael 1841; C. Broughton 1847; C. North Aston 1848–51; C. Adderbury 1851–58. In *Crockford* 1889.

Marshall, William John, 1821–? Queens', Cambridge, 1839, BA 1843; D. 1844, Peterborough, P. 1845, Peterborough; C. Claybrook, Leics. 1845–46; P.C. Oughtibridge,Yorkshire 1846–50; C. Christ Church, West Bromwich 1852–53; C. Fleetmarston 1853; R. Grendon Underwood 1855–62; C. Much Marcle, Hereford 1862–69; V. Godney, Bath & Wells, 1869–99.

Marsham, Charles, 1788–1867, Christ Church, 1805, BA 1809, MA 1811; R. Ilsington, Devon 1812–6; V. Caversfield 1812–67; V. Stoke Lyne 1812–66.

Marter, Richard, 1788–1871, Exeter, Oxford, 1807; D. 1816, Salisbury, P. 1817, Gloucester; R. Bright Waltham 1841–1871.

Martin, Henry John, 1830–1903, Trinity, Cambridge, 1843, BA 1852, MA 1861; D. 1853, Oxford, P. 1855, Oxford; C. Shirburne 1853–56; C. Holy Trinity w St.Thomas, Exeter 1856–62; Diocesan Secretary C.M.S. 1862–66; V. West Hartlepool, Durham 1866–71; V. Newcastle-upon-Tyne 1871–82; R.D. 1872–82; Surrogate; Hon. Canon, Durham Cathedral 1874–88; Archdeacon, Lindisfarne, 1882–1903; v. Eglingham, Northumberland, 1882–1903; Hon.Canon, Newcastle-on-Tyne.

Martyn, Claudius Robert, 1816–73, Lincoln, Oxford, 1834, BA 1838, MA 1841; R. Ludgershall 1869–73. *Foster.*
Martyn, Thomas, R. Ludgershall 1821–69. *Clergy List.*
Master, William, 1796–1878, New College 1815, BCL 1821, Fellow 1815–34; D. 1819, Hereford, P. 1821, Hereford; R. Bucknell 1833–78.
Matthews, Andrew Hughes, 1782–1854, Jesus, Oxford, 1794 (*aet* 12), BA 1798, MA 1801, BD 1809, Fellow until 1812: D. 1805, Oxford, P. 1806, Oxford; R. Stanton Harcourt 1810–54; V. Weston on the Green 1822–54; R.Tilbrook, Beds. 1829–54.
Matthews, Joseph, D. 1848, Chichester, P. 1850, Oxford; C. Hailsham, Sussex 1848–49; C. Chenies 1850–62; C. Trunch, Norfolk 1864–65; C. Haughley, Suffolk 1865–68; C. Hailsham 1868–69; R. Chesham Bois 1868–92; General Preacher 1892.
Mayne, James, M A, V. Hanslope 1841–1851.
Mavor, John, 1796–1853, Wadham 1802, BA 1806, MA 1808, BD 1816, Fellow of Lincoln until 1826; D. 1808, Oxford, P. 1809, Oxford; C. Fritwell w N. Aston 1810; C. Forest Hill 1821–23; P.C. Forest Hill 1823–48; R. Hadleigh, Essex 1825–48. Died in his cell on the Debtors' side, Oxford County Goal.
Mayor, Charles, 1820–? St.John's, Cambridge, 1838, BA 1842, MA 1845; D. 1845, Norwich, P. 1846, Norwich; C. South Cove, Suffolk 1845–48; C. Wavendon 1848–76. Disappears from *Crockford* 1877.
McCreight, William Walkinshaw, Trinity, Dublin, BA 1821; D. 1827, Down & Connor, P. 1827, Dromore; V. Winslow 1841–62.
Meakin, John Alexander Deverell, 1804–1873, St.John's, Cambridge, 1822, BA 1826, MA 1829; D. 1827, Norwich, P. 1828, Norwich; C. Speen 1840–44; P.C. Speenmanland 1845–73.
Meech, William John, 1802–1858, New College 1823, BA 1827, MA 1832, Fellow 1823–37; V. Whaddon, Bucks. 1836–?1850; R. Hammoon, Dorset 1832–1858.
Meeres, Henry, 1818–? Clare Hall, Cambridge, 1836, BA 1840, MA 1843; D. 1841, London, P. 1842, London; C. Highgate, London 1843–44; C. Cuddington 1845–48; Chaplain to the Buckingham County Gaol 1848; Minister St.Bartholomews Ch. Rochester 1854; V. Rolvenden, Kent 1854–55; V. Haddenham 1855–98.
Menteath, Granville Wheler Stuart, 1811–1887, Magdalen Hall, Oxford, 1828, BA 1833, MA 1835; D. 1834, Lincoln, P. 1835, Lincoln; V. Rauseby, Lincoln 1843–54; R. Hascomb, Winchester 1854 60; P.C. Grazeley 1861–63; R. Morcott, Rutland 1868–72. Chaplain to the Earl of Caithness, Mar & Kellie.
Menzies, Frederick, 1815–? Brasenose, 1833, BA 1837, MA 1840, Fellow 1837–67; D. 1839, Winchester, P. 1840, Winchester; C. Hambledon, Hants. *circa* 1845; C. Ackhampstead 1846; R. Great Shefford 1866–1887; Hon. Canon, Christ Church 1883.
Meredith, Richard E., 1796–1886, St.Edmund Hall, 1819, BA 1823, MA 1826; D. 1823, Worcester, P. 1824, Hereford; V. [& Patron] Hagbourne 1825–68; R. Westborough & Dry Doddington 1868–1885.
Merry, William Walter, 1835–? Balliol, 1852, BA 1857, MA 1860, BD & DD 1886, Fellow 1859–84; D. 1860, Oxford, P. 1861, Oxford; V. All Saints, Oxford 1861–84; Select Preacher, Oxford 1878–79; Surrogate.
Michell, Thomas Hungerford, 1828–? Oriel, Oxford, 1846, BA 1850, MA 1853; D. 1850, Oxford, P. 1851, Oxford; C. Sparsholt 1850; C. Histon 1852–56; V. Histon, dio. Ely 1865–? General Preacher, 1872.

Miller, Joseph Augustus, D. 1856, Oxford, P. 1857, Oxford; C. Windsor 1856–62; V. Ile-Brewers, dio. Bath & Wells 1862–79; St.Benedict, Glastonbury, 1879–? In *Crockford* 1880.

Miller, William Saunderson, 1822–? New College 1840, SCL 1841, BA 1853, MA 1854, Fellow 1840–48; D. 1845, Oxford, P. 1846, Oxford; P.C. Sibford Gower 1848–60; C. Bishop's Itchington, dio. Worcester 1865–67; V. Morton Murrell, Warks. 1880–84; R. Whatcote, dio. Worcester 1887–? R.D. South Kineton 1896.

Mills, William, 1818–1874, Queens', Cambridge, 1836, BA 1840, MA 1844; D. 1845, Peterborough, P. 1846, Peterborough; C. Witney 1847–64; Chaplain, Witney Union 1855; C. Burton Agnes,Yorkshire 1865–70; C. Bempton w Speeton,Yorks. 1870–74.

Milne[r], John Haworth, 1828–? Brasenose 1846, BA 1850, MA 1854; D. 1851, Canterbury, P. 1852, Canterbury; C. West Farleigh,Kent 1851–52; C. Hammersmith, London 1853; V. Midgham 1855–58; V. Greenham 1855–59; V. Thatcham 1855–62; R. Ithingfield, Sussex 1862–73; Assistant Chaplain, Dinan 1873–76; Assistant Chaplain, Avranches 1876–? In *Crockford* 1889.

Monkhouse, John, 1834–1879, Queen's, Oxford, 1852, BA 1856, MA 1859, Fellow 1858–62; D. 1858, Oxford, P. 1859, Oxford; C. Wargrave 1858; R. Church Oakley, dio. Winchester 1862–79.

Monro, Horace George, 1831–1920, Trinity, Cambridge, 1850, BA 1854, MA 1857; D. 1855, Winchester, P. 1856, Winchester; C. Holy Trinity, Winchester 1855–58; P.C. Highmore, Henley on Thames 1859–71; R. Clapham, Worthing 1871–73; R. Strathfieldsaye, Hants. 1878–1903.

Montagu, George, 1821–? Worcester, Oxford, 1839, BA 1843; C. Epwell 1857; R. Thenford, Peterborough 1883–?

Moore, Edward, 1792–1880, Brasenose, 1810, BA 1817, MA 1817; D. 1814, Canterbury, P. 1817, Canterbury; C. Norwood; C. Heston; R. Gisleham, Suffolk 1817–40; R. Whitchurch, Oxford 1840–80; Domestic Chaplain to the Rt. Hon. Lord Brougham & Vaux.

Moore, The Hon. Edward George, 1798–1876, St.John's, Cambridge, 1817, MA 1819; R. West Ilsley 1842–73; Canon of Windsor 1843–72.

Morrell, Thomas Baker, 1815–1877, Balliol, 1832, BA 1836, MA 1839, BD & DD; D. 1839, Chester, P. 1840, Chester; P.C. Sibford 1841–48; R. Henley-on-Thames 1852–63; R.D. Bishop of Edinburgh 1863–69.

Morres, Thomas, 1796–1877, Brasenose, 1813, BA 1817, MA 1820; D. 1819, Salisbury, P. 1820, Salisbury,; P.C. Wokingham 1820–72; Surrogate; Master of Lucas Hospital, Wokingham 1872.

Moultrie, Gerard, 1830–1885, Exeter, Oxford, 1848, BA 1852, MA 1856; D. 1853, Lichfield, P. 1858, Durham; Assistant Master, Shrewsbury School 1852–55; Chaplain to the Dowager Marchioness of London 1855–64; Headmaster, Royal Kepler Grammar School 1855–? C. Brightwalton 1859; Chaplain to the Duke of Barrow Gurney 1864–69; V. South Leigh, 1869–8; Warden, St.James' College, Southleigh 1873–1885.

Murray, David Rodney, 1791–1878, Christ Church, 1810, BA 1814; R. Brampton Bryan, dio. Hereford 1826–78; R. Cusop, Hereford 1826–78; V. Beedon 1828–74.

Murray, George William, 1828–? Queen's, Oxford, 1846, BA 1850, MA [Jesus] 1853; D. 1851, Winchester, P. 1852, Winchester; C. Redhill, Surrey 1851–54; R.Welton-le-Wold, Lincs. 1854–59; V. Shrivenham w Watchfield 1859–90; Surrogate; Chaplain to the Earl of Cork & Orrery; Inspector of Schools, Vale of the White Horse Deanery 1882; R.D. 1887.

Musgrave, Sir William Augustus, Bart. 1792–1875; Christ Church, 1809, BA 1812, MA 1815; D. 1814, Gloucester, P. 1815, Gloucester; R. Chinnor 1816–1875; R. Emmington 1827–72.

Napier, The Hon. Henry Alfred, 1798–1871, Christ Church, 1817, BA 1820, MA 1822; D. 1821, Oxford, P. 1821, Oxford; C. Stonesfield 1821; C. Ewelme 1821; R. Swyncombe 1826–71.

Nash, Zachariah, 1816–1883, St.Catherine's, Cambridge, 1836, BA 1841, MA 1846; D. 1843, Lincoln, P. 1844, Lincoln; C. Denham 1843–44; C. Langley Marish 1847–56; Senior Curate, Christchurch, Hants. 1857–71; V. Christchurch, Hants.1871–83. Surrogate, Dio. Winchester.

Neate, Arthur, 1803–1870, Trinity, Cambridge, 1823, BA 1827, MA 1829; C. Alvescot 1828; R. Alvescot 1829–70; V. Shilton 1829–70.

Nepean, Evan Yorke, 1826–? Queen's, Oxford, 1844, BA 1848, MA 1851; D. 1847, Salisbury, P. 1852, Salisbury; C. & Evening Lecturer, Midgham 1855; C. Bucknall, Lincolnshire, 1859–68; V. Applesham, dio. Winchester 1868–? In *Crockford* 1889.

Nicholson, Mark Anthony, University of Durham, Licen. Th, 1837, MA 1837; D. 1837, Chester, P. 1838, Chester; V. Hanslope-cum-Castlethorpe 1851–92.

Nicholson, William, 1805–1878, Trinity, Oxford, 1824 BA 1829, MA 1831; D. 1832, P.1833; R. (& Patron),Welford w Wickham Chapel 1836–78.

Nind, Philip Henry, 1806–1886, Christ Church, 1823, BA 1829, MA 1831, Student 1827–31; D. 1829, Oxford, 1830, P. Gloucester & Bristol; V.Southstoke w Woodcote 1844–1886.

Niven, James, *ob* 1879, MA; C. Harrogate,Yorks. *Circa* 1852; V.Swanborne 1853–67; R. Adstock, 1867–79.

Noble, William, 1805–1882, St.John's, Cambridge, 1829, BA 1833, MA 1837; D. 1833, Rochester for York; C. Sedgbrook w West Allington, Lincoln 1841–43; P.C. Winster, Kendal 1844–47; R. Pitchcott 1847–82.

Noel, The Hon. Augustus William, 1816–1884, Trinity, Cambridge, 1837, MA 1840; D. 1840, Gloucester, P. 1841, Gloucester; C. Wollastone, Gloucester 1840–43; C. Hurstpierpoint, Sussex 1844–45; V. Cropredy 1851–60; R. Stanhoe w Barwick, Norfolk 1861–84.

North, John North Ouvry, 1817–? Trinity, Cambridge, 1844, BA 1849, MA 1852; D. Oxford, 1848, P. Oxford, 1848; V. Mentmore 1848–60. Disappears from *Crockford* 1876.

Nourse, Ain Henry, *ob* 1868, C. Llangattoc Lingoid, Mon; C. Standlake 1856–63; P.C. Cogges 1863–68.

Nucella, Thomas, 1772–1856, Trinity Hall, Cambridge, 1807, BA 1809, MA 1812; D. 1809, P. 1810; R. Glympton,1818–56.

Nutting, George Horatio, 1807–1874, Trinity Hall, Cambridge, 1825, BA 1829; D. 1829, Norwich, P. 1830, Norwich; C. Bletchingley, Surrey 1841–43; C. Hatch Beauchamp, Somerset 1844–45; C. Charlynch, Bath & Wells 1846–48; R. Chedzoy, Bath & Wells 1849–55; R. Chastleton 1863–74.

Ogle, James Ambrose, 1825–? Brasenose, 1842, BA 1846, MA 1849, D. 1848, Gloucester & Bristol, P. 1849, Gloucester & Bristol; C. Icomb, Gloucs. 1848–51; C. Writtle, St.Alban's 1851; C. Begbrooke 1853–55; C. Letheringsett, Norfolk 1855–56; V. Sedgeford, Norfolk 1858–74; R. Southmere w Sedgeford, Norfolk 1874–?

Ormerod, Arthur Stanley,1822–1884, Exeter, Oxford,1840, BA 1843, MA 1846; D. 1844, Lincoln, P. 1845, Lincoln; C. Hitchendon *circa* 1845; V. Halvergate, Norfolk 1853–8; Surrogate, dio. Norwich 1853.
Ouvry, Peter Thomas, 1811–1891, Trinity, Cambridge,1830, BA 1834, MA 1837; D. 1836, Lincoln for Peterborough, P. 1837, Gloucester for Peterborough; C. Mears-Ashby, Northampton 1836–37; C. St.John's, Paddington, London 1828–47; P.C. Linslade, Gloucs. 1847–5; V. Wing 1850–85; R. Grove 1860–85. J.P. for Buckinghamshire.
Owen, Brisco, 1807–1864, Jesus, Oxford, 1824, BA 1829, MA 1831, BD 1838, Fellow 1832–4, Vice Principal; D. 1835, Oxford, P. 1836, Oxford; R. Remenham 1841–64.
Owen, Edward, 1784–? Trinity, Cambridge, 1802, migrated to Corpus Christi 1804, BA 1806, MA 1809; P.C. St.Leonard's 1810–58; P.C. Aston Clinton 1848–58; Professor of Rhetoric, Gresham College, London. Disappears from *Clergy List* 1866. Father of the next entry.
Owen, Edward, 1820–1904, Sidney Sussex, Cambridge, 1839, BA 1844, MA 1847; D. 1843, Lincoln, P. 1844, Lincoln; C. St.Leonard's, Wendover 1843–46; R. Halton, Bucks. 1846–57; Incumbent Laura Chapel, Bath 1857–61; R. Sedlescombe, Sussex, 1861–1870; R. Bradwell-juxta-Mare, dio. Rochester 1870–1904. J.P. for Buckingham.
Palmer, George Horsley, 1833–1881, Exeter, Oxford, 1843, BA 1847, MA 1850; D.1850, Oxford, P. 1851, Oxford; C. Mixbury 1850–52; R. Mixbury 1852–1881.
Palmer, Richard, 1796–1874, Christ Church, 1813, BA 1816, MA 1819, Student 1813–25; D. 1822, Oxford, P. 1823, Oxford; R. Blaby, Leics. 1824–45; R. Purley, Berks. 1844–74.
Palmer, William Jocelyn, 1778–1853, Brasenose, 1796, BA 1799, MA 1802, BD 1811; R. Mixbury 1802–53; R. Finmere 1814–53.
Parker, Edwin James, 1796–1873, Pembroke, Oxford, 1810, BA 1814, MA 1817, BD 1847, Fellow 1823–54; D. 1819,Oxford, P. 1820, Oxford; V. Waltham St.Lawrence 1834–73.
Parsons, Henry, 1798–1878, Balliol, 1816, BA 1820, MA 1823; D. 1820, Peterborough, P. 1822, Peterborough; P.C. Upton St.Leonards,Gloucs. 1833–4; R. Sandhurst, 1850–78.
Partridge, Charles Francis, 1811–1860, Trinity, Cambridge, 1830, BA 1834, MA 1838; D. 1835, P. 1836; V. Chicheley 1852–60.
Partridge, William Edward,1809–1886, Brasenose, 1827, BA 1830; D. 1832, Lincoln, P.1833, Lincoln; V. Ilmer 1833–86; R. Horsendon 1844–86.
Passand, Henry John, 1802–1867, St.Alban Hall, Oxford, 1820, BA 1824, MA 1827; D. 1825, Oxford, P. 1826, Oxford; C. Noke 1826; R. Shipton on Cherwell 1831–1867.
Payne, Edward, 1810–1886, New College, 1826, BA 1829, MA 1832, Fellow; D. 1832, Oxford, P. 1833, Winchester; C. Old Alresford, Hants. 1832–33; C. Padgham, Surrey 1834; C. St.Michael, Winchester 1835–36; V. Swalcliffe w Shutford & Epwell 1837–86; R.D. Deddington 1847–75; Surrogate; Hon.Canon, Christ Church 1869–86.
Payne, William, 1828–1892, Corpus Christi, Cambridge, 1847, BA 1851, MA 1854; D. 1851, Ely, P. 1852, Ely; C. St.Andrew the Great, Cambridge 1851–54; C. St.John w St.Stephen, Reading 1854; V. St.John's, Reading 1857–92.

Pears, Edmund Ward, 1814–1878, Magdalen, Oxford, 1830, BA 1833, MA 1836; C. Marshwood, Devon; C. Stoke Goldington *circa* 1860; R. St.Peter's, Dorchester, Dorset 1864–78.

Pearse, George Wingate, 1824–? Corpus Christi, Oxford, 1841, BA 1845, MA 1848, Fellow 1849–51; D. 1848, Oxford, P. 1849, Oxford; R. Walton, nr Fenny Stratford, 1851–?93; Licensed to Sympson 1859.

Pearse, William, 1786–1861, Corpus Christi, Cambridge, 1804, BA 1808, MA 1811; P. 1810, London; P.C. Struston, Norfolk 1814–16; R. Hanwell 1816–61.

Pearson, Hugh, 1817–1882, Balliol, 1834, BA 1839, MA 1841; D. 1841, P. 1841; V. Sonning 1841–1882; R.D. Henley-on-Thames 1864–74; R.D. Sonning 1874–76; Chaplain to Bishop of Manchester 1870; Canon of Windsor 1876; Deputy Clerk to the Closet 1881–82.

Peel, Charles Steers, 1821–1873, Worcester, Oxford, 1839, BA 1843, MA 1847; D. 1845, Lichfield, P. 1846, Lichfield; R. Syresham, dio. Peterborough, 1850–59; R. Rousham 1859–73.

Peel, Edmund, 1818–1877, Brasenose, 1836, BA 1839, MA 1845; D. 1848, Bath & Wells, P. 1849, Bath & Wells; V. West Pennard, Somerset 1849–50; V. Wargrave 1850–54; V. Toot–Baldon 1860–71.

Peers, John, 1772–1855, Magdalene, Cambridge, 1789, BA 1793, MA 1796; C. Ackhampstead 1833; P.C. Lane End 1832–55.

Peers, John Witherington, 1804–1876, St.Catherine's, Cambridge, 1828, BA 1833, MA 1836; D. 1832, Chichester, P. 1833, Chichester; C. Old Shoreham, Sussex 1832–41; Lecturer, Portslade 1832–41; Chaplain, Shoreham Union 1837–41; V. Tetsworth 1841–76.

Pegus, Frederick Edward, 1799–1848, St.John's, Oxford, 1817, BA 1822, MA 1825; C. Little Missenden to 1848.

Pennefather, William, Trinity, Dublin, BA 1841; D. 1841, Chester, P. 1842, Chester; C. Holy Trinity, Aylesbury; P.C. Walton 1848–52; P.C. Christ Church, Barnet 1852–64; P.C. St.Jude's, Islington 1864–?

Perkins, William, 1796–1874, Lincoln, Oxford, 1812, BA 1818, MA 1820; D. 1819, Salisbury, P. 1820, Chester; C. Goddington 1820–66; V. Twyford 1820–74.

Phelps, William Whitmarsh, 1797–1867, Corpus Christi, Oxford, 1815, BA 1819, MA 1822, Fellow 1822–24; D. 1822, P. 1822; C. St.Lawrence, Reading 1840; C. Sulhampstead 1842; P.C. Holy Trinity, Reading 1845–64; Archdeacon, Carlisle 1863–67; Canon of Carlisle 1863–67.

Phillimore, George, 1808–1886, Christ Church, 1825, BA 1829, MA 1832, Student 1825–33; D. 1831, Oxford, P. 1832, Lincoln; C. Little Linford 1846; V. Willen 1832–51; V. Newport Pagnell 1832–51; R. Radnage 1851–1886.

Pinckney, William Philip, 1810–1898, Trinity, Cambridge, 1828, BA 1832, MA 1836; Gray's Inn, 1836; D. 1842, Lincoln, P. 1843, Lincoln; C. Moulsoe 1843–47; P.C. Rotherfield Grays (Holy Trinity) 1848–89.

Pigott, Randolphe Henry, 1837–1900, St.John's, Cambridge, 1856, BA 1860; D. 1861, Oxford, P. 1862, Oxford; C. Chipping Norton 1861–62; R. Grendon Underwood 1862–1900.

Pigott, William, 1811–1881, New College, 1831, B.C.L. 1835, Fellow 1831–51; D. 1836, Oxford, P. 1837, Lincoln; V. Whaddon 1850–81.

Pigou, Francis, Trinity, Dublin, BA 1853, BD 1878, DD 1878; D. 1855, Oxford, P. 1856, Oxford; C. Stoke Talmage 1855–56; Chaplain to Bishop Spencer [Paris]

1856–58; Chaplain, Marboeuf [France] 1856–58; C. St.Philip's, Regent St. London 1858–60; C. St.Mary, Kensington 1858–60; P.C. St.Philip's, Regent St. London 1860–69; V. Doncaster 1869–75; R.D. Doncaster 1870–75; V. and R.D. Halifax 1875-98; Hon Canon Carlisle 1885-88; Dean of Chichester 1888-91; Dean of Bristol 1891. In *Crockford* 1903.

Pinder, North, 1829–1901, Trinity, Oxford, 1846, BA 1850, MA 1853, Fellow 1851– 61; D. 1855, P. 1856; R. Rotherfield Greys 1860–1901; R.D. Henley on Thames 1874; Hon. Canon, Christ Church 1892.

Pinwill, William James, 1796–1885, Trinity, Cambridge, 1820, BA 1824, MA 1828; C. Horley w Horton 1849–53; V. Horley w Horton 1853–78; Chaplain to Lord Kingsale.

Pooley, James, 1825–1901, Christ's, Cambridge, 1847, BA 1851; D.1851, Lincoln, P. 1852, Lincoln; C. Great Limber, dio. Lincoln 1851–56; C. Hambledon, Bucks. 1856–63; C. in charge Standlake 1863–68; C. Lane End 1868; C. Quainton 1869–72; V. Little Milton, 1875–1901.

Porter, Charles Fleetwood, 1830–1914, Caius, Cambridge, 1849, BA 1853, MA 1856; Cuddesdon College, 1854; D. Oxford, 1855, P. Oxford,1855; C. Cropredy 1854– 56; C. Bisham 1857–59; C. Raunds, Northants. 1859–62; C. Slapton 1862–66; C. St.Anne, Dropmore 1866; V. St.Anne, Dropmore 1867–81; Inspector of Schools 1867; R.D. Burnham 1876–81; V. Banbury w Neithrop 1881–1905; R.D. Deddington 1898–1905; Hon. Canon, Christ Church 1896–1914.

Porter, Reginald, 1833–? Exeter, Oxford, 1851, BA 1855, MA 1857; C. Wantage 1856– 57; R. Kenn, dio. Exeter 1858–?

Porter, Richard Ibbetson, 1837–? Corpus Christi, Cambridge, 1855, BA 1858, MA 1862; D. 1860, Oxford, P. 1861,Oxford; C. Stewkley 1860–62; C. in charge South Stoke 1862–68; R. Chipping Ongar, dio. Rochester 1869–78; R. Crowmarsh Gifford 1878–93.

Powell, William Charles Bolton, Sidney Sussex, Cambridge, 1844, a "Ten Year Man "; C. Minster Lovell 1850. Disappears from the *Clergy List,* 1867.

Power, John, 1817–1887, St.Edmund Hall, 1843, BA 1847, MA 1853; D. 1847, Ripon, P. 1848, Ripon; C. Buttershaw, dio. Ripon 1847–48; P.C. Shelf, dio. Ripon; C. St.John, Portsea, dio. Winchester 1853–57; Chaplain, Missions to Seamen, 1857–62; Incumbent St.Margaret's, Tylers Green 1862–68; P.C. Bedford Chapel, Exeter 1868–71; R. Dodbrooke, dio. Exeter 1872–79; V. Altarnum, Cornwall 1879–87.

Powys, Richard Thomas, 1798–1877, University, Oxford, 1816, BA 1820, MA 1823; D. 1821, Oxford, P. 1822, Oxford; C. Whitchurch 1821–22; C. Caversham 1823–27; Chaplain, Goring Heath Almhouses 1828–64; C. Rotherfield Peppard 1840–49; C. Purley, Berks. 1854–64; V. Hullavington, dio Gloucester & Bristol 1864–77.

Powys, Thomas Arthur, D. 1826, Oxford, P. 1826, Oxford; R. Sawtry St.Andrew, Hunts.1831–? R. Medmenham 1837–52.

Powys [Powis],William Percy, 1838–? University, Oxford, 1857, BA 1862, MA 1864; D. 1862, Oxford, P. 1864, Oxford; C. St.Mary, Reading 1862–73; R. Ashow, dio. Worcester 1873–77; R. Thorp Achurch, Northants 1877–94.

Prater, Thomas,1813–? Exeter, Oxford, 1830, BA 1833, MA 1836; D. 1836, Winchester, P. 1838, Winchester; R. Tusmore 1841–56; R. Hardwick 1841–56; V. Leighton-under-Wrekin 1856–62.

Price, Aubrey Charles, 1788–1848, New College,1806, BA 1820, MA 1815, Fellow 1806–1827; V. Chesterton 1826–48.

Price, Robert Cholmeley, Christ Church, MA; D. 1842, Oxford, P. 1843, Oxford; C. Littleworth 1843.
Price, William Henry, 1813–? Pembroke, Oxford,1831, BA 1835, MA 1838, Fellow 1840–59; D.1836, Oxford, P. 1837, Oxford; Chaplain, Wantage Union 1837; C. Fawley, Berkshire 1838–55; C. Farnborough, Berkshire 1837–60; R. Farnborough 1860; R. Somerton 1861–74; R. Coln St.Dennis, Gloucester 1874–?
Pring, Joseph Charles, 1800–1876, Jesus, Oxford, 1820, BA 1824, MA 1826; Chaplain, New College 1825–73; V. Headington 1835–76; Chaplain, Headington Union 1842.
Prosser, James, 1890–1877, St.Catherine's, Cambridge, 1828, BA 1832, MA 1835; D. 1832, Lincoln, P. 1833, Lincoln; P.C. Loudwater 1833–40; V. Thame 1841–71.
Quartley, Henry Reade, 1788–1869, Queen's, Oxford, 1803, BA 1808, MA 1811; D.1812, Oxford, P. 1813, Oxford; C. Stratton Audley 1812–55; V. Wolverton 1838–55; V. Stantonbury 1842–55.
Raine, William, 1784–1858, Queen's, Oxford, 1791, BA 1795, MA 1798; P.1798, Oxford; P.C. Lemington, Glos. 1810–57; R. Widford, Glos. 1812–57; C. Swinbrook 1838; P.C. Swinbrook 1838–57.
Randall, James, 1790–1882, Trinity, Oxford, 1809, BA 1813, MA 1816, Fellow 1818–21; D. 1828, P. 1829; R. Binfield 1831–59; Archdeacon of Berks.1855–69; Chaplain to the Bishop of Oxford 1846–69; Hon. Canon, Christ Church 1866; Chaplain to the Bishop of Winchester 1869–73; Canon of Bristol 1873–75.
Randall, James Leslie, 1829–1922, New College, 1848, BA 1852, MA 1855, Fellow 1848–56; D. 1852, Oxford, P. 1853, Oxford; C. Warfield 1852–57; R. Newbury 1857–78; R.D. Newbury 1867; Surrogate; R. Sandhurst 1878–80; R. Mixbury 1881–85; Hon. Canon, Christ Church 1878–95; Archdeacon of Buckingham 1880–95; Archdeacon of Oxford 1895–1902; Bishop of Reading 1889–1908.
Randolph, Francis Charles Hingeston,1833–? Exeter, Oxford, 1851, BA 1855, MA 1858; D. 1856, Oxford, P. 1859, Oxford; C. St.Cross, Holywell 1856–58; P.C. Hampton Gay 1859–60; R. Ringmore, Devon 1860–? C. Deopham, Norfolk 1872–73; R.D. Woodleigh, 1879; Preb. of Exeter 1885.
Randolph, Levenson Cyril, 1825–1876, Christ Church, 1842, BA 1845, MA 1848, Student 1842–53; D. 1849, Oxford, P. 1850, Oxford; V. East Garston 1852–70; V. St.Luke's, Lower Norwood 1870–76.
Ranking, John Harvey, 1828–1866, Gonville & Caius, Cambridge, 1854, BA 1858, MA 1861; D. 1858, Chester, P. 1859, Chester; C. St.Mary's, Birkenhead; 1858–62; C. Chipping Norton 1863–66. *Venn.*
Rawlings, William, 1795–1862, Magdalen Hall, Oxford, 1824, BA 1829, MA 1831; D. 1830, Peterborough, P. 1831, Peterborough; Chaplain to the Bicester Union, 1829; V. Fritwell 1838–62; R. Thenford, Northants. 1843–62.
Rawnsley, Robert Drummond Burrell, 1818–1882, Magdalen, Oxford, 1836, BA 1840, MA 1843, Fellow 1840–42; D. 1841, P. 1842; V. Shiplake 1849–61; R. Halton Holgate, dio. Lincoln 1861–82; R.D. Candleshoe 1873 & 1877; Surrogate; Preb. of Lincoln Cathedral 1877.
Reade, Compton, 1834–? Magdalen, Oxford, 1852, BA 1857, MA 1859; D. 1857, Oxford, P. 1858, Oxford; C. Burford 1858; Chaplain, Magdalen Coll.1858–79; Chaplain, Christ Church 1860–67; C. Summertown 1861; V. Cassington 1867–69; R. Elton, Durham,1883–84; Lecturer, Curzon Chapel, London 1886.

Reade, Joseph Bancroft, 1801–1870, Trinity, Cambridge, 1819, Caius, 1822, BA 1825, MA 1828, F.R.S.; D. 1825, Lincoln, P. 1826, Lincoln; C. Kegworth, Leics. 1825–29; C. Halifax,Yorks. 1829–32; P.C. Harrow Weald, Middx. 1832–34; V. Stone 1839–59; Chaplain, Stone Asylum 1853; R. Ellesborough 1859–63; V. Bishopsbourne, Kent 1863–70. One of the orginal members of the Microscopical Society & sometime President; discovered a means of separating Heat-rays from those of light & effected several improvements in photographic methods; invented the "Reades Kettledrum", a hemispherical condenser for the microscope.

Redifer, Alfred, 1830–1902, St.Mary Hall, Oxford, 1848, BA 1852, MA 1855; D. 1853, Peterborough, P. 1854, Peterborough; C. Daventry 1853–59; C. Hurstpierpont, Sussex 1859; C. Quainton 1860–63; V. Finstock 1863–1902.

Reed, George Vareene, 1816–1889, Jesus, Cambridge, 1833, BA 1837, MA 1840; D.1837, P.1838; C. Hayes 1837–39; C. Tingewick 1839–54; R. Hayes, dio. Canterbury, 1854–86; R.D. West Dartford; Secretary to the S.P.G.

Rees, Samuel George, 1826–? Jesus, Oxford,1844,BA 1848, MA 1853; D.1848, Lincoln, P.1851, Lincoln; C. Attenborough, Notts. 1852; C. Wasing 1853; R. Wasing 1857–80; R. Abb Kettleby, Leics 1880–?

Rendall, Henry, 1818–? Trinity, Oxford, 1836, BA 1840, MA 1843, Fellow of Brasenose 1840–56; D. 1841, Oxford, P. 1842, Oxford; P.C. Holy Trinity, Stepney, 1847–55; V. Great Rollright 1855–1893.

Rew, Charles, 1814–1884, St.John's,Oxford, 1830, BA 1834, MA 1838, BD 1843, Fellow,1830–60; D. 1837,Oxford, P. 1838, Oxford; C. All Saint's, Maidstone 1838–46; V. St.Giles, Oxford 1846–54; R. Cranham, Essex 1859–84; 2nd Master, Highgate Grammar School 1836–68.

Reynolds, Henry, 1806–1869, Jesus, Oxford 1823, BA 1827, MA 1829, BD 1841, Fellow 1831–49; P. 1832, Oxford; R. Rotherfield Peppard 1848–69.

Reynolds, Osborne, 1814–1890, Trinity, Cambridge 1833, migrated to Queens', BA 1837, MA 1840, Fellow of Queens' 1838–45; D. 1838, Ely, P. 1839, Ely; C. Chesham 1844–45; Headmaster, Dedham Grammar School, Essex 1846–54; C. Pettistree, Suffolk about 1860; R. Rockland St.Mary, Norfolk 1880–89; sometime also a Schoolmaster in Belfast.

Riadore, James Evans, 1830–1904, Peterhouse, Cambridge 1848, BA 1852; D. 1853, Lichfield, P. 1855, Oxford; C. St.Alkmund's, Derby 1853–55; C. Sutton Courtney 1859–60; C. Canon's Ashby, Northants 1860–61; C. Higher Broughton, Manchester 1864; C. St.Andrew's, Westminster 1865; C. Turnham Green, London 1866–68; C. Upton 1867; C. Gargrave, Ripon 1870–71; C. Rickmansworth 1872; C. St.Alphege, London 1873–79. *No other Cures identified.*

Rice, Richard John Howard, 1828–1902, Exeter, Oxford, 1846, BA 1850, MA 1853; C. High Wycombe; V. Sutton Courtney 1855–1902.

Rich, Edward John George Henry, 1816–? New College 1837, BA 1841, MA 1845, Fellow 1837–51; D. 1841,Oxford, P. 1842, Oxford; Minister of St.Paul's Chapel, Wittle about 1843; C. Hardwick ?

Ridley, William Henry, 1816–1882, Christ Church 1834, BA 1838, MA 1840, Student 1836–41; D. 1839, Oxford, P. 1840, Oxford; R. Hambledon, Bucks. 1840–82; R.D. Wycombe 1859; Hon. Canon, Christ Church 1871.

Riggs, George,1799–1855,Queen's, Oxford 1819, BA 1824, MA 1828, Chaplain 1833–45, Fellow 1836–46; P. 1829, Oxford; R. Charlton-on-Otmoor 1846–55.

Risley, John, 1771–1853, New College 1787, BA 1791, MA 1808; P. 1796, Oxford; C. Upper Heyford 1796; R. Aston, Northants. 1818–53; R. Thornton 1819–53.

Risley, William Cotton, 1833–1908, Exeter, Oxford 1852, BA 1856, MA 1857; D. 1858, Oxford, P. 1860, Oxford; C. Hambledon, Bucks. 1858–60; C. Burford 1860; C. Fulbrook & Kidmore End 1862; C. St.John's, Paddington 1864–67; C. St.Michael's, Paddington 1867–76; V. Titley, Herefordshire 1876–77; R. Shalstone 1878–1907.

Roberts, John Lindfield, Queen's, Oxford, MA, Fellow; C. Bradenham 1846; C. Crowell w Shirburn 1848; C. Pyrton 1851; C. South Weston 1855; C. Maidenhead 1856; Chaplain, Cookham Union 1859; Chaplain, Ascot Heath Hospital 1865.

Roberts, Richard, 1784–1859, Merton, 1801, BA 1805, MA 1815; Minor Canon, Worcester Cathedral 1814; V. Stewkley 1830–59. *Foster.*

Robertson, George Samuel, 1825–1874, Exeter, Oxford 1843, BA 1847, MA 1850; D. 1849, P. 1850; C. Sywell, Northampton 1850–? P.C. Pitstone 1854–55; C. East Hendred 1862.

Robinson, Francis, 1805–1886, Corpus Christi, Oxford, 1819, BA 1823, MA 1826, Fellow 1826–31; D. 1828, Oxford, P. 1829, Oxford; Staughton Parva, Beds. 1831–81; R. Stonesfield 1834–82.

Robinson, John Ellill, 1808–? Christ Church 1825, BA 1829, MA 1832; D.1832, Oxford, P.1833,Oxford; C. Kirtlington 1832; C. Blechingdon w Kirtlington 1833; C. Bicester 1834; C. Charlton-on-Otmoor 1835; V. Chieveley 1837–1881; C. Curridge, 1837–81; R. Oare, Winterbourne1837–? R. Leckhampstead 1837–81

Rogers, James Edward Thorold, 1823–1890, Magdalen Hall, 1843, BA 1846, MA 1849; D.1846; C. St.Paul's, Oxford, 1846; C. Headington 1859; Drummond Professor of Political Economy 1862–68 & 1888; M.P.for Southwark 1880–85; M.P.for Bermondsey District 1885–86. Instrumental in obtaining the Clerical Disabilities Relief Act and the first to avail himself of it in 1870. *DNB.*

Rogers, Josiah, Trinity, Dublin, BA 1844; D.1844, P.1844; C. Haversham 1849; C. North Stoke w Newnham Murren & Ipsden 1873.

Rolfe, George Crabb, 1811–1893, St.John's, Cambridge, 1830, BA 1834; D. 1834, Oxford, P. 1835, Oxford; C. Witney 1834; C. Hailey 1838; V. Hailey w Crawley 1839–93; Chaplain to the Witney Union 1845.

Romanis, William, 1824–1899, Emmanuel, Cambridge 1842, BA 1846, MA 1849; D. 1847, Gloucester & Bristol, P. 1848, Gloucester & Bristol; C. Axminster, Devon 1856–58; Senior Curate St.Mary, Reading 1858–63; V. Wigston Magna, dio. Peterborough 1863–68; V. Twyford, Hants.1888–95.

Roundell, Henry Dawson, 1786–1852, Brasenose 1804, BA 1808, MA 1810, BD 1818, Fellow of Magdalen 1819; D. 1809, Oxford, P. 1810, Oxford; C. Mixbury 1809; C. Fringford 1811; R. Fringford 1815–33.

Routh, John William, 1818–1905, Magdalen, Oxford 1835, BA 1839, MA 1841; D. 1840, Oxford, P. 1841, Oxford; C. Tilehurst 1841–46; R. & V. Tilehurst 1855–1905. Surrogate 1855.

Rowton, Rupert James, 1820–1894, St.John's, Cambridge 1838, BA 1842, MA 1845; D. 1842, Salisbury, P. 1843, Salisbury; C.Hazelbury Bryan, Dorset 1842–45; C. Wendover 1845–47; R. Southwood & V. Limpinhoe 1847–58; Chaplain, Clifton Union, Bristol 1857–59; C. St.James', Shaftesbury, Dorset 1859–68; Chaplain, Brussels 1862–64; C. St.Philip's, Kennington, Surrey 1865–68; C. Herriard, Hants. 1868–70; V. Wessington, Derbyshire 1870–76; V. Penkhill,

Staffs. 1876–80; C. Plungar, Notts. 1880–83; C. St.Philip's, Kennington 1884–86; C. Ashendon 1886–88; R. Eynsham 1888–93.

Rudd, Leonard Hampson, 1817–1888, Pembroke, Oxford 1833, BA 1837, MA 1840; D. 1839, Worcester, P. 1840, Worcester; C. Wick, nr Pershore, Worcs. 1839–44; P.C. Ruscombe & Polehampton 1844–64; Chaplain, Twyford Hospital 1844–64; C. Twyford 1848.

Rush, John, 1770–1855, St.John's, Oxford 1788, BCL 1795; R. Hartwell & Little Hampden 1803–55; V. Chelsea Old Church, London 1824–55.

Rushton, John Richard, 1800–1881, Clare, Cambridge 1834, BD 1834; D. 1822, Chester, P. 1823, Chester; C. Crosthwaite, Cumberland 1822–27; C. Ormside, Westmorland 1827–30; C. Banbury 1830–41; Chaplain, Banbury Union 1836; P.C. Hooknorton 1840–81.

Russell, Richard Norris, 1809–1896, Caius, Cambridge 1828, BA 1832, MA 1835; D. 1833, Ely, P. 1834, Lincoln; R. Beachampton 1834–83; R.D. Buckingham 1865–78; Hon. Canon, Christ Church 1877–96; J.P. for Bucks.& Northants.

Russell, Samuel Henry, 1814–1873, St.John's, Oxford 1832, BA 1836, MA 1840, BD 1845; D. 1837, Oxford, P. 1838, Oxford; C. St.John's, Hoxton, Middlesex; Master, Merchant Taylor's School 1836–57; V. Charlbury w Shorthampton 1857–73.

Russell, Thomas, 1830–? St.John's, Oxford 1848, BA 1852, MA 1854; D. 1853, Oxford, P. 1855, Oxford; C. St.Thomas the Martyr, Oxford 1853–56; C. Horley w Horton 1856–57; C. Shotteswell, Warws. 1858–59; C. Drayton 1859–61; Master, Banbury Grammar School 1861–65; Master, Brackley Grammar School 1865–70; C. Sherwell, dio. Exeter 1878–?

Russell Lord Wriothesley, 1804–1886, Trinity, Cambridge 1828, MA 1829; R. Chenies 1829–86; R. Streatham, Surrey 1830–35; Canon, St.George's Chapel, Windsor 1840–86; Hon. Chaplain to Queen Victoria 1850–86; Deputy Clerk to the Closet 1850–86; Chaplain to Prince Albert; Chaplain in Ordinary to the Queen 1862–66

Ruston, James, 1829–? Jesus, Cambridge 1847, BA 1851, MA 1856; D. 1851, P. 1852; C. Bensington 1851–54; C. Fritwell 1855–56; C. St.Thomas, Stamford Hill, Middx. 1856–61; V. Hordle, Hants. 1861–75. Disappears from *Crockford* 1902.

Sabin[e], John Edward, 1792–1863, Lincoln, Oxford 1809, BA 1813, MA 1818; D.1815, P.1816; R. Preston Bissett 1823–63; Minister, Eaton Chapel.

Sabin, John Edward, 1822–1891, Emmanuel, Cambridge 1840, BA 1840; D. 1844, Lincoln, P. 1846, Oxford; C. Preston Bissett 1847–49; C. St.Michael's, Pimlico 1850; R. Warfield 1850–54; Chaplain, Crimea 1854–56; Hon. Canon, Gibraltar, and Chaplain to the Bishop of Gibraltar,1882–91.

St.John, Edward,1805–1891, Downing, Cambridge 1827, LLB 1831; D. 1835, Worcester, P. 1836, Norwich; R. Barkham 1842–62; R. Finchampstead 1842–91.

Salmon, Henry Thomas,1827–? Exeter, Oxford 1844, BA 1848, MA 1851; D. 1849, Norwich, P. 1850, Norwich; C. Morston, Norfolk 1849–51; C. Hinton-Waldrist 1851–53; C. Shutford 1854–55; C. Twickenham, Middlesex 1855–59; C. Bilton, Warcs.1859–62; C. Balwell, Leics. 1862–65; V. Milford, Surrey 1865–85; Chaplain, Hambledon Union,1878.

Salter, Edward, C. St.Marks, Dukinfield Cheshire; C. Chievely 1856.

Salter, Frederick, 1811–1881, Exeter, Oxford 1831, BA 1835, MA 1866; D. 1836, P.1837; R. Hethe 1855–81.

Samuel, John, 1803–1878, Jesus, Oxford 1823, BA 1829; D. 1837, Salisbury, P.1839, Oxford; C. Chipping Norton 1837; Chaplain to Viscount Dillon,1843–? R. Heythrop 1845–78; Chaplain, Chipping Norton Union.

Sandwith, Henry, 1828–1896, St.Catherine's, Cambridge 1847, BA 1852, MA 1866; D. 1852, York, P. 1853, Oxford; C. Adlingfleet,Yorks. 1852–53; C. Charlbury 1853–55; C. Harthill, Cheshire 1855–59; P.C. Norley 1859–62; C. Cawthorne,Yorks 1862–66; R. Todwick, Sheffield 1866–76; Chaplain, Dunmore, Stirling, Scotland 1876–78; V. Thorpe-Salvin,Yorks. 1878–88.

Sankey, Richard, 1802–63, Corpus Christi, Oxford 1820, BA 1824, MA 1827, Fellow 1828–29; D. 1827, Oxford, P. 1828, Oxford; C. Farnham, Surrey, R. Witney, 1852–63.

Sankey, William Thompson, 1829–1875, Exeter, Oxford 1847, BA 1852, MA 1854; D. 1853, Rochester, P. 1855, Rochester; C. St.Stephen's, St.Alban's, V. Stony Stratford 1859–75.

Saulez, Theophilus, D. 1841, P. 1842; Incumbent Grazeley 1850–54; Incumbent (& Patron), All Saints, Islington, dio. London 1853–? Hon. Chaplain, Great Northern Hospital.

Sawyer, Duncombe Herbert, 1837–1913, Trinity, Cambridge 1855, BA 1859, MA 1862; D. 1860, Oxford, P. 1862, Oxford; C. Hambledon, Bucks. 1860–63; C. West Harnham, Salisbury, 1863–65; C. Farnham & Chettle, Dorset 1865–67; C. Hammoon, Dorset 1867–84; R. Hammoon 1884–1911.

Sawyer, George Herbert, 1826–? Trinity Hall, Cambridge 1844, LL.B 1851; D. 1849, Oxford, P. 1850, Oxford; C. Faringdon 1849–52; C. Woughton-on-the-Green 1851; R. Sunningwell 1854–66. No other cures found; disappears from *Crockford* 1912.

Sawyer, William George, 1829–1917, Trinity Hall, Cambridge 1848, BA 1852, MA 1855; D. 1852, Salisbury, P. 1854, Oxford; C. Wilton, dio. Salisbury 1852–54; C. Wantage 1854–60; V. Little Milton 1860–74; V. St.Luke's, Maidenhead 1874–90; R. Taplow 1890–97.

Scobell, Edward, 1785–1860, Balliol 1801, BA from Magdalen Hall 1814, MA 1827; D. 1815, P. 1817; V. Turville 1823–60; Incumbent St.Peter,Vere Street, London 1831–60.

Scobell, George Richard, Cuddesdon Theological College; D.1857, Oxford, P.1859, Oxford; C. Great Milton 1857; C. Prestwood 1857–59; C. Fenny Stratford 1859–60; C. Madron, Cornwall 1860–67; V. Shaugh-Prior, dio. Exeter 1867–77; V. Bickleigh, dio. Exeter 1877–?

Scurr, Robert William, 1801–1866, Magdalene, Cambridge 1819, BA 1825; D. 1824, Lincoln, P. 1825, Peterborough; V. Aldeburgh, Suffolk 1833–39; R. Addington 1839–65; R. Shenley 1839–65.

Sendall, Simon, 1796–1871, Caius, Cambridge 1819, BA 1824, MA 1827; D. 1822, Norwich, P. 1824, London; C. East Acklan,Yorks; C. Langham, Suffolk 1841–45; C. St.John's, Portland, Dorset 1852–54; C. Cookham 1853; C. Scremby, Lincs.1857–64; P.C. Scampton,Yorks. 1865–71.

Sergeant, Oswold Pattinson, 1830–1908, Trinity, Cambridge 1849, BA 1853, MA 1858; D. 1853, Oxford, P. 1854, Oxford; C. Somerton 1853–56; C. Milton, Berks.1858; R. Syresham, Northants. 1859–89; R. Chesterton, Oxford 1889–97.

Sharpe, Lancelot Arthur,1807–1891, St.John's, Oxford 1824, BA 1828, MA 1832, BD 1837, Fellow, 1824–40; Select Preacher, Oxford 1840; D. 1829, P. 1831; P.C. Northmoor 1834; R. Tackley 1839–91; Surrogate.

Shaw, John, 1803–1866, St.John's, Cambridge 1822, BA 1826, MA 1834, Fellow, Jesus College, Cambridge; D. 1826, Ely, P. 1827, Ely; C. Marsh, Cambs. 1826–41; R. Connington 1830–41; V. Stoke Poges 1841–66.

Shuldam, Naunton Lemuel, 1832–1874, Magdalen, Oxford 1850, BA 1854, MA 1856, Fellow 1865–67; D. 1858, Oxford, P. 1860, Oxford; C. White Waltham w Shottesbrooke 1858–60; C. St.Giles, Oxford 1860–62; Conduct & Assistant Master, Eton College 1862–67; Classics Tutor to H.R.H. Prince Leopold 1863–66; V. Scawby, dio. Lincoln 1867–1874.

Shurlock, John Russell, 1809–1868, Queens', Cambridge 1828, BA 1832, MA 1840; D. 1834, London, P. 1835, London; C. Witney 1837; P.C. Attleborough, Warws. 1842–45; C. Hethe 1846–50; R. Hethe 1850–54; P.C. East Teignmouth, Devon 1855–56; P.C. Bassenthwaite, Cumberland 1857–68.

Simcox, Henry Kingdom, 1840–? Lincoln, Oxford 1857, BA 1860, MA 1860; D. 1862, Oxford, P. 1865, Exeter; C. Holy Trinity, Windsor 1862–65; C. Honiton, Devon 1865–68; C. Bampton 1868–72; C. Shrivenham 1872–73; R. Patney, dio. Salisbury 1873–? Dio. Insp. Schools, Enford Rural Deanery,1885; R. Ewelme 1889–1901

Slatter, John, 1817–1899, Lincoln, Oxford 1835, BA 1838, MA 1841; D. 1840, Chester, P. 1841, Chester; C. St.James, Leeds; P.C. Sandford on Thames 1852–61; V. Streatley 1861–80; Hon. Canon, Christ Church 1876; R. Whitchurch, Berkshire 1880–99.

Slocock, Samuel, 1780–1847, St.John's, Oxford 1798; R. Wasing 1812–47; R. Shaw-cum-Donnington 1838–47. *Foster* only.

Sloper, George Stokes, 1774–1854, Emmanuel, Cambridge 1794, BA 1795, MA 1798; D. & P. 1798, Salisbury; C. Combe, Berks; R. West Woodhay 1798–1854.

Small, Harry Alexander, 1804–1880, Downing, Cambridge 1823, LL B 1829; D. 1827, Lincoln, P. 1828, Ely; R. Haversham 1827–56; R. Clifton Reynes 1832–63. Name appears in *Crockford* until 1869; "died aged 76 years" *Venn*.

Smith, Charles, 1818–1855, Christ Church 1836, Student 1836–47, BA 1840, MA 1842; D. 1843, Oxford, P. 1844, Oxford; C. Amersham; V. East Garston 1846–51; R. Boothby Graffoe, Lincs. 1851–55.

Smith, Edward Langdale, 1811–1895, St.John's,Cambridge 1830, BA 1835, MA 1838; D. 1837, Lincoln, P. 1838, Lincoln; P.C. Barton-Hartshorn w Chetwode 1839–95.

Smith, Francis Edward, 1830–1916, Clare Hall, Cambridge 1848, BA 1852, MA 1855; D. 1854, Oxford, P. 1855, Oxford; C. Bracknell 1854–57; Chaplain, Easthampstead Union 1854–57; C. Bletchingley 1856–63; C. Harlington, Middx. 1863–70; R. Harstock, Essex 1870–1916.

Smith, Joseph, 1794–1886, Trinity, Oxford 1811, BA 1815, MA 1818, BD 1827, Fellow 1824–52; D. 1818, Gloucester, P. 1825,Oxford; R. Rotherfield Greys 1851–60.

Smith, Samuel Mountjoy, 1830–1908, Emmanuel,Cambridge, a "Ten Year Man", BA 1849, MA 1852; D. 1850, P. 1851; C. Studley, Warws. 1850–52; C. Chelwood, Somerset 1852–56; V. Harwell 1856–1906.

Speke, Benjamin,1830–1881, Christ Church, BA 1853, MA 1859; D. 1853, Oxford, P. 1854,Oxford; C. Banbury 1853–57; R. Washfield, Exeter 1857; R. Dowlish Wake w West Dowlish 1857–81.

Spencer, Charles Vere,1828–1898, Christ Church 1845, BA 1849, MA 1852; D. 1851, Peterborough, P. 1852, Peterborough; C. St.Peter's, Northampton 1851–52; C. Adwell 1852–1898; R. (& Patron) Wheatfield 1852–1898.

Springett, William John,1824–? Wadham 1842, BA 1846, MA 1848; D. 1846, Oxford, P. 1847, Oxford; C. Grove & Eynsham 1846–48; C. Brightwell 1849–51; C. Brabourne with Monk's Horton, Kent 1851–54; V. Dunkirk, dio. Canterbury 1854–? In *Crockford* 1889.

Spurrell, Benjamin, 1803–1877, St.John's, Cambridge 1825, BA 1829, MA 1832; D.1829, York; C. Scarborough, Yorks. 1829; C. Holt, nr Bradford,Wilts. 1833–38; C. St.Philip's, Birmingham 1838–44; C. Deddington 1845–47; R. Drayton Parsloe 1847–77.

Stanhope [The Hon.] Henry William, 1790–1872, Trinity Hall, Cambridge, 1812, MA 1814; V. Chesham, Bucks. 1826–47; R. Gawsworth, Cheshire 1827–72.

Stephenson, Lawrence, 1802–1889, St.John's, Cambridge 1819, BA 1823, MA 1826, BD 1833, DD 1844, Fellow 1826–35; D. 1826, Ely, P. 1826, Lincoln for Ely; R. Souldern 1835–1889.

Sterry, Francis, 1832–? Exeter, Oxford 1853, BA 1856, MA 1859; D.1858, Oxford, P.1859, Oxford; C. Holy Trinity,Windsor 1858–60; C. Upminster, Essex 1860–62; C. Stockland, Devon 1864–67; C. Chilton Canteloe, dio. Bath & Wells 1868–69; R. Poltimore w Huxham, dio. Exeter 1869–?

Stevens, Henry Bingham, 1835–1924, Emmanuel, Cambridge. 1853, BA 1857, MA 1890; D. 1858, Oxford, P. 1859, Oxford; C. Thatcham 1858–61; C. Chieveley 1861; C. Curridge, nr Newbury 1861–67; C. St.Lawrence, Reading 1867–68; R. St.Mary, Chatham, Kent 1868–83; V. Darenth, Kent 1883–1911; Hon. Canon Rochester 1906.

Stevens, Thomas, 1810–1888, Oriel 1827, BA 1832, MA 1835; D. 1839, Chichester, P. 1839, Winchester; Assisant Poor Law Commissioner 1836–39; P.C. Keele, Staffs. 1839–41; C. Bradwell 1841; R. Bradfield 1842–82; Warden St.Andrew's College 1847–81; Commissary for the Bishop of Christ Church, New Zealand; R. Newton w Toft, Lincs. 1883–88.

Stevens, William Everest, 1804–1870, St.John's, Cambridge 1822, BA 1826, MA 1829; D. & P. 1834, Oxford; C. Salford 1834; C. Little Rollright 1834; R. Salford 1834–70; R. Little Rollright 1836–70.

Steward, John, ob 1856, P.C.Fenny Stratford 1847–56.

Stillingfleet, Henry James William, 1827–1887, Brasenose 1844, BA 1848, MA 1850; D. 1851, Oxford, P. 1853, Oxford; C. Wantage 1851–59; ? C. Lambourne Woodlands *circa* 1857; C. Clehonger, Hereford 1859–68; R. Hampton Bishop, Hereford 1868–87.

Stoddart, William Wellwood, 1810–1856, St.John's 1828, BA 1832, MA 1836, BD 1841, Fellow 1828–53; D. 1832, Oxford, P. 1832, Oxford; Chaplain St.John's College 1853–56; V. Charlbury 1853–56.

Stokes, William Henry, 1816–1884, Wadham 1832, BA 1837, MA 1844; Fellow, Caius College, Cambridge; D. 1842, P. 1843; V. Goring 1851–84; Chaplain, Sherburn Hospital,Durham.

Ston[e]house, Henry, 1802–1860, New College 1820, Fellow 1820–35, BCL 1826; R. Stanton St.John 1835–60.

Sturges, Simon, 1818–1890, Hertford [Magdalen Hall] 1842; BA 1845, MA 1848; D. 1845, Oxford, P. 1847, Oxford; C. Knowle Hill 1845; P.C. Knowle Hill1852–59; V. Wargrave 1859–90.

Styles [*sic*], Charles Montague, 1831–? St.John's, Oxford 1849, BA 1854, MA 1857, BD 1862, DD 1880, Fellow 1849–67; D. 1855, Oxford, P. 1856, Oxford; C. Hardwick 1855; R. Hardwick 1856–66; R. South Warnborough, Hants.1866–?

Suckling, Henry Edward, 1827–1907, Caius, Cambridge 1846; Cuddesdon College 1857–58; D. 1858, Oxford, P. 1859, Oxford; C. Shrivenham 1858–62; C. Reepham, Norfolk 1862–72; C. Roydon, dio. Norwich 1872–81; R. North Wootton, dio. Norwich 1881–1907.

Sugden, Arthur Maitland,1823–? Wadham 1846, BA 1850, MA 1857; D. 1850, Bath & Wells, P. 1851, Salisbury for Bath & Wells; C. Midsomer Norton, Somerset, 1850–52; C. All Saints Chapel, Walcot, nr Bath 1853–55; C. St.George's, Hanover Square, London 1857–60; C. Turville 1860; R. Mollington 1863–73; C. St.John, Bathwick, Somerset 1874–79; C. in Charge Holy Rood, Carnostie 1881–86; C. St.Mary, Walton in Gordano 1882–85; R. Markshall, St.Alban's, 1885–?

Swaine, James, 1814–1882,Wadham 1832, BA 1836; D.1837, London, P. 1838, London; C. Barking, Essex ? 1845; Minister, St.Thomas's Chapel, Baswich, Staffs. *circa* 1852, C. Stewkley 1856; C. Whaplode Drove, Lincs.

Swinney, Henry Hutchinson, 1814–1862, Trinity, Cambridge 1831, Magdalene, Cambridge 1832, BA 1836, MA 1839, Fellow 1836–40; D. 1837, Ely, P. 1838, London; V. St.Giles w St.Peter, Cambridge 1840–44; C. Mortlake, Surrey 1847–49; P.C. Mortlake 1850–55; V. Wargrave 1855–59; Principal Cuddesdon Theological College & V. Cuddesdon 1859–62.

Symons, Jelinger, 1776–1851, St.John's, Cambridge 1793, BA 1797, MA 1800; D. 1799, Durham, P. 1801, Durham; C. Whitburn, Durham 1799; V. Monkland, Hereford 1808–51; C. West Ilsley 1809; Chaplain to the British Residents, Boulogne 1821; R.Radnage 1833–51; J.P. for Hereford.

Talbot, James Hale, 1809–1880, Pembroke, Oxford 1827, BA 1830, MA 1834; D. 1831, Lincoln, P. 1832, Lincoln; C. Hardmead; R. Newton Blossomville 1846–1880.

Talman, William, 1819–1876, King's, Cambridge 1839, BA 1843, MA 1846, Fellow 1842–56; D. 1844, Lincoln, P. 1845, Salisbury; C. Hilperton, Wilts.1845; C. Cottisford 1847–51; P.C. Wattisham, Suffolk 1851–56; P.C. Thames Ditton, Surrey 1857–60; R. Haddiscoe w Toft Monks, Norfolk 1860–76.

Tarver, Joseph, 1824–1904, Worcester, Oxford 1843, BA 1848, MA 1858; D. 1849, Oxford, P. 1850, Oxford; C. Tyringham 1849; R. Filgrove w Tyringham 1850–1904.

Taylor, Henry, V. North Moreton 1824–55.

Templer, Henry Skinner, 1813–1877, Exeter & New Inn Hall, Oxford 1831, BA 1845, MA 1847; D. 1842, Exeter, P. 1843, Exeter; C. Ashford, nr. Barnstaple, Devon; R.Thornton 1853–61; V. Great Coxwell 1861–77.

Thelwell, John Hampden, 1800–1874, Trinity, Cambridge 1818, BA 1823, MA 1826; R.Oving 1831–74.

Thompson, Charles Edward, 1818–? Trinity, Oxford 1837, BA 1841, MA 1865; D. 1841, Worcester, P. 1842,Worcester; C. Westbury, Bucks. 1860; V.Radston, nr Brackley 1868–74; V. Ken, Somerset, 1875–76; V. South Clevendon, dio. Bath &Wells, 1876–82.

Thompson, Edward, 1808–1891, St.Catherine's, Cambridge 1839, a "Ten Year Man", BD 1841; V. Lambourne 1832–1851; V. Chaddleworth 1851–1887. *Venn* only; *Crockford* confuses him with Edward Thompson, Clare Hall, Cambridge.

Thompson, James, 1802–1860, Lincoln, Oxford 1820, BA 1823, MA 1826, BD 1833, DD 1852, Fellow 1823–46; D. 1824, Oxford, P. 1825, Oxford; R. Cublington 1845–53; R. Twyford, Berks. 1851–60; Rector, Lincoln College, 1851–60.

Thornton, Francis Vansittart, 1816–1895, Trinity, Cambridge 1834, BA 1838, MA 1841; D. 1839, Chichester, P. 1840, St.Albans; C. Hodnet, Salop 1839–40; V. Bisham 1840–48; R. Brown Candover, Hants. 1848–64; R. South-Hill w Callington, Cornwall 1864–86; Hon. Canon, Truro Cathedral 1882.

Thornton, Spencer, 1814–50,Trinity, Cambridge 1832; BA 1836, MA 1839; V. Wendover 1837–50.

Tilbury, Robert, 1838–? Emmanuel, Cambridge, 1858, BA 1860, MA 1864; D. 1860, Oxford, P. 1861, Oxford; C. Langford w Little Faringdon 1860–64; C. Totworth, Gloucs. 1864–76; Chaplain to the Earl of Ducie; C. Brignall,Yorks. 1876–78; V. Hutton Magna 1878–84; C. Barningham 1879–84; R. Brignell 1884–1910. Disappears from *Crockford* 1911.

Tillbrook, William John, 1834–? St.John's, Oxford,1852, BA 1858, MA 1859; F.R.G.S. D. 1859, Oxford, P. 1862, Chichester; C. Lacey Green 1859; Fellow & Tutor, St.Augustine's College, Canterbury 1861–62; C. Barlavington, Sussex 1862–64; V. Comberton, dio. Ely, 1867–89; Chaplain, Weem, dio. Dunkirk, 1889–?

Tooke, Thomas Hammond, 1824–1888, Trinity, Cambridge 1842; BA 1848, MA 1851; D. 1848, Oxford, P. 1849, Oxford; C. Iver 1848–50; C. Upton w Chalvey 1850–58; R. St.Edmunds, Salisbury 1858–63; R. Monkton-Farley, dio. Salisbury 1865–88.

Towns[h]end, Abraham Boyle, 1791–1860, Christ Church 1809, BA 1813, MA 1817, Student 1809–27; D. & P. 1819; R. Easthampstead 1826–1860.

Townsend, Samuel Thomas, 1797–? Trinity,Cambridge 1822, BA 1826, MA 1830; D. 1828, P. 1829; V. Chicheley 1830–50; R. Farndish, Bedfordshire 1832–52. Disappears from *Crockford* 1876.

Trench, Francis Chenevix, 1806–1886, Oriel 1824, BA 1834, MA 1859; D. 1835, Winchester, P. 1836, Salisbury; C. Hound w Burlesdon Hants; C. St.Giles, Reading; P.C. St.John, Reading 1837–57; R. Islip 1857–75.

Trotman, Fiennes Samuel, 1796–1863, Sidney Sussex, Cambridge 1815, BA 1819; D. 1819, London, P. 1820, Coventry & Lichfield; V. Dallington, Northants. 1822–63; R. Gayhurst w Stoke Goldington 1822–1863; R.D. Northampton.

Tubbs, George Ibberson, D. 1847, P.1848; P.C. St.Giles, Reading 1848; Chaplain, Reading Union; C. Holy Trinity, Southwark 1852.

Tucker, John, 1793–1873, Corpus Christi, Oxford 1810, BA 1813, MA 1817, BD 1825, Fellow 1820–53; D. 1818, P. 1819; V. West Hendred 1852–73.

Tufnell, George, 1796–1868, Emmanuel, Cambridge 1821, BA 1825; D.1824, London, P.1825, London; V. Wormingford, Essex 1825–40; Chaplain, Boulougne 1842; C. Pleshay, Essex 1843; V. Uffington 1847–52; P.C. Baulking & Woolstone 1852 [Uffington separated in 1852]; R. Thornton-Watlass, Yorks. 1852–68.

Turner, Alfred, 1815–1876, St.John's, Oxford 1833, BA 1837, MA 1840; V. Whitchurch, Bucks. 1843–1876.

Turner [Tanner], Isaac Biass,1818–1870, Trinity, Cambridge 1837, BA 1841, MA 1845; D. 1843, P.1845; C. Hathersage, Derbyshire 1844–45; C. New Mills, Glossop,1845–46; C. Bartholomew's Chapel, Sydenham 1846; V. Marsworth 1847–70.

Tweed, John Edward, 1822–? Christ Church 1841, BA 1845, MA 1847; D. 1845, Oxford, P. 1846, Oxford; Chaplain, Christ Church 1845–57; V. Stratton Audley 1857–98.

Twopenny, Thomas Newell, 1820–1869, Oriel 1838, BA 1841, MA 1844; D. 1843, Peterborough, P. 1844, Peterborough; C. Little Casterton, dio. Peterborough, 1851–59, R. South Weston 1859–62.

Tyndale, Henry Annesley, 1816–1891, Wadham 1834, BA 1838, MA 1841; D. 1839, Oxford, P. 1840, Oxford; C. Marsh Baldon 1839–42; R. Tatsfield, Surrey 1842–56; R. Holton 1856–91.

Tyndale, Thomas George, 1797–1865, Trinity, Oxford 1795, BA 1799, MA 1802; V. Wooburn 1819–56; R. Holton 1820–56.

Uthwatt, Eusebius Andrewes, 1807–1891, St.John's, Cambridge 1826, BA 1830; D.1831, P.1832; R. Foxcote 1843–1886.

Uthwatt, William Andrewes, 1793–1879, St.Johns', Cambridge 1812, BA 1816, MA 1819; R. Lillingstone Dayrell 1832–48; V. Stowe 1833–75; R. Maid's Moreton 1848–78. J.P. Lord of the Manors of Maids Moreton & Great Linford.

Vane, Frederick, 1793–1865, Queen's, Oxford 1811, BA 1815, MA 1818, Fellow 1815–38, Chaplain 1818; C. Elsfield 1824; R. Blechingdon 1837–46.

Vansittart, Charles, 1820–1878, Oriel 1838, BA 1842, MA 1845; D. 1844, P. 1845; V. White Waltham 1848–56.

Waddington, Herbert, 1829–? Trinity, Cambridge 1847, BA 1851, MA 1854; D. 1851, Canterbury, P. 1852, Canterbury; C. Newington-next-Hythe, Kent 1851–59; C. Pusey 1859–60; C. Longworth 1860–62; V. Steventon 1862–72; R. Ranmore, Surrey 1872–99. Disappears from *Crockford* 1905.

Wale, Alexander Malcolm, 1797–1884, St.John's, Cambridge 1815, BA 1819, MA 1822, BD 1819, Fellow 1821–31; D. 1827, Lincoln, P. 1829, Ely; Chaplain, Horningsey, Cambridge 1829–30; V. Sunninghill 1830–84.

Walker, Frederic John, 1824–1913, Magdalene, Cambridge 1842; BA 1846, MA 1849; D.& P. 1846, Chester; C. Farnworth, Lancs. 1846–49; C. St.George's, Liverpool 1852–53; R. Finmere 1853–66; V. Good Easter, Essex 1867–78, V. Albrighton, Salop 1878–91; R. Frodesley, Salop 1892–98.

Walsh, William Percival, 1819–? Worcester, Oxford 1837, BA 1840, MA 1844; D. 1841, P. 1842; C. Stanton Harcourt 1841; V. South Leigh 1845–68; V. Stanton Harcourt 1845–?

Walters, Charles, 1810–1877, Merton 1829, BA 1833, MA 1836; D. 1834, Winchester, P. 1835, Winchester; C. Corhampton, Hants; P.C. Littlemore 1848–51; V. Wardington 1851–77.

Wapshare, Charles, 1776–1859, Merton 1793, BA 1797; R. East Hendred 1806–1858.

Warriner, George, 1814–? St.Edmund Hall 1835, BA 1838, MA 1841; D. 1839, P. 1840; C. Epwell w Shutford 1839–41; C. Bodicote 1841–55.

Watkins, Daniel, ob. 1890, MA; D. 1826, St.David's, P. 1827, St.David's; V. Thornborough 1834–79; Chaplain, Buckingham Union 1855; R. Adstock 1879–90.

Watts, George Edward Oscar,1832–? Trinity, Oxford 1851,BA 1855, MA 1864; F.R.Astr.S.; F.R.M.S; D. 1857, Oxford, P. 1858, Oxford; C. Ducklington 1857–59; C. Newquay, Cornwall 1859; C. St.Mary's, Leeds,1862–63; C. Sherburn 1863. In *Crockford* 1889.

Watts, John William, 1807–1885, Magdalen Hall 1825, BA 1828, MA 1838; D. 1829, Bath & Wells, P. 1831, Bath & Wells; Minister, St.James, Guernsey 1834–38; P.C. Downside, Bath, Somerset 1838–40; Minister, Kensington Chapel, Bath 1840–42; V. Bicester 1843–81; Chaplain, Bicester Union 1852–81. Surrogate 1843.

Weighell, John, 1803–1853, Pembroke, Cambridge 1826, BA 1832; V. Marsworth 1837–45; R. Cheddington 1846–53; P.C. Pightlestone 1846–53.

Welburn, John Edward Brown, 1836–1918, St.Catherine's, Cambridge 1854, BA 1858; D. 1859, Oxford, P. 1860, Oxford; C. Ducklington w Alvescot 1859–61; C. Shilton 1861; C. St.Stephen, Kearsley Moor 1861–77; V. Orby, dio. Lincoln 1877–1918.

Wellford, George, 1786–1861, Exeter, Oxford 1809, BA 1813, MA 1815; C. Bray & Chaplain, Jesus Hospital, Bray *circa* 1855; V. Cookham 1855–?

Wells, George, 1803–1872, Magdalen, Oxford 1821, BA 1825, MA 1828, Fellow 1829–35; D. 1826, Chichester, P. 1827, Chichester; C. Tadmarton 1827–29; C. Boxford 1830–42; R. Boxford 1842–72.

West, Joseph, 1799–1876, New College 1818, BA 1823, MA 1826; D.1823, Oxford, P. 1824, Oxford; Chaplain, New College 1823–66; Chaplain, Magdalen College 1826–69; Chaplain, Radcliffe Infirmary 1830–44; "Barge" Chaplain, St.Thomas, Oxford 1839; P.C. Holy Trinity, Oxford 1844–69; R. Standlake 1868–76.

Westmacott, Horatio, 1809–1862, Corpus Christi, Cambridge 1827, BA 1832, MA 1835; D. 1831, P.1832; R. Chastleton 1838–62.

Wethered, Florence James, 1807–1867, King's, Cambridge 1827, BA 1831, MA 1834, Fellow 1830–39; D.1831, P. 1832; C. Ibstone 1831–32; C. Hurley 1832–38; V. (& Patron) Hurley 1838–67.

Wetherell, William, 1815–1864, New College 1837, BCL 1843, MA 1856, Fellow 1837–60; D. 1842, Oxford, P. 1843, Oxford; R. Heyford Warren 1860–64.

Whately, Charles, 1815–? St.Mary Hall 1833, BA 1837, MA 1840; R.Rise,Yorks. 1839–50; R. Taplow 1850–? R.D. Burnham 1855–73.

Whately, Thomas, 1773–1864, Christ's, Cambridge 1791, BA 1795, MA 1800; D. 1795, Norwich, P. 1797, London; V. Cookham 1797–1837; R. Chetwynd, Salop. 1837–64.

Whelpton, Henry Robert, 1833–1902, St.John's, Cambridge 1853, BA 1857, MA 1860; D. 1857, London, P. 1858, London; C. All Saints, Dalston 1857–59; C. Upton w Chalvey 1859–62; C. St.Edmund's, Salisbury 1862–65; P.C. St.Saviour's, Eastbourne 1867–97; Preb. Chichester Cathedral 1882–1902.

Whinfield, Henry Wrey, 1793–1848, Peterhouse, Cambridge 1810, BA 1815, MA 1818; R. Battlesden, Beds. 1821–48; R. Tyringham & Filgrove 1822–48.

White, Adolphus Leighton, 1823, Balliol 1841, BA 1845, MA 1848; D. 1848, Oxford, P. 1849, Oxford; C. Arborfield 1848–52; P.C. Leavesden, Herts. 1853–55; V. St.Saviour, Mortimer 1856–?

White, Glyd, 1790–1869, Oriel 1808, BA 1812, MA 1815, D.1812, Oxford, P.1813, Oxford; C. Brightwell Baldwin 1812; C. Ewelme 1817–18; C. Easington 1820; C. Swyncomb 1823; C. Nettlebed 1823; C. Mongewell *circa* 1852. Resided at Ewelme.

White, Herbert, 1795–1868, Corpus Christi, Oxford 1811, BA 1816, MA 1819, BD 1829, Fellow 1821–38; D. 1819, Oxford, P. 1828, Oxford; P.C. Warborough 1837–68.

White, Stephen Morgan, 1800–? St.Edmund Hall 1823, BA 1827; D. 1827, Bath & Wells, P. 1828, B & W; C. Marshfield, Gloucs. about 1845; C. Winslow 1853; Residing in Bath, 1889.

Whitehead, Thomas Clarke,1818–1873, Wadham 1836, BA 1840, MA 1844; D. 1840, London, P. 1841, London; P.C. Holy Trinity, Mount Albion, Ramsgate ? Incumbent Gawcott 1849–64; Headmaster, Christ's College, Finchley, London 1864–73.

Whitfield, Henry John, 1808–1855, Magdalene, Cambridge 1826, BA 1830, MA 1843; V. Granborough 1845–55; Chaplain to the Earl of Mornington; Chaplain, Scutari 1854–55.

Whittingham, Samuel, 1783–1874, Corpus Christi, Oxford 1799, BA 1803, MA 1806, BD 1815, DD 1833, Fellow until 1841; D. 1806, Oxford, P. 1807,Oxford; R. Childrey 1840–74.

Whittle, Charles,1823–? Trinity, Oxford, 1841, SCL 1846, BA 1846; D. 1848, York, P. 1849, York; C. Granton,Yorks. 1848–50; C. Church Knowle, Dorset 1850–52; C. Thatcham & Midgham 1852–59; P.C. Greenham 1852–59; C. Stoke Abbas, Dorset 1859–61; C. Nassington w Yarwell, Northants. 1861–69; C. Belgrave, Leics. 1861–69; Chaplain to the Sevenoaks Union, Kent, 1870–74.

Whorwood, Thomas Henry, 1812–1885, Magdalen, Oxford 1829, BA 1833, MA 1836, BD 1843, DD 1847, Fellow 1833–50; D. 1835, Oxford, P. 1836, Worcester; V. Marston 1836–49; V. Willoughby, dio. Worcester 1849–?85.

Wilberforce, Samuel, 1805–1873, Oriel 1823, BA 1826, MA 1829, DD 1845; Hon. Fellow All Souls 1871; D. 1828, Oxford, P. 1829, Oxford; C. Checkendon 1828–1830; R. Brighstone, IoW 1830–1841; Archdeacon of Surrey 1839–45; R. Alverstoke 1841–1845; Canon, Winchester 1841–1845; Dean of Westminster 1845; Bishop of Oxford 1845–1869; Bishop of Winchester 1869–1873.

Wilberforce, William Francis, 1834–? University, Oxford 1852, BA 1856, MA 1858; D. 1857, Oxford, P. 1859, Oxford; C. Dalton-Holme,York 1857–59; C. St.Giles, Reading 1859–62; V. Royston,Yorks. 1862–73; V. St.Mary's, Oldham 1873–76; V. St.John, Ousebridge,York 1876–82; V. Fulford, York 1882–89.

Wilder, John, 1801–1892, King's, Cambridge 1820, BA 1824, MA 1828, Fellow 1828–31; D. 1824, P. 1825; R. Sulham 1836–92; R.D. Bradfield.

Williams, James Reynold, 1828–1900, St.John's, Cambridge 1849, BA 1853; D. 1853, Oxford, P. 1854, Oxford; C. Langley St.Mary's 1853–54; C. Kempston, Beds. 1854–55; C. Chievely 1857–59; R. Hedsor 1860–70; R. Pulford, Cheshire 1870–1900.

Williams, John, 1799–1873, Christ Church 1816, BA 1820, MA 1822, Student 1816–40; D. 1828, Oxford; P.C. Tring 1839–41; V. Spelsbury 1841–55; Lecturer, Rhayader,Radnorshire.

Williams, John, 1810–1872, Jesus, Oxford 1827, BA 1831, MA 1833, BD 1841, Fellow 1833–44; R. Wigginton 1843–72.

Williams, Thomas Edmunds, 1782–1849, St.Mary Hall 1809; C. Caversham 1832; V. Bucklebury 1832–49.

Williamson, Thomas Pym, St.Bees 1850; D. 1852, Oxford, P. 1854, Oxford; C. Fenny Stratford 1852; P.C. Fenny Stratford 1856–60; V. Little Brickhill 1860–76.

Willis, John, 1799–1855, St.John's, Cambridge 1817, BA 1821, MA 1824; D. 1822, Lincoln for Rochester, P. 1823, Winchester; V. Haddenham & P.C. Cuddington 1826–55.

Willoughby, Hugh Pollard, 1801–1858, Exeter, Oxford 1819, BA 1826, MA 1829; D. 1826, Oxford, P. 1827, Oxford; C. Noke 1826; R. Burthorpe, Glos. 1827–? R. Marsh Baldon 1830–1858.

Wilson, Francis Garrett, 1826–1885, Corpus Christi, Cambridge 1844, BA 1848; D. 1849, Worcester, P. 1850, Oxford;C. Duddeston, Birmingham 1849–50; C. Deddington 1850–53; C. St.Paul's, Banbury 1853–56; P.C. Nether Worton 1850–67; C. Simpson 1860–68; R. Over Worton 1862–67; V. East & West Rudham, Norfolk 1867–85.

Wilson, John, 1790–1873, Trinity, Oxford 1806, BA 1810, MA 1814, BD 1826, DD Cantab 1845, DD 1852; F.S.A., F.R.S. 1845; D. 1817, Oxford, P. 1821, Oxford; President, Trinity College, 1850–66; R. Garsington 1850–67.

Wintle, Thomas, 1774–1855, St.John's, Oxford 1791, Fellow 1791–1841, BA 1795, MA 1799, BD 1804; D. 1802, Oxford, P. 1802, Oxford; R. Tidmarsh 1814–54; R. Leckford, Hants. 1840–55.

Woods, Henry Horatio, 1805–1880, Emmanuel, Cambridge 1823, BA 1827, MA 1830; D. & P. 1829, Winchester; C. East Woodhay w Ashmansworth, dio. Winchester 1841–54; R. Tidmarsh 1855–80.

Wordsworth, Christopher, 1807–1885, Trinity, Cambridge 1826, BA 1830, MA 1833, BD & DD 1839, Fellow, 1830–36, Hon. DCL [Oxford] 1870; D. 1833, Lincoln, P. 1835, Carlisle; Headmaster, Harrow School 1836–44; Canon of Westminster 1844; V. Stanford in the Vale w Goosey 1850–69; Archdeacon of Westminster 1865–68; Bishop of Lincoln 1869–85.

Worsley, John Henry, 1814–? Magdalen, Oxford 1831, BA 1836, MA 1838; D. 1837, Oxford, P. 1838, Oxford; C. Tilehurst 1838; P.C. Seer Green, 1847–48; C. South Moreton 1850; C. Churchill[*dates unknown*] P.C. Leafield,1857–69; Chaplain, Bromley College 1874–84.

Wroth, William Bruton, 1785–1863, St.John's, Cambridge 1804, BA 1806, MA 1809; D. 1810, Lincoln, P. 1811, Salisbury; V. Edlesborough 1815–63; V. Tottenhoe, Beds. 1819–63; R.D.

Wyatt, Charles Francis, 1795–1877, Jesus, Cambridge 1815 [from Oriel, Oxford, 1813], BA 1818, MA 1821; D. 1818, Oxford, P. 1819, Oxford; C. Broughton 1818; R. Broughton 1819–70.

Wyatt, Charles Francis, 1820–1906, Christ Church 1838, BA 1842, MA 1845; D. 1844, Oxford, P. 1845, Oxford; V. Foresthill 1848–70; R. Broughton w North Newington 1870–1906.

Yates, Samuel Wildman, 1794–1862, Balliol 1812, BA 1831, MA 1836; V.St.Mary, Reading 1835–61.

Yonge, Denys Nelson, 1836–1920, Christ's, Cambridge 1855, BA 1859; D. 1860, Oxford, P. 1861, Oxford; C. Holy Trinity, Windsor 1860; C. Shottesbrooke w White Waltham 1860–64; C. Lamorbey, Kent 1864–65; C. Englefield 1865–69; V. Broxted, dio. Rochester 1869–85; Dio. Inspector of Schools, Essex 1880–85; V. Boreham, dio. St.Albans 1885–1918.

Yonge, William Wellington, 1836–1920, Exeter, Oxford 1848, BA 1851; D. 1853, Norwich, P. 1854, Norwich; C. Southwold, Suffolk 1853–54; C. Filby, Norfolk 1853–54; V. White Waltham w Shottesbrooke 1857–78.

York, Samuel,1835–?, Exeter, Oxford 1854, BA 1857, MA 1859, Fellow; D. 1858, Manchester, P. 1859, Manchester; C. Preston, dio. Manchester 1858–61; C. Christ Church, Luton, Beds. 1861–62; V. Fritwell 1863–76; V. Ascot under Wychwood 1876–83; R. Fifield w Idbury 1883–1904.

Youlden, Abraham, 1803–1860, St.John's, Cambridge 1821, BA 1825, MA 1828; D. 1825, Lincoln, P. 1825, Lincoln; R. Hedsor 1841–60.

Young, Edward Newton, 1796–1885, Christ Church 1814, BA 1818; D. 1819, London, P. 1820, London; Assistant Master, Charterhouse; R. Quainton 1822–85. Chaplain to the Duke of Buckingham; Chaplain, Blean Union, Canterbury.

Young, Frederick,1826–? Queen's, Oxford 1844, BA 1848; D.1848, Oxford, P. 1850, Oxford; C. Holy Trinity, Reading 1848–54; C. St.Paul's, Ball's-pond, Islington 1854–56; V. Walton, Aylesbury 1858–93.

Young, William Boyter, 1794–? St.John's, Oxford 1813, BA 1816, MA 1819; D.1817, P.1818; Surrogate, dioceses of Oxford & Salisbury. Residing 1870 at Oxford House, Reading.

Young, William Henry, 1831–? Pembroke, Oxford 1849, BA 1853, MA 1857; D. 1858, Oxford, P. 1860, Oxford; C. Little Milton 1858–60; C. Great Milton 1860; C. Benson 1860–63; C. in Charge, Sunningwell 1863–72; C. in Charge, Oving 1866–72; V. North Moreton 1873–?

INDEX OF NAMES AND PLACES

The editor has made every effort to identify persons with the same surnames and those mentioned only by surname. In cases where he has not been successful the persons concerned are identified by surname only.

n = note   Biographical Appendix (pp 341-389) not indexed

Abdon (Salop) 280
Aberdare (Glam) 221
Abingdon (Berks)
  chapel 43
  Deanery 39–40, 43–51
  Lepine of 259
  St Helen 39, 43, 97
  St Nicholas 39, 43, 97
  school 48
Abingdon, Lord 8, 16, 17, 166, 293
Abrahall, J Hoskyns 156
Ackhampstead (Oxon) 25, 97, 218
Acland, - 262
Adams, Dacres 27, 29, 116, 134, 269, 338, 339
Adams, H C 339
Adams, J 202
Adams, John 281
Adams, Simon Thomas 31, 33, 82, 92, 295
Adams, William Fulford 169, 315
Addams, Dr, 214
Adderbury (Oxon) 11, 97–8, 275, 323, 324, 330
Addington (Bucks) 33, 81, 98, 339
Addison, - 274
Addison, J F 17
Addison, John Cranmer 320
Addison, P C 165
Addison, William Fountaine 164–5, 259, 261, 334
Adstock (Bucks) 33, 81, 98–9, 274
Adwell (Oxon) 24, 99, 109
Ainger, Edward B 159
Akeley (Bucks) 80–1, 89, 99, 216, 223
Akroyd, Jonathan 157
Albert, Prince xvi
Albury (Oxon) 16, 85, 99, 195
Alcock, Charles 11

Alcock, J 97
Aldborough 43
Alderman, - 62
Alderman, F C 163
Aldermaston (Berks) 40, 41, 55, 99–104, 133, 252, 306, 319
Aldershot (Surrey) 182
Alderson, Baron 158
Aldis, J 260
Aldridge, R 212
Aldworth (Berks) 40, 69, 104
Aldworth, John 274
Alectus 141
Alford, - 191
Alford, George 31, 109
Alford, Lady Miriam 108, 255, 313
Alfred, King 107
Alkerton (Oxon) 12, 104
Allan, George 196
Allan, Hugh 196
Allan *see also* Allen
Allen, - 152
Allen, H 290
Allen *see also* Allan
Allsop, R W 155
Almack, Henry 31, 76, 178
Alton (Hants) 223
Alvescot (Oxon) 26, 29, 30, 83, 85, 104, 130, 269
Ambrosden (Oxon) 6, 105, 122
Amersham (Bucks) 31, 105, 155
Amesbury, Lord 64
Andrews (Andrewes), - 63, 81, 82, 84
Andrews, Arthur 185
Andrews, J 28
Andrews, John 185
Andrews, Martha 186
Andrews (Andrewes), Thomas 154

Andrews, William 305
Annesley, Misses 125
Ansted, Mrs and Miss - 286
Ansted, Joseph Boord 286
Anstice, - 85
Anstis, - 22
Antigua, Bishop of 98
Appleford (Berks) 40, 44, 105
Appleton (Berks) 40, 44, 105, 298
Apsley Guise (Beds) 307
Apthorp (Apthorpe), - 73, 89
Arborfield (Berks) 42, 56, 105–6, 261, 285
Archer, Mary 3
Arden, - 32
Ardington (Oxon) 27, 106
Ardley (Oxon) 6, 90, 106, 138, 228, 282
Ardrighetti, Caroline 59n
Armagh (Co Armagh) 154, 184
Armistead, John R 308
Armstrong, - 123
Armstrong, J H 258, 259, 261
Armstrong, Skeffington 166
Arnold, Edward 77, 86, 222
Arnold, G 87
Arrowsmith, James 283
Ascott under Wychwood (Oxon) 9, 11, 106–7
Ash (Kent) 5
Ashampstead (Berks) 39, 51, 87, 107
Ashbury (Berks) 45, 107
Ashby, E Q 168
Ashendon (Bucks) 107–8
Ashley (Bucks) 222
Ashley, F B 317–18
Ashley, Thomas 62, 91
Ashpitel, Francis 187, 213
Ashridge (Bucks) 34, 146, 147, 169, 195, 233, 255, 272
Ashton, Ellis 21
Ashurst, - 18, 228, 295
Ashurst, Miss - 19
Ashurst, J 18, 43, 229
Ashurst, J H 83
Ashurst, Jas 162
Ashurst, William 43
Ashwell, Canon - ix, xiii, 288
Ashwell, A K 338
Ashworth, John A 164

Askridge 313
Astbury (Berks) 39, 41
Asthall (Oxon) 27, 30, 90, 108, 139
Asthall Lye (Oxon) 108
Astley, T 200
Aston (Oxon) 24–6, 27, 30, 92, 114, 115, 160
Aston, - 127
Aston Abbotts (Bucks) 108, 112, 123
Aston Clinton (Bucks) 74, 84, 93, 108, 138, 217
Aston Park (Bucks) 74
Aston Rowant (Oxon) 24, 109
Aston St Leonards (Bucks) 31, 74, 93, 108, 138, 217
Aston Sandford (Oxon) 31, 109
Aston Tirrold (Oxon) 39, 51, 110, 164, 199
Aston Upthorpe (Berks) 70, 110, 128, 334
Astwood (Bucks) 36, 93, 110, 148
Athawes, John 32, 36, 80, 81, 91, 222
Atkins, - 212
Atkins and Todman 259
Atkinson, - and child 212
Atkinson, Peter Righton 220, 257, 338
Attey, - 169
Attwood, - 25
Audland, W F 15
Aughton 86
Augustus, J 212
Aulus Plautus 211
Austen (Austin), John Thomas 40, 69, 104
Austen (Austin), Joseph Mason 160
Avebury (Wilts) 267
Avington (Berks) 40, 62, 64, 110–11
Aylesbury (Bucks)
   church consecrated 89
   church reopened 97
   clergy 71, 72, 73, 126, 202, 226, 227, 231
   clergy in vicinity 31
   prison 114
   special services 112
   Wilberforce at 113, 139, 160, 167, 184, 186, 199, 202, 213, 217, 312
Aylward, Adolphus Frederick 87, 146–7

Baber, C 157
Back, - 12

INDEX OF NAMES AND PLACES

Back, Henry 116, 117
Bacon, John 61, 213
Bagot, Charles ix, 11, 27, 49, 60, 91, 287
Bagpath (Glos) 118
Bagshot (Wilts) 267
Baines, John 225
Baines, R H 113
Baird, James Skerett 184
Baker, - 52, 273
Baker, George 76, 206
Baker, H 44, 51
Baker, J 199
Baker, James 19
Baker, Robert Lowbridge 257, 265, 311, 335
Baker, William Innes 7
Baker, William John 310
Bakewell 35
Ball, John 53, 260
Ballard, J and Mrs 85
Ballard, John 13, 19, 83
Balscote (Oxon) 14, 321–2, 323
Baly, J 302
Bampton (Oxon) 27, 30, 106, 114, 115–16, 124, 210, 216, 338, 339
Banbury (Oxon) 10, 11, 13, 14–15, 32, 96, 116–17, 323, 324; see also South Banbury
Bandinel (Bandinell), James 43, 152, 155, 171, 175, 314, 328
Bangor (Gwynedd) 171
Banister, - 55
Bannersley (Glos) 25
Barbury, - 90
Barff, Albert 232
Barford (Oxon) 97, 324, 325, 330
Barford St John (Oxon) 11, 12, 98, 117, 323
Barford St Michael (Oxon) 12, 117
Baring, C 306
Baring, N L C 11
Barker, - 19
Barker, Miss - 35
Barker, George 205
Barker, Thomas Childe 276
Barkham (Berks) 42, 57, 118, 119
Barnard, - 311
Barnard, - and Son 151

Barne, - 186, 305
Barne, H 175, 176
Barnes, - 81
Barnes, Ralph 27, 38, 106, 114, 116
Barnet (G London) 109
Barnett, Old 181
Barnett, Jnr 181
Barnett, J W 86
Baron, J 133
Baron, William Joseph 204, 205
Barr, Sophia C 106
Barrett, - 284
Barrington see Great Barrington; Little Barrington
Barrington, Lord - 271
Barrington, - 299
Barrington, Augusta 155
Barrington, Percy 142
Barrington, William Aug Curzon 308
Barrow, Lady - 194
Barrow, H W 338
Barter, C H 10, 11, 69, 83, 85, 106, 114, 139, 153, 157, 200, 213, 216, 235, 264, 265, 266, 270, 276, 292
Barter, Henry 213
Bartholomew, C M 181
Barton, - 275
Barton, H 295
Barton, Mary Ann 3
Barton, Thomas 300
Barton with Chetwode (Bucks) 35
Barton Hartshorne (Bucks) 79, 81, 118
Barwis, William Cuthbert 152
Basildon (Berks) 39, 51, 118–19
Bassett, Francis Tilney 138
Bates, - 199
Bath (Som) 21, 76, 106, 138, 309
  and Wells 184, 255
Bathurst, Lord - 329
Bathurst, F 223
Bathurst, W 83
Baulking (Berks) 40, 47, 119
Bavis, George 185
Bavis, Moses 185
Baxter, William G 118
Bayfield, Mrs - 270
Bayfield, B 56, 270
Baylee, - 152

Bayley, - 38, 200
Bayley, C 135
Bayley, E 87, 110
Bayley, Thomas 253
Baylis, Edward 79, 196–7
Baynes, - 105
Baynes, A 33, 98–9
Baynes, R H 338
Bazeley, H C B 258
Beachampton (Bucks) 31, 80, 81, 119, 310
Beaconsfield (Bucks) 31, 78, 119, 253
Beaminster (Dorset) 196
Beamish, Adam Newman 223
Bearwood (Berks) 95, 119–20
Beasley, - 331; see also Beazley
Beauchamp, - 8
Beauchamp, H T 76
Beauchamp, Henry William Johnson 25, 263
Beauchamp, James 25, 76, 160, 270
   wife of 160
Beauchamp, Jesse 270
Beaumont, Sir G 160
   sister of 160
Beavis, Letitia 185
Beavoir, Benion de 51
Beazley, - 108, 313; see also Beasley
Beckenham, Harriot 185
Beckenham, Thomas 185
Beckett, - 110
Beckley (Oxon) 17, 120, 144
Beddingfield, - 60
Bedford (Beds) 298
Bedford, Duke of 110, 146, 196, 307
Bedford, H 140
Beech Newbury (Berks) 90
Beedon (Berks) 6, 40, 68, 120–1
Beenham (Berks) 40, 55, 67
Beenham Vallance (Berks) 121
Begbie, A G 301
Begbroke (Oxon) 21, 121, 125
Bell, - 9, 11
Bell, Alexander 258
Bell, C D 54
Bell, G 12
Bell, G R 86
Bell, W 35, 80, 84

Bell, William 218
Bellairs, - 153
Bellairs, Septimus 55
Bellis, R 87
Bennett, - 175, 285
Bennett, Miss - 101, 143
Bennett, Joshua 19, 142, 224
Bennitt, Joseph 126
Benson (Bensington) (Oxon) 17, 121–2, 288
Benson, Henry 198
Benson, R M 158, 339
Bent, - 139
Bent, Major - 310
Benthall, John 311
Benyon, R 284, 285
Beral, Sir G 75
Berens, - 39, 43, 45, 46, 51, 52, 54, 55, 155, 219, 271
Beresford, W M 303
Berkeley, Lady Mary 130
Berrick Prior (Oxon) 122
Berrick Salome (Oxon) 121, 122, 143
Bertie, F 16, 43, 83, 85, 328
Bessels Leigh (Berks) 40, 44, 122, 162
Besswell, Sarah 236
Best, William 97, 116, 293
Bests, S 255
Betteridge, - 17
Bew, Elijah 181
Bibby, Miss - 63
Bicester (Oxon) 6, 57, 86, 122–3, 223, 254, 282, 331–4
Bickersteth, Edward 108, 113, 119, 135, 142, 143, 152, 168, 194, 215, 218, 226, 231, 248, .253, 261, 263, 269, 272, 274, 285, 290, 295, 301, 305, 308, 309, 331, 338
   neice of 273
Bickersteth, John 53
Bicknoller (Som) 258
Biddlesden (Bucks) 80, 81, 123
Biddulph, H 276, 277
Biddulph, T 29
Bierton (Bucks) 73, 89, 91, 93, 112, 123, 313
Binfield (Berks) 42, 60, 61, 123, 288
Binney, H 63, 144, 233, 272

INDEX OF NAMES AND PLACES 393

Binsey *see* Oxford
Birch, - 77, 292, 295, 309
Birch, Augustus Frederic 169
Birch, James 57
Birch, Thomas Frederick 38
Bird, Roger 300
Birkenhead (Wirral) 152
Birkett, A H 270
Birkett, W 195
Birkett *see also* Burkit
Bisham (Berks) 41, 58, 124, 198
Bisham Abbey (Berks) 124
Bishop, - 47
Bishop, Freeman H 183
Bishop, James 185
Bishop, Maryan 185
Bishop, William 55–6, 185
Bishop's Itchington (Warks) 236
Bishopston (Bucks) 91
Bix (Oxon) 19, 124
Black Bourton (Burton Abbotts) (Oxon) 27, 30, 116, 124, 304
Blackman, Charles 87, 147
Blackstone, - 160, 165, 221
Bladon (Oxon) 21, 90, 124–5
Blagden, - 140, 170, 267
Blagden, Henry Charles 251–2
Blake, Vernon 116
Bland, P D 208
Blandford, Lord 118, 125, 328
Blandy, - 258
Blandy, Major and Mrs 220
Bleamire, Thomas 36
Bledlow (Bucks) 73, 93, 125–6
Blenheim Palace (Oxon) 328
Blenkin, Fred B 259, 260
Bletchingdon (Oxon) 6, 14, 84, 125, 212
Bletchley (Bucks) 32, 35, 93, 126
Blewbury (Berks) 39, 40, 70, 110, 127–8, 334
Blick, - 104
Bligh, Squire 319
Blissard (Blizard), John 69, 187, 188
Blomfield, Alfred 235, 248, 261, 338
Blomfield, H 122
Blomfield, James Charles 198, 215
Blount, William 224
Bloxham (Oxon) 12, 92, 128–9, 140, 251, 323, 324
Blunt, J H 250
Blunt, James St John 261, 312
Blunt, Mary 312
Board, B 279
Boarstall (Bucks) 129, 133
Bode, T G 309–10
Bodicote (Oxon) 11, 97, 129, 323, 324, 330
Boissier, P Henry 225
Bolney (Oxon) 129, 194
Bolton, - 15
Bond, - 36
Bond, Jane 185
Bonham, John 142n
Bonus, Edward 138, 330
Booth, James 284
Boothby, C 200
Boston, Lord 197
Boswell, Squire 36
Bosworth, -, sister of 159
Bosworth, Joseph 286, 287
Boulogne (France) 64
Boultbee, R M 164
Bourton 136
Bourton (Berks) 271
Bourton (Oxon) 13, 324; *see also* Great Bourton; Little Bourton
Bourton on the Water (Glos) 107
Bouverie, - 114
Bouverie, Bertie 45
Bouverie, Edmund 45, 155
Bouwens, T 37, 282
Boveney (Bucks) 129, 139
Bowden, - 200
Bowles, - 21
Bowles, Col - 22, 109
Bowman, John 66
Bowyer, - 258
Bowyer, Henry 43
Bowyer, Isobel Atkins 264
Boxford (Berks) 40, 62–3, 129
Boyce, - 32, 72
Boyce, Mrs - 237, 238
Boyce, H Le Grand 237
Boyle, A 60
Boyne Hill (Berks) xi, 129, 140–1, 157, 283

Brackley (Oxon) 231
Bracknell (Berks) 42, 61, 90, 96, 129, 130, 304, 313
Bradenham (Bucks) 75, 76, 129, 258, 327
Bradfield (Berks) 41, 54, 95, 129–30, 171, 261
Bradford, C W 134
Bradshaw, G Y 138
Bradwell (Bucks) 35, 80, 84, 93, 131, 269, 292; *see also* New Bradwell
Brafield (Bucks) 36, 93
Braithwaite, F 116
Brampton Bryan (Herefs) 68, 91
Bramston, W Monteford 213
Brancker, - 44
Brancker, Henry 279
Brandryth, - 78
Bray (Berks) 41, 57, 131, 156, 261, 288
Braybrooke, Lord 59, 60, 305
Braywood Lodge (Berks) 140
Brazier, John Henry 61
Breedon, Capt - 252, 253
Breedon, Henry 54, 252
Brickersley 86
Brickhill Bow (Bucks) 132; *see also* Great Brickhill; Little Brickhill
Bricknell, William Simcox 22, 49, 86, 87, 118, 171, 173, 174–5, 183–4, 246, 314
Brickness, Jonah 160
Bridgewater, Lord and Lady 233, 255
Brighthampton (Oxon) 277
Brighton (Sussex) 162, 195
Brightwalton (Berks) 40, 68–9, 90, 142, 302–3
Brightwell (Berks) 39, 51, 86, 132–3, 261
Brightwell Baldwin (Oxon) 24, 133
Brill (Bucks) 133, 206, 237
Brimpton (Berks) 41, 42, 65, 133
Briscoe, - 55
Briscoe, Owen 58
Bristow, T 123
Bristow, W J 141
Britwell Prior (Oxon) 92, 133, 234
Britwell Salome (Oxon) 6, 24, 92, 133, 234
Brize Norton (Oxon) 27, 28, 30, 116, 134, 153, 209
Broad, Eliza 186
Broad, John 185
Broad, Thomas 185
Broad, William 185
Broadhead, George 327
Broadwell (Oxon) 27, 30, 91, 95, 130–1, 134
Brogden, J 97, 163
Bromley College (Kent) 339
Brooke, A 45
Brookes, Henry 109–10
Brookes, T 263
Broom Park (Kent) 100
Brougham, Lord 32, 60
Broughton (Bucks) 36, 37, 92, 104, 134, 230
Broughton (Northants) 13
Broughton (Oxon) 6, 12, 134, 209, 214, 269, 289, 324, 325, 335
Broughton, - 285
  sister of 36
Broughton, Thomas Delves 32, 126, 272
Broughton Pogges (Oxon) 28, 30, 83, 130, 131, 134–5
Brown, - 21, 75, 90, 122, 128, 283
Brown, Miss - 142
Brown, Arthur 109
Brown, E Jun 260
Brown, G M 8, 122
Brown, J 196
Brown, J T 157
Brown, John 109
Brown, R 2
Brown, Stephen 62, 268
Brown, W L 307–8
Brown Willis 141
Browne, Benjamin Hayward Huddleston 109
Browne, G W 125
Browne, Henry 223
Browne, J G 10, 22, 23, 24, 171, 210, 328
Browne, John 186
Browne, Robert 22
Browne, Thomas 199
Browne, Sir W 106
Bryan, - 29
Bryant, - 50
Buccleuch, Duke of 30
Buchanan, Alexander 106

Buckingham (Bucks)
  clergy 35, 80, 212
  clergy in vicinity 31
  Deanery 80–3, 89, 92
  school 141
  special services 135–6
  vicarage accounts 136–7
  Wilberforce at 137, 144, 188, 218, 252, 257
  see also Gawcott
Buckingham, Duke of 73, 74, 91, 302, 320
Buckland (Berks) 40, 46, 47, 137–8
Buckland (Bucks) 73, 108, 112, 123, 138, 221, 330
Buckland Common (Bucks) 217, 330
Buckle, - 216
Buckle, R 24
Bucklebury (Berks) 41, 66, 90, 91, 121, 138, 179, 188, 277, 329
Bucknell (Oxon) 6, 138, 228
Budd, Joseph 219
Bull, - 12, 79, 89, 154, 165, 193
Bull, J 32n, 71
Bull, John 182
Bullock, - 8, 170
Bullock, G F 245, 246
Bullock, George 69, 104
Bullock, John 185, 186
Bullock, Joseph 90
Bulteel, - 244
Bunbury, - 72
Bunbury, Mrs - 66, 138
Burdett, Halford B 13
Burford (Oxon) 28, 30, 138–9, 153, 187, 200, 279, 291, 292, 309
Burge, R B 113
Burgess, - 125, 154, 245, 329
Burgess, Bryant 215, 341
Burgess, Frank 29, 31, 83, 85, 144, 167, 180, 236, 276, 277
Burgess, Henry 154
Burgess, J R 52, 287
Burgess, John Hugh 139, 163
Burgess, R B 301, 302
Burgess, Bishop Thomas 45, 52, 64, 70
Burgess, W J 74
Burghfield (Berks) 56, 139, 288
Burghfield Hurst (Berks) 42

Burgon, J W 2n, 135, 194, 224, 300, 305
Burkit, - 18; *see also* Birkett
Burlton, F T 20
Burnaby, Henry F 120
Burne, Edward 99
Burne, I B 99, 100, 104
Burney, H 307
Burnham (Berks) 41
Burnham (Bucks) 31, 38, 78–9, 88, 92, 139
Burr, Mrs - 100, 101
Burr, Higford (Highford) 100, 101
Burridge, Thomas W 281
Burrow, Samuel 334
Burrows, - 165
Burrows, H W 248, 261
Burrows, Joseph 23, 85, 109, 110, 265
Burrows, Thomas 110
Burton, - 221
Burton Abbotts *see* Black Bourton
Buscot (Burwestcot) (Oxon) 39, 45, 140, 335
Bush, - 100, 311
Bushell, - 102
Bushnell, T H 121
Bushnell, William 55, 121
Bussell, - 238
Bussell, Fred 77, 224, 225, 287
Bussell, J 287
Butcher, - 311
Butler, - 64, 78, 142, 151, 163, 194, 210, 218, 305
Butler, Miss - 237–8
Butler, A S 253
Butler, E 143
Butler, H 44
Butler, John 38, 44, 64, 207
Butler, T 295
Butler, W James 105, 298, 338
Butler, W John 113, 135, 142, 163, 187, 194, 210, 218, 248, 261, 303–4, 305
Butt, John Molesworth (Martin) 313
Butt, Martin 61
Buttenshaw (really Buttanshaw), Francis 152
Butterfield, William 180, 215
Butterfield, T G 148, 149
Buttermere 297
Button, - 49

Byron, Hon W 218, 283

Cadmore End (Bucks) 96, 141
Cadogan, - 54
Cadwallader, - 317
Caffin, Benjamin Charles 246
Caffin, George Benjamin 42, 65, 133
Calcot, J 16
Calcutta (India) 238
Calverley, H C 113, 261, 262
Calverton (Bucks) 80, 141
Cambridge (Cambs) 59, 104, 303
Cameron, Archibald Allen 60, 205–6, 299
Cameron, G D 244
Camilleri, Michael 278
Camoys, Lord - 19
Campbell, - 74, 108, 140
Campbell, A 72
Campbell, J J 15, 293
Campden, - 138
Candy, B 252
Canterbury (Kent) xii, 5n, 19, 75, 248, 284, 295
Capetown (S Africa) 267
Caractacus 211
Carausius 141
Carden, Lionel 54
Carden, R 270
Cardew, John Haydon 255
Carey, A 288
Carey, C 90, 276
Carey, O H 97
Carey, T 149
Carlisle (Cumbria) 58, 60
Carlisle, Lord 255
Carlyle, John 19, 235
Carpenter, George 144, 270, 275
Carrington, Lord 234
Carrington, - 76, 231
Carter, - 31, 79, 105, 221, 306
Carter, Ellen Elizabeth 270
Carter, T 139
Carter, T T 58, 113, 135, 154, 178, 216, 248, 261, 274
Carter, W 84
Carter, W D 270, 275, 329
Carter, W E D 311

Cartwright, - 71, 72
Cartwright, F W 84, 85, 237
Casey, Charles 68
Cassington (Oxon) 22, 90, 125, 141
Castlethorpe (Bucks) 35, 141, 189, 192–3
Caterer, I 260
Catmore (Cattemore; Catmere) (Berks) 68, 141
Cattermole, Richard 225
Caunter, Richard MacDonald 165, 193
Cauntle, Batey 267
Cautley, George Spencer 233
Cave, - 163
Cavendish, - 91, 295, 296
Cavendish, Mrs - 296
Cavendish, Charles Compton 215
Caversfield (Oxon) 8, 35, 81, 90, 122, 141–2
Caversham (Berks) 19–20, 41, 142, 224, 261, 262
Cecil, - 251
Cecil, Lord R 231
Cerdic 145
Chaddleworth (Berks) 40, 69, 70, 142
Chadlington (Oxon) 9, 142, 143–4, 162, 276
Chalfont St Giles (Bucks) 142–3, 187
Chalfont St Peter (Bucks) 31, 143, 164, 224n, 267
Chalgrove (Oxon) 25, 122, 143
Challis, Nathan 293
Challow (Berks) 163; *see also* East Challow; West Challow
Chalsfield (Glos) 69n
Chalvey (Bucks) 79, 96, 273, 301
Chamberlain, Thomas 16, 201, 246, 250, 338
Chambers, Magd 11
Chambers, W 39, 45, 46, 107, 206
Champnes, E 88, 301
Champneys, - 78, 194
Champneys, C C 87
Champneys, C F 135, 308
Champneys, E T 84
Chandos, Lord 108, 136, 165, 279, 320
Chandos, Lady 320
Chaplin, Edward Morland 151
Chaplin, J E 83, 85

Chapman, - 74, 132, 225, 280
Charlbury (Oxon) 9, 143–4, 276, 284, 335
Charles, W W 108
Charlton (Oxon) 6, 227, 304, 318
Charlton on Otmoor (Oxon) 144–5
Charney (Oxon) 40, 48, 145, 220
Chase, Drummond Percy 247
Chasledon 291
Chastleton (Oxon) 9, 145
Chatteris, - 276
Chatteris, W 133
Cheakle, - 139
Cheales, - 305
Chearsley (Bucks) 3, 71, 112, 145–6
Checkendon (Oxon) 20, 146, 297
Checkley, - 193
Cheddington (Bucks) 34, 37, 97, 146, 169, 209
Chedwin, - 105
Chelmsford, Lord 271, 311
Cheltenham (Glos) 66n
Cheney, George C 204
Chenies (Bucks) 146
Chepmell, W 16
Cherry, - 64, 91
Cherry, Henry Curtis 56, 139
Chesham (Bucks) 87, 88, 146–7, 195, 283
Chesham Bois (Bucks) 87, 147
Chester, - 110, 215
Chester, Anthony 84, 148
Chester, J B 170
Chesterfield, Earl of 88
Chesterton (Oxon) 6, 147, 228, 307
Chetwode (Bucks) 35, 79, 148, 256, 287
Chetwode, G 84, 151
Chetwode, Sir J 70
Chetwode, Pigott Alfred 71
Chetwode, R 85
Chetwode, Sir T 151
Chetwode, Walter 212
Chicheley (Bucks) 36, 89, 93, 110, 148, 159, 215, 320
Chicheley Hall (Bucks) 148n
Chicheley Hill (Bucks) 84
Chichester (Sussex) 62, 66n, 70, 97, 207, 217, 238, 284, 292
Chiddington (Bucks) 31
Chieveley (Berks) 23, 41, 65, 69, 90, 120, 148–9, 150, 198, 312
Childrey (Oxon) 39, 50, 151, 217
Chilton (Berks) 40, 42, 67, 90, 151
Chilton (Bucks) 71, 84, 151
Chilton (Oxon) 30, 276
Chilton, R 205
Chinnor (Oxon) 25, 151–2
Chipping Norton (Oxon) 9–10, 85, 145, 152, 199, 200, 264, 265
Chirol, Alexander 140
Chislehampton (Oxon) 17, 152
Chislehurst (Kent) 26
Chittenden, Thomas Knapp 20, 212
Cholesbury (Bucks) 138, 152–3
Cholmley, Charles Humphrey 201
Cholsey (Oxon) 39, 51–2, 86, 153
Christie, C M 286
Christie, John F 56, 300
Christopher, Alfred Millard William 238
Churchill (Oxon) 10, 11, 153, 211, 266
Churchill family 143
    Lord - 106
    Clementina 125
    Cornelia 125
Churton, H B Whitaker 66
    sister of 67
Churton, T T 268
Chute, - 30
Clanfield (Oxon) 28, 30, 86, 153
Clarke, - 126, 136, 142, 213, 219
Clarke, Cecil Jarvis 277
Clarke, Charles William Barnett 115, 285
Clarke, J Erskine 338
Clarke, John Alexander 284–5
Clarke *see also* Clerke
Clarkson, - 37
Claughton, T C 109, 135, 142, 187, 194, 248, 261
Claydon (Oxon) 13, 117, 153, 324, 325; *see also* East Claydon; Steeple Claydon
Clayton, E 8, 287
Clayton, E F 274
Clayton, Rice 196–7
Cleaver, - 167
Cleaver, Misses 158
Cleaver, Jn Francis 46, 90, 158
Clementi, Vincent 38, 66

Cleminson, W 65, 306
Cleobury, - 8, 122
Clerke, Archdeacon Charles C 20, 45, 98, 228, 241-2, 311, 331
Clerke, 122; *see also* Clarke
Clewer (Berks) 26, 41, 58, 154, 226
Clifton (Glos) 176
Clifton (Oxon) 15, 28, 96, 97, 163, 164, 220, 324, 325
Clifton, C R 8, 108–9
Clifton, R C 108, 273, 274
Clifton Hampden (Oxon) 17, 154, 162
Clifton Reynes (Bucks) 36, 93, 154, 195
Clive, - 57
Clive, Mrs - 57, 118
Cliveden (Bucks) 157, 292
Clode, Maria 218
Clonmell, Lord and Lady Louisa 269
Cloudesley, - 170
Cloyne, Bishop of 279
Clubbe, - 202
Clutterbuck, H 45
Clutterbuck, J 315
Cobb, John Wolstenholme 210
Coblers Hill (Bucks) 194
Cockell, T W 277
Cockerill, Miss - 64
Cockerton, Jas 31, 80, 298–9
Cocking (Sussex) 286
Cockle, - 267
Cockle, R J 87
Codd, A 195, 196
    wife of 195
Codrington, - 249
Cogges (Oxon) 27, 28, 30, 154–5, 314
Coker, Mrs - 82
Coker, C 122, 268
Coker, J 35, 82, 91, 297
Coker, John 83, 85, 257
Cokethorpe (Oxon) 28, 30, 166–7
Cold Brayfield (Bucks) 132, 215–16
Cole, - 81
Coleman, G 79, 82, 84, 286
Coleridge, - 141
Coleridge, E 84, 224
Coles, - 19
Coles, Edward Norman 72
Coles, John B 302

Coleshill (Bucks) 105, 155
Coleshill (Berks) 39, 45, 158
Coley, - 17–18, 165, 166
Colles *see* Collis
Collings, P B 130
Collins, - 36, 49; *see also* Collyns
Collinson, - 33
Collinson, George John (G T) 87
Collis (Colles), Thomas William Sandes 274–5
Collyns, Fernando 219
Collyns, J M 121, 166
Collyns *see also* Collins
Colnbrook (Bucks) 78, 88, 96, 155–6
Colvill, J H 263
Combe (Oxon) 284; *see also* Long Combe
Comely, - 105
Compton (Berks) 40, 69
Compton, - 210, 224
Compton, Lord Alwyne 288
Compton, Sir H and daughter 74
Compton Beauchamp (Berks) 40, 47, 156
Compton Parva (Berks) 156
Conroy, - 206
Conroy, Sir E 105
Conroy, Sir John 56
Conybeare, C 160, 257, 291
Conynghame, Lady 3, 285
Cooke, G T 120
Cooke, H Pennant 234
Cooke, S 121
Cooke, T Leigh 17
Cookersley, W G 86
Cookes, T H 14, 276
Cookes, Thomas 85
Cookham (Berks) 38, 41, 57, 86, 131, 156, 157, 317
Cookham Dean (Berks) 41, 58, 95, 157
Cookson, W 63, 204
Coombe Hill (Berks) 207
Cooper, - 17
Cooper, E 125
Cooper, Edward Philip 28, 30
Coote, Algernon 31, 87, 225
Cope, Sir W 117
Copeland, W 16
Copeman, Philip W 29, 30
Corbett, G O 182

Corker, - 132
Cornish, A A 312
Cornish, H H 239
Cornwal, Allan 122
Cornwall, - 61
Cornwell (Oxon) 10, 153, 157
Cote (Oxon) 115
Cotechings, John 274
Cotes, Septimus 234
Cotmore (Berks) 40
Cottenham, Lord 21
Cotter, Charles Purcell 279
Cotterell-Dormer family 264
    Squire - 23
    Charles 23n
    Elizabeth 23
Cotterill, - 144
Cottisford (Oxon) 6, 157–8, 179
Cottle, T 49
Cotton, - 21, 44, 49, 50
Couch, F 200
Coulthard, Robert 55, 288
    wife of 288
Coupland, Edward 236
Court, James Charles Lett 132
Coutts, Messrs 3
Covey, Richard 326, 327
Cowan, - 258, 262
Cowleech, - 66
Cowley (Oxon) 17, 158, 206
Cox, - 69
Cox, F 3, 135, 312
Cox, Thomas 187, 207
Cox, W Haywood 15, 86, 87
Coxe, - 17, 91
Coxe, C B 62, 64
Coxe, H O 328
Coxwell, T T 3, 77
Coxwell (Oxon), *see* Great Coxwell; Little Coxwell
Cozens, - 238
Crabtree, W 20, 146
Cranborne School (Dorset) 313
Cranbourne (Berks) 158–9
Cranmer, J S G 174, 183
Crases Hill (Berks) 305
Craven, Lord and Lady 65, 213
Crawley (Oxon) 95, 110, 186, 314–15

Cree, John Adams 301
Creslow (Bucks) 159
Crewe, H H 166
Crickland, - 314
Crole, - 35
Crookham (Berks) 295
Cropredy (Oxon) 13, 19, 124, 159–60, 231–2, 304, 323, 324
Cross, John 144, 233
Cross, Stock (Berks) 63
Crow, - 81
Crowdy, F 128
Crowell (Oxon) 25, 160
Crowley, - 67
Crowmarsh Gifford (Oxon) 20, 121, 160, 302
Cruse, Francis 156
Crutch, Stephen Spicer 216
Cublington (Bucks) 33, 92, 112, 123, 160, 313
Cuddesdon (Oxon) xi, xiv, xv, 3n, 16, 17, 118, 139, 152, 155, 160–1, 162, 165, 168, 170, 178, 183, .196, 197, 199, 202, 213, 216, 221, 222, 225, 248, 275, 279, 291, 296, 297, 303, 307, 309, 339
Cuddington (Bucks) 73, 99, 112, 161, 184, 311
Cuffe, - 231
Culham (Callum) (Oxon) xi, 17, 18, 47, 124, 133, 162, 224
Cumberledge, Charles 110
Cumberledge, S F 36, 110
Cumnor (Berks) 7, 39, 43, 162
Cunningham, A H 189
Cunningham, F M 314
Cunobeline 211
Curbridge (Oxon) 95, 162, 314–15
Cure, C 249
Cureton, - 299
Curme, Thomas 10, 23, 87, 92, 118, 163, 171, 265–6
Curridge (Berks) 148
Currie, - 220
Currie, Sir F 303
Currie, Frederic L 302–3
Currie, M W 113
Currie, Maynard 227

Currie, Messrs and Co 317
Curtis, - 153
Curtis, Edith 267
Curtis, Francis H 252
Curtis, G W 55, 252
Curwen, J 260
Curwen, Spedding 259–60
Curwen, T T 260
Cust, A P 108, 146, 152, 169, 218, 233, 255, 262, 272, 273, 274
Cuthred 107
Cuthwulph 113
Cuxham (Oxon) 25, 162
Cuxson, George Appleby 33, 186
Cynric 145

Dacres, F 317
Dagnall (Bucks) 169
Dalby, - 70
Dale, - 195
Dalton, - 165, 230
Dand, Thomas 6, 14, 125
Dandridge, George 23, 109, 264
Dartmouth, Lord 237
Dashwood, - 212, 292
Dashwood, Lady - 212
Dashwood, Sir G 7, 327
Dashwood, Sir George, son of 22
Dashwood, Sir H 167
Dashwood, Henry 75
Dashwood King, Sir J 75
Datchet (Bucks) 59, 79, 162, 163, 201
Daubeny, F 167
Daubeny, John 113
Daubeny, Thomas 318
Dauncey, - 202
Davenport, John M xv, 115, 157, 170, 173, 183, 220, 221, 245, 258, 264, 272, 273, 279
Davies, Miss - 200
Davies, A E 63
Davies, E 124
Davies, Matthew Watkin 223
Davis, - 120, 277
Davis, E 260
Davis, Frederick 317
Davis, George 144
Dawkins, - 152, 265

Dawson, F A 140
Day, - 217
Day, G 133
Day, George (J) 24, 69, 133
Day, Sister Harriet 303
Day, Sarah 185
Day, William 185
De Salis, Henry Jerome 179
De Tessier, A 147
De Vitre, G E D 157
Dean, - 25
Deane, J H (should be R W) 298
Deane, T H 85
Dearlove, Alfred 185
Dearlove, Daniel 185
Dearlove, Emma 185
Dearlove, Ezra 185
Dearlove, Hannah 186
Dearlove, Isaac 185
Dearlove, Jane 186
Dearlove, John 185
Dearlove, Martha Ann 185
Dearlove, William 186
Dearney, - 75
Deddington (Oxon) 11, 15, 96, 97, 163, 323, 324, 325
Delabeech family 69
Delaware, Lord 13
Denchworth (Berks) 39, 50, 96, 163
Denford (Dinford) (Berks) 91, 204
Denham (Bucks) 84, 90, 164
Denman, Lord 64
Dennis, - 48
Dent (Cumbria) 230
Dent, C 160
Dent, Cartwright 54
Denton, - 313
Denton, N 236
Derby, Lord 309
Derle, Philip 87
Derry, Bishop of 184
Devizes (Wilts) 98
Dew, - 220
Dewar, D E 169, 170
Dickerson, R C 113
Dickinson, T G 25
Dickson, W R 307; *see also* Dixon
Didcot (Berks) 39, 40, 42, 70, 164

Dillon, Lord 10, 11, 171, 199, 276
Dingford, - 315
Dinton (Bucks) 31, 73, 93, 164
Dinton, J 38
Dixon, - 51; *see also* Dickson
Dobree, Delisle 265
Dodd, - 7
Dodd, Henry A 50, 212, 275
Dodson, Joseph 188
Dodson, Nathaniel 39, 43, 49, 97, 162, 289, 315, 330
Donnington (Berks) 63, 268
Dorchester (Oxon) 17, 164–5, 166
Dorney (Bucks) 79, 88, 165
Dorton (Bucks) 165
Douglas, Lord - 13
Douglas, Alexander 169
Douglas, Sir C 117
Dover (Kent) 301
Down, Lord 89
Down Ampney (Glos) 6n
Downshire, Lord 60, 61n, 62, 69, 168, 169
Drake, John T and family 105
Drake, T 217
Drake, Walter 35, 37, 84, 232
Dran, - 17
Drawbridge, William Barker 139
Drayton (Berks) 39, 43, 97, 165–6
Drayton (Oxon) 13, 17–18, 164, 165, 200, 324
Drayton Beauchamp (Bucks) 3, 34, 37, 166
Drayton Parslow (Bucks) 33, 92, 166, 234
Dredge, William 103
Druce, Joseph 174–5
Drummond, Miss - 216
Drummond, Lady Elizabeth 82
Drummond, H 31, 81, 82, 195, 216
Drummond, Mortimer 164
Drury, H 118, 248
Dry, W L (J) 124, 308
Dry Sandford (Berks) 330
Dryden, L G 6, 11, 83, 105, 122
Du Pre *see* Dupre
Ducane, - 146, 196
Ducklington (Oxon) 28, 30, 155, 166–7, 236, 277, 314, 318

Dudley, - 42
Duffield, C 44, 224
Dugdale, - 279
Dukinfield, Sir H 164
Duncan, - 279, 302
Duncombe, - 132, 275
Duncombe, Sir P 132
Dundas, Admiral - 64
Dundas, J W D 38, 64, 211
Dundridge, G 87
Duns Tew (Oxon) 22, 108, 167
Dunsden (Oxon) 274
Dunster (Som) 13
Dunton (Bucks) 33, 92, 168, 313
Dupre, - 78
Dupre, Miss - 267
Dupre, Henry R 48, 268
Dupre, James 209
Dupuis, G T 84
Durell, T V 20, 25, 232
Dyke, - 6
Dynevor, Lord - 30

Eagles, - 160
Earle, Robert E 230
Earley (Berks) 168, 261, 330
Easington (Oxon) 25, 168
East, Lady - 183
East, Lady Clayton 205
East, Sir Gilbert 205
East, Lady Gilbert 205
East Challow (Berks) 39, 50, 143
East Claydon (Bucks) 32, 153, 154, 209
East Farleigh (Kent) 4n
East Garston (Berks) 40, 61, 181
East Hendred (Berks) 39, 49, 160, 197
East Ilsley (Berks) 40, 67, 128, 151, 156, 207, 329n
East Lockinge (Berks) 39, 49, 219
East (Little) Shefford (Berks) 40, 62, 91, 268
East Tisted (Hants) 36n
East Worldham (Hants) 36n
Eastbury (Berks) 96, 213
Easthampstead (Berks) 42, 60–1, 90, 168–9
Easthampstead Park (Berks) 60
Easton, - 68

Eaton, W 163
Eaton Hastings (Berks) 39, 46, 169
Ecclesiastical Commissioners, 115, 214
Eddlesborough (Bucks) 31, 33, 92, 169
Eden, - 6
Eden, C P 15, 248
Edgcott (Bucks) 32, 35, 78, 81, 169–70, 318
Edington (Berks) 204, 205
Edmonds, - 220
Edward, King 206
Edwardes, S 320
Edwards, J 152
Edwards, Lambert Campbell 165
Egerton, - 163
Egerton, C C 315
Egerton, P Reginald 129
Eldridge, Robey 10
Eliot, Edward 272
Elkington, - 36
Ellames, - 225
Ellerton, - 18, 56
Ellesborough (Bucks) 74, 93, 146, 170, 284
Ellice, - 326
Elliott, - 61, 158, 159
Elliott, C J, 313
Elliott, Charles Jno 59
Elliott, Florence May 313
Ellis, - 31
Ellis, Conyngham 158–9, 313
Ellis, T 18
Ellis, W May 206
Ellison, H J 156, 212, 312
Elliston, - 44
Elmley (Yorks) 155
Elsfield (Oxon) 18, 170
Elton, E 310
Elwes, C 224
Ely (Cambs) 104, 249, 307
Emberton (Bucks) 36, 93, 170, 269, 299
Emmington (Oxon) 25, 152, 170
Enborne (Berks) 41, 65, 171, 187
England, W H 74, 170, 284
England, W T 232
Englefield (Berks) 41, 54, 171, 253, 261, 297
English, W W 115

Enraght, - 226
Enstone (Oxon) 10, 23, 87, 171
Epsom (Surrey) 238
Epwell (Oxon) 13, 171, 272, 289, 290, 324
Erck, - 69
Erle, Christopher 33, 193–4
Erle, Robert 29
Espin, - 210
Essex, Diana 185
Essex, William 185
Estcourt, - 122
Etchilhampton (Wilts) 277
Ethelred 107
Eton College (Berks)
   chapel 171
   clergy 84, 90, 157
   confirmation 97
   dissenters 86, 87
   fellows 54, 58
   master 253, 312
   patronage 12, 27, 28, 29, 140, 154, 155, 158, 284
   provost 6, 251
   pupil 192
Ettrick, - 90
Evans, - 14
Evans, Mr and Mrs Capt - 11
Evans, A B 135
Evans, Evan 83
Evans, George 47–8
Evans, J W 113
Evans, W 48, 256
Everett, C W 319
Everett, Charles 50
Everett, Charles Dundas 122
Everett, G F 63, 268
Evetts, - 105
   widow and daughter of 292
Evetts, T 256
Ewelme (Oxon) 25, 84, 85, 121, 133, 172
Exeter (Devon) 14, 107, 235
Eyfley *see* Iffley
Eynsham (Oxon) 22, 87, 172–5, 314
Eyre, - 62, 143, 307
Eyre, C 68
Eyre, C J P 261
Eyre, Francis John 54, 171

wife of 171
Eyre, G (W T) 32, 82, 252
   wife of 32
Eyre, Henry S 171
Eyton, - 108

Faber, - 24
Faber, F A 78, 125, 267
Fairbairn, Henderson 305
Fairbrother, W 259
Fairthorne, - 271
Faithful, Charles H 198
Faithful, G D 7, 83, 85, 109, 198
Falcon, T W 134, 144
Falkner, F B 231; *see also* Faulkner
Falmouth, Lord 164
Falwasser, J F 130
Fane family 19
Fanshawe, H L 154, 309
Farley, - 73
Farley, Thomas 28, 30, 166–7
Farmer, - 330
Farnborough (Berks) 40, 67, 91, 142, 176–7, 178
Farnborough Park (Oxon) 13
Farnham Castle (Surrey) xii
Farnham Royal (Bucks) 79, 95, 177, 282, 314
Farrar, J M 135, 335
Farrell, Maurice 321
Farringdon (Berks) 39, 46, 48, 140, 169, 175–6, 219, 271
Faulkner, Allan 139; *see also* Falkner
Faussett, Godfrey 85
Fawkes, F F 310
Fawley (Berks) 41, 67, 92, 142, 178
Fawley (Bucks) 31, 76, 92, 178
Fazeley (Bucks) 87
Felix, - 38
Fell, - 253
Fell, G 52, 86
Fell, Hunter F 20
Fenner, - 143
Fenny Stratford (Bucks) 3, 37, 92, 135, 285
Fenton, J A 291
Fenwick, Lewis G 258
Fereman, G 134
Ferguson, - 122

Ferguson, Mary Roma 313
Fermor family 274
Fern Hill (Berks) 158
Fernham (Berks) 219
Ferrey, - 233
Ferris, Godfrey Richard 202, 203
Few, William Seth 262
Fewcot (Oxon) 90, 106, 282
Fiddler, - 68
Fidler, Amos 186
Fidler, Caroline 186
Fidler, Hannah 186
Fidler, Isaac 25, 168
Fidler, John 185
Fidler, T D 256
Field, - 35, 163, 195, 196, 285
Field, Matthew 56
Fielding, - 272
Fifield (Oxon) 10, 178, 329
Filgrave (Filgrove) (Bucks) 32, 178, 299
Filkins (Oxon) 27, 134, 135, 214, 269, 335
Finch, - 230
Finch, Robert 252, 253
Finchampstead (Finchamstead) (Berks) 38, 42, 57, 178
Finden, G S 263
Fingest (Bucks) 76, 87, 88, 178
Finmere (Oxon) 6, 178–9
Finstock (Oxon) 9, 10, 11, 143–4, 179, 257, 335
Firth, W 50, 217
Fish, James C 117
Fish, John D 116
Fisher, John 85
Fisher, R B 39, 51, 52, 118, 119
Fisher, Wilfred 310
Fiske, Robert W 235
FitzClarence, Lord Augustus 20
Fitzgerald, Mrs - 299
Fitzgerald, Geraldine 268
Fitzgerald, Richard Purefroy 308
Fitzgerald family 268
Fixsen, F F 198, 224
Flackwell Heath (Bucks) 225
Fleet Marston (Bucks) 32, 71, 89, 113, 179, 183, 226
Fleming, - 210, 240

Flemyng, - 271
Fletcher, W 42, 70
Flint, C R 130, 213, 264, 288
Floyd, Thomas 128
Follett, - 179
Foot, R Gorges 201–2
Foots Cray (Kent) 225
Forbes, A P 16
Forbes, C 11, 15, 117
Ford, - 33
Ford, Edward Alex 47
Ford, R R 81
Fordyce, A T D 143
Forest Hill (Oxon) 18, 179, 279
Formoys House (Berks) 157
Forster, - 22, 141
Fort, C 121
Fortescue, William F 147
Fosbery, T V 175, 233, 258, 261, 262, 277, 288, 312, 338
Foulis, Sir H 36, 132
Foulke, - 66
Foulkes, Dr. 30, 44, 122
Fountain, Bernard 209
Fowler, Charles 123, 331, 332, 334
Fox, C F 20
Fox, G F 100
Fox, John 83
Foxcote (Foscot) (Bucks) 82, 89, 179
Foxfield Chapel (Berks) 91
Francis, T 228
Frankam, - 294
Frankland, Lady 74, 217, 284
Franklin, - 172
Franks, - 321
Fraser, James 300
Frazer, Arthur Bruce 195
    wife of 195
Freemantle (Fremantle), Mrs - 280, 301
Freemantle (Fremantle), Sir T 33, 227, 296
Freemantle (Fremantle), W R 31, 32, 72, 87, 113, 135, 137, 142, 153, 154, 169, 183, 194, 209, 210, 214, 225, 226, 227, 302, 309, 338
Freemantle (Fremantle), William Henry 218
Frere, Miss - 277

Frieth (Bucks) 187
Frilsham (Berks) 41, 71, 179
Fringford (Oxon) 6, 179, 235, 282
Frith, James 232
Frith, W C 53, 302
Fritwell (Oxon) 6, 108, 179–80
Fry, - 88
Fry, John 87
Fry, T 114, 115, 170, 215
Fulbrook (Oxon) 28, 30, 138–9, 180
Fullegar, Hugh Scales 113
Fulmer (Bucks) 180
Furlong, C J 304–5
Fyfield (Berks) 40, 44, 180, 277
Fyrstone (Bucks) 87

Gainsborough, Lord 215
Gaisford, Charles 30, 31, 42, 67, 151
Gaisford, Thomas 30
Galloway, William 193
Gane, Brisco Morland 235
Gardiner, E 108, 165
Gardner, - 165, 226
Garfield Hundred 39
Garford (Berks) 181
Garnier, Mrs A E 303
Garnier, Edward 303
Garrard, - 47
Garratt (Garrett), Charles Foster 300
Garrett, J Jnr 86
Garrett, W 260
Garsington (Oxon) 18, 181, 308
Garth, Mrs - 205, 206
Gaseley, R C 61
Gaskell, - 210
Gaulin 113
Gawcott (Bucks) 4n, 35, 81, 136, 181
Gayhurst (Bucks) 36, 93, 181
Geare, E 48, 125, 328
Geckby, - 8
Genge, George 136
George, Horace 264
George, John 74
Gerrards Cross (Bucks) 181, 331
Gibbings, Robert 258
Gibbons, James 174
Gibbs, Jos 17, 154
Gibbs, Walter 301

Gibbs, Wesley Henry 154
Gibson, - 26, 219, 266
Gilbert, - 18
Gilbert, Mrs - 17
Gilbert, Edward A 258
Gilbert, William 255
Gilchrist, Mrs - 100
Giles, - 27, 90, 115, 184
Gill, - 55, 121
Gill, Mrs - 294
Gill, Dugald Campbell 319
Gill, Francis Turner 305
Gillam (Gilliam), Isaac 87, 235, 314
Gillam, T Henry 121, 162, 172
Gillett, - 29
Gilliam, V 140
Gilliatt, - 158
Gladstone, W E xii, xvi, 197
Glandville, - 24
Glanville, - 26
Gleed, William (G) 31, 143
Glympton (Oxon) 22, 171, 181, 210
Goalen, Alex 97, 188
Goddard, Daniel Ward 138, 139, 200
Goddard family 98, 134
Goddington (Oxon) 6–7, 179, 181
Godfrey, - 9
Godfrey, R S 258
Godfrey, William 36, 258
Goffin, John H 286–7
Goldie, - 182, 202
Goldie, C D 113, 155–6, 338
Golding, Edward 133; *see also* Goulding
Golightly, Charles P 2, 16, 196, 226, 231, 309
Gooch, C 210, 318
Goodall, - 73
Goodenough, - 104
Goodenough, James Joseph 28, 30, 83, 130, 134
Goodheart, C J 54, 86
Goodlake, - 49, 50, 175
Goodlake, Thomas W 27, 30, 130–1, 134, 135, 335
Goodrich, Bartlett George 187, 193
Goosey (Berks) 40, 48, 181, 277–8
Gordon, - 18
Gordon, Miss - 20

Gordon, Edward 179
Gordon, H D 98
Gordon, O 105
Gordon, Osborne 169
Gordon, R 170, 226, 279
Gordon, Robert 64, 110, 275
Gore, John 86, 267
Goring (Oxon) 20, 182
Goring Heath (Oxon) 182
Gosport (Hants) 98
Gosset (Gossett), Isaac 59, 312
Gough, H 144, 145
Goulburn, - 130
Goulburn, Mrs - 22
Goulburn, E M 16, 243
Gould, - 59, 109
Gould, Hussey 119
Gould, J A 322
Gould, J Aubrey 330
Gould, John 78, 119
Gould, R J 59, 285
Goulding, - 259; *see also* Golding
Gower, Eliza 3
Gower, Lord J Leveson 205, 283
Grace, O J 125, 267
Graffham (Sussex) 238
Grafton (Oxon) 182
Grainger, Mrs - 253
Grainger, Cecil 54, 258
Grainger, F 253, 312
Grainger, J C 54, 258, 259, 260
Grampound (Devon) 281
Grandborough (Bucks) 33, 182
Grant, Alexander 258
Grant family 69
Grantham, G F 57
Grantham, J J 57, 86, 157
Graves, - 129
Gravesend (Kent), Longfield Court 20
Gray, C E 74, 78, 84, 263; *see also* Grey
Grazeley (Berks) 95, 182–3
Great Barford *see* Barford St Michael
Great Barrington (Glos) 30
Great Bourton (Oxon) 13, 159, 160
Great Brickhill (Bucks) 36, 37, 92, 132
Great Coxwell (Berks) 39, 46, 90, 155, 158
Great Hampden (Bucks) 31, 38, 75, 91, 93, 164, 187

Great Haseley (Oxon) 18, 195
Great Horwood (Horwood Magna) (Bucks) 31, 33, 82, 92, 202
Great Kimble (Bucks) 75, 91, 93, 112, 187, 211
Great Linford (Bucks) 35, 89, 218
Great Marlow (Bucks) 3, 77, 92, 96, 224–5, 287
Great Milton (Oxon) 18, 195, 212, 228–9
Great Missenden (Bucks) 31, 38, 74, 75, 76, 93, 230–1, 256
Great Rollright (Oxon) 10, 263–4
Great (West) Shefford (Berks) 40, 62, 65, 91, 268
Great Tew (Oxon) 15, 96, 118, 293, 323, 324
Great Woolston (Bucks) 37, 92, 311, 319, 320
Greaves, - 195
Greaves, J A 114
Greaves, Josh 230
Greaves, Tudor 154
Green, M J 16
Green, Vernon 98, 129
Green, William 118
Greene, Dawson J 258
Greene, Thomas Huntley 226
Greene, W S 258
Greenham (Berks) 41, 66, 86, 90, 183, 184, 294–5, 329
Gregory, Henry 27, 28, 30, 108, 314
Gregory, R 338
Gregson, J 44, 288–9
Grendon Underwood (Bucks) 35, 78, 183
Gresley, William 140, 153
Greville, - 68
Grey, - 68; *see also* Gray
Griffith, - 252
Griffith, Samuel 245
Griffith, T H 144, 162, 276
Griffiths, G Sandham 115
Griffiths, H B 258
Grove (Berks) 183–4
Grove (Bucks) 34, 37, 184, 313
Grove (Oxon) 39, 49, 175
Grove, - 290
Grover, H M 79, 88
Guest, - 265–6

Guillemard, J 7, 212
Gurdon (Guerdon; Guordon), William M 1–2, 35, 80, 89
Gurney, Henry Peter 300
Gurney, J H 156
Gwynne, J 26

Hacher, Mrs Marshall 106
Hackman, A 16, 246, 248, 249, 261
Haddenham (Bucks) 73, 89, 93, 112, 161, 184, 321
Hadleigh 210
Hadlow (Kent) 279
Hagbourne (Berks) 39, 40, 42, 70, 185–6; *see also* West Hagbourne
Hailey (Oxon) 28, 30, 186, 314–15
Hales, R C 87, 246, 249
Halford (Warks) 40
Halifax, Joseph 130, 134, 209, 291
Halifax, Kelly 202
Hall, - 20, 118, 167, 252
Hall, Col - 12
Hall, C A 84, 164
Hall, H 162, 163
  wife of 162
Hall, H W 11, 12
Hall, J 205
Hallward, J L 154
Halton (Bucks) 75, 93, 186
Halton, - 36, 151
Halton, L Miles 42, 55, 319
Hambleden (Bucks) 76, 87, 95, 178, 186–7, 227, 277
Hamilton, Archibald Robert 184
Hamilton, W J 31, 34, 37, 38, 209
Hamletts, - 6
Hammersley, - 18, 130–1, 209, 257, 306
Hammond, - 153
Hampden *see* Great Hampden; Little Hampden
Hampden, - xi, 1n, 25, 172
Hampstead Norreys (Berks) 40, 41, 69, 90, 188
Hampton Gay (Oxon) 7, 188
Hampton Poyle (Oxon) 7, 188, 212
Hamstead Marshall (Berks) 41, 65, 187, 319
Hanbury, John 66, 295

INDEX OF NAMES AND PLACES

Hancock, Thomas 217
Handborough (Oxon) 22, 24, 188
Handy Cross (Bucks) 225
Hanmer, Col - 272
Hanmer, T W 37, 76, 84, 231, 272, 275
Hannah, John 22
Hannam family 164
Hannan, Francis 238
Hanney (Berks) 39, 44, 51, 92, 188–9
Hannington, - 102
Hansell, Edward Halifax 329
Hansell, H 16
Hanslope (Bucks) 35, 93, 135, 189–93
Hanslope Park (Bucks) 192
Hanson, Samuel 238
Hanwell (Oxon) 13, 83, 193, 200, 324
Harcourt, - 155, 164, 277, 331
Harcourt, Mrs - 234
Harcourt, Barnes Adam 115
Harcourt, G 279
Hardman, - 167
Hardmead (Bucks) 36, 93, 193
Hardwick (Oxon) 7, 8, 90, 167, 194, 228
Hardwicke (Bucks) 33, 92, 112, 193–4
Harley, William 280, 299
Harnett, Francis William 276, 317
Harper, - 45
Harper, E T H 97
Harper, H J C 55, 284
Harpsden (Oxon) 20, 194, 261
Harrington, H D 14, 234
Harrington, H T 163
Harrington, R 83, 85
Harris, - 106, 216, 227, 233
Harris, Henry 201
Harris, Thomas 18, 83, 85, 291
Harrison, - 198, 269
Harrison, C S 157–8, 179
Harrison, J 31, 72, 73, 93, 164, 309
Harrison, Michael 14
Harrison, W A 314–15
Hart, John 34, 37, 38, 99, 274
Hartley, - 114, 138
Hartley, J S 115
Hartwell (Bucks) 73, 91, 93, 194
Harvey, - 4, 27, 200, 214
Harvey, Mrs - 214
Harvey, Richard 124, 304

Harwell (Berks) 39, 40, 42, 70, 151, 194
Harwood, - 68
Haslemere (Bucks) 87, 88, 195, 301
Hatford (Berks) 48, 195
Haverfield, T T 6
Haversham (Bucks) 35, 93, 154, 195, 218
Haviland (Havilland), - 155, 156
Hawker, John Manley 330
Hawker, W Manley 168
Hawkins, - 15
Hawkins, W 46
Hawridge (Bucks) 146, 195–6, 300
Hawthorne, William 193
Hawtrey, - 171
Hawtrey, E C 224
Hawtrey, Henry 58, 312
Hawtrey, Stephen 58
Hayes, Sir John Warren 105, 106
Haygarth, - , daughter of 54
Hayter, C F 283
Hayton, Amos 3, 71, 88–9, 146
Hayton, G 309
Hayton, T 71, 84, 159, 311
Hayward, - 213
Hayward, H R 175, 178
Hayward, John Wheeler 182
Hayward, Lee 225
Hazel, F 86
Hazel, Jas 19, 20, 233, 302
Hazel, W 302
Hazelgrove (Oxon) 196
Hazelwood, - 271
Heading, Miss - 188
Headington (Oxon) 18, 170, 196
Headington Quarry (Oxon) 95, 179, 196
Heard, Thomas J 120; *see also* Hurd
Hearne (Hearn), J B 49
Hearne (Hearn), James 48, 195
Heath, Christopher 33
Heaton, C W 15
Hedgerley (Bucks) 79, 96, 196–7
Hedges, - 166
Hedsor (Bucks) 31, 38, 197
Heigh 77
Hemel Hempstead (Herts) 140
Heming, H 29, 30, 167, 236
Hempton (Oxon) 15, 97, 163, 323, 324, 325

Hemsted, John 206, 321
Hemsted, Stephen 206
Henderson, Julius 209–10
Hendred (Berks) 68; *see also* East Hendred; West Hendred
Henley, Francis George 162
Henley Park 309
Henley-on-Thames (Oxon) 19–21, 59, 76, 97, 125, 142, 152, 197–8, 259, 281, 286
Hensley, Edward 146
Herbert, Miss - 307
Herbert, G 124
Herbert, Henry 267
Herbert, Sidney 141
Hereford (Herefs) 1n, 56, 91
Hermitage Chapel (Berks) 40, 41, 70, 198
Hervey, - 131
Heslop, W 302
Hester 306
Hethe (Oxon) 7, 158, 179, 198
Heurtley, Louis 301
Hewett (Hewitt), J 293
Hewett (Hewitt), W H 116, 128, 129, 228, 293
Heyford, *see* Lower Heyford; Upper Heyford
Heyford Bridge (Oxon) 7
Heyford Warren (Oxon) 7, 199
Heythrop (Oxon) 10, 84, 85, 199
Heywood Lodge (Berks) 140
Hibbert, F 331
Hibbert, J 140
Hicks, - 100
Higgs, - 188
Higgs, Griffith 92
High Moor (Oxon) (*sic*) 264
High Wycombe (Bucks) xi, 31, 65, 87, 88, 91, 93, 212, 216, 301, 325–7
Highlands (Berks) 182
Highworth (Wilts) 67
Hill, - 7, 10, 33, 272
  daughter of 210
Hill, Mrs - 254
Hill, B 33
Hill, C J 258
Hill, Charles 10, 254–5, 272
Hill, E 319, 320
Hill, John Smith 164

Hill, Justly 31, 32, 35, 79, 297
Hill, W 131
Hillesden (Bucks) 32, 82, 154, 199
Hilliard, F S 45
Hilliard, John Ashby Stafford 275, 315
Hinde, - 35
Hinde, John Fitz-richard 298
Hindhead (Surrey) 178
Hingeston, F C 188
Hinton (Berks) 40, 47–8
Hinton Waldrist (Berks) 199, 312
Hippersley, H 114
Hippisley, H 213
Hissey, Mrs - 220, 221
Hissey, James 220
Hitcham (Bucks) 79, 88, 139, 199
Hitchenden *see* Hughenden
Hitchings, James 59
Hitchman, - 201
Hoare, E H 168
Hobart, - 18
Hobhouse, E 16, 114, 247, 249, 250, 252
Hockley, - 21
Hodges, - 30, 246
Hodges, James 152–3, 214
Hodgkinson, J 70
Hodgson, - 140, 297
Hodgson, F 6, 251
Hodhson, James 128
Hodson, George 58, 130, 157
Hoggeston (Bucks) 33, 92, 199–200
Hogshaw (Bucks) 200, 209
Hogston *see* Hoggeston
Holbech, C 153, 231–2
Holbeck, C 116
Holbeck, W 13
Holden, Jno 107
Hole, C 86
Holland, John Murray 279
Hollinshed, Richard Edward 232
Holloway, Miss - 140, 251, 252
Holloway, Charles 71, 277
Holmes, Edward 153, 157, 266
Holt, R 87, 166, (A) 233
Holt, T B 202
Holton (Oxon) 18, 86, 200
Holton, - 65
Holwell (Oxon) 27, 30, 91, 200

INDEX OF NAMES AND PLACES 409

Holyoake, - 244
Honneywill (Honeywell), J B 86
Hook Norton (Oxon) 10, 200, 251, 263, 291
Hooke, Alfred 321
Hooker, R 61
Hookins, P 97, 98, 117, 128, 140, 251, 330
Hooper, R H 46, 176, 256, 296
Hooper, Richard 334
Hopkin, Squire 54
Hopkins, A 312
Hopkins, J 107
Hopkins, Robert John 252–3, 296, 297
    wife of 253
Hopkins, W T 20, 236
Horan, Arthur Rikey 306–7
Horley (Oxon) 14, 92, 104, 193, 200–1, 321
Hormer Hundred 39
Horn, T 31, 33, 34, 37; *see also* Horne
Hornbuckle, Mrs and Miss 76
Horne, - 330
Horne, J 261
Horne *see also* Horn
Horner 96
Hornton (Oxon) 92, 200–1
Horsenden (Bucks) 73, 84, 93, 201
Horsley, G 231
Horspath (Oxon) 18, 201
Horton (Bucks) 79, 162, 201–2
Horton, V E 50, 163
Horwood *see* Great Horwood; Little Horwood
Horwood, E R 84
Hoskyns, Sir Hungerford 51
Hoskyns, J L 51, 110, 127, 128, 133, 232, 302
Hoste, Philip 160
Houblon, J 68
Houblon, Thomas A 68, 253
Hough, George 329
Housman, - 208
Howard, John Florey 71, 86, 179, 329
Howe, Lord - 57, 231, 253
Howes, Herbert Taylor 130, 157
Howley, Archbishop William 1, 329
Howman, A 21

Hubbard, - 98
Hubbard, Langston 129
Hubert, Henry Samuel Musgrave 114
Huddersfield (Yorks) 201
Hudson, - 45
Huggins, - 215
Hughenden (Hitchenden) (Bucks) 3, 31, 72, 77, 88, 95, 199, 202
Hughes, - 78, 90
Hughes, Miss - 245, 256
Hughes, E 12
Hughes, Frederick G 202
Hughes, H E 85
Hughes, J R 32, 37, 113, 166, 234, 309
Hughes, J W 15
Hughes, John 63, 213, 219
Hughes, Robert E 12, 83, 104
    son of 12
Hulcott (Bucks) 73, 112, 123, 202–3
Hulme, G 25
    son of 54
Hulme, Samuel Joseph 246
Hulme, T H 97
Hulme, W 25, 54, 270, 296–7
Hulton, Campbell Grey 170
Hulton, H E 274
Humfrey, Salisbury 71
Humphreys, S M 226
Hungerford (Berks) 38, 40, 63, 204–5, 252
Hunt, - 202
Hunt, Jos 83
Hunt family 231
Hunter, - 50
Hunter, W 15, 236
Huntingford, G W 154, 219
Hurd, - 106; *see also* Heard
Hurle, - 21
Hurley (Berks) 41, 58, 205, 261
Hurst (Berks) 60, 95, 131, 205–6, 261, 299
Hurst, J C 320
Hurstmonceaux (Sussex) 156
Hussey, - 49, 197, 206, 266
    nephew of 166
Hussey, Edward 157
Hussey, J A 135
Hussey, Robert 15, 132

Hutchins, G 20
Hutchinson, Charles R 255
Hutchinson, L 97

Ibstone (Bucks) 76, 178, 206
Ickford (Bucks) 31, 206, 321
Idbury (Oxon) 10, 206, 329
Iffley (Oxon) 19, 206–7
Iles, J H 338
Ilmer (Bucks) 71, 207
Image, William Thomas 312
Inkpen (Berks) 38, 41, 64, 207
Ipsden (Oxon) 21, 95, 207, 236
Ipstone (Oxon) 25
Irby, Miss - 288
Irby, Llewelyn 288
Irving, John William 134, 218, 230
Irwin, J J 33, 37, 87
Isham, Arthur 31, 74, 76, 93, 113, 309
Isleworth (G London) 210
Islip (Oxon) 7, 86, 114, 144, 207–8, 274
Itchen Stoke (Hants) 257
Iver (Bucks) 79, 208, 334
Iver Heath (Bucks) 208
Ivinghoe (Bucks) 31, 34, 37, 112, 146, 209

Jackson, J Marshall 37, 132
Jackson, W 71, 89
Jacob, - 155, 223, 288
Jacobson, - 52, 172
James, - 202
James, Charles Anderston 171
James, Edward Stanley 217, 218
    wife of 218
James, George Burder 195n
James, John 110, 196
James, Samuel B 313
James, William 52, 232
Jenkins, Blandy 211
    mother of 220
    wife of 211, 220
Jenkins, C A 154
Jenkins, John D 312
Jenkins, Owen 38, 48, 220, 221–2
Jenkins *see also* Jenkyns
Jenkinson, J H 262
Jenkyns, T 275; *see also* Jenkins
Jenner, - 166

Jennings, R M 258
Jephson, J Hilton 148, 149, 150, 312
Jephson, W 199, 312
Jerningham family 43
Jerram, - 314
Jerram, Charles J 28, 30, 31, 86
Jerram, J T 86
Jerram, S J 30, 31
Jersey, Lord 12, 228
Jeston, Henry P 152, 153
Jeudwine, W 110, 148
Jeune, Dr. 60
Johnson, - 133, 326
Johnson, C A 171, 187
Johnson, Charles Thomas 65, 187n
Jones, E 37, 132, 230
Jones, P 69
Joplen, Mrs - 100
Jordan, - 19
Jordan, John 10, 87, 171
Jordan, S W 87
Joscelyne, Henry 97, 282
Jowett, J F 211
Joy, Charles Ashfield 184
Joyce, - 34
Joyce, G 138, 139
Judge, - 16

Kaye, John, Bishop of Lincoln 1–4, 88–9
Keefe, Sarah 99
Keene, - 21
Keene, C E R 233, 255
Keep, Mrs - 100
Kelk (Kelke), W H 34, 37, 166
Kelmscott (Oxon) 28, 30, 91, 130–1, 209
Kelson, Francis 83
Kempe, A A 38, 310
Kencot (Oxon) 28, 30, 104, 130, 131, 140, 209
Kennett, - 141
Kennington (Berks) 40, 43, 209–10, 258
Kent, Charles 38
Kentucky, Bishop of 310
Kenwalch 107
Kerby, C L 24, 25, 27, 115, 116, 283
Kerr, C W J 33, 34
Kerr, M 33, 84
Kersey, - 220

INDEX OF NAMES AND PLACES 411

Kewley, Francis 298
Kewley, G R 79
Kiddington (Oxon) 10, 22, 171, 210
Kidlington (Oxon) 2, 21, 22, 90, 210, 292
Kidmore End (Oxon) 96, 210, 224, 261, 318
Killmaster, Robert 104, 269
Kimble *see* Great Kimble; Little Kimble
King, - 195, 304
King, A 36, 269
King, Edward 160, 327
King, Isaac 75, 76, 129
King, James 20
King, John G 121
King, Samuel 215
King, William Robert 103
King, William Wilson 226
Kingdon, R H 105
Kingham (Oxon) 10, 85, 153, 157, 211
Kings Sutton (Oxon) 136
Kingscote, H 208, 282
Kingsey (Bucks) 71, 75, 89, 211
Kingston (Oxon) 109, 160
Kingston Bagpuize (Berks) 211
Kingston Lisle (Berks) 39, 50, 211, 212, 275, 319
Kingston Lodge (Oxon) 109
Kinsey, W M 20
Kintbury (Berks) 38, 41, 64, 91, 110, 163, 207, 211
Kintbury Eagle Hundred 40
Kirkham 166
Kirtlington (Oxon) 7, 125, 167, 212, 283, 308
Kitcat, John 291
Kitson, Francis 44, 85
Knapp, - , daughters of 218
Knapp, Miss - 80
Knapp, Squire - 269
Knapp, C J 201
Knight, G 42, 70
Knight, R 226–7
Knights Enham (Hants) 309
Knipe, C 160
Knipe, John 89
Knoll House (Berks) 42
Knollis, Jas 57, 78, 223, 253
Knollys, W E 258

Knowl (Knoll) Hill (Berks) 41, 59, 212
The Knowle (Berks) 41
Knox, Henry 88, 90
Kyrke, Richard 66

Labouchere, - 283
Lacey Green (Bucks) 74, 213, 263
Lambe, Alice 294
Lambe, Edward 294
Lambourn (Berks) 40, 61, 213
Lambourn Hundred 40
Lambourn Woodlands (Berks) 40, 61, 96, 213
Lambwood Hill (Berks) 261
Lamphier, H 338; *see also* Lanphier
Lancaster, - 321
Landon, - 74
Lane End (Bucks) 77, 86, 87, 153, 186, 213–14
Lanfear, Charles 128
Langford (Oxon) 30, 130, 214
Langford, William 26, 306–7
Langley, Dr. 36, 237
Langley, Mrs - 237, 258
Langley, J P 237
Langley, John 53, 86, 302
Langley Marish (Bucks) 214, 327, 328
Langston (Oxon) 9
Langston (Langstone), - 10, 11, 144
Lanphier, H 261; *see also* Lamphier
Lansdowne, Lord 133, 234
Laprimdayes family 238
Lathbury (Bucks) 32, 36, 93, 329
Latimer (Bucks) 88, 215
Latimer, Edward William 32, 301
Latter, A 151, 152
Laugharne, Mary 141
Launton (Oxon) 7, 122, 215, 287
Laurence, G 143
Laurence, Robert French 122
Lavendon (Bucks) 3, 215–16
Lavington House (Sussex) xii, 165, 183, 206, 222, 226, 284, 295, 302, 305, 321
Lawrell, J 135, 187, 248, 261, 274, 305, 338
Lawrence, - 25
Lay, - 168
Layton, G D Turner 139, 291, 311
Layton, Thomas Charles Litchfield 238

Le Geyt, - 154
Lea, Thomas 14, 236, 292; *see also* Lee; Leigh
Leaborough 136
Leafield (Oxon) 9, 11, 93, 106, 216
Leak, Richard 252
Lear, - 225
Leckhampstead (Berks) 41, 65, 148–51, 216
Leckhampstead (Bucks) 31, 81, 82, 216
Lee (Bucks) 75, 216
Lee, - 329; *see also* Lea; Leigh
Lee, F 209–10, 288
Lee, Henry 107
Lee, W Blackstone 24, 285, 320
Lefevre, J S 134
Legg, W 260
Leicester (Bucks) 146–7
Leicester (Leics) 293
Leigh, - 210
Leigh, J E Austen 41, 59, 60, 131, 140, 156, 261
Leigh *see also* Lea; Lee
Leighton, - 132–3
Leighton, F K 19, 194, 219, 256
Leighton, Frank 194
Leighton Buzzard (Beds) 37
Lemann (Leman), Francis G 130, 214
Lenny, H S N 139
Lenthall, - 329
Leonard, - 170
Lepine, S 259
Letcombe Bassett (Berks) 39, 50, 217
Letcombe Regis (Berks) 39, 50, 217–18
Levett, Walter 41, 55, 56, 57, 58, 262
Levy, F B 85
Levy, T Bagley (Bayley) 308–9
Lew (Oxon) 27, 115, 218
Lewes, Thomas 30, 31, 83, 85, 139, 292
Lewis, - 27, 50
Lewis, W I 307
Lewknor (Oxon) 25, 97, 109, 218
Ley, Jacob 15, 247
Ley, John 15
Lichfield, Bishop of, 37, 106, 226, 236, 276
Lichfield, F 82, 89, 218
Liddell, - 152
Liddell, Dean - , brother of 257

Liddon, H P 113, 248
Lightfoot, - 210
Lillingston Dayrell (Bucks) 81, 218
Lillington Lovell (Bucks) 7, 218
Linchlade *see* Linslade
Lincoln (Lincs)
  Bishop 25, 71, 82, 88, 162, 166, 240, 248, 261
  Corporation 35
  Dean 123
Lindsey, Col - 121
Lindzee (Linzee), E Hood 130, 168
Linford (Bucks) 82, 269; *see also* Great Linford; Little Linford
Linger, - 193
Lingwood, - 122
Lingwood, Thomas John 223
Linslade (Linchlade) (Beds) 34, 37, 95, 112, 135, 218–19, 274, 313
Linton, Henry 249
Linton, Herbert 292
Linton, Hewett Jun 292n
Lipscombe House (Bucks) 34, 275
Little, Thomas 226, 273
Little Barford *see* Barford St John
Little Barrington (Glos) 30
Little Bourton (Oxon) 13
Little Brickhill (Bucks) 37, 92, 132
Little Casterton (Rutland) 309
Little Coxwell (Berks) 39, 46, 158, 175
Little Faringdon (Berks) 214
Little Hampden (Bucks) 73, 91, 187, 194
Little Horwood (Bucks) 82, 92, 202
Little Kimble (Bucks) 75, 91, 93, 211, 223, 267
Little Linford (Bucks) 36, 218
Little Marlow (Bucks) 77, 225, 327
Little Milton (Oxon) 18–19, 195, 229–30
Little Missenden (Bucks) 76, 231
Little Rollright (Oxon) 10, 264
Little Shefford *see* East Shefford
Little Tew (Oxon) 15, 91, 96, 293, 300, 323, 324, 325
Little Wittenham (Berks) 40, 45, 164, 275, 315
Little Woolstone (Bucks) 37, 80, 92, 320
Little Worton (Oxon) 97
Littledale, Miss - 268

Littlehales, - 80, 81, 82
Littlejohn, William Douglas 26, 291
Littlemore *see* Oxford
Littleworth (Berks) 39, 46, 47, 219
Litton, E A 244
Liverpool (Lancs) 235
Livingston, T G 128
Llandaff (Glam) 118, 120, 155
Lloyd, - 7, 104, 105, 154
Lloyd, Mrs - 142
Lloyd, Charles 31, 75, 108, 114, 132, 135, 142–3, 166, 170, 187, 200, 201, 211, 213, 223, 227, 258, 269, 286, 291
Lloyd, Emma Frances 187
Lloyd, Francis Llewellyn 104
Lloyd, H W 51, 86, 153
Lloyd, William 13, 165, 218
Lloyd-Lindsay, Col - 219
Lockinge *see* East Lockinge
Lockwood, John William 10, 85, 153, 211
Lockyer, Edmund L 118, 293
Locock, - 69
London
    Bethnal Green 286
    Bishop of xii, 119, 184, 218, 248, 261, 286
    Bloomsbury 110
    Chelsea 10
    Gresham College 74
    Haggerston 196
    Hanover Square 298
    Haverstock Hill 225
    Islington 303
    Kensington Palace 287
    Pall Mall 291
    St Mary Le Strand 226
    St Mary Marylebone 156
    Southwark, St Jude 156
    Waterworks 21
    Westminster 248, 261, 277
    Whitechapel 286
    see also Barnet; Isleworth; Richmond; Uxbridge
Long, James 89
    daughter of 81
Long Combe (Oxon) 22, 156
Long Crendon (Bucks) 71, 84, 88–9, 112, 159

Long Wittenham (Berks) 40, 45, 164, 315
Longcot (Berks) 40, 46, 219
Longford, (Langford?) W 306
Longlimbs, J E 208
Longmore, Philip A 198
Longworth (Berks) 38, 40, 48, 220–2, 257
Lord, - 47
Lott, Frederick Edwin (G) 106, 115
Lott, S 216
Loudwater (Bucks) 77, 86, 87, 91, 92, 222
Loughton (Bucks) 32, 36, 80, 81, 93, 222, 269
Lousley, Joseph 185
Loveday, - 231–2
Loveday, T 40, 67, 68, 69, 70, 207
Lovekin, A P 301
Lovell, - 175
Lovett (Lovet), Capt - 274
Lovett (Lovet), Miss - 34
Lovett (Lovet), Squire - 275
Lovett (Lovet), Robert 274
Lowe, John 6, 90, 106, 138, 307
Lower Heyford (Oxon) 83, 85, 109, 198
Lower Worton (Oxon) 15
Lowndes, - 217
Lowndes, Miss - 296
Lowndes, Mrs - 146
Lowndes, Charles 34, 36, 73, 84, 194
Lowndes, Charles Selby 159
Lowndes, G 147
Lowndes, Thomas 36, 159
Lowndes, V T Selby 233
Lowndes, W 217, 283
Lowndes, W Selby 159
Lowndes, William 147n
Lowry, Charles 308
Lowry, John 32
Lucas, - 313
Luce, E J 105
Luce, E F 105
Ludgershall (Bucks) 32, 35, 222
Ludlow, T B 272, 273
Lupton, James 27, 30, 116, 124
Lush, Alfred 271
Lush, Vicesimus 46, 271
Lushington, - 64
Luxmoore, - 213
Lyford (Berks) 39, 40, 44, 48, 92, 222

Lyminster (Leominster) (Sussex) 226
Lyneham (Oxon) 11, 329
Lyttelton, Lady - 110
Lyttledale, Gertrude Harriet 313

Maberton, Sir Pulteney 22
Macbride, Dr. 250
Macclesfield, Lord 218, 257, 283, 306
McCreight, W W 87, 314
Macdonald, Jacob 70, 127, 128
Macdonald, James 188
MacDougall, - 16, 51
MacDougall, Wilson V 181
Macfarlane, - 20
Macfarlane, W C 165
Mackarness, J 248
Mackonochie, A H 304
Macnamara, - 36
Macray, - 247
Madden, W H 86
Magee, W C 248
Maiden Earley (Berks) 41, 42, 60
Maidenhead (Berks) 41, 57, 131, 140, 157, 223, 259
Maids Moreton (Bucks) 81, 82, 84, 89, 99, 179, 216, 218, 223, 284
Maine, L G 113
Maitland, E Fuller (T Fuller) and wife 223
Majendie, - 213, 286
Majendie, H 275–6, 281
Majendie, Henry (W) 40, 42, 61, 63, 66, 68, 90, 110, 121, 130, 275–76, 281
Major, Simon Edwin 119
Malcolm, Archibald 167
Malcolm, Gilbert 22
Mallam, - 238
Mallard, Charles E 5
Manchester 8
Manclarke, R P 129
Mangin, Samuel Waring 164, 196
Manley, Lord and Lady de 214
Mapledurham (Oxon) 20, 41, 187, 224, 261
Marah, - 153
March, - 33
March, Lord - 312
Marcham (Berks) 40, 44, 97, 220, 224
Mardon, - 15

Marlborough, Duke and Duchess 23, 124, 125, 129, 188, 301, 302, 328
Marlow (Bucks) 58, 79, 213; *see also* Great Marlow; Little Marlow
Marlston (Berks) 41, 66, 90, 91, 138
Marriott, C 247
Marriott, J 130
Marsden, J B 31, 76, 87
Marsh (Bucks) 91
Marsh, - 61
Marsh, E G 43
Marsh, John 297
Marsh Baldon (Oxon) 16, 114
Marsh Gibbon (Bucks) 31, 82, 154, 225–6, 273
Marshall, - 171
Marshall, E 15, 163, 247
Marshall, George 257
Marshall, James 117
Marshall, Junior 85
Marshall, S F 177
Marshall, W J 183
Marshall's charity 96
Marsham, - 78
Marsham, C 8, 35, 83, 122, 142, 282
Marsham, C D B 170
Marston (Oxon) 170, 226
Marsworth (Bucks) 34, 37, 146, 227
Marten, - 35; *see also* Martin; Martyn
Marter, R 68
Marter, R and family 302
Martin, H 270; *see also* Marten; Martyn
Martyn, Claude 32, 169, 183
Martyn, T 222
Martyn *see also* Marten; Martin
Mason, J 291
Master, William 138
Matson, Robert 98
Matthews, - 7, 37, 260
Matthews, Andrew (Jun) 8, 83, 85
Matthews, Henry 83
Mattews, Joseph 146
Maul, John Compton 218
Maunder, - 31
Maurice, Peter 328
Mavor, John 18, 58
Mawgan, - 237
May, James T 126

INDEX OF NAMES AND PLACES 415

May St Quentin 67
Mayne, James 35
Mayne, L G 338
Maynooth, - 59
Mayo, - 194
Mayo, R 194
Mayor, Charles 307
Meade, John 8, 179, 235
Meaken, - 208
Meakin, J A D 63, 276
Medd, P G 338
Medley, Edward 111
Medmenham (Bucks) 77, 87, 227
Meech, J W 34, 84, 91
Meeres, H 73, 184
Menheniot (Cornwall) 22
Menteath, G W Stuart 183
Mentmore (Bucks) 34, 37, 112, 146, 227
Menzies, F 25, 76, 103
Meredith, C 83
Meredith, J 15
Meredith, Richard E 70, 128, 185
Mereweather, - 53
Merley, - 36
Merry, W 183
Merrymouth, - 10
Merton (Oxon) 7, 227
Messing (Essex) 209, 210
Metcalfe, F 248
Mexborough, Lord 51
Michel, - , neice of 69
Michell, - 205
Michell, Richard 232
Michell, T P 267
Mickletone, Rowland 83
Middle Claydon (Bucks) 32, 153
Middleton Stoney (Oxon) 7, 8, 125, 228
Midgham (Berks) 41, 66, 90, 228, 294–5, 300
Midhurst (Sussex) 200
Milcombe (Oxon) 12, 92, 128–9, 140, 228, 251, 324, 325
Mildmay, Sir H 45
Milford, Robert Newman 133
Millais, - 119
Miller, Aug J 312
Miller, Henry 107
Miller, Thomas 136
Miller, W S 14, 272, 310
Milliar, F 109
Millman, R 338; *see also* Milman
Mills, - 109
Mills, W 86, 314
Mills, William 48
Milman, R 70, 181, 187, 212, 225, 261, 338
Milman, Robert 213
Milman *see also* Millman
Milner, John Henry 295
Milton (Berks) 40, 45, 96, 228; *see also* Great Milton (Oxon); Little Milton (Oxon)
Milton, W 225, 327
Milton in Adderbury (Oxon) 97, 98, 117, 323, 325, 330
Milton Keynes (Bucks) 37, 92, 230, 232
Milton-under-Wychwood (Oxon) 178, 228, 329
Minster Lovell (Oxon) 27, 29, 30, 86, 230, 314
Missenden (Bucks) *see* Great Missenden; Little Missenden
Mixbury (Oxon) 8, 178, 231, 299
Moberley, H C 206
Mollington (Oxon) 13, 153, 159, 207, 231–2, 324, 325, 330
Molloy, Edward 258
Mongewell (Oxon) 20, 232
Monins, - 34
Monk, J B 235
Monkhouse, John 305
Monks Risborough (Bucks) 25, 76, 263
Monro, - 164
Monro, H 264
Monro, R 109
Monsell, J S B 192
Montagu, G 290
Montagu family 22
Moody, N 243, 244
Moody, W 71, 75
Moor, John 54
Moore, - 223, 237, 307
Moore, Mrs - 138
Moore, D 248, 261, 338
Moore, Edward 21, 310
Moore, Edward George 67, 85, 207

Moore, Joseph 45, 46, 47, 137
Moore, William Joseph Bramley 331
Moorehouse, J 338
Morant, Henry J 207
Morell, - 10
Morell, B 51–2
Morell *see* Morrell
Moreton, - 231
Moreton Hundred 39, 51
Morgan, - 25
Morgan, W 202
Morland, - 67, 72, 151, 207
Morland, Benjamin 50
Morley, G 235
Morrall, Cyrus 235
Morrell, - 221
Morrell, F 245
Morrell, G K 232
Morrell, James 162
Morrell, Mary 232
Morrell, R 92
Morrell, T B 14, 197, 198 , 271, 274
Morrell family 161, 178
Morres, Thomas 60, 315
Morrice, - 37
Morris, A J 230
Morrison, A W 315
Morrison, Bertie W 199
Morriss, Peter 209
Mortimer (Berks) 42
Mortimer, - 37
Mortimer, T G 97
Moullin, G A 318–19
Moulsey, - 201
Moulsford (Moulsey) (Berks) 39, 51, 182, 232, 261
Moulsoe (Bucks) 35, 37, 84, 92, 232
Moultrie, Gerard 302
Mount, - 65, 66, 295, 306
Mount, C 291
Mount, William 100
Mount Cashel, Lord 67
Mozley, - 178
Munn, H 328
Murray, D Rodney 68, 91, 120–1
Murray, Fred 210
Murray, George William 271
Murray, John 321, 323

Murray, Scott 77
Murray, T 200
Mursley (Bucks) 31, 33–4, 37, 92, 166, 233
Musgrave, Sir J 25
Musgrave, Sir W 25, 151–2

Nalder, Miss - 236
Napier, A H 21, 291
Nash (Bucks) 91, 119, 233, 295
Nash, Z 90, 214, 328
Neale, - 58, 197; *see also* Niel
Neate, Arthur 26, 29, 30, 31, 83, 85, 104, 130, 131, 269
Neithrop (Oxon) 116, 117, 323, 325
Nelson, Lord - 315
Nelson, B 231
Nelson, J 50
Nelson, Jno 38, 39, 49
Nepean, Evan Yorke 183, 295
Nether Winchendon (Bucks) 72, 311
Nether Worton (Oxon) 293, 321, 325
Nettlebed (Oxon) 19, 20, 86, 95, 233, 236, 255, 302
Nettleden (Bucks) 34, 38, 112, 233, 255
New Bradwell (Bucks) 279, 317
New Windsor (Berks) 41, 59, 261, 312
New Wolverton (Bucks) 36, 135, 316
New Zealand, Bishop of 171
Newbottle (Northants) 170
Newbury (Berks)
　clergy 224, 233–4, 327
　Deanery 40–1, 61–8
　Donnington Square 329
　draper 102
　private memoranda 90, 91
　Wilberforce at 184, 233–4, 300
Newdigate, A 111
Newington (Oxon) 19, 121, 122, 234
Newman, John Henry ix, 116
Newnham Courtney *see* Nuneham Courtenay
Newnham Murren (Berks) 21, 234, 236
Newport (Mon) 118
Newport Pagnell (Bucks) 32, 35, 36, 89, 93, 135, 193, 218, 230, 235, 285
Newton Blossomville (Bucks) 32, 36, 93, 235

Newton Longville (Bucks) 32, 37, 92, 166, 234
Newton Purcell (Oxon) 8, 90, 179, 235
Newton Underwood (Bucks) 36
Nicholson, M A 189, 192, 193
Nicholson, William 62, 307
Niel, 'Butcher' 226; *see also* Neale
Nightingale, Miss - 245
Nind, Philip Henry 21, 275
Nisbett, J M 153
Nisbett, J W 135
Niton (IOW) 309
Niven, James 290
Nixson, - 165, 246, 315
Noble, W 256
Noel, A 159, 160, 257
Noke (Oxon) 19, 170, 235
Norice, Thomas 185; *see also* Norris
Norman, E 315
Norris, - 234
Norris, Mrs - 289
Norris, Annie 290
Norris, H 322
Norris, James 185
Norris, John Thomas 288, 289
Norris, Mary Elizabeth 289
Norris, Naomi 185
Norris, W Foxley 137
Norris *see also* Norice
North, - 34
North, Col - 14, 195, 322
North, John North Ouvry 227
North, Lady Susan 14, 18
North Aston (Oxon) 2, 21, 22, 90, 108–9, 273
North Crawley (Bucks) 36, 84, 93, 148, 159, 193
North End (Bucks) 91, 298
North Hinksey (Oxon) 39, 43, 162, 199
North Leigh (Oxon) 87, 235, 314
North Marston (Bucks) 32, 72, 78, 226–7
North Moreton (Berks) 39, 52, 232, 306
North Newington (Oxon) 12, 323, 324
North Stoke (Oxon) 21, 92, 236
Northmoor (Oxon) 29, 30, 167, 236, 277
Nott, - 16
Nottley, William George 122, 213

Nourse, A H 155, 277
Nucella, Thomas 22, 171, 181
Nuffield (Oxon) 20, 160, 233, 236
Nuneham Courtenay (Oxon) 19, 92, 162, 164, 234
Nuneham Minor (Oxon) 92
Nunn, - 27
Nutting, G H 145

Oakley (Bucks) 84, 152, 237
Oakley (Oakeley), - 2, 23
Oare (Berks) 41, 65, 148–9, 237
O'Brien, - 154
Ock Hundred 39
Odcombe (Som) 223
Oddington (Oxon) 8, 144, 237
Ogle, Octavius 240
Old Windsor (Berks) 41, 59, 312
Old Wolverton (Bucks) 141
Old Woodstock (Oxon) 320
Oldfield, - 224
Oldham, J O 230n
Olney (Bucks) 36, 93, 135, 154, 170, 215, 235, 237, 258
Onslow, T G 141
Oram, - 321
Ormerod, - 13, 223
Ormerod, A 77
Ormond, John 211, 223
Oughton, Mrs - 100
Ousley, Sir F 118
Ouvry, Peter 34, 313
Over Norton (Oxon) 152
Over Worton (Oxon) 321, 325
Overstone, - 108, 134, 304
Overy, - 298
Oving (Bucks) 32, 72, 93, 112, 237–8
Owen, - 8
Owen, Brisco 263
Owen, Charlotte 281
Owen, E 31, 74, 75
Owen, E Jun 186, 217, 223
Owen, L 105
Oxenham, J M 321
Oxford (Oxon)
    Boatmen's Chapel 16
    Bodleian Library xii, xiv
    Carfax 22, 174, 246

Oxford (Oxon) (cont.)
  colleges: All Souls 25, 43, 49, 113,
    248, 261, 301, 328, 338; Balliol
    247; Brasenose 10, 13, 42, 66n,
    83, 85, 160, 322; Christ Church
    11, 17, 22, 26, 27, 60, 64, 65, 67,
    108, 117, 124, 134, 165, 238, 241,
    246, 247, 249, 257, 272, 276, 287,
    321, 322; Corpus Christi 18, 49,
    50; Exeter 19, 106, 227, 247, 249;
    Jesus 20, 44, 48, 58, 74, 84, 85,
    108, 140; Lincoln 15, 16, 18, 22,
    33, 83; Magdalen 13, 17, 18, 44,
    51, 52, 56n, 67, 78, 83, 84, 85,
    105, 244; Merton 15, 16, 25, 142,
    169, 242, 320; New College 6, 11,
    13, 18, 19, 22, 24, 32, 33, 34, 80,
    83, 84, 85, 91; Oriel 23, 46, 55,
    63, 300; Pembroke 60, 69, 71, 83,
    155–6; The Queen's 26, 50, 55,
    83, 84, 85, 134, 248, 308, 309; St
    Edmund Hall 7; St John's 29, 47,
    53, 54, 83, 84, 85, 212; St Mary
    Hall 44; Trinity 5, 17, 18, 43, 58,
    322; Wadham 17, 153; Worcester
    33, 83, 92, 267
  County Prison 251
  Earl of 68n
  parishes: All Saints 15, 238–9, 240;
    Binsey 15, 123, 339; Holy Trinity
    15, 251; Holywell/St Cross 2, 16,
    239, 240–3; Littlemore 16, 95,
    206, 219, 339; St Aldate 15, 238;
    St Clement 15, 243–4; St Ebbe 15,
    244–5; St George 247; St Giles
    15, 245, 248, 271; St John Baptist
    15, 245–6; St Martin 15, 86, 246;
    St Mary Magdalen 15, 96, 247;
    St Mary the Virgin 15, 247–8; St
    Michael 16, 96, 240, 248; St Paul
    16, 248–9; St Peter in the East
    16, 249; St Peter le Bailey 16,
    249–50; St Thomas 16, 250, 339;
    Summertown 15, 125, 251

Padbury (Bucks) 32, 82, 154, 252
Paddon, H 87, 187, 212, 325–7
Padworth (Berks) 41, 55, 252

Pakenham, A 118
Paley, - 246
Palin, Edward 251
Palmer, - 179, 304
Palmer, G H 198
Palmer, Henry 79, 88, 165
Palmer, Hor C 165
Palmer, Richard 38, 54, 205, 206, 231,
  256, 330
Palmer, W J 6, 8
Palmerston, Lord xi, xii, 182
Pangbourne (Berks) 41, 54, 252–3, 261
Pannall (Yorks) 207
Parker, - 207, 236
Parker, Edward (Edwin) James 60
Parker, Edwin 303
Parker, George 264
Parker, J H 210
Parker, Michael 226
Parr, T 159
Parry, Frederick R 141
Parsons, - 17
Parsons, Andrew Everard 53
Parsons, H 266
Parsons, John 207
Partington, - 138, 330
Partridge, C F 148, 263
Partridge, Mrs - 201, 207
Partridge, W E 71, 73, 84, 201, 207
Passand, J H 23, 83, 270
Paterson, - 11
Patterson, J L 16
Paul, Charles K 171
Paulet, - 257
Paxton, - 20, 123, 332
Payne, E 13, 117, 163, 272, 289, 292
  sister of 303
Payne, William 259
Pearce see also Pearse; Peers
Pears, E W 181
Pearse, A H 168
Pearse, G W 113, 221, 272, 303
Pearse, Vincent 193, 200
Pearse, W 13, 83, 193
Pearse see also Pearce; Peers
Pearson, - 63, 143, 330
Pearson, Mrs - 59
Pearson, C 253

Pearson, Hugh 60, 261, 274, 330
Pearson, Pavitt 30
Pearson *see also* Penson
Pease, George Clifford 204–5
Peasemore (Berks) 40, 68, 253
Pechell, Lady Caroline 19
Pechell, H P 19, 124
Peel, - 306
Peel, Charles S 264
Peel, Edmund 115, 305
Peel, Sir Robert xvi, 46
Peers, - 17
Peers, Mrs - 293
Peers, J 77, 86, 213
Peers, J W 26, 86, 291, 293
Peers *see also* Pearce; Pearse
Pegus, Mrs - , sister of 208
Pegus, T 76
Pelham, Bishop of Lincoln 3
Pember, - 105
Pember, Frederick 217
Penn (Bucks) 3, 78, 88, 95, 119, 253, 301
Penn Street (Bucks) 231, 253–4
Penniston, Miss - 157
Penny, Edward 5
Pennyfather, W 72, 87
Penrose, - 63
Penson, - 16
Penson, John Pavitt , 28, 30, 86, 153
Penson, Pavitt 27, 28, 30, 116, 134
Penson *see also* Pearson
Peppard (Oxon) 263
Pepper, T Staples 231
Perceval, Mrs - 316
Perceval, Arthur 80
Perceval, Charles G 80, 141, 296
Perkins, William 6, 7, 35, 179, 181
Perry, - 143, 212
Petch, George 237
Peterborough (Cambs) 179
Peyton, Sir H 282
Phelps, W W 262
Phillimore, - 9, 11, 21, 61, 171
Phillimore, Amy 258
Phillimore, G 32, 36, 37, 280
Phillimore, George and wife 258
Phillimore, J 202
Phillimore, R 174, 205, 274

Phillipps, J 18, 162
Phillips, Herbert J 267
Phillips, Richard 100
Phipps, - 208, 330
Pickard, J A 330
Pickering, - 311
Pickford, J 178
Piddington (Oxon) 8, 122, 254–5
Pierpont, E G 179
Piggott, - 145
Pigott, - 35, 80, 91
Pigott, Jno David 35
Pigott, John 31, 72, 76, 77, 78, 93, 183
Pigott, Randolph Henry 183
Pigott, W 310
Pigou, Francis 283
Pinder, - 271
Pinder, North 264
Pinfold, Fanny 303
Pinnegar, - 267
Pinwell, W O 14, 200, 201
Pishill (Oxon) 20, 233, 255, 291
Pitchcott (Bucks) 32, 72, 93, 256
Pitstone (Pightelsthorne) (Bucks) 34, 38, 146, 233, 255, 256
Plummer, - 98
Plumptre, - 4, 225
Plumptre, William A 172
Pollen, J H 16
Polson, - 47
Poole, Miss - 9
Pooley, James 187, 277
Popham, - 62, 256
Porter, C F 124, 159, 273
Porter, R 304
Porter, R Ibbetson 275
Portsmouth (Hants) 105, 302
Pott, Alfred 106, 114, 160, 176, 194, 197
Potter, Coterill 128
Powell, - 198
Powell, Harriaut 185
Powell, Harriot 185
Powell, James 185
Powell, Kezia 185
Powell, Sarah 186
Powell, T E 124
Powell, Thomas 185
Powell, W C Bolton 86

Powell, William 186
Power, John 301
Powys, - 13, 65, 224
Powys, C 187
Powys, Francis Arthur 251
Powys, R T 20, 182
Powys, T A 77
Powys, William 262
Poyntz, - 104
Prater, Thomas 7, 194
Prebend End Summerfield (Bucks) 136
Prentice, Henry 139
Preston, A M 154
Preston Bissett (Bucks) 35, 78, 82, 256
Prestwich 295
Prestwood (Bucks) 91, 95, 187, 253, 256
Pretyman, - 72
Pretyman, F 83
Pretyman, G 142
Pretyman, R 7, 8, 228
Prevost, Sir G 113, 118, 168, 224, 261, 297, 339
Price, - 24, 25, 32, 66, 72, 122
Price, A 6n
Price, Aubrey 6
Price, Mrs Barrington 46
Price, Edmund 176
Price, J M 113, 338
Price, James Mansel 161, 184, 338
Price, Robert 46, 47
Price, Robert Morgan 335
Price, W H 67, 90, 176, 178
Price, W W 176, 178, 274
Prichard, R 20
Prince, - 233, 255
Princes Risborough (Bucks) 74, 78, 84, 93, 211, 263
Pring, J 18, 196
Priorspark, - 69
Pritchard, H 58
Proctor, - 255
Proctor, Miss - 255
Prosser, James 26, 86, 291, 293
Prout, - 123
Punter, - 273
Purdue, G 143
Purley (Purleigh) (Berks) 41, 54, 256, 261

Purrier, Henry S 47
Pusey (Berks) 40, 48, 256–7
Pusey, E B 2, 3n, 19, 248
Pusey, Miss - 256
Pusey, W 18, 295
Pyncombe's charity 96
Pyrton (Oxon) 25, 257

Quainton (Bucks) 32, 72, 93, 112, 257, 335
Quarrendon (Bucks) 123, 257
Quartley, H J 80, 84
Quartley, H R 36, 80, 84, 315–16
Quartley, R 279

Radclive (Bucks) 35, 79, 82, 257
Radford, - 35
Radley (Berks) 40, 44, 164, 258, 330, 339
Radnage (Bucks) 78, 258, 327
Radnor, Lord 155, 158, 271
Radstone (Northants) 80
Radway (Warks) 107
Raikes, R J 258
Rainby, John H 152
Raine, William 29–30, 31, 291, 311
Rains, Richard Edward 295
Ramsay family 274
Ramsden (Oxon) 11, 257, 258, 265, 270, 311, 335
Ramsgate (Kent) 4, 5
Randall, Mrs - 266
Randall, James 60, 61, 113, 116, 123, 131, 140, 153, 187, 205, 248, 261, 264, 266, 273, 285, 338
Randall, K 339
Randall, Leslie 234, 304, 338
Randolph, Herbert 44, 224
Randolph, John 292
Randolph, Leveson 181, 268
Ranelagh, Lord 313
Ratcliffe (Radcliffe), John 44
Ravenstone (Bucks) 36, 93, 258
Rawlings, William 6, 179, 180
Rawlins, T S F 163
Rawlinson, - 7
Rawnsley, R D B 270
Rawson, William 126

Raymond family 211
Read, W T 201
Reade, - (really Reed G V) 35, 79, 81
Reade, Compton 139
Reade, Eleanor 78
Reade, Sir John 10, 68, 120
Reade, Joseph Bancroft 31, 74, 170, 283–4
Reading (Berks)
  brewer 47, 313
  chapels 259, 260
  churches: All Saints 262; St Giles 41, 54, 86, 258–9, 261; St John 41, 54, 86, 259–60, 303; St Lawrence 41, 53, 260; St Mary 41, 86, 261, 262; St Mary Chapel 41, 54, 259, 262; Trinity 41, 262, 303
  confirmation 130
  Deanery 41–2, 53–61
  game list 38
  gaol 66, 263, 285
  Mission 261
  Royal Berkshire Hospital 101, 103
  Wilberforce at 234
  see also Caversham
Reddell, E 125
Rede, Miss - 331
Redesdale, Lord 29, 92, 291, 311
Redhead, - 227
Redifer, Alfred 113, 257, 335
Redwood, Isaac 185
Reed, G V 297
Rees, George Samuel 306
Remenham (Berks) 41, 58, 263
Rendall, H 264
Rew, Chas 83, 85
Reynardson, - 309
Reynolds, - 326
Reynolds, H 84, 264
Reynolds, O 88
Reyroux, F 21
Rhodes, H C 48
Rhyl (Denbigh) 275
Riadore, James Evans 289
Ricardo, - 22
Ricardo, Mrs - 210
Ricardo, Squire - 210
Rice, Miss - 292
Rice, H 80
Rice, Richard 46, 169
Rice, T Howard 288–9, 325–6
Rich, - 38, 73
Rich, H 193
Richards, - 21, 22, 331, 333
Richardson, - 298
Richardson, W E 218–19
Richings (Bucks) 208
Richings, Alfred Cornelius 196
Richmond (G London) 238
Rickards, Miss - 130
Riddell, J 261
Ridley, - 261–2
Ridley, Ella Frances 187
Ridley, W B 187 (probably W H)
Ridley, W H 133, 178, 186–7, 298
Rigaud, - 244
Riggs (Rigges), G 6, 144
Ripon (Yorks) 230
Ripon, Mrs - 233
Riseholme (Lincs), letters from 1, 8
Risley, J H 80–1, 83, 89, 99, 187, 296
Risley, W 15, 85, 97, 117
Risley, William Cotton 80, 83, 139, 163, 210
Ritwell, W 86
Rivington, L 338
Rixon, - 298
Robarts, A 320
Roberts, - 57, 98, 225
  sister of 57
Roberts, Arthur 118
Roberts, C L 308
Roberts, Horace 119, 168
Roberts, J Lindfield 223
Roberts, R 33, 88, 280
Robertson, George S 197, 255
Robeson, Hemming 131
Robey, - 151
Robinson, - 220, 255
Robinson, F 23, 284
Robinson, J E 65, 148, 149, 150–1
  wife of 150
Robinson, John 130
Robson, H 252
Roby, - 197
Rochester (Kent) 74, 140, 161, 166, 235, 253, 295, 339

Rockbourne (Hants) 271
Roe, - 143
Rogers, I 196
Rogers, J 157
Rogers, Josiah 36, 195, 279
Roke (Oxon) 122
Rolfe (Rolf), George Crabbe (Crabb) 28, 30, 186, 314
Rollright *see* Great Rollright; Little Rollright
Romaine, - 32
Romanis, William 261, 262
Romsey (Hants) 223
Roper, T H 171
Rose, F 37, 80, 184, 320
Rose, Sir G 296
Rose, W 326
Rosebery, Lord 45
Ross, George Gould 113, 119, 238, 256
Ross, H 298
Ross, John Lockhart 267
Rotherham (Yorks) 240
Rotherfield Greys (Oxon) 20, 95, 264
Rotherfield Peppard (Oxon) 20, 264
Rothschild, Baroness - 227
Rothschild, Sir Anthony 138, 186
Rothschild, Baron Lionel Nathan 186, 202, 227
Roundell, H D 6
Roundell, Miss - 179
Roundell, Henry 136, 137
Rousby, - 158
Rousham (Oxon) 23, 34, 38, 87, 109, 188, 198, 199, 264
Routh, John William 56, 297
Rowden, - 25, 65
Rowland, J 259
Rowton, Rupert 75, 76
Royce, David 17
Ruck-Keene, Charles Edmund 291
Rudd, Leonard H 60, 264, 299
Rugby (Warks) 234
Ruscombe (Berks) 41, 42, 60, 264
Rush, John 194
Rushton, Jn 10, 291
Rushton, John Richard 200
Russell, - 256
Russell, Lady Frankland 170

Russell, Sir R Frankland 74
Russell, R N 31, 80, 81, 119, 137, 279
Russell, Samuel Henry 144
  sister of 144
Russell, Thomas 201
Russell, Lord Wriothesley 87, 146, 162
Ryde (IOW) 301
Ryder, Bishop 48
Ryman, - 251

Sabine, J E 82, 256
Sabine, J E jun 35, 82, 256
St Bees (Cumb) 80
St Davids (Pemb) 152
St John, Edward 38, 57, 118, 178
St John, G W 124, 125, 328
St John, Henry 38, 57
St John, J 38
St John family 57
St Lawrence (Kent) 4
St Leonards (Bucks) 186
Salford (Oxon) 10, 11, 265
Salisbury (Wilts) 49, 56, 59, 63, 64, 70, 130, 176, 186, 188, 196, 301, 319
Salkeld, C E 258
Salmon, H T 289
Salter, Edward 149
Salter, F 198
Samuel, John 10, 84, 85, 199
Samuel, T (probably J) 84
Sanders, - 48, 139
Sanders, Harrington S 128
Sanders, W S 97, 98, 328
Sandford-on-Thames (Oxon) 19, 23, 85, 97, 118, 171, 206, 265–6, 293, 321, 339
Sandhurst (Berks) 42, 61, 261, 266
Sandwith, H 186, 217
Sankey, R 314
Sankey, William Thompson 113, 286, 335
Sanson, John 251
Sapcote (Leics) 53
Sargent, H W 245, 246
Sarsden (Oxon) 11, 85, 153, 266
Saulez, T 183
Saunders, - 223, 283
Saunders, G 12
Saunderstead, - 292

Saunderton (Bucks) 78, 90, 267
Savory, Edmund 123
Sawyer, - 55, 57, 271
Sawyer, Charles 140
Sawyer, Duncombe Herbert 187
Sawyer, G 219, 258, 288
Sawyer, William George 229, 304
Saye, Lord 134
Scarletts (Berks) 41, 59
Scher[], - 36
Schierz, - 86
Sclater, W 319
Scobell, E 78, 88, 298
Scobell, G R 285
Scoones, - 214
Scott, - 90
Scott, E D 84
Scott, F 26
Scott, Gilbert 103, 237, 250, 270, 381
Scott, W A 125, 185, 328
Scratchley, B 53
Scurr, R W 33, 36, 81, 269
Scurr, Mrs - 269
Scurr, T (really R W) 98
Seagrave, - , daughter of 118
Searle, - 237
Seckham, - 188
Secretan, C F 338
Sedgwick, Mrs - 230
Seer Green (Bucks) 95, 267
Segrave, - 24
Selborne (Hants) 19
Selby, Bulwith 86
Selwyn, Edward John 335
Send (Hants) 286
Sendall, Simon 157
Serle, - 8; *see also* Searle
Sevenhampton (Glos) 56n
Sewell, - 25
Sewell, Mrs - 131
Sewell, Arthur 258
Seymour, Misses 61
Seymour, Sir J 14, 210
Seymour, Neville 327
Shabbington (Bucks) 72, 93, 267
Shadwell, Julius 210
Shaftesbury, Lord xi
Shakespeare, - 213

Shalbourne (Wilts) 40, 64, 86, 205, 267
Shalford (Surrey) 260
Shallington 50
Shalstone (Bucks) 80, 82, 122, 268, 298
Shardeloes (Bucks) 105
Sharpe, - 245
Sharpe, John 128
Sharpe, L A 24, 292
Shaugh (Devon) 193n
Shaw (Berks) 40, 42, 63, 268
Shaw, John 31, 140, 177, 282–3
Sheard, - 44, 51
Shedden, E 193
Shedden, William George 193
Shefford *see* Great Shefford; East Shefford
Sheldon, R W 86
Shellingford (Berks) 40, 268; *see also* Shillingford
Shelswell (Oxon) 8, 90, 179, 198, 235, 269
Shelswell House (Oxon) 269
Shenington (Oxon) 4, 83, 85
Shenley (Bucks) 36, 80, 81, 93, 135, 222, 269
Shephard, - 18
Shephard, J L 280
Sheppard, - 119
Sheppard, Tim T 81
Sheppard, Walter 70
Sherfield (Hants) 145
Sherington (Bucks) 36, 93, 269, 291, 299
Shewen, - 215
Shiffner family 21
Shifford (Oxon) 27, 30, 115, 269
Shillingford (Berks) 48; *see also* Shellingford
Shilton (Oxon) 29, 31, 104, 130, 269
Shinfield (Berks) 42, 91, 105, 165, 178, 183, 270, 273, 291
Shiplake (Oxon) 19, 21, 91, 270
Shippon (Berks) 97
Shipton on Cherwell (Oxon) 23, 83, 270
Shipton under Wychwood (Oxon) 9, 11, 257, 270, 275, 329
Shipton Court 68
Shipton Estate 216
Shirburn (Oxon) 25, 270
Shirley, - 33

Short, - 43
Shorthampton (Oxon) 9, 143–4, 271
Shottesbrooke (Berks) 41, 58, 90, 271
Shottoner, Charles 85
Showell (Oxon) 271, 291
Shower, - 192
Shrewsbury, Lord 10, 56
Shrivenham (Berks) 39, 40, 46, 219, 271
Shuldam, Naunton 271
Shurlock, J R 7, 198
Shute, - 24
Shute, H 229, 338
Shutford (Oxon) 13, 272, 289, 290, 324, 325
Shuttleworth, Bishop of Chichester 37, 326
Sibford Gower (Oxon) 14, 272, 324
Sibtoft 10
Sicklemore, - 4
Sidebotham, - 224
Silver, - 9, 236
    nephew of 10
Silvester, - 80
Simcox, Henry T 312
Simmonds family 199
Simmons, Thomas 38
Simonds, St J Jn 38
Simpson (Bucks) 37, 84, 92, 272, 285
Sinclair, - 227
Skinner, J S 338
Skinner, James 338
Skirmetts (Bucks) 187
Skrine, W H 287
Slade, James 230
Slapton (Bucks) 34, 38, 146, 272–3, 311
Slather (Berks) 176–7
Slatter, - 7, 207
Slatter, J 266, 287
Slatter, W 43
Slight, - 18
Slocock, Samuel 42, 63, 65, 178
Sloper, George 64, 318
Sloper, John 38, 64
Slough (Bucks) 84, 273
Small, H A 35, 154, 195
Smith, - 17, 37, 73, 80, 105, 182, 335
Smith, Miss - 274, 286
Smith, Mrs - 286

Smith, C 61
Smith, C B 195
Smith, E L 35, 79, 81, 87, 148, 256
Smith, Goldwin 283
Smith, H 80, 85
Smith, John 194
Smith, Joseph 264
Smith, Mary 119
Smith, Payne 71
Smith, R 252
Smith, Samuel Mountjoy 194, 194n
Smith, W 84
Smyth, William 36, 37
Smythe, Fish 250
Sneyd, - 219
Somerton (Oxon) 8, 108, 109, 167, 179, 273–4, 275
Sonning (Berks) 38, 60, 261, 267, 274, 330
Sonning Eye (Berks) 274
Soper, - 102
Soper, Mrs - 100
Sotheby, - 138
Sotwell (Berks) 39, 53, 274, 302
Soulbury (Bucks) 34, 37, 38, 274–5
Souldern (Oxon) 8, 275
South Banbury (Oxon) 323, 324, 325
South Hinksey (Oxon) 39, 43, 199
South Leigh (Oxon) 22, 167, 275, 279
South Moreton (Berks) 39, 52, 232
South Newington (Oxon) 14, 128, 129, 234, 293, 311, 323
South Stoke (Oxon) 20, 21, 92, 95, 182, 261, 275, 315
South Weston (Oxon) 26, 308
Southcot (Beds) 274
Southey, - 309
Sparsholt (Berks) 38, 39, 49, 212, 275
Sparsholt House (Berks) 39, 49
Speck, - 36
Speen (Berks) 40, 63, 66, 204, 275–6, 281
Speenhamland (Berks) 40, 63, 276
Speke, - 36
Spelsbury (Oxon) 11, 276
Spencer, Bishop 283
Spencer, Lord - 110, 279
Spencer, Charles Frederick Octavius 162
Spencer, Charles Vere 26

Spencer, L 218
Spraggett, W 207
Spring, - 125
Spring, - , widow of 210
Springett, W J 86
Springs, - 71
Spurgeon, - 268
Spurrell, Benjamin 15, 166
Stackpoole, Mrs - 148
Stadhampton (Oxon) 17, 143, 152, 276
Stair, - 102
Standhill (Oxon) 25
Standlake (Oxon) 29–30, 31, 155, 167, 276–7
Stanford Dingley (Berks) 41, 71, 277
Stanford le Hope (Essex) 235
Stanford in the Vale (Berks) 40, 48, 195, 277–8
Stanhope, H W 88
Stanhope, Lord - 200
Stanhope, Miss Spencer 247
Stanlake Park (Berks) 205
Stanley, Canon A P 248, 261
Stanton Harcourt (Oxon) 22, 23, 167, 279
Stanton St John (Oxon) 19, 84, 179, 199, 279
Stantonbury (Bucks) 36, 93, 131, 279
Stapley, - 123
Starkey, Arthur 236
Statter, J 320–1
Steele, George 124–5, 328
Steeple Aston (Oxon) 23, 85, 109–10, 167, 198, 264, 265
Steeple Barton (Oxon) 2, 23, 91, 118, 125, 264
Steeple Claydon (Bucks) 31, 32, 33, 78, 81, 87, 92, 154
Stephens, - 73, 277
Stephens, B R 28; (RR) 30
Stephens, Richard Ruding 98
Stephens, W 125–6
Stephens *see also* Stevens
Stephenson, - 143
Stephenson, Dr. 8, 275
Stephenson, L 275
Sterry, Francis 312
Stert Devizes (Wilts) 186
Steuart *see* Stewart

Stevens, - 73
Stevens, Henry B 295
Stevens, Jno 32, 71
Stevens, Thomas 54, 129
Stevens, W E 10, 11, 264, 265
Stevens *see also* Stephens
Steventon (Berks) 40, 45, 86, 280, 299
Steward, John 285
Stewart (Steuart), C A (Jas) 59; *see also* Stuart
Stewkley (Bucks) 33, 88, 92, 112, 135, 280–1, 307, 313
Stillingfleet, H W 213
Stockcross (Berks) 40, 281
Stockholt (Bucks) 99
Stoddart (Stoddard), W W 143–4, 162; *see also* Stoddart
Stoddart, William 329
Stoke Goldington (Stoke Goldey) (Bucks) 36, 93, 181, 281
Stoke Hammond (Bucks) 37, 92, 281–2
Stoke Lyne (Oxon) 8, 90, 106, 142, 194, 282
Stoke Mandeville (Bucks) 73, 112, 123, 138, 221, 282, 330
Stoke Park (Berks) 214
Stoke Poges (Bucks) 31, 79, 140, 177, 273, 282–3
Stoke Row (Oxon) 21, 95, 283
Stoke Talmage (Oxon) 10, 25, 218, 283
Stokenchurch (Oxon) 24, 109, 281
Stokes, W H 182
Stone (Bucks) 31, 74, 91, 93, 112, 283–4
Stone, L 24
Stone family 287
Stonehouse (Stonhouse), 19, 199, 279
Stonesfield (Oxon) 23, 284
Stony Stratford (Bucks) 93, 135, 141, 286, 335
Store, Mr and Mrs - 256
Stothart, Mrs - 144
Stow (Stowe) (Bucks) 81, 82, 91, 284
Stowmarket (Suffolk) 223
Strange, Mrs - 100
Stratfield Mortimer (Berks) 55, 261, 284–5
Stratfield Saye (Hants) 138
Stratton, - 299

Stratton Audley (Oxon) 8, 106, 287
Streatley (Berks) 39, 52, 261, 287
Street, George Edmund, work at
    Akeley 99
    Ascot under Wychwood 106
    Brightwalton 303
    Buckland 138
    Chadlington 144
    High Wycombe 327
    Iffley 207
    Ipsden 236
    Longcote 219
    Oxford 248
    Padworth 252
    Shalstone 268
    Sherrington 269
    Shrivenham 271
    Thornton 295
    Winkfield 313
    Wroxton 322
Strickland, Mrs - 167
Strickland, W 28, 166
Strickland family 277
Stuart, Miss - 200–1
Stuart, E 200–1
Stuart, James 219
Stuart *see also* Stewart (Steuart)
Stubbings (Berks) 95, 287
Studley (Studleigh) (Berks) 223, 287
Stupart, - 7, 227
Sturges, Edward 209
Sturges, Simon 104, 168–9, 212, 270, 305
Styles, Admiral - 282
Styles, Capt - 122
Styles, Charles Montague 194
Suckling, H 271
Suckling, S 27, 30
Sugden, Arthur Maitland 298
Sulham (Berks) 41, 54, 287
Sulhampstead (Berks) 139, 300
Sulhampstead Abbotts (Berks) 42, 55, 288
Sulhampstead Banister (Berks) 288
Summerfield, *see* Prebend End
Summertown *see* Oxford
Sumner, Charles Richard xii, 238
Sumner, John 170
Sumner, R 132–3, 232

Sunninghill (Berks) 41, 59, 288
Sunninghill Dale (Berks) 42, 288
Sunningwell (Berks) 40, 43, 199, 288
Sutherland, Lady - 305
Sutton, Miss - 217
Sutton, Robert 217, 330
Sutton Courtenay (Berks) 40, 44, 288–9
Swabey, H 214, 238
Swaine, James 280, 281; *see also* Swayne
Swainson, - 286
Swalcliffe (Oxon) 13, 14, 289–90, 323, 324, 325
Swallowfield (Berks) 42, 56, 91, 261, 270, 273, 290, 291
Swan, - 3, 4
Swan, Bellingham 126
Swanbourne (Bucks) 33–4, 92, 290
Swayne, - 262; *see also* Swayne
Swerford (Oxon) 11, 85, 200, 291
Swift, - 122
Swinbrook (Oxon) 29, 31, 92, 139, 291, 311
Swincombe (Swyncombe) (Oxon) 21, 291
Swinney, J H (really H H) 305
Swinney (Swinny), Henry Hutchinson 160, 238, 261, 275, 305, 310
Sydenham (Oxon) 26, 109, 291
Sykes, E J 119
Sykes, W 51
Sylvester, - 35, 81
Symons, J 78
Symons, Eliz 264
Symons *see also* Simmons
Sympson (Bucks) 303, 321

Tackley (Oxon) 24, 292
Tadmarton (Oxon) 14, 134, 236, 292, 325
Tait, Mrs - 231
Tait, T H 153, 231
Talbot, James H 32, 36, 231, 235
Talbot, M P 276
Talmage, Mayow 178
Talman, W 6
Taplow (Bucks) 79, 292
Tarbutt, Arthur Charles 106
Tarring, - 99
Tarry, - 193
Tarver, Jos 299

Tatham, - 37
Tattenhoe (Bucks) 92, 292
Taunton (Som) 258
Taylor, Henry 52, 232
Taylor, John 245
Taynton (Oxon) 30, 31, 83, 85, 292
Teape, D W 290
Teignmouth (Devon) 76
Temperley House (Oxon) 201
Temple 124
Templer, Henry Skinner 158, 295–6
Tench, - 10
Tetsworth (Oxon) 26, 77, 86, 293
Teulin, - 149
Tew, Mrs - 100
Tew under Bampton (Oxon) 31; *see also* Great Tew; Duns Tew; Little Tew
Thame (Oxon) 26, 71, 86, 293–4
Thatcham (Berks) 38, 41, 66, 90, 207, 294–5, 300
Thatcher, William 185
Theale (Berks) 41, 56, 261, 295, 297
Thelwall, Black Patch 32
Thelwall, J H 32, 72, 237
Theobald, - 288
Thesiger, Sir Fred 294
Thomas, G J 210
Thomas, Henry 210
Thomas, J 87
Thomas, Vaughan 24, 328
Thompson, - 33, 175, 219
Thompson, C 308
Thompson, E 61, 142
Thompson, Marmaduke 51
Thompson, Sylvester and Co 164
Thompson, W 86
Thompson *see also* Thomson; Tompson
Thomson, - 134; *see also* Thompson; Tompson
Thorley (Isle of Wight) 72
Thornborough (Bucks) 83, 295
Thornton (Bucks) 83, 158, 295–6
Thornton, Spencer 76
Thornton, V 58
Thorold, A W 135, 248, 261
Thorold, J 108, 209
Thorold, James 28, 30, 130
Thorpe, - 148

Thorpe, C 13
Thoyts, Mortimer 55
Thring, Godfrey 105–6
Throckmorton, Sir R 138
Thurland, - 18
Thursley, - 279
Thwaites, - 288
Tickell, Walsh 36
Tiddeman, G 43
Tiddeman, R P G 199
Tiddington (Oxon) 16, 85
Tidmarsh (Berks) 41, 54, 91, 261, 296–7
Tidmarsh Manor (Berks) 252n, 296n
Tilbrook, - 263
Tilbury, R 214
Tilehurst (Berks) 41, 56, 261, 297
Timsbury (Hants) 196
Tingewick (Bucks) 35, 79, 80, 81, 83, 135, 297
Todenham (Glos) 22n
Togodumnus 211
Tomkins, W 36, 215
Tompson, Edward 208; *see also* Thompson; Thomson
Tooke, T H 301
Toot Baldon (Oxon) 16, 51, 114–15, 162, 200
Torquay (Devon) 171, 234, 280
Tottenhoe (Bucks) 33, 34
Tower, - 208
Tower, Beatrice 208
Towersey (Oxon) 26, 86, 298
Townsend, Miss - 206
Townsend, A B 60–61, 168, 169
Townsend, Richard 206
Townsend family 77
Townshend, S T 36, 89, 148
Travers, C H 105, 113, 141, 164, 223, 280, 316, 338
Tregony (Cornwall) 300
Trench, Francis 54, 86, 155, 207, 208, 259, 261
Trench, G 207
Trench, Mary Eliza 208
Trevelyan, - 316
Trevelyan, Mrs - 279, 286, 304
Trevelyan, William Pitt 141, 316
Trinder, - 248, 300

Tring (Herts) 11
Tripp, H 163
Trollope, John 20, 160, 302
Trotman, F S 36, 181
Troyte, C A W 258
Truro (Cornwall) 164
Tubbs, G I 259, 262
Tubney (Berks) 40, 44, 95, 298
Tucker, - 11
Tucker, John 197, 217–18
Tudor, - 227
Tudor, Henry 293
Tuffnell (Tuffnall), - 47, 300
Tull, - 68, 102
Turfield (Bucks) 76
Turner, - 24, 151
Turner, Alfred 34, 311
Turner, Sir E 123
Turner, George H 226
Turner, I B 37, 227
Turner, James 163
Turner, W B 131
Turner, W N 207
Turrell, - 249
Turton, H M 212, 228, 325–6
Turvey (Beds) 216
Turville (Bucks) 78, 87, 88, 91, 298
Turville Park (Bucks) 298
Turweston (Bucks) 31, 80, 83, 89, 280, 298–9
Tusmore (Oxon) 7, 8, 90, 194, 228, 299
Tutchen End (Berks) 131
Tweed, John Edward 287
Tweedy, Robert 106
Twopenney, R T 21, 236
Twopenney, T Nowell 309
Twyford (Berks) 42, 95, 205–6, 264, 299
Twyford (Bucks) 35, 83, 154, 299
Twyford (Oxon) 7
Tylers Green (Bucks) 223, 253, 299, 301
Tyndale, Henry Annesley 200
Tyndale, T G (T R) 18, 86, 200
Tyndall, J 260
Tyrrel (Tyrrell), - 201, 202, 296
Tyrringham (Bucks) 36, 93, 269, 299
Tyrwhitt, Richard St John 247

Uffington (Oxon) 40, 47, 300, 319

Ufton (Upton) Nervet (Berks) 55–6, 261, 288, 300
Underhill, - 207
Upper Basildon (Berks) 119
Upper Heyford (Oxon) 109, 199
Upper Winchendon (Bucks) 113, 312
Upper Worton (Oxon) 15, 293
Upton cum Chalvey (Bucks) 79, 88, 90, 96, 164, 273, 301
Upton (Berks) 39, 70, 128, 185, 334
Upton Nervet *see* Ufton Nervet
Uthwatt, Andrewes 82, 223
Uthwatt, E A 89, 179
Uthwatt, William 284
Uxbridge (G London) 208, 226

Valentine, Lord 125
Valpy, Gab 86, 138
Vane, R 6
Vansittart, - 58
Vansittart, C 271
  wife of 271
Vaughan, - 162, 261
Venables, - 188, 248
Verney, D 274
Verney, Sir Harry 209
Vesey, - 132
Victoria, Queen xvi
Vidler, Mrs - 100
Villars (Villar), J G 33, 199
Vincent, Edward Odell 167
Vincent, William 45, 86
Vizard, - 30, 214

Waddesdon (Bucks) 32, 71, 72, 88, 93, 112, 301–2, 312, 320
Waddington, Herbert 257, 280
Wade, - 252
Wade, Nugent C 258
Wait, - 193
Walcot (Bucks) 89
Wale, Alex M 59, 288
Walker, Francis J 178
Walker, R 17, 162
Walker, R Z 212
Walling, - 11
Wallingford (Berks) 19, 39, 51–3, 70, 86, 95, 122, 166, 200, 302

INDEX OF NAMES AND PLACES

Wallington (Berks) 261
Wallis, Miss - 73
Walmer (Kent) 4, 5
Walmsley, H 132
Walpole, Mr and Mrs 192
Walsh, - 207
Walsh, Old - 23, 279
Walsh, Digby 272
Walsh, W P 23, 167, 279
Walter, J 119, 120, 205
Walters, Charles 304
Walters, J 315
Waltham St Lawrence (Berks) 41, 60, 261, 303
Walton (nr Aylesbury) (Bucks) 303
Walton (nr Fenny Stratford) (Bucks) 37, 272, 303
Walton, - 183, 237, 257
Walton, W 87, 301, 302, 312, 320
Walton, W W (H B) 239, 241, 243
Wanklyn, - 177
Wanklyn, Hibbert 226
Wantage (Berks) 39, 49, 124, 138, 229, 303–4, 339
Wapshare (Wapshire), C 49, 197
Warborough (Berks) 19, 304
Warburton, - 206, 207
Ward, W S 208
Wardington (Oxon) 13, 159, 304, 323, 324
Warfield (Berks) 61, 96, 138, 304–5, 313
Warfield House (Berks) 60
Wargrave (Berks) 41, 59, 223n, 261, 263, 270, 305
Warner, C 261, 339
Warnham (Sussex) 202
Warpsgrove (Oxon) 305
Warren (Oxon) *see* Heyford Warren
Warrener, R 252
Warriner (Wariner), G 11, 97
Wart, - 248
Warwick (Warks) 313
Wasey, - 69
Wasey, Miss - 150
Wasey, John Spearman 156
Wasing (Berks) 41, 63, 65, 90, 295, 306
Watchfield (Berks) 38, 219, 271
Water Eaton (Oxon) 22, 210, 306

Water Stratford (Bucks) 35, 79, 82, 84, 92, 286–7
Wateringbury (Kent) 29
Waterperry (Oxon) 306
Waterstock (Oxon) 18, 19, 306
Watkins, D 82, 83, 135, 295
Watkins, W 87
Watlington (Oxon) 26, 85, 270, 306–7
Watson, W W 135
Watts, - 138, 168, 192, 314
Watts, G E 167
Watts, John William 86, 87, (M) 122–3, 215, 331–4
Wavendon (Bucks) 37, 92, 95, 307
Way, - 164, 264
Way, Ben 164
Wayne, W 221
Ways, C D 75
Weale, - 10
Weatherhead, F J (T) 58
Webb, - 198, 255
Webb, Mrs - 304
Webb, D G 198
Webb, John M 218
Weddell, - 312
Weighill (Weighell; Weyghell), J 31, 34, 37, 38, 255
Weight, G 316–17
Weippert, - 85
Welburn, Edward B 104, 167, 269
Welby, W H E 120
Welford (Berks) 40, 62, 68, 91, 129, 268, 307, 319, 327
Welford, George 57, 157
Wellington College (Berks) 164
Wells (Som) 106, 116
Wells, Francis 202
Wells, George 62–3, 129
Welsh, T 260
Welton le Wold (Lincs) 271
Wendlebury (Oxon) 8, 122, 307–8
Wendover (Bucks) 72–6, 87, 89, 93, 112, 308
Wenman (Wennman), Lady - 26, 293
Wesley, J 50
West, Jos 15, 251
West, Richard Temple 140–1
West, W W 238–9, 248

West Challow (Berks) 39, 50, 143, 275
West Hagbourne (Berks) 128, 185–6
West Hendred (Berks) 39, 49, 197
West Ilsley (Berks) 40, 67, 207
West Shefford *see* Great Shefford
West Woodhay (Berks) 38, 41, 64, 318–19
West Wycombe (Bucks) 327
Westbury (Bucks) 1, 35, 80, 83, 89, 268, 299, 308
Westbury, Lord Chancellor 266
Westcombe, Thomas 50
Westcote Barton (Oxon) 24, 91, 118, 293
Westcott (Bucks) 302
Western family 277
Westerton, - 160
Westmacott, Horatio 9, 145
Westminster *see* London
Weston on the Green (Oxon) 8, 83, 85, 212, 308
Weston Turville (Bucks) 31, 76, 112, 154, 186, 309
Weston Underwood (Bucks) 93, 309
Westwell (Oxon) 30, 31, 309–10
Wetherall, - 287; *see also* Wetherell
Wethered, - 225
Wethered, F 205
Wethered, Owen 225
Wetherell, William 84, 85, 199; *see also* Wetherall
Wexham (Berks) 38, 310
Weyland, - 318
Whaddon (Bucks) 34, 36, 84, 91, 92, 119, 159, 296, 310
Whaddon Chase (Bucks) 34
Wharton, J C 123
Whateley, C 292
Whateley, John 211
Whateley, Tom 57
Wheatfield (Oxon) 26, 310
Wheatley (Oxon) 19, 179, 310
Wheeler, R and J 317
Wheelers End (Bucks) 214
Wheelwright, - 115
Whelpton, H R 301
Whinfield, H W 32
Whishaw, A 152
Whishaw, Helen 152
Whitaker, - 254, 314

Whitchurch (Bucks) 3, 34, 112, 227, 238, 311
Whitchurch (Oxon) 21, 224, 310–11
Whitcock, - 55
White, A L 285
White, Glyd 84, 85
White, H T 234
White, Herbert 19, 304
White, S M 314
White, W 274
White Waltham (Berks) 41, 58, 90, 271, 303
Whitehaven, 256
Whitehead, - 210
Whitehead, J C 87
Whitehead, Thomas C 4, 5, 27, 181, 299
Whitehead, W 27, 31
Whitfield, H J 33, 182
Whitfield, Amie 146
Whitley Hill (Berks) 258, 334
Whitmore, Miss - 144
Whitmore family 291
Whittingham, Sam C 50, 151
Whittle, Charles 184, 329
Whytt, James 214
Wickham (Berks) 40, 62, 91, 307, 311
Wickham (Hants) 286
Wickham, Mr and Mrs - 152
Widford (Oxon) 30, 92, 291, 311
Wigginton (Oxon) 12, 14, 92, 311, 323, 324
Wilberforce, Emily 97
Wilberforce, Ernest Roland xii
Wilberforce, Henry 4
Wilberforce, Octavia xii, xiii
Wilberforce, Samuel ix–xiii, xiv–xvi
Wilberforce, W F 259, 261
Wilcote (Wilcot) (Oxon) 24, 257, 311, 335
Wilde, - 114
Wilder, H W 287
Wilder, John 54, 252, 287
Wilkinson, - 290
Wilkinson, Walter George 222
Wilks, - 73
Willen (Bucks) 32, 37, 92, 311
Willes, - 205
Willes, Mrs - 6

INDEX OF NAMES AND PLACES

Williams, - 24, 35, 36, 44, 48, 124, 125, 208
Williams, Col - 201, 202
Williams, Miss - 110
Williams, Mrs - 110, 159
Williams, A J 166
Williams, E S 176, 178
Williams, J 26, 338
Williams, James Reynolds 197
Williams, John 14, 313
Williams, John 11, 276
Williams, T 109
Williams, T E 66, 90
Williams, T J 113, 224
Williams, W 9, 11, 338
Williams, William 222
Williamson, - 316
Williamson, Thomas Pym 132, (T H) 285
Willis, Charles Francis 217
   wife of 217
Willis, J 89, 184
Willmott, R A 119, 120
Willoubey, John 256
Willoughby, Hugh 16, 114
Willoughby, John 114
Willoughby family 188
Wills, Miss - 299
Wilson, - 37
Wilson, Bishop 238
Wilson Dr. 321
Wilson, Edward S 237
Wilson, Francis Garratt 15, 272, 293, 321
Wilson, J 84
Wilson, N 22
Wilson, W 116, 117
Wilson, W Jun 321
Wilson family 300
Wimball, - 100
Winchendon (Bucks) 3, 93; *see also* Nether Winchendon; Upper Winchendon
Winchester (Hants) xii, xiii, 50, 51, 238, 284, 297, 309
Windsor (Berks) 18, 21, 44, 49, 67, 72, 78, 91, 156, 226; *see also* New Windsor; Old Windsor
Wing (Bucks) 38, 112, 280, 313
Wingrave (Bucks) 34–5, 38, 112, 313

Winkfield (Berks) 41, 59, 95, 159, 313
Winslow (Bucks) 33, 84, 135, 233, 290, 314
Winstanley, - 27
Winterborne (Berks) 41, 65, 148–9, 314
Winterbourne Bassett (Wilts) 201
Winterbourne Monkton (Wilts) 267
Wintle, J 84
Wintle, Richard 17, 47
Wintle, Thomas 54, 91
Wiseman, Lady - 146
Witney (Oxon)
   church consecrated 95
   Deanery 26–7, 29–31
   dissenters 86
   private memoranda 90, 91, 93
   Wilberforce at 108, 155, 230, 314–15
Wittley, Raymond 211
Woburn (Beds) (Wooburn, Bucks) 78, 110, 146–7, 317
Woburn Sands (Bucks) 307
Wokingham (Berks) 42, 57, 60, 261, 315, 335
Wollaston, W M 227
Wolvercote (Oxon) 16, 320, 339
Wolverhampton (W Mids) 208
Wolverton (Bucks) 36, 80, 84, 93, 141, 195, 223, 279, 315–17; *see also* New Wolverton; Old Wolverton
Wood, - 6, 300
Wood, Col - 107
Wood, Cyril 108
Wood, J 113
Wood, J A 298
Wood (Woodd), Mary 3
Wood Green (Oxon) 95, 314
Wood Hay 297
Woodall, - 301
Woodcote (Oxon) 21, 92, 95, 275, 318
Woodeaton (Oxon) 18, 19, 83, 170, 318
Woodford, J R 113, 116, 129, 142, 168, 210, 248, 261, 274, 338
Woodger, - 311
Woodlands (Berks) 319
Woodley, Abraham 185, 186
Woodley, Amos 186
Woodley, Edwin 186
Woodley, Ephraim 186

Woodley, Francis 185
Woodley, George 185
Woodley, Hannah 185
Woodley, Igal 185
Woodley, Jacob 185
Woodley, John 185
Woodley, Mary 185
Woodley, Sarah 185
Woodley, Thomas 185
Woodley, William 185
Woodman, - 131
Woodman, F T 131, 269
Woods, - 88
Woods, H H 297
Woodstock (Oxon) 19, 21–2, 23, 24, 90, 125, 188, 319, 328
Woodyer, - 121
Woolcombe, - 222
Woolcombe, H 19
Woolhampton (Berks) 40, 41, 42, 55, 65, 67, 319
Woolley (Berks) 67, 142
Woolley, W 260
Woolstone (Oxon) 40, 47, 320; *see also* Great Woolstone; Little Woolstone
Wootton (Berks) 39, 43, 162, 320
Wootton (Oxon) 24, 125, 199, 222, 284, 285, 320, 328
Wootton Underwood (Bucks) 33, 320
Worcester (Worcs) 179, 222, 236
Wordsworth, - 197
Wordsworth, Christopher 195, 268, 277
Wordsworth, Mary 278
Worley, - 286
Worminghall (Bucks) 89, 320–1
Wormsley (Oxon) 19
Worsley, John Henry 56, 213, 216, 296
Worthing (Sussex) 253
Worthy (Hants) 36
Worton (Oxon) 325; *see also* Little Worton; Lower Worton; Over Worton; Upper Worton
Woughton on the Green (Bucks) 80, 321
Wrangler, Senior 69
Wray, Cecil 235
Wraysbury (Wyrardisbury) (Bucks) 38, 201, 214, 327, 328
Wrey, Arthur B 212

Wright, - 22, 23, 227
Wroth, - 31, 33, 34, 37
Wroth, Charles B 37, 169
Wroth, W B 31, 33, 34, 169
Wroughton (Bucks) 37, 92
Wroughton, Bartholomew 67, 69, 70, 92, 142, 176
Wroughton, Mary Anne 142n
Wroughton, P 178, 303
Wroxton (Oxon) 14, 134, 200, 321–2
Wulphur 107
Wyatt, - 179, 270, 296
Wyatt, C F (senior) 12, 14, 134
Wyatt, C F (junior) 12, 84, 160, 179
Wyatt, Lawrence 250
Wyatt, T 14
Wychwood (Oxon) 216
Wycombe, *see* High Wycombe; West Wycombe
Wynter, Dr. 22
Wynter, - 3
Wynter, Hannah 146
Wytham (Oxon) 39, 43, 328

Yarnton (Oxon) 24, 125, 328
Yates, Edmund 186
Yates, S W 53, 262
Yattendon (Berks) 40, 71, 86, 138, 188, 329
Yeffley *see* Iffley
Yelford (Oxon) 29, 30, 31, 329
Yeo, - 56
Yonge, Denys W 271
Yonge, W Wellington 271
Yonge *see also* Young
York (Yorks) xii, 58
Yorke, Richard 167
Yorke, Samuel 179–80
Youlden (Youldon), A 31, 197
Young, Lady - 157
Young, E N 31, 32, 72, 257
Young, Frederick 303
Young, N B 85
Young, Sir W 24
    brother of 24
Young, W B 84
Young, William Henry 122, 288